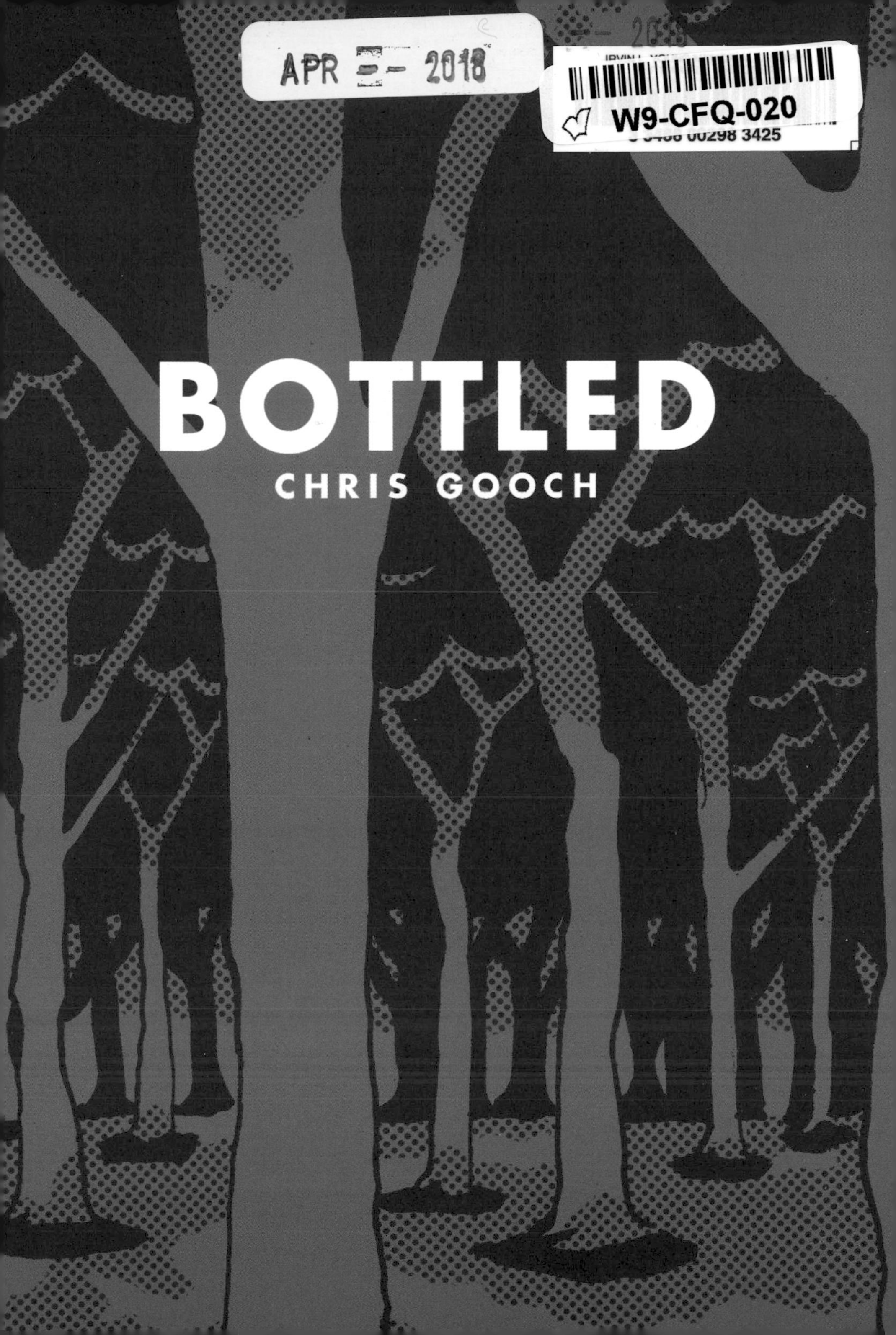

BOTTLED

CHRIS GOOCH

BOTTLED

CHRIS GOOCH

ISBN: 978-1-60309-420-7   20 19 18 17   1 2 3 4

Published by Top Shelf Productions, PO Box 1282, Marietta, GA 30061-1282, USA. Top Shelf Productions is an imprint of IDW Publishing, a division of Idea and Design Works, LLC. Offices: 2765 Truxtun Road, San Diego, CA 92106. Top Shelf Productions®, the Top Shelf logo, Idea and Design Works®, and the IDW logo are registered trademarks of Idea and Design Works, LLC. All Rights Reserved. With the exception of small excerpts of artwork used for review purposes, none of the contents of this publication may be reprinted without the permission of IDW Publishing. IDW Publishing does not read or accept unsolicited submissions of ideas, stories, or artwork.

Editor-in-Chief: Chris Staros.
Edited by Chris Staros & Leigh Walton.
Designed by Gilberto Lazcano.
Visit our online catalog at www.topshelfcomix.com.

Printed in Korea.

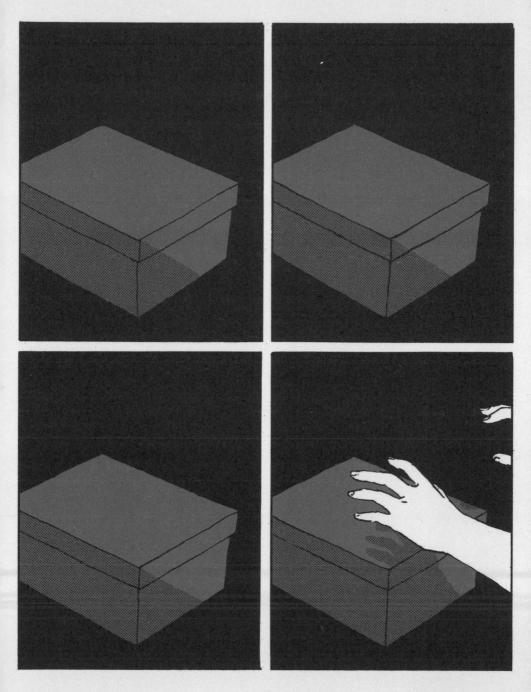

3

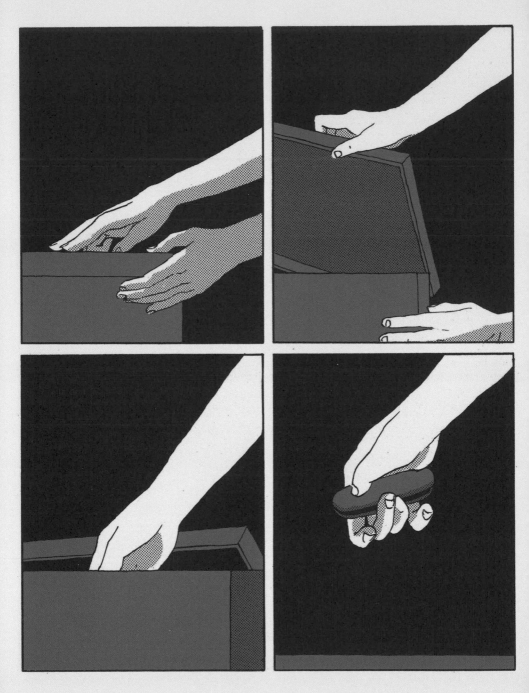

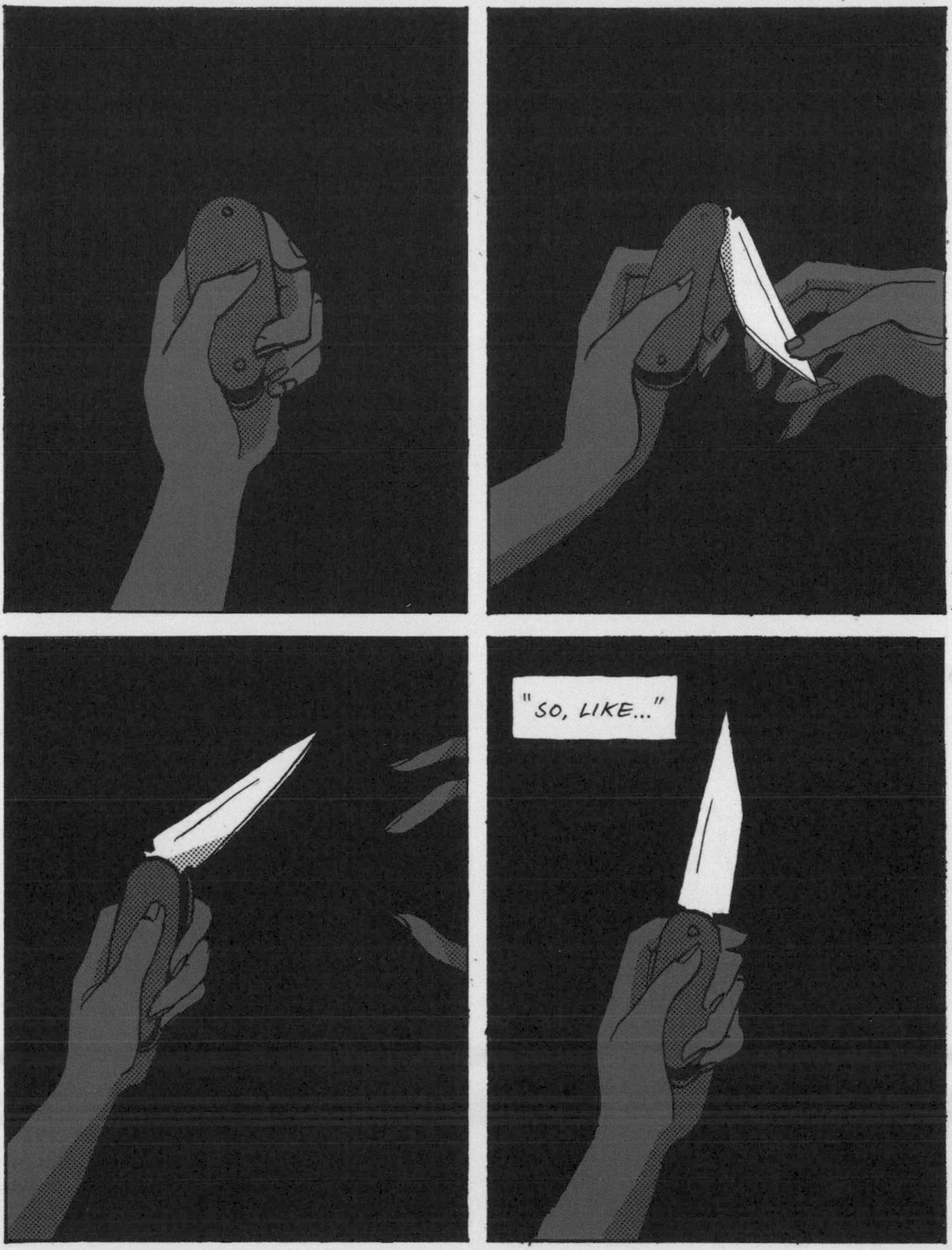
"SO, LIKE..."

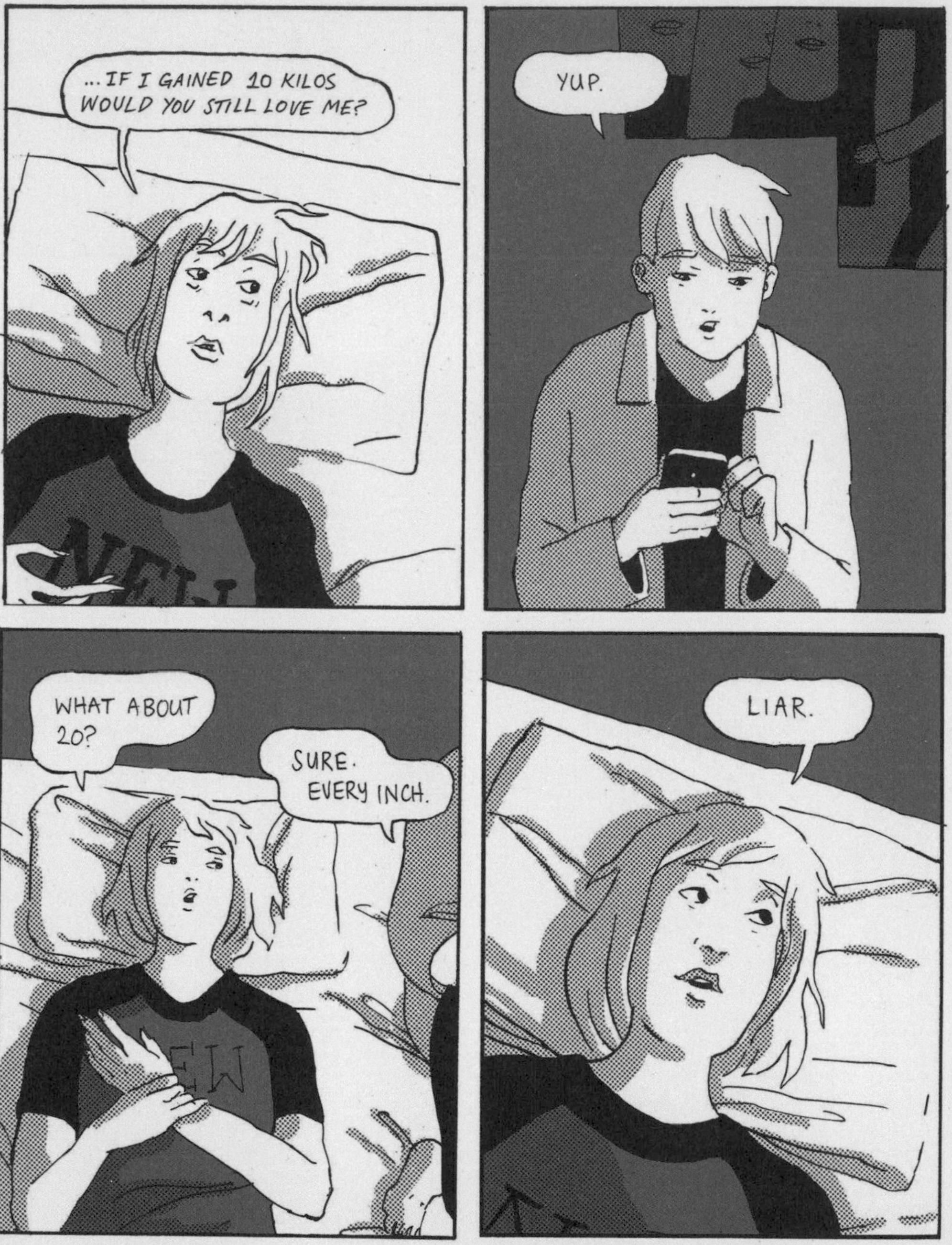
...IF I GAINED 10 KILOS WOULD YOU STILL LOVE ME?
YUP.
WHAT ABOUT 20?
SURE. EVERY INCH.
LIAR.

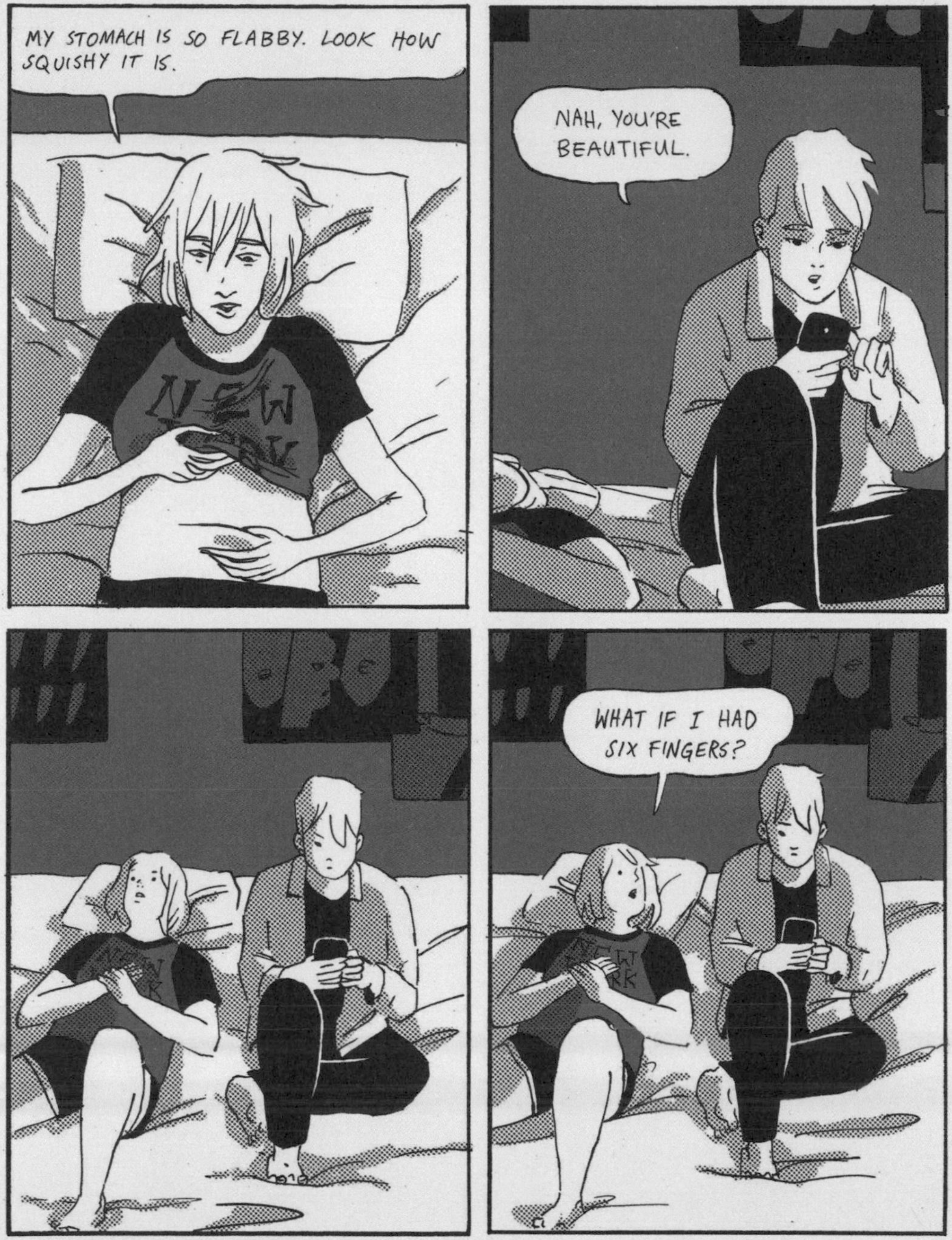
MY STOMACH IS SO FLABBY. LOOK HOW SQUISHY IT IS.
NAH, YOU'RE BEAUTIFUL.
WHAT IF I HAD SIX FINGERS?

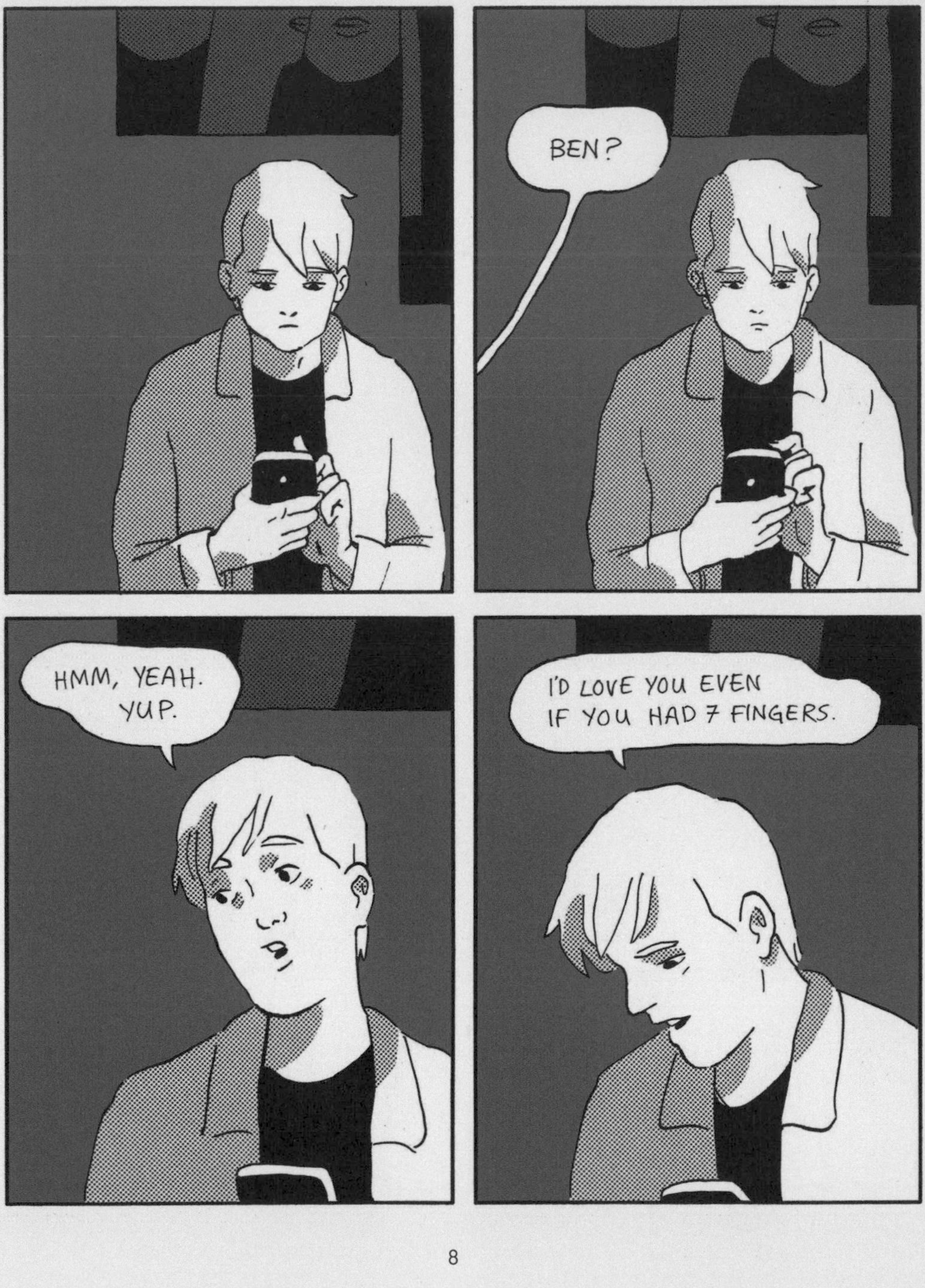
BEN?
HMM, YEAH. YUP.
I'D LOVE YOU EVEN IF YOU HAD 7 FINGERS.

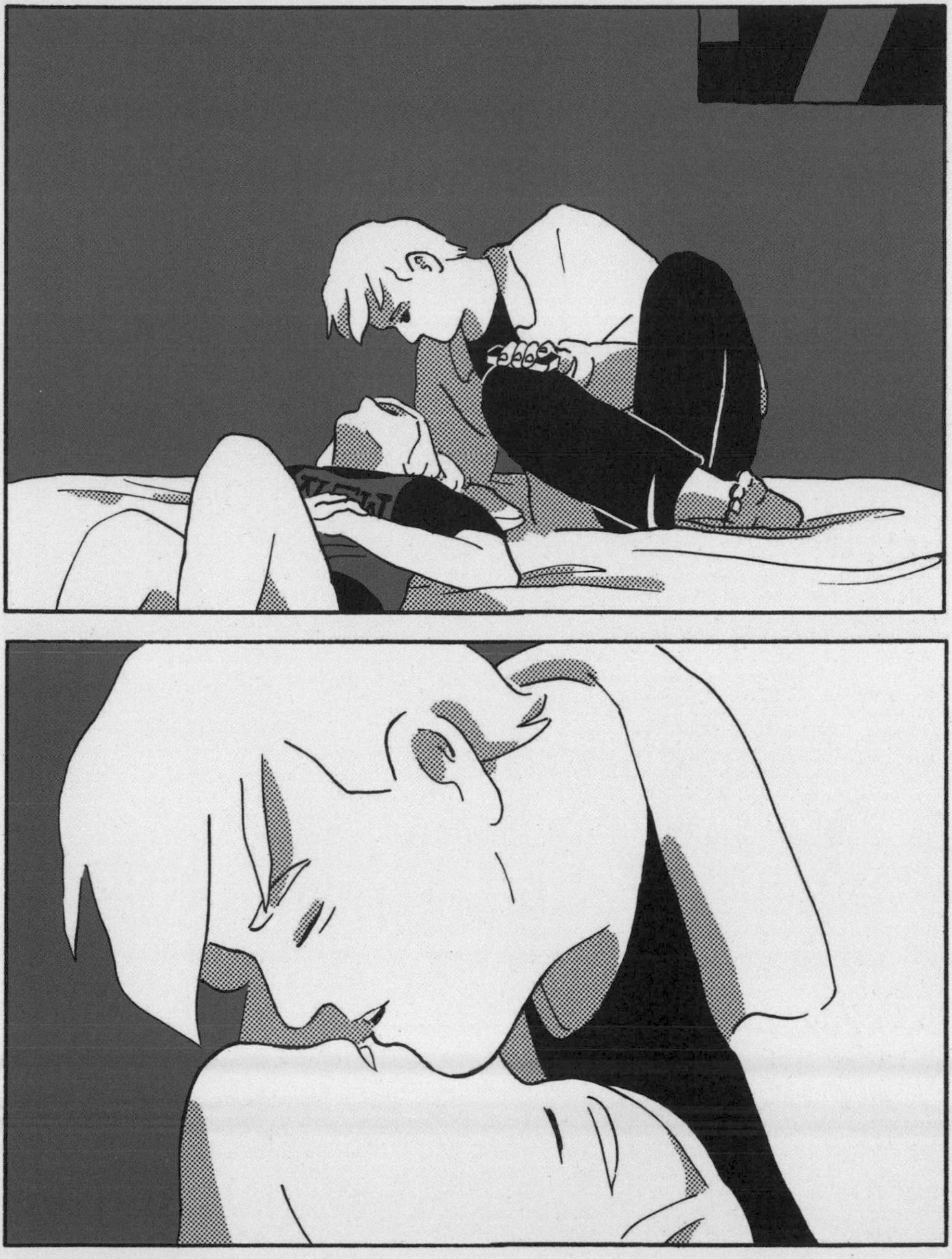

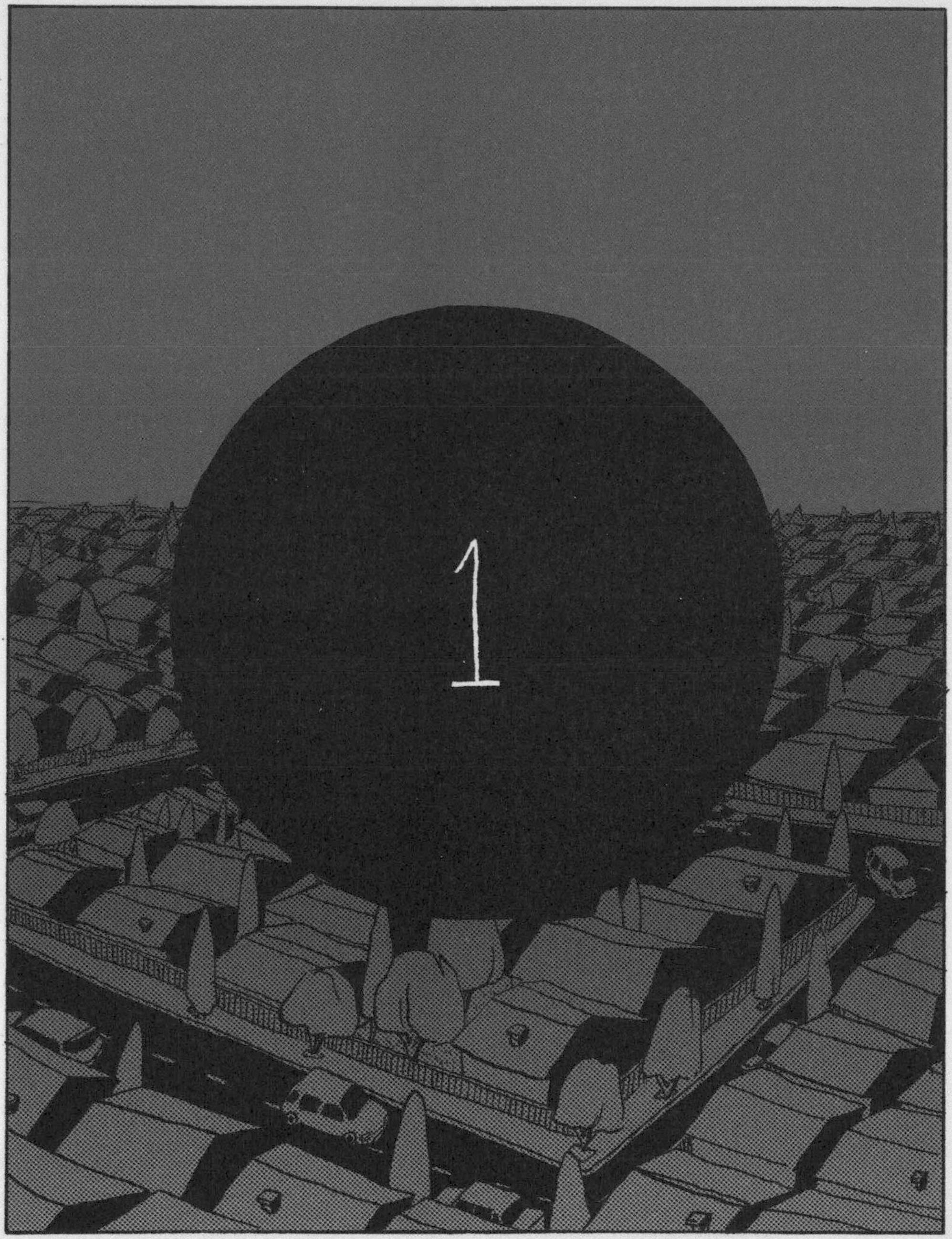
1

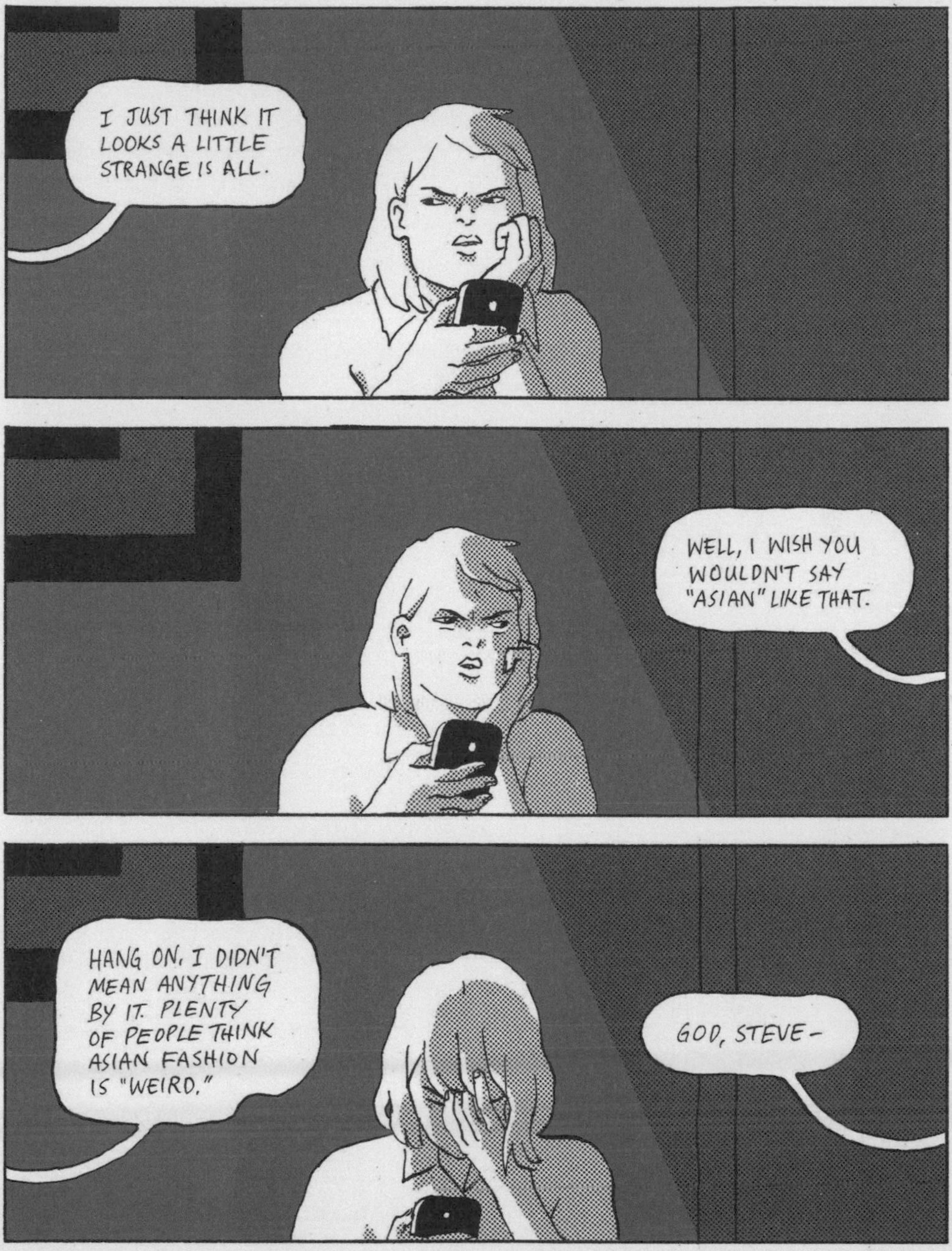
I JUST THINK IT LOOKS A LITTLE STRANGE IS ALL.
WELL, I WISH YOU WOULDN'T SAY "ASIAN" LIKE THAT.
HANG ON. I DIDN'T MEAN ANYTHING BY IT. PLENTY OF PEOPLE THINK ASIAN FASHION IS "WEIRD."
GOD, STEVE-

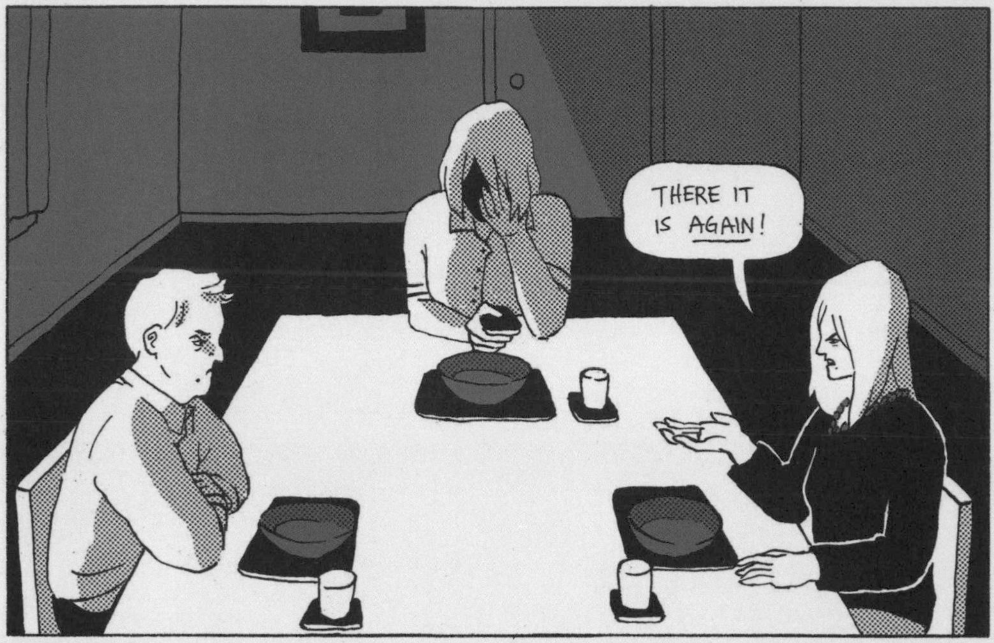
THERE IT IS AGAIN!

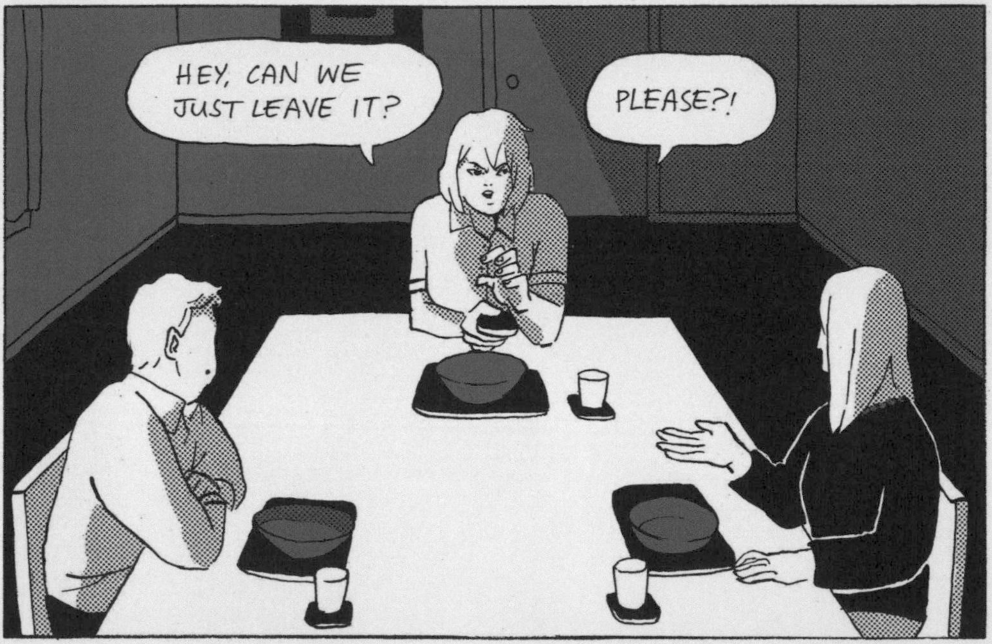
HEY, CAN WE JUST LEAVE IT?
PLEASE?!

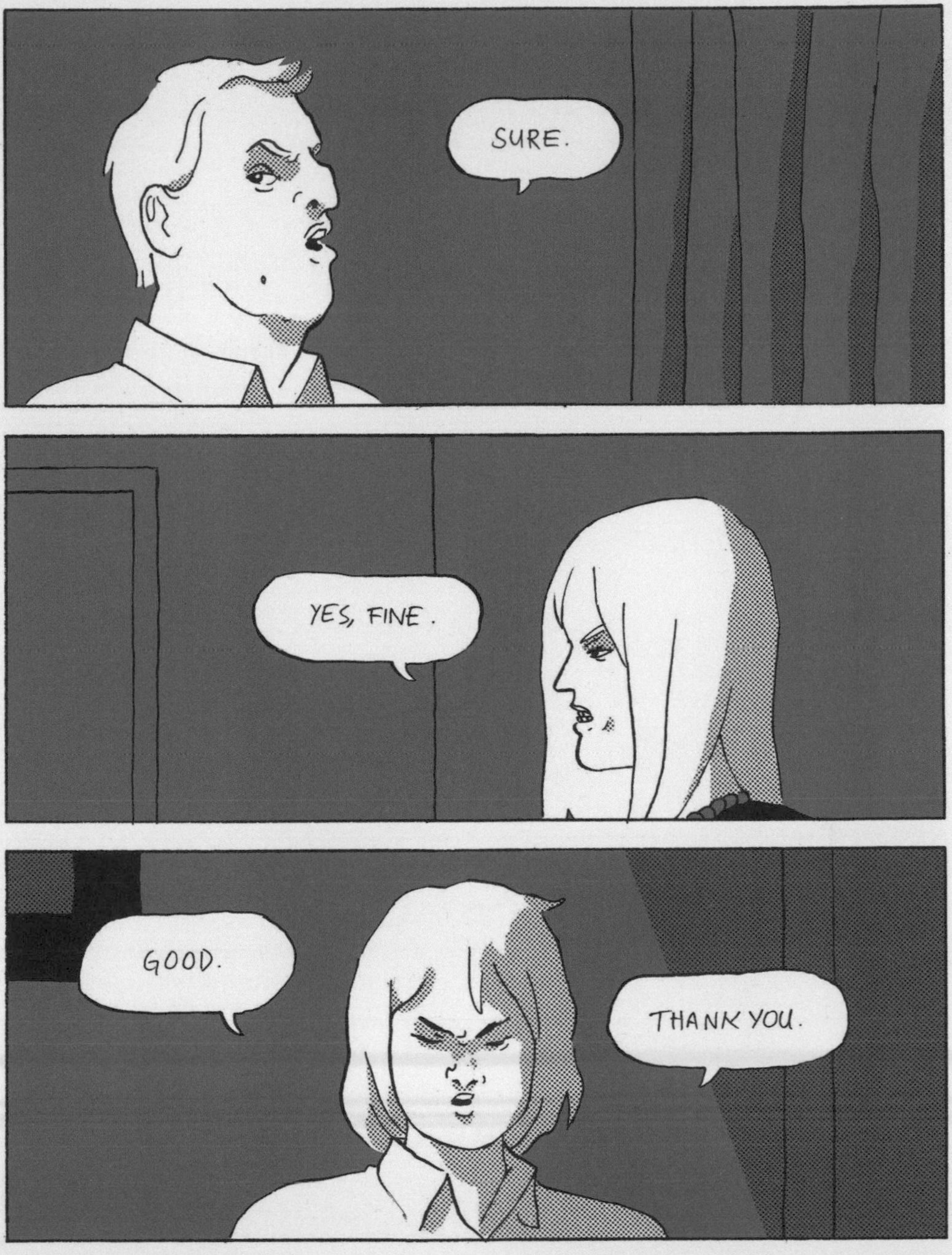
SURE.
YES, FINE.
GOOD.
THANK YOU.

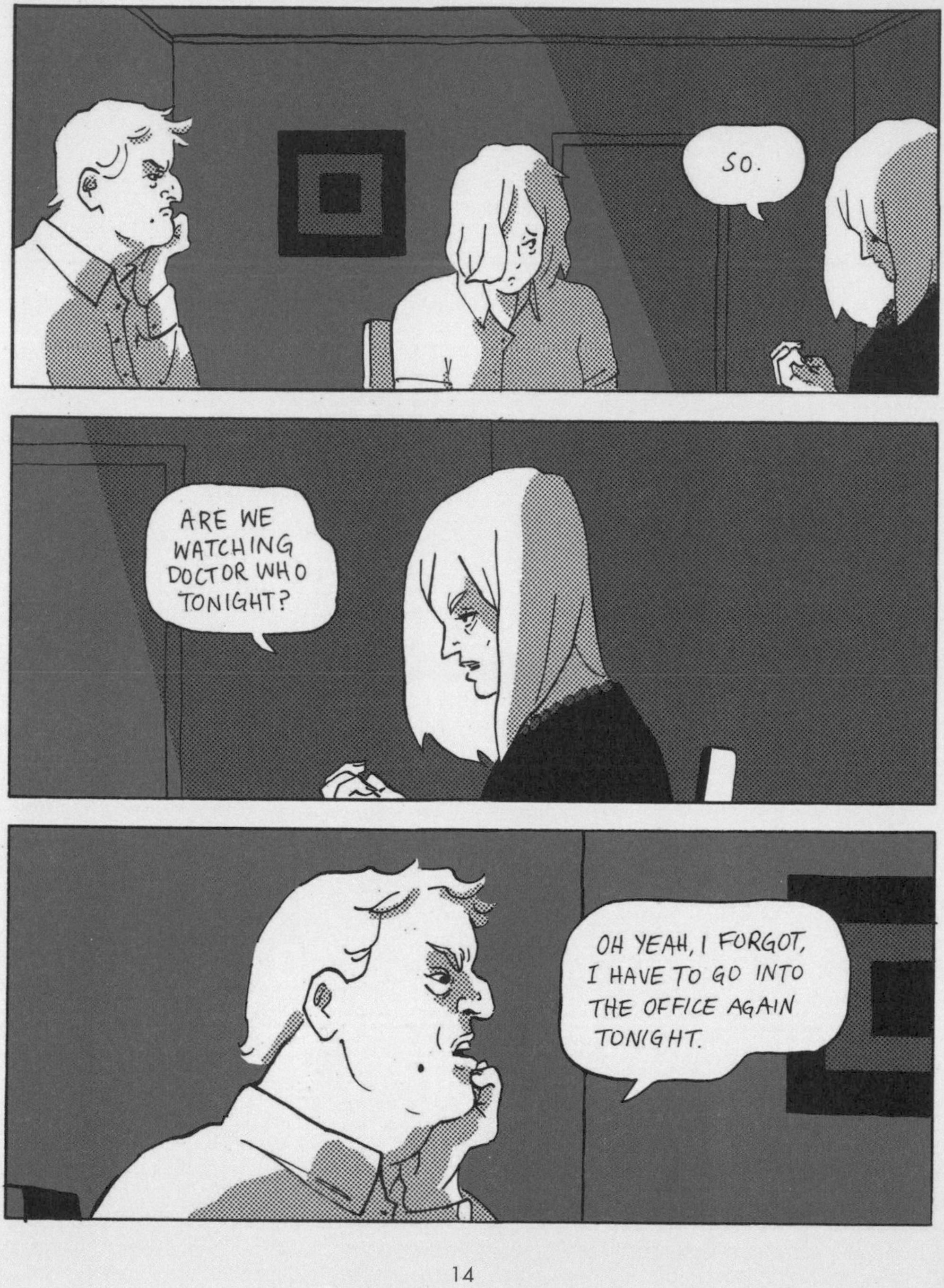
SO.
ARE WE WATCHING DOCTOR WHO TONIGHT?
OH YEAH, I FORGOT, I HAVE TO GO INTO THE OFFICE AGAIN TONIGHT.

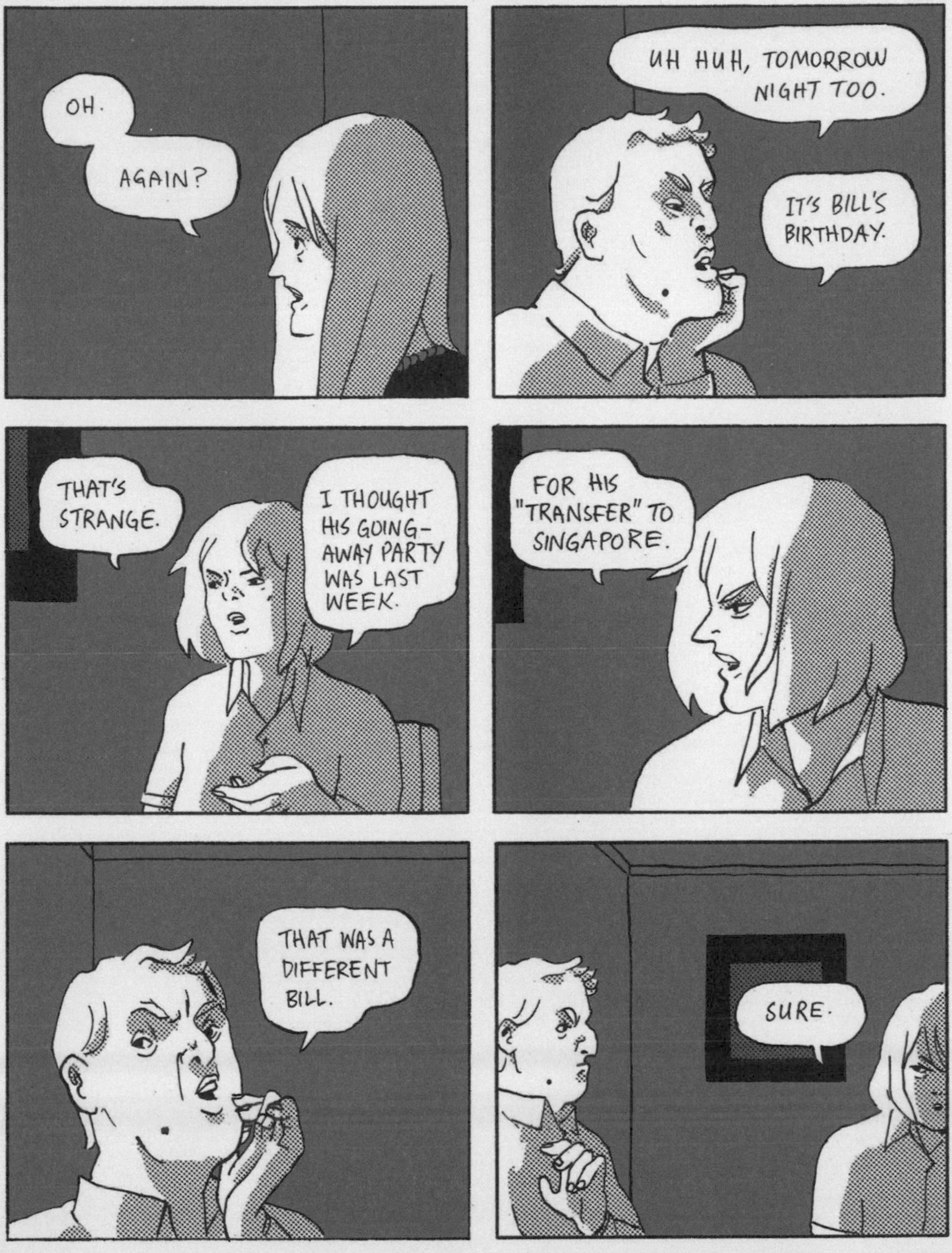
OH.
AGAIN?
UH HUH, TOMORROW NIGHT TOO.
IT'S BILL'S BIRTHDAY.
THAT'S STRANGE.
I THOUGHT HIS GOING-AWAY PARTY WAS LAST WEEK.
FOR HIS "TRANSFER" TO SINGAPORE.
THAT WAS A DIFFERENT BILL.
SURE.

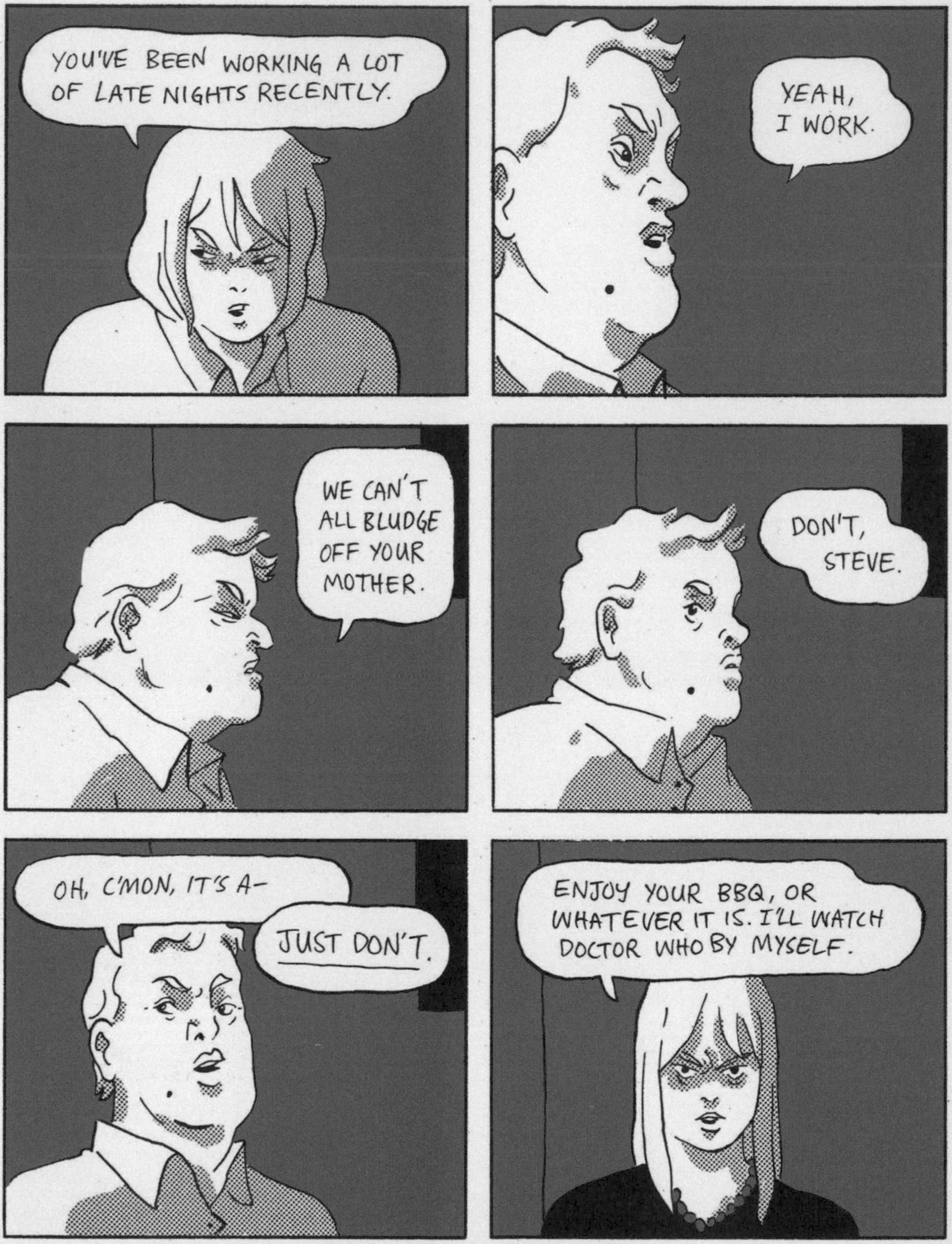
YOU'VE BEEN WORKING A LOT OF LATE NIGHTS RECENTLY.
YEAH, I WORK.
WE CAN'T ALL BLUDGE OFF YOUR MOTHER.
DON'T, STEVE.
OH, C'MON, IT'S A-
JUST DON'T.
ENJOY YOUR BBQ, OR WHATEVER IT IS. I'LL WATCH DOCTOR WHO BY MYSELF.

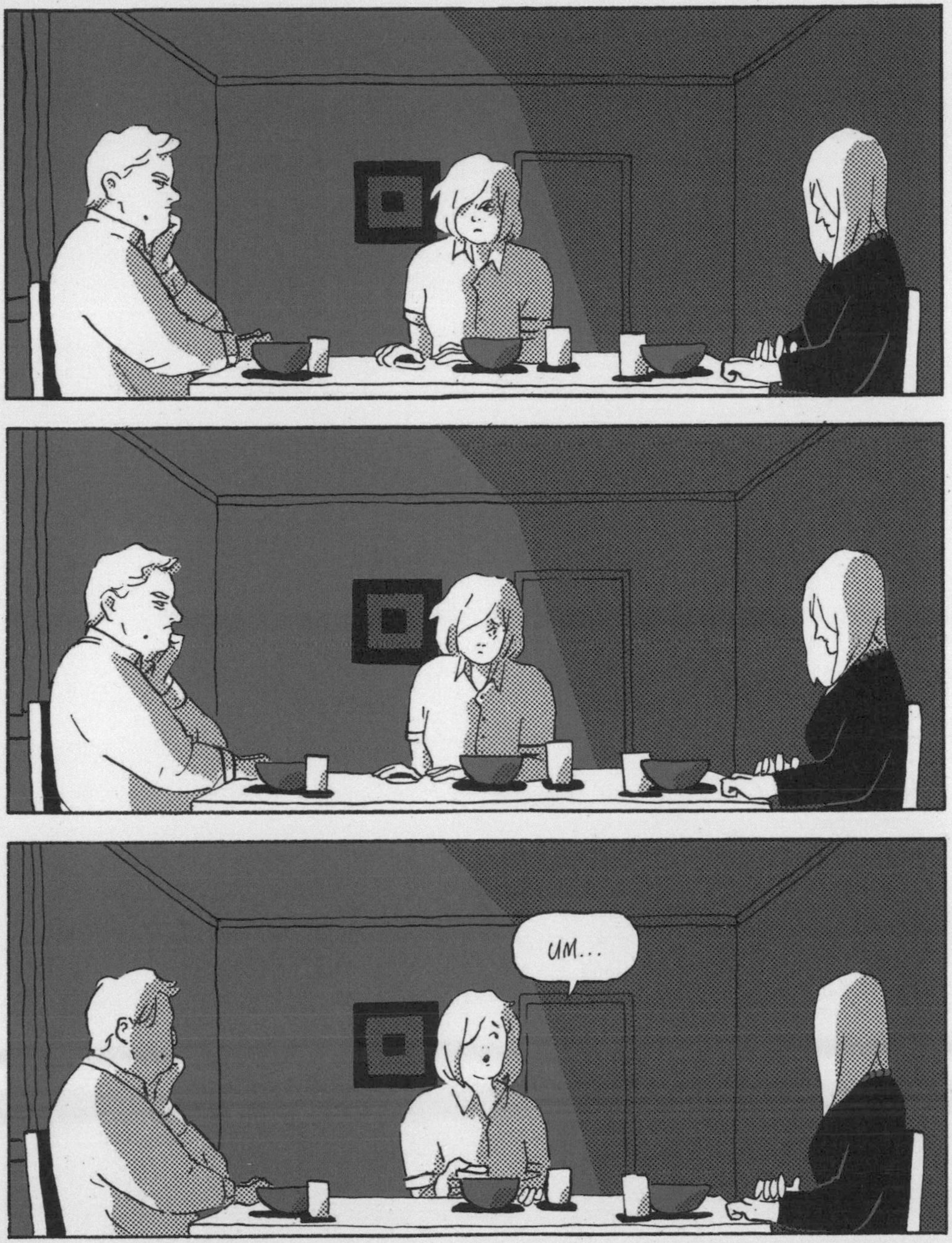
UM...

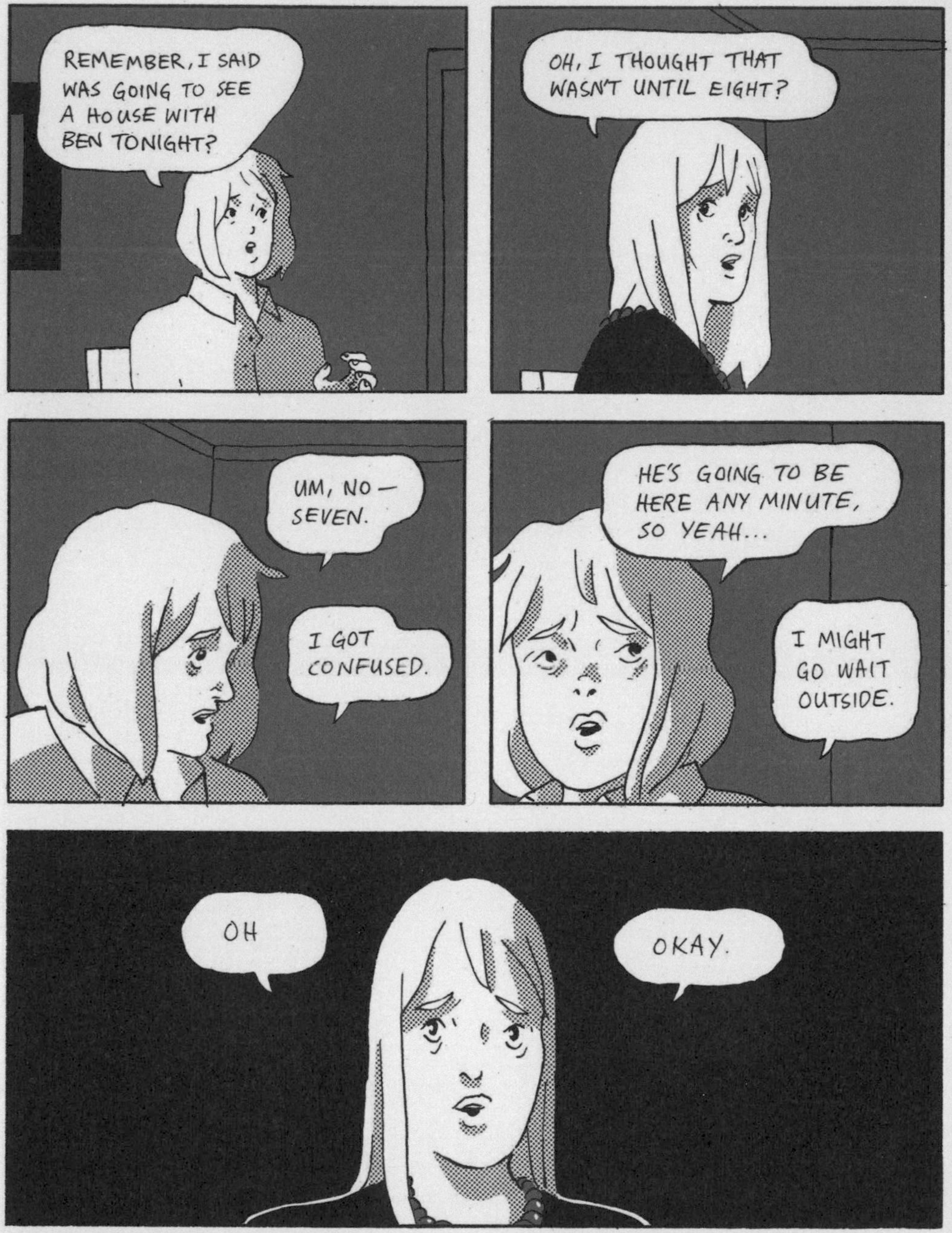
REMEMBER, I SAID WAS GOING TO SEE A HOUSE WITH BEN TONIGHT?
OH, I THOUGHT THAT WASN'T UNTIL EIGHT?
UM, NO— SEVEN.
I GOT CONFUSED.
HE'S GOING TO BE HERE ANY MINUTE, SO YEAH...
I MIGHT GO WAIT OUTSIDE.
OH
OKAY.

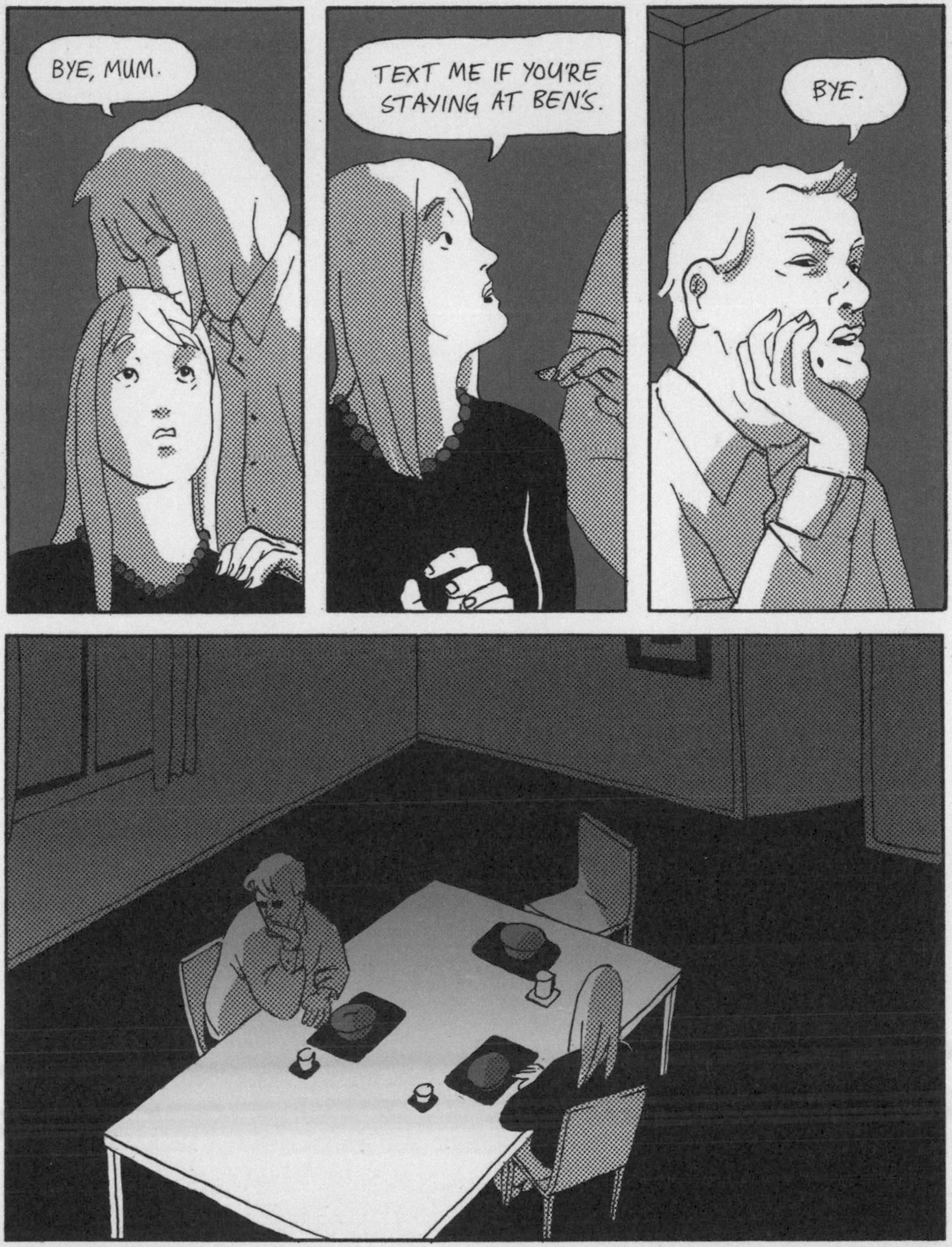
BYE, MUM.
TEXT ME IF YOU'RE STAYING AT BEN'S.
BYE.

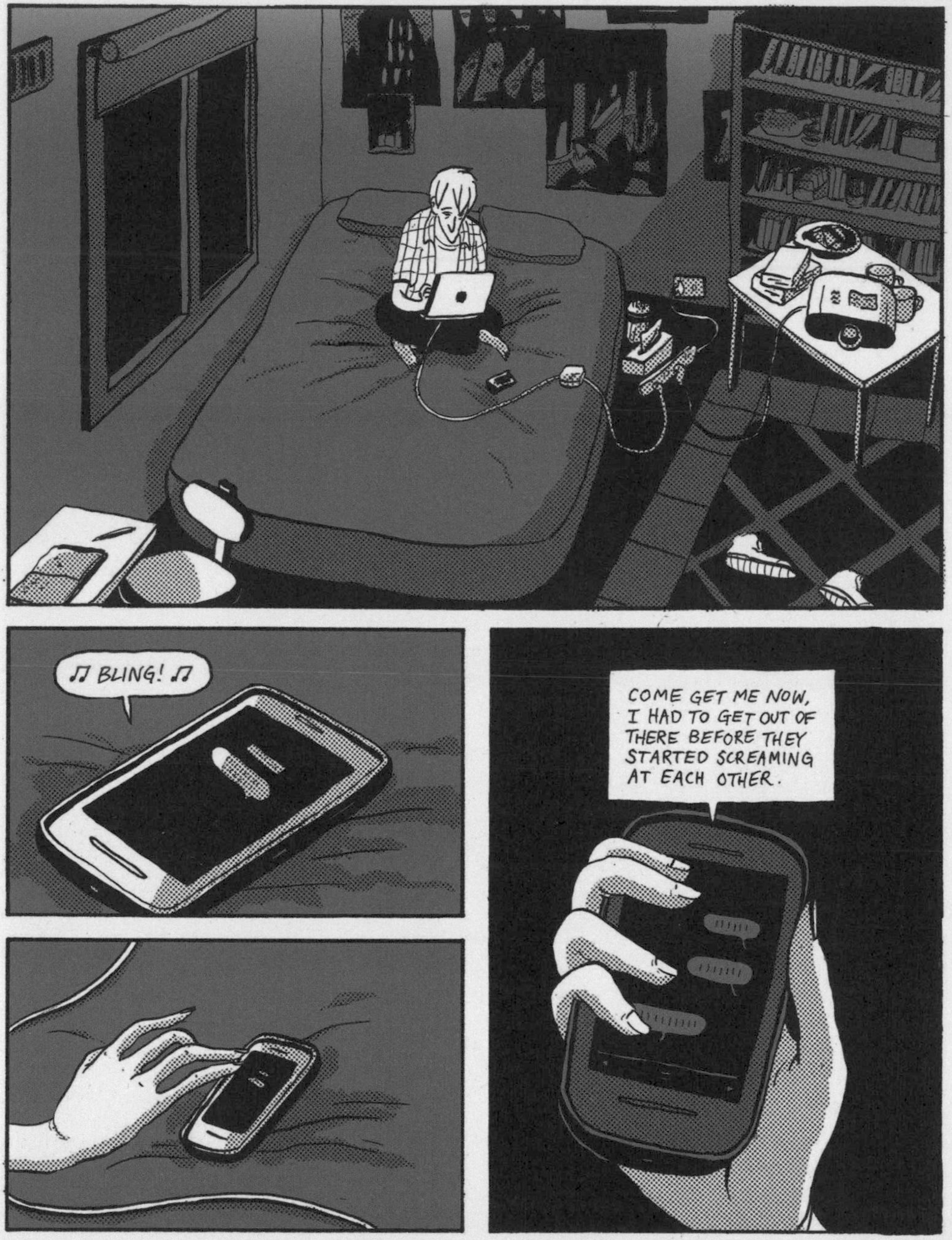
♫ BLING! ♫
COME GET ME NOW, I HAD TO GET OUT OF THERE BEFORE THEY STARTED SCREAMING AT EACH OTHER.

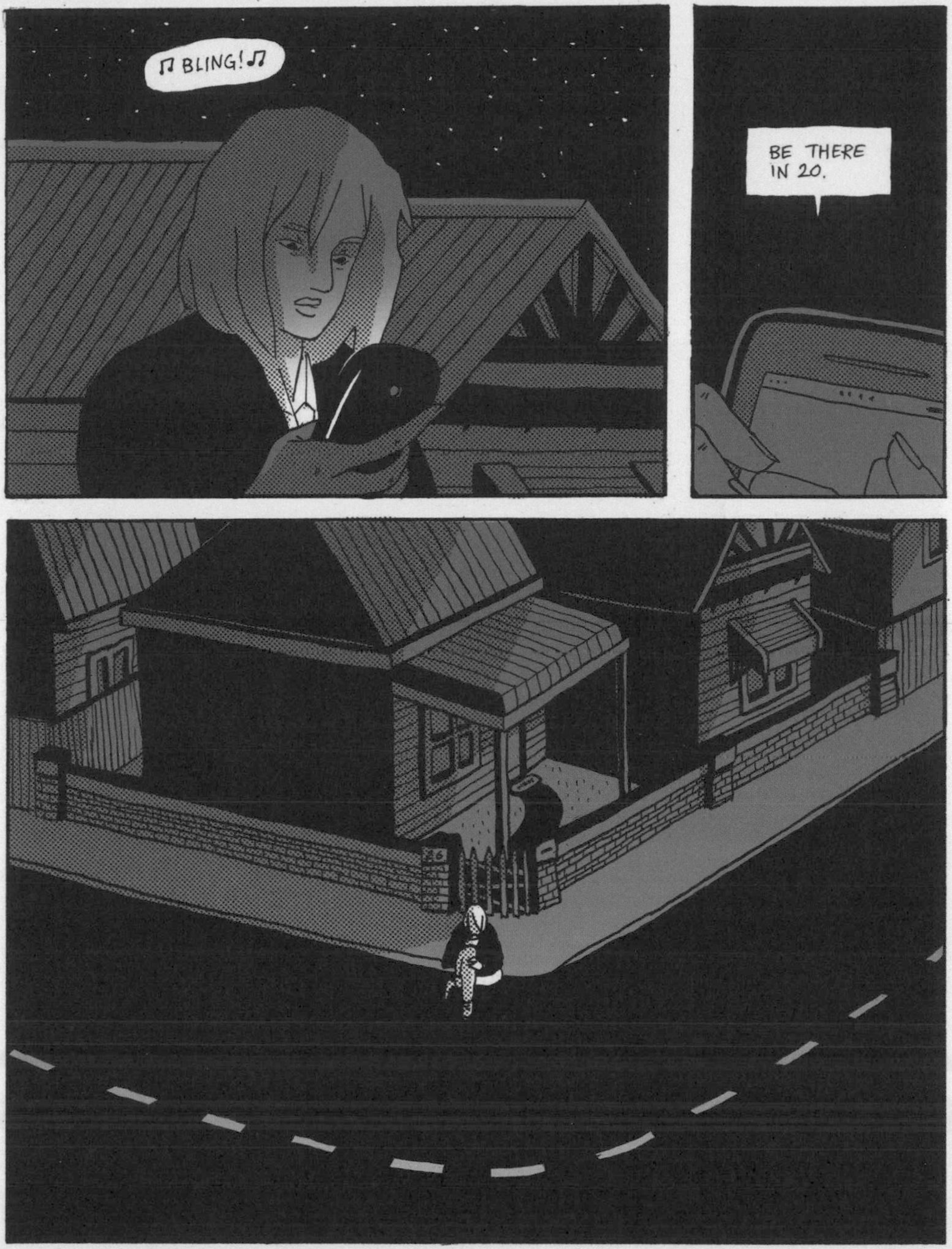
♫ BLING! ♫
BE THERE IN 20.
26

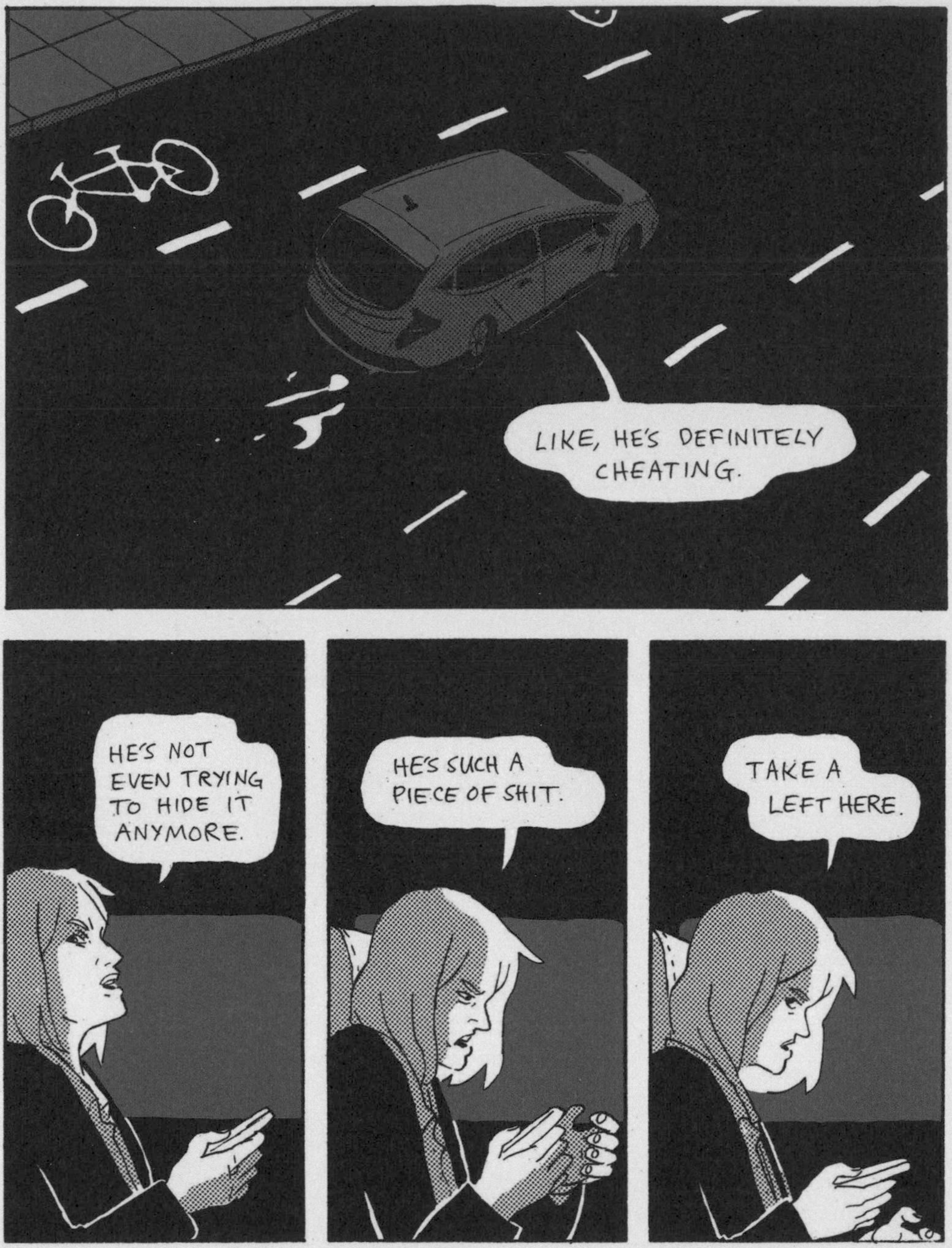
LIKE, HE'S DEFINITELY CHEATING.
HE'S NOT EVEN TRYING TO HIDE IT ANYMORE.
HE'S SUCH A PIECE OF SHIT.
TAKE A LEFT HERE.

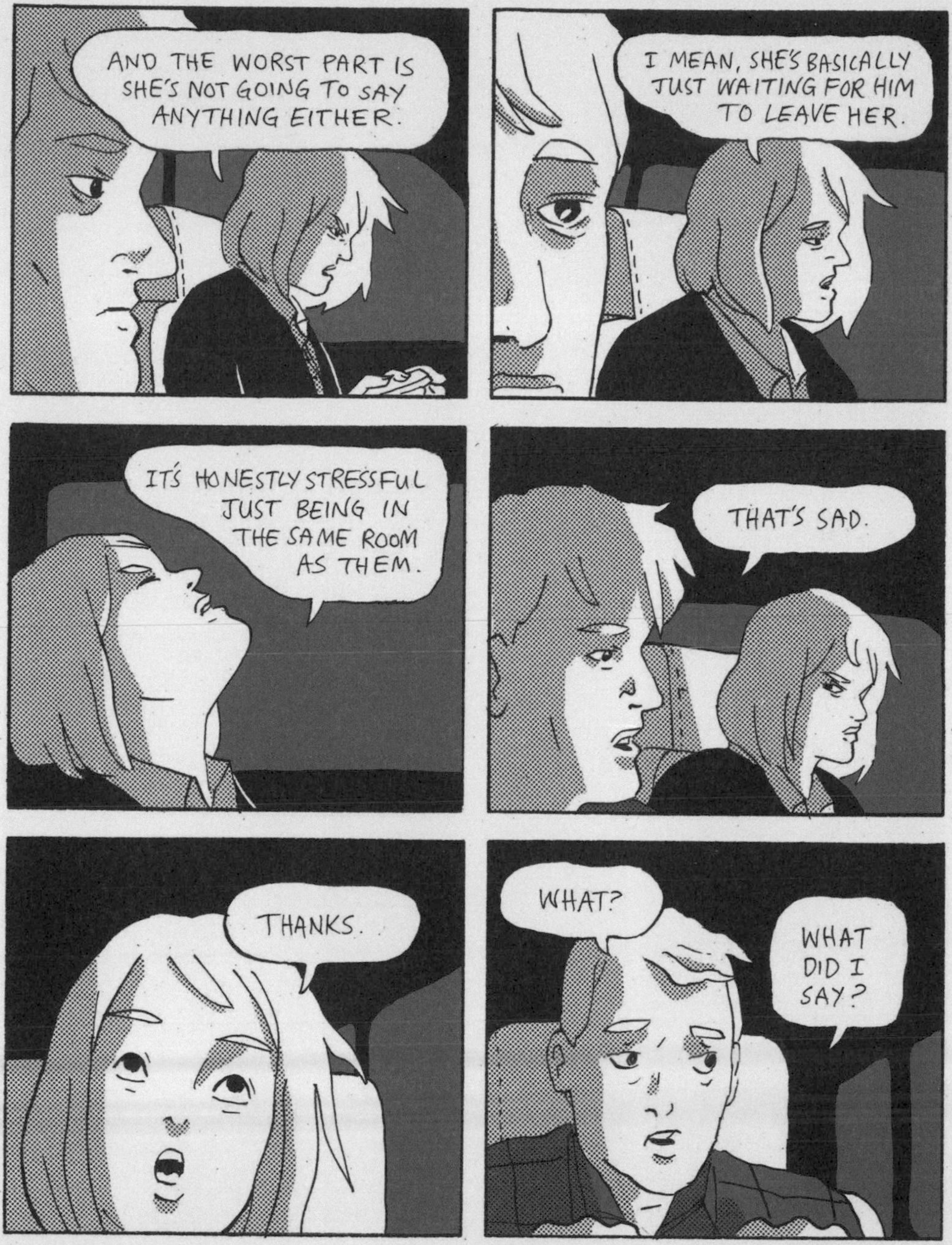
AND THE WORST PART IS SHE'S NOT GOING TO SAY ANYTHING EITHER.
I MEAN, SHE'S BASICALLY JUST WAITING FOR HIM TO LEAVE HER.
IT'S HONESTLY STRESSFUL JUST BEING IN THE SAME ROOM AS THEM.
THAT'S SAD.
THANKS.
WHAT?
WHAT DID I SAY?

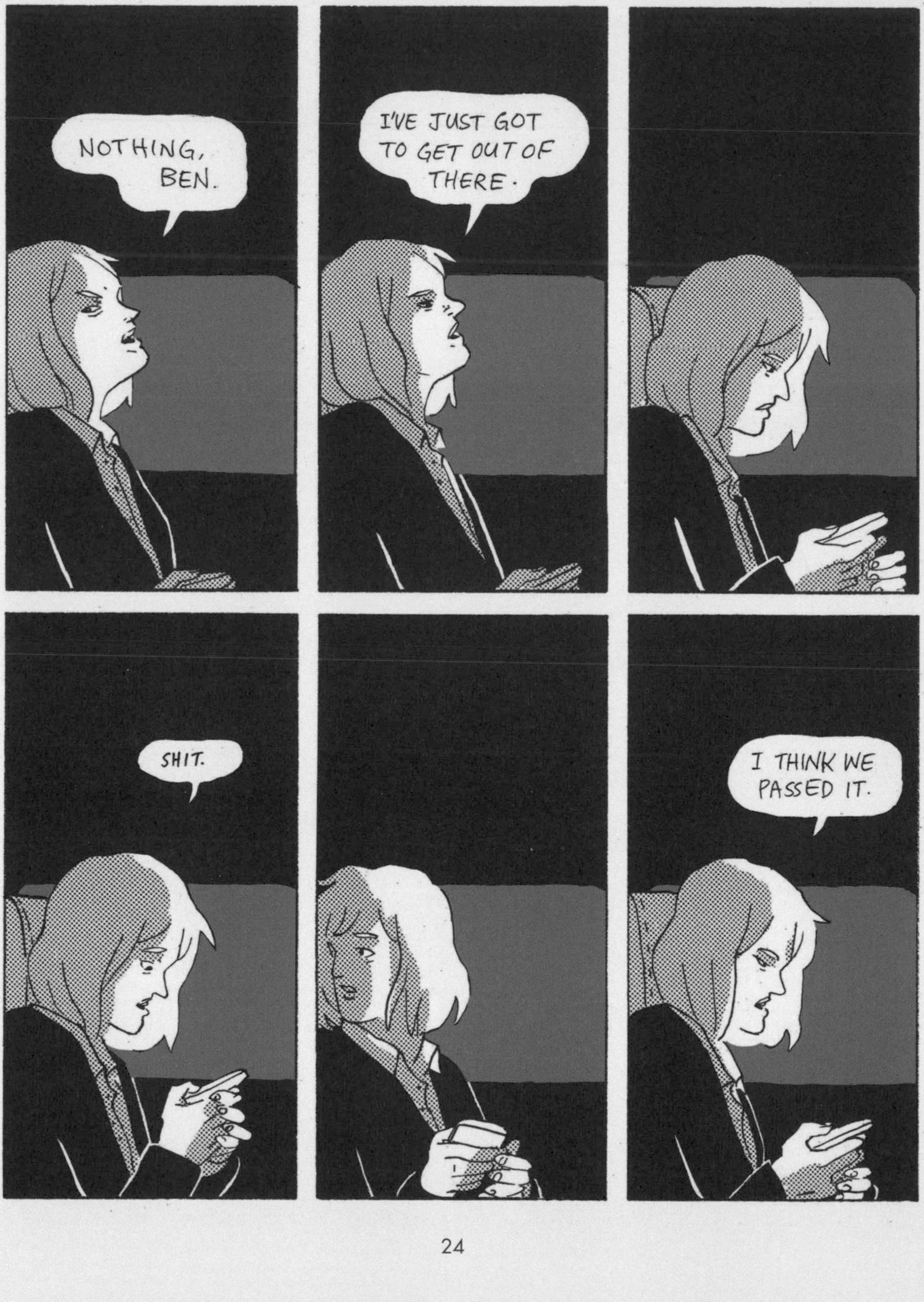
NOTHING, BEN.
I'VE JUST GOT TO GET OUT OF THERE.
SHIT.
I THINK WE PASSED IT.

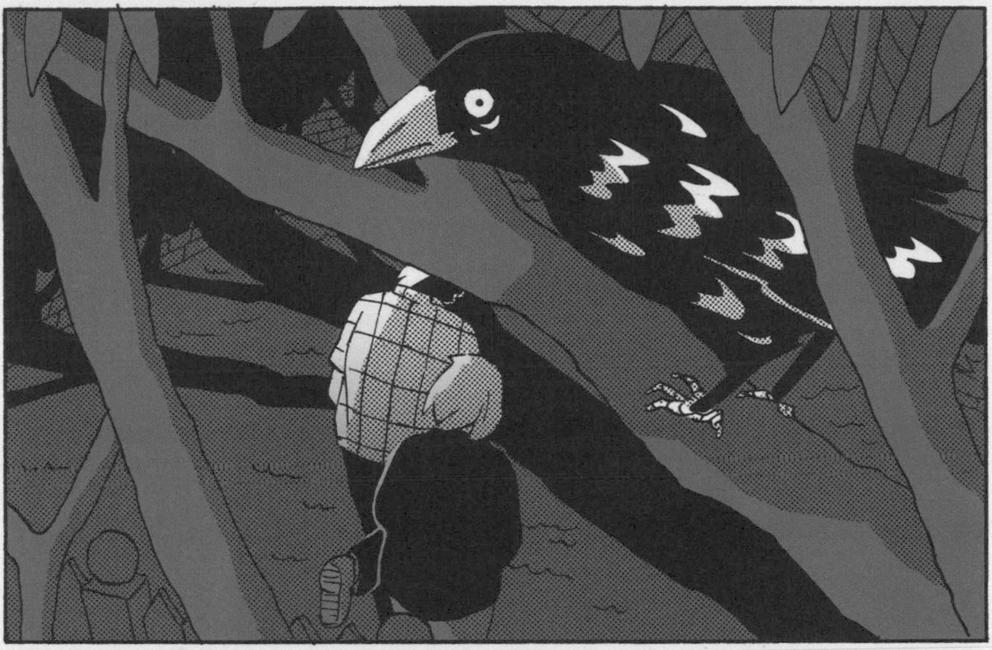

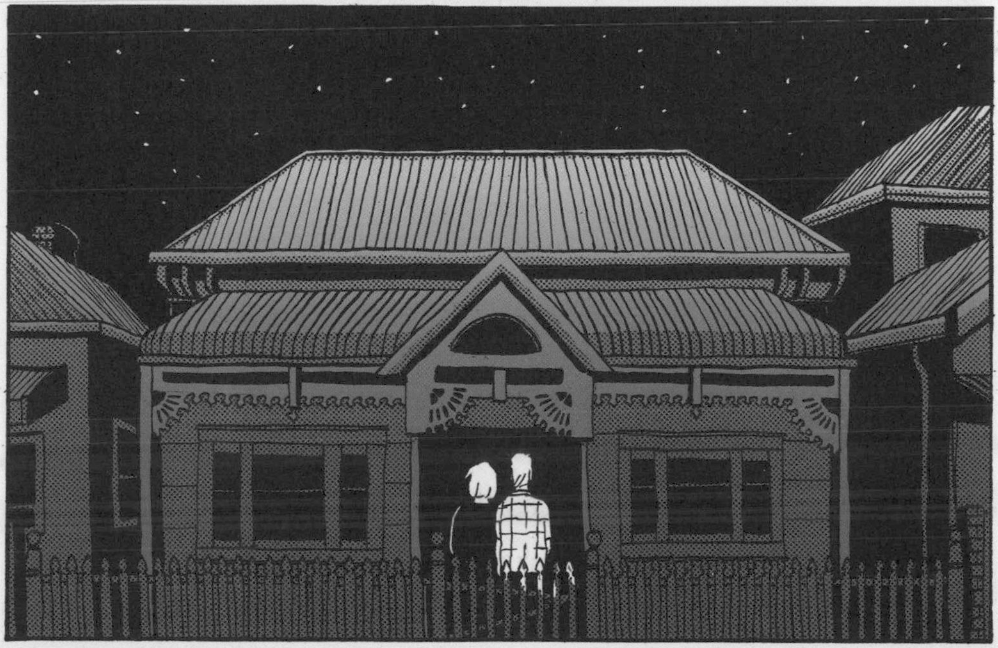

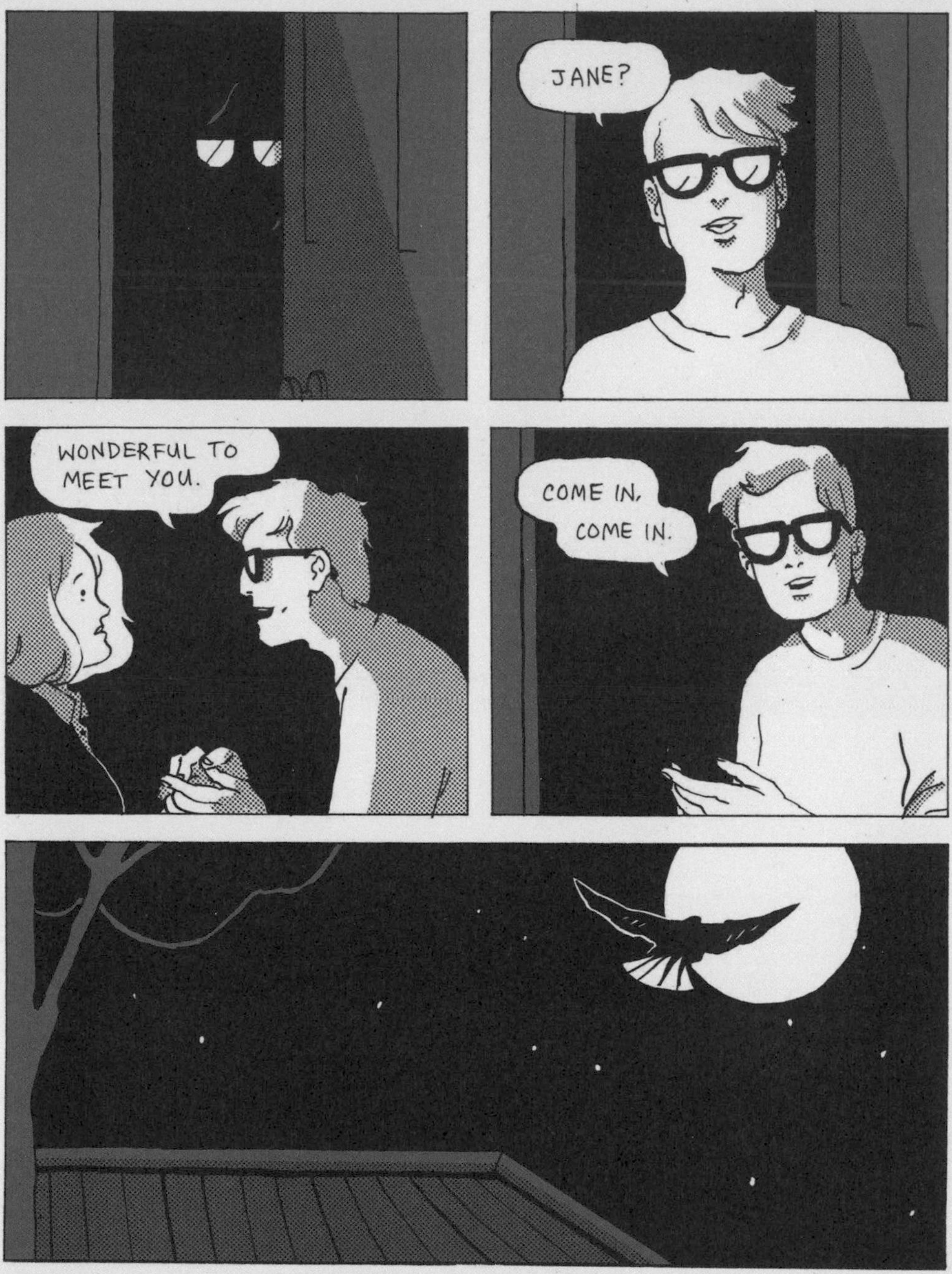
JANE?
WONDERFUL TO MEET YOU.
COME IN, COME IN.

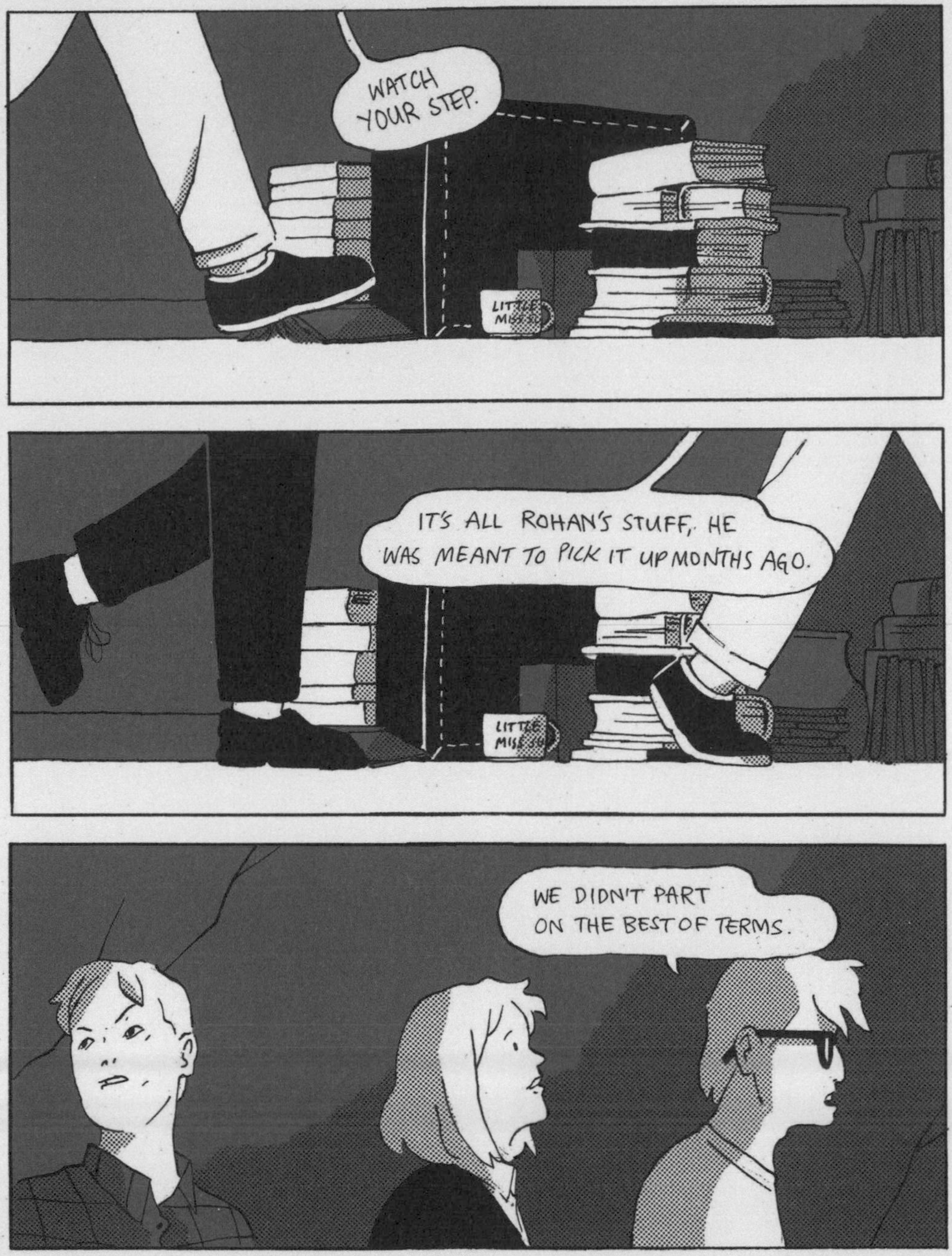
WATCH YOUR STEP.
IT'S ALL ROHAN'S STUFF, HE WAS MEANT TO PICK IT UP MONTHS AGO.
WE DIDN'T PART ON THE BEST OF TERMS.

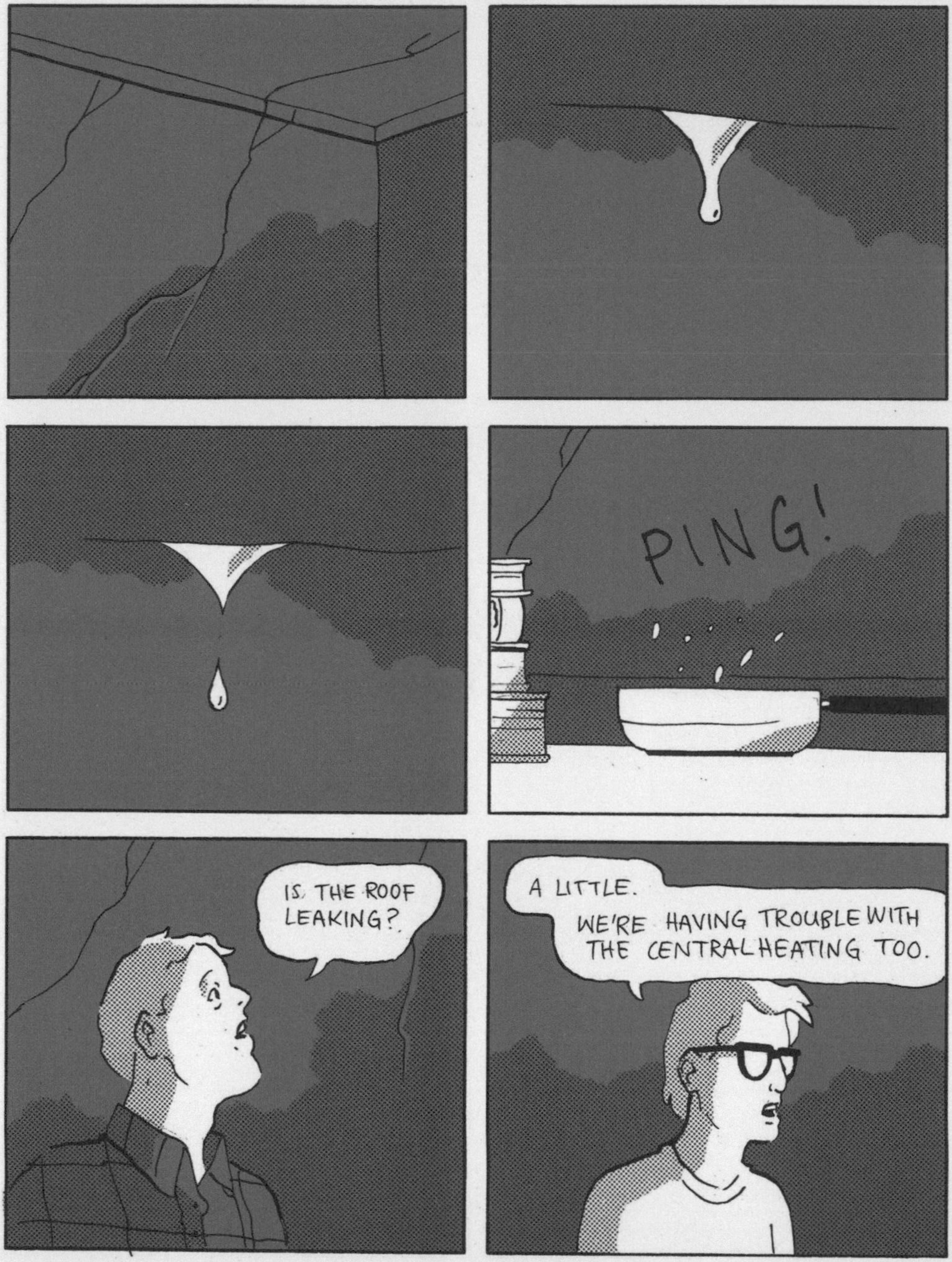
PING!
IS THE ROOF LEAKING?
A LITTLE.
WE'RE HAVING TROUBLE WITH THE CENTRAL HEATING TOO.

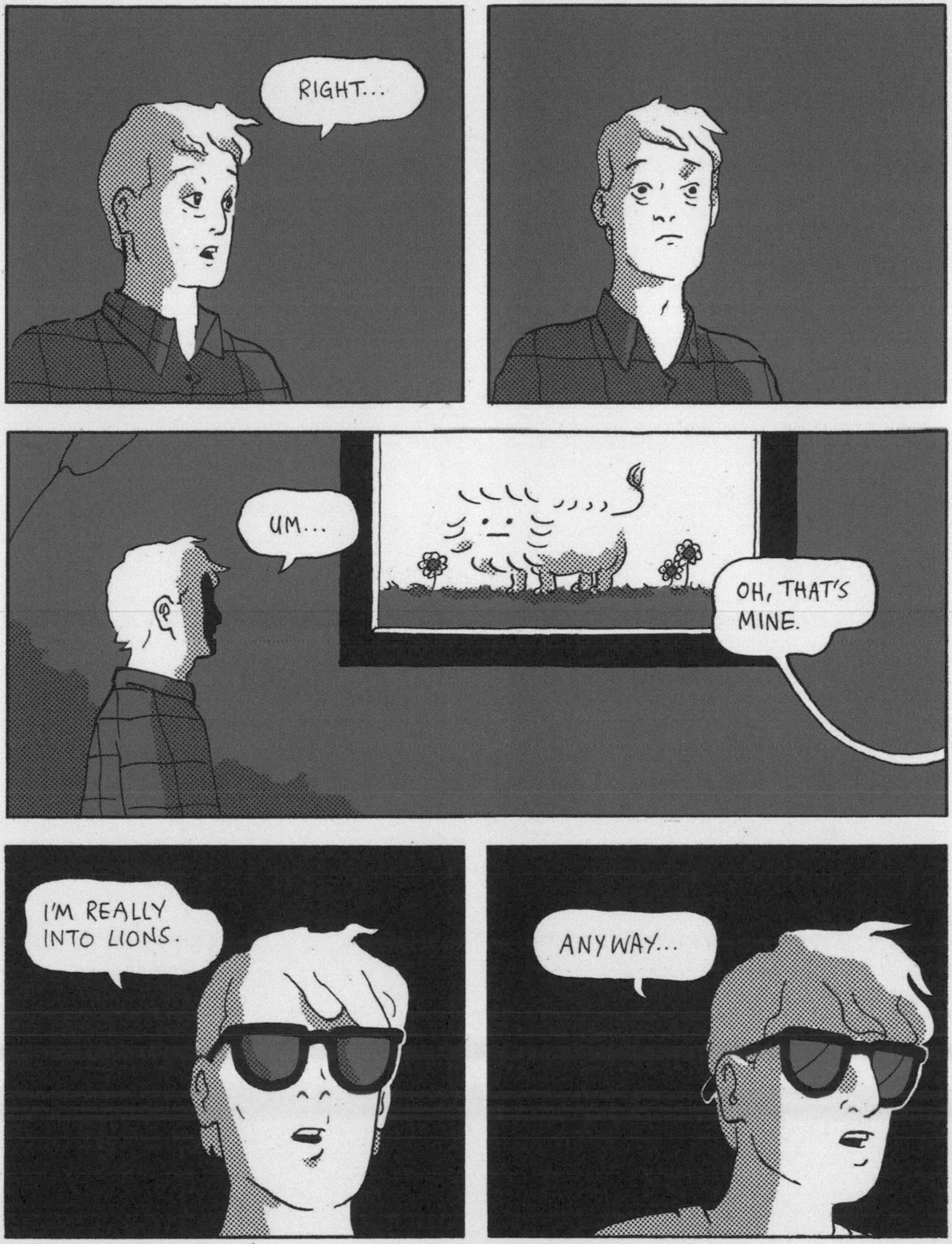
RIGHT...
UM...
OH, THAT'S MINE.
I'M REALLY INTO LIONS.
ANYWAY...

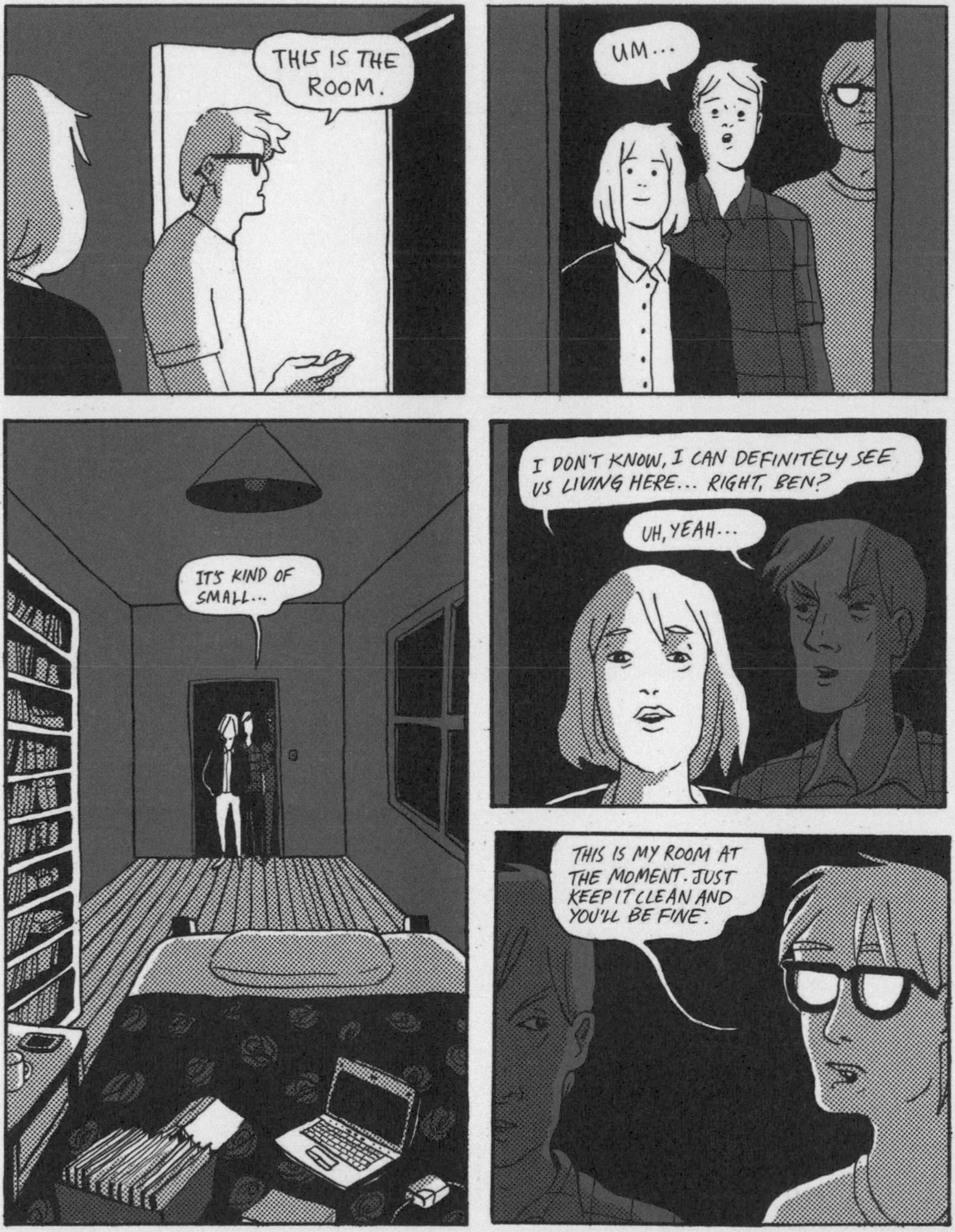
THIS IS THE ROOM.
UM...
IT'S KIND OF SMALL...
I DON'T KNOW, I CAN DEFINITELY SEE US LIVING HERE... RIGHT, BEN?
UH, YEAH...
THIS IS MY ROOM AT THE MOMENT. JUST KEEP IT CLEAN AND YOU'LL BE FINE.

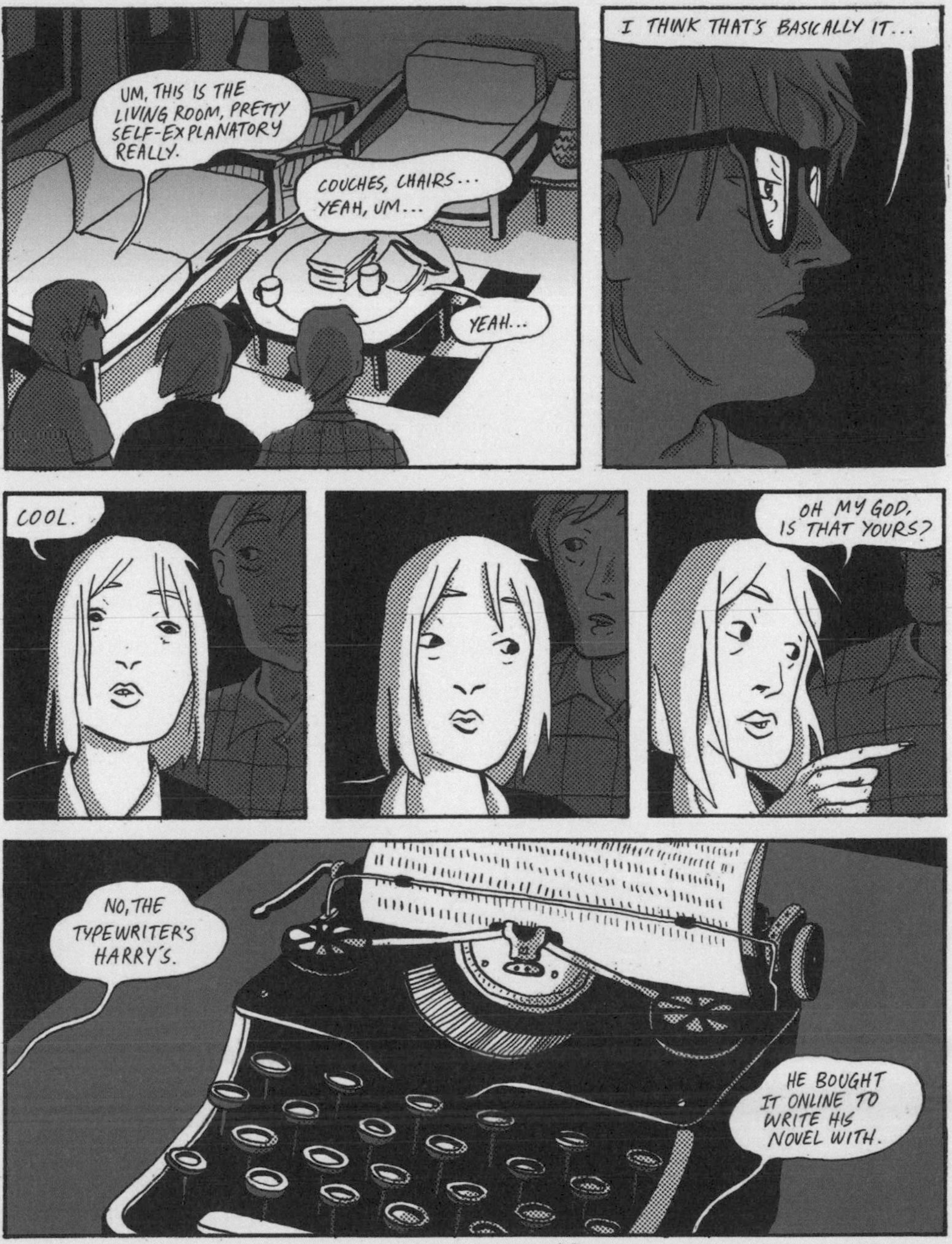
UM, THIS IS THE LIVING ROOM, PRETTY SELF-EXPLANATORY REALLY.
COUCHES, CHAIRS... YEAH, UM...
YEAH...
I THINK THAT'S BASICALLY IT...
COOL.
OH MY GOD, IS THAT YOURS?
NO, THE TYPEWRITER'S HARRY'S.
HE BOUGHT IT ONLINE TO WRITE HIS NOVEL WITH.

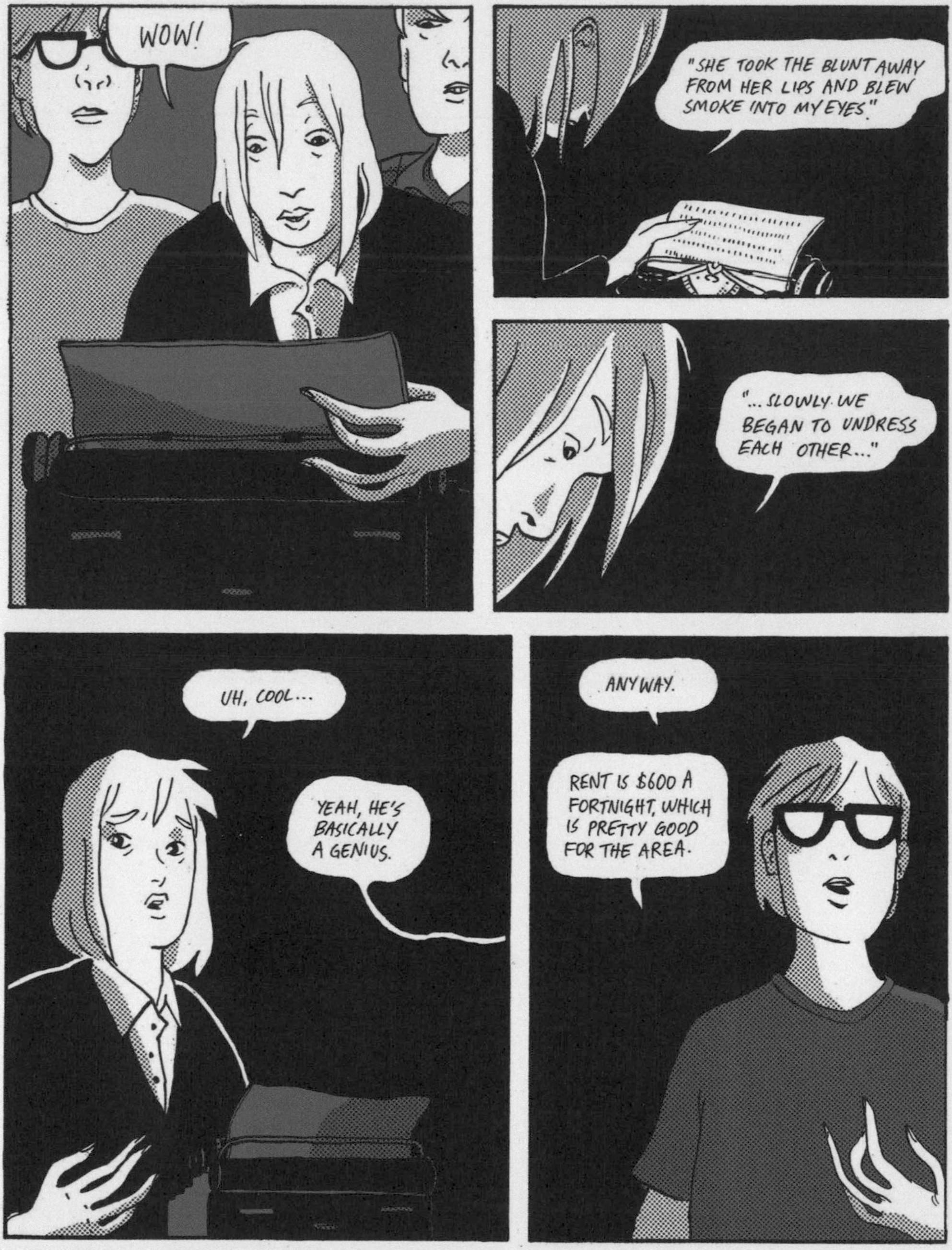
WOW!
"SHE TOOK THE BLUNT AWAY FROM HER LIPS AND BLEW SMOKE INTO MY EYES."
"... SLOWLY WE BEGAN TO UNDRESS EACH OTHER..."
UH, COOL...
YEAH, HE'S BASICALLY A GENIUS.
ANYWAY.
RENT IS $600 A FORTNIGHT, WHICH IS PRETTY GOOD FOR THE AREA.

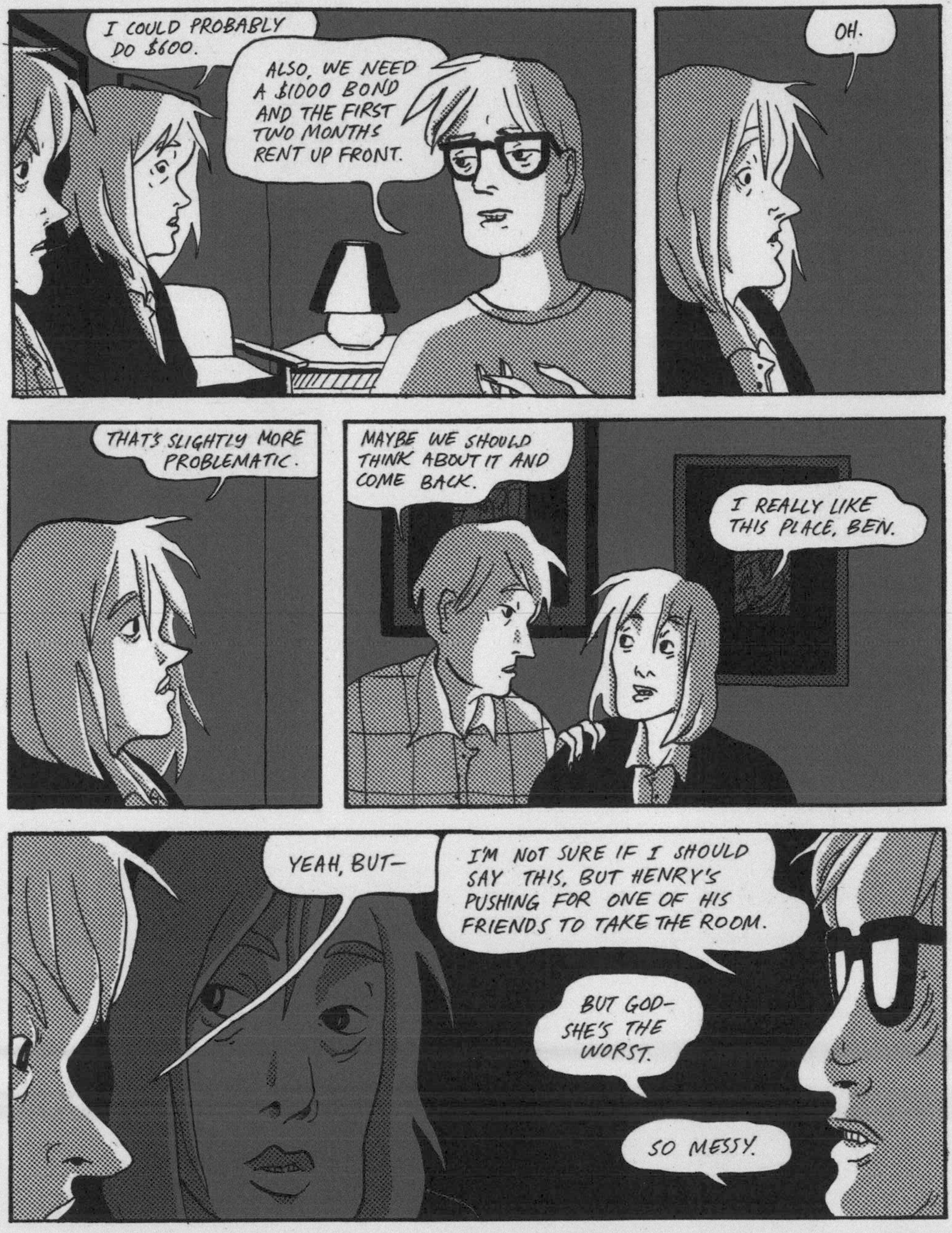
I COULD PROBABLY DO $600.
ALSO, WE NEED A $1000 BOND AND THE FIRST TWO MONTHS RENT UP FRONT.
OH.
THAT'S SLIGHTLY MORE PROBLEMATIC.
MAYBE WE SHOULD THINK ABOUT IT AND COME BACK.
I REALLY LIKE THIS PLACE, BEN.
YEAH, BUT—
I'M NOT SURE IF I SHOULD SAY THIS, BUT HENRY'S PUSHING FOR ONE OF HIS FRIENDS TO TAKE THE ROOM.
BUT GOD— SHE'S THE WORST.
SO MESSY.

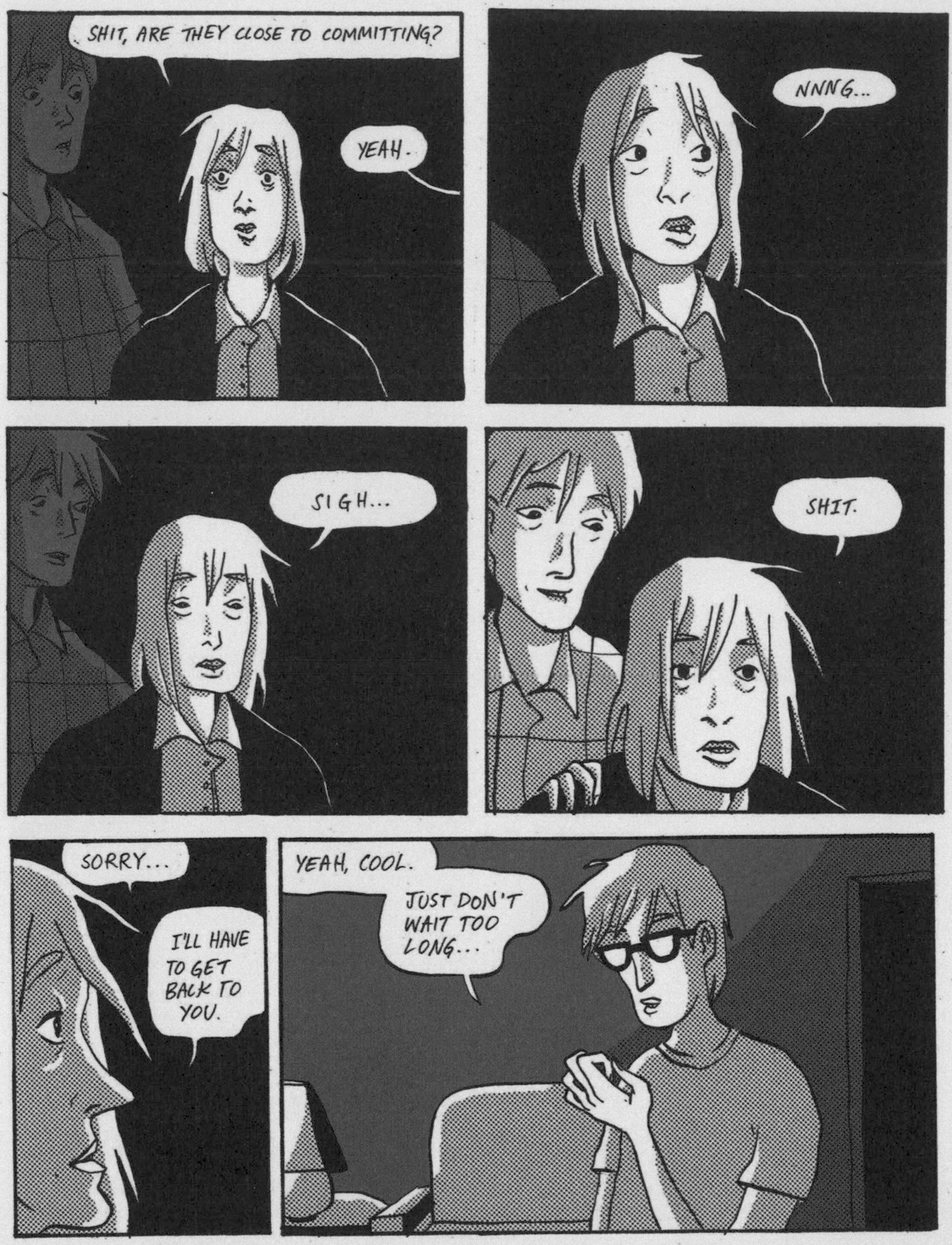
SHIT, ARE THEY CLOSE TO COMMITTING?
YEAH.
NNNG...
SIGH...
SHIT.
SORRY...
I'LL HAVE TO GET BACK TO YOU.
YEAH, COOL.
JUST DON'T WAIT TOO LONG...

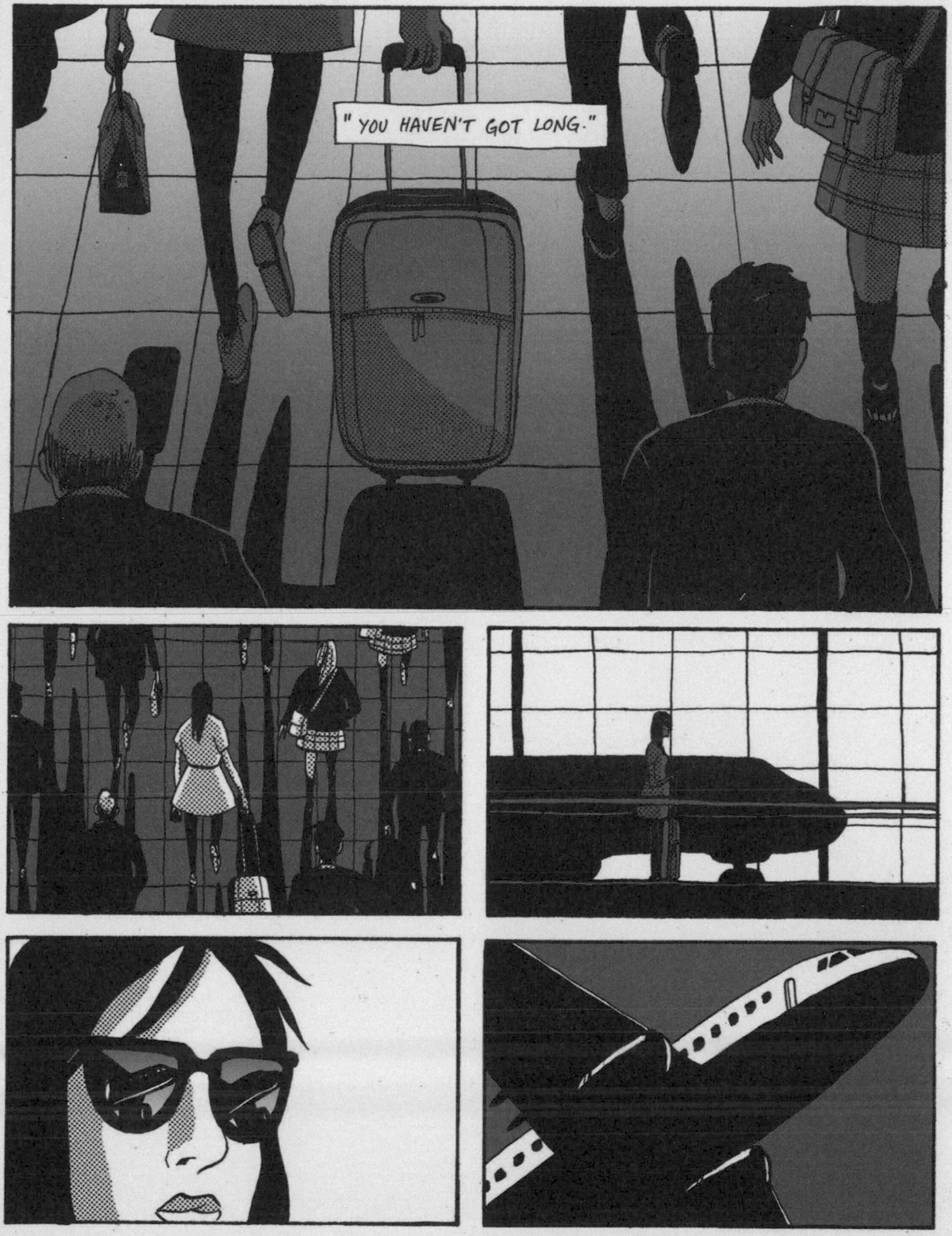
"YOU HAVEN'T GOT LONG."

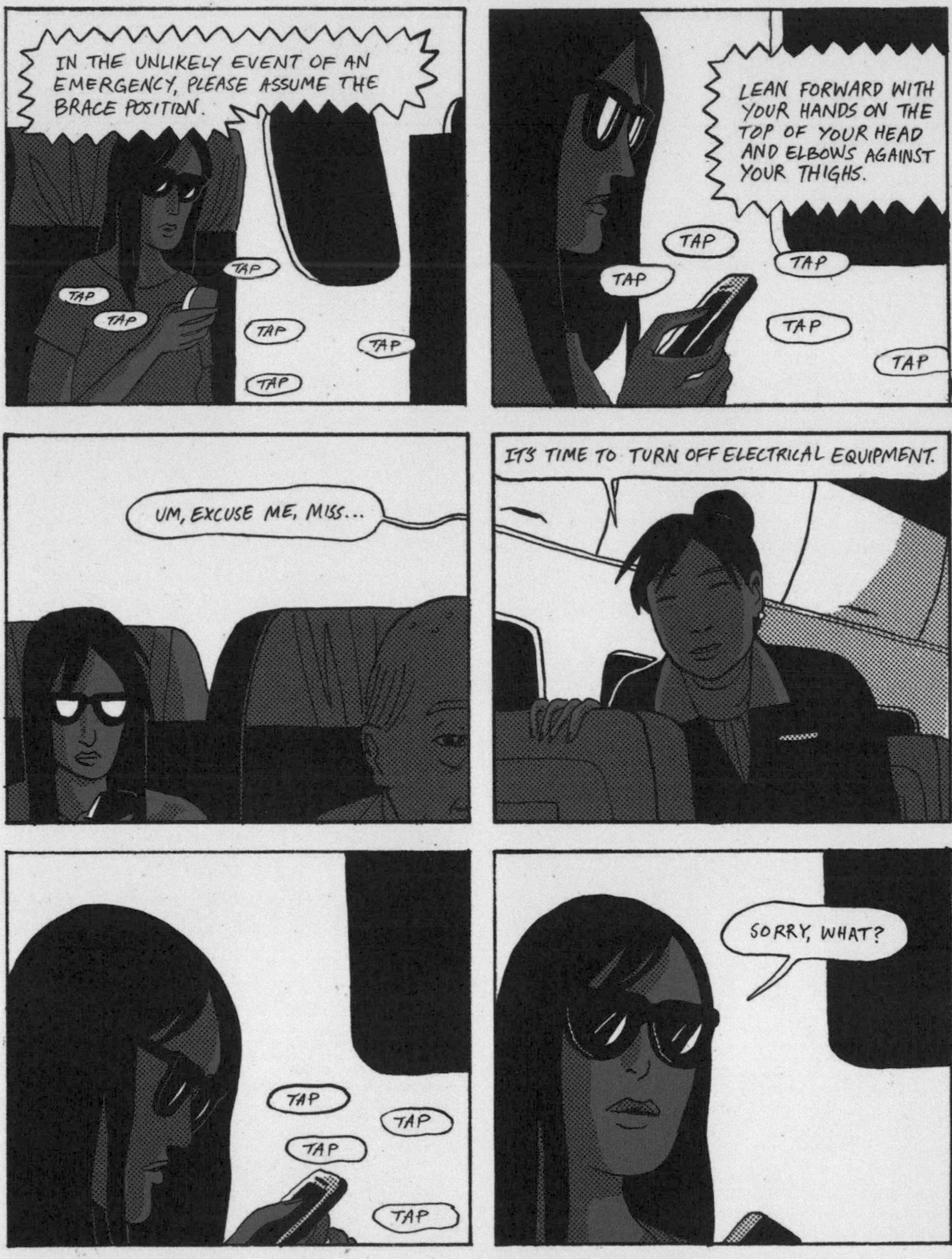
IN THE UNLIKELY EVENT OF AN EMERGENCY, PLEASE ASSUME THE BRACE POSITION.
TAP
TAP
TAP
TAP
TAP
TAP
LEAN FORWARD WITH YOUR HANDS ON THE TOP OF YOUR HEAD AND ELBOWS AGAINST YOUR THIGHS.
TAP
TAP
TAP
TAP
TAP
UM, EXCUSE ME, MISS...
IT'S TIME TO TURN OFF ELECTRICAL EQUIPMENT.
TAP
TAP
TAP
TAP
SORRY, WHAT?

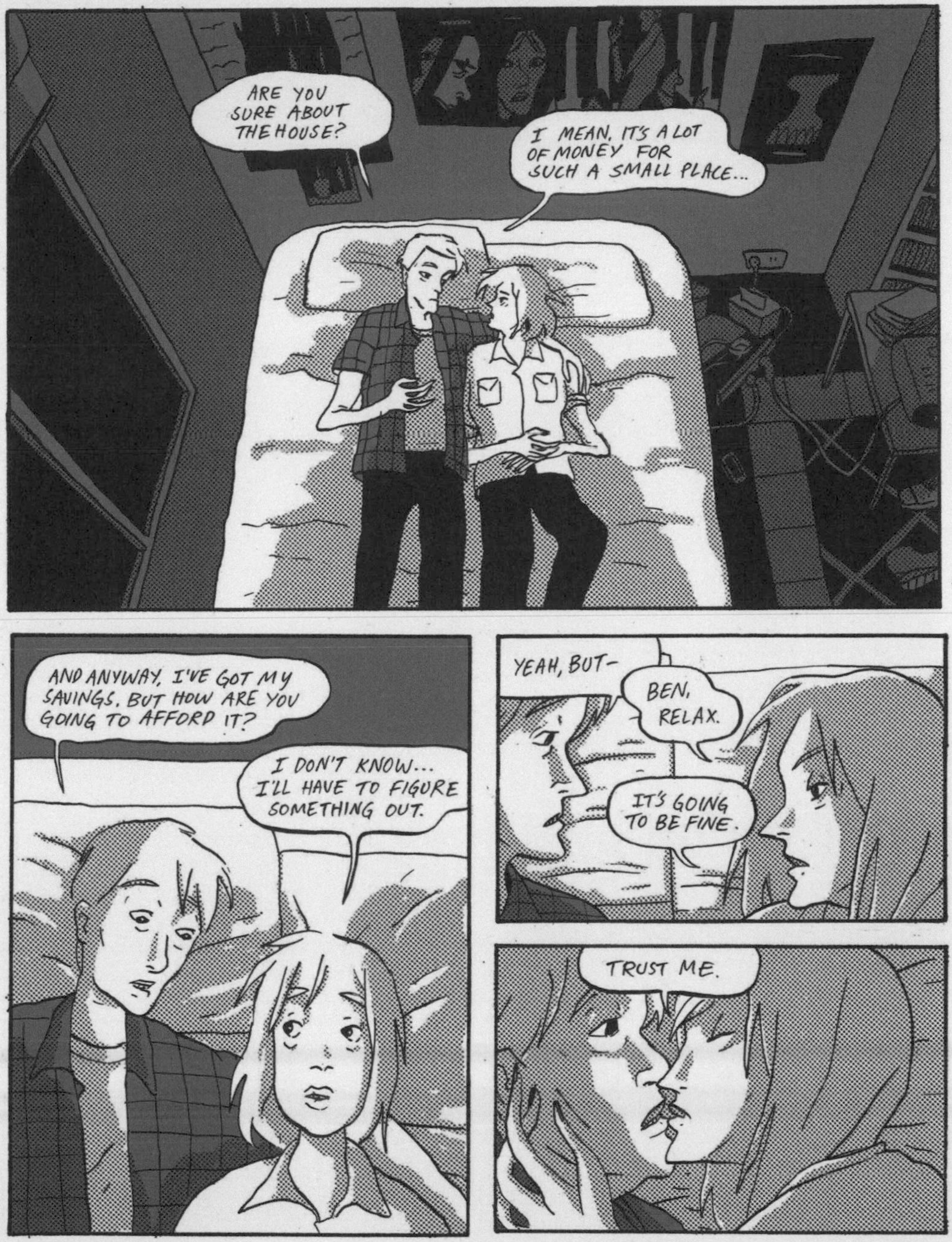
ARE YOU SURE ABOUT THE HOUSE?
I MEAN, IT'S A LOT OF MONEY FOR SUCH A SMALL PLACE...
AND ANYWAY, I'VE GOT MY SAVINGS. BUT HOW ARE YOU GOING TO AFFORD IT?
I DON'T KNOW... I'LL HAVE TO FIGURE SOMETHING OUT.
YEAH, BUT-
BEN, RELAX.
IT'S GOING TO BE FINE.
TRUST ME.

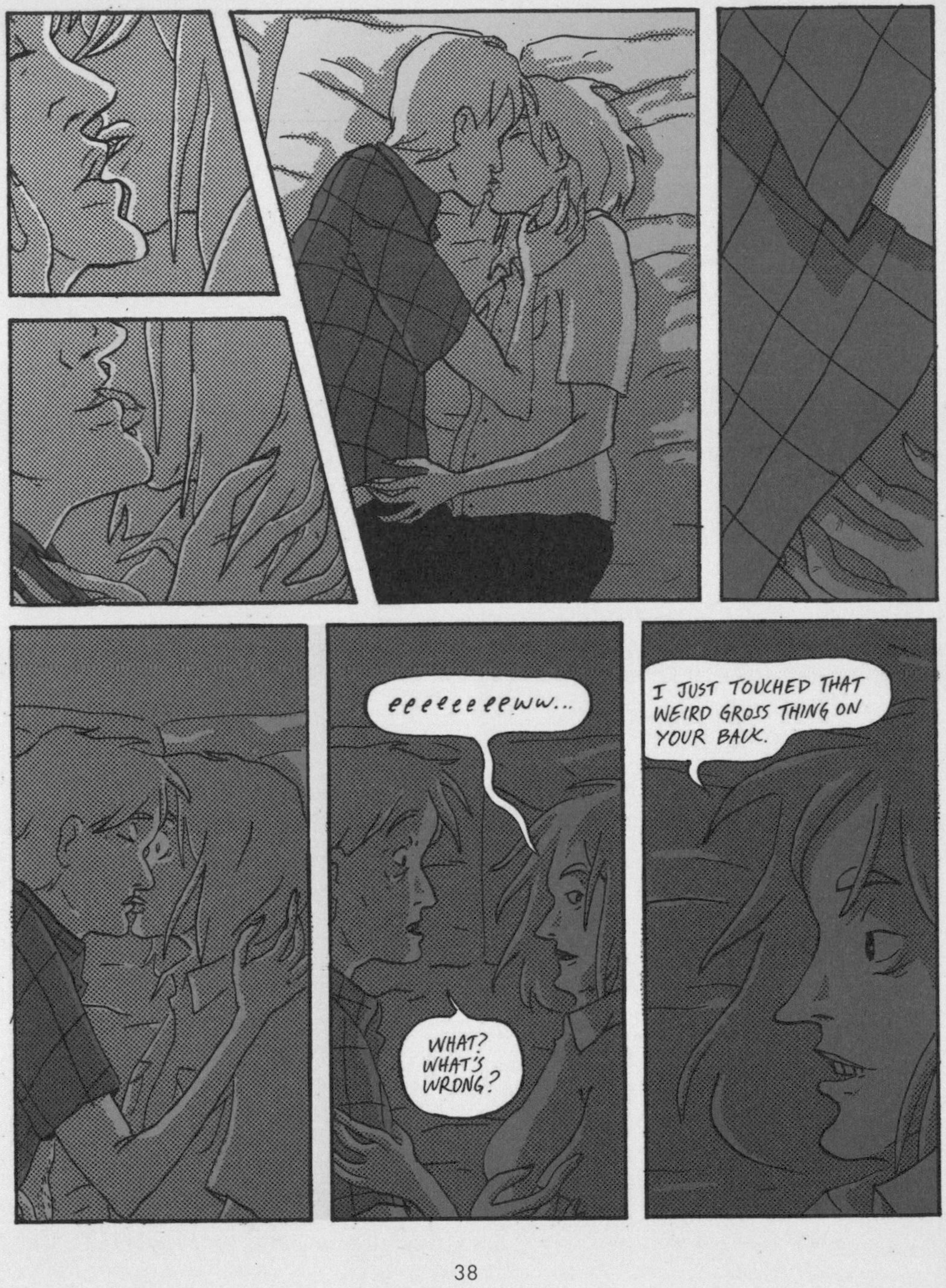
eeeeeeeeww...
WHAT? WHAT'S WRONG?
I JUST TOUCHED THAT WEIRD GROSS THING ON YOUR BACK.

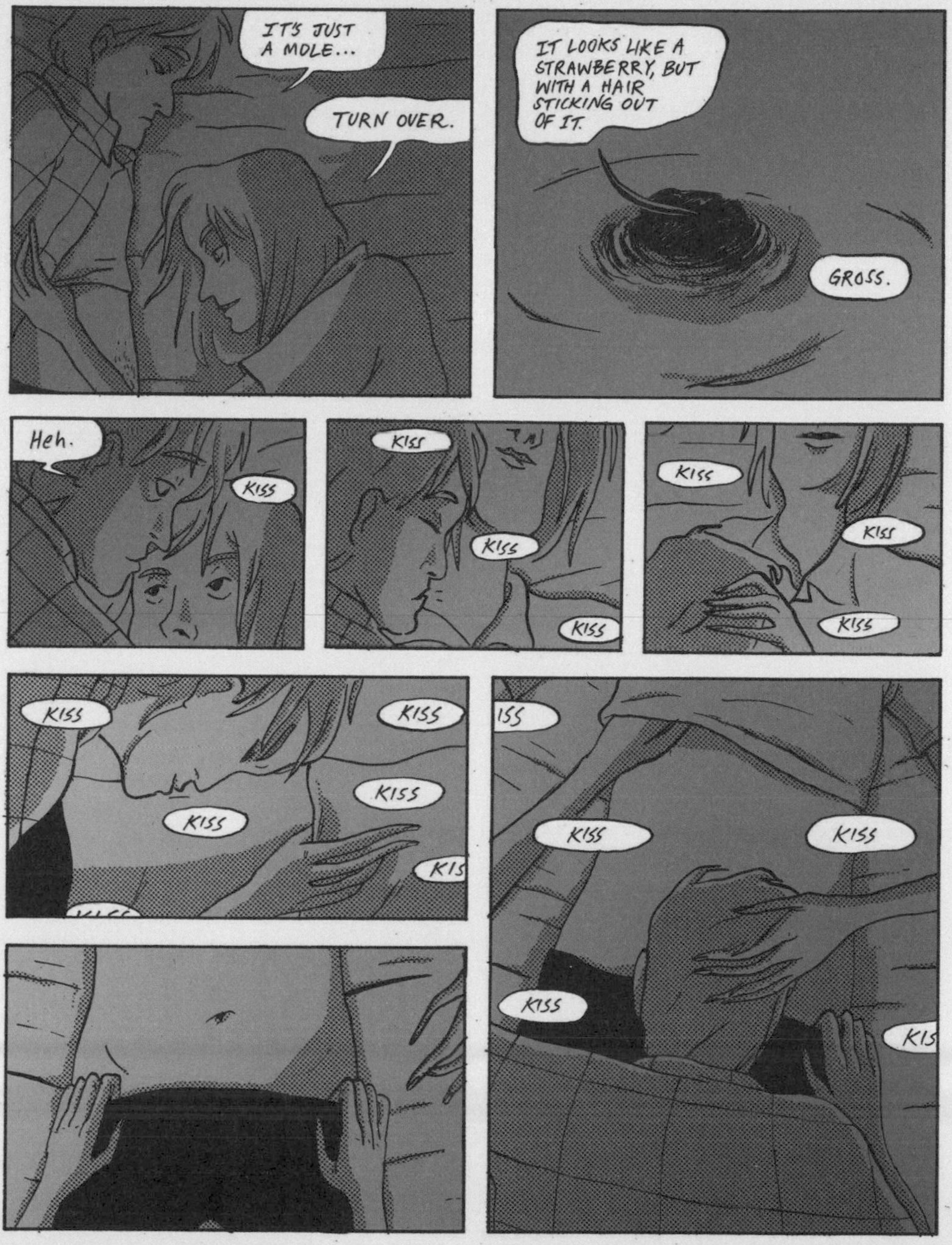
IT'S JUST A MOLE...
TURN OVER.
IT LOOKS LIKE A STRAWBERRY, BUT WITH A HAIR STICKING OUT OF IT.
GROSS.
Heh.
KISS
KISS
KISS
KISS
KISS
KISS
KISS
KISS
KISS
KISS
KISS
KISS
KIS
ISS
KISS
KISS
KISS
KIS

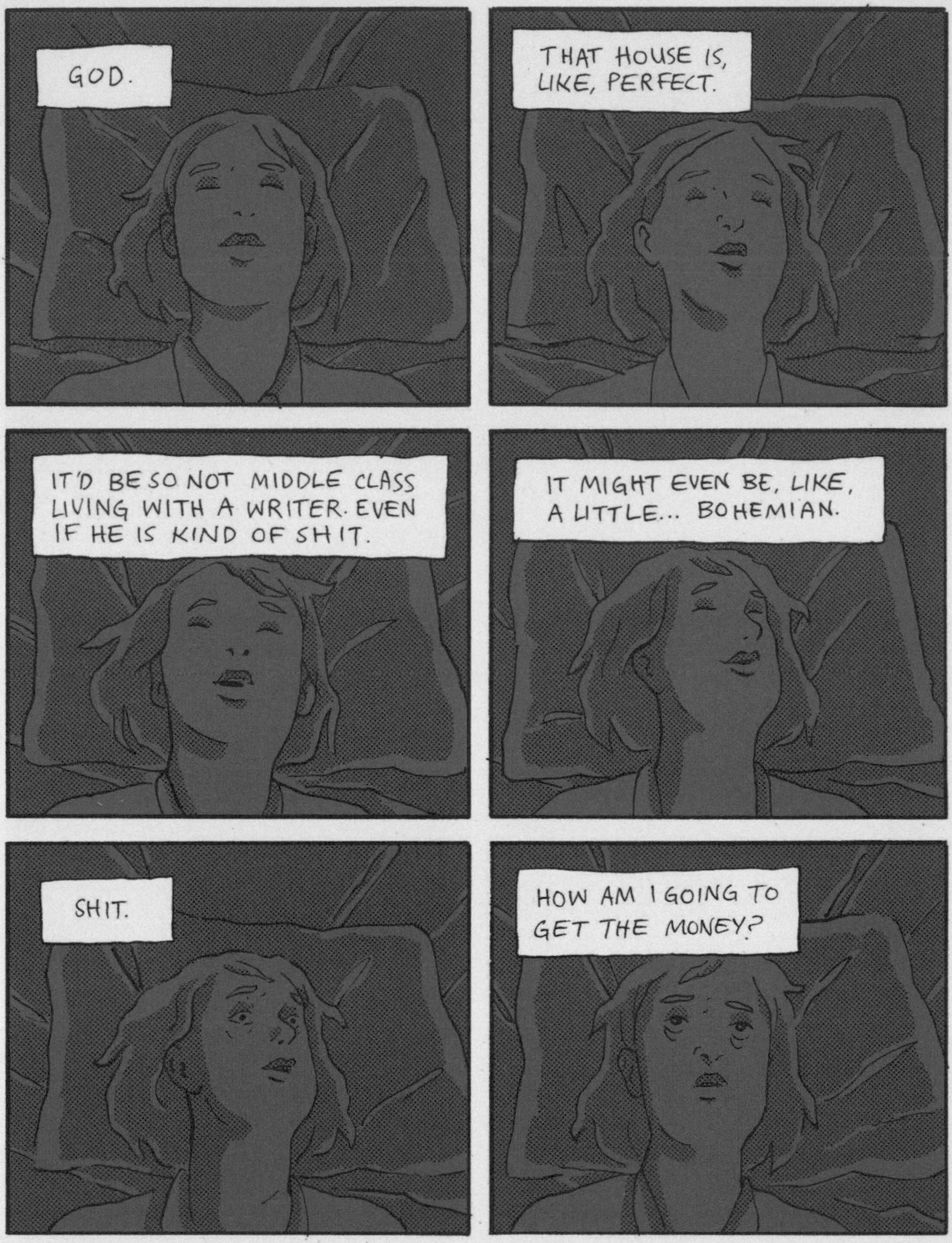
GOD.
THAT HOUSE IS, LIKE, PERFECT.
IT'D BE SO NOT MIDDLE CLASS LIVING WITH A WRITER. EVEN IF HE IS KIND OF SHIT.
IT MIGHT EVEN BE, LIKE, A LITTLE... BOHEMIAN.
SHIT.
HOW AM I GOING TO GET THE MONEY?

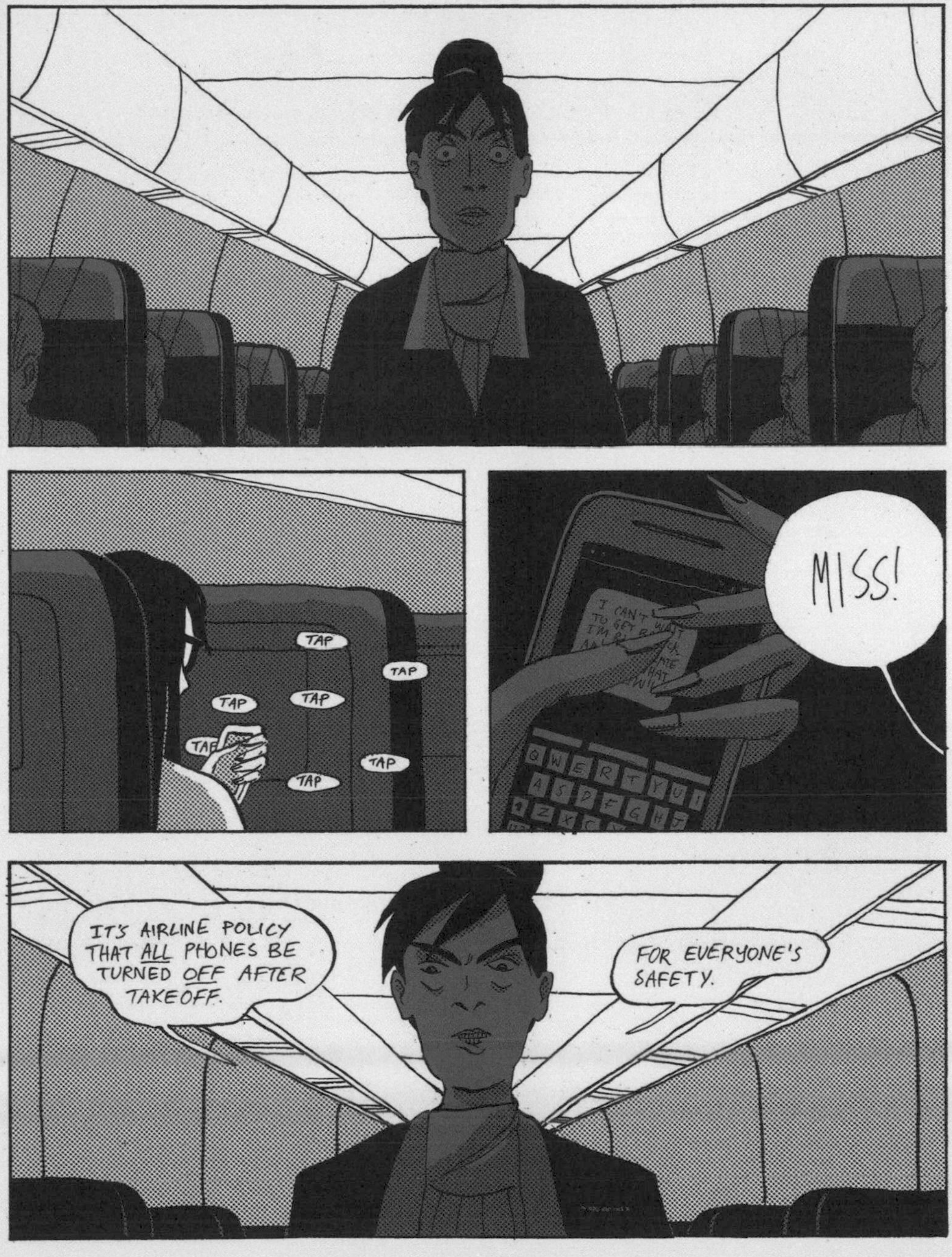
TAP
TAP
TAP
TAP
TAP
TAP
MISS!
IT'S AIRLINE POLICY THAT ALL PHONES BE TURNED OFF AFTER TAKEOFF.
FOR EVERYONE'S SAFETY.

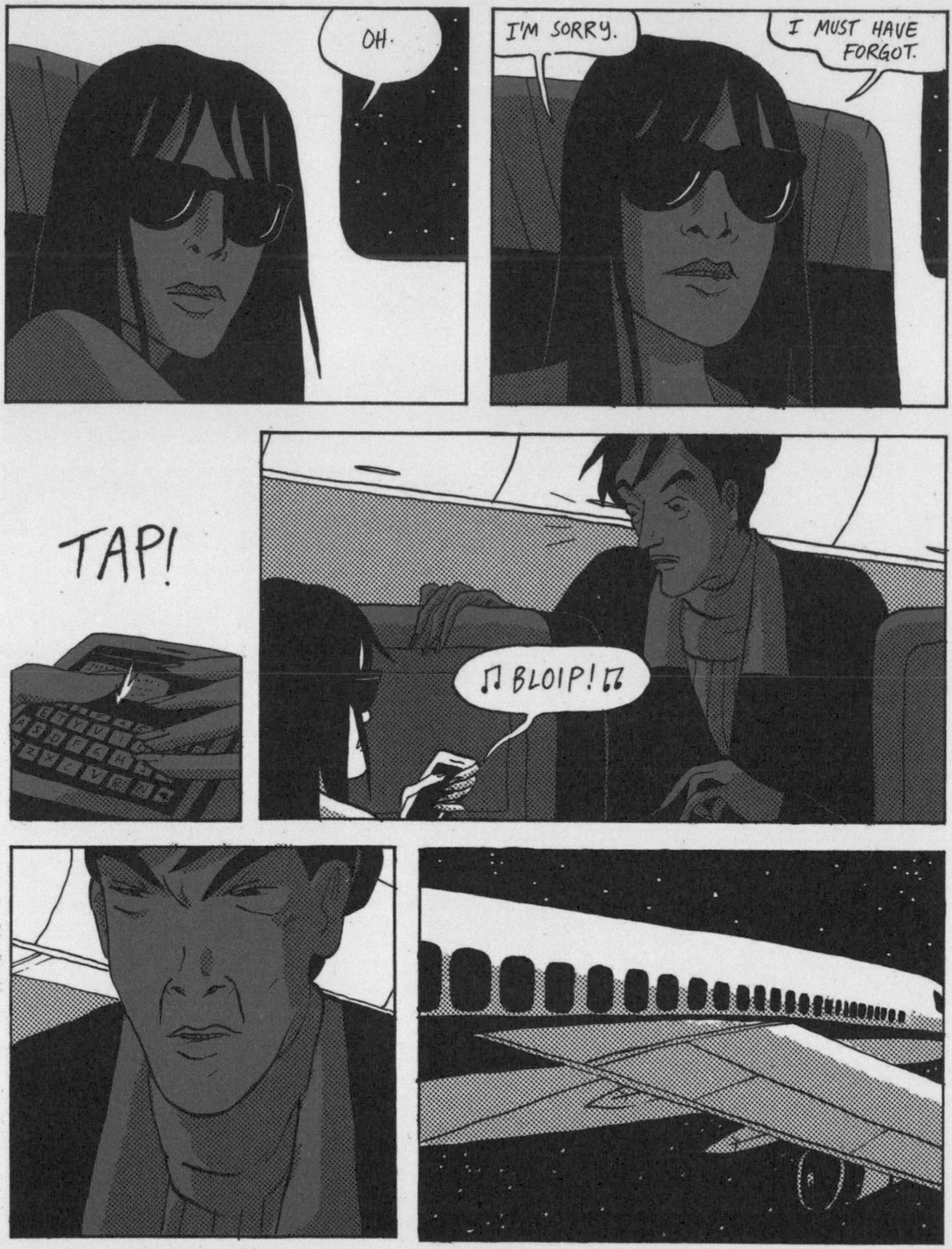
OH.
I'M SORRY.
I MUST HAVE FORGOT.
TAP!
♫ BLOIP! ♫

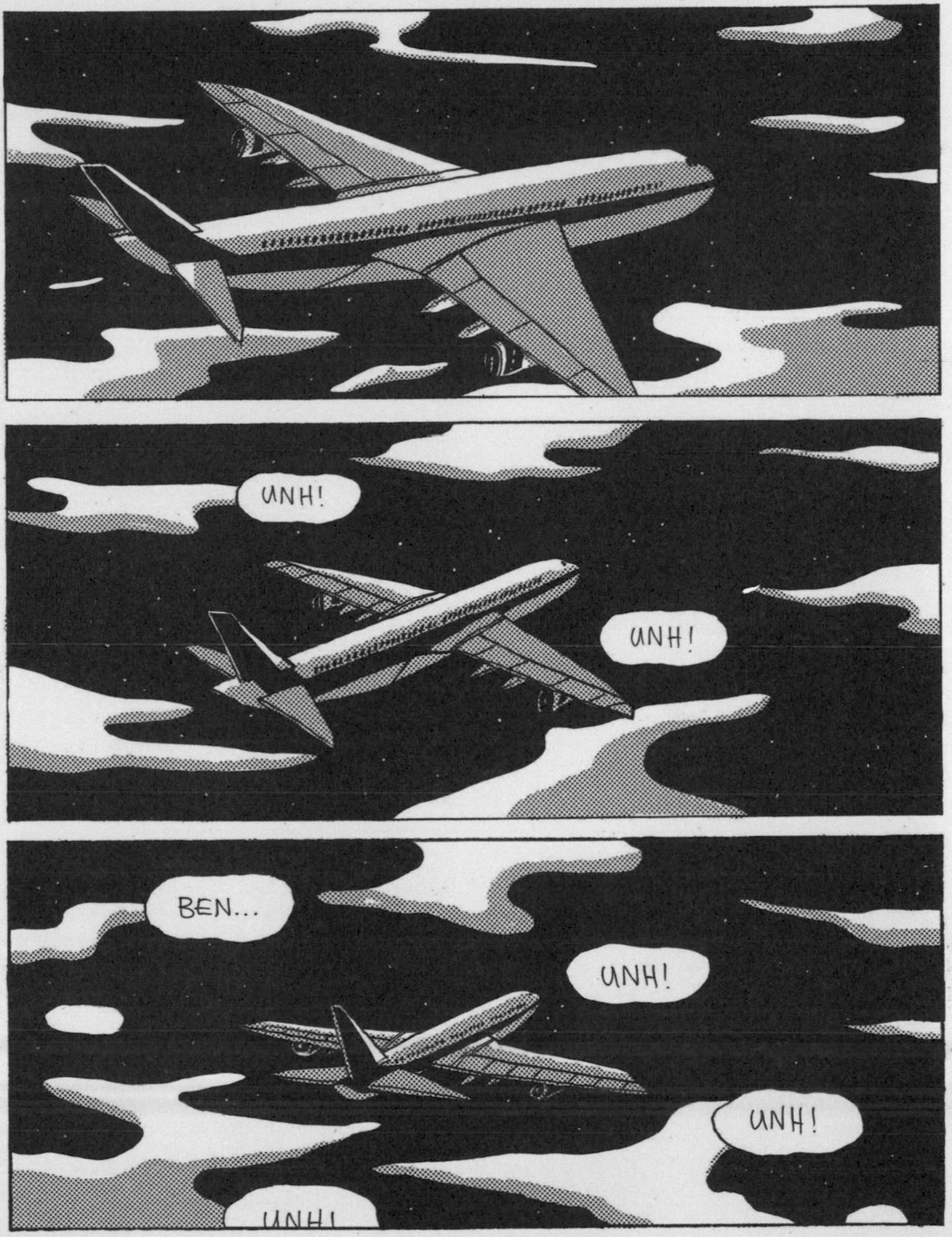
UNH!
UNH!
BEN...
UNH!
UNH!

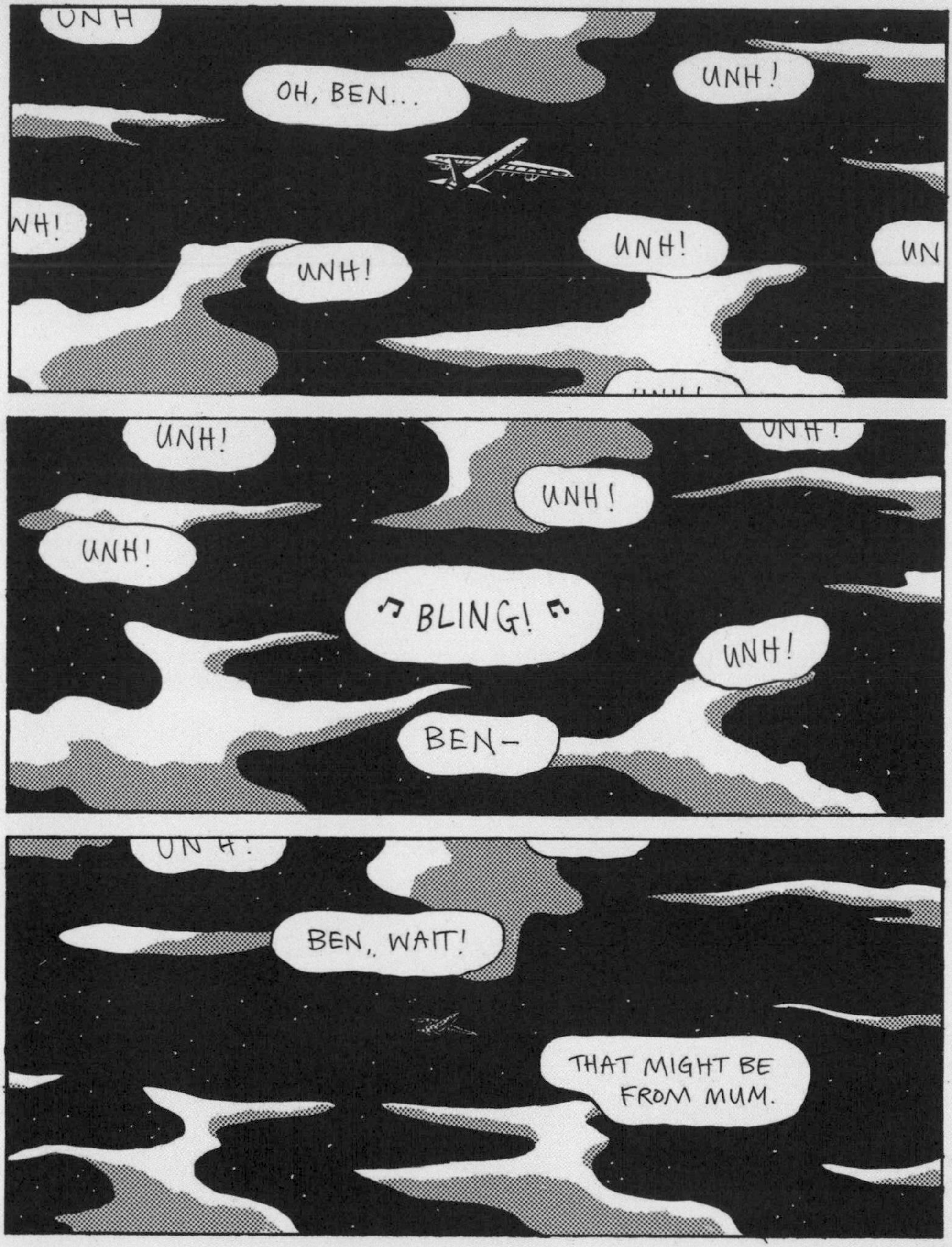
UNH
OH, BEN...
UNH!
UNH!
UNH!
UNH!
UNH!
UNH!
BLING!
UNH!
BEN-
BEN,, WAIT!
THAT MIGHT BE FROM MUM.

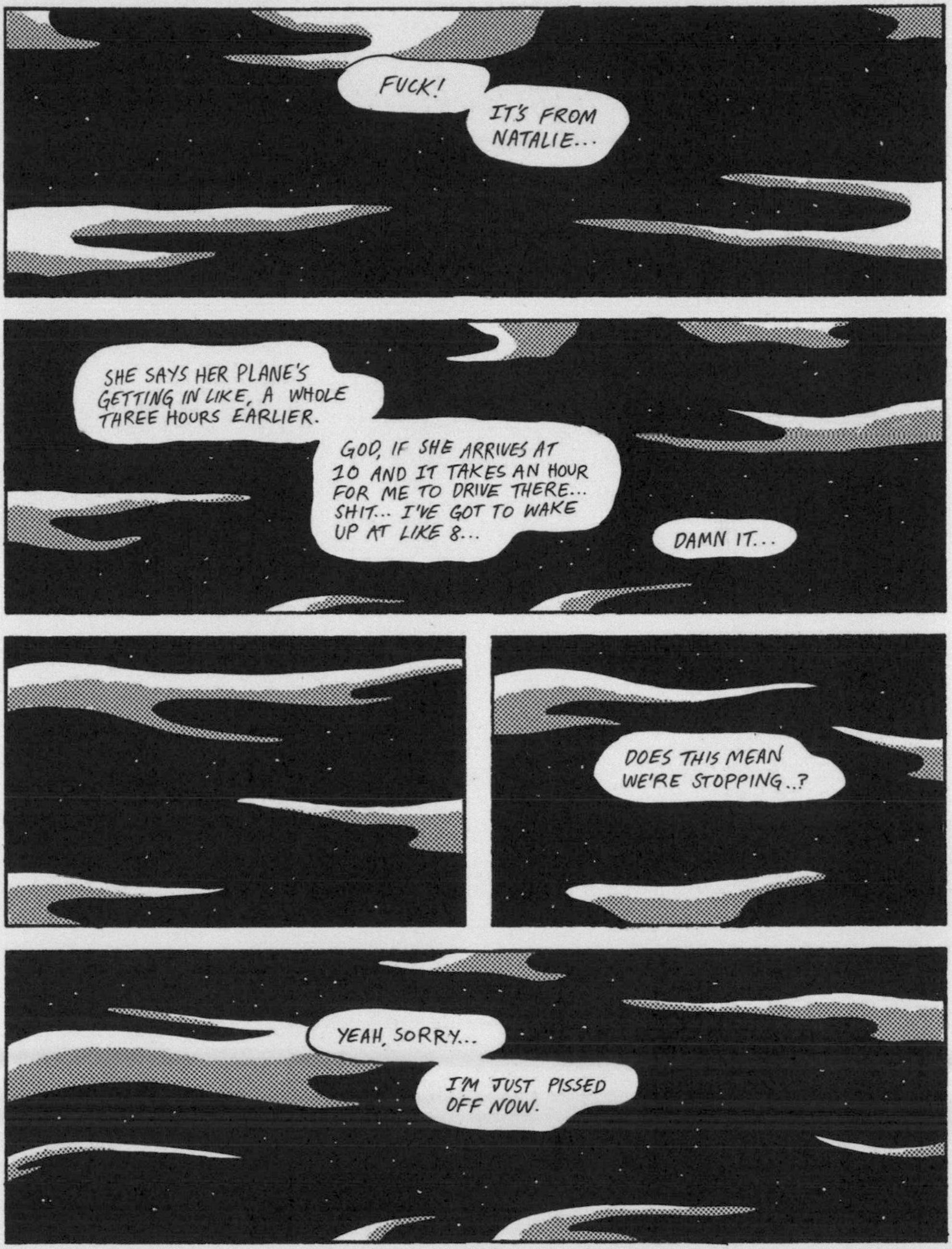
FUCK!
IT'S FROM NATALIE...
SHE SAYS HER PLANE'S GETTING IN LIKE, A WHOLE THREE HOURS EARLIER.
GOD, IF SHE ARRIVES AT 10 AND IT TAKES AN HOUR FOR ME TO DRIVE THERE... SHIT... I'VE GOT TO WAKE UP AT LIKE 8...
DAMN IT...
DOES THIS MEAN WE'RE STOPPING..?
YEAH, SORRY...
I'M JUST PISSED OFF NOW.

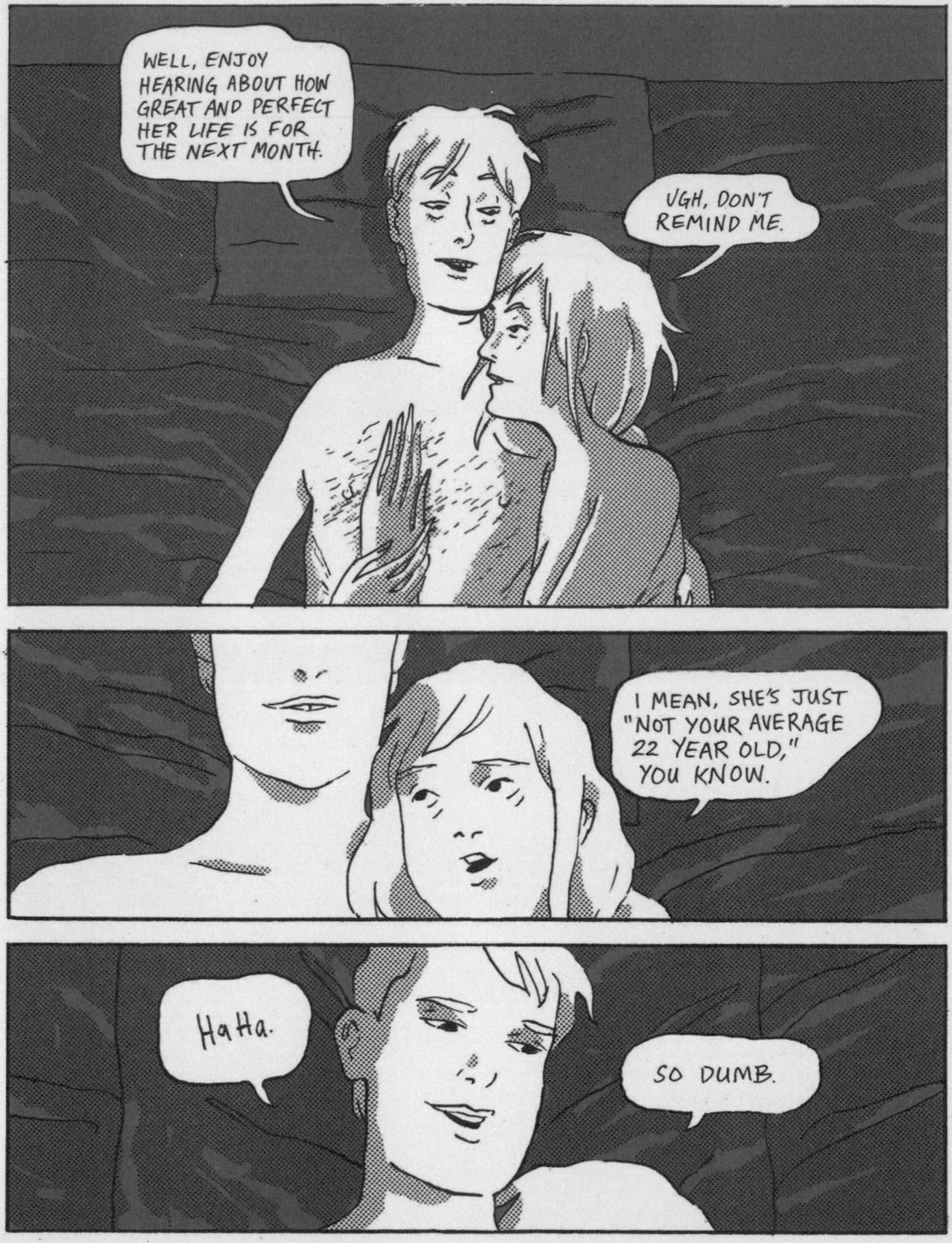
WELL, ENJOY HEARING ABOUT HOW GREAT AND PERFECT HER LIFE IS FOR THE NEXT MONTH.
UGH, DON'T REMIND ME.
I MEAN, SHE'S JUST "NOT YOUR AVERAGE 22 YEAR OLD," YOU KNOW.
HaHa.
SO DUMB.

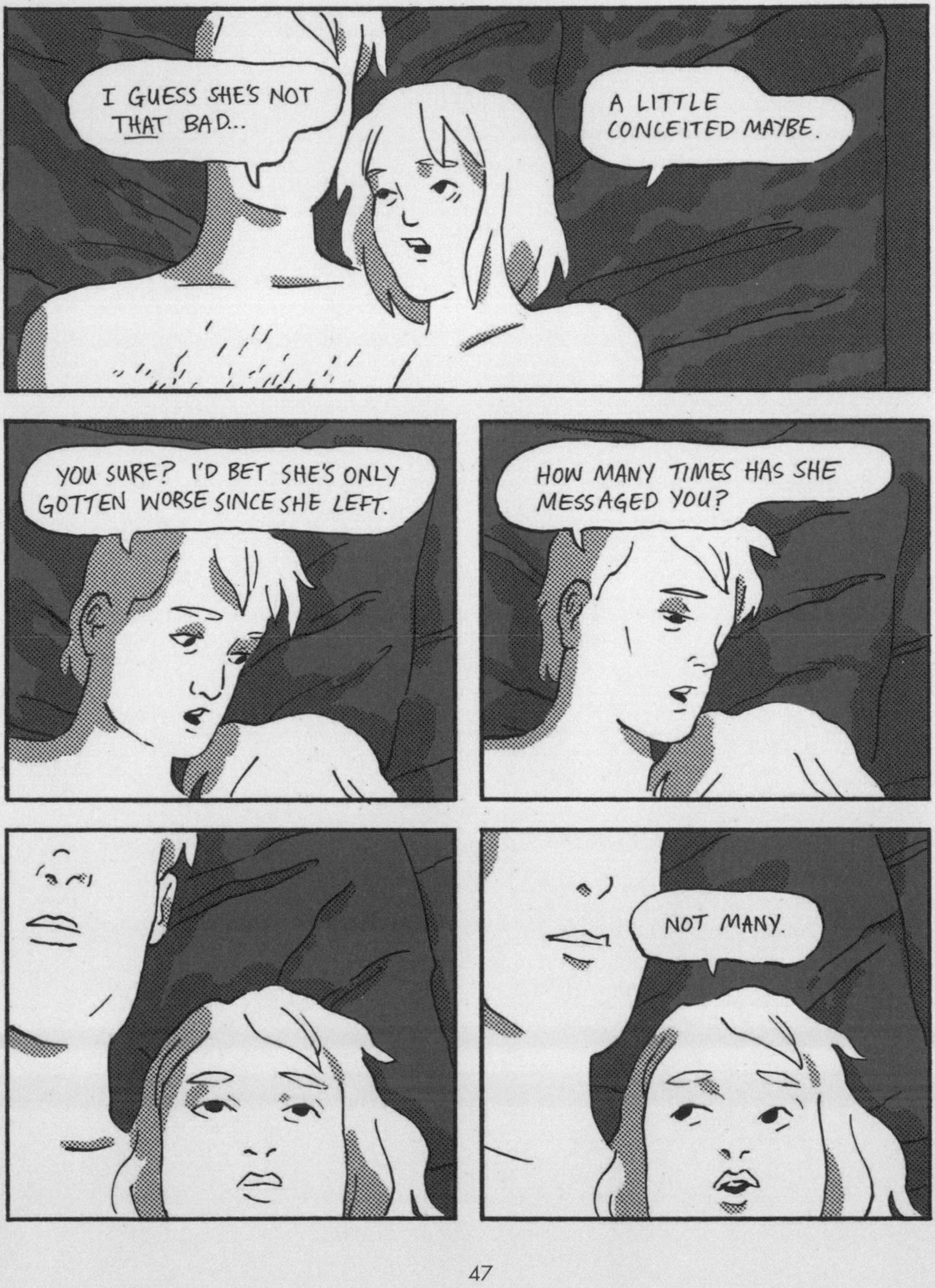
I GUESS SHE'S NOT THAT BAD...
A LITTLE CONCEITED MAYBE.
YOU SURE? I'D BET SHE'S ONLY GOTTEN WORSE SINCE SHE LEFT.
HOW MANY TIMES HAS SHE MESSAGED YOU?
NOT MANY.

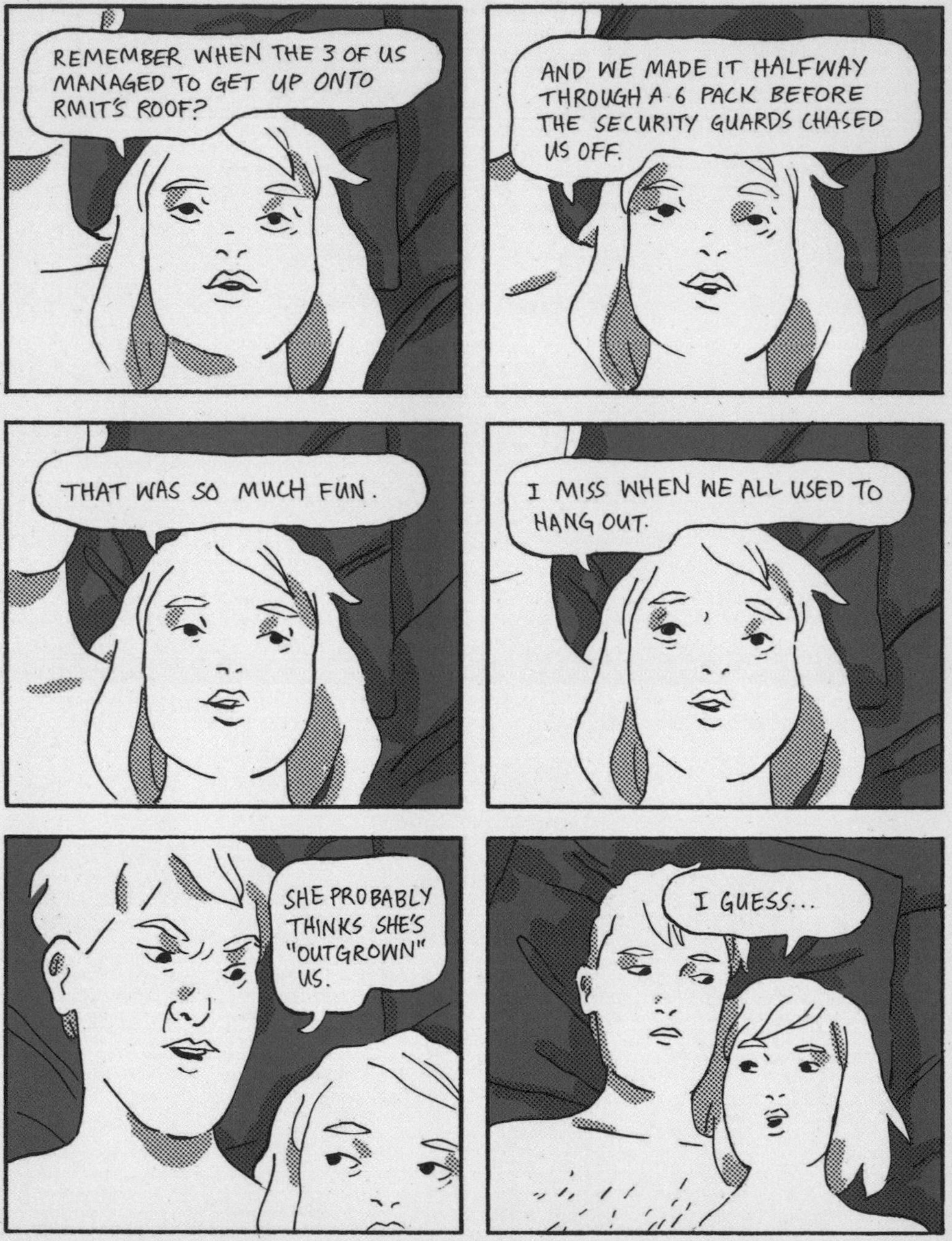
REMEMBER WHEN THE 3 OF US MANAGED TO GET UP ONTO RMIT'S ROOF?
AND WE MADE IT HALFWAY THROUGH A 6 PACK BEFORE THE SECURITY GUARDS CHASED US OFF.
THAT WAS SO MUCH FUN.
I MISS WHEN WE ALL USED TO HANG OUT.
SHE PROBABLY THINKS SHE'S "OUTGROWN" US.
I GUESS...

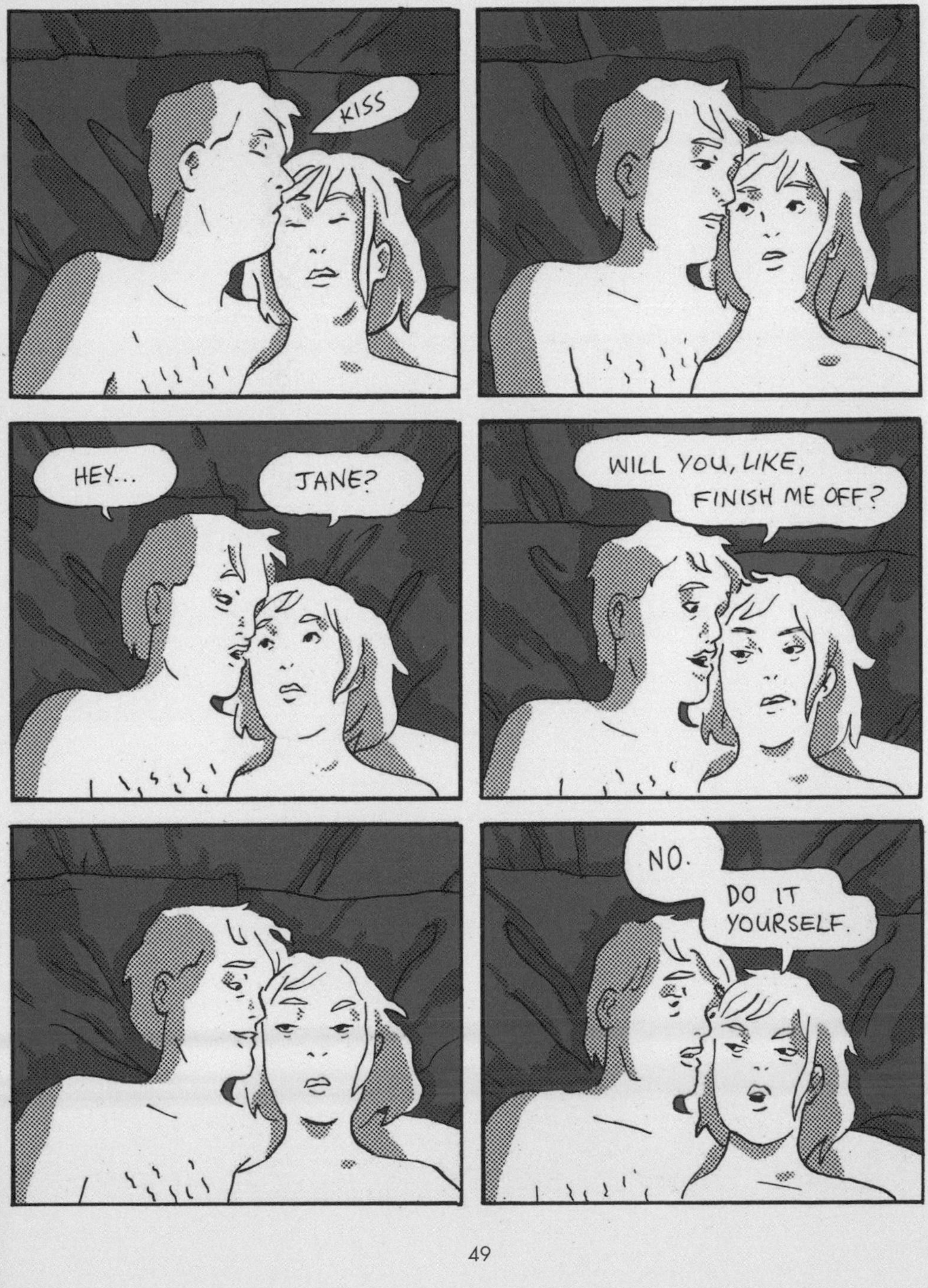
KISS
HEY...
JANE?
WILL YOU, LIKE, FINISH ME OFF?
NO.
DO IT YOURSELF.

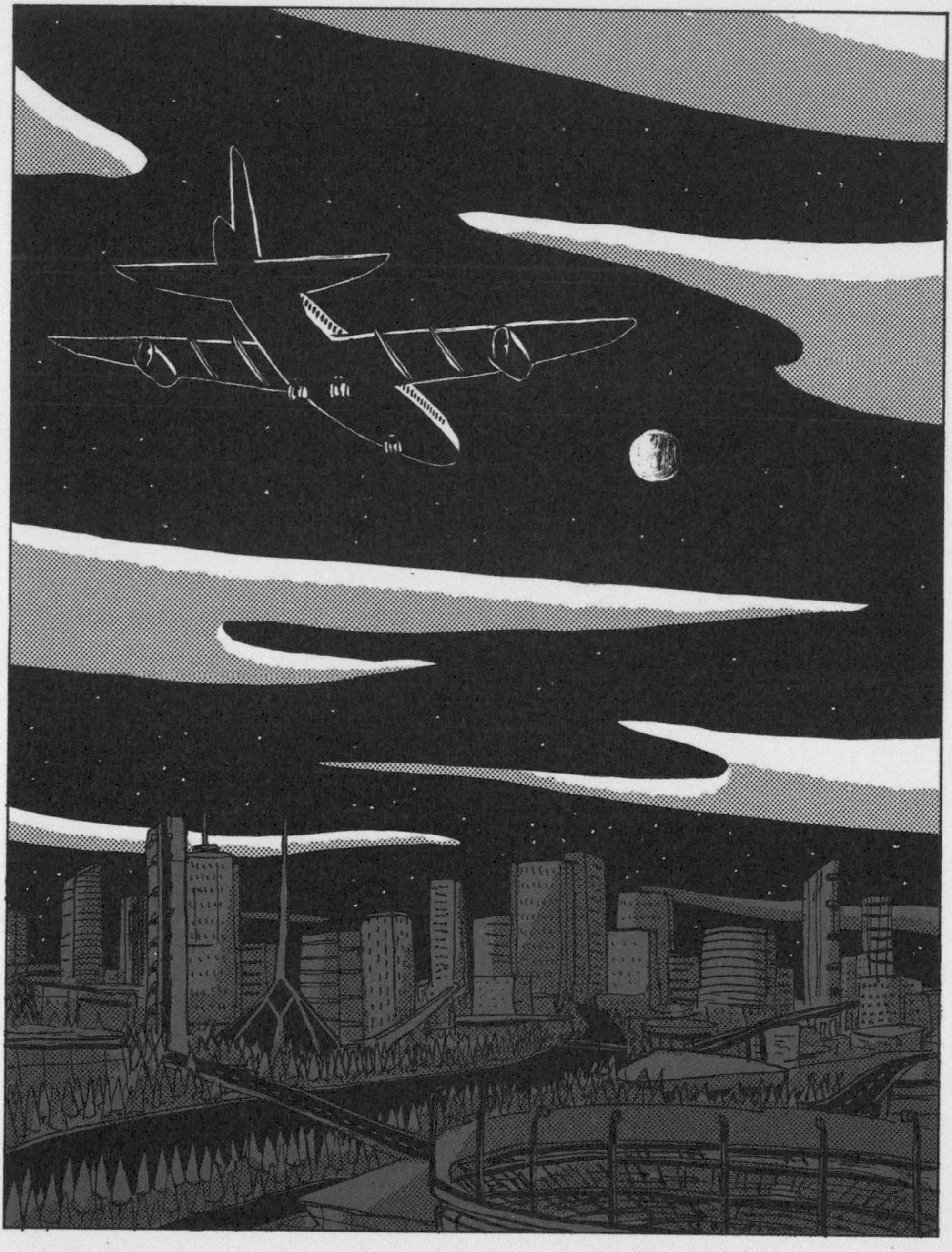

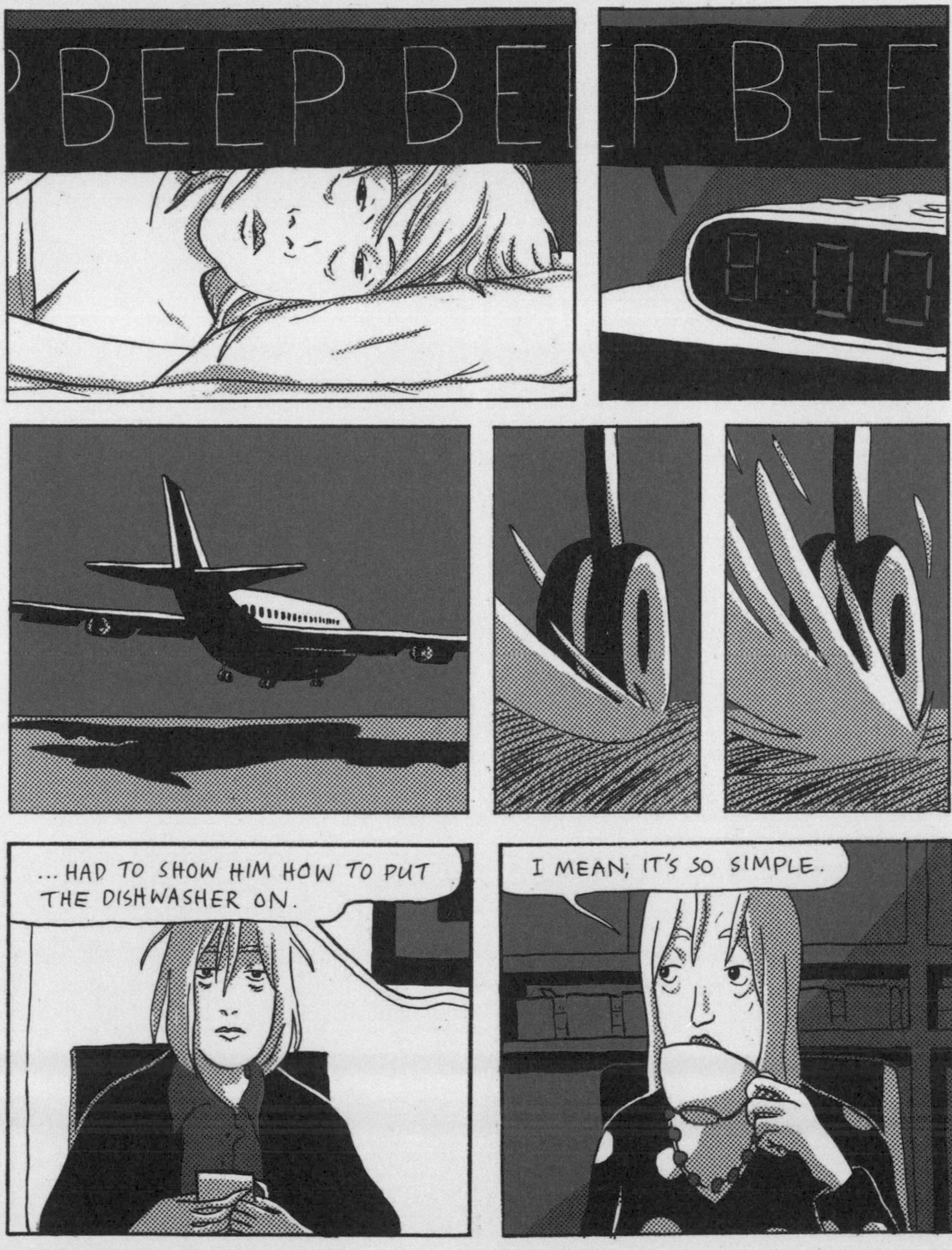

BEEP BEEP BEEP BEE
8:00
...HAD TO SHOW HIM HOW TO PUT THE DISHWASHER ON.
I MEAN, IT'S SO SIMPLE.

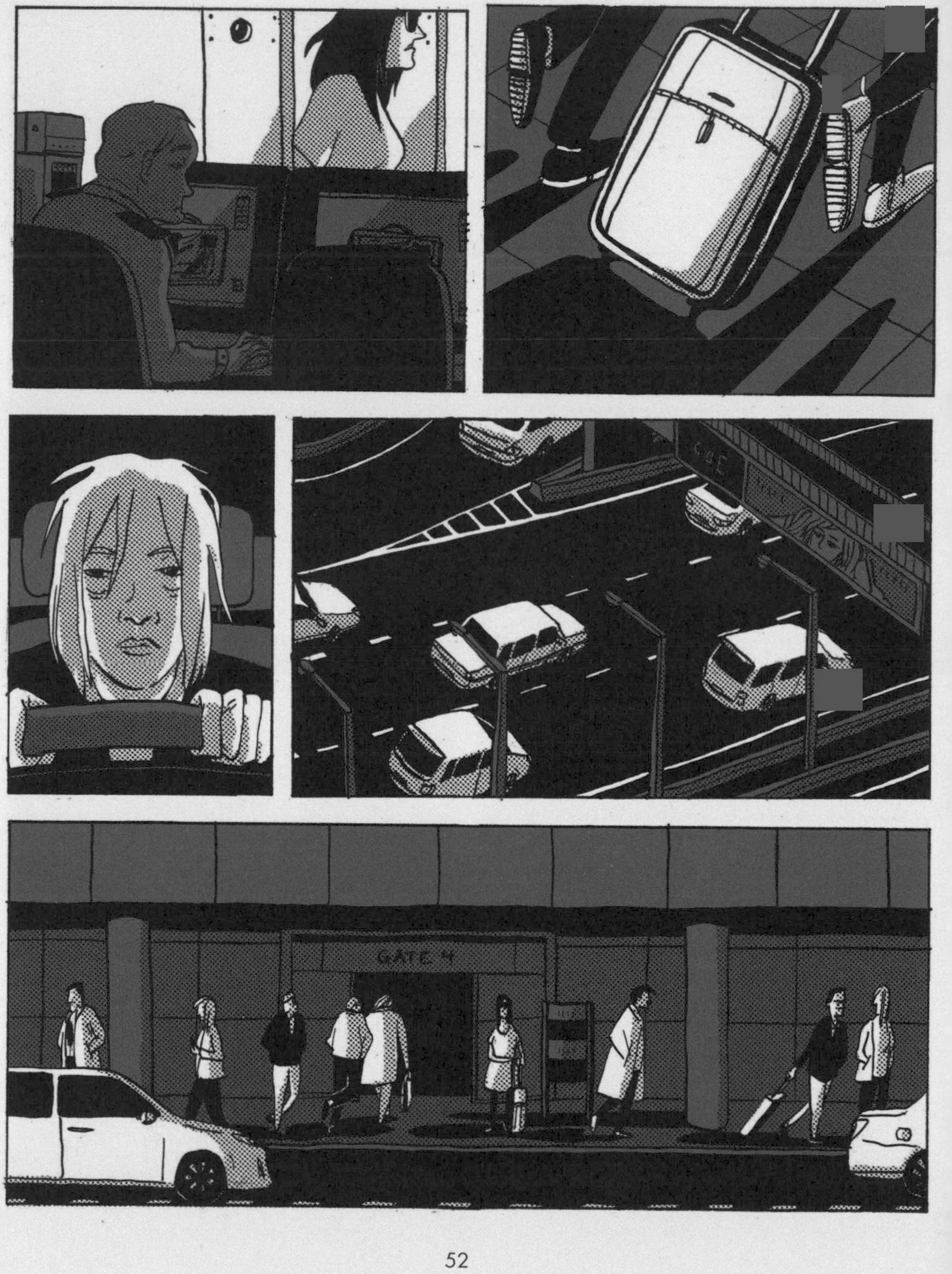
GATE 4

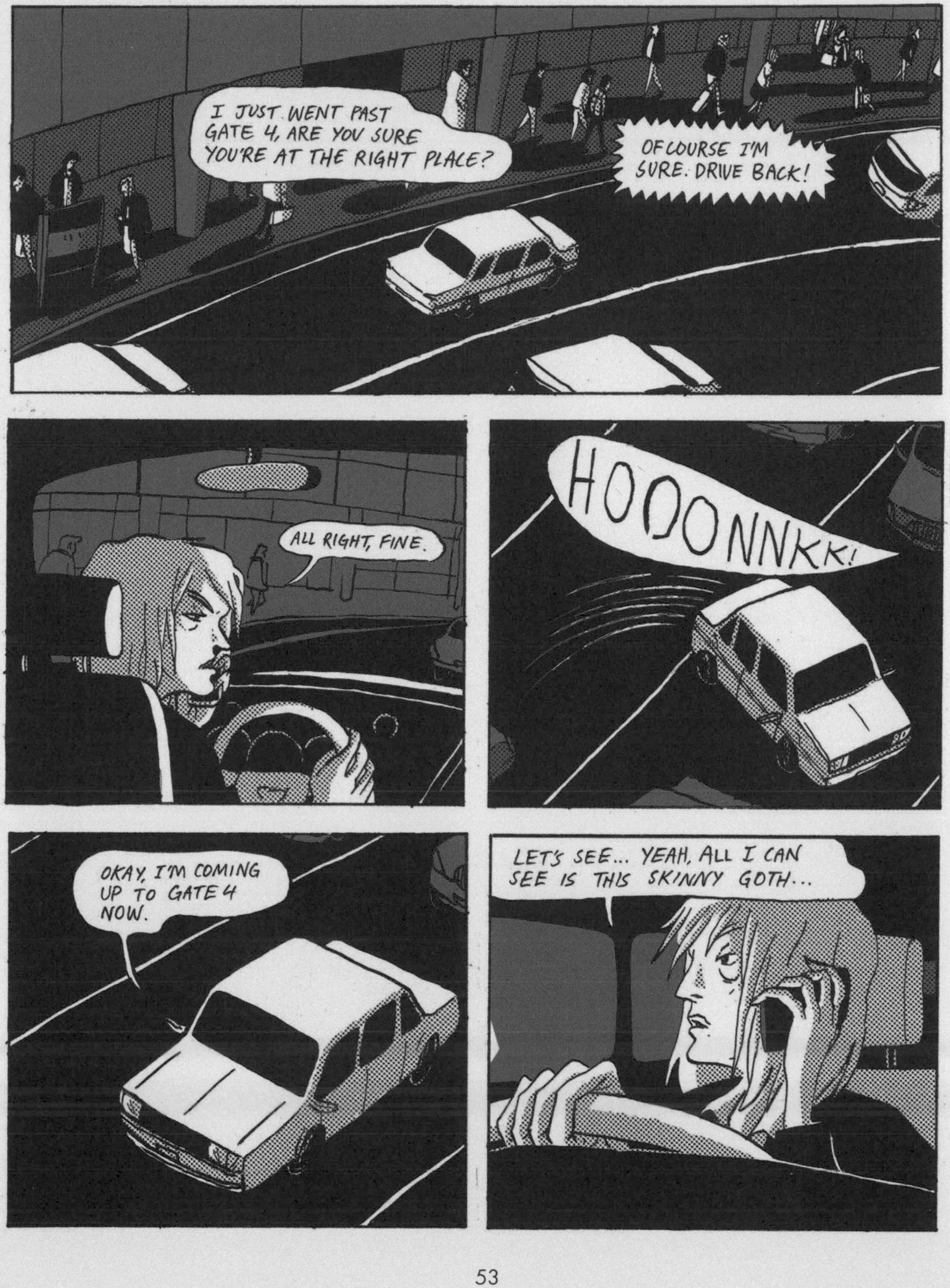
I JUST WENT PAST GATE 4, ARE YOU SURE YOU'RE AT THE RIGHT PLACE?
OF COURSE I'M SURE. DRIVE BACK!
ALL RIGHT, FINE.
HOOONNKK!
OKAY, I'M COMING UP TO GATE 4 NOW.
LET'S SEE... YEAH, ALL I CAN SEE IS THIS SKINNY GOTH...

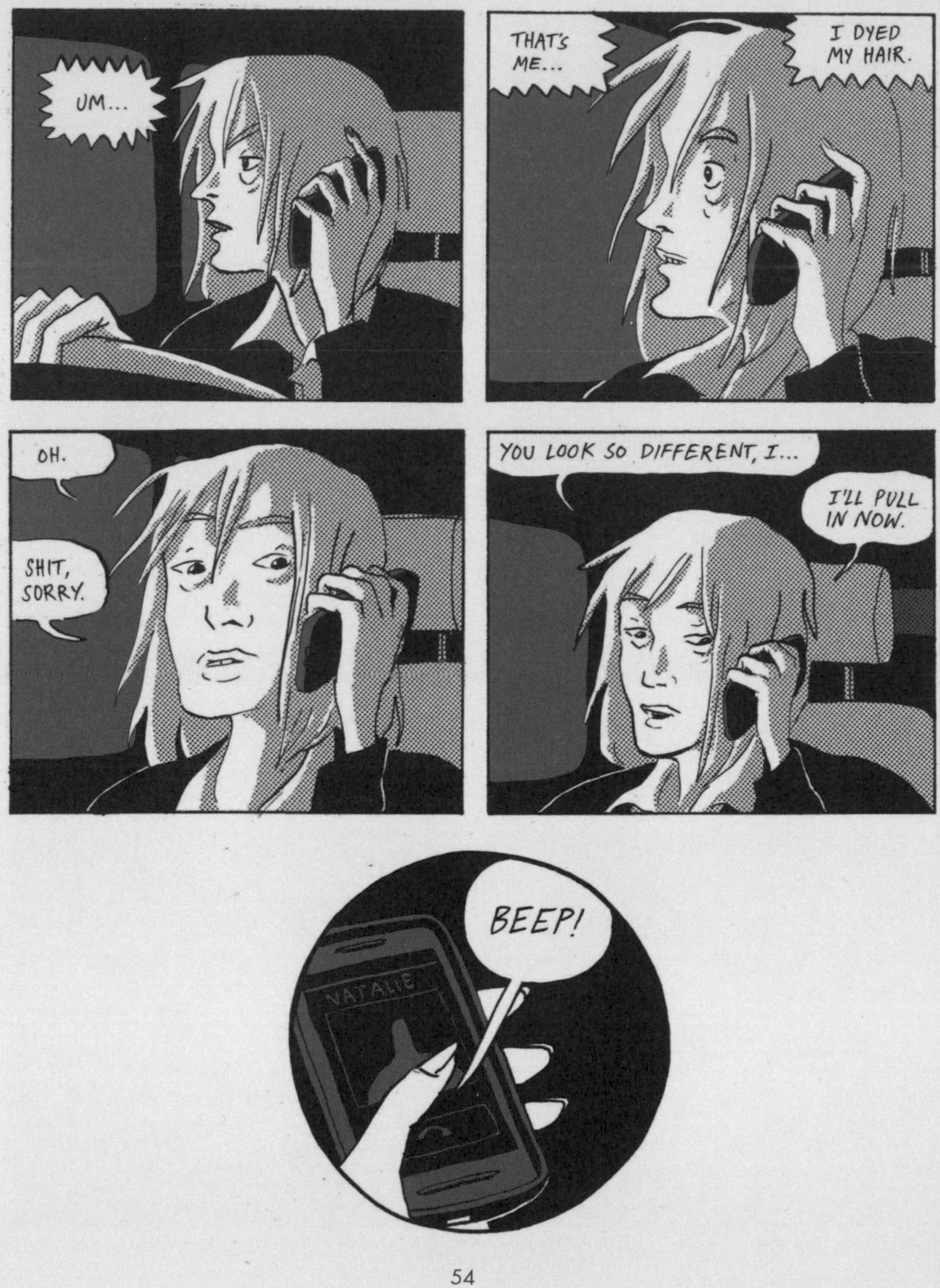
UM...
THAT'S ME...
I DYED MY HAIR.
OH.
SHIT, SORRY.
YOU LOOK SO DIFFERENT, I...
I'LL PULL IN NOW.
BEEP!
NATALIE

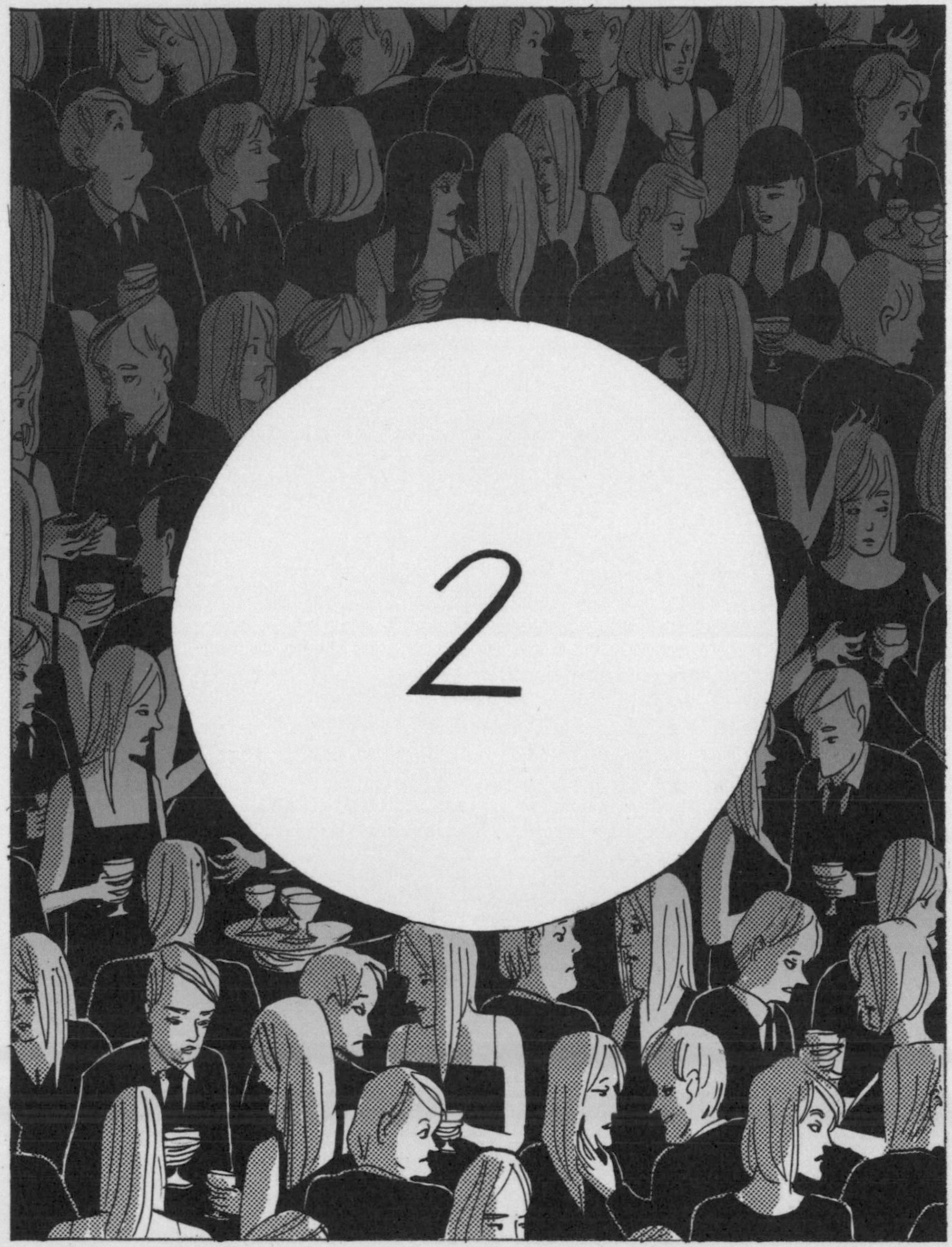
2

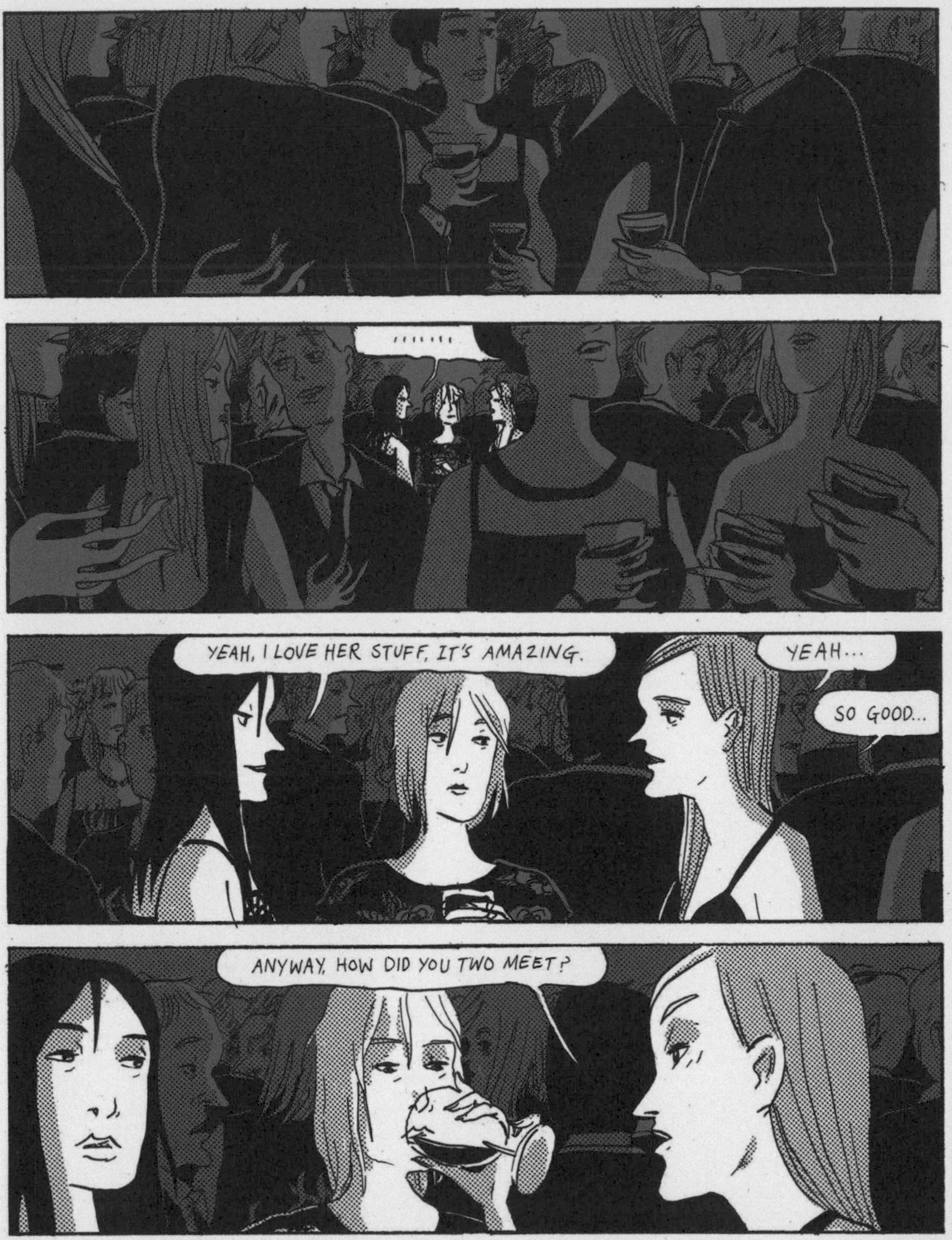

......
YEAH, I LOVE HER STUFF, IT'S AMAZING.
YEAH...
SO GOOD...
ANYWAY, HOW DID YOU TWO MEET?

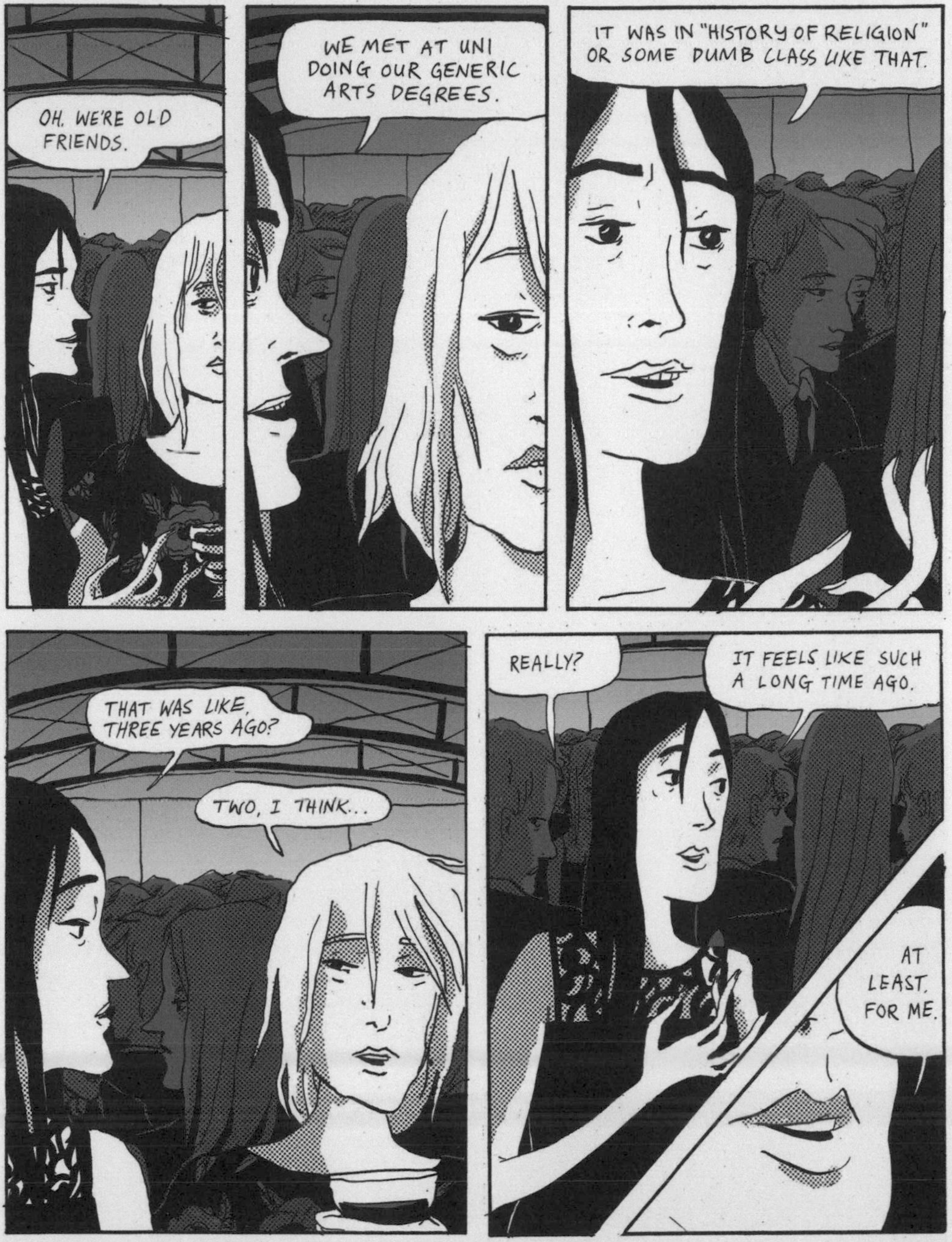
OH. WE'RE OLD FRIENDS.
WE MET AT UNI DOING OUR GENERIC ARTS DEGREES.
IT WAS IN "HISTORY OF RELIGION" OR SOME DUMB CLASS LIKE THAT.
THAT WAS LIKE, THREE YEARS AGO?
TWO, I THINK...
REALLY?
IT FEELS LIKE SUCH A LONG TIME AGO.
AT LEAST, FOR ME.

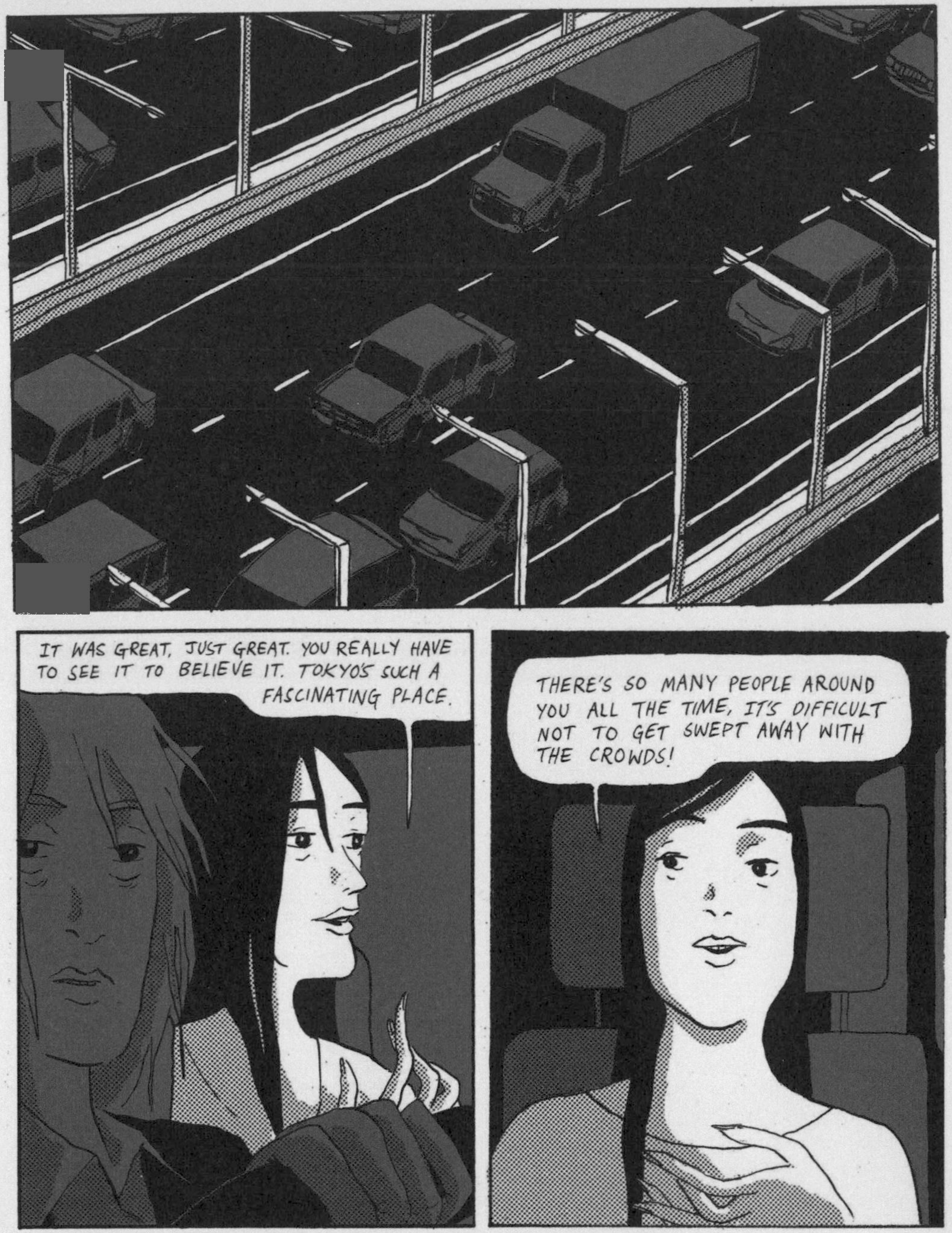
IT WAS GREAT, JUST GREAT. YOU REALLY HAVE TO SEE IT TO BELIEVE IT. TOKYO'S SUCH A FASCINATING PLACE.
THERE'S SO MANY PEOPLE AROUND YOU ALL THE TIME, IT'S DIFFICULT NOT TO GET SWEPT AWAY WITH THE CROWDS!

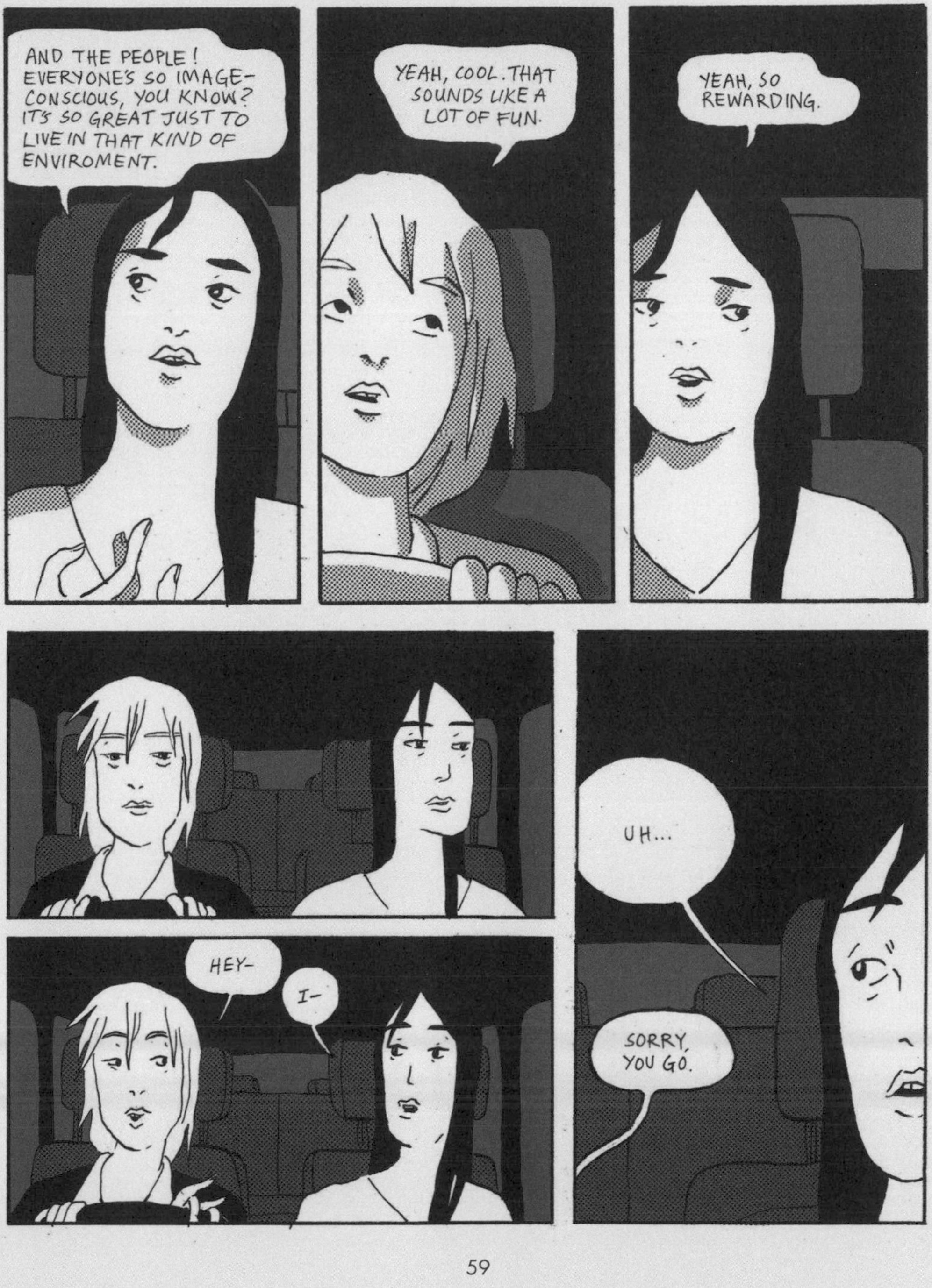
AND THE PEOPLE! EVERYONE'S SO IMAGE-CONSCIOUS, YOU KNOW? IT'S SO GREAT JUST TO LIVE IN THAT KIND OF ENVIROMENT.
YEAH, COOL. THAT SOUNDS LIKE A LOT OF FUN.
YEAH, SO REWARDING.
HEY-
I-
UH...
SORRY, YOU GO.

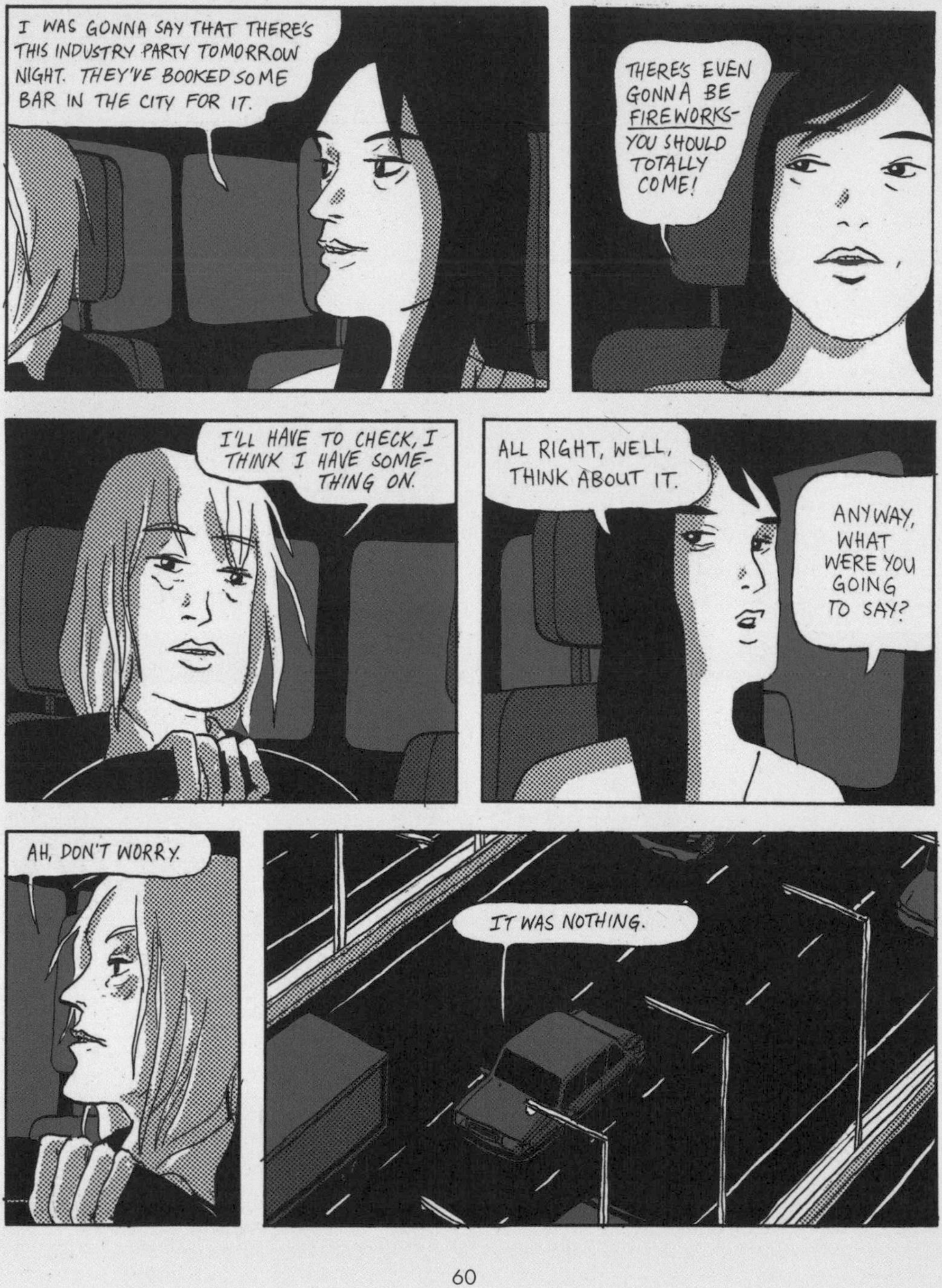
I WAS GONNA SAY THAT THERE'S THIS INDUSTRY PARTY TOMORROW NIGHT. THEY'VE BOOKED SOME BAR IN THE CITY FOR IT.
THERE'S EVEN GONNA BE FIREWORKS- YOU SHOULD TOTALLY COME!
I'LL HAVE TO CHECK, I THINK I HAVE SOMETHING ON.
ALL RIGHT, WELL, THINK ABOUT IT.
ANYWAY, WHAT WERE YOU GOING TO SAY?
AH, DON'T WORRY.
IT WAS NOTHING.

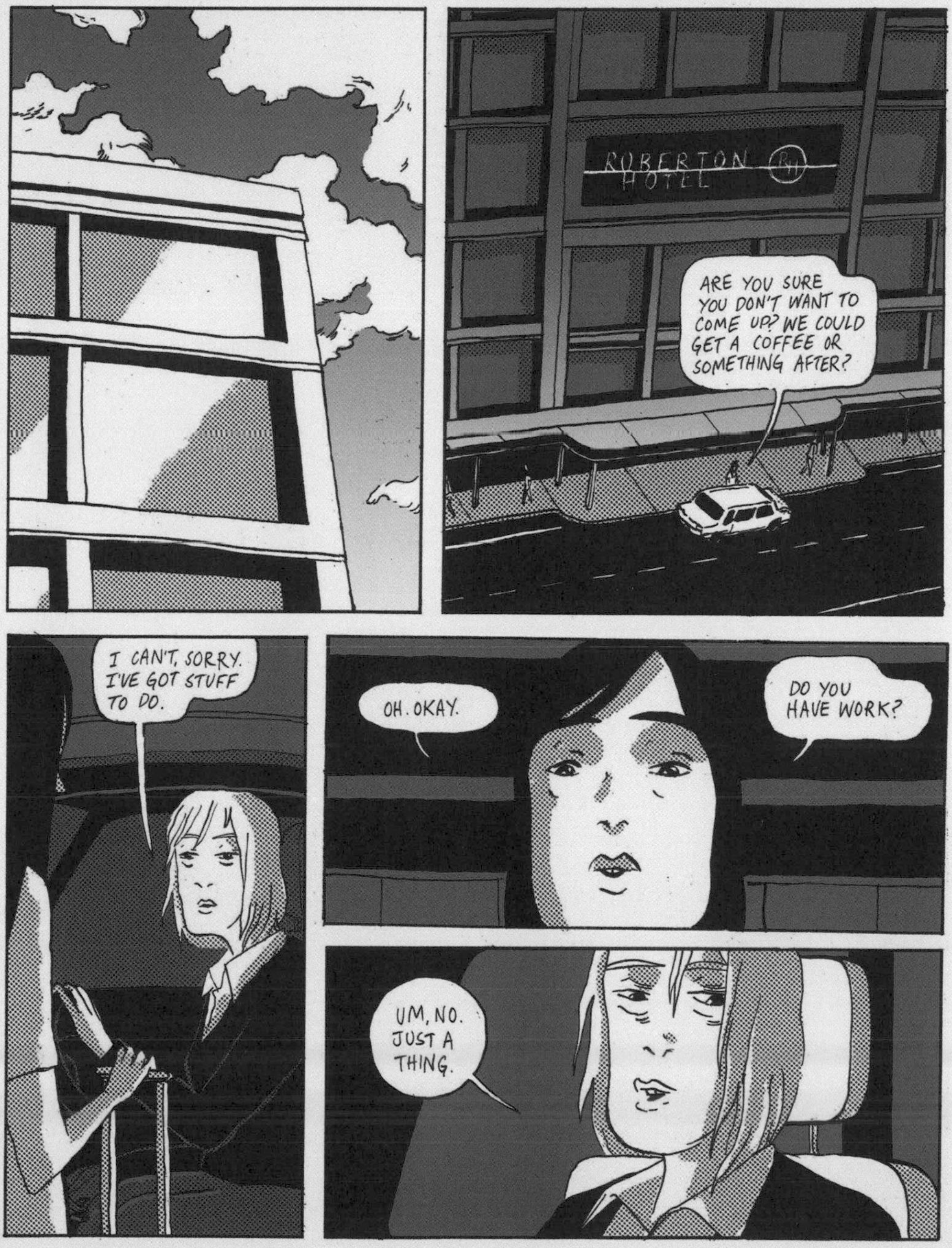
ROBERTON HOTEL
ARE YOU SURE YOU DON'T WANT TO COME UP? WE COULD GET A COFFEE OR SOMETHING AFTER?
I CAN'T, SORRY. I'VE GOT STUFF TO DO.
OH. OKAY.
DO YOU HAVE WORK?
UM, NO. JUST A THING.

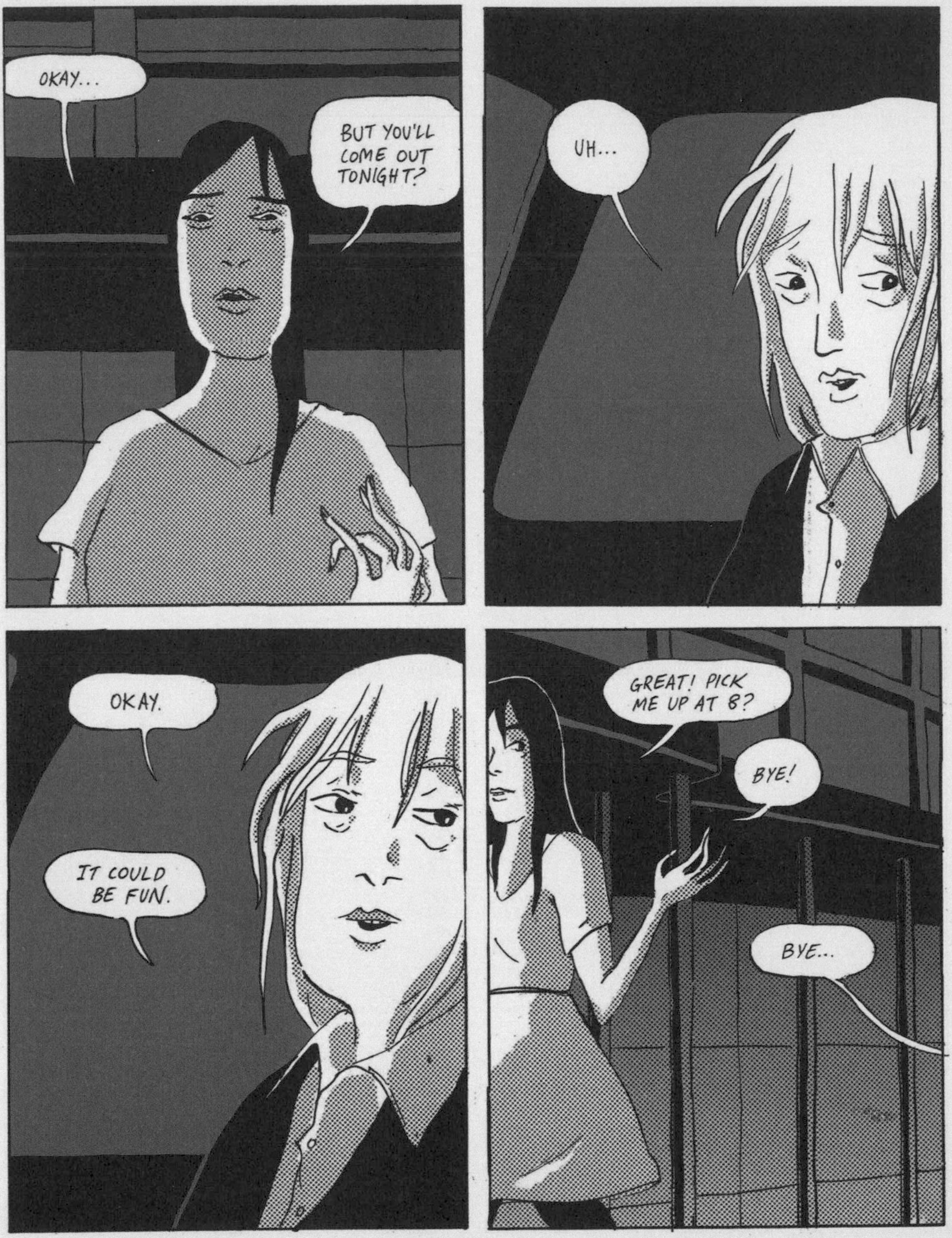
OKAY...
BUT YOU'LL COME OUT TONIGHT?
UH...
OKAY.
IT COULD BE FUN.
GREAT! PICK ME UP AT 8?
BYE!
BYE...

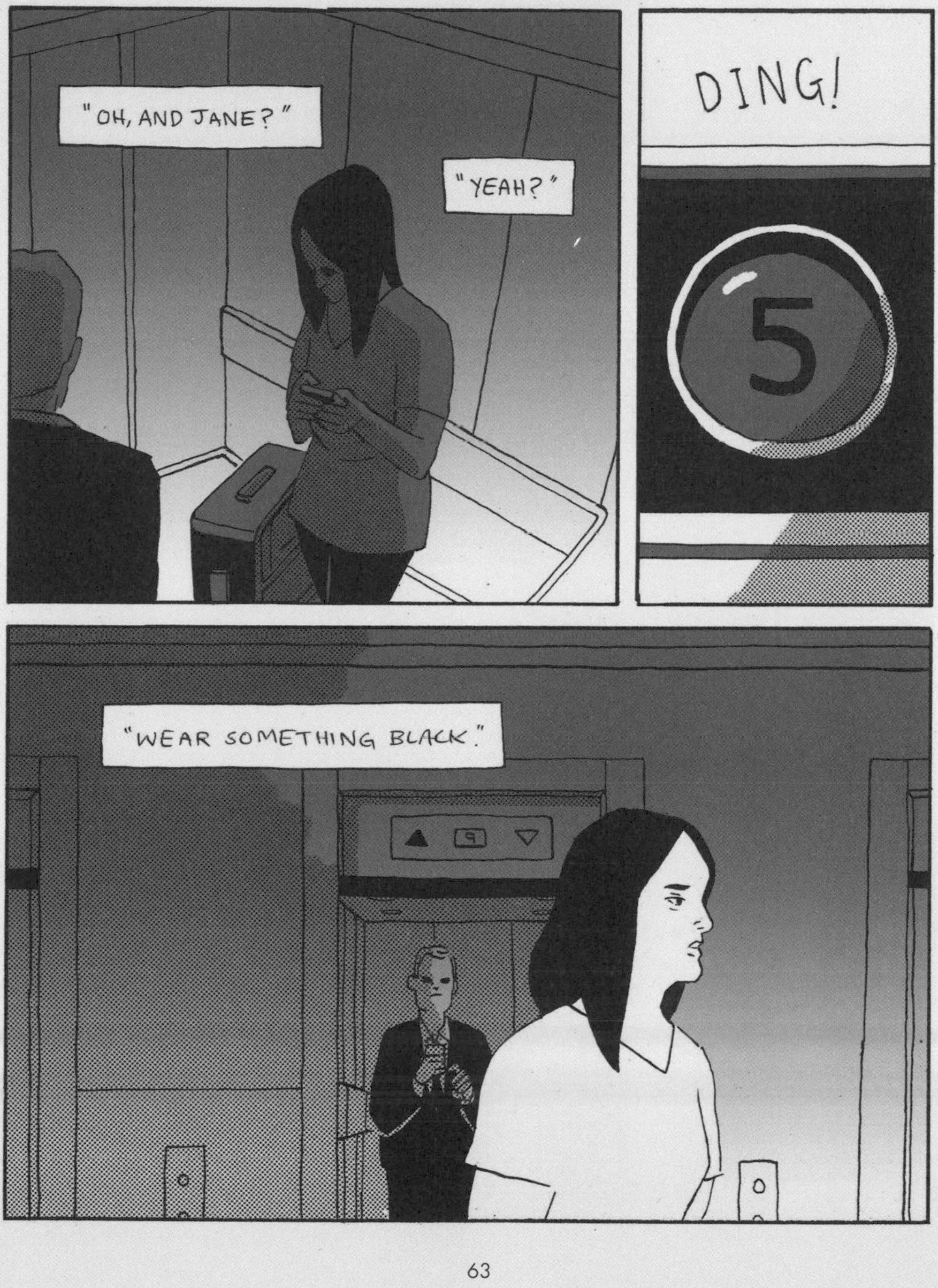
"OH, AND JANE?"
"YEAH?"
DING!
5
"WEAR SOMETHING BLACK."

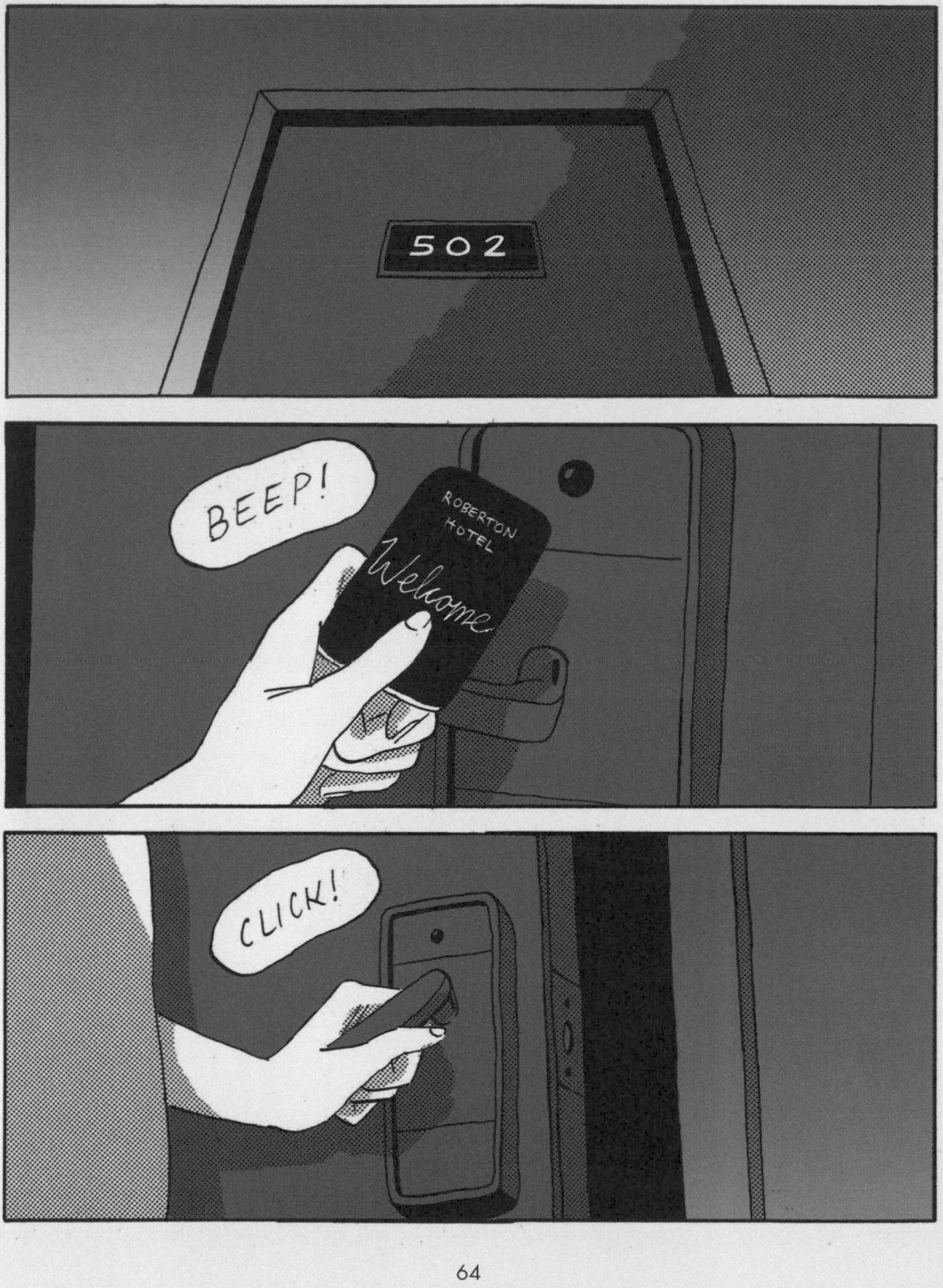
502
BEEP!
ROBERTON HOTEL
Welcome
CLICK!

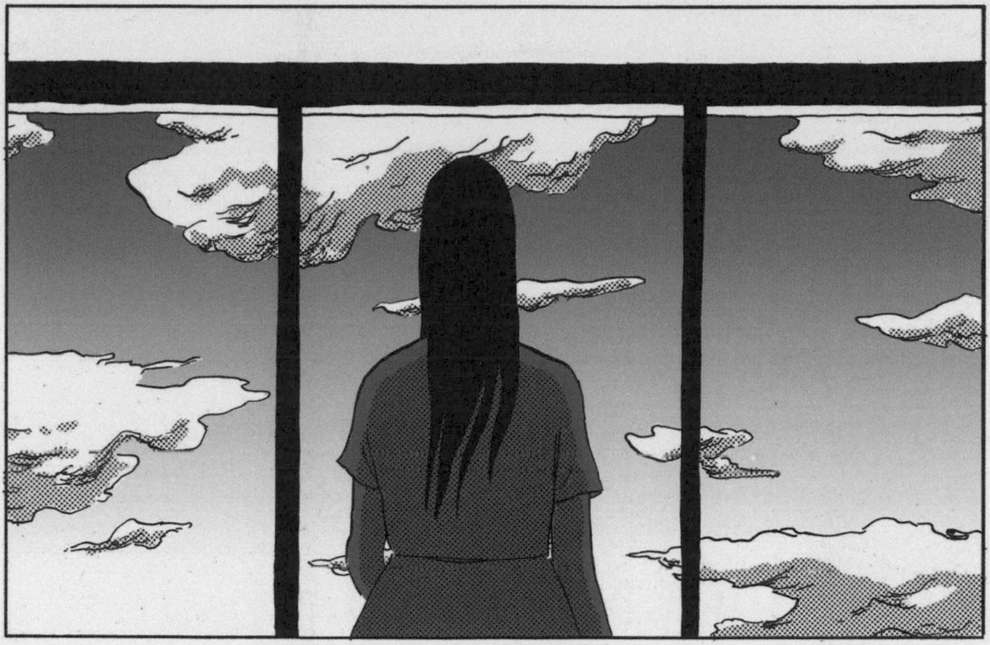

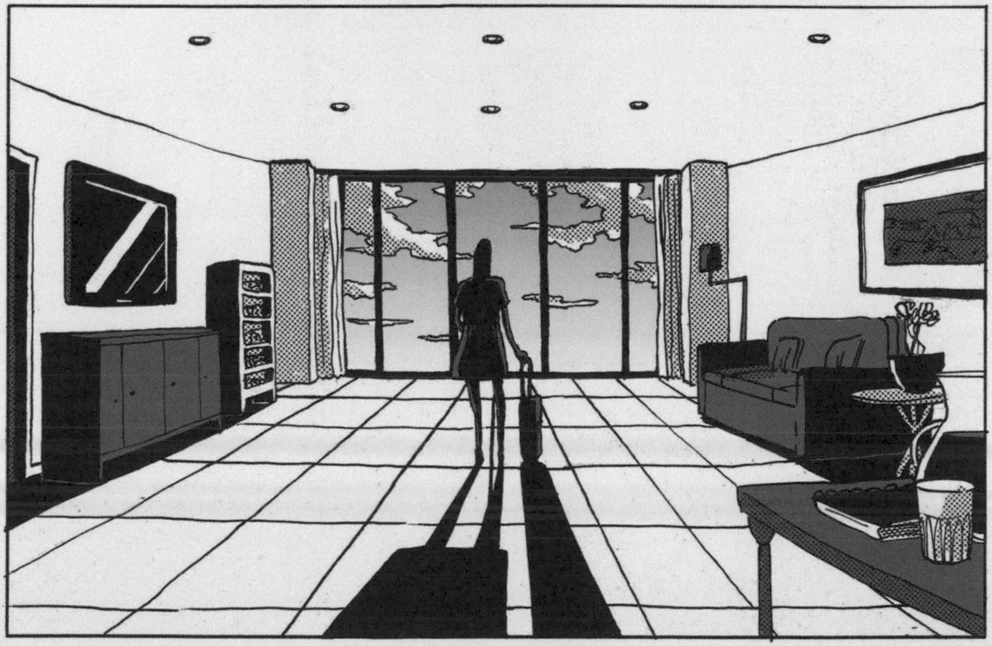

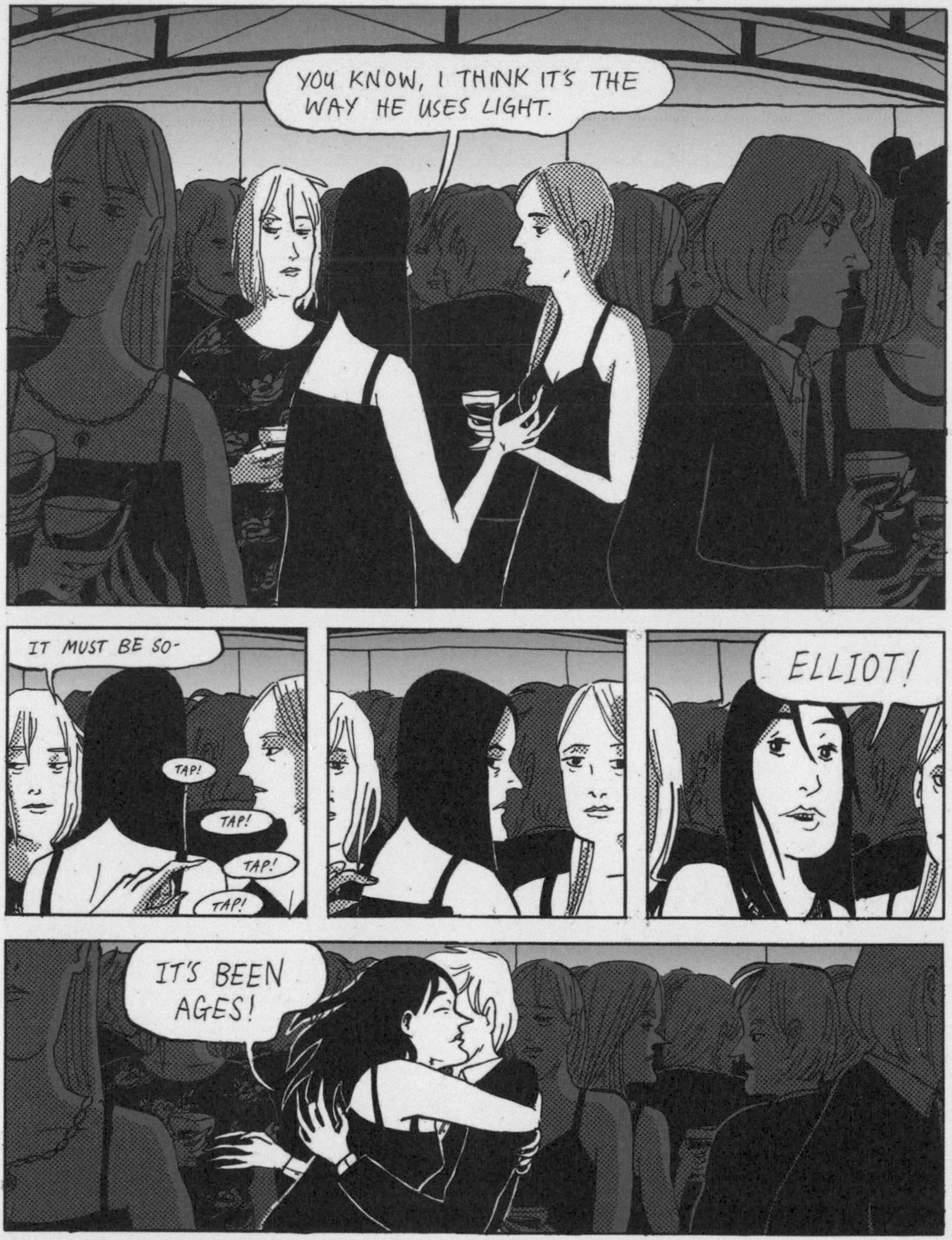
YOU KNOW, I THINK IT'S THE WAY HE USES LIGHT.
IT MUST BE SO-
TAP!
TAP!
TAP!
TAP!
ELLIOT!
IT'S BEEN AGES!

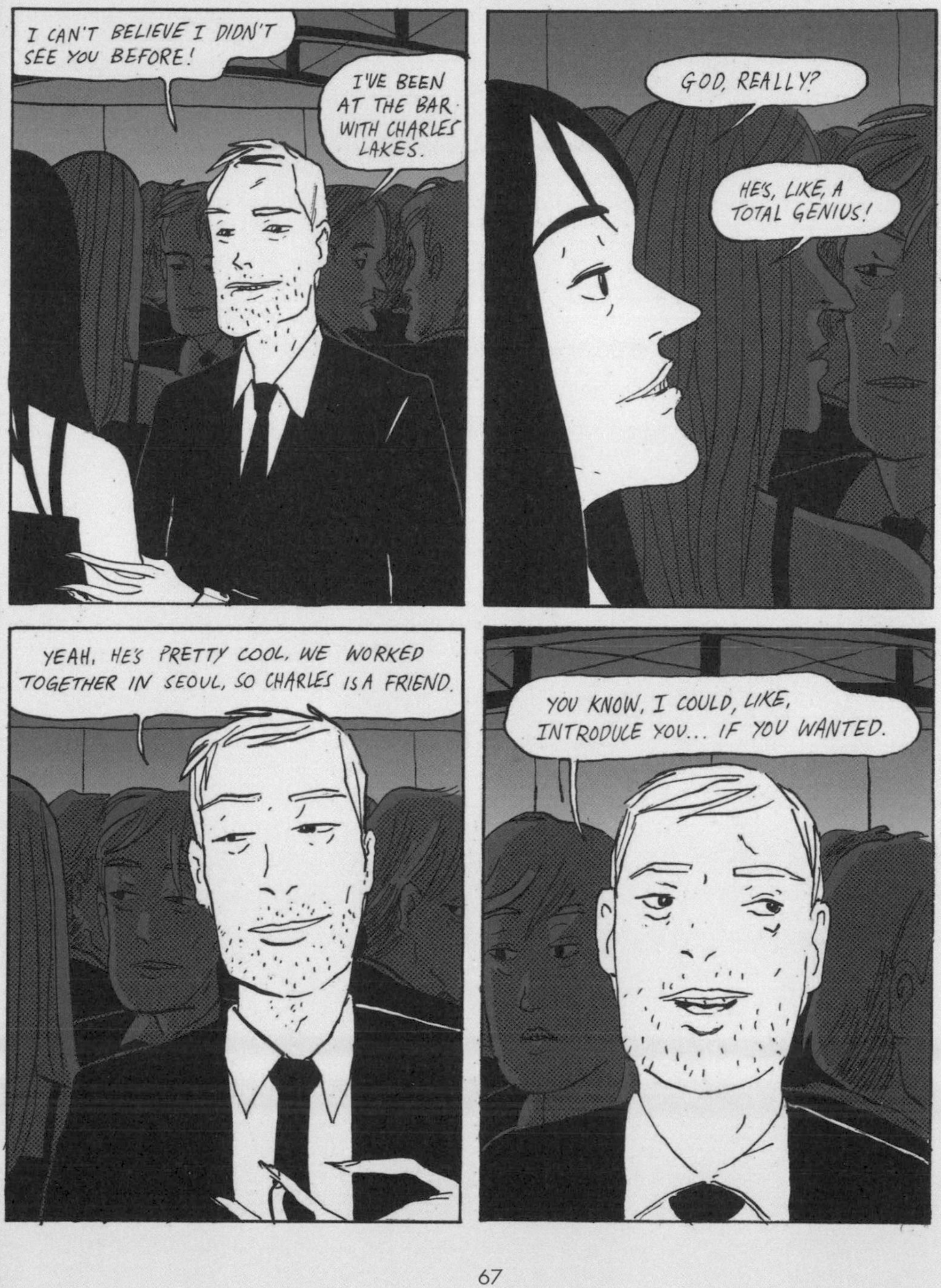
I CAN'T BELIEVE I DIDN'T SEE YOU BEFORE!
I'VE BEEN AT THE BAR WITH CHARLES LAKES.
GOD, REALLY?
HE'S, LIKE, A TOTAL GENIUS!
YEAH. HE'S PRETTY COOL. WE WORKED TOGETHER IN SEOUL, SO CHARLES IS A FRIEND.
YOU KNOW, I COULD, LIKE, INTRODUCE YOU... IF YOU WANTED.

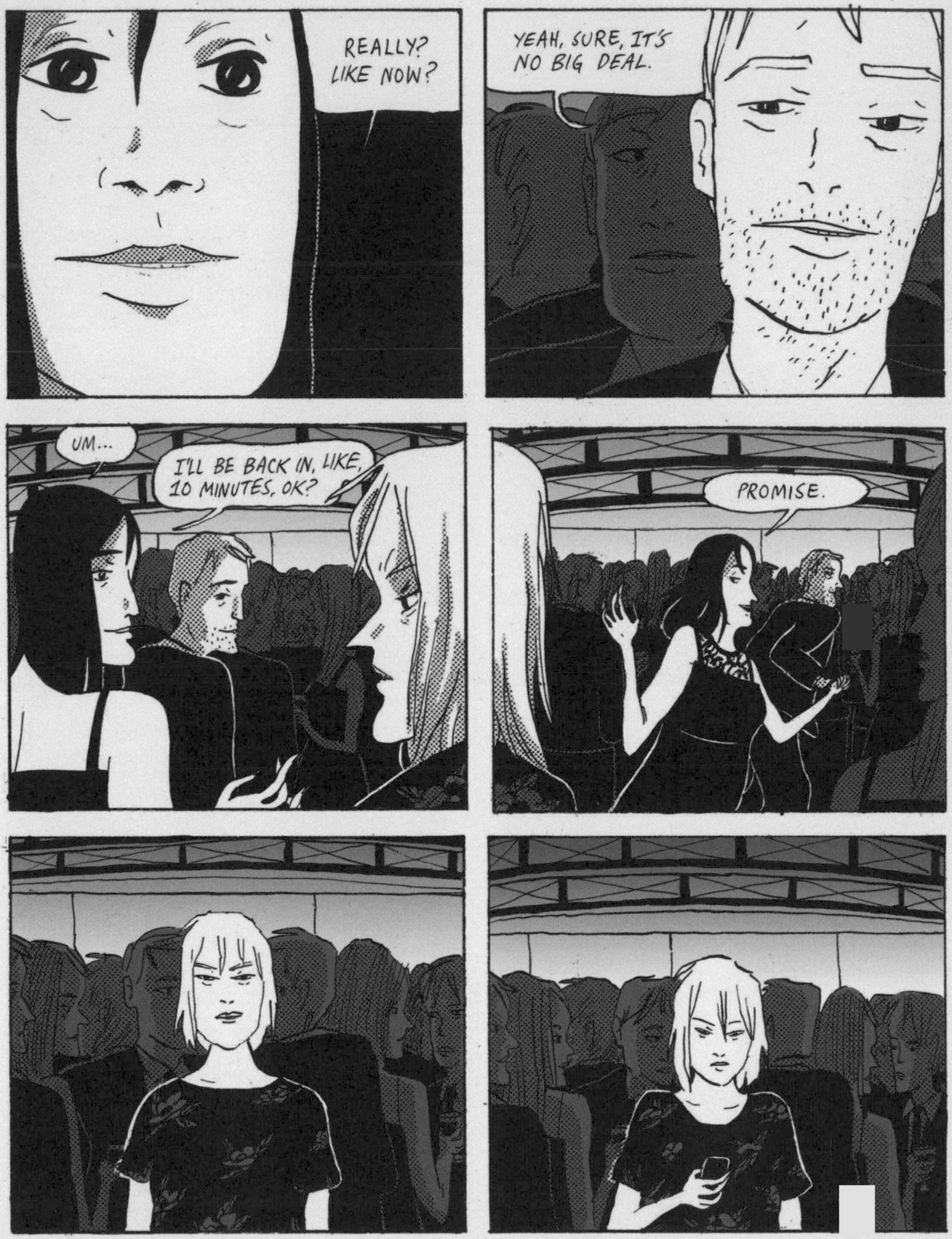
REALLY? LIKE NOW?
YEAH, SURE, IT'S NO BIG DEAL.
UM...
I'LL BE BACK IN, LIKE, 10 MINUTES, OK?
PROMISE.

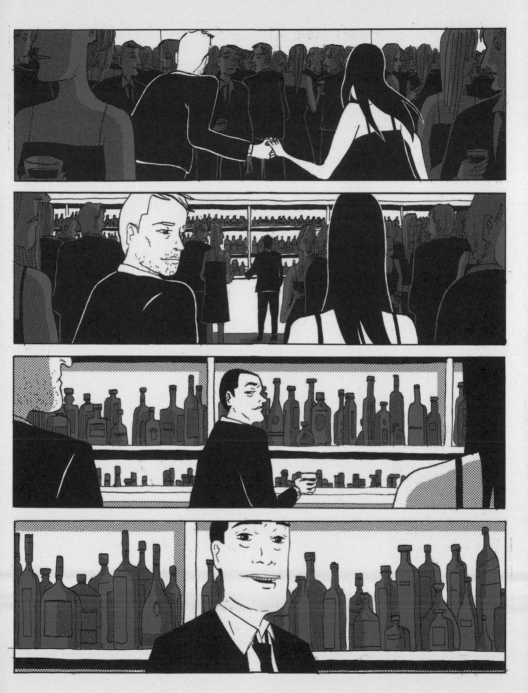

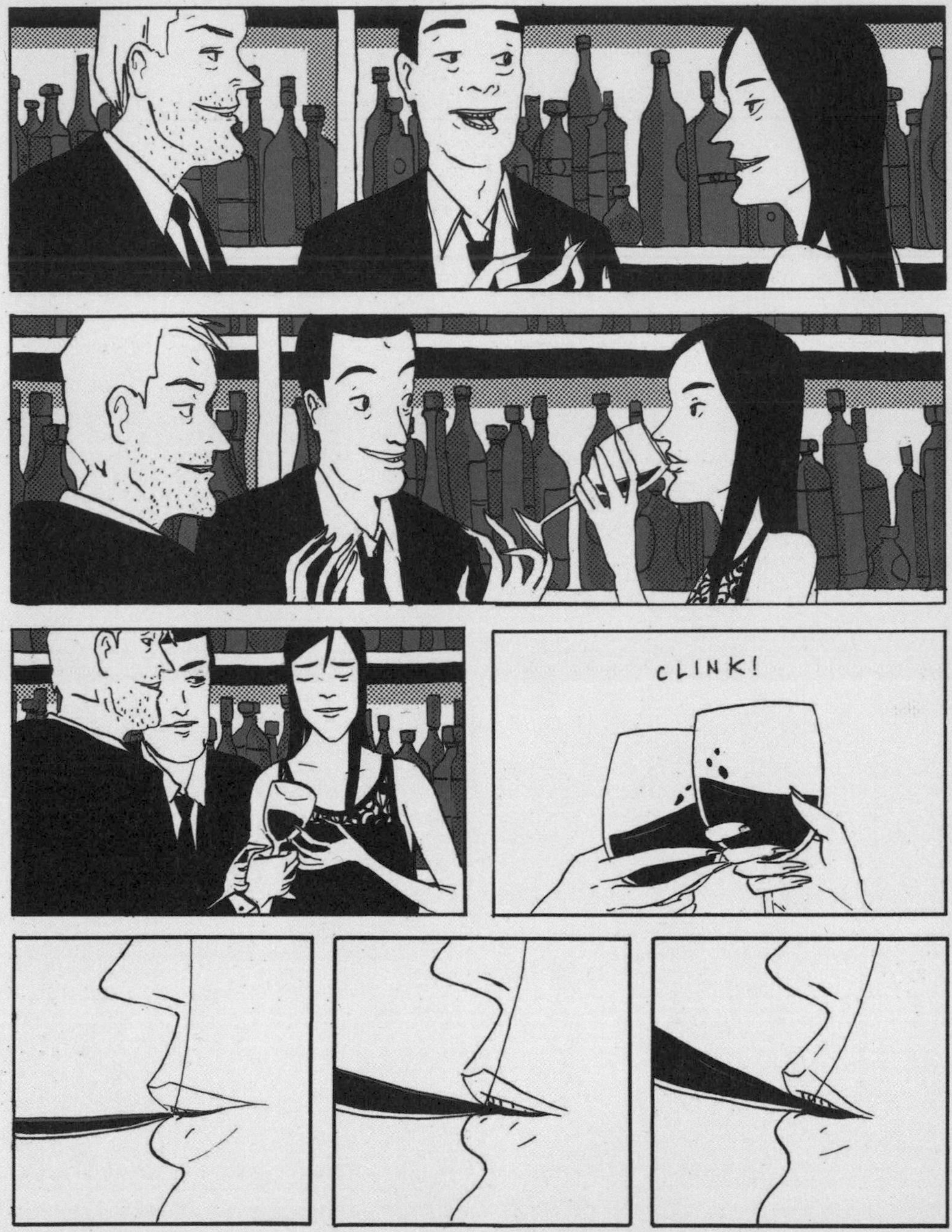
CLINK!

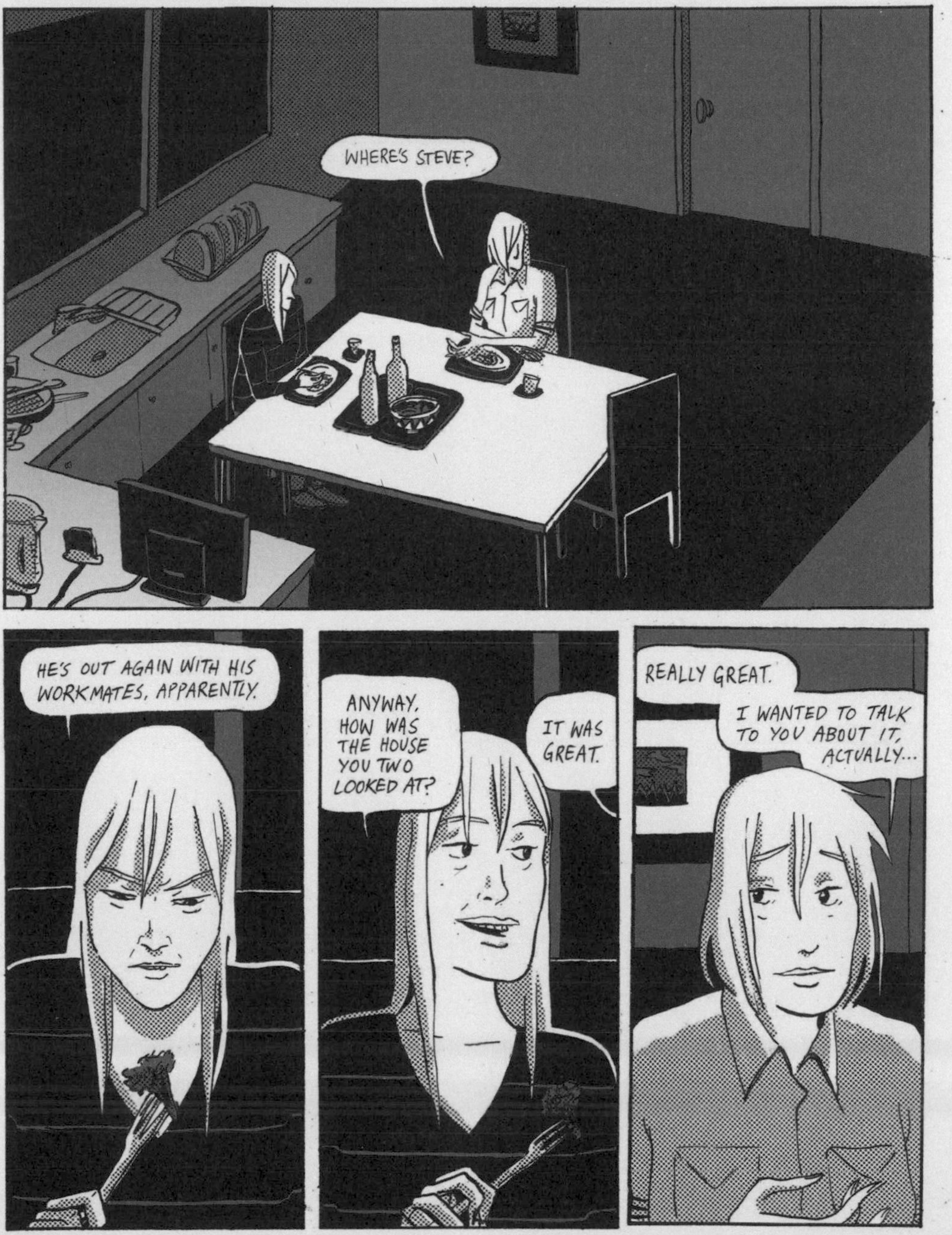
WHERE'S STEVE?
HE'S OUT AGAIN WITH HIS WORKMATES, APPARENTLY.
ANYWAY, HOW WAS THE HOUSE YOU TWO LOOKED AT?
IT WAS GREAT.
REALLY GREAT.
I WANTED TO TALK TO YOU ABOUT IT, ACTUALLY...

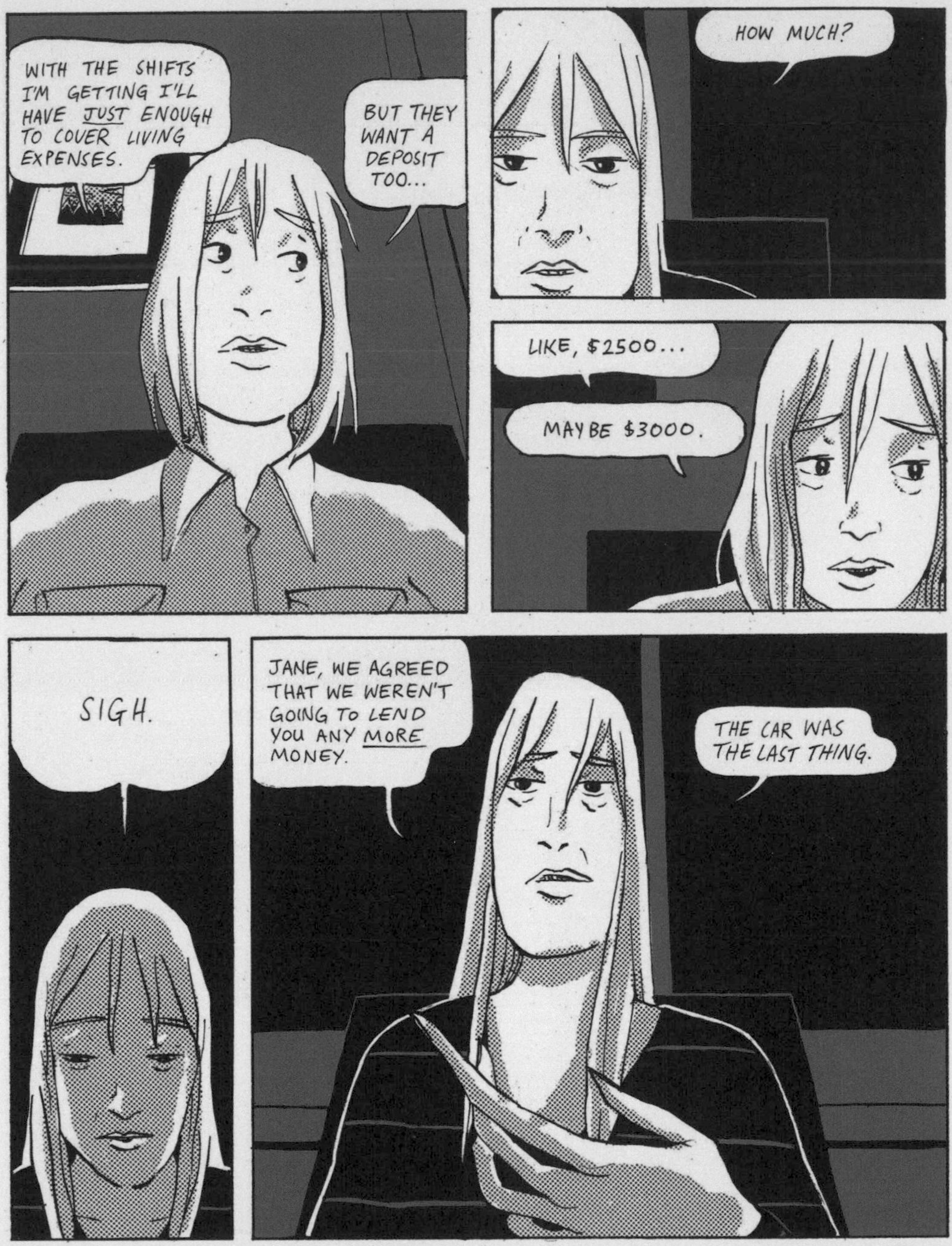
WITH THE SHIFTS I'M GETTING I'LL HAVE JUST ENOUGH TO COVER LIVING EXPENSES.
BUT THEY WANT A DEPOSIT TOO...
HOW MUCH?
LIKE, $2500...
MAYBE $3000.
SIGH.
JANE, WE AGREED THAT WE WEREN'T GOING TO LEND YOU ANY MORE MONEY.
THE CAR WAS THE LAST THING.

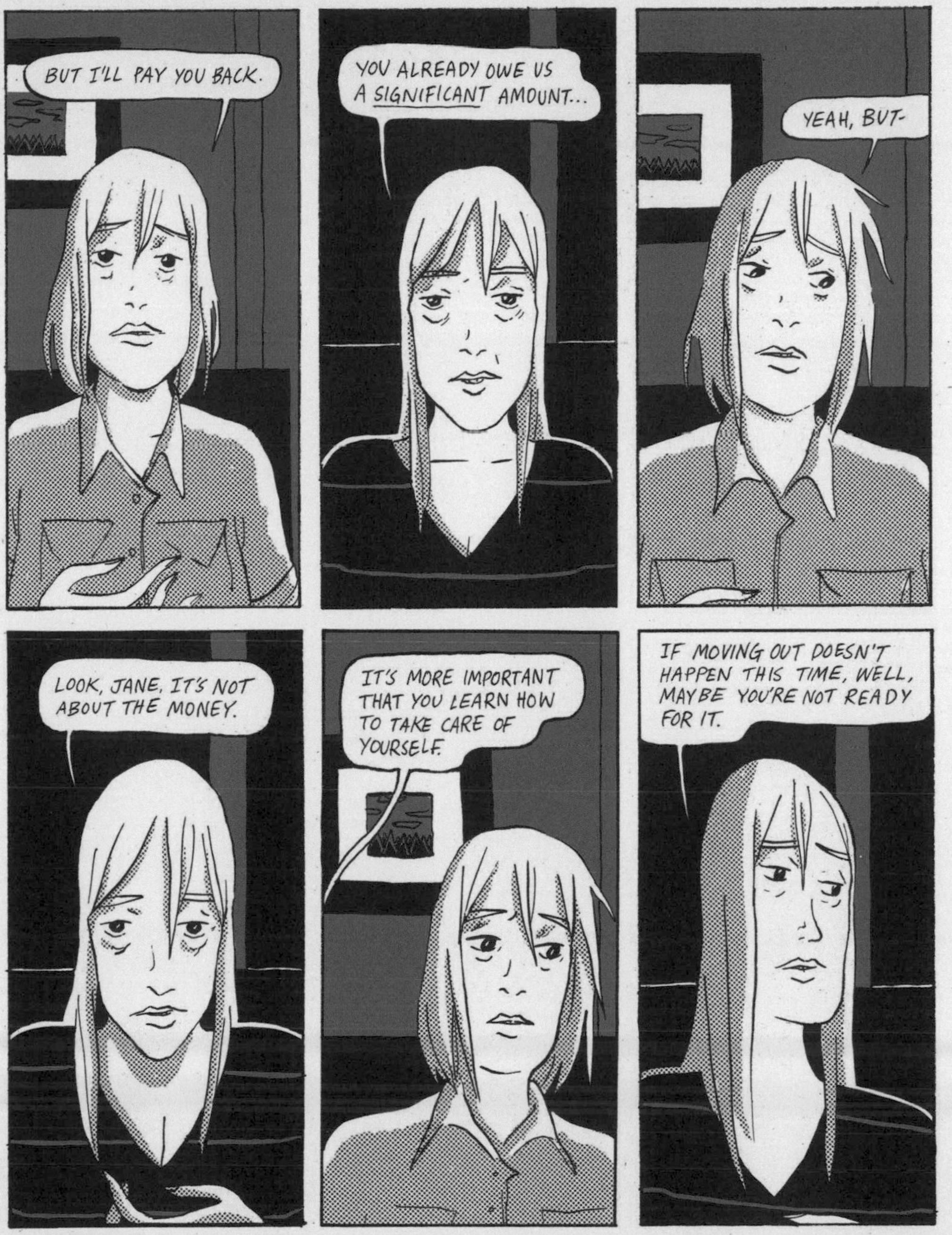
BUT I'LL PAY YOU BACK.
YOU ALREADY OWE US A SIGNIFICANT AMOUNT...
YEAH, BUT-
LOOK, JANE, IT'S NOT ABOUT THE MONEY.
IT'S MORE IMPORTANT THAT YOU LEARN HOW TO TAKE CARE OF YOURSELF.
IF MOVING OUT DOESN'T HAPPEN THIS TIME, WELL, MAYBE YOU'RE NOT READY FOR IT.

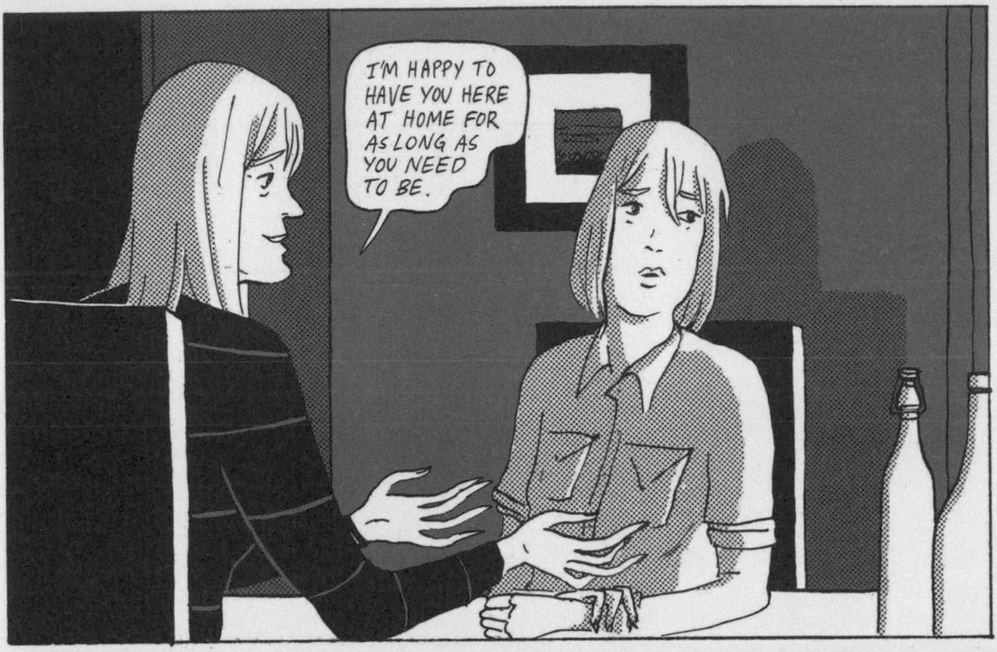
I'M HAPPY TO HAVE YOU HERE AT HOME FOR AS LONG AS YOU NEED TO BE.

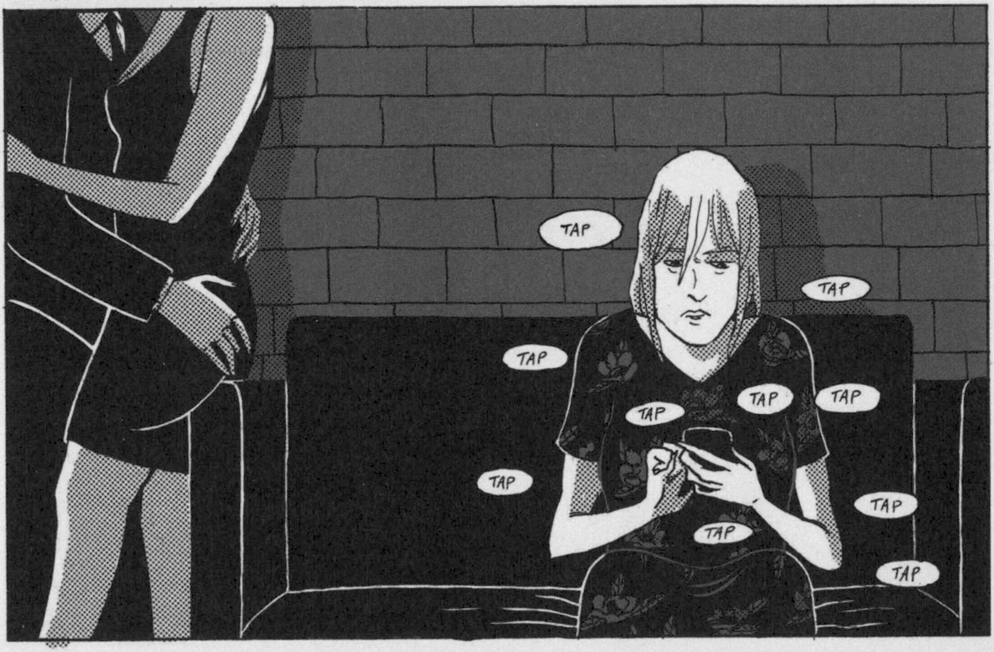
TAP
TAP
TAP
TAP
TAP
TAP
TAP
TAP
TAP
TAP

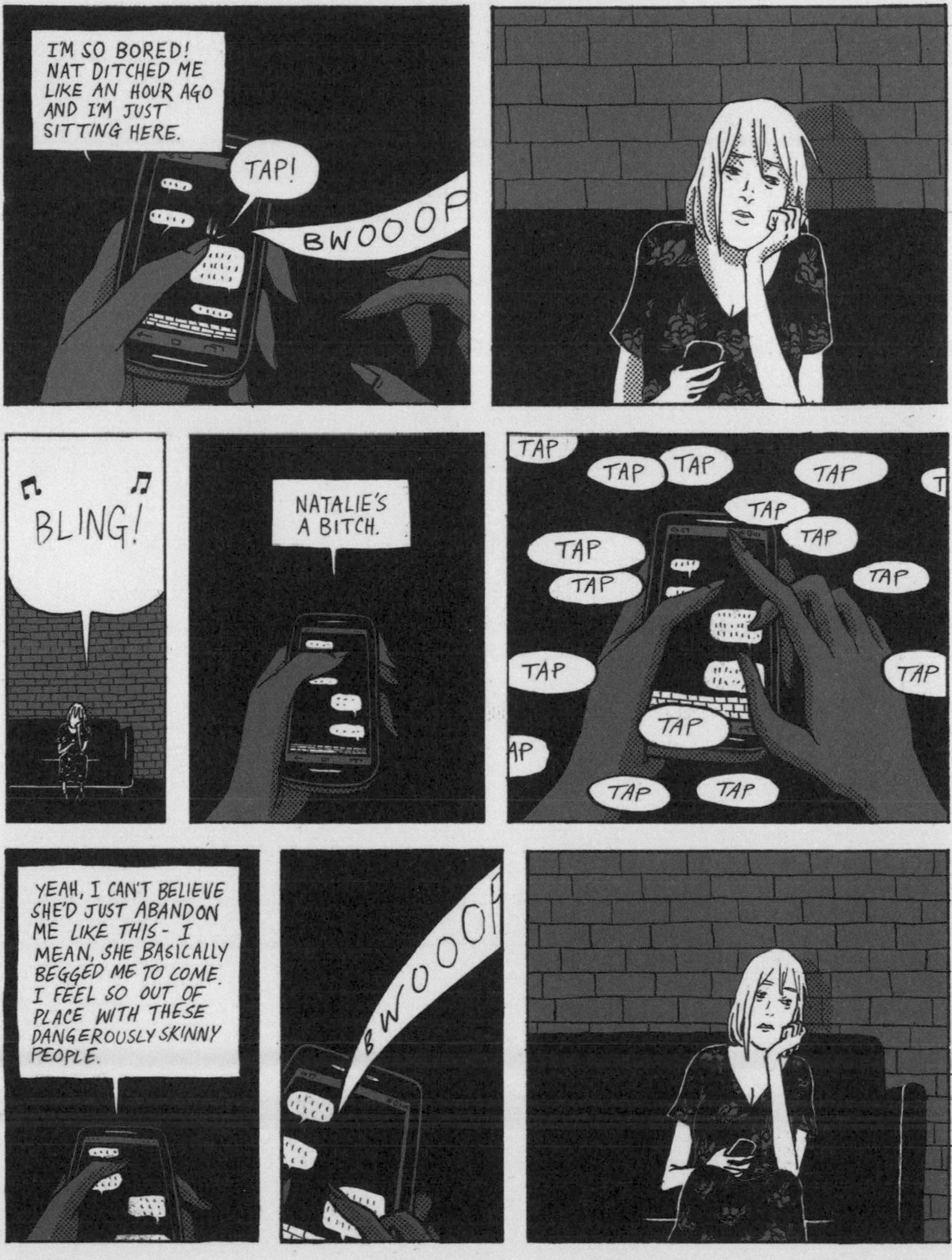
I'M SO BORED! NAT DITCHED ME LIKE AN HOUR AGO AND I'M JUST SITTING HERE.
TAP!
BWOOOP
BLING!
NATALIE'S A BITCH.
TAP TAP TAP TAP TAP TAP TAP TAP TAP TAP TAP TAP TAP TAP
YEAH, I CAN'T BELIEVE SHE'D JUST ABANDON ME LIKE THIS - I MEAN, SHE BASICALLY BEGGED ME TO COME. I FEEL SO OUT OF PLACE WITH THESE DANGEROUSLY SKINNY PEOPLE.
BWOOOP

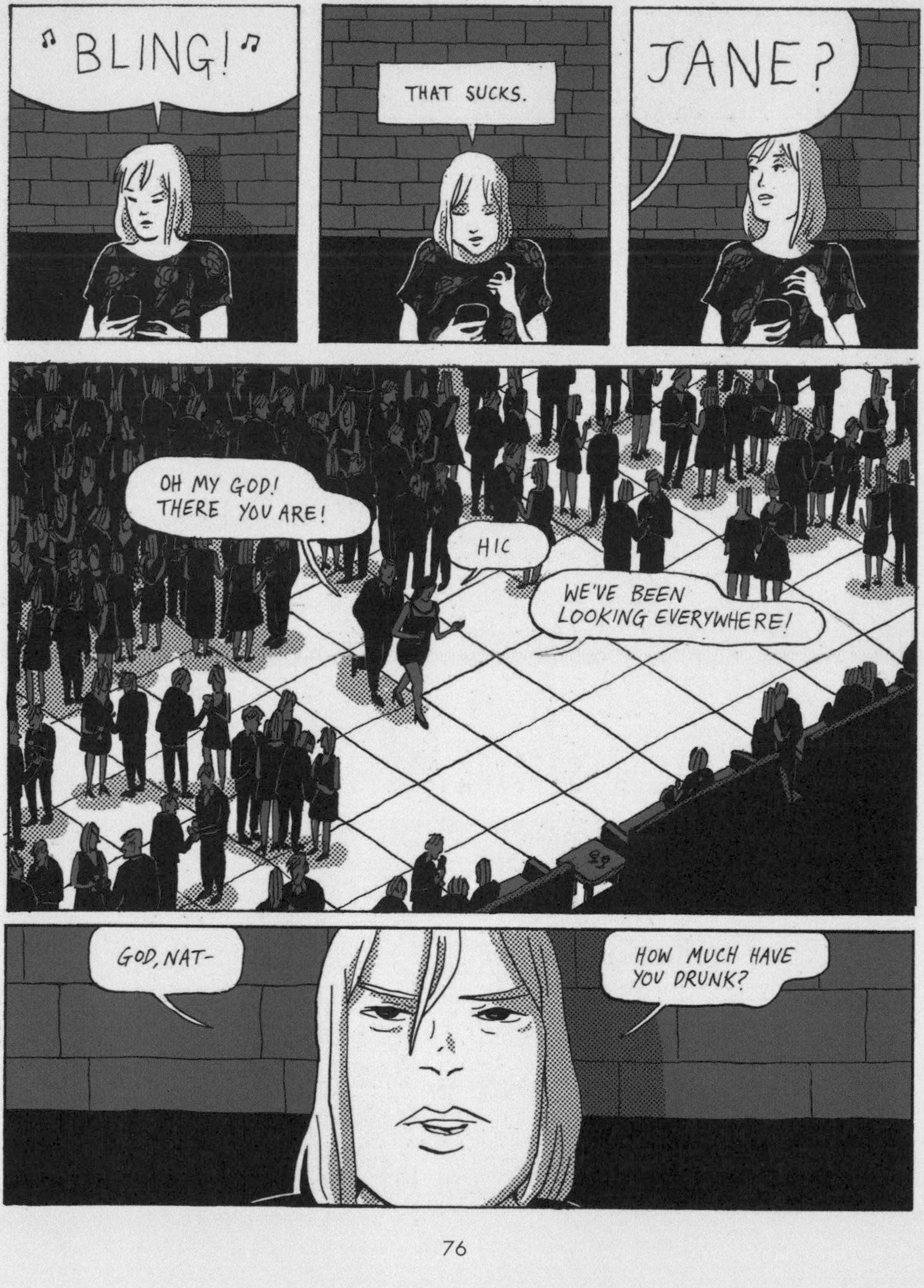
♪ BLING! ♪
THAT SUCKS.
JANE?
OH MY GOD! THERE YOU ARE!
HIC
WE'VE BEEN LOOKING EVERYWHERE!
GOD, NAT-
HOW MUCH HAVE YOU DRUNK?

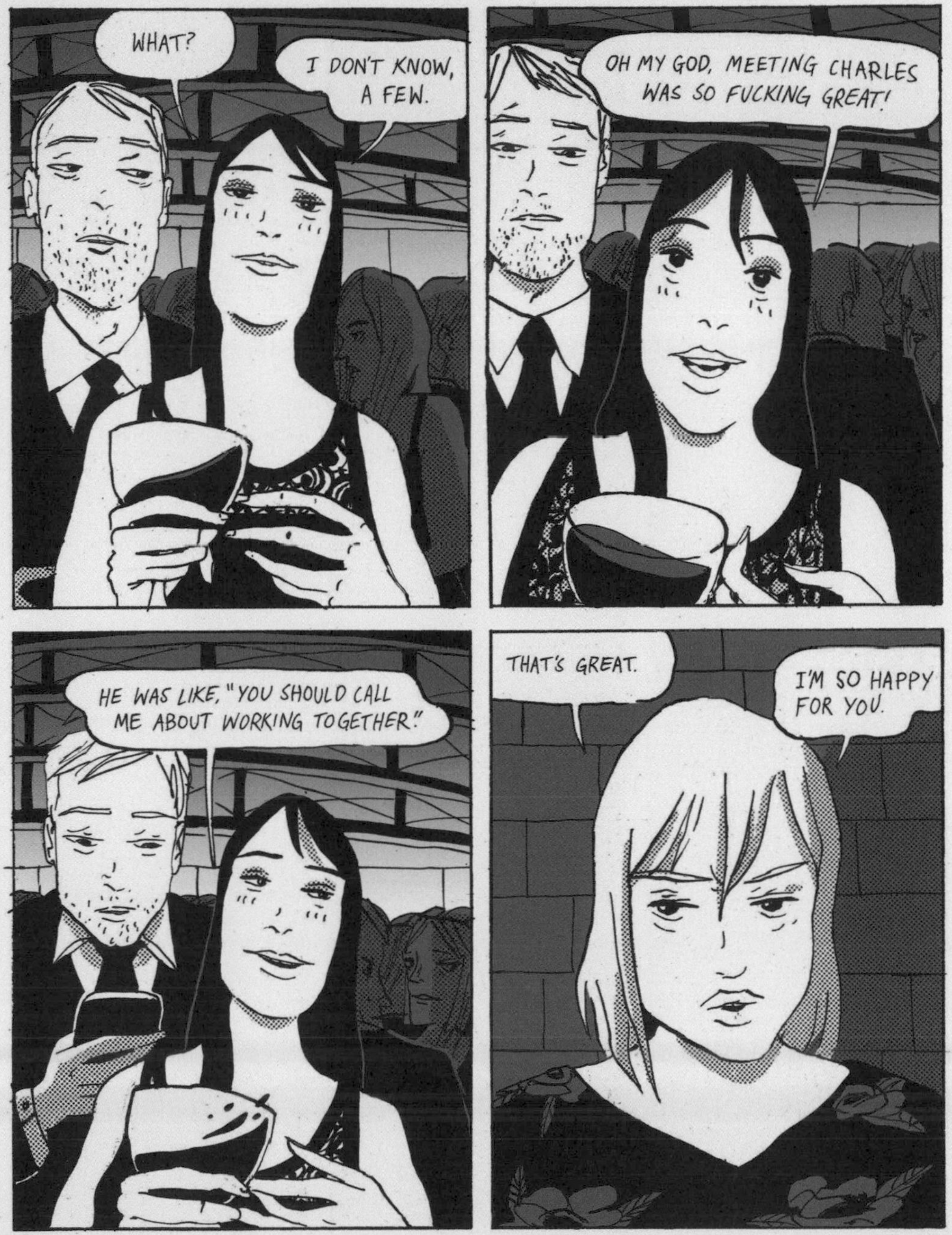
WHAT?
I DON'T KNOW, A FEW.
OH MY GOD, MEETING CHARLES WAS SO FUCKING GREAT!
HE WAS LIKE, "YOU SHOULD CALL ME ABOUT WORKING TOGETHER."
THAT'S GREAT.
I'M SO HAPPY FOR YOU.

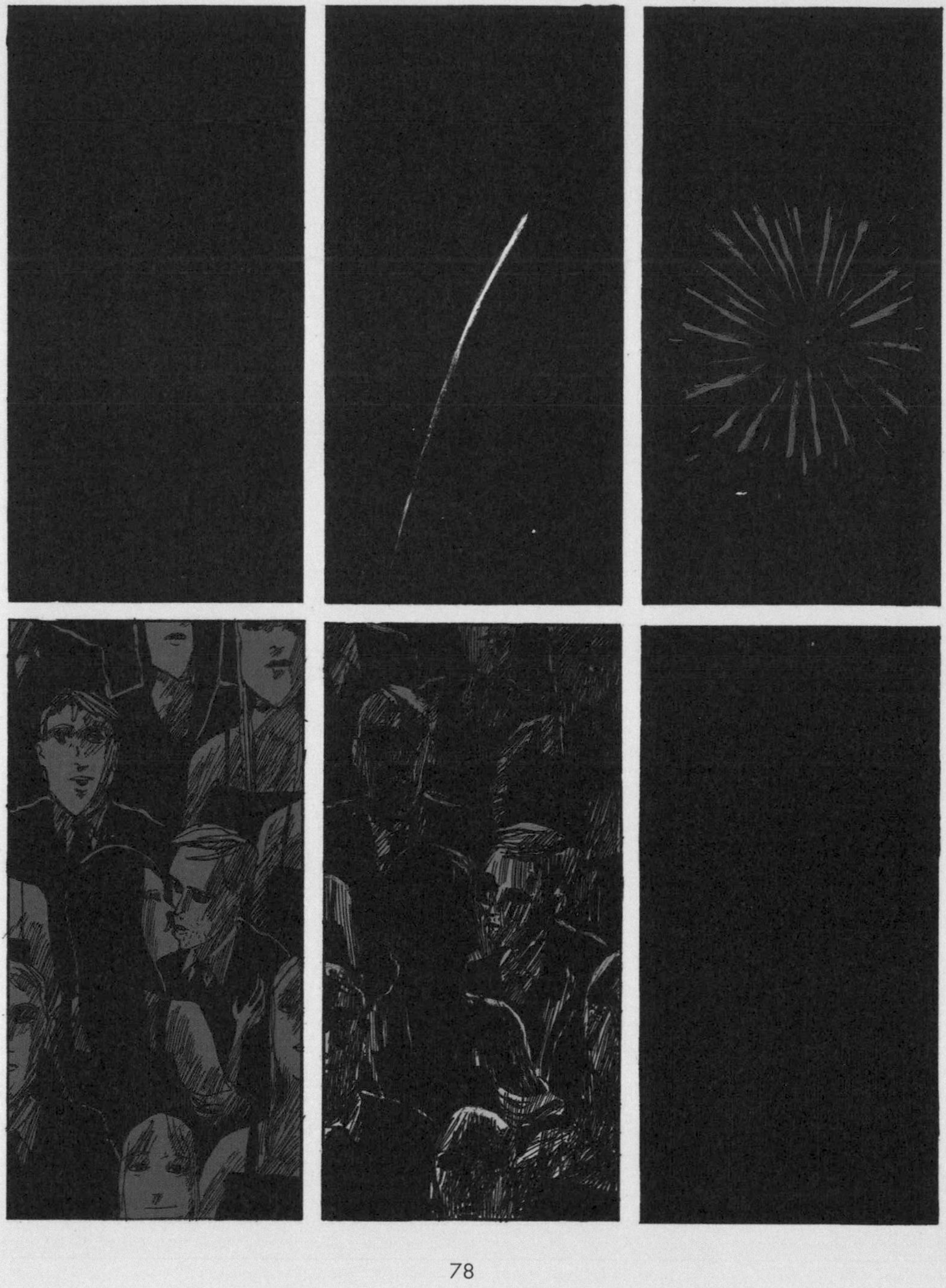

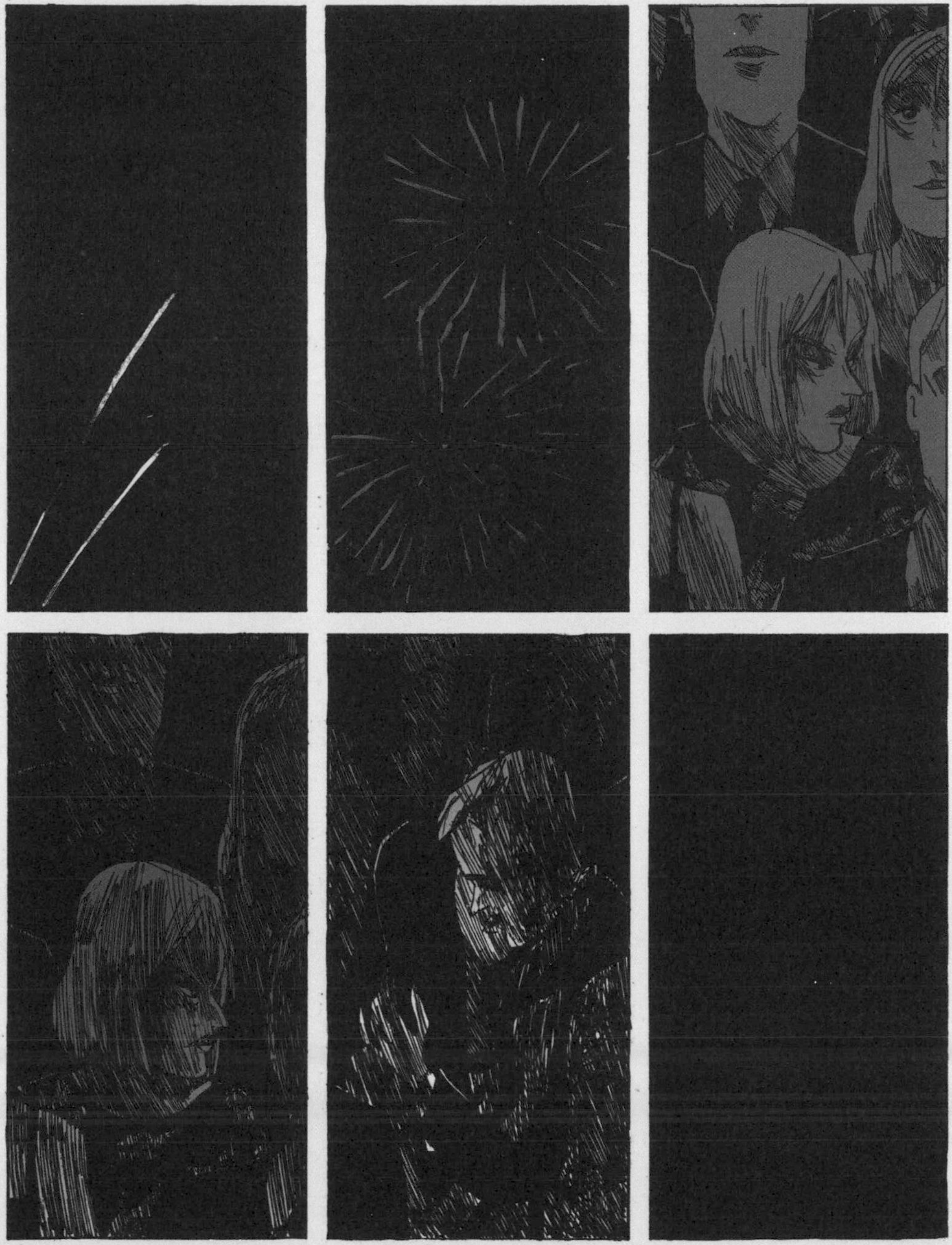

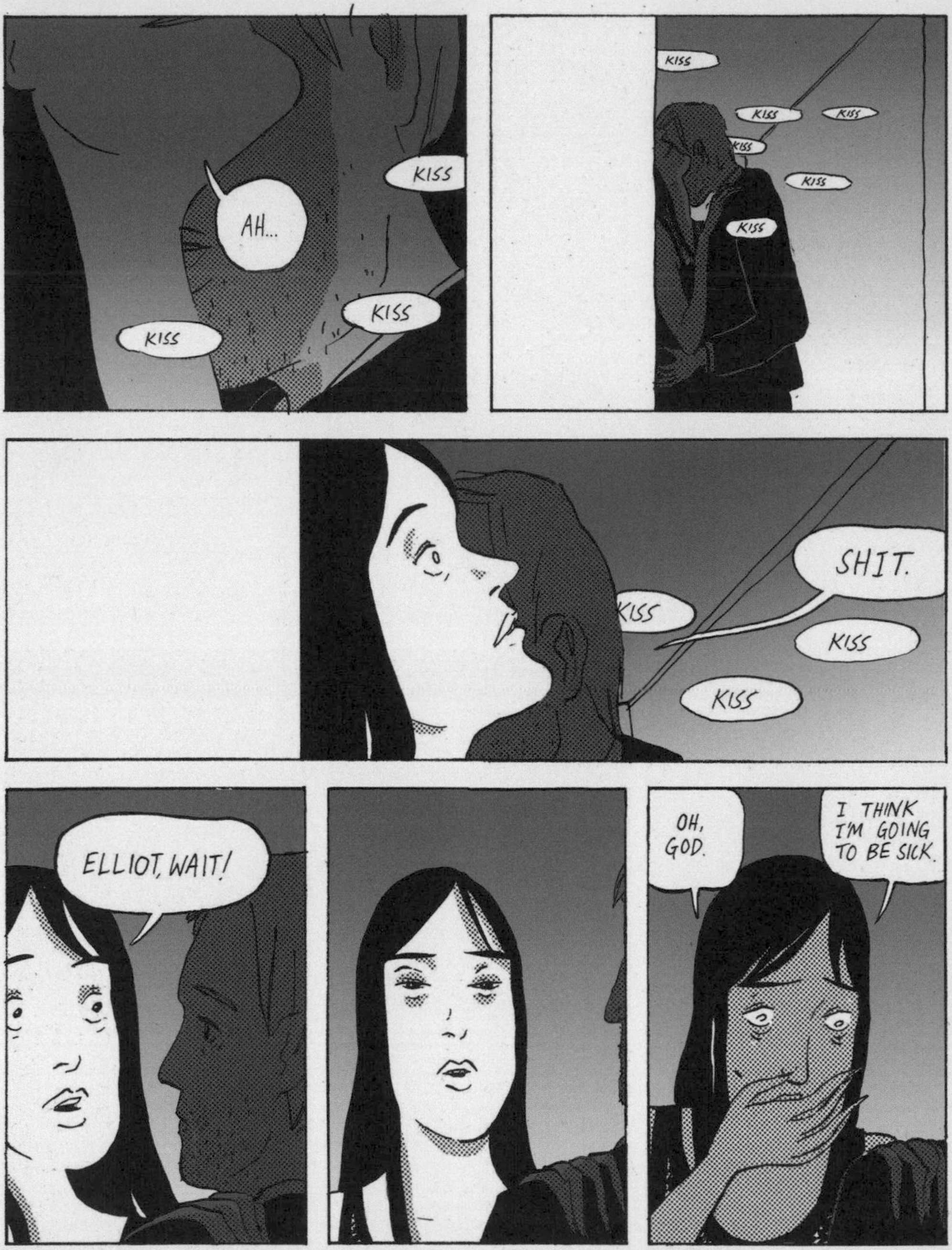
KISS
AH...
KISS
KISS
KISS
KISS
KISS
KISS
KISS
KISS
KISS
SHIT.
KISS
KISS
KISS
ELLIOT, WAIT!
OH, GOD.
I THINK I'M GOING TO BE SICK.

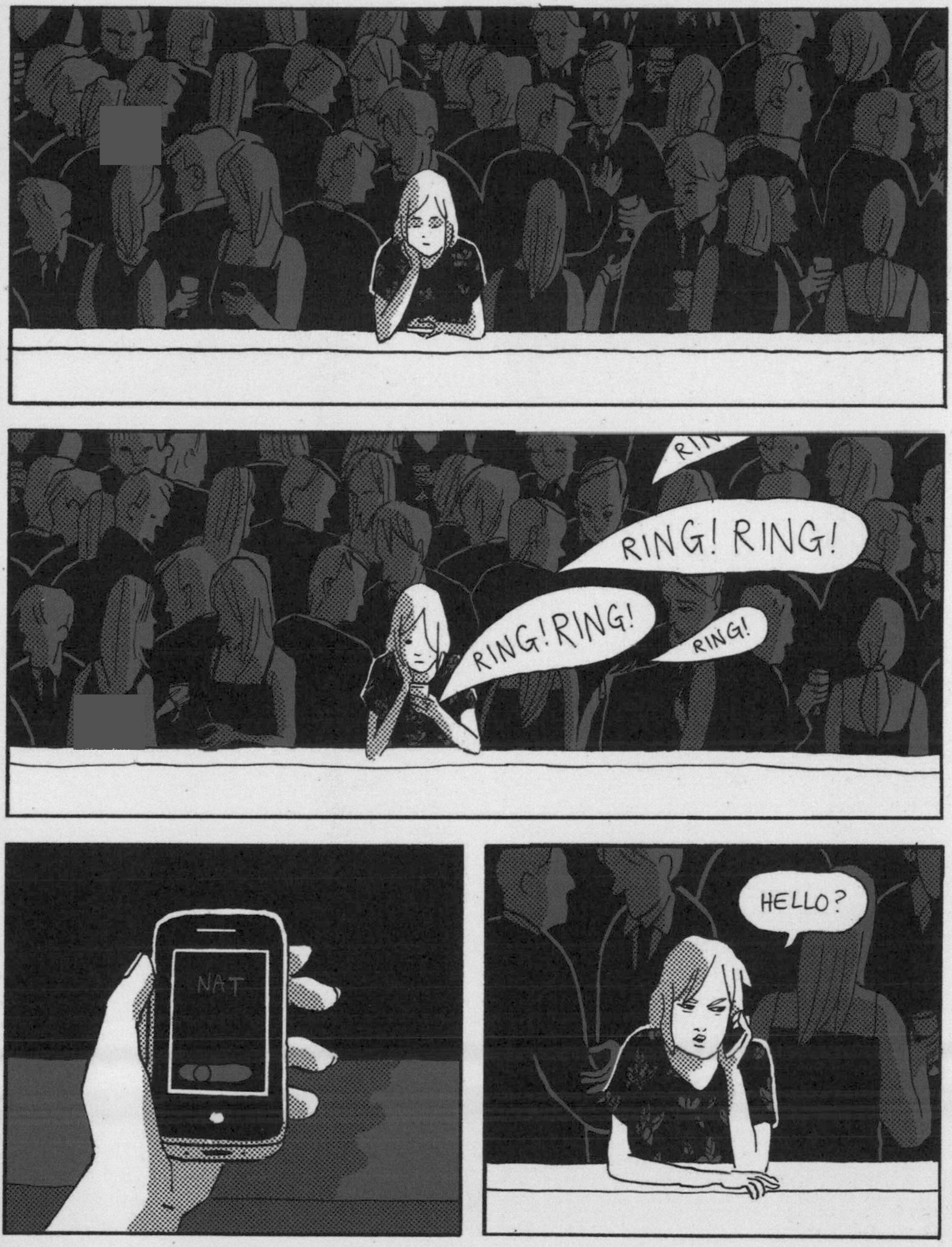
RING! RING!
RING!RING!
RING!
NAT
HELLO?

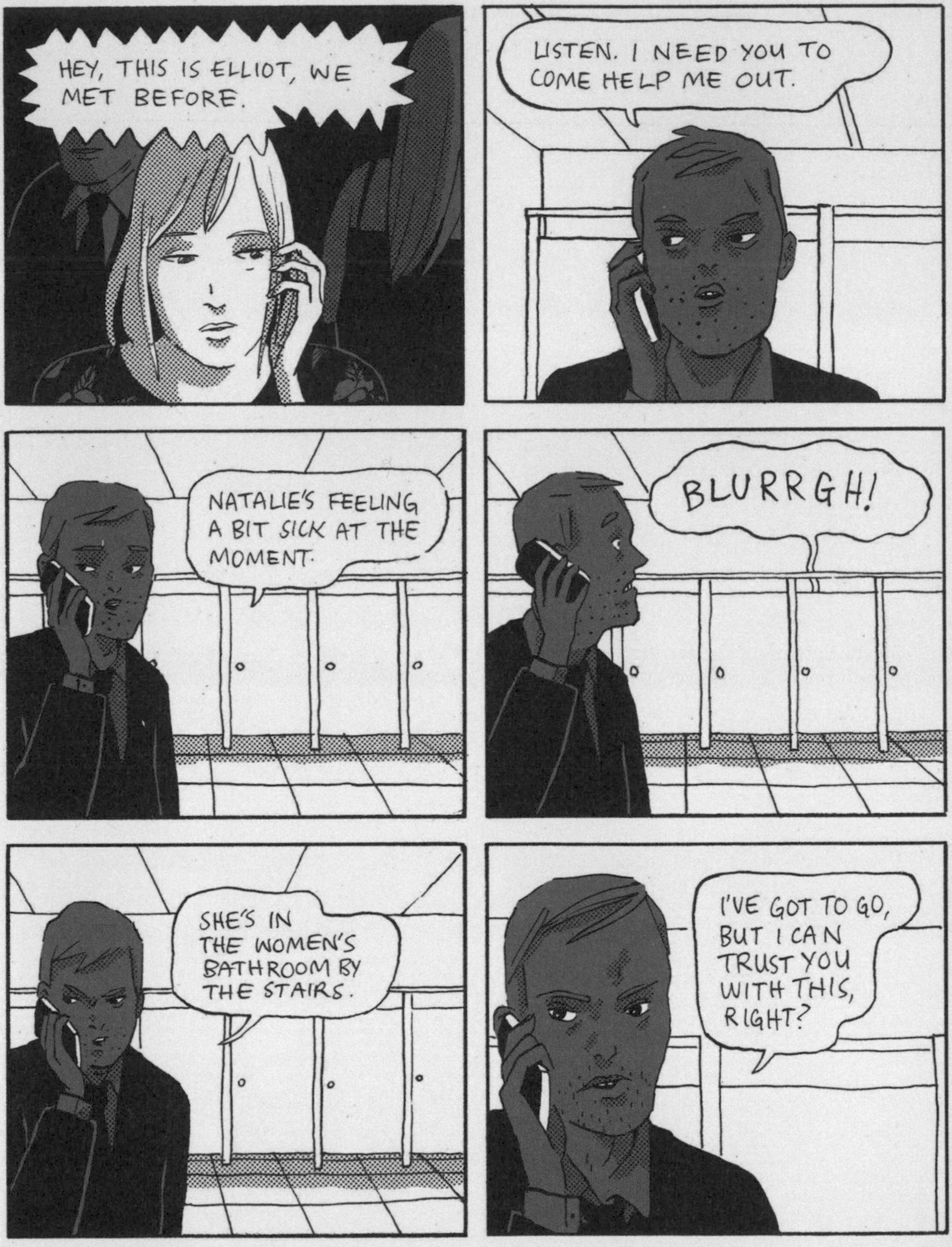
HEY, THIS IS ELLIOT, WE MET BEFORE.
LISTEN. I NEED YOU TO COME HELP ME OUT.
NATALIE'S FEELING A BIT SICK AT THE MOMENT.
BLURRGH!
SHE'S IN THE WOMEN'S BATHROOM BY THE STAIRS.
I'VE GOT TO GO, BUT I CAN TRUST YOU WITH THIS, RIGHT?

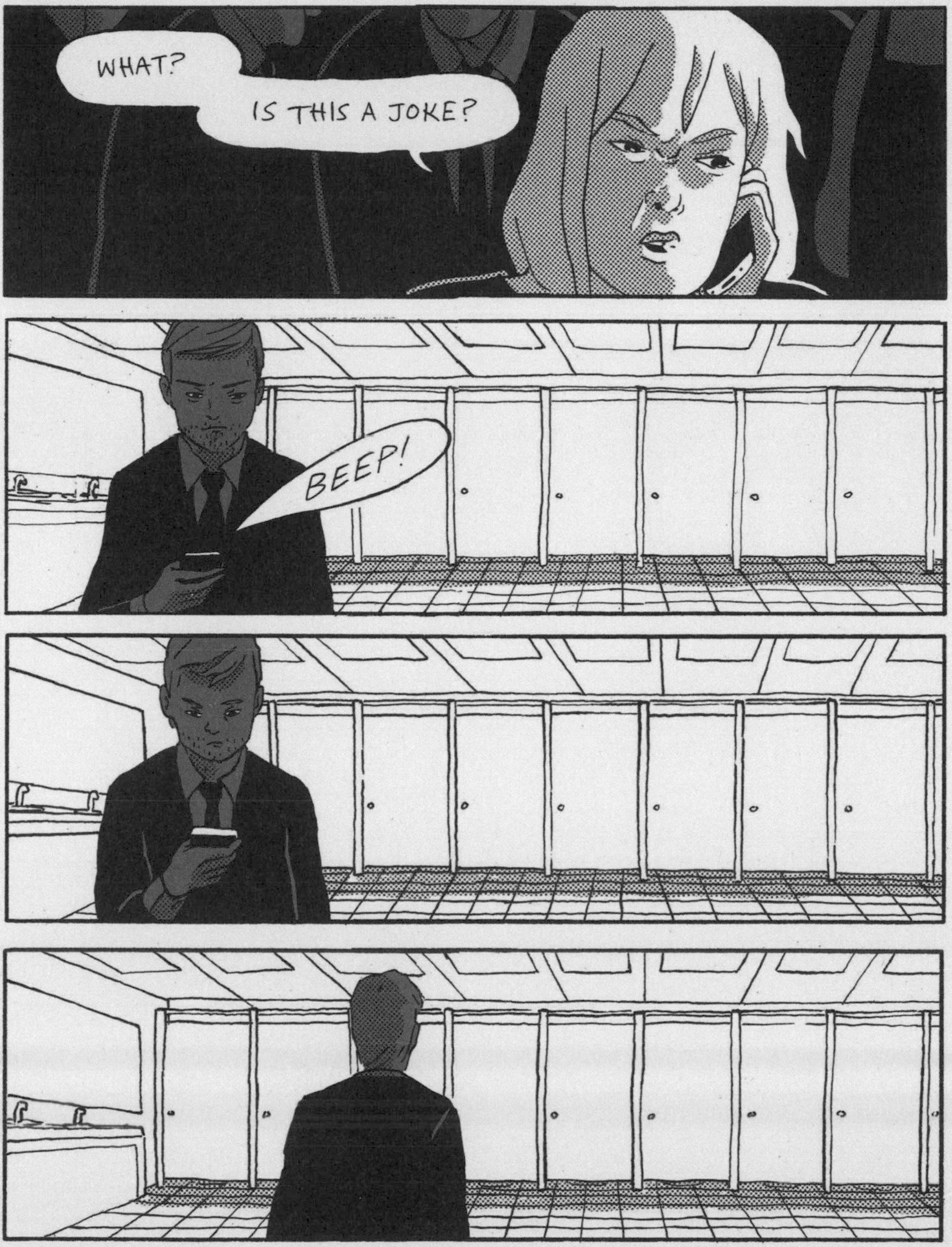
WHAT?
IS THIS A JOKE?
BEEP!

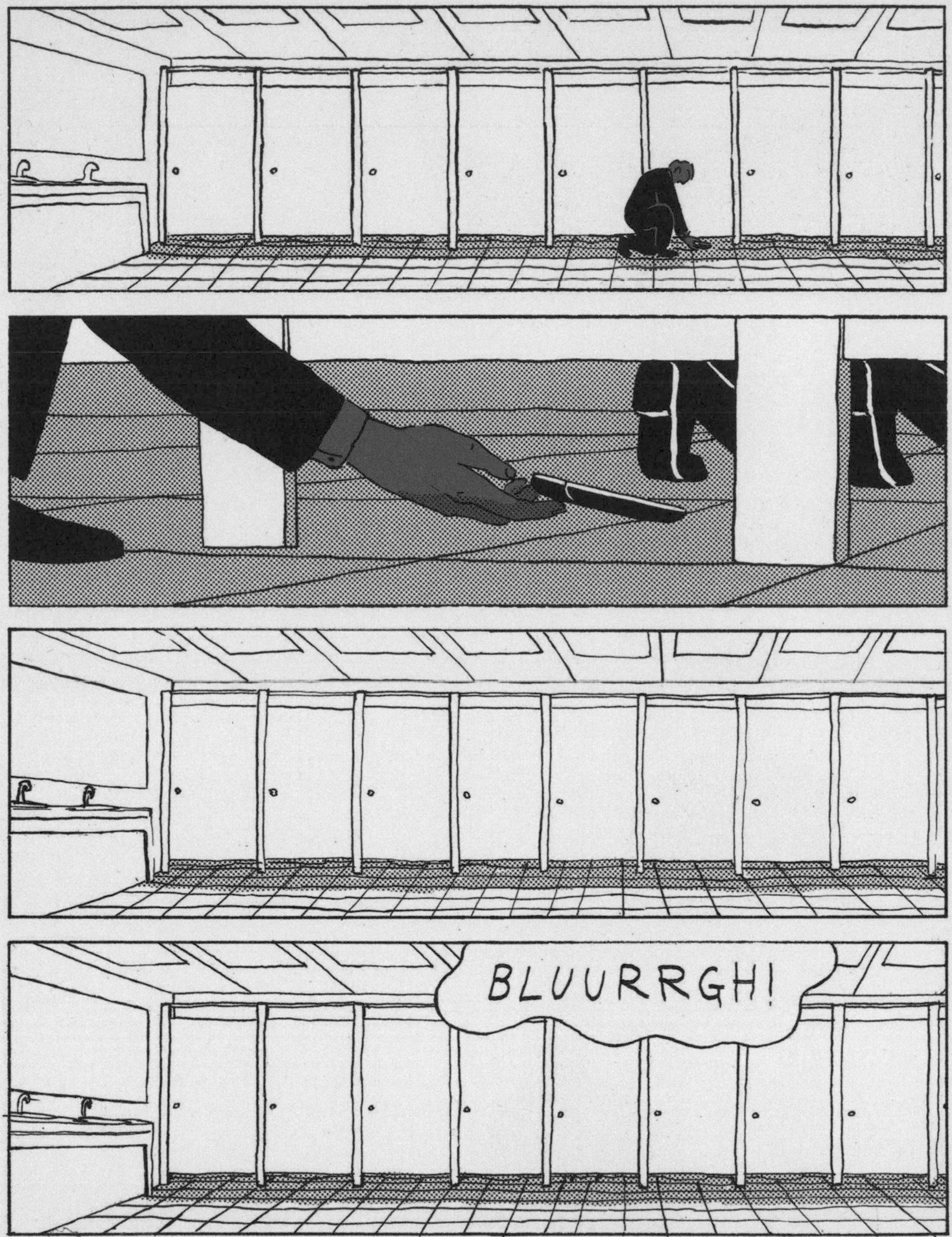
BLUURRGH!

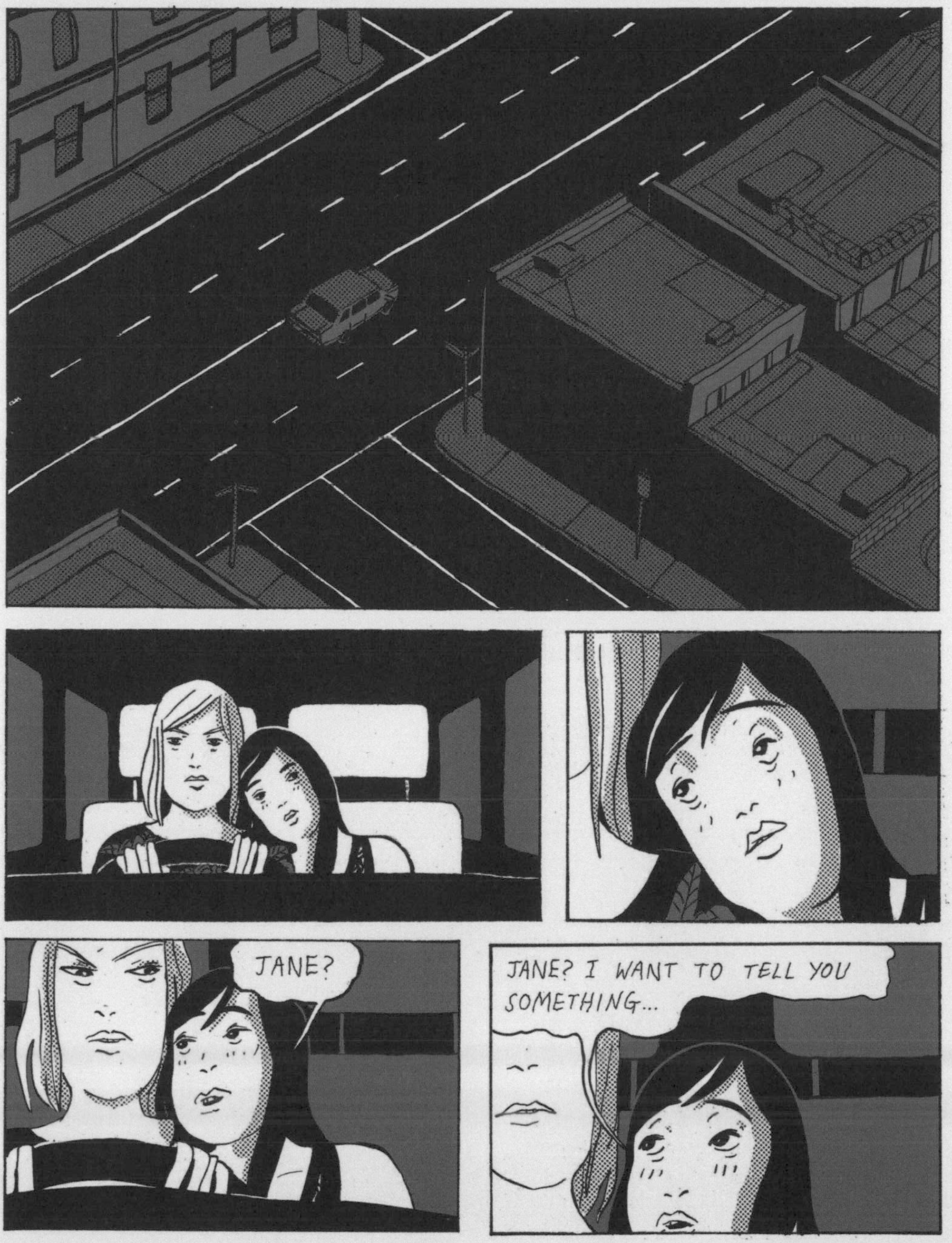
JANE?
JANE? I WANT TO TELL YOU SOMETHING...

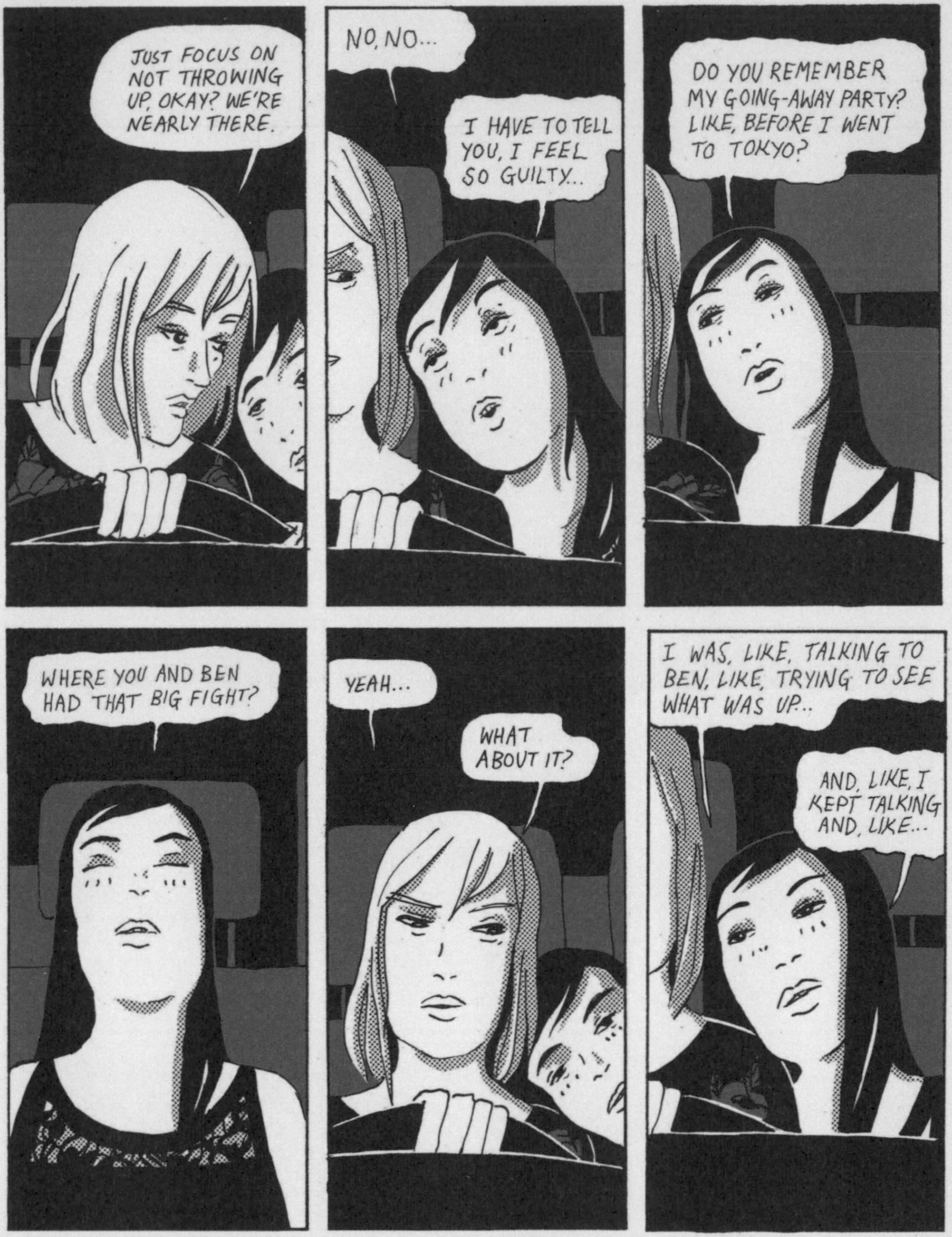
JUST FOCUS ON NOT THROWING UP, OKAY? WE'RE NEARLY THERE.
NO, NO...
I HAVE TO TELL YOU, I FEEL SO GUILTY...
DO YOU REMEMBER MY GOING-AWAY PARTY? LIKE, BEFORE I WENT TO TOKYO?
WHERE YOU AND BEN HAD THAT BIG FIGHT?
YEAH...
WHAT ABOUT IT?
I WAS, LIKE, TALKING TO BEN, LIKE, TRYING TO SEE WHAT WAS UP...
AND, LIKE, I KEPT TALKING AND, LIKE...

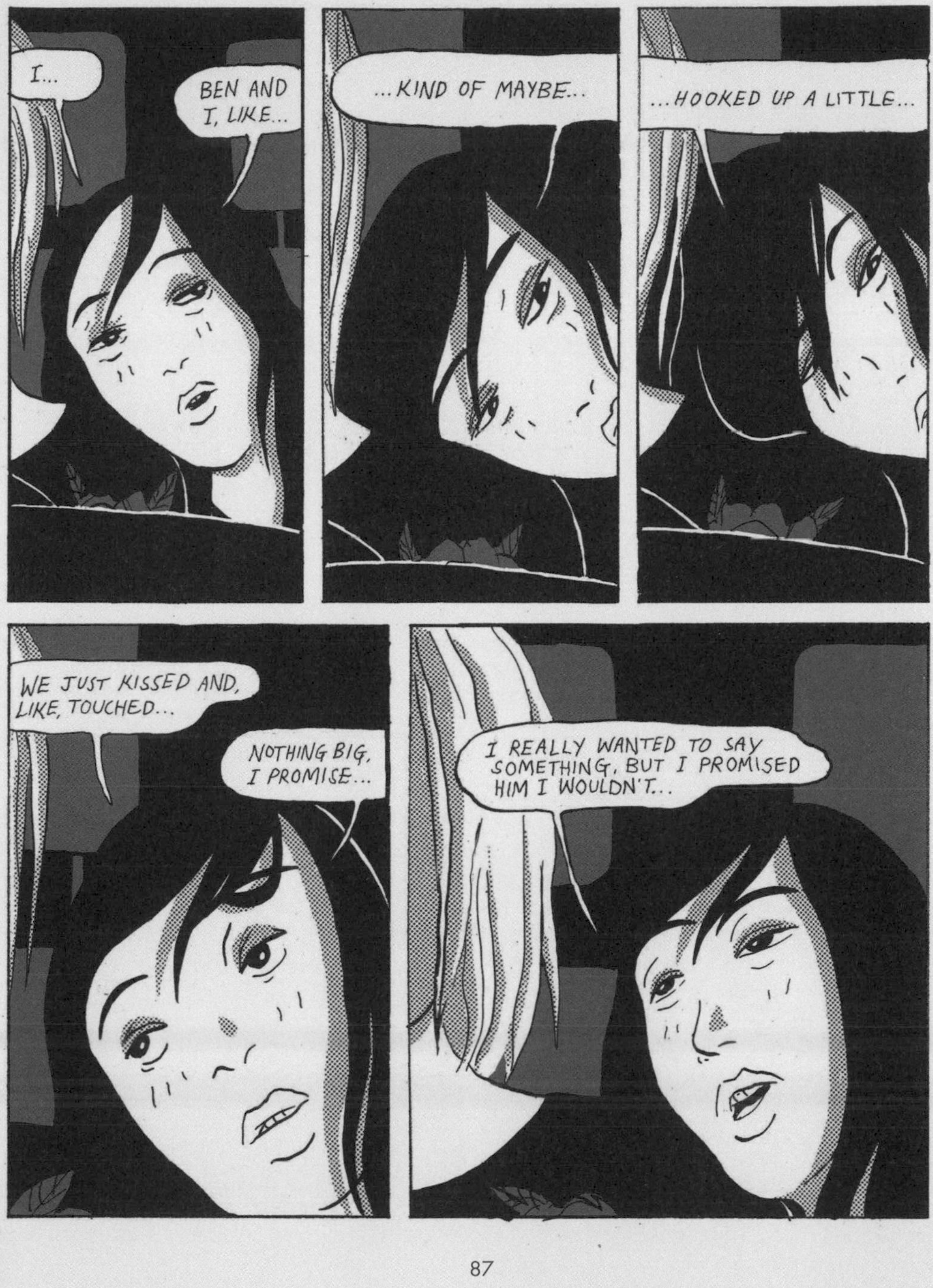
I...
BEN AND I, LIKE...
...KIND OF MAYBE...
...HOOKED UP A LITTLE...
WE JUST KISSED AND, LIKE, TOUCHED...
NOTHING BIG, I PROMISE...
I REALLY WANTED TO SAY SOMETHING, BUT I PROMISED HIM I WOULDN'T...

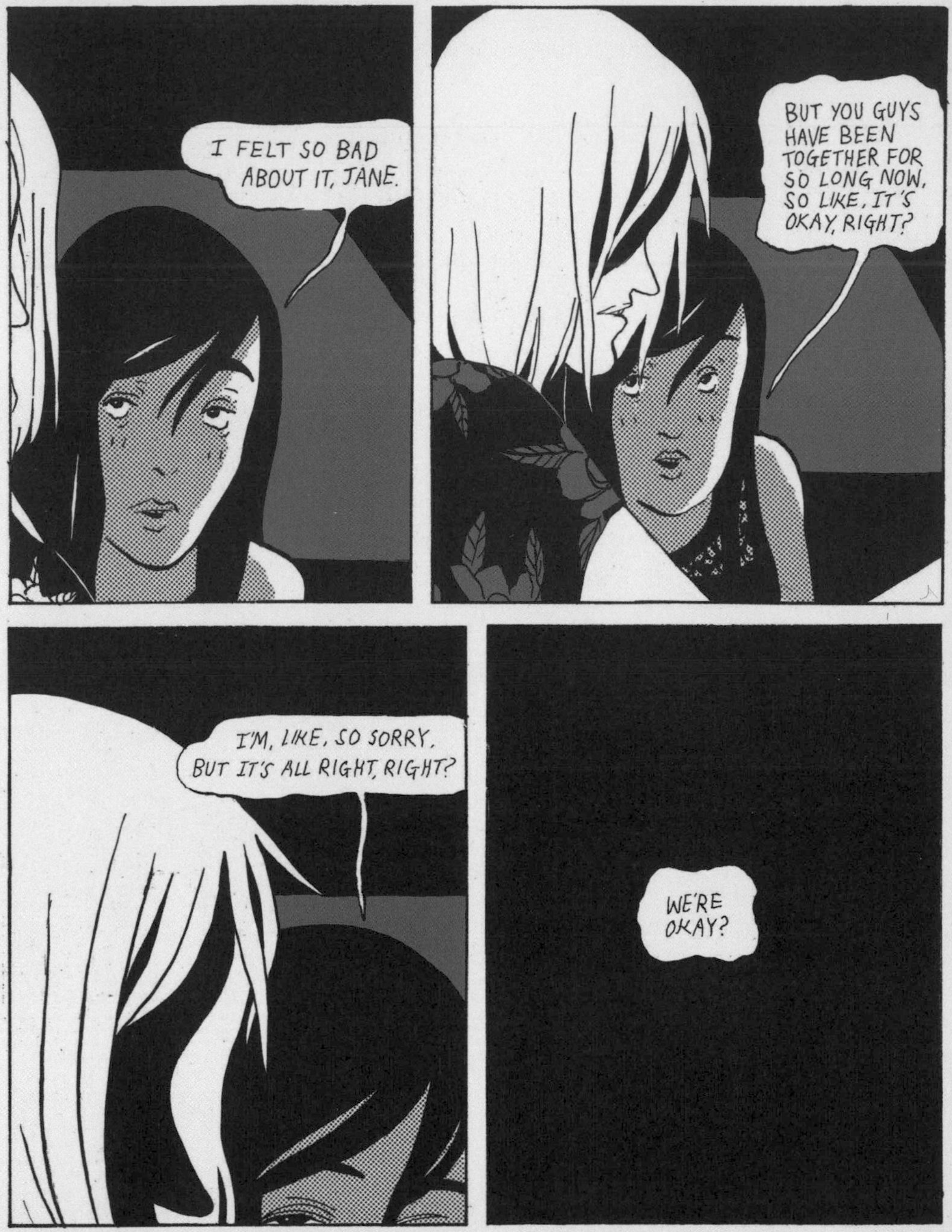
I FELT SO BAD ABOUT IT, JANE.
BUT YOU GUYS HAVE BEEN TOGETHER FOR SO LONG NOW, SO LIKE, IT'S OKAY, RIGHT?
I'M, LIKE, SO SORRY. BUT IT'S ALL RIGHT, RIGHT?
WE'RE OKAY?

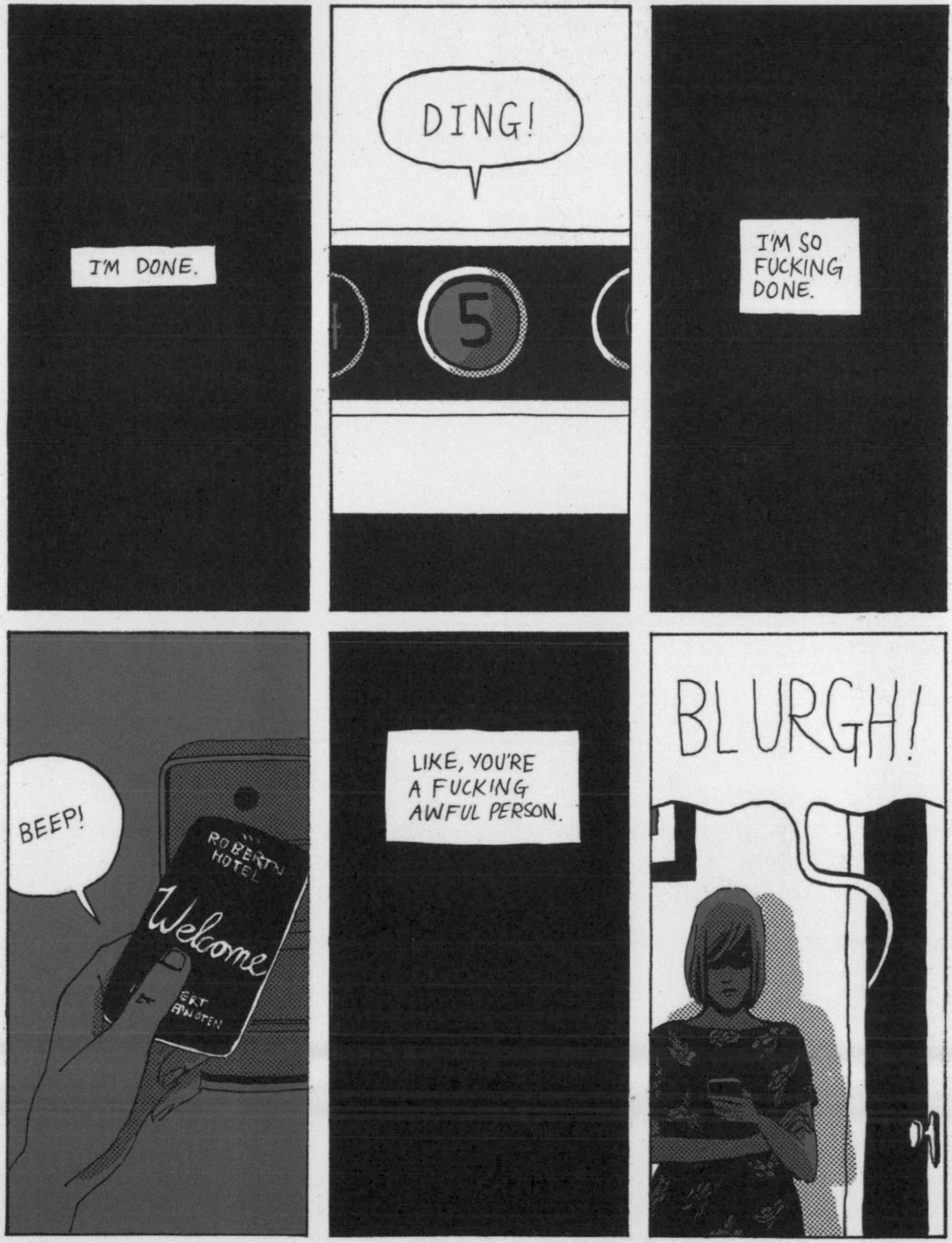
I'M DONE.
DING!
5
I'M SO FUCKING DONE.
BEEP!
HOTEL
Welcome
LIKE, YOU'RE A FUCKING AWFUL PERSON.
BLURGH!

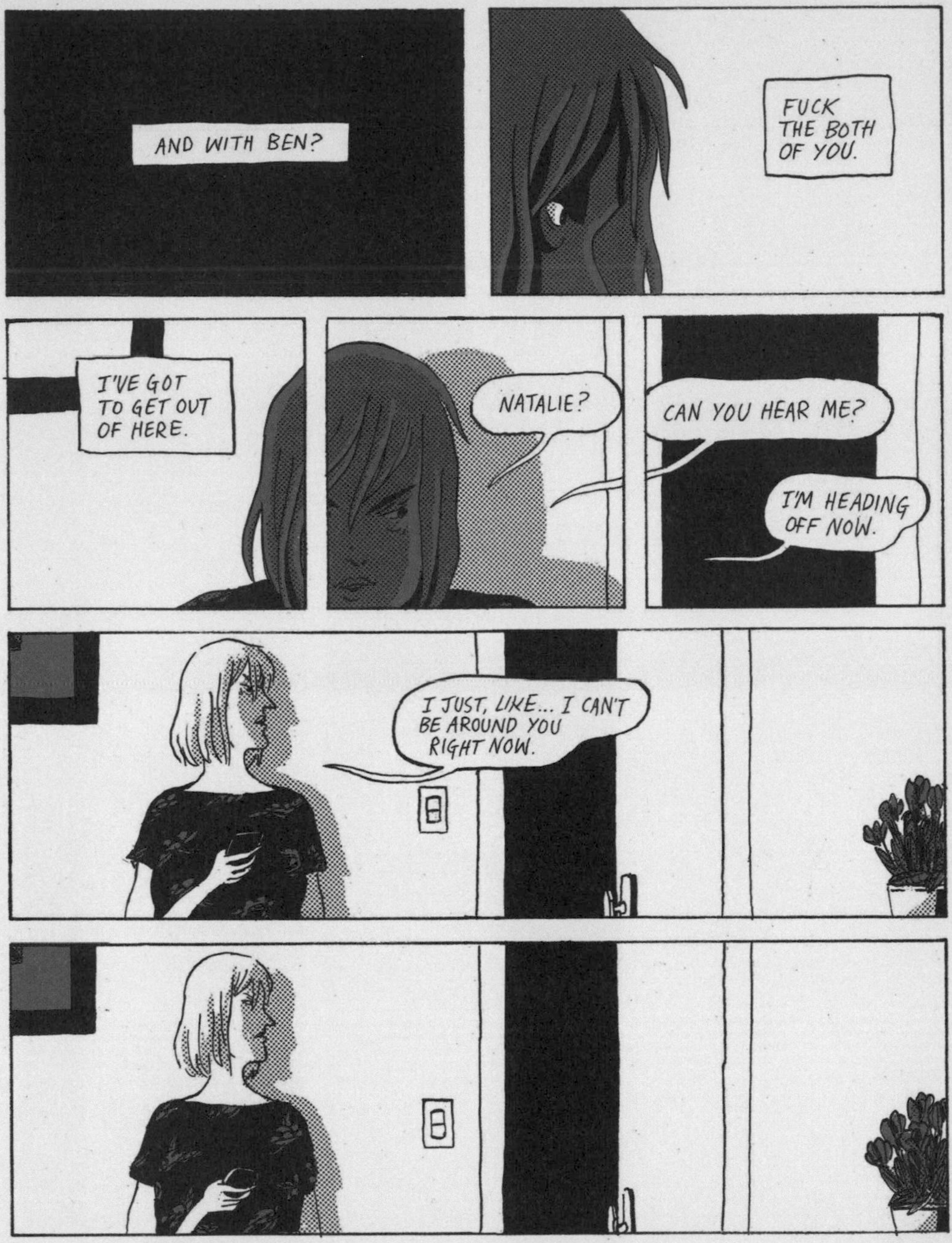
AND WITH BEN?
FUCK THE BOTH OF YOU.
I'VE GOT TO GET OUT OF HERE.
NATALIE?
CAN YOU HEAR ME?
I'M HEADING OFF NOW.
I JUST, LIKE... I CAN'T BE AROUND YOU RIGHT NOW.

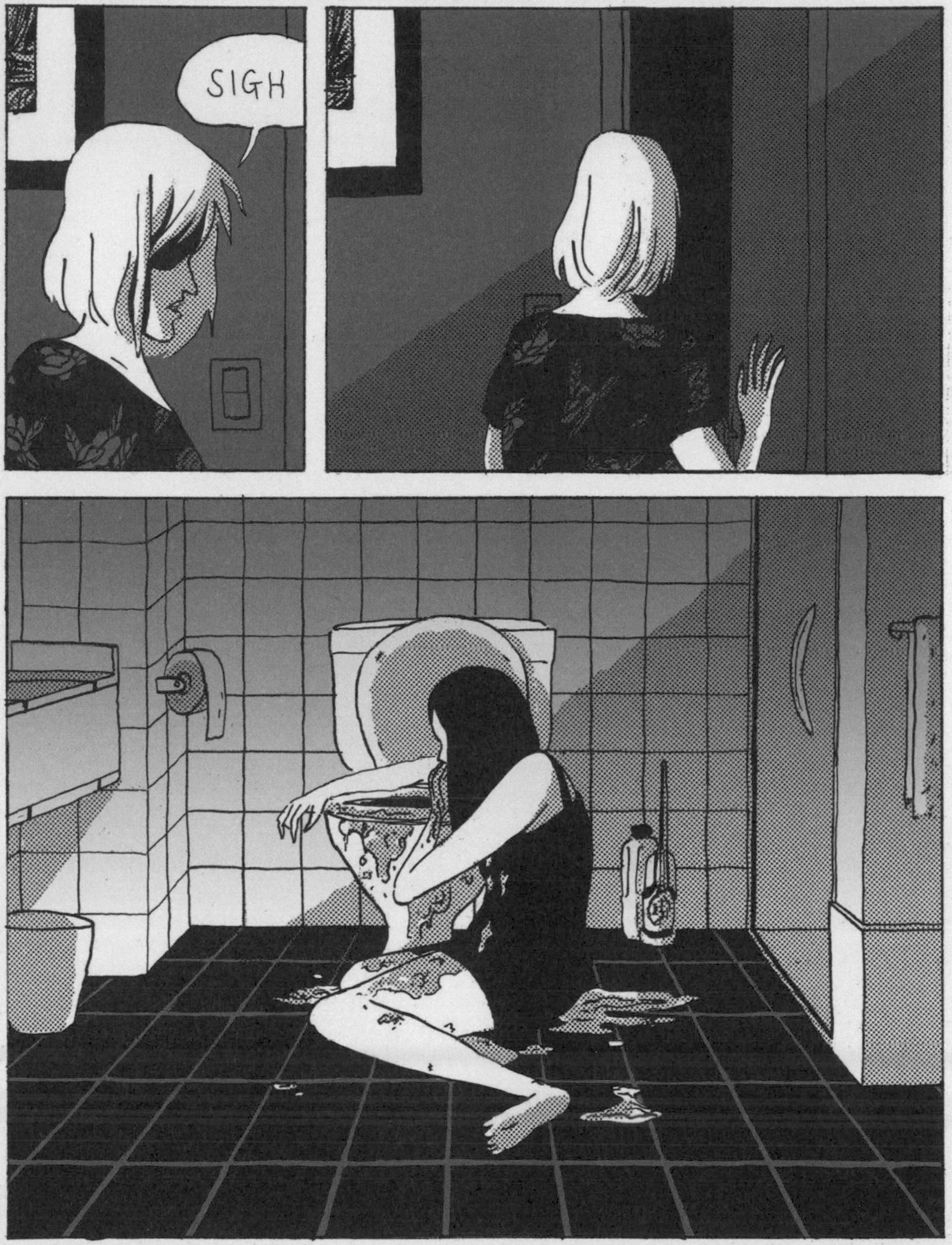
SIGH

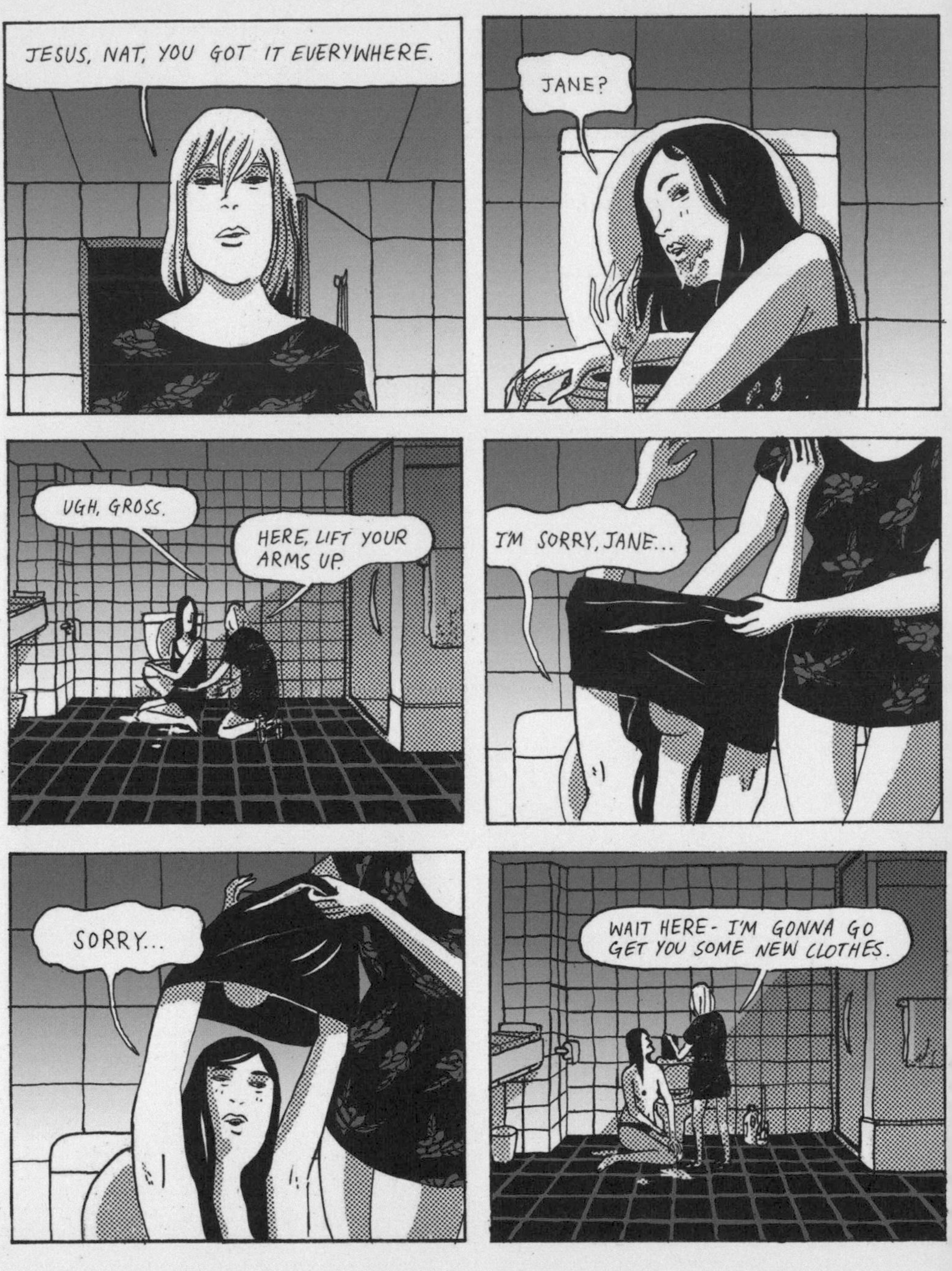
JESUS, NAT, YOU GOT IT EVERYWHERE.
JANE?
UGH, GROSS.
HERE, LIFT YOUR ARMS UP.
I'M SORRY, JANE...
SORRY...
WAIT HERE- I'M GONNA GO GET YOU SOME NEW CLOTHES.

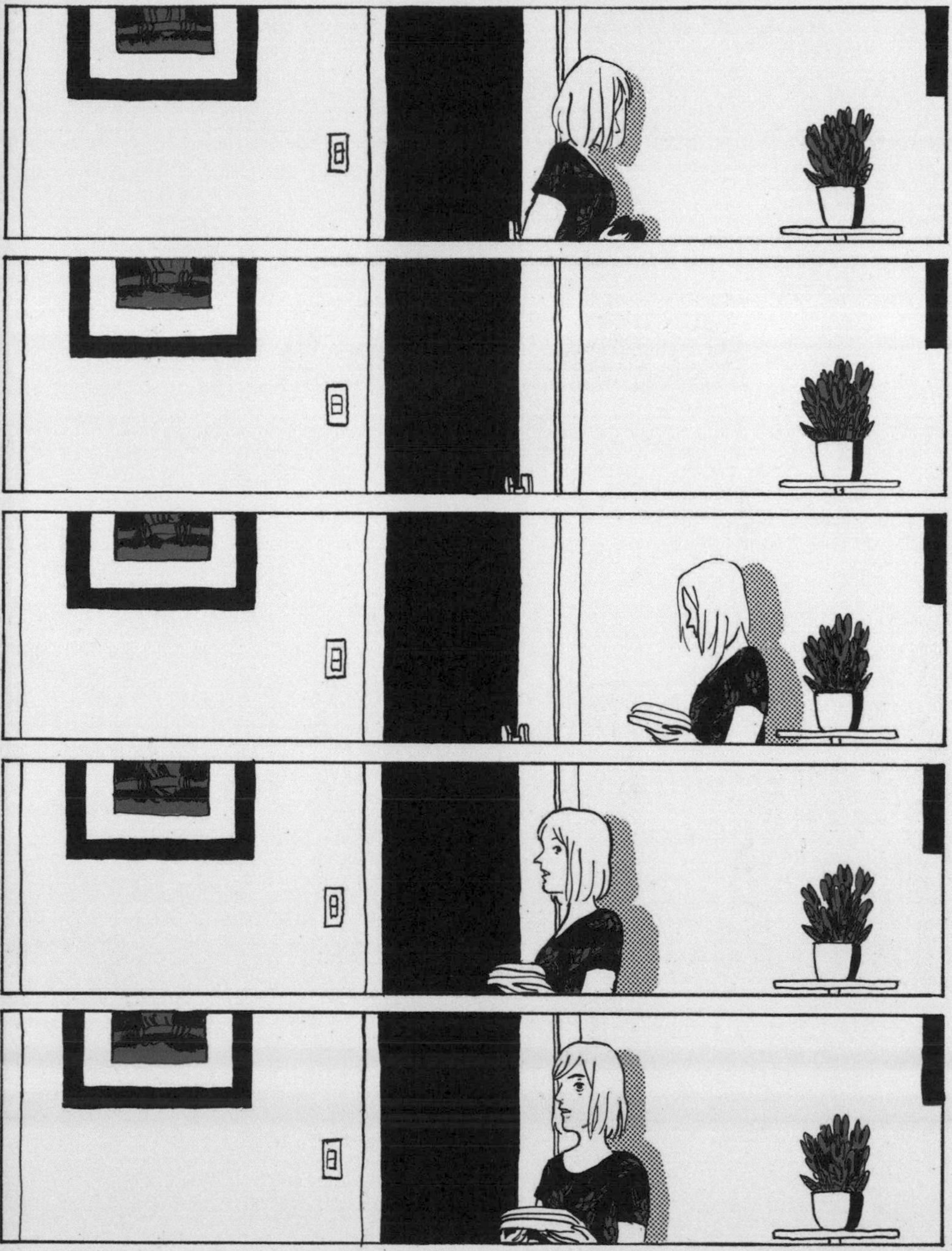

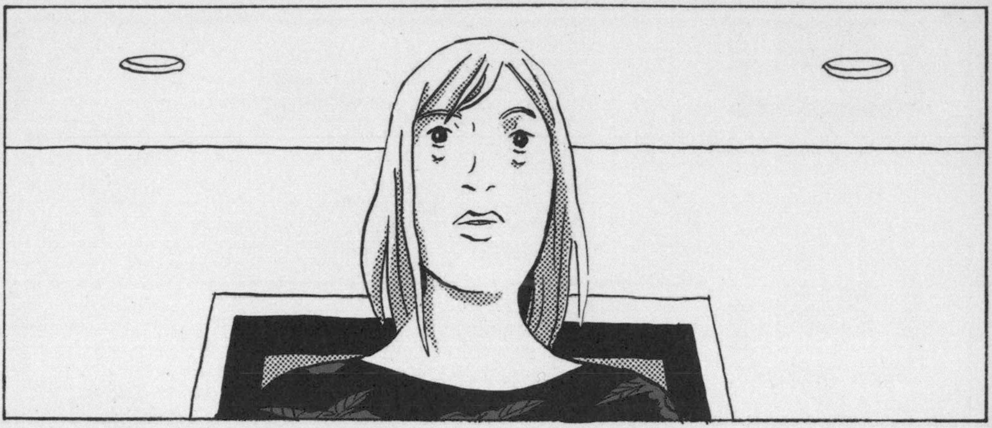

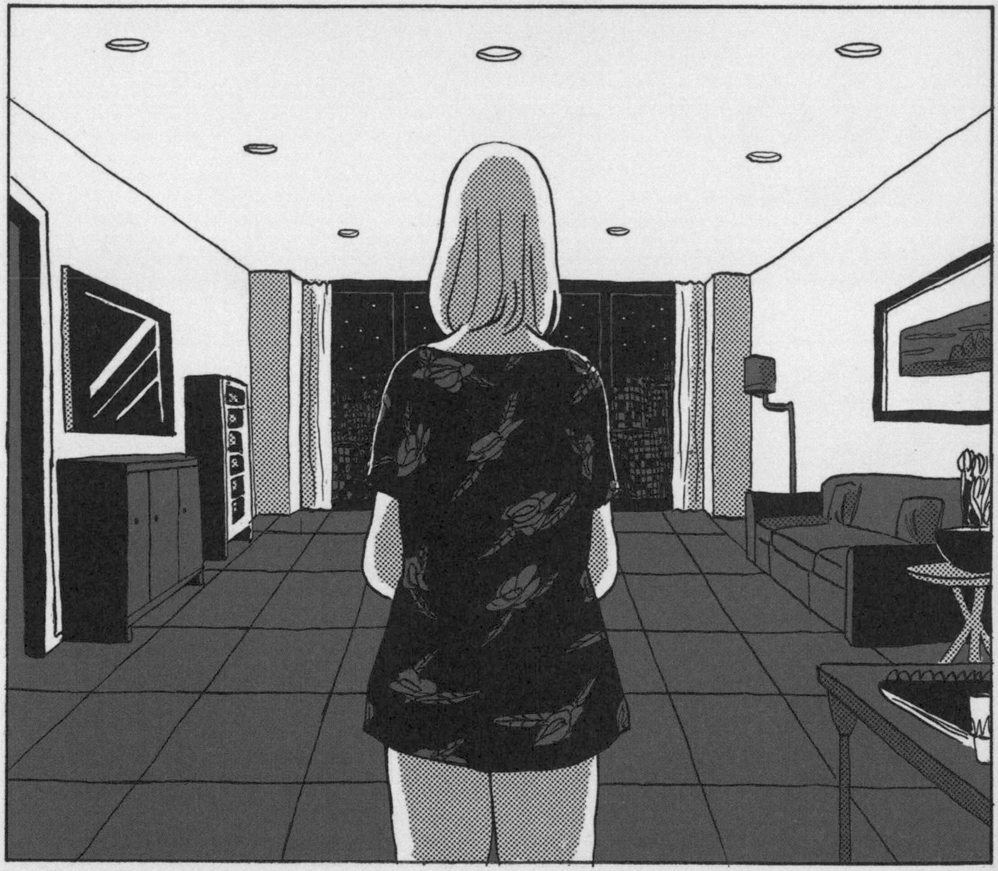

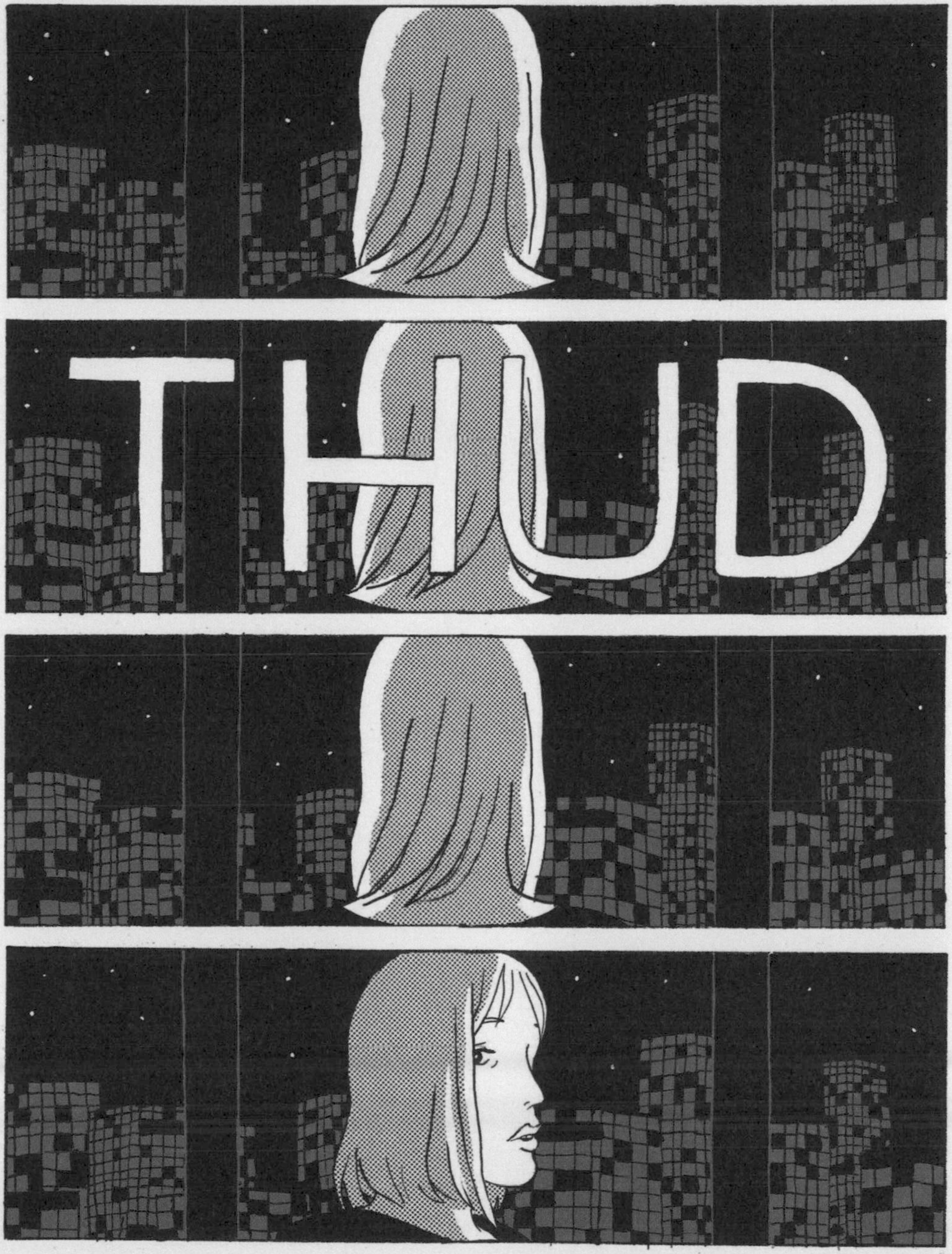
THUD

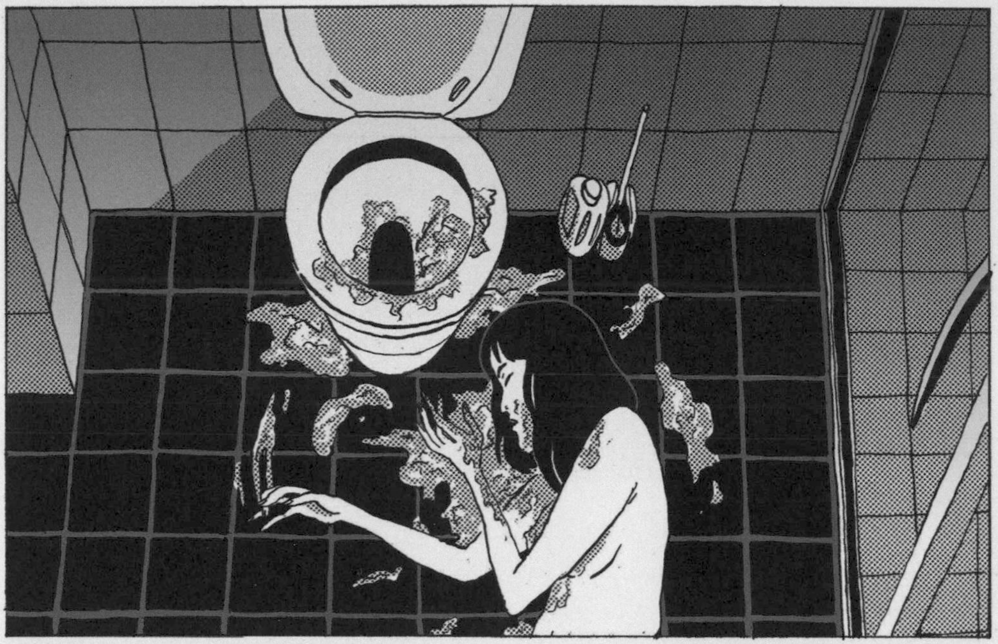

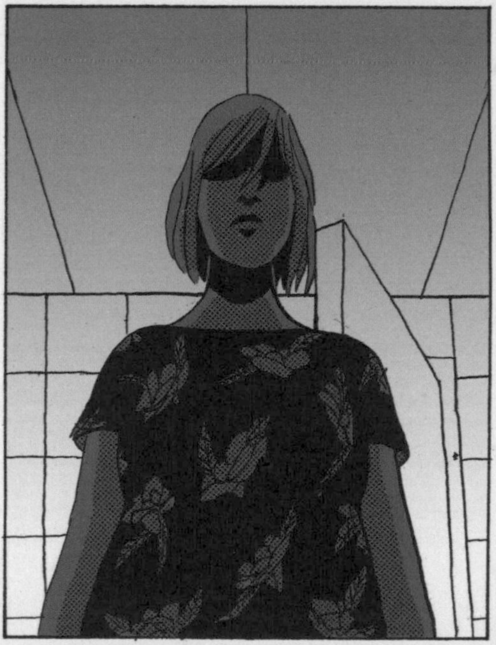

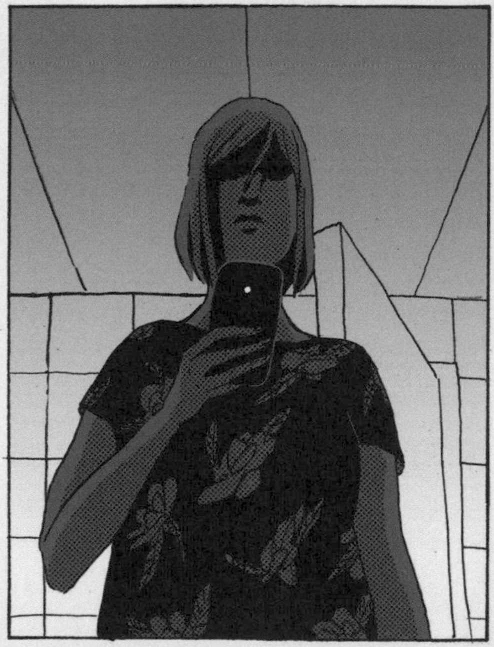

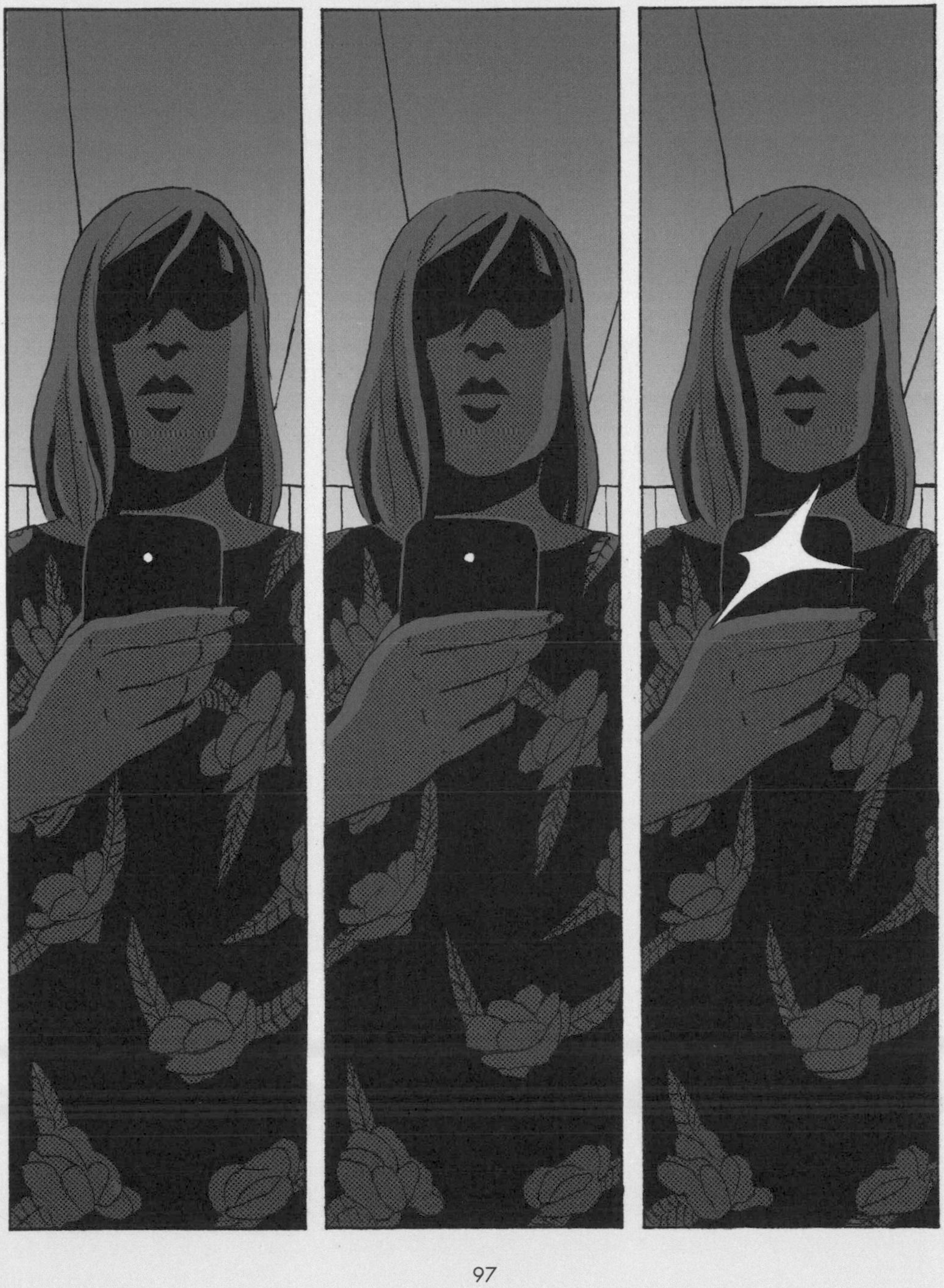

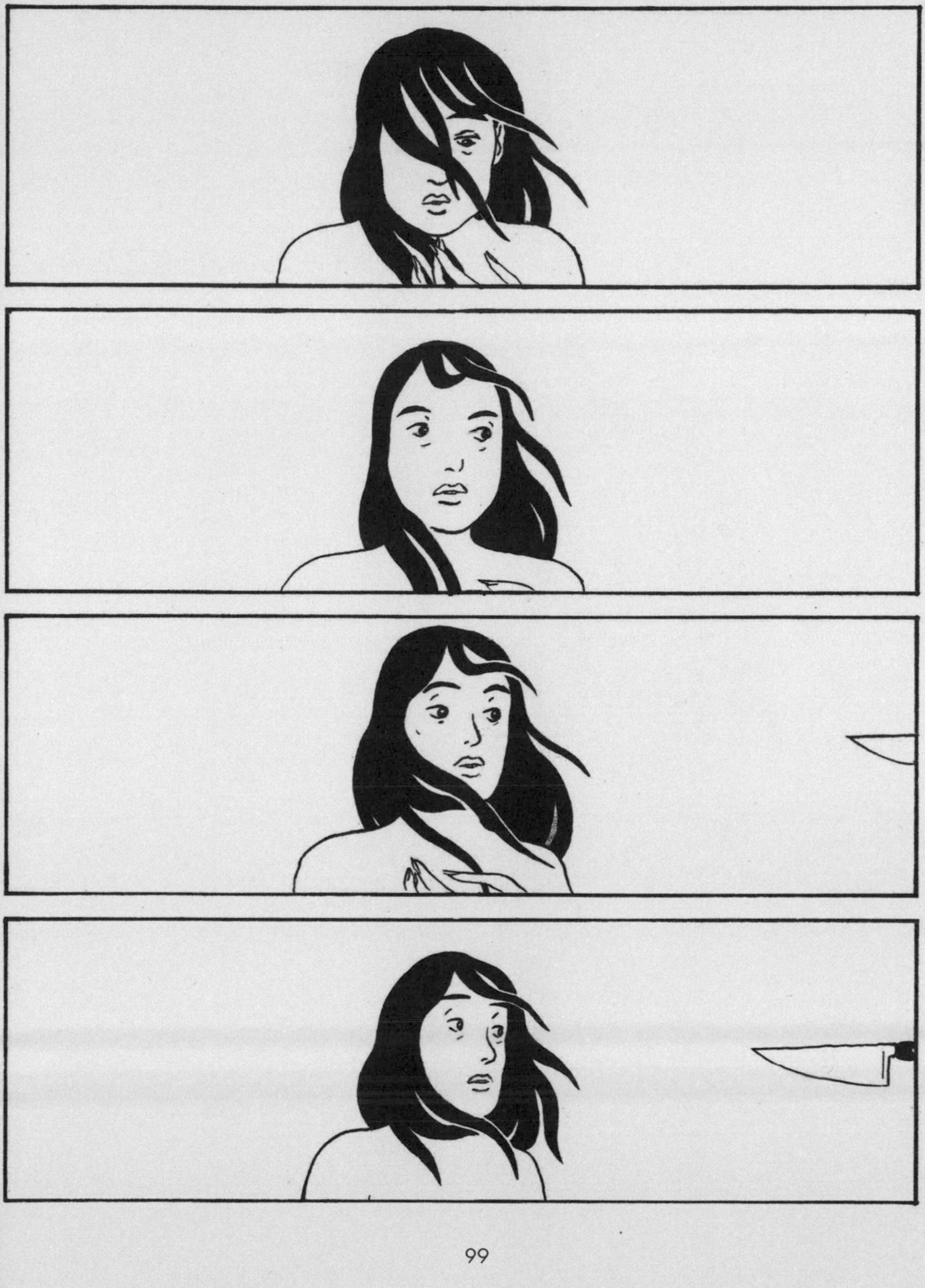

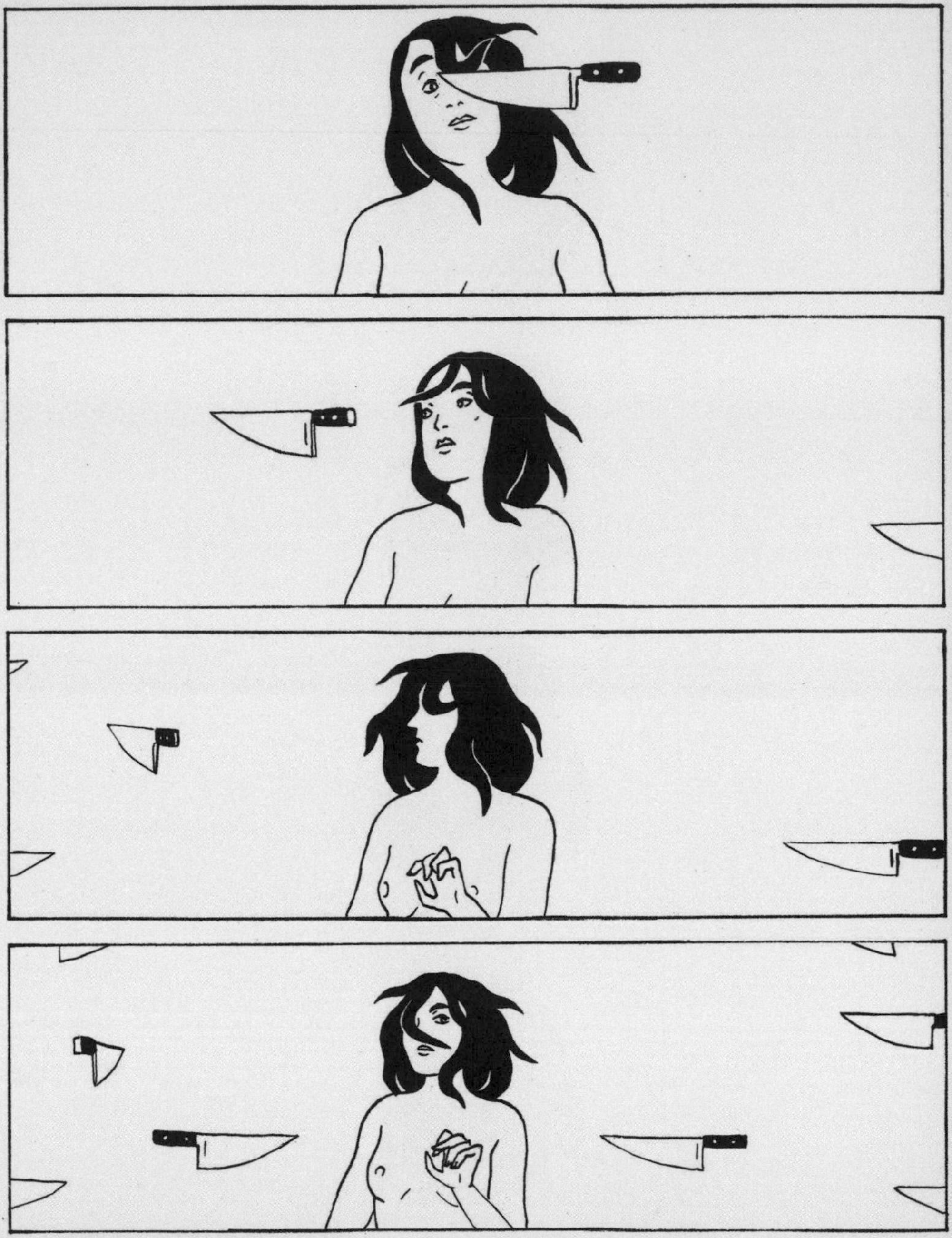

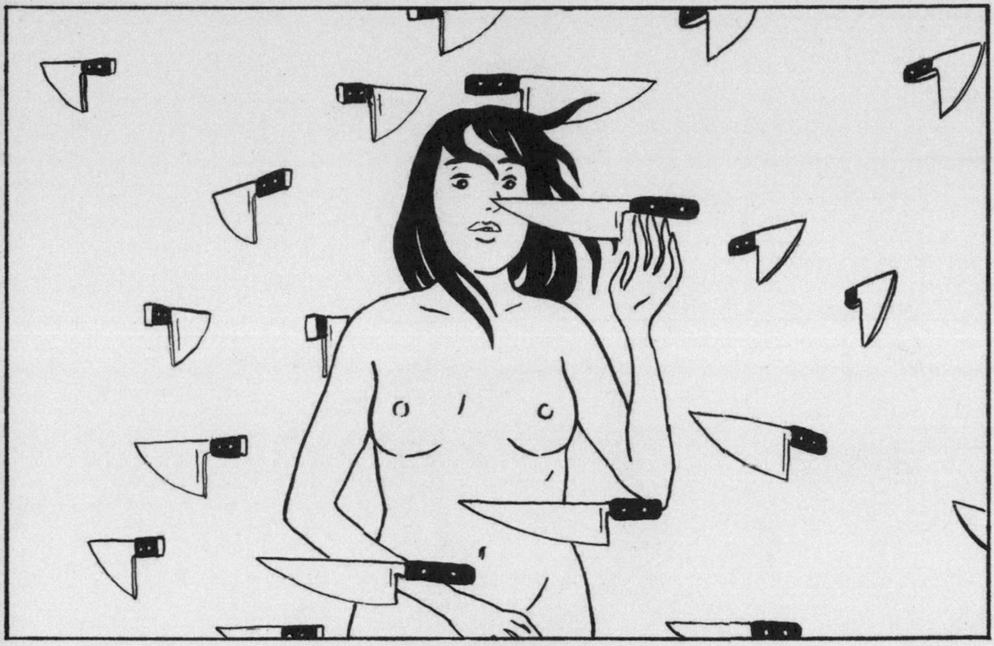

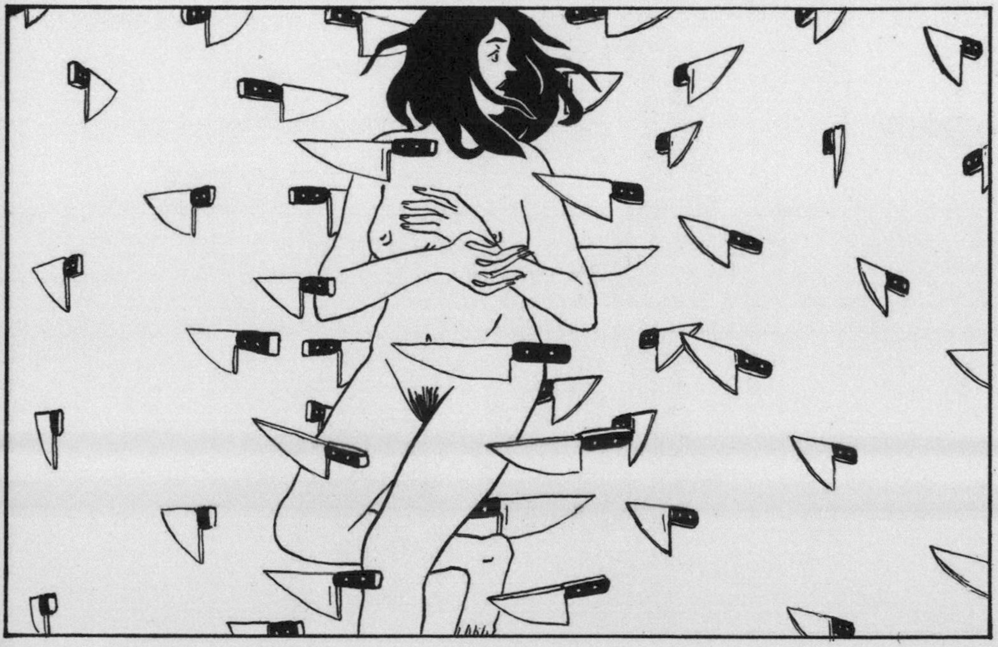

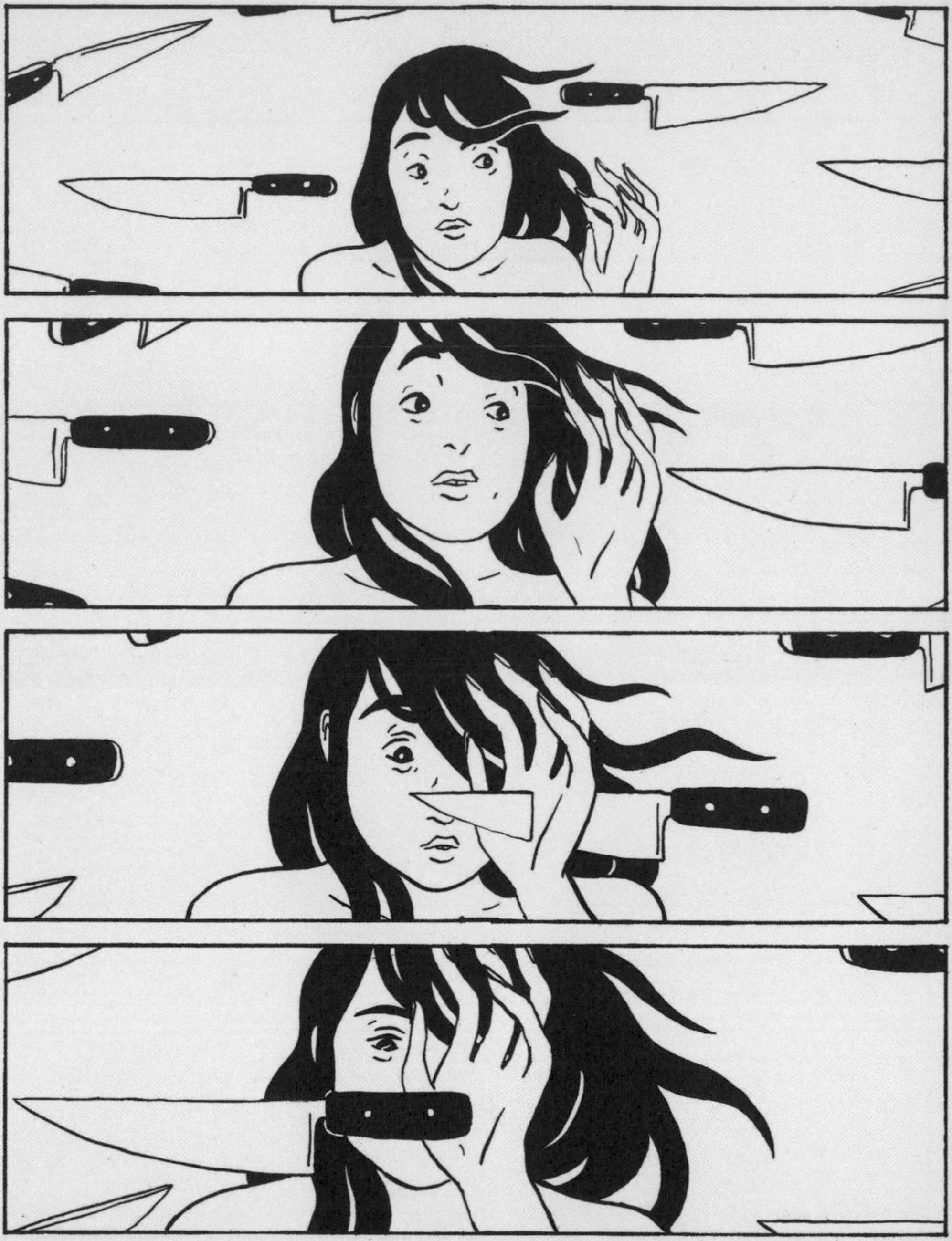

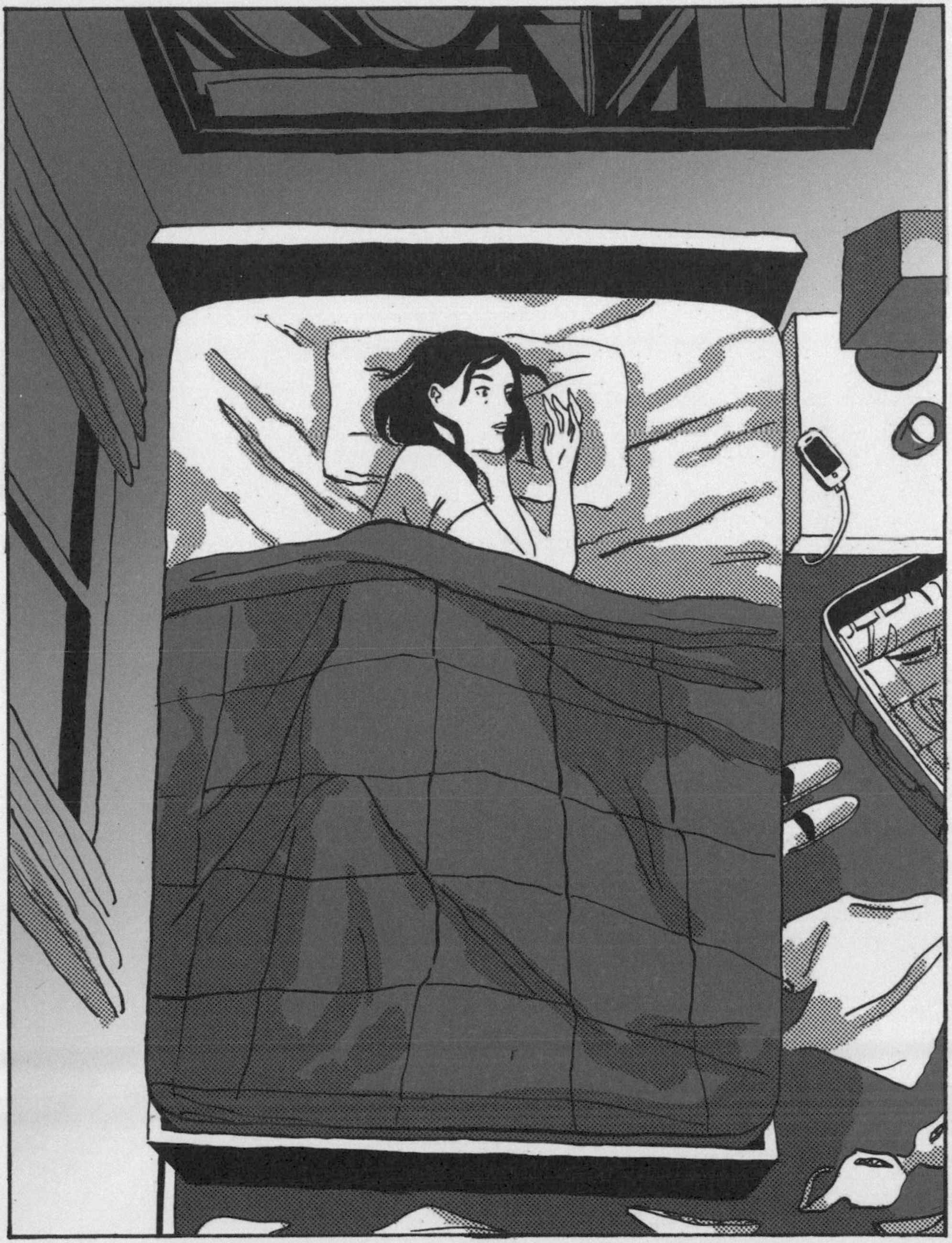

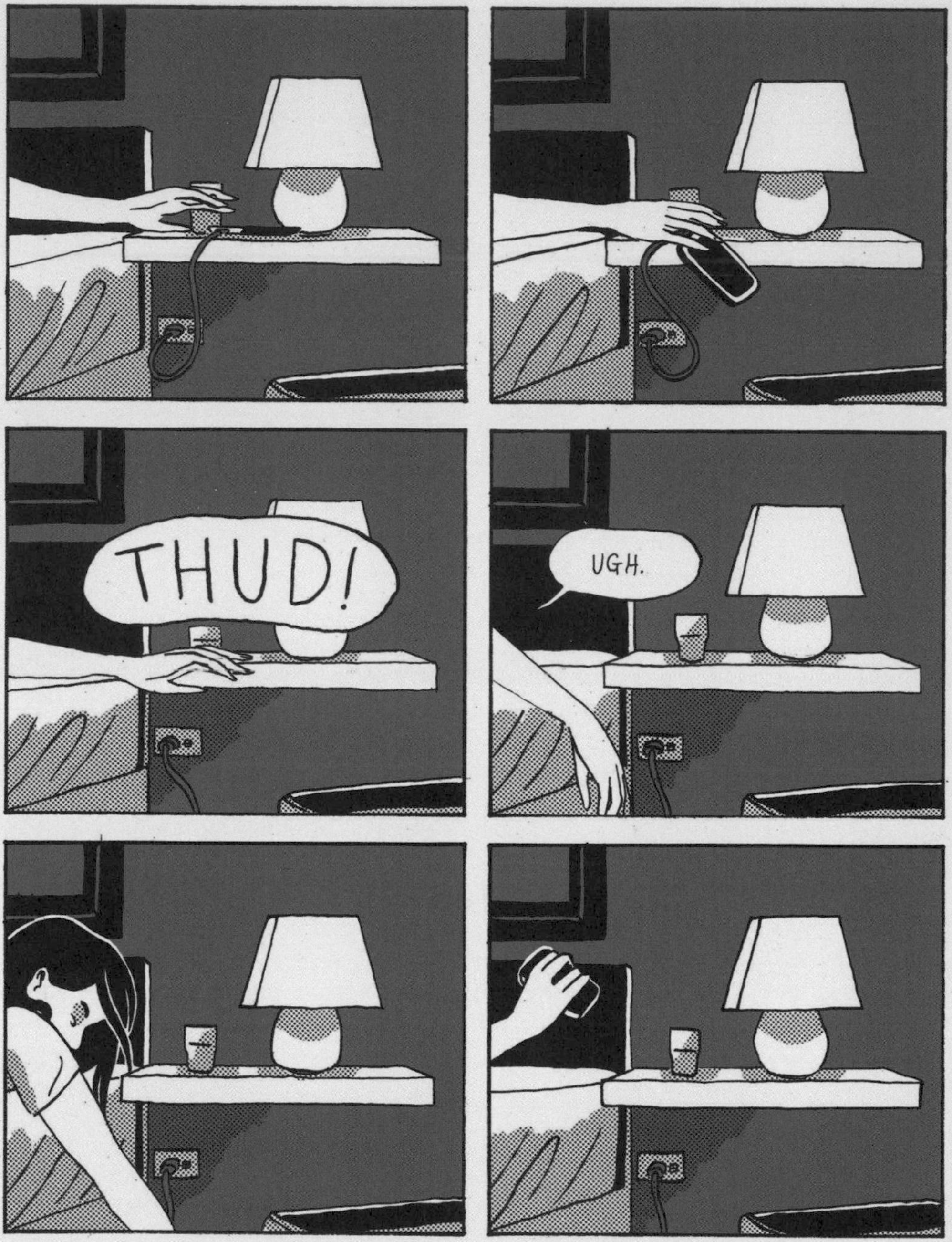
THUD!
UGH.

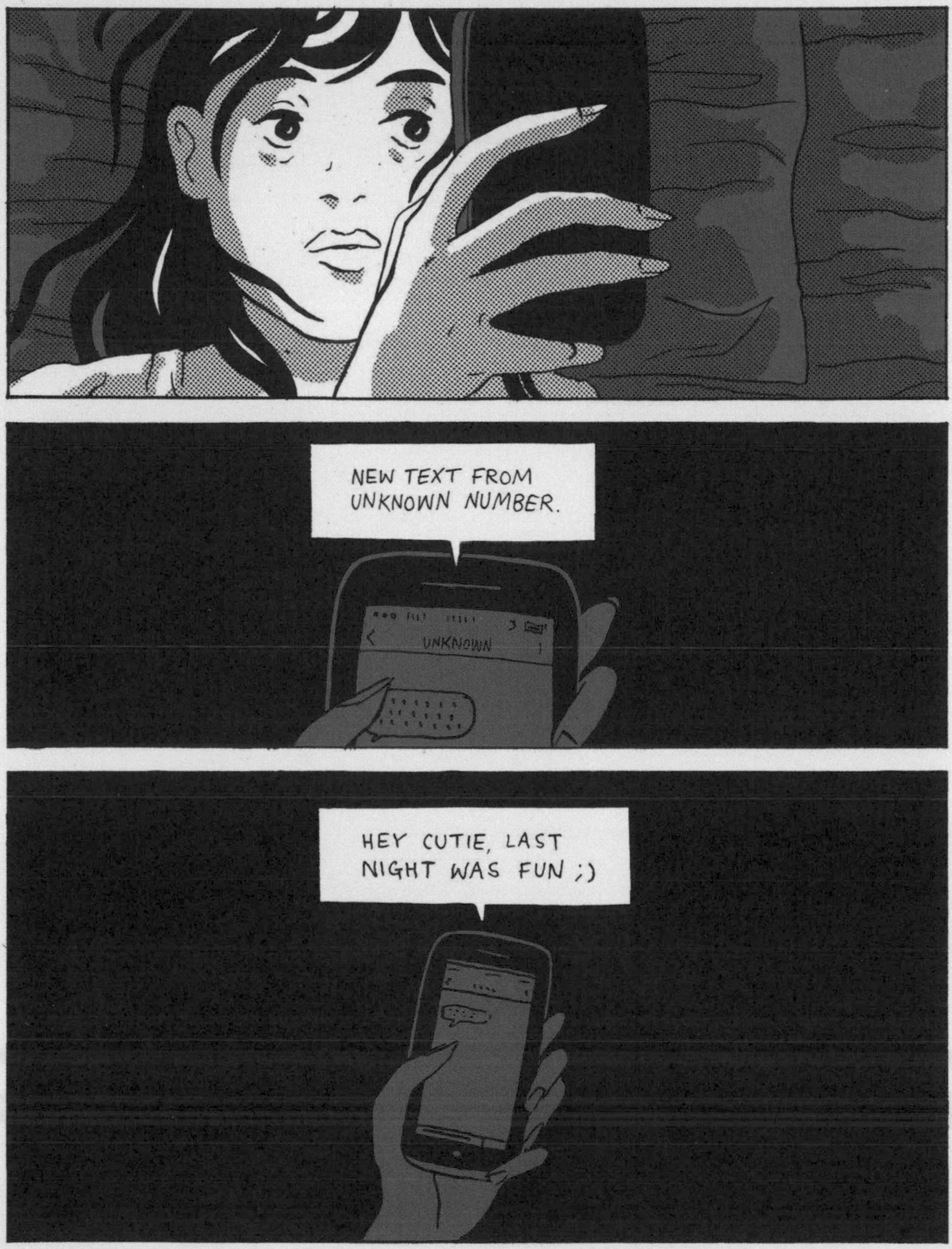
NEW TEXT FROM UNKNOWN NUMBER.
UNKNOWN
HEY CUTIE, LAST NIGHT WAS FUN ;)

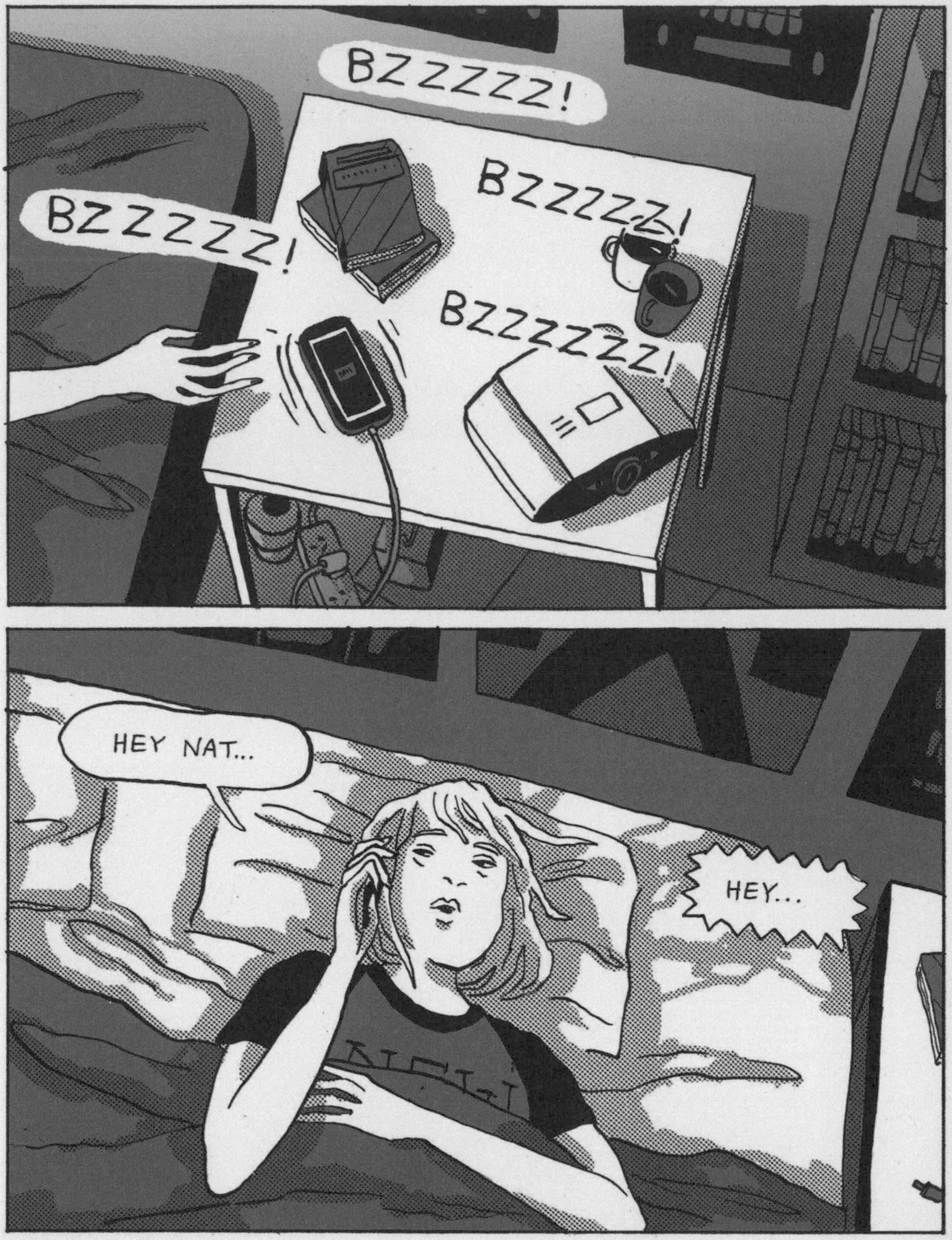
BZZZZZZ!
BZZZZZZ!
BZZZZZZ!
BZZZZZZZZ!
HEY NAT...
HEY...

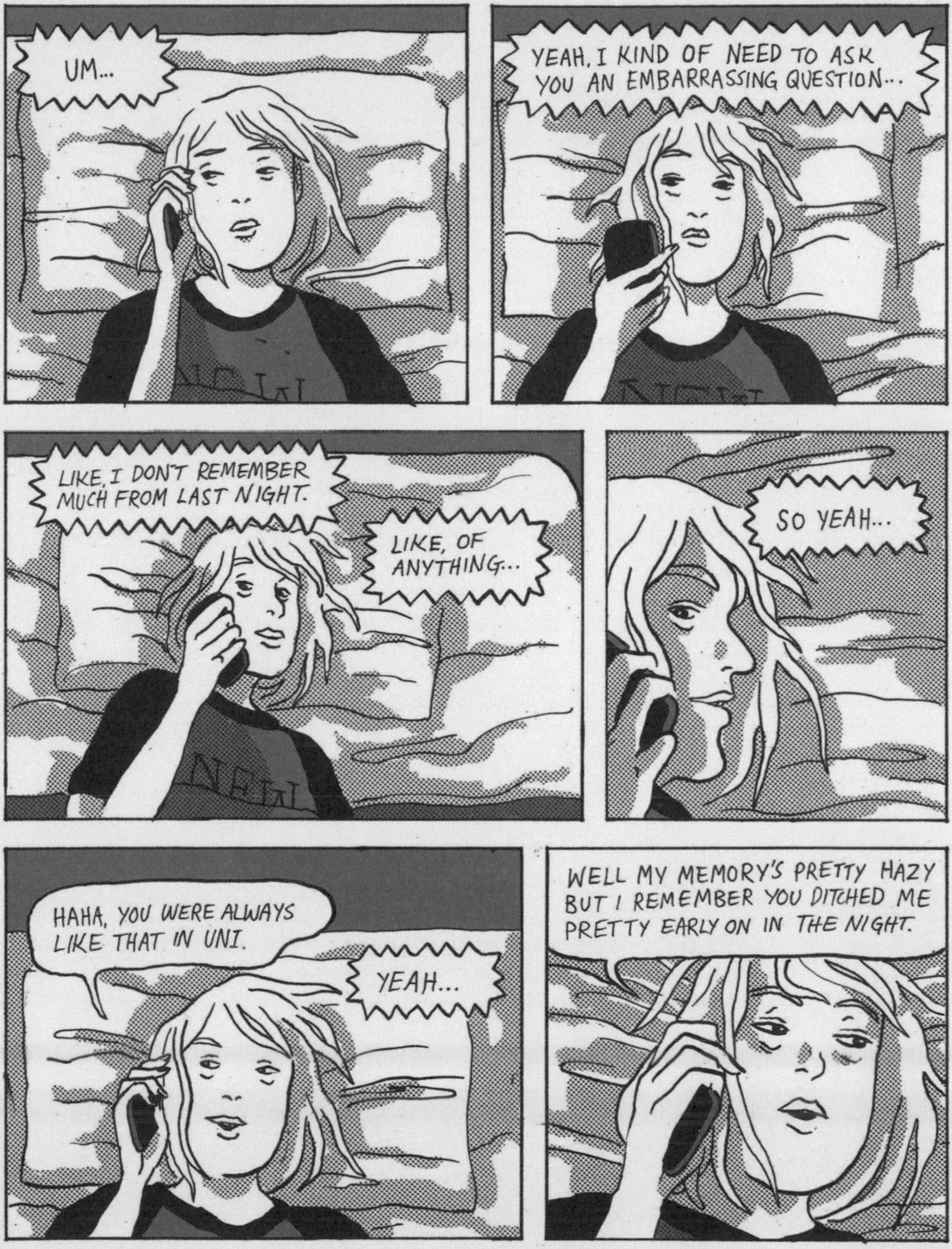
UM...
YEAH, I KIND OF NEED TO ASK YOU AN EMBARRASSING QUESTION...
LIKE, I DON'T REMEMBER MUCH FROM LAST NIGHT.
LIKE, OF ANYTHING...
SO YEAH...
HAHA, YOU WERE ALWAYS LIKE THAT IN UNI.
YEAH...
WELL MY MEMORY'S PRETTY HAZY BUT I REMEMBER YOU DITCHED ME PRETTY EARLY ON IN THE NIGHT.

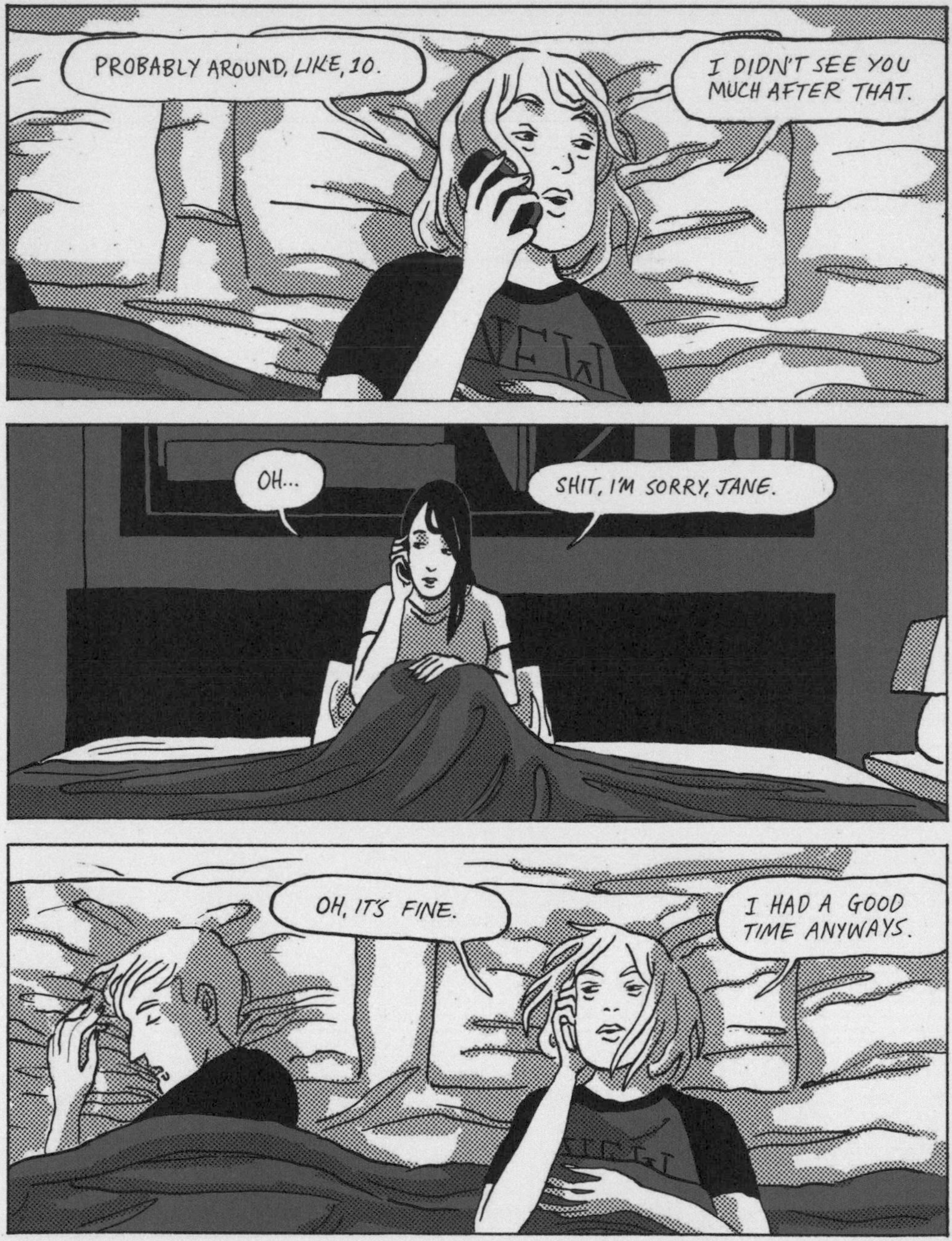
PROBABLY AROUND, LIKE, 10.
I DIDN'T SEE YOU MUCH AFTER THAT.
OH...
SHIT, I'M SORRY, JANE.
OH, IT'S FINE.
I HAD A GOOD TIME ANYWAYS.

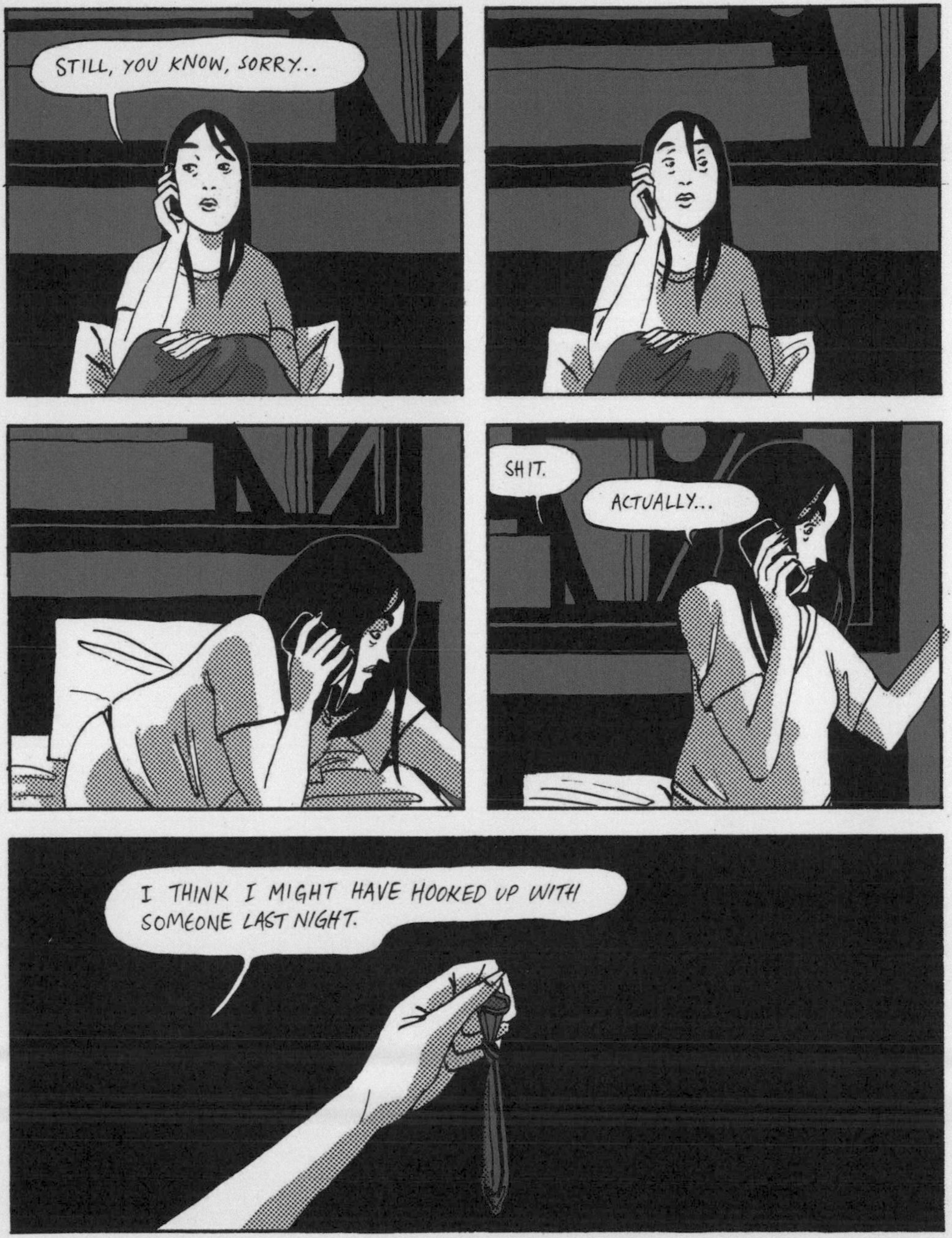
STILL, YOU KNOW, SORRY...
SHIT.
ACTUALLY...
I THINK I MIGHT HAVE HOOKED UP WITH SOMEONE LAST NIGHT.

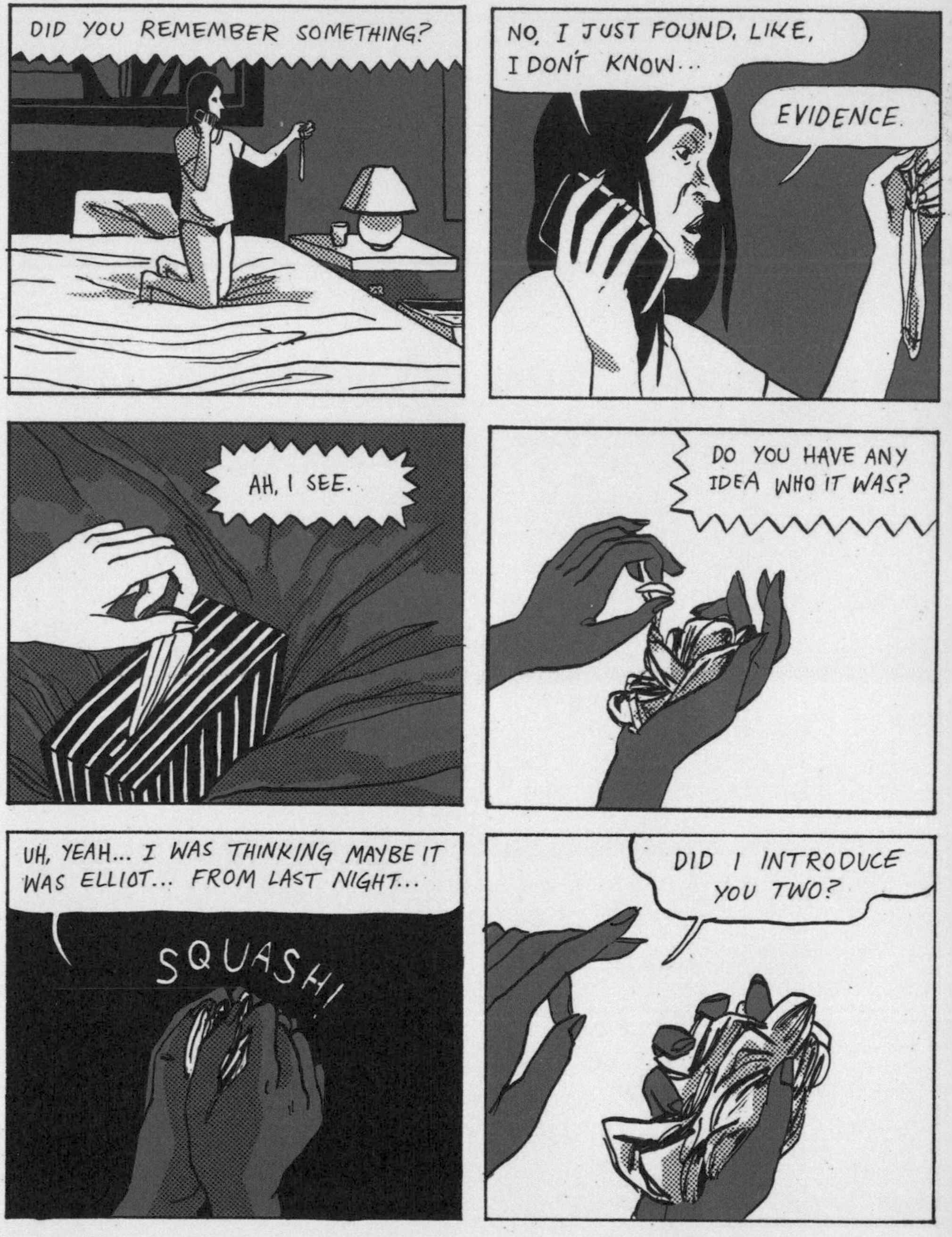

DID YOU REMEMBER SOMETHING?
NO, I JUST FOUND, LIKE, I DON'T KNOW...
EVIDENCE.
AH, I SEE.
DO YOU HAVE ANY IDEA WHO IT WAS?
UH, YEAH... I WAS THINKING MAYBE IT WAS ELLIOT... FROM LAST NIGHT...
SQUASH!
DID I INTRODUCE YOU TWO?

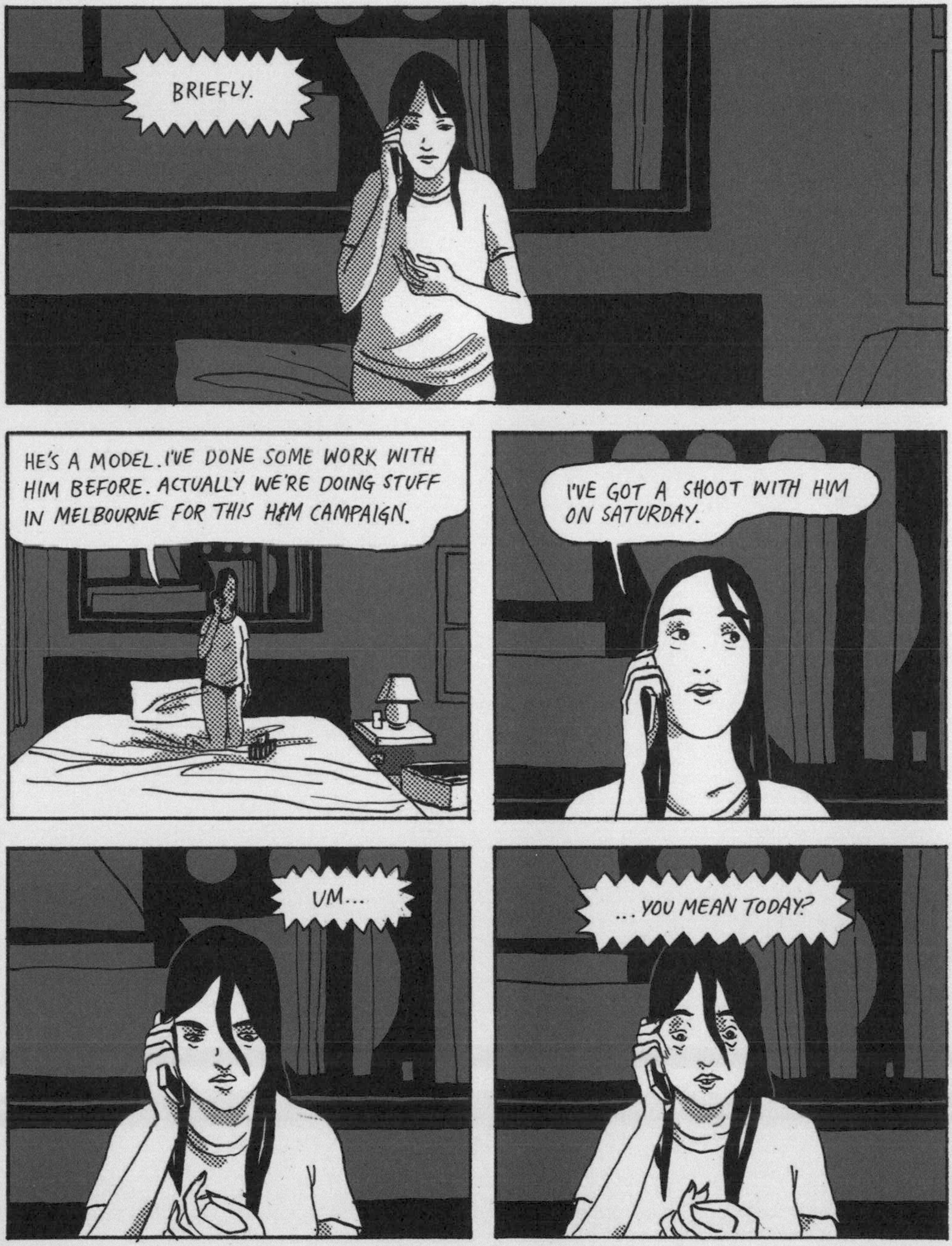
BRIEFLY.
HE'S A MODEL. I'VE DONE SOME WORK WITH HIM BEFORE. ACTUALLY WE'RE DOING STUFF IN MELBOURNE FOR THIS H&M CAMPAIGN.
I'VE GOT A SHOOT WITH HIM ON SATURDAY.
UM...
...YOU MEAN TODAY?

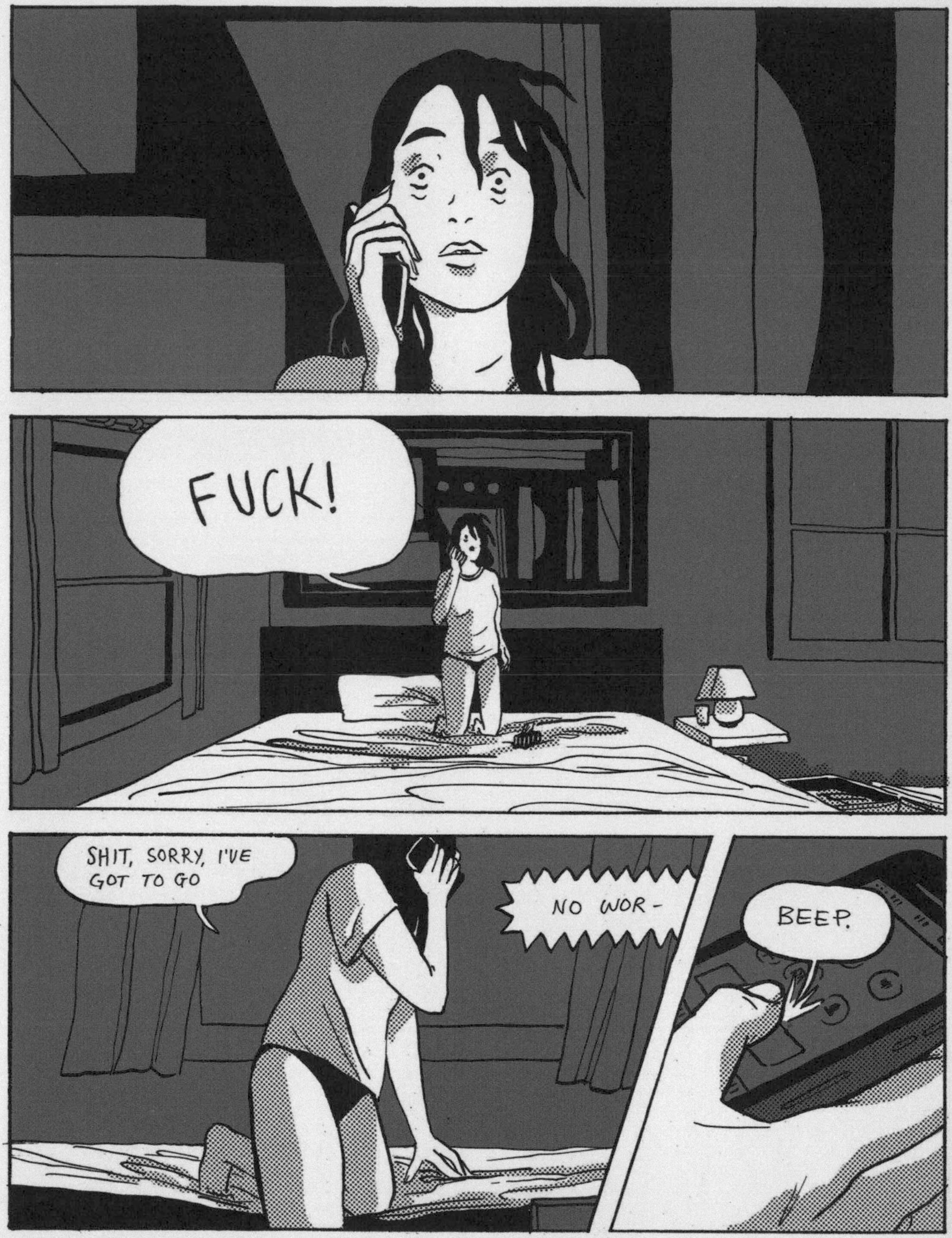
FUCK!
SHIT, SORRY, I'VE GOT TO GO
NO WOR-
BEEP.

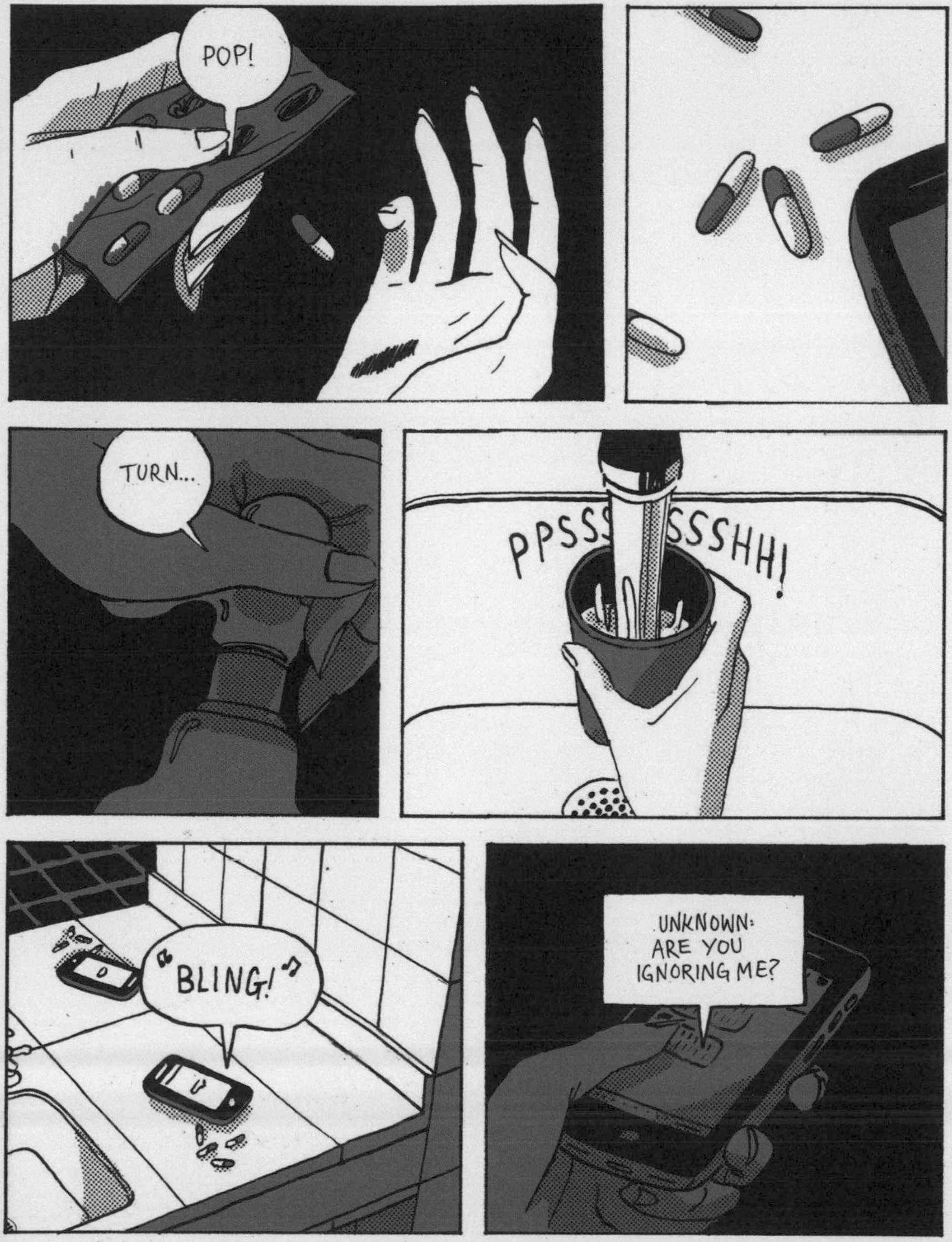
POP!
TURN...
PPSSSSSSHH!
BLING!
UNKNOWN:
ARE YOU
IGNORING ME?

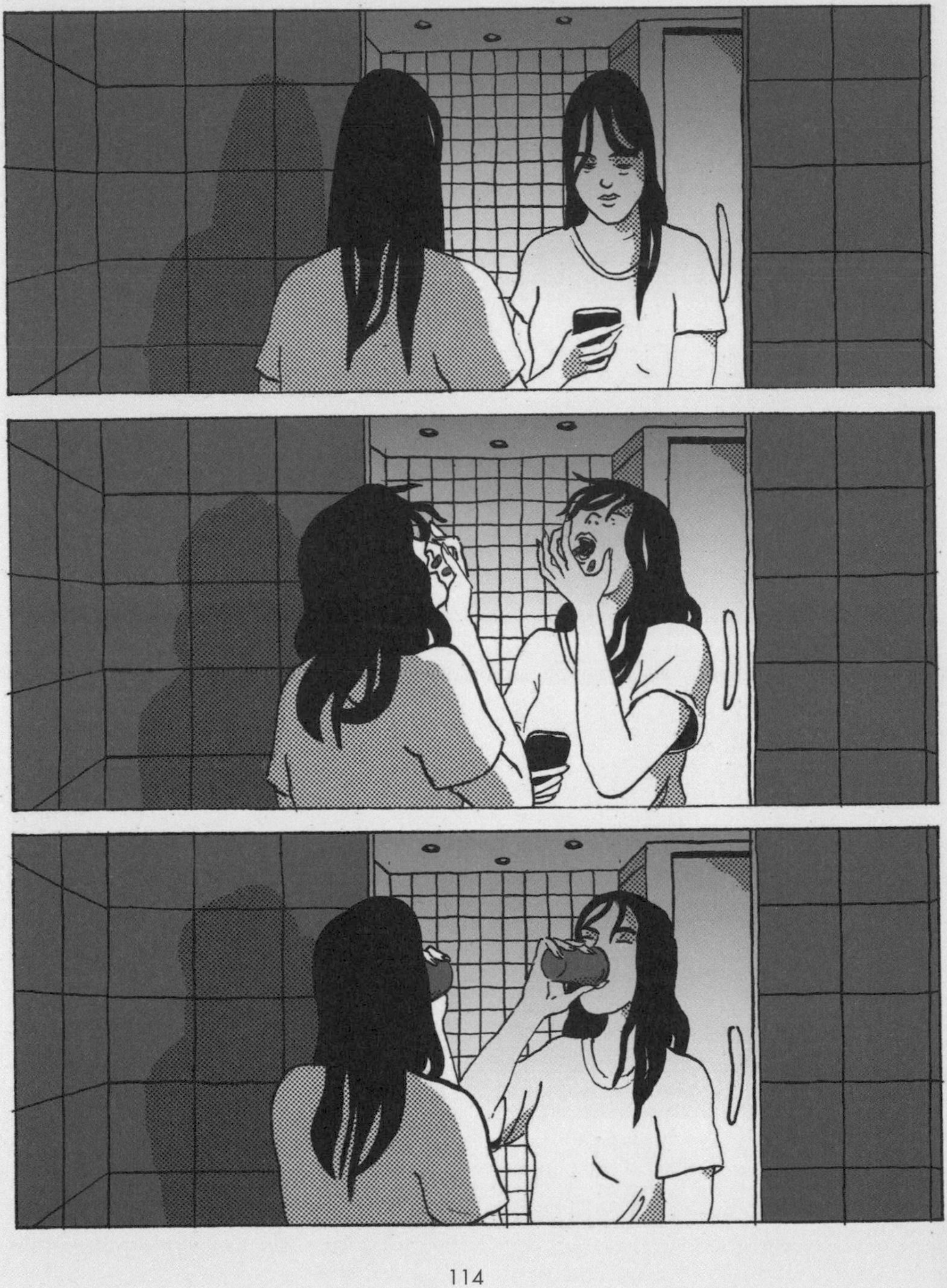

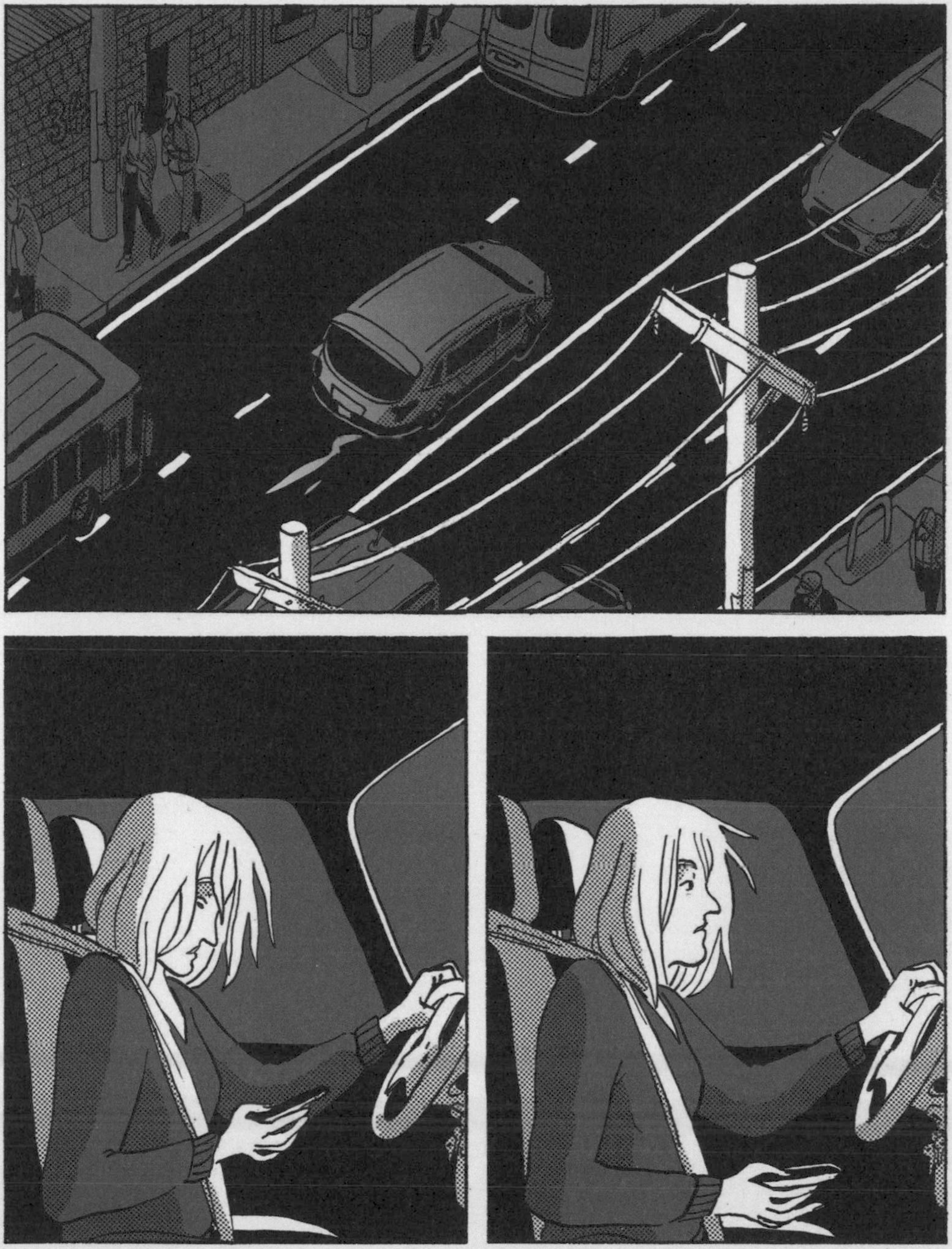

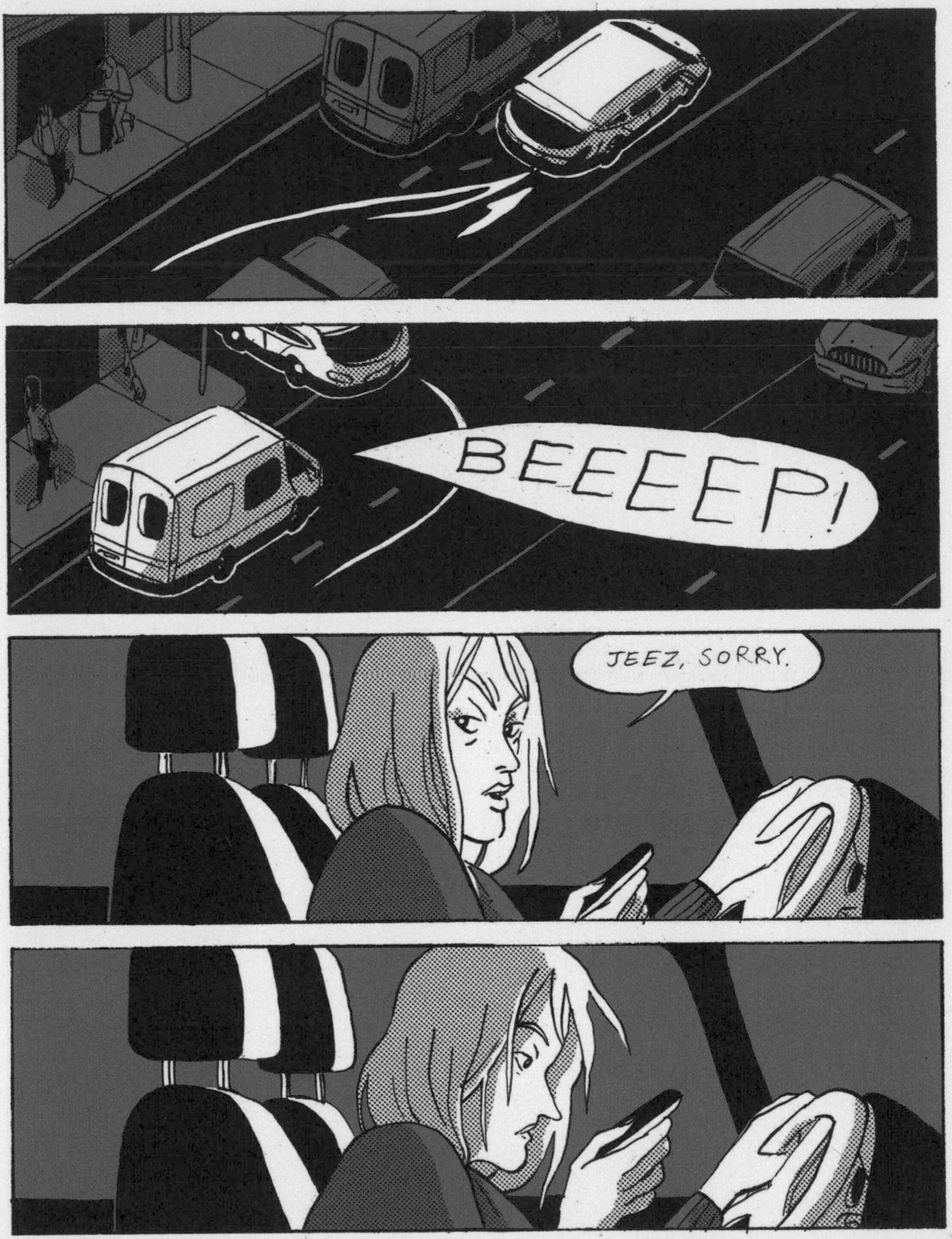
BEEEEP!
JEEZ, SORRY.

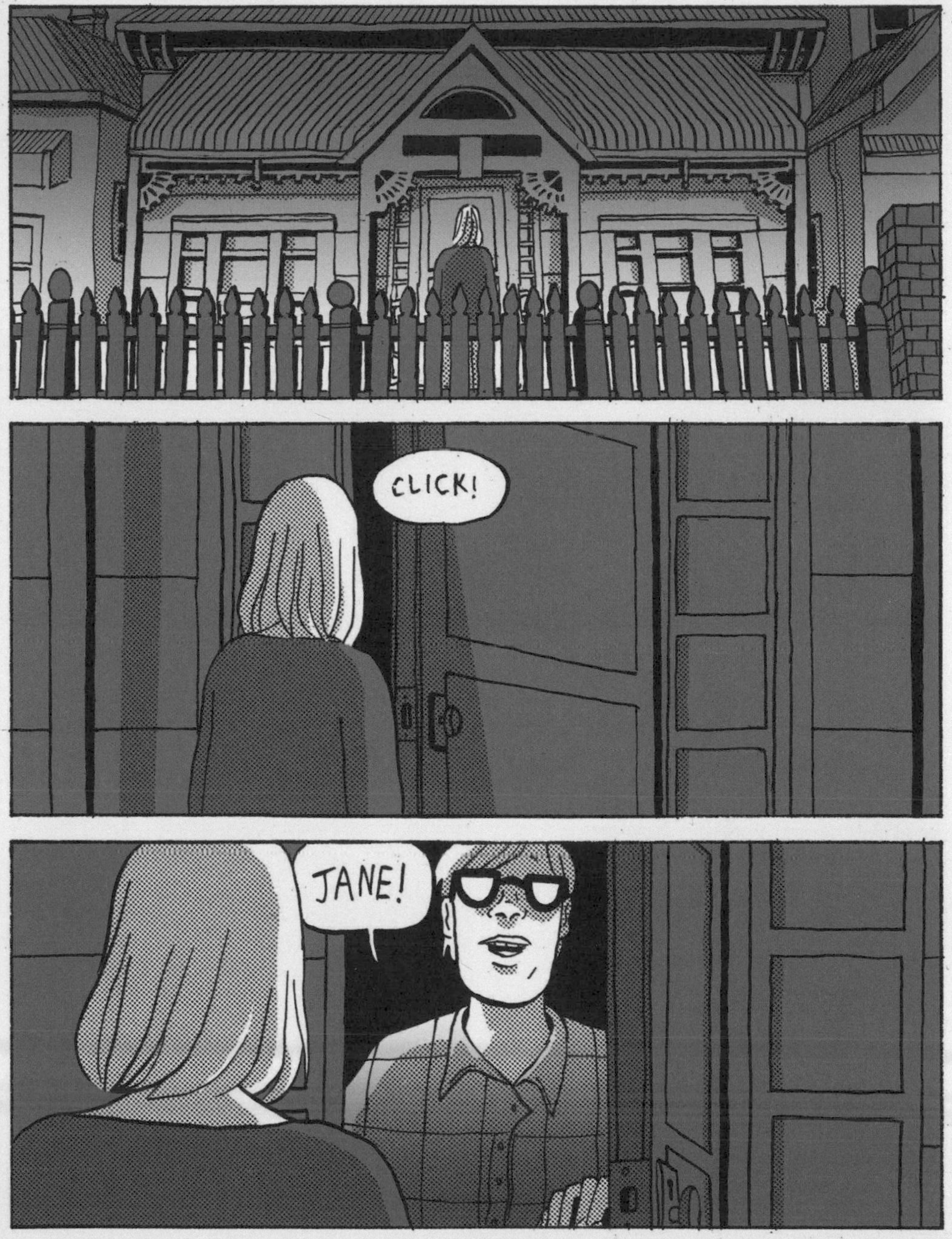
CLICK!
JANE!

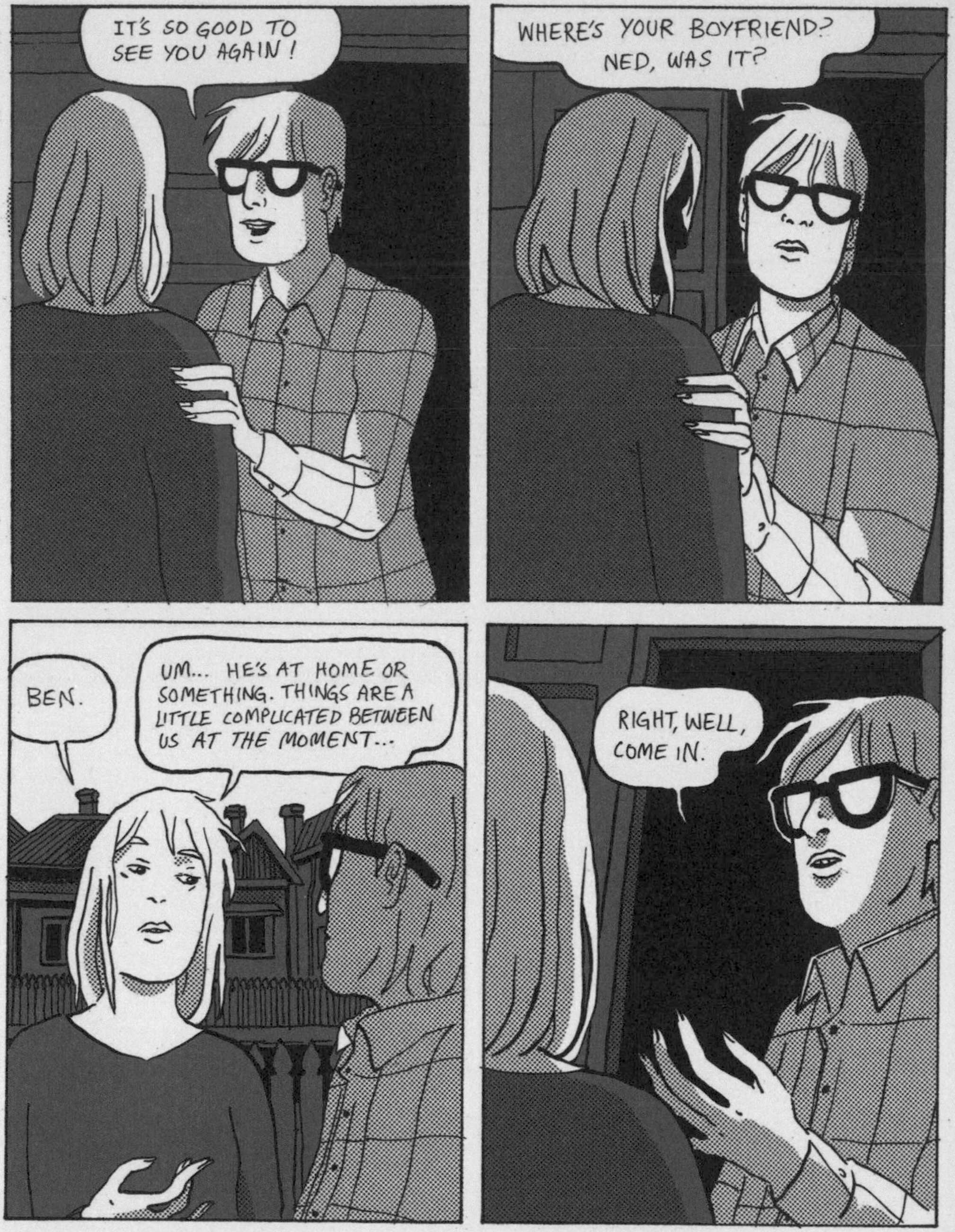
IT'S SO GOOD TO SEE YOU AGAIN!
WHERE'S YOUR BOYFRIEND? NED, WAS IT?
BEN.
UM... HE'S AT HOME OR SOMETHING. THINGS ARE A LITTLE COMPLICATED BETWEEN US AT THE MOMENT...
RIGHT, WELL, COME IN.

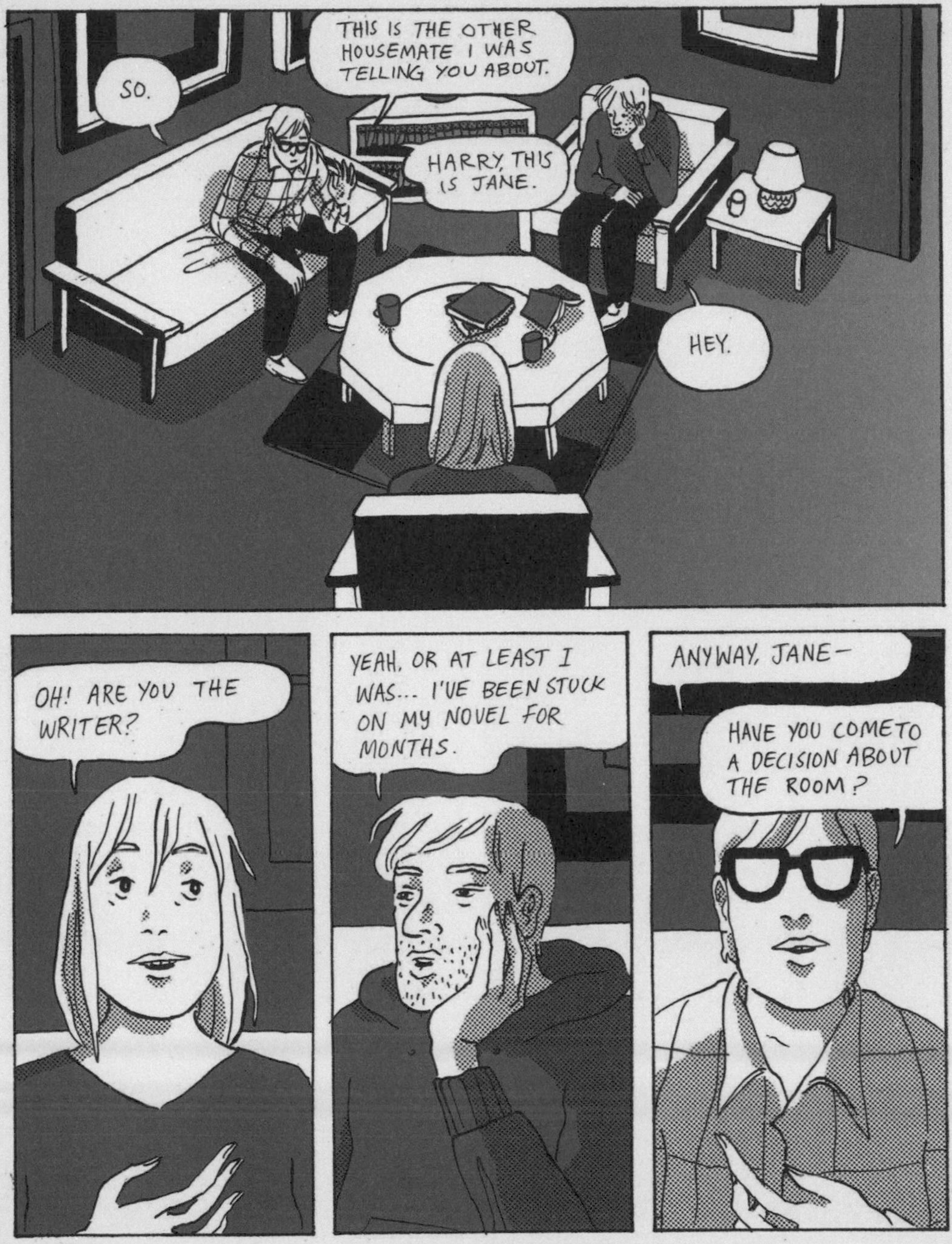
SO.
THIS IS THE OTHER HOUSEMATE I WAS TELLING YOU ABOUT.
HARRY, THIS IS JANE.
HEY.
OH! ARE YOU THE WRITER?
YEAH, OR AT LEAST I WAS... I'VE BEEN STUCK ON MY NOVEL FOR MONTHS.
ANYWAY, JANE–
HAVE YOU COME TO A DECISION ABOUT THE ROOM?

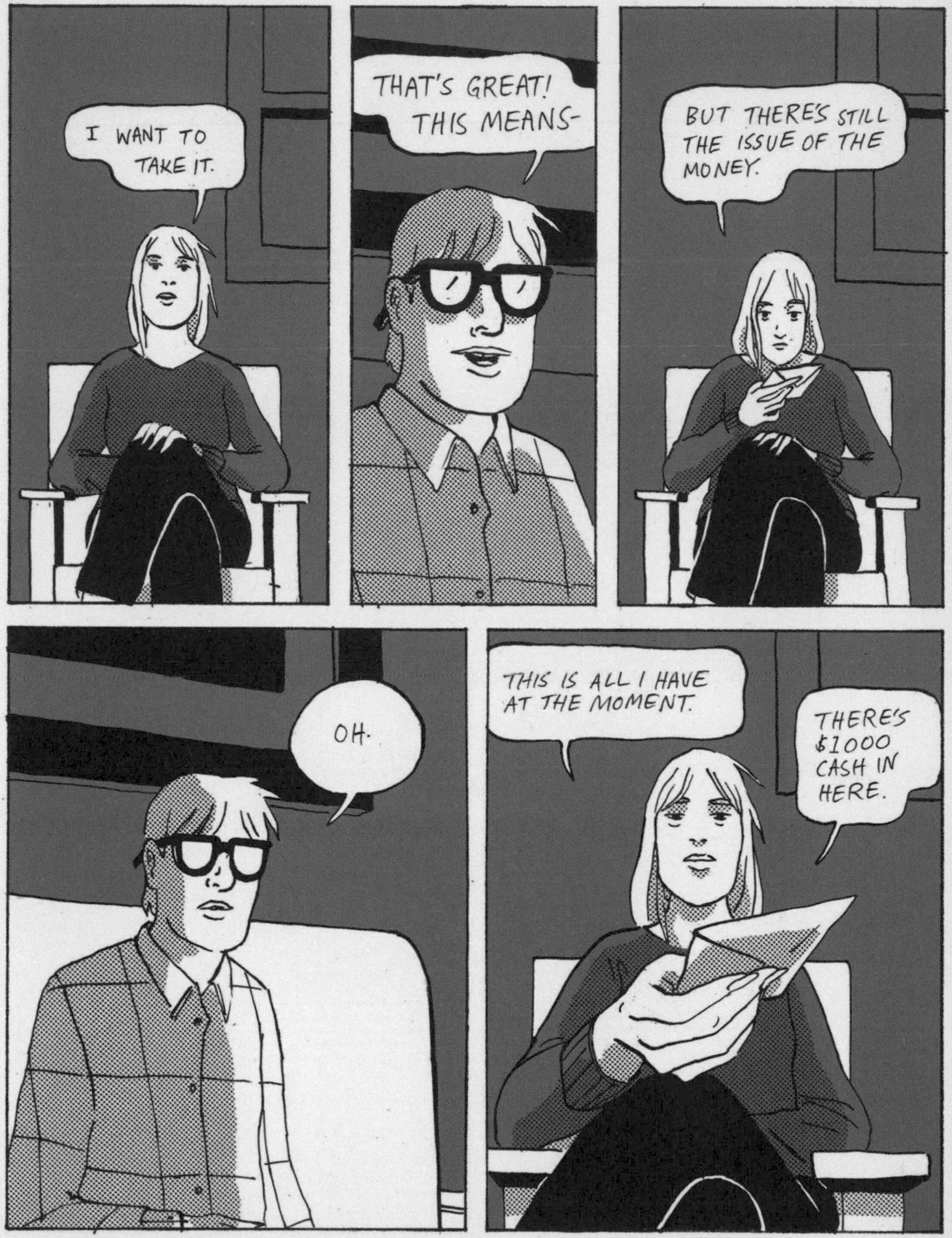
I WANT TO TAKE IT.
THAT'S GREAT! THIS MEANS-
BUT THERE'S STILL THE ISSUE OF THE MONEY.
OH.
THIS IS ALL I HAVE AT THE MOMENT.
THERE'S $1000 CASH IN HERE.

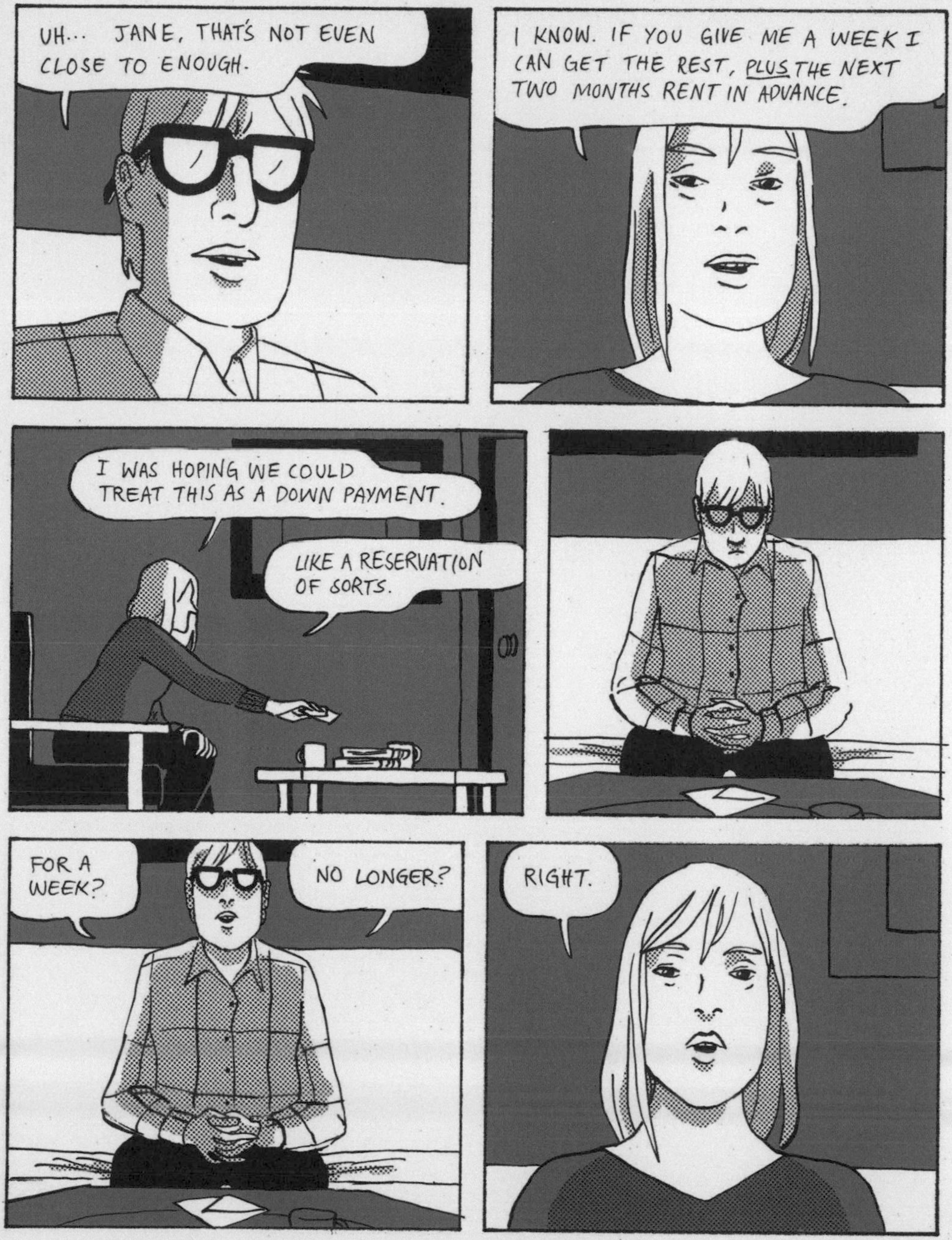
UH... JANE, THAT'S NOT EVEN CLOSE TO ENOUGH.
I KNOW. IF YOU GIVE ME A WEEK I CAN GET THE REST, PLUS THE NEXT TWO MONTHS RENT IN ADVANCE.
I WAS HOPING WE COULD TREAT THIS AS A DOWN PAYMENT.
LIKE A RESERVATION OF SORTS.
FOR A WEEK?
NO LONGER?
RIGHT.

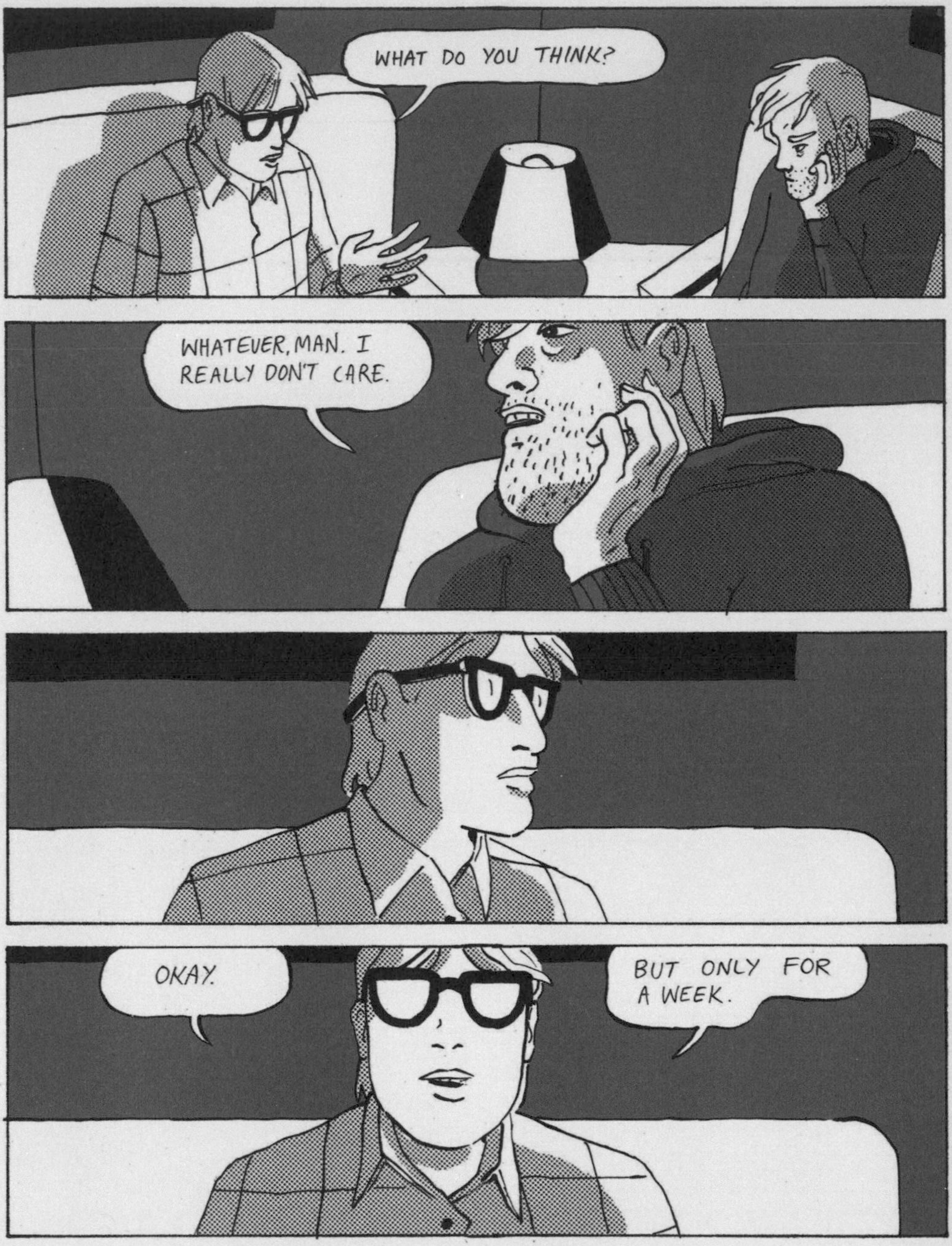
WHAT DO YOU THINK?
WHATEVER, MAN. I REALLY DON'T CARE.
OKAY.
BUT ONLY FOR A WEEK.

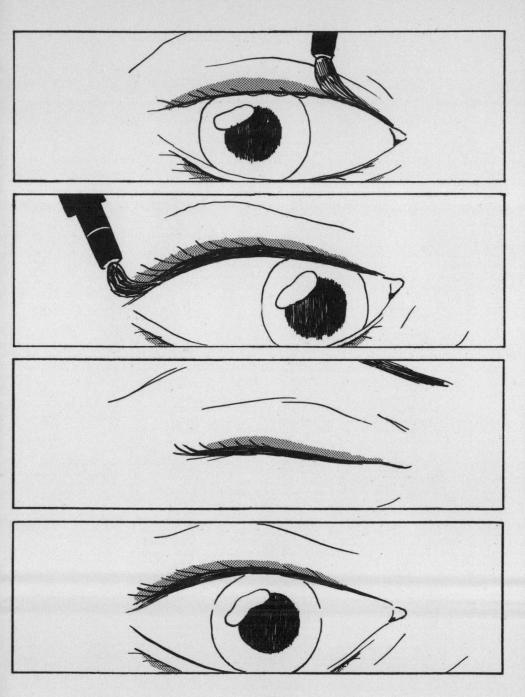

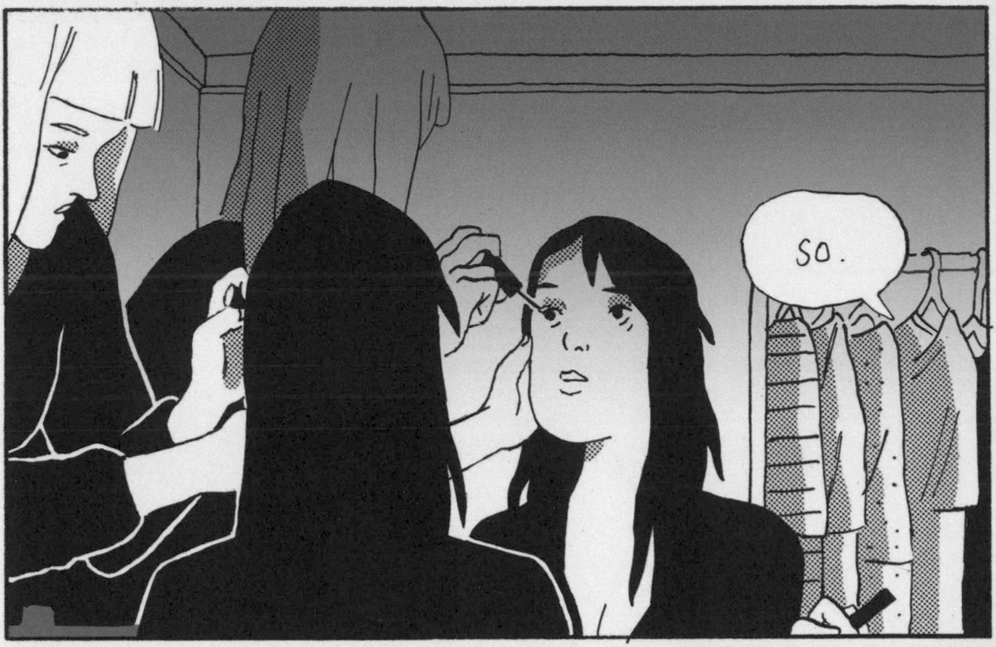
SO.

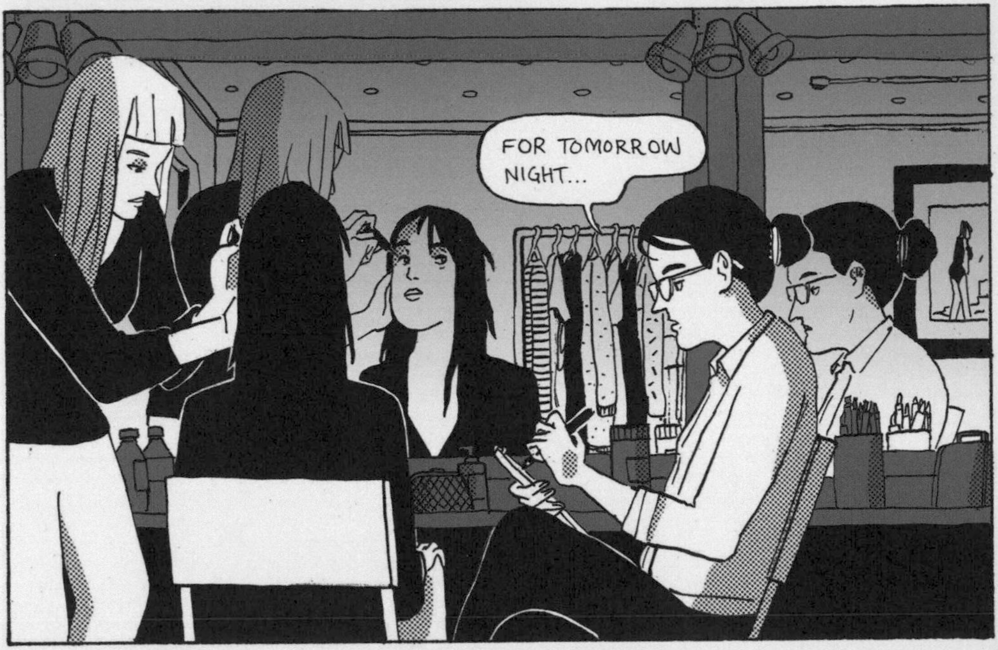
FOR TOMORROW NIGHT...

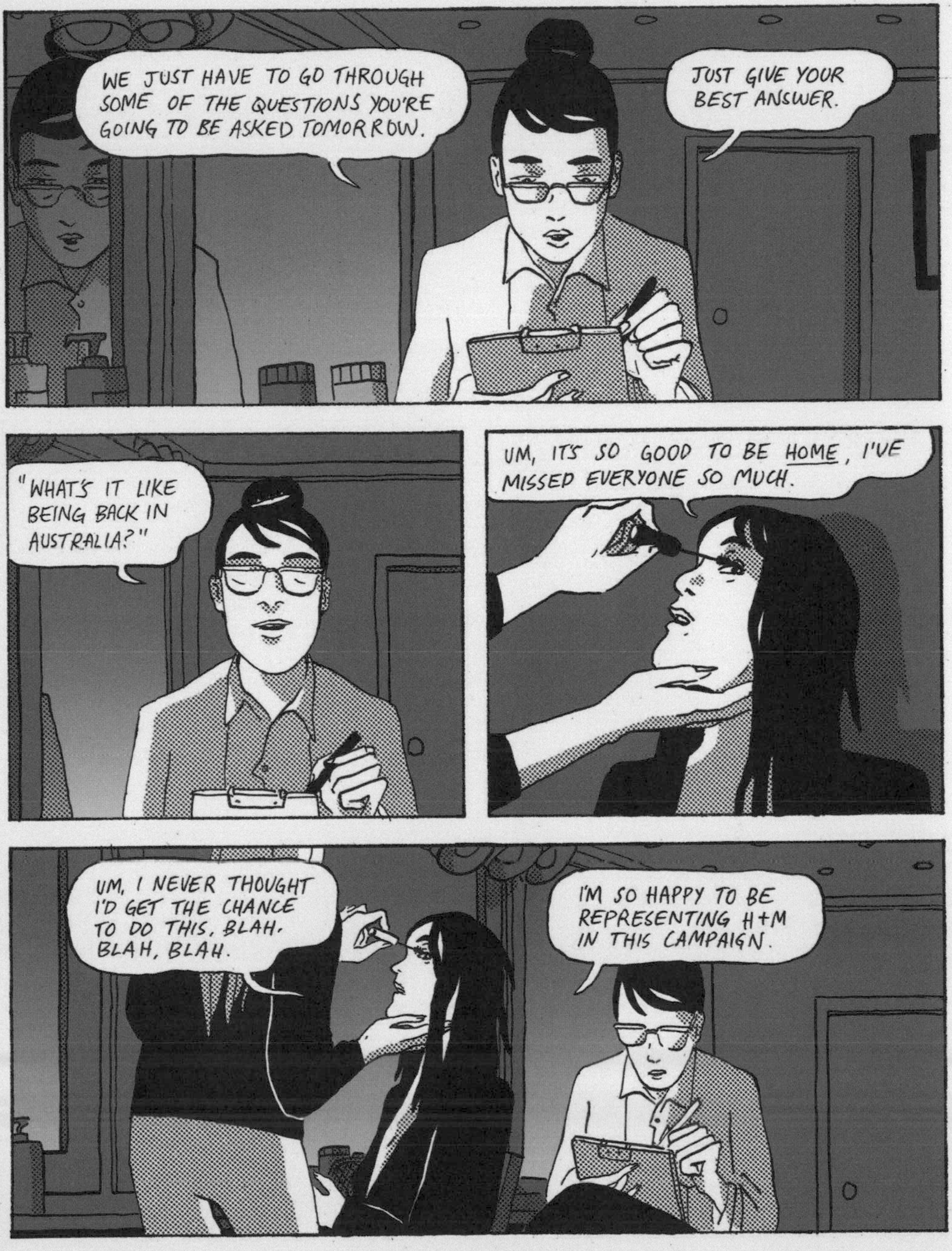
WE JUST HAVE TO GO THROUGH SOME OF THE QUESTIONS YOU'RE GOING TO BE ASKED TOMORROW.
JUST GIVE YOUR BEST ANSWER.
"WHAT'S IT LIKE BEING BACK IN AUSTRALIA?"
UM, IT'S SO GOOD TO BE HOME, I'VE MISSED EVERYONE SO MUCH.
UM, I NEVER THOUGHT I'D GET THE CHANCE TO DO THIS, BLAH, BLAH, BLAH.
I'M SO HAPPY TO BE REPRESENTING H+M IN THIS CAMPAIGN.

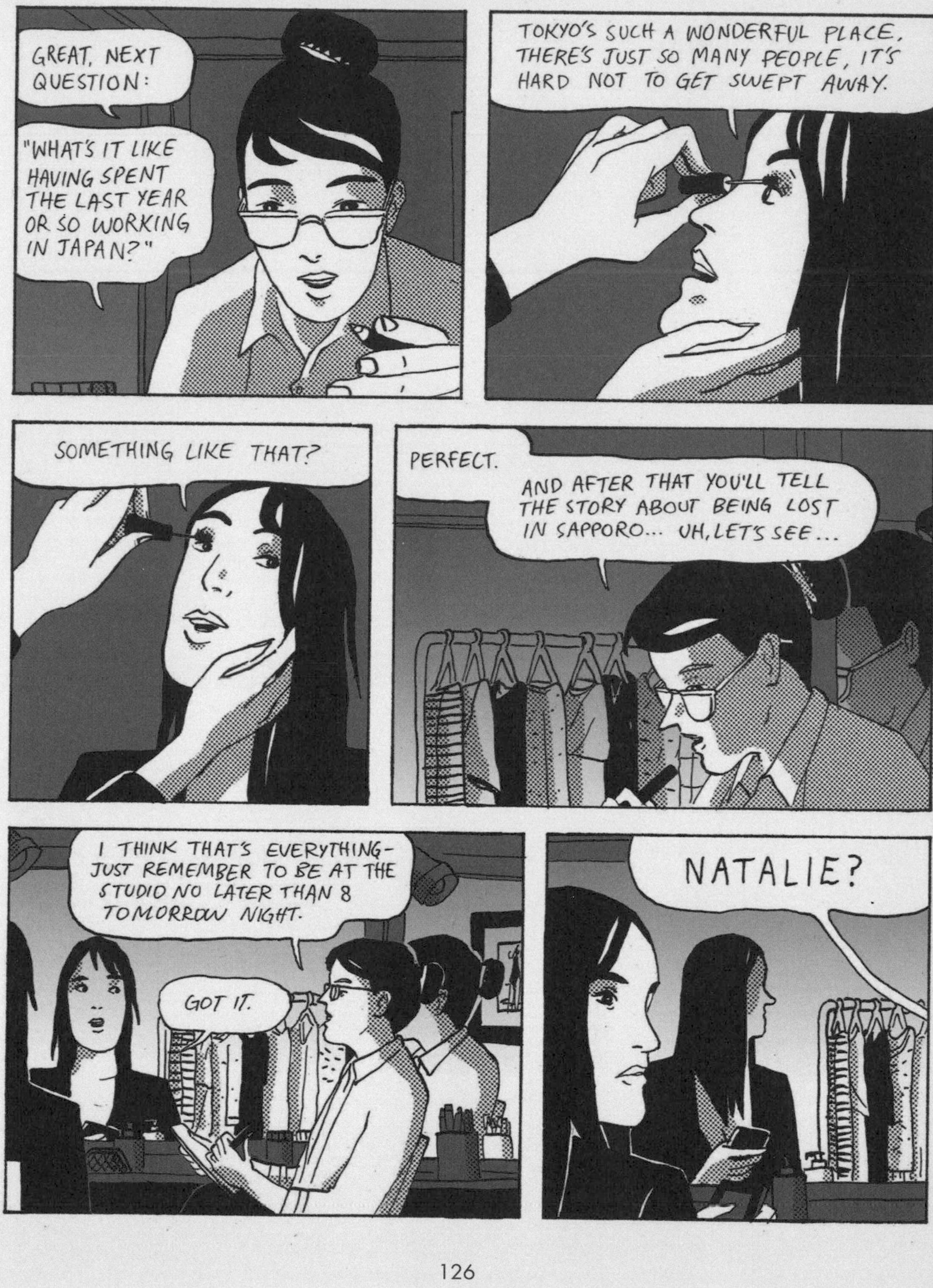
GREAT, NEXT QUESTION:
"WHAT'S IT LIKE HAVING SPENT THE LAST YEAR OR SO WORKING IN JAPAN?"
TOKYO'S SUCH A WONDERFUL PLACE. THERE'S JUST SO MANY PEOPLE, IT'S HARD NOT TO GET SWEPT AWAY.
SOMETHING LIKE THAT?
PERFECT.
AND AFTER THAT YOU'LL TELL THE STORY ABOUT BEING LOST IN SAPPORO... UH, LET'S SEE...
I THINK THAT'S EVERYTHING- JUST REMEMBER TO BE AT THE STUDIO NO LATER THAN 8 TOMORROW NIGHT.
GOT IT.
NATALIE?

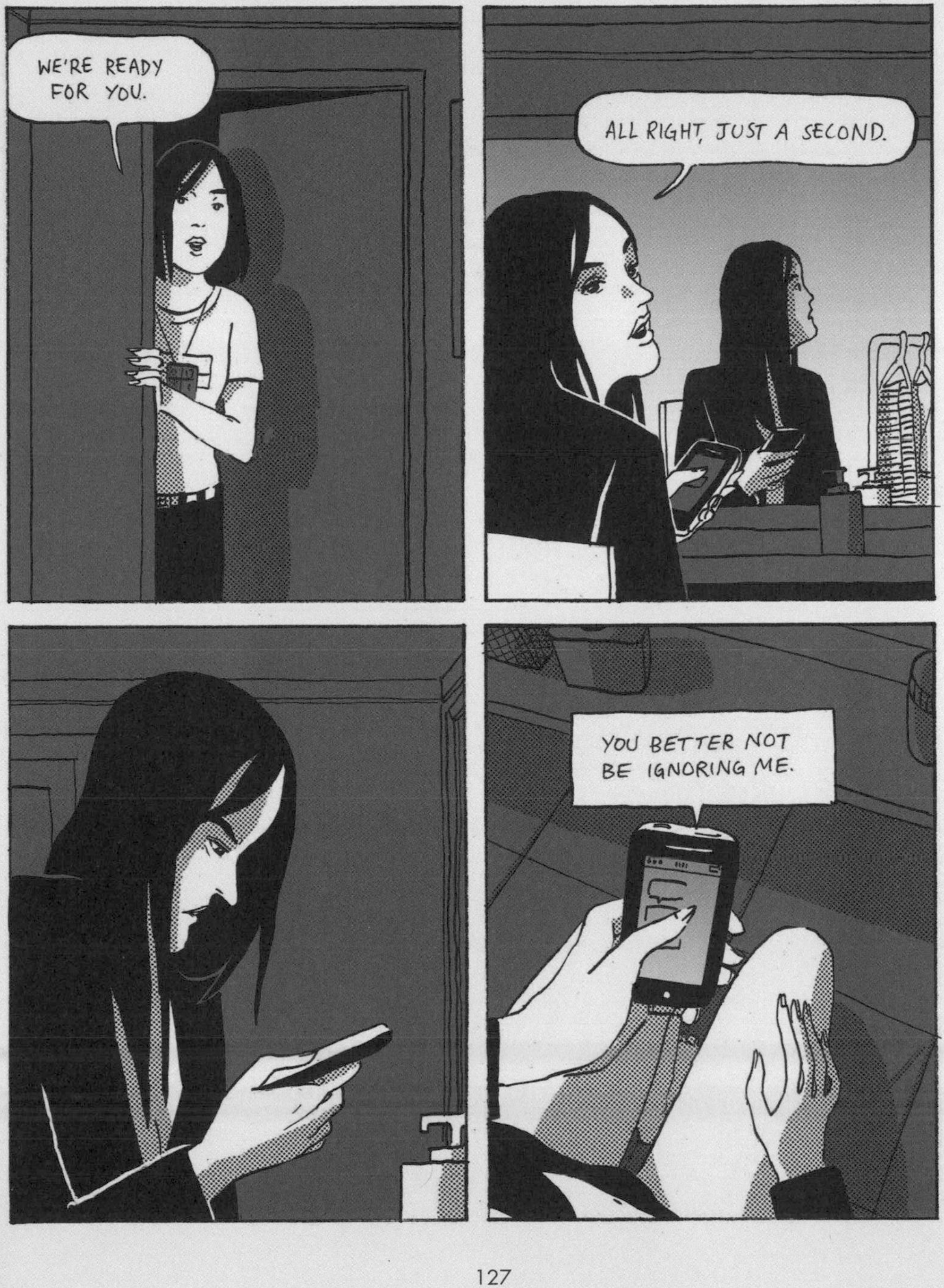
WE'RE READY FOR YOU.
ALL RIGHT, JUST A SECOND.
YOU BETTER NOT BE IGNORING ME.

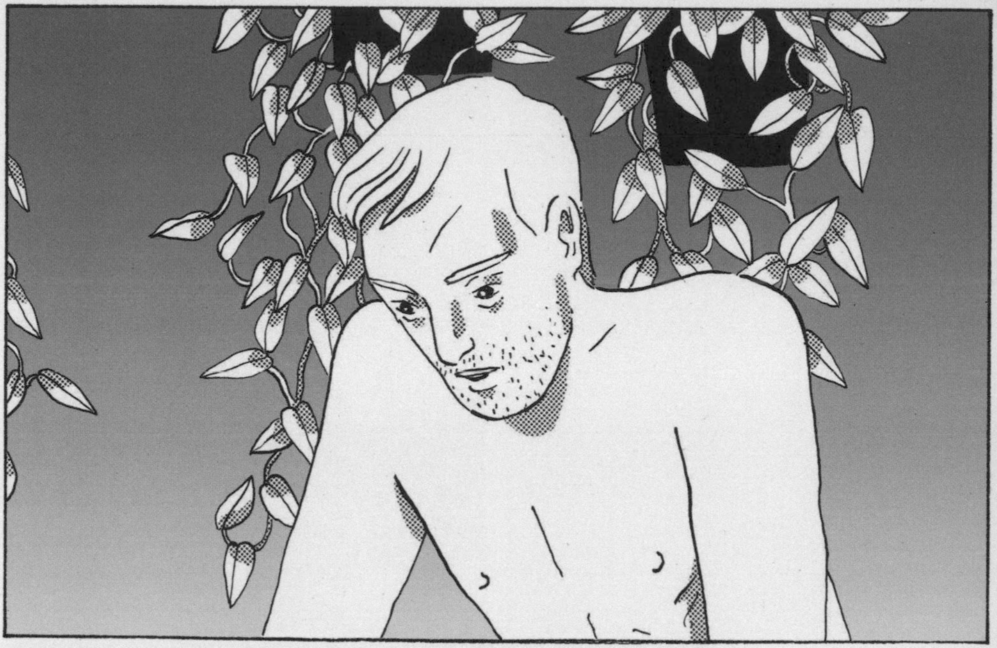

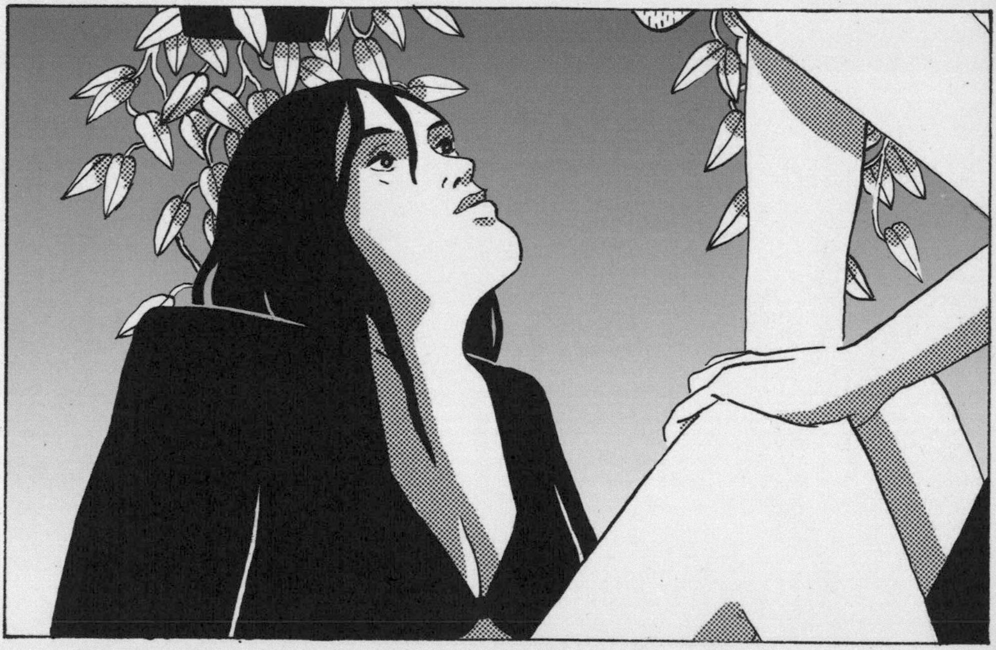

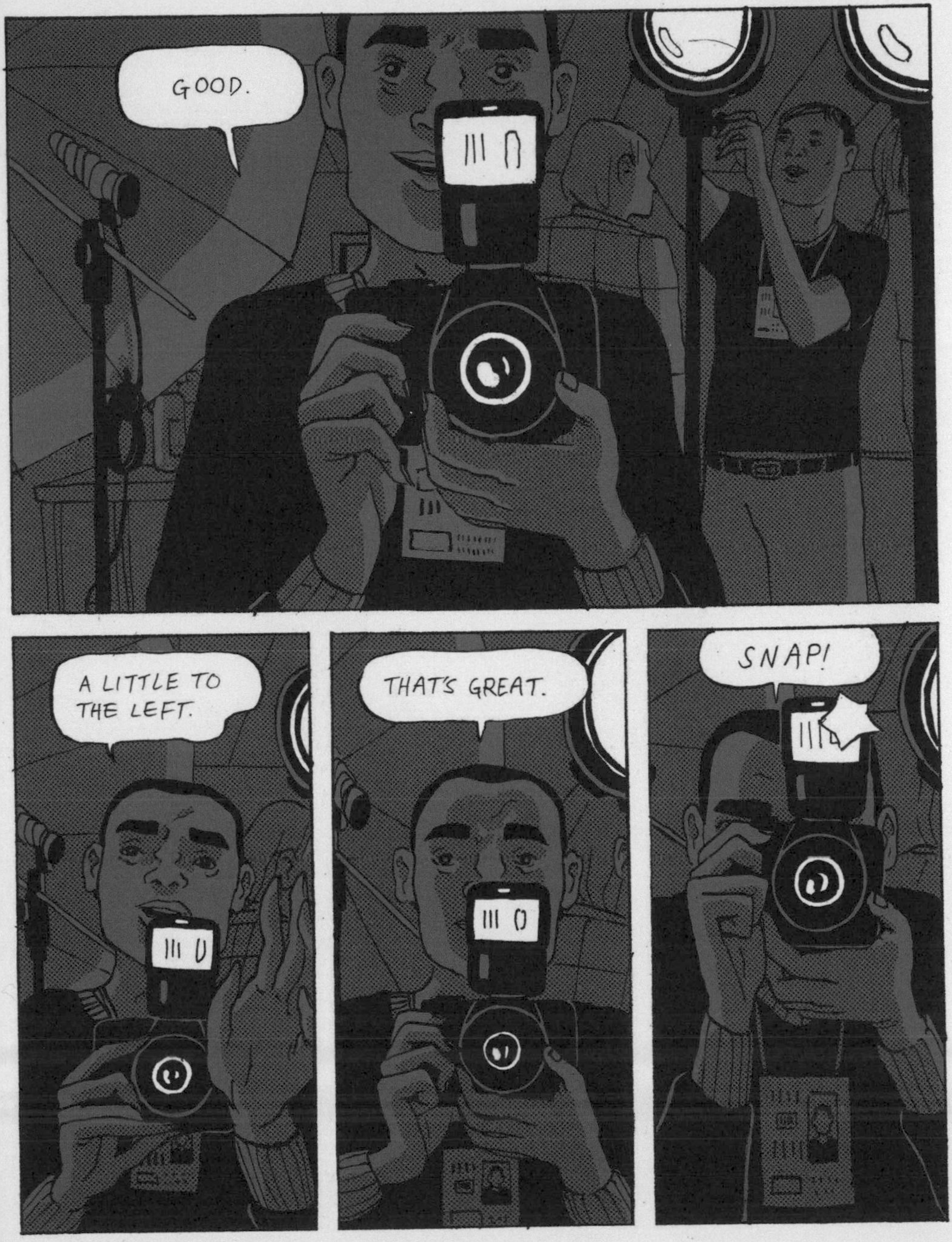
GOOD.
A LITTLE TO THE LEFT.
THAT'S GREAT.
SNAP!

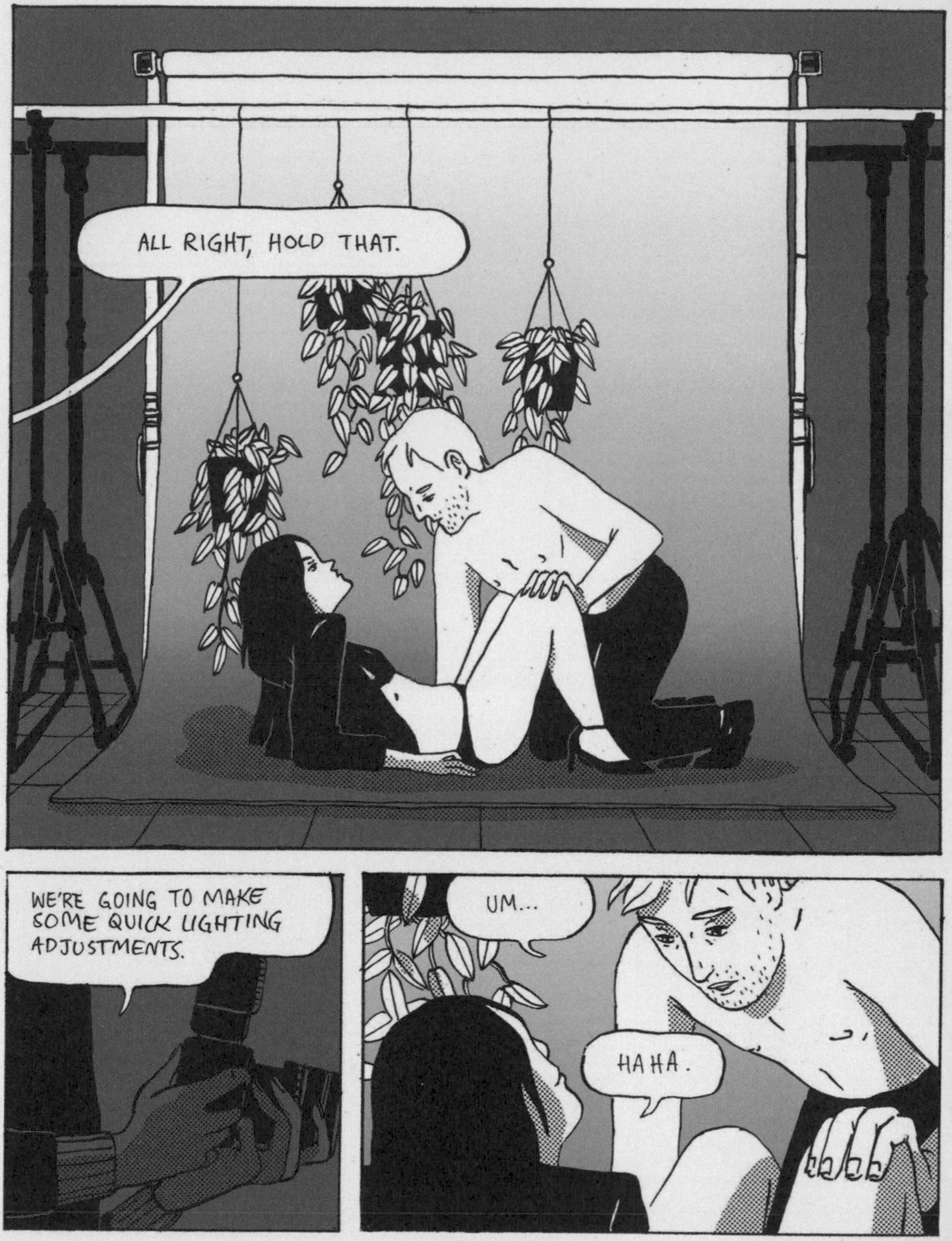
ALL RIGHT, HOLD THAT.
WE'RE GOING TO MAKE SOME QUICK LIGHTING ADJUSTMENTS.
UM...
HA HA.

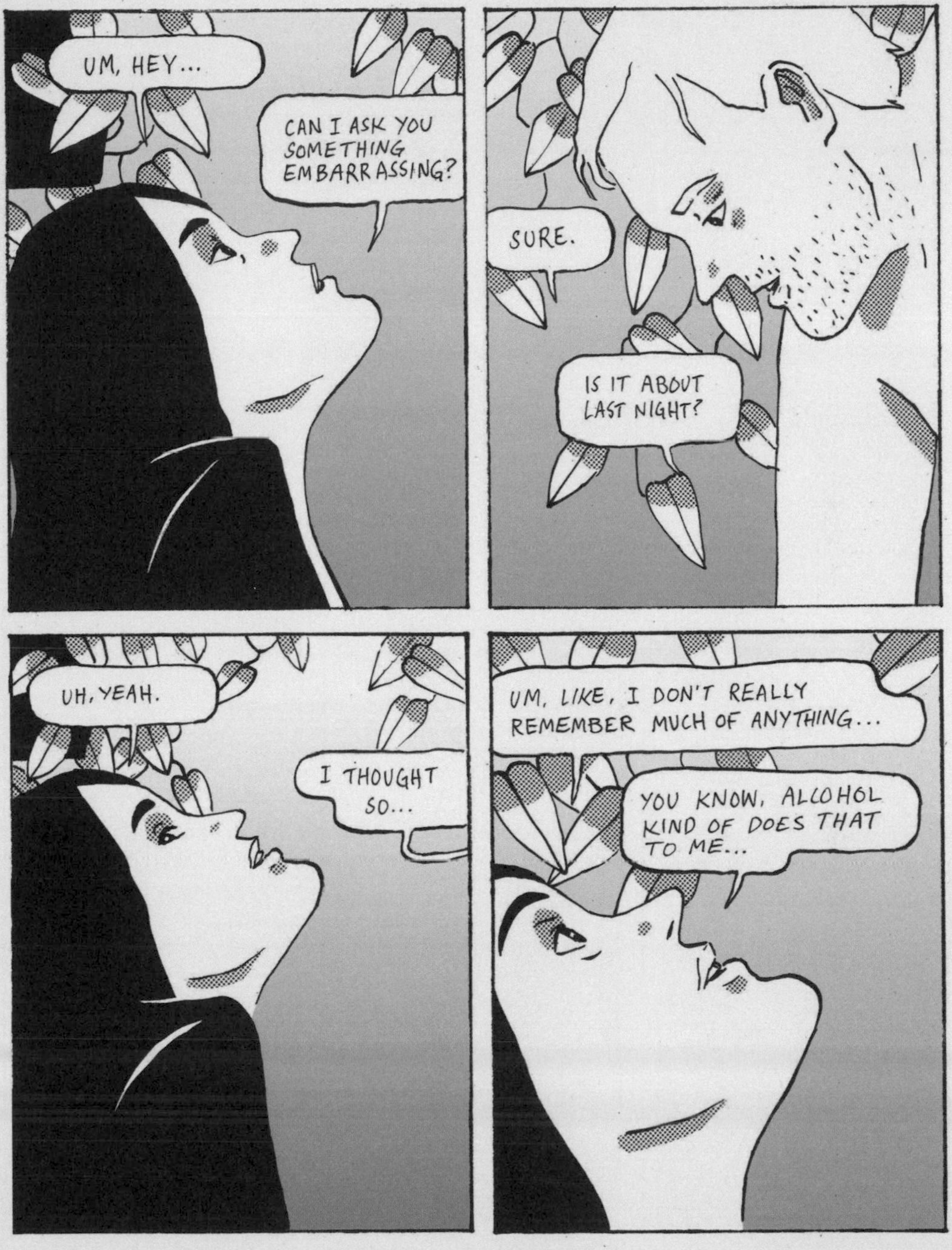
UM, HEY...
CAN I ASK YOU SOMETHING EMBARRASSING?
SURE.
IS IT ABOUT LAST NIGHT?
UH, YEAH.
I THOUGHT SO...
UM, LIKE, I DON'T REALLY REMEMBER MUCH OF ANYTHING...
YOU KNOW, ALCOHOL KIND OF DOES THAT TO ME...

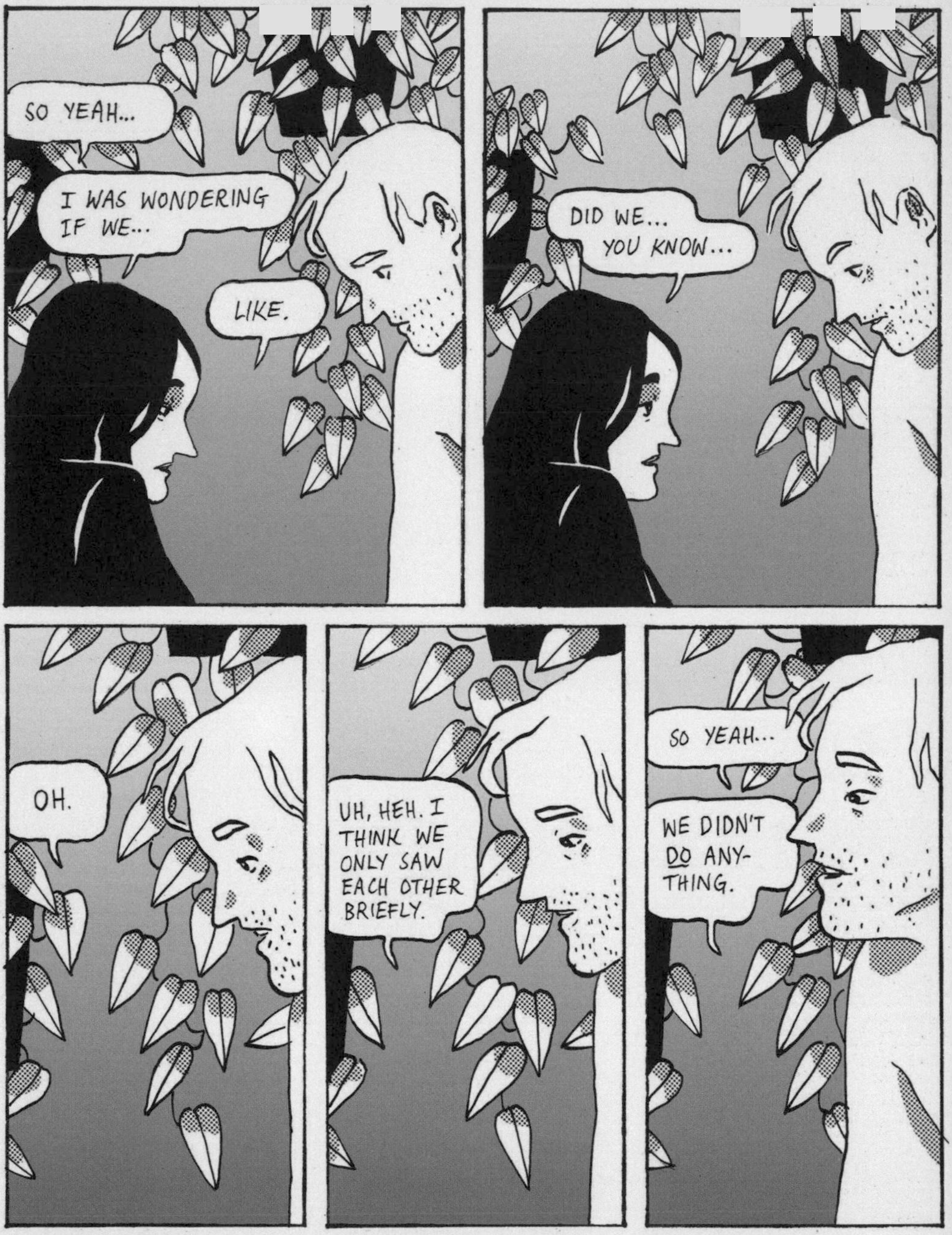
SO YEAH...
I WAS WONDERING IF WE...
LIKE.
DID WE... YOU KNOW...
OH.
UH, HEH. I THINK WE ONLY SAW EACH OTHER BRIEFLY.
SO YEAH...
WE DIDN'T DO ANYTHING.

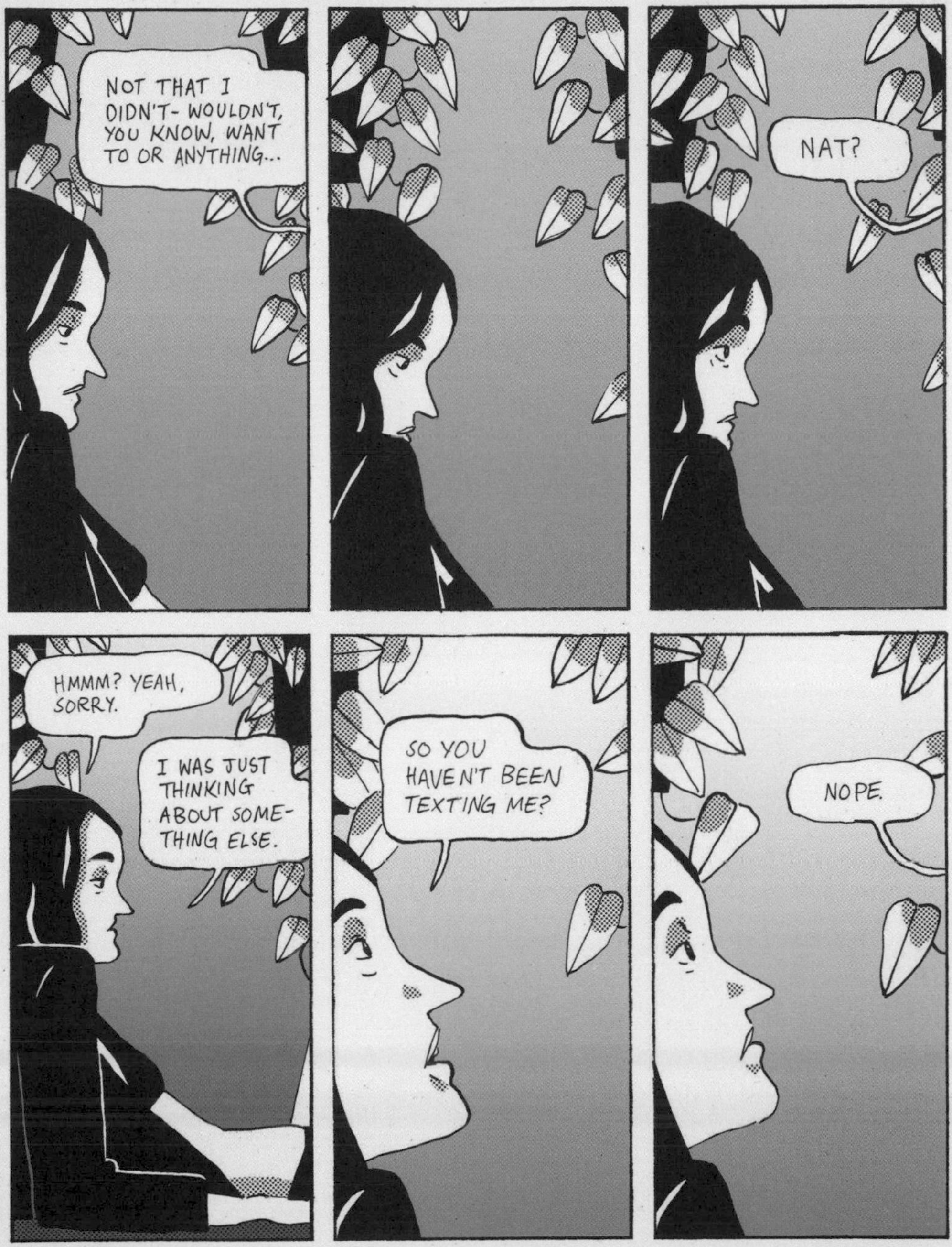
NOT THAT I DIDN'T- WOULDN'T, YOU KNOW, WANT TO OR ANYTHING...
NAT?
HMMM? YEAH, SORRY.
I WAS JUST THINKING ABOUT SOME-THING ELSE.
SO YOU HAVEN'T BEEN TEXTING ME?
NOPE.

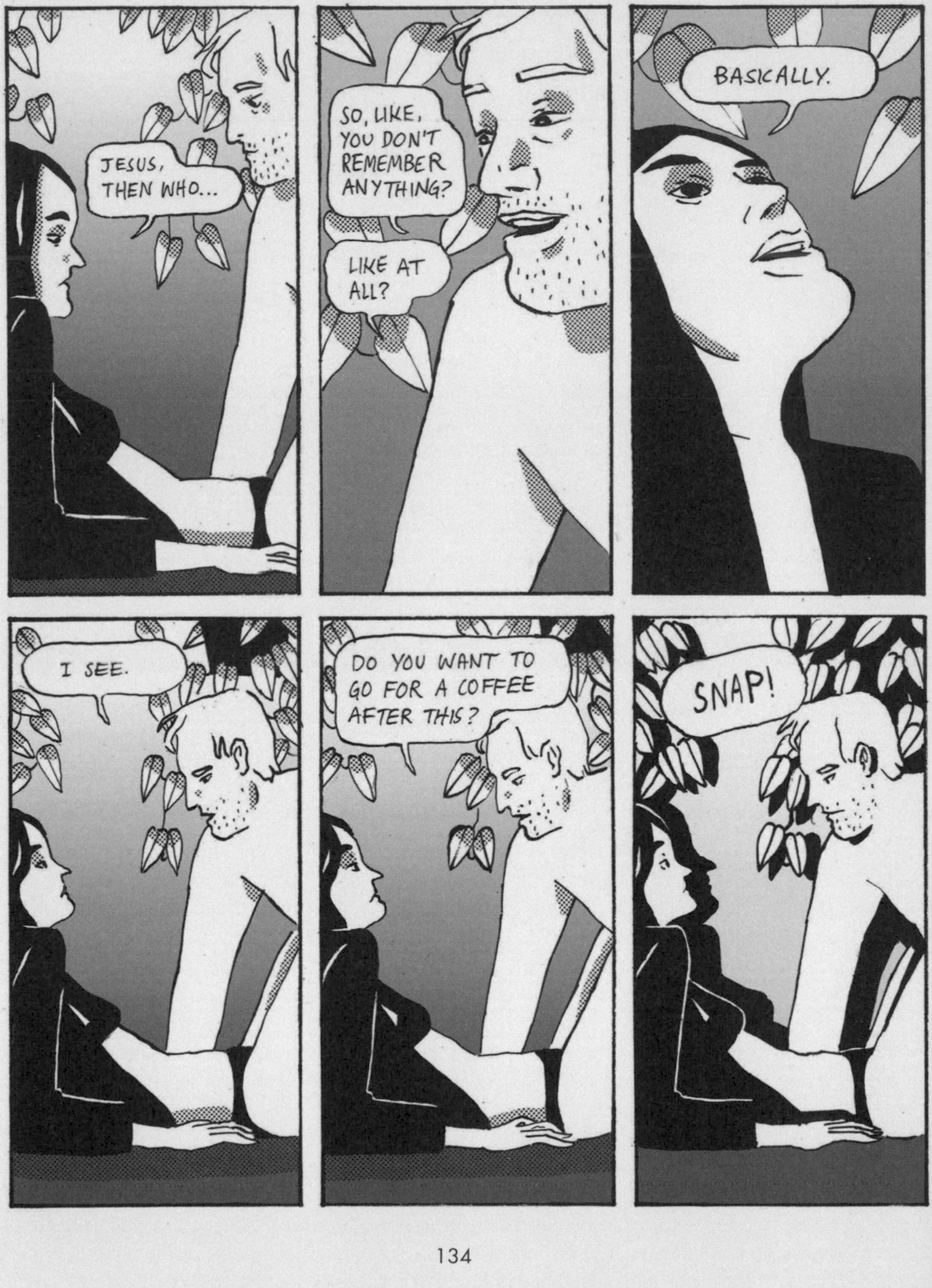
JESUS, THEN WHO...
SO, LIKE, YOU DON'T REMEMBER ANYTHING?
LIKE AT ALL?
BASICALLY.
I SEE.
DO YOU WANT TO GO FOR A COFFEE AFTER THIS?
SNAP!

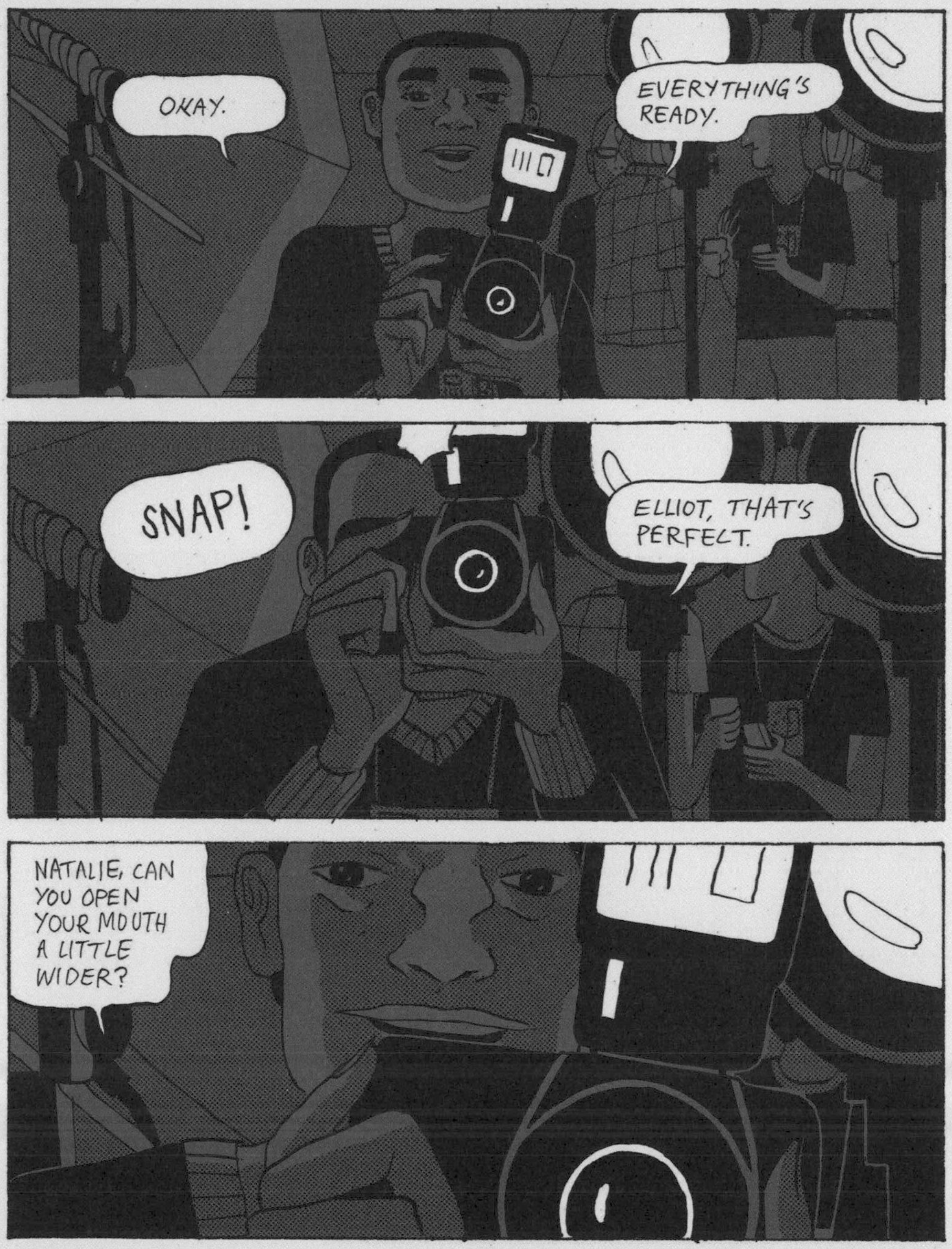
OKAY.
EVERYTHING'S READY.
SNAP!
ELLIOT, THAT'S PERFECT.
NATALIE, CAN YOU OPEN YOUR MOUTH A LITTLE WIDER?

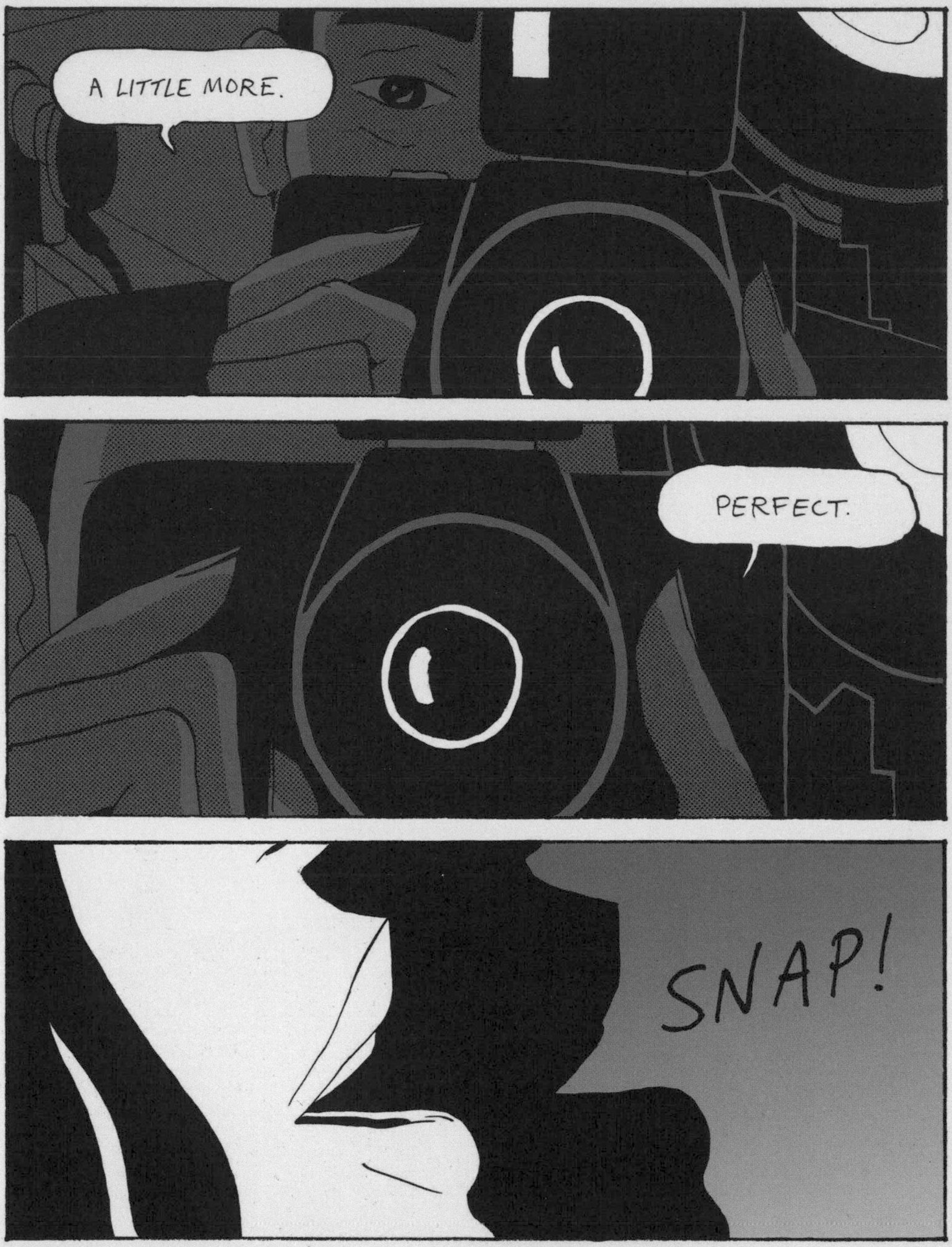
A LITTLE MORE.
PERFECT.
SNAP!

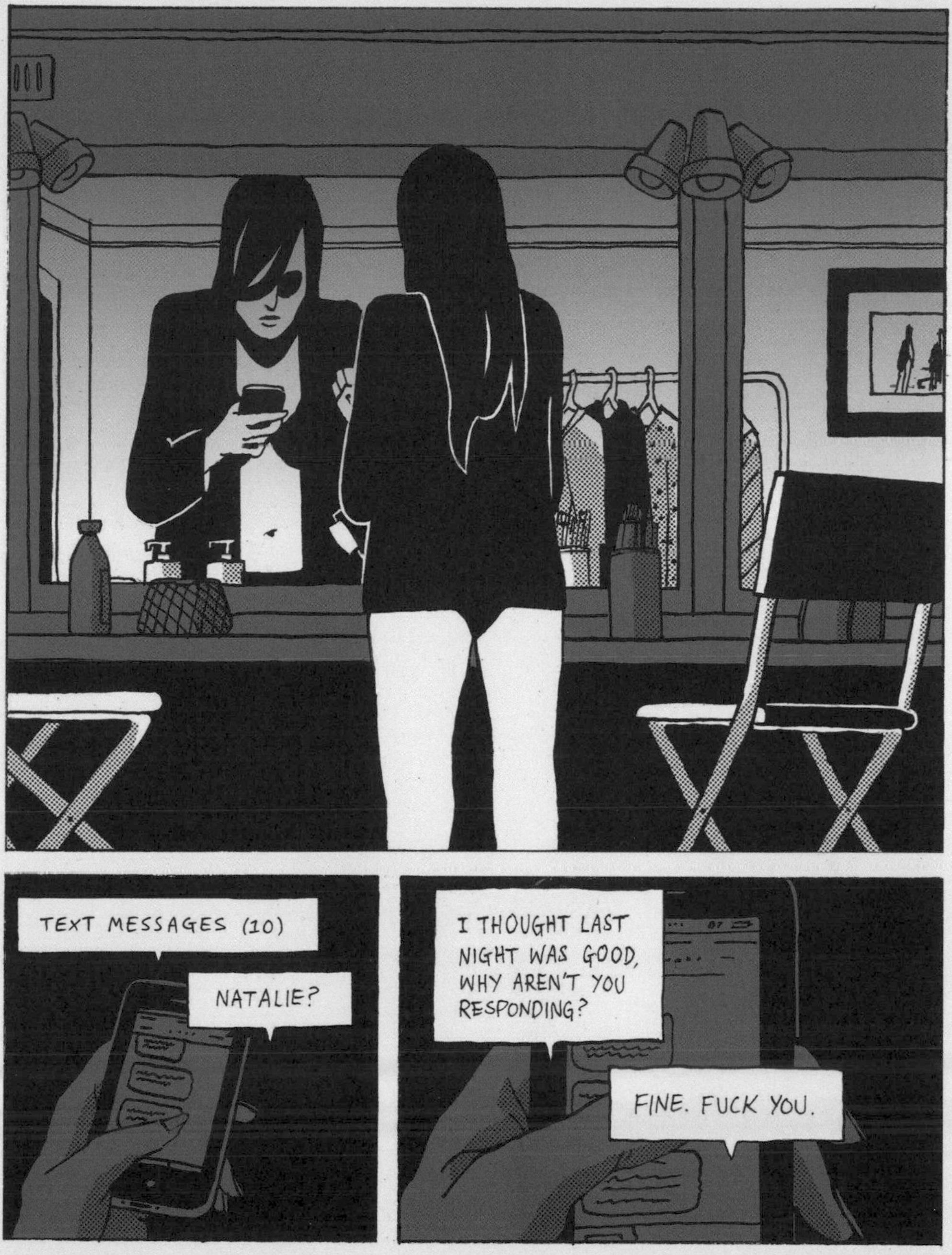
TEXT MESSAGES (10)
NATALIE?
I THOUGHT LAST NIGHT WAS GOOD, WHY AREN'T YOU RESPONDING?
FINE. FUCK YOU.

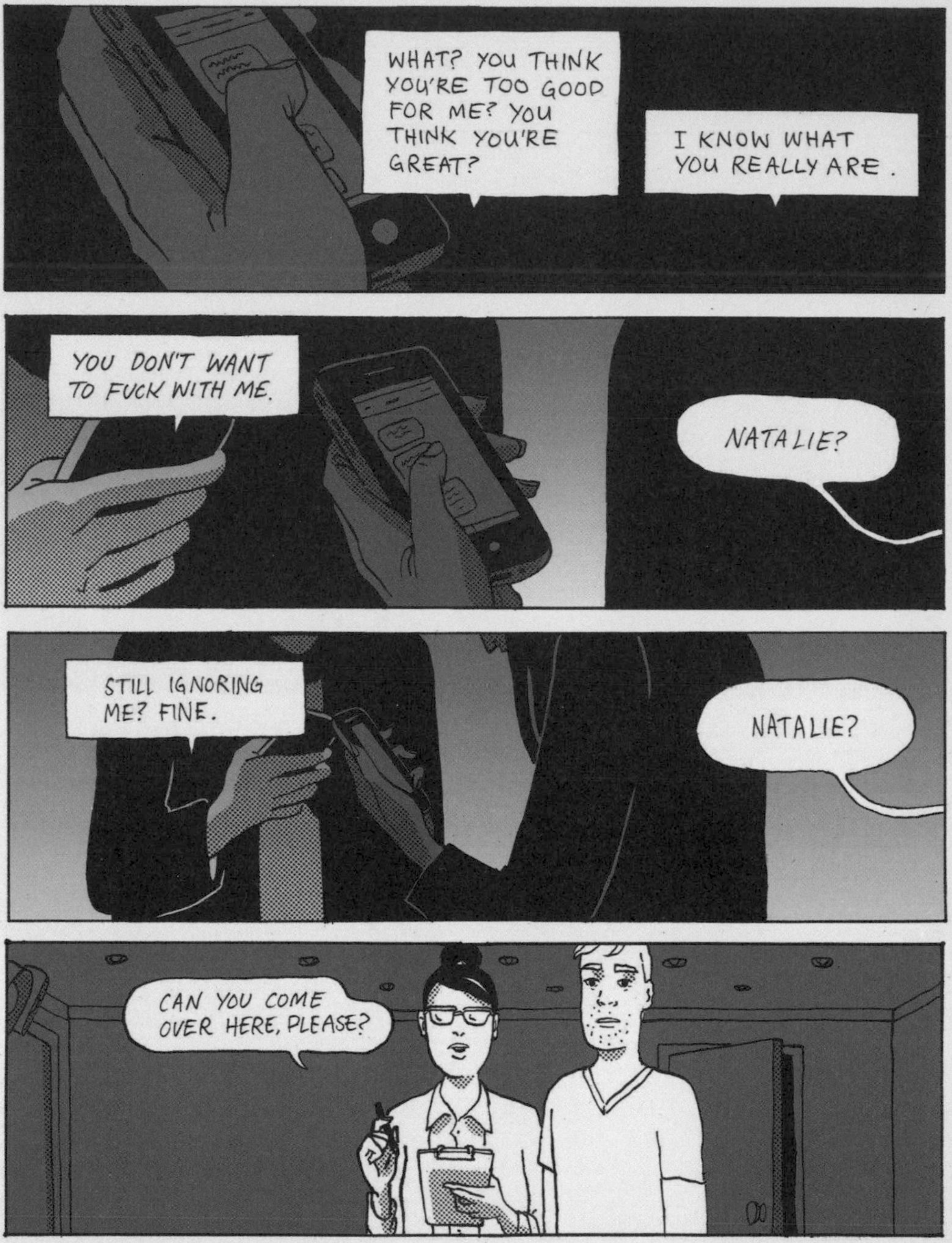
WHAT? YOU THINK YOU'RE TOO GOOD FOR ME? YOU THINK YOU'RE GREAT?
I KNOW WHAT YOU REALLY ARE.
YOU DON'T WANT TO FUCK WITH ME.
NATALIE?
STILL IGNORING ME? FINE.
NATALIE?
CAN YOU COME OVER HERE, PLEASE?

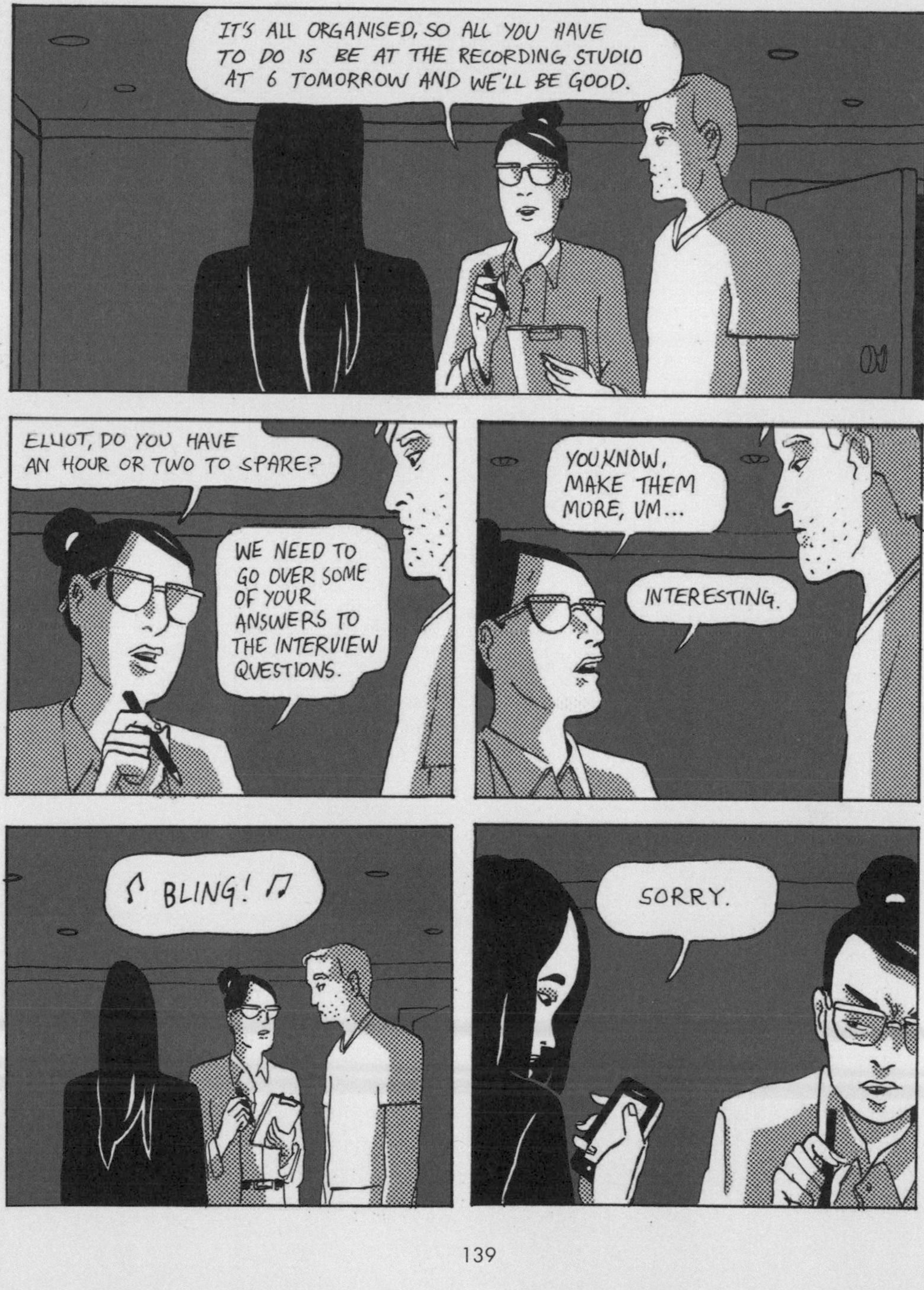
IT'S ALL ORGANISED, SO ALL YOU HAVE TO DO IS BE AT THE RECORDING STUDIO AT 6 TOMORROW AND WE'LL BE GOOD.
ELLIOT, DO YOU HAVE AN HOUR OR TWO TO SPARE?
WE NEED TO GO OVER SOME OF YOUR ANSWERS TO THE INTERVIEW QUESTIONS.
YOU KNOW, MAKE THEM MORE, UM...
INTERESTING.
♪ BLING! ♫
SORRY.

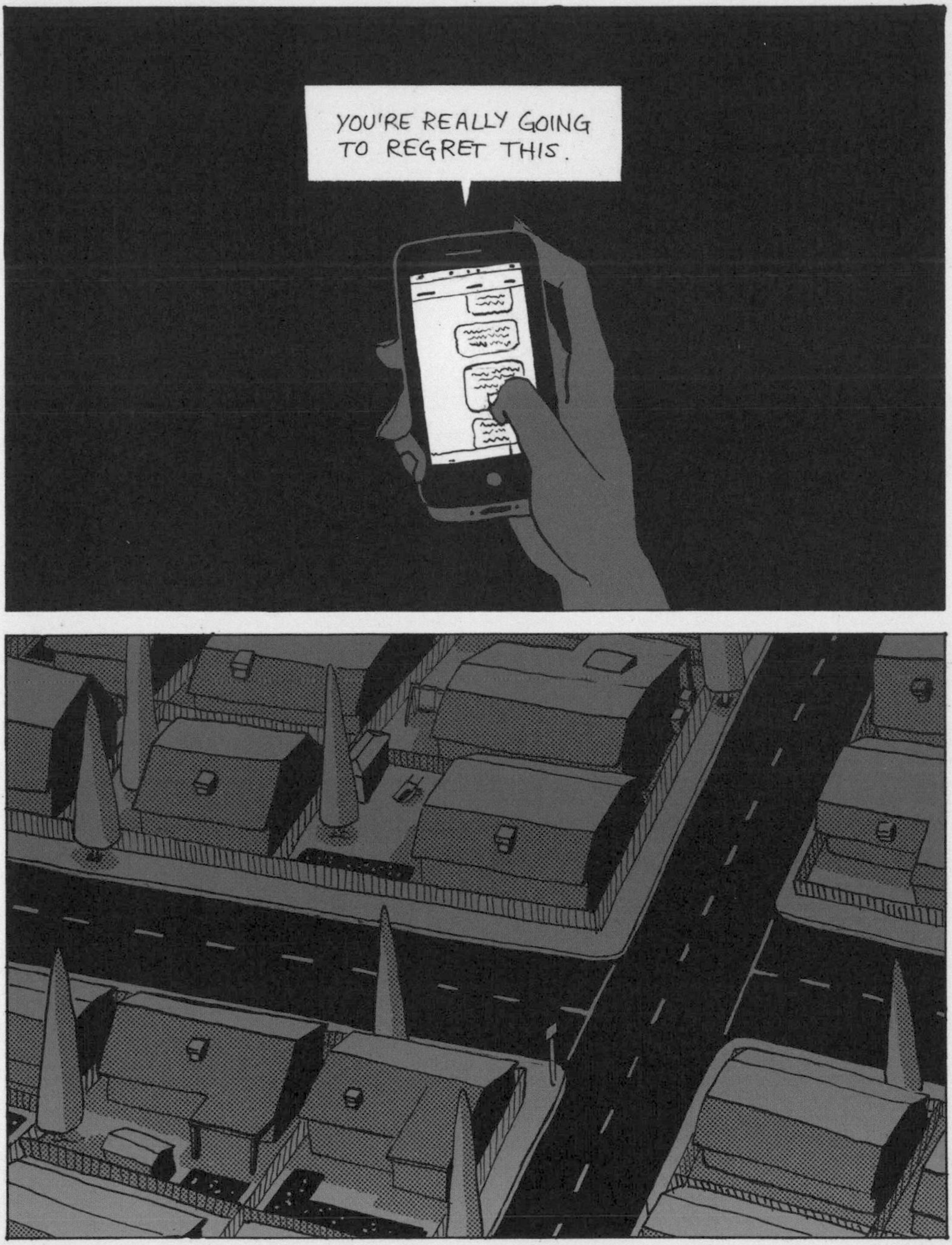
YOU'RE REALLY GOING TO REGRET THIS.

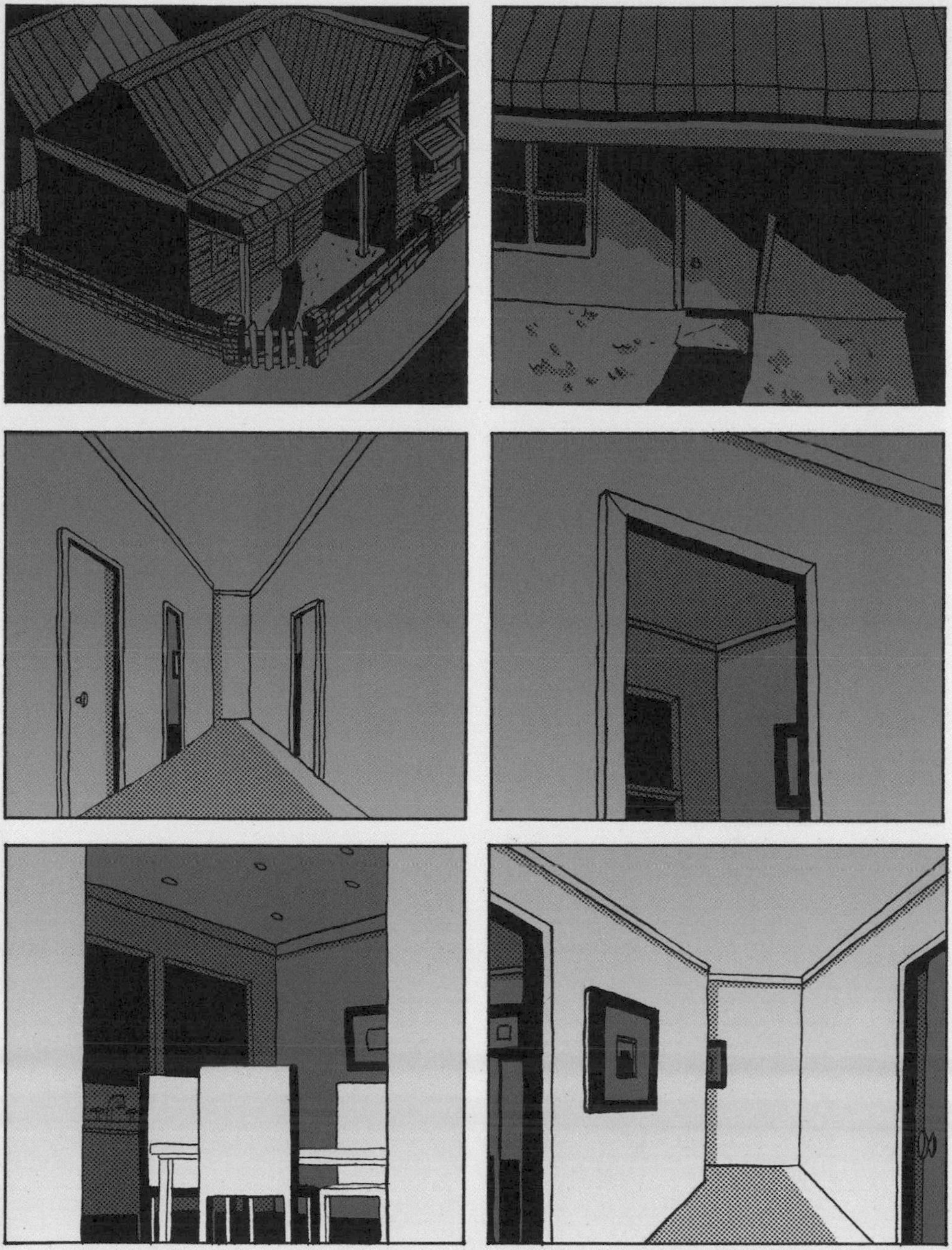

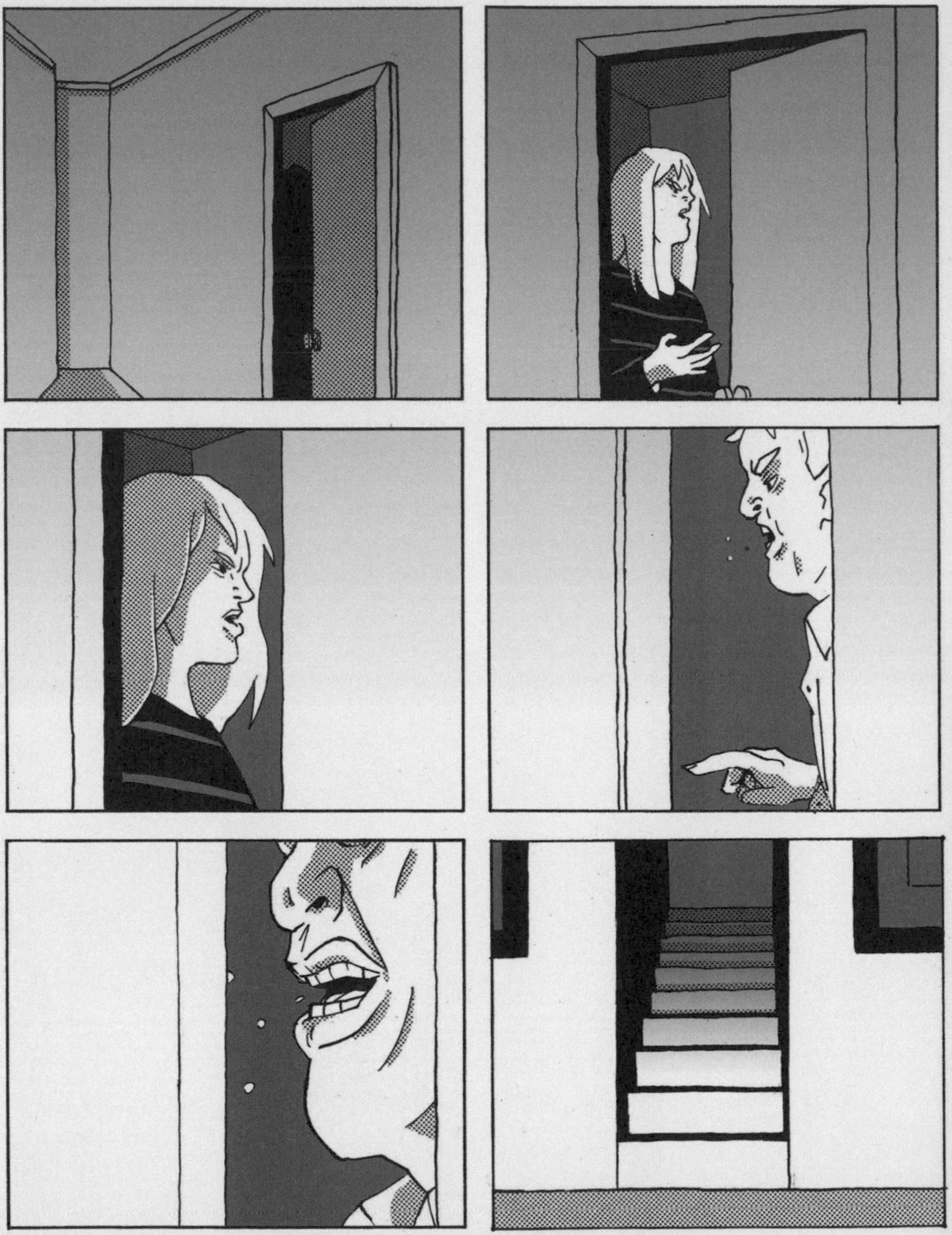

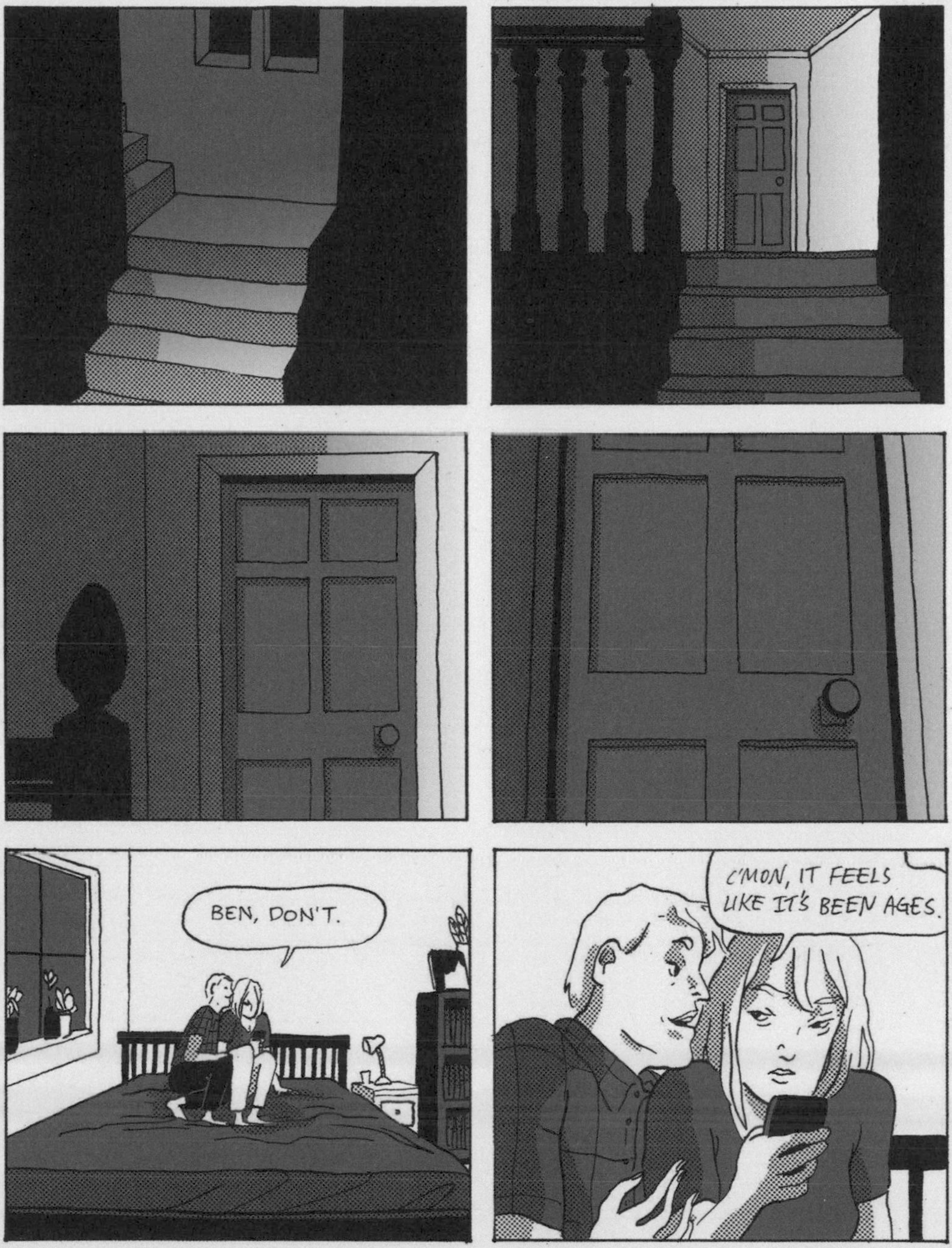
BEN, DON'T.
C'MON, IT FEELS LIKE IT'S BEEN AGES.

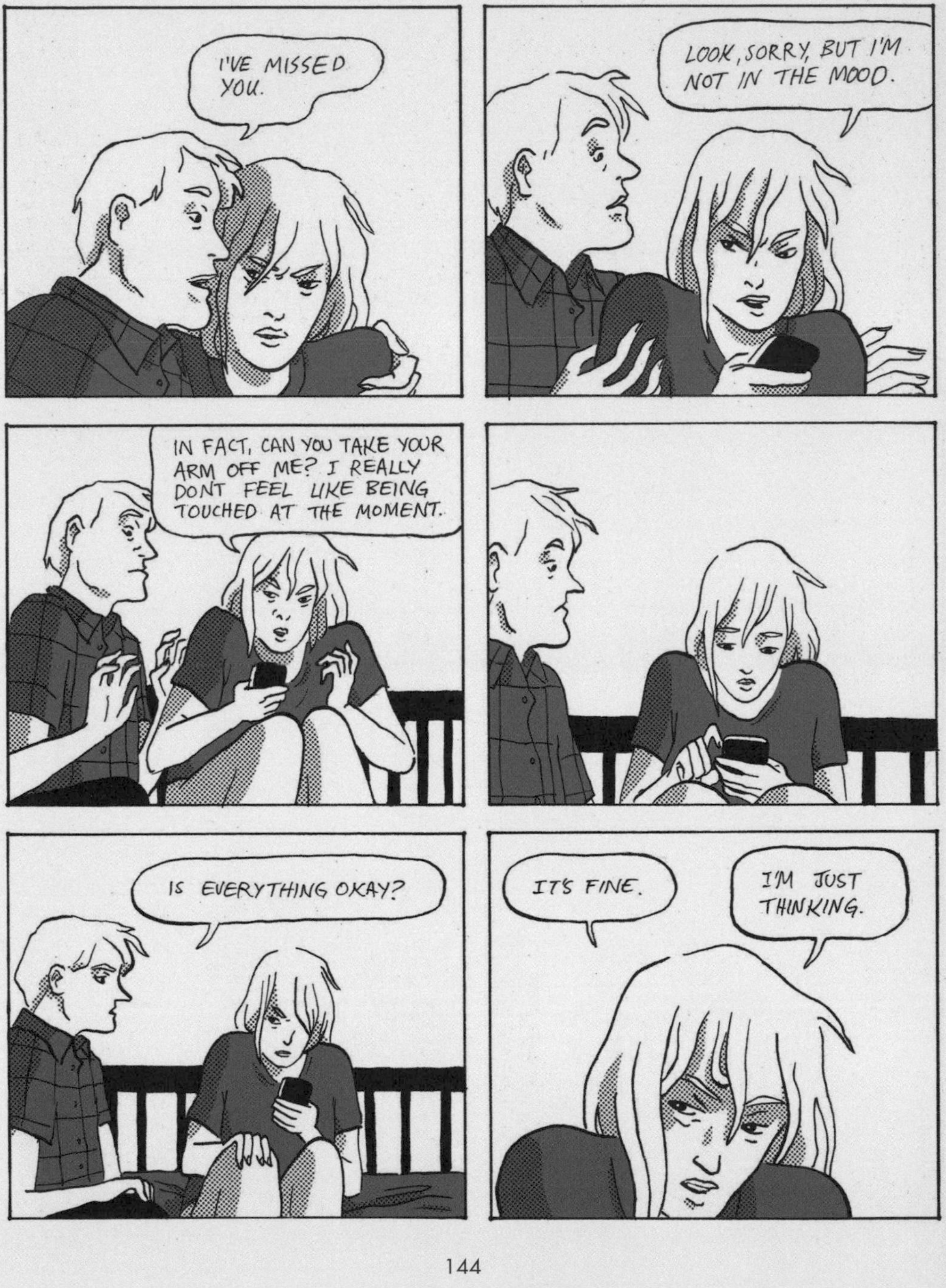
I'VE MISSED YOU.
LOOK, SORRY, BUT I'M NOT IN THE MOOD.
IN FACT, CAN YOU TAKE YOUR ARM OFF ME? I REALLY DONT FEEL LIKE BEING TOUCHED AT THE MOMENT.
IS EVERYTHING OKAY?
IT'S FINE.
I'M JUST THINKING.

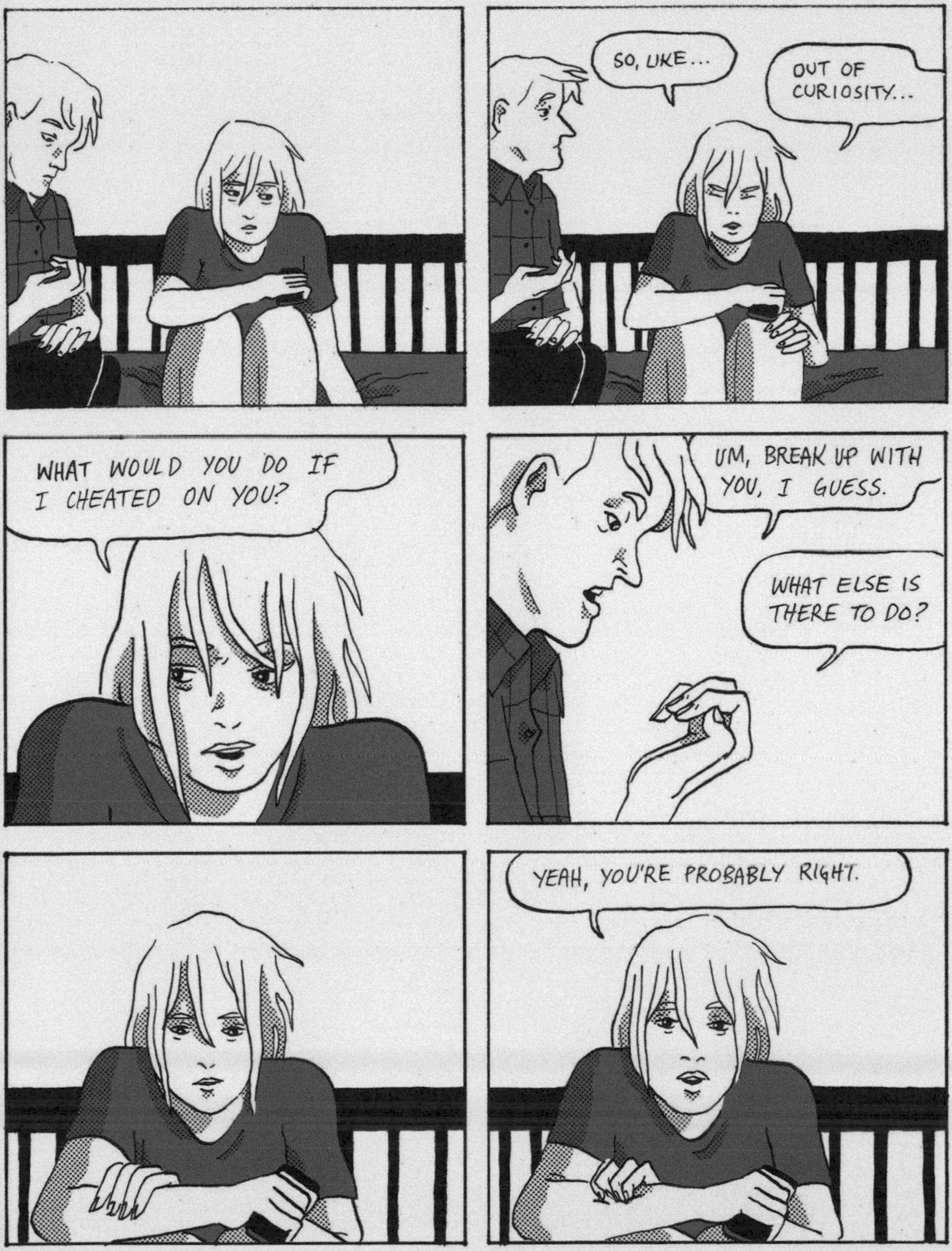
SO, LIKE...
OUT OF CURIOSITY...
WHAT WOULD YOU DO IF I CHEATED ON YOU?
UM, BREAK UP WITH YOU, I GUESS.
WHAT ELSE IS THERE TO DO?
YEAH, YOU'RE PROBABLY RIGHT.

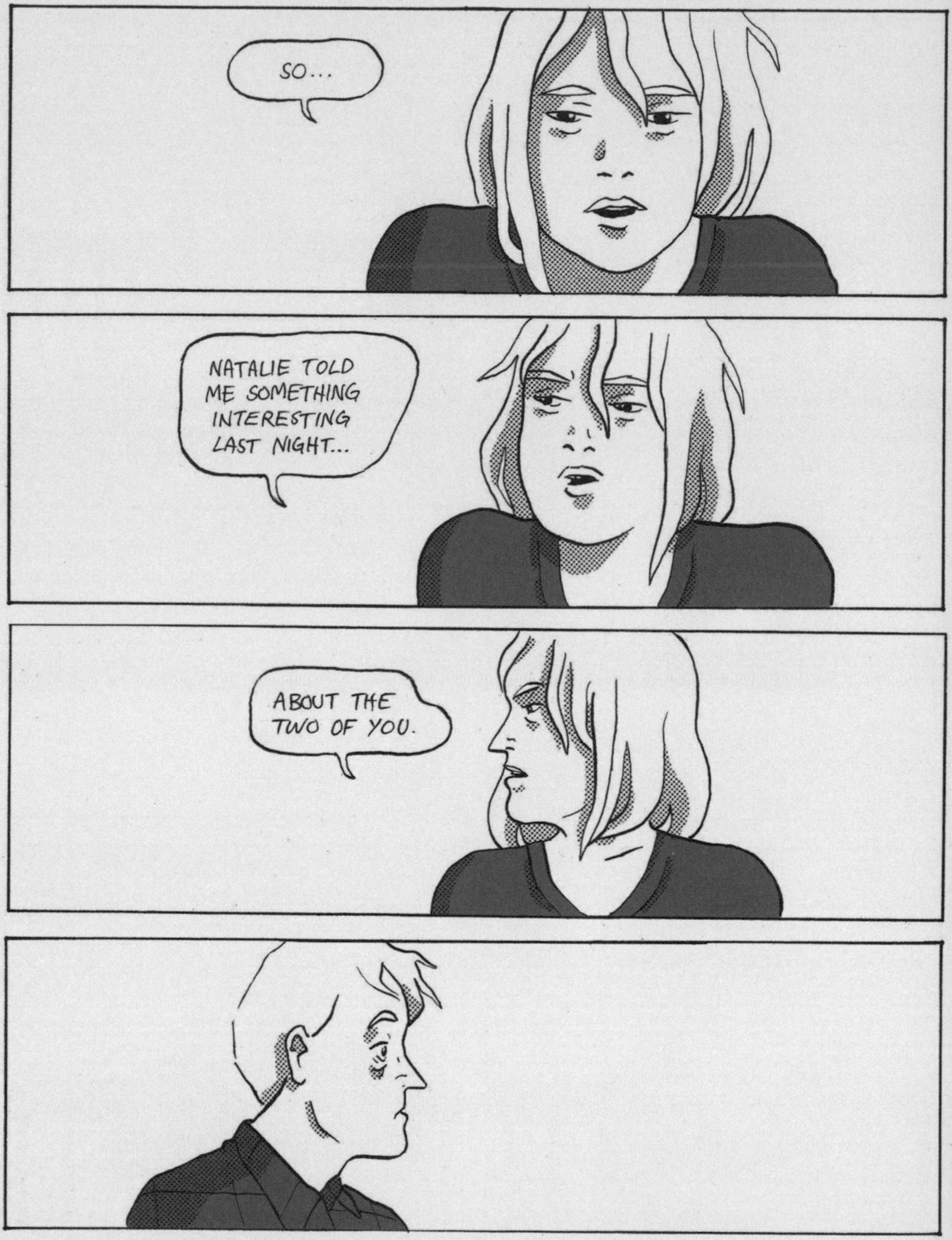
SO...
NATALIE TOLD ME SOMETHING INTERESTING LAST NIGHT...
ABOUT THE TWO OF YOU.

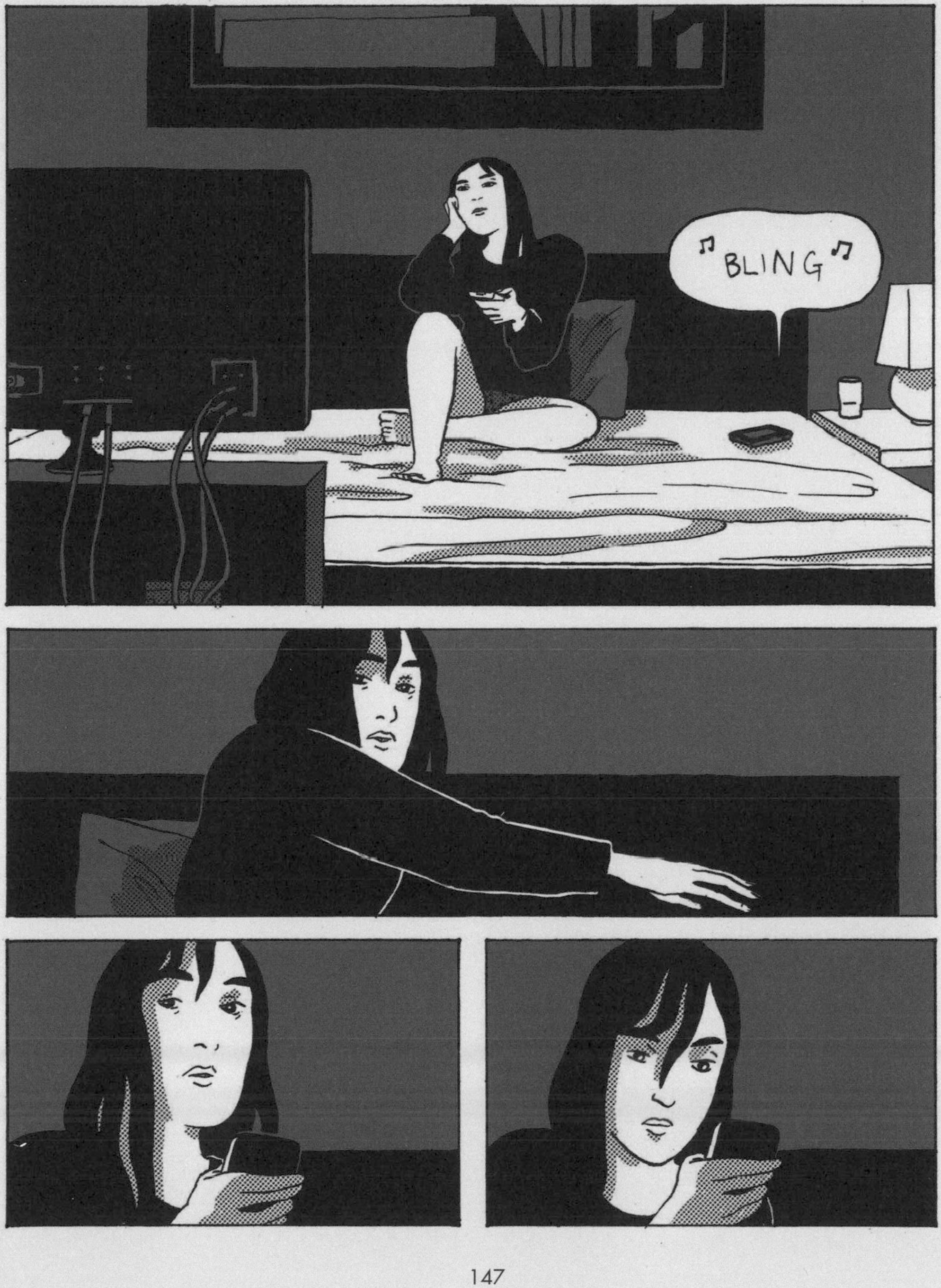

♫ BLING ♫

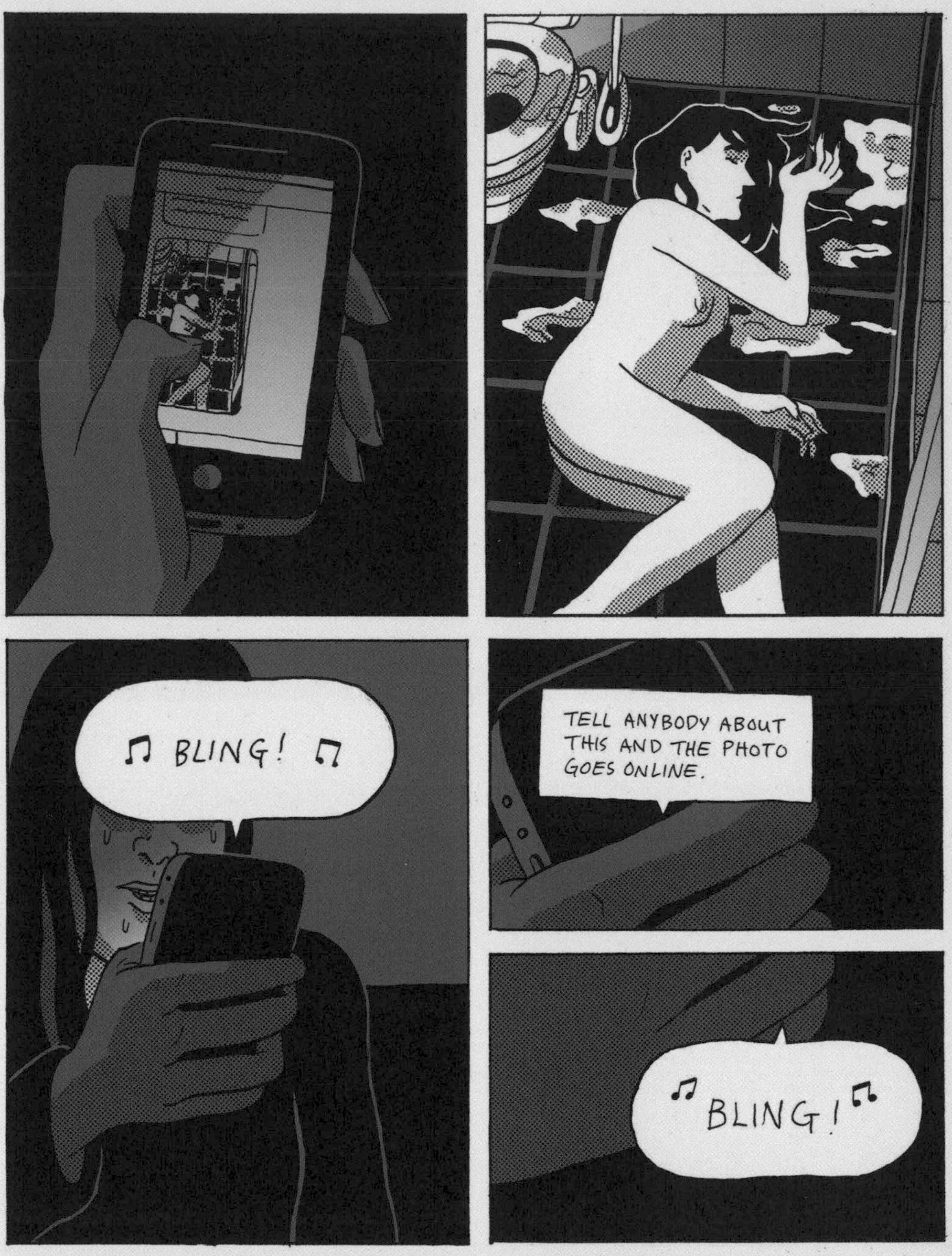
♫ BLING! ♫
TELL ANYBODY ABOUT THIS AND THE PHOTO GOES ONLINE.
♫ BLING! ♫

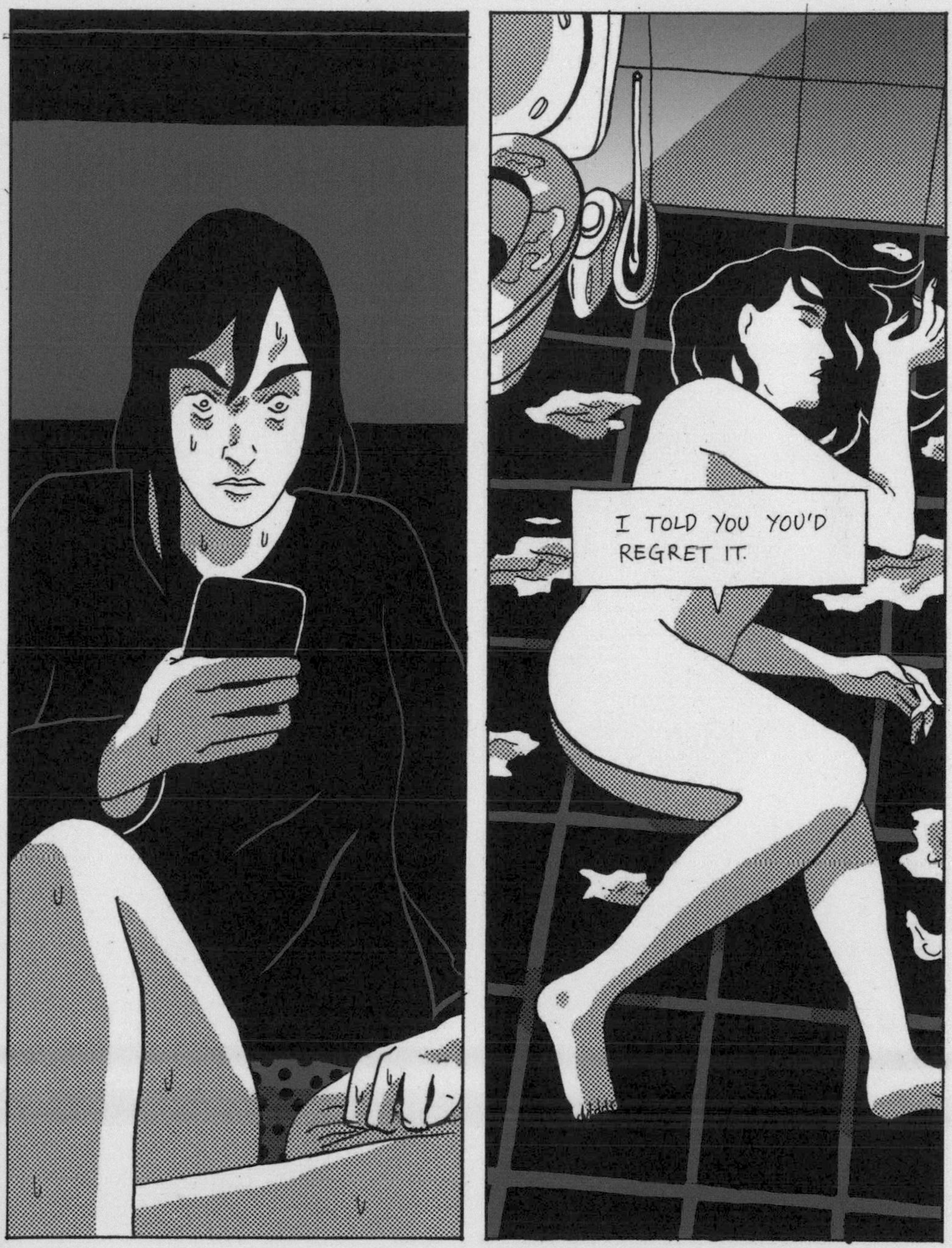
I TOLD YOU YOU'D REGRET IT.

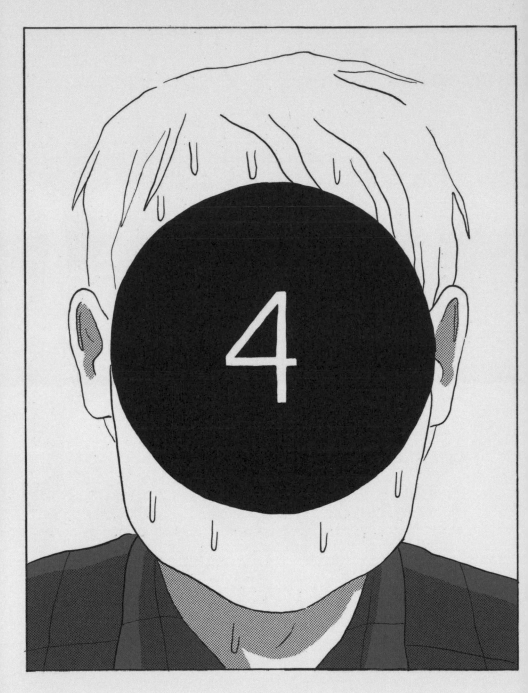

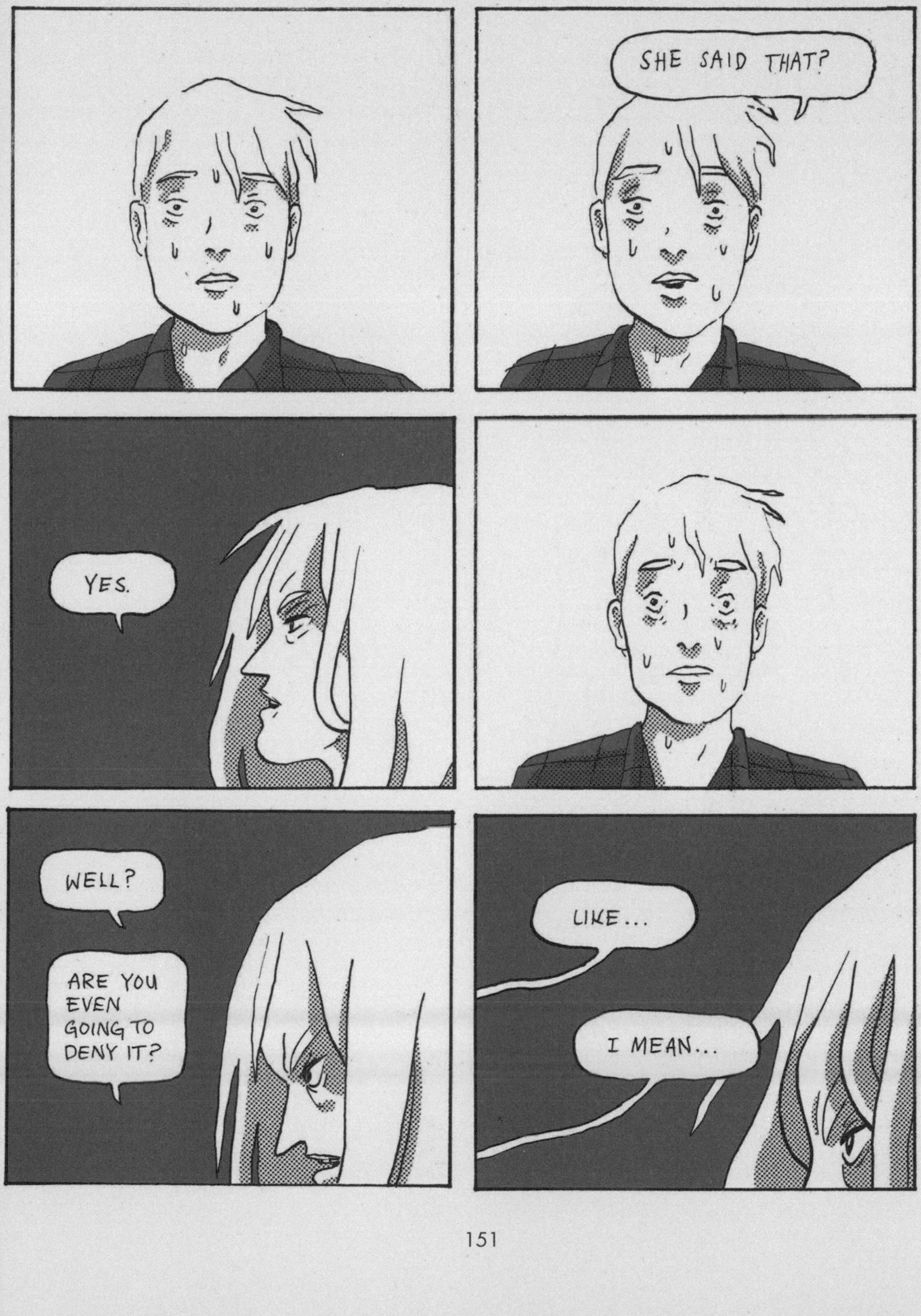
SHE SAID THAT?
YES.
WELL?
ARE YOU EVEN GOING TO DENY IT?
LIKE...
I MEAN...

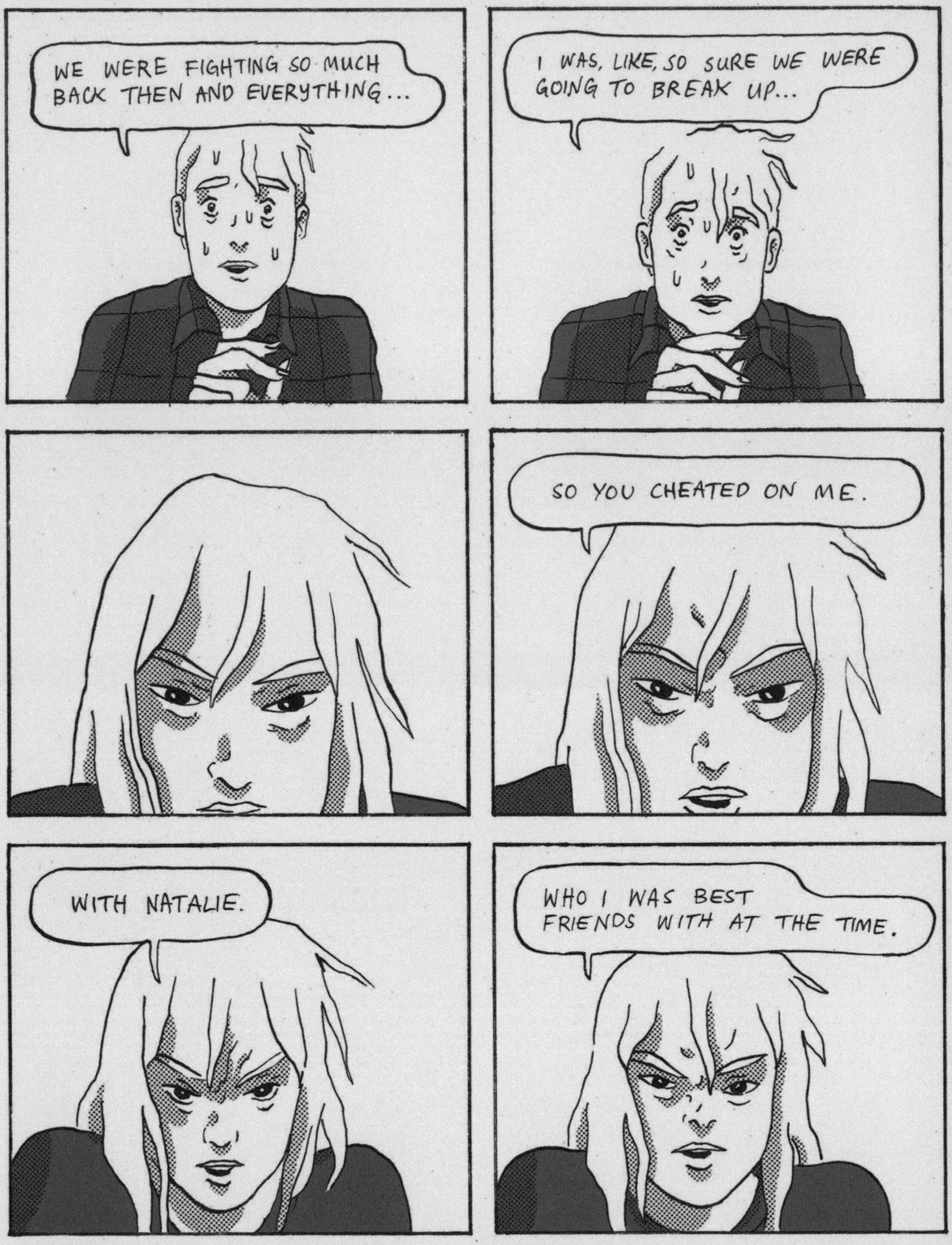
WE WERE FIGHTING SO MUCH BACK THEN AND EVERYTHING...
I WAS, LIKE, SO SURE WE WERE GOING TO BREAK UP...
SO YOU CHEATED ON ME.
WITH NATALIE.
WHO I WAS BEST FRIENDS WITH AT THE TIME.

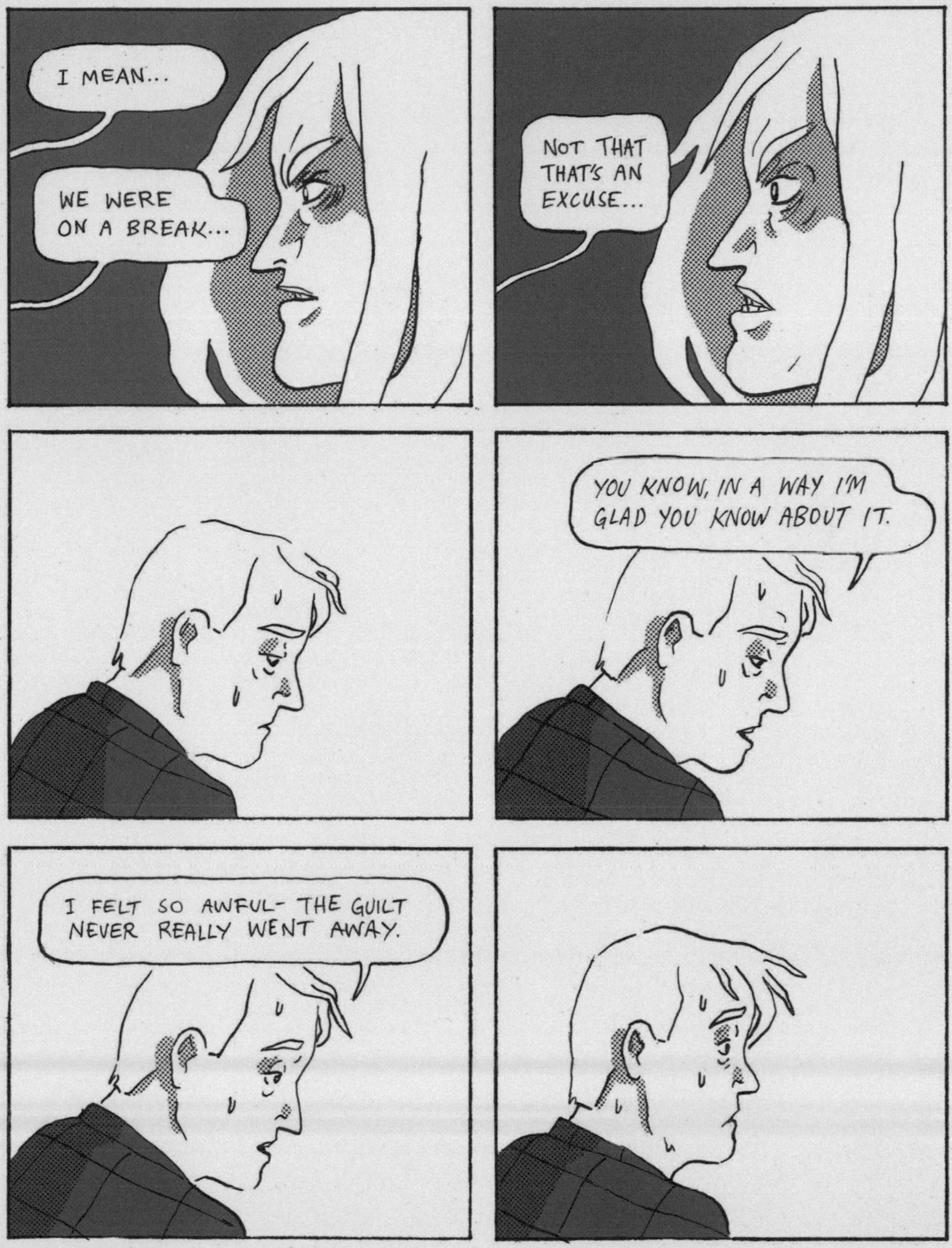
I MEAN...
WE WERE ON A BREAK...
NOT THAT THAT'S AN EXCUSE...
YOU KNOW, IN A WAY I'M GLAD YOU KNOW ABOUT IT.
I FELT SO AWFUL- THE GUILT NEVER REALLY WENT AWAY.

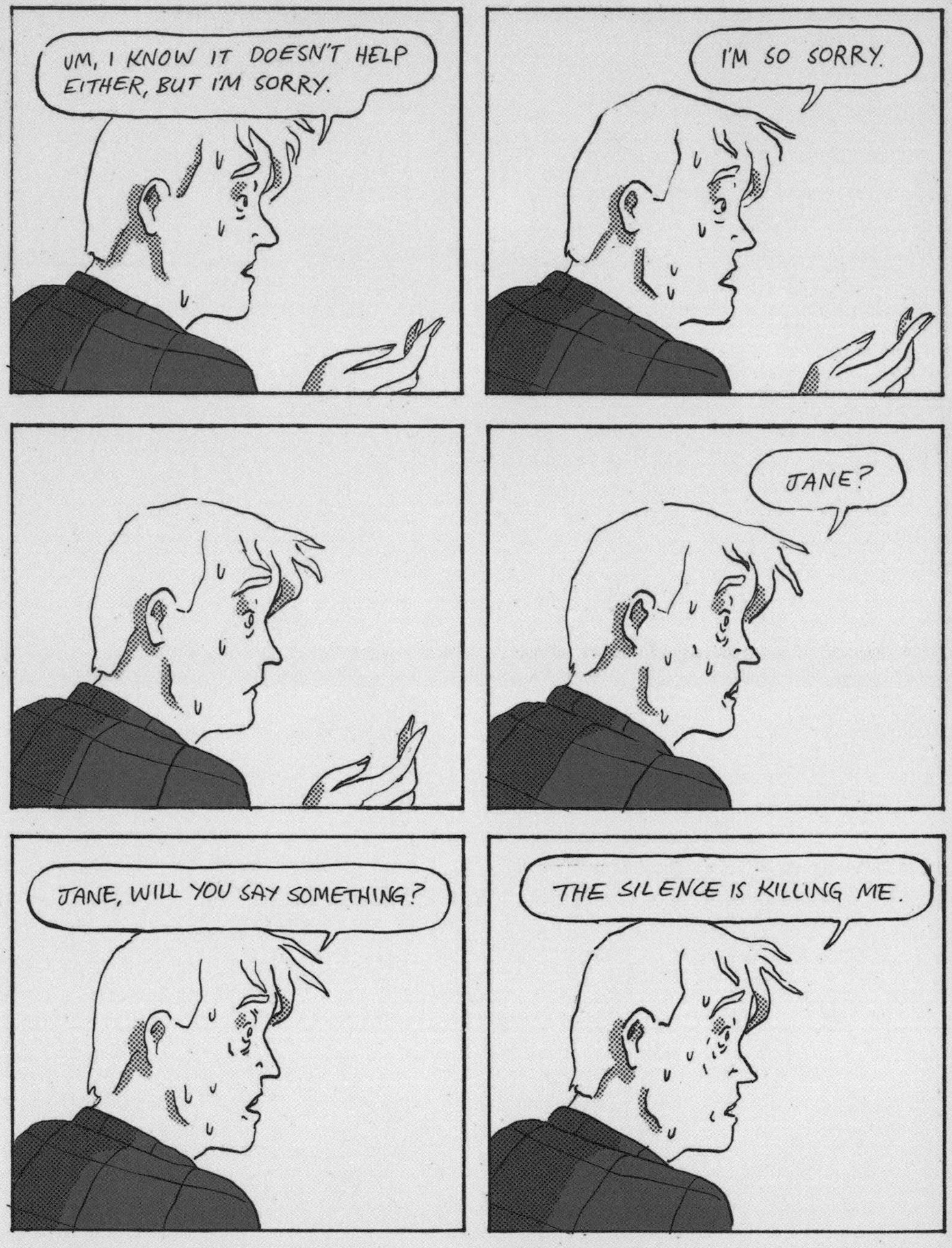
UM, I KNOW IT DOESN'T HELP EITHER, BUT I'M SORRY.
I'M SO SORRY.
JANE?
JANE, WILL YOU SAY SOMETHING?
THE SILENCE IS KILLING ME.

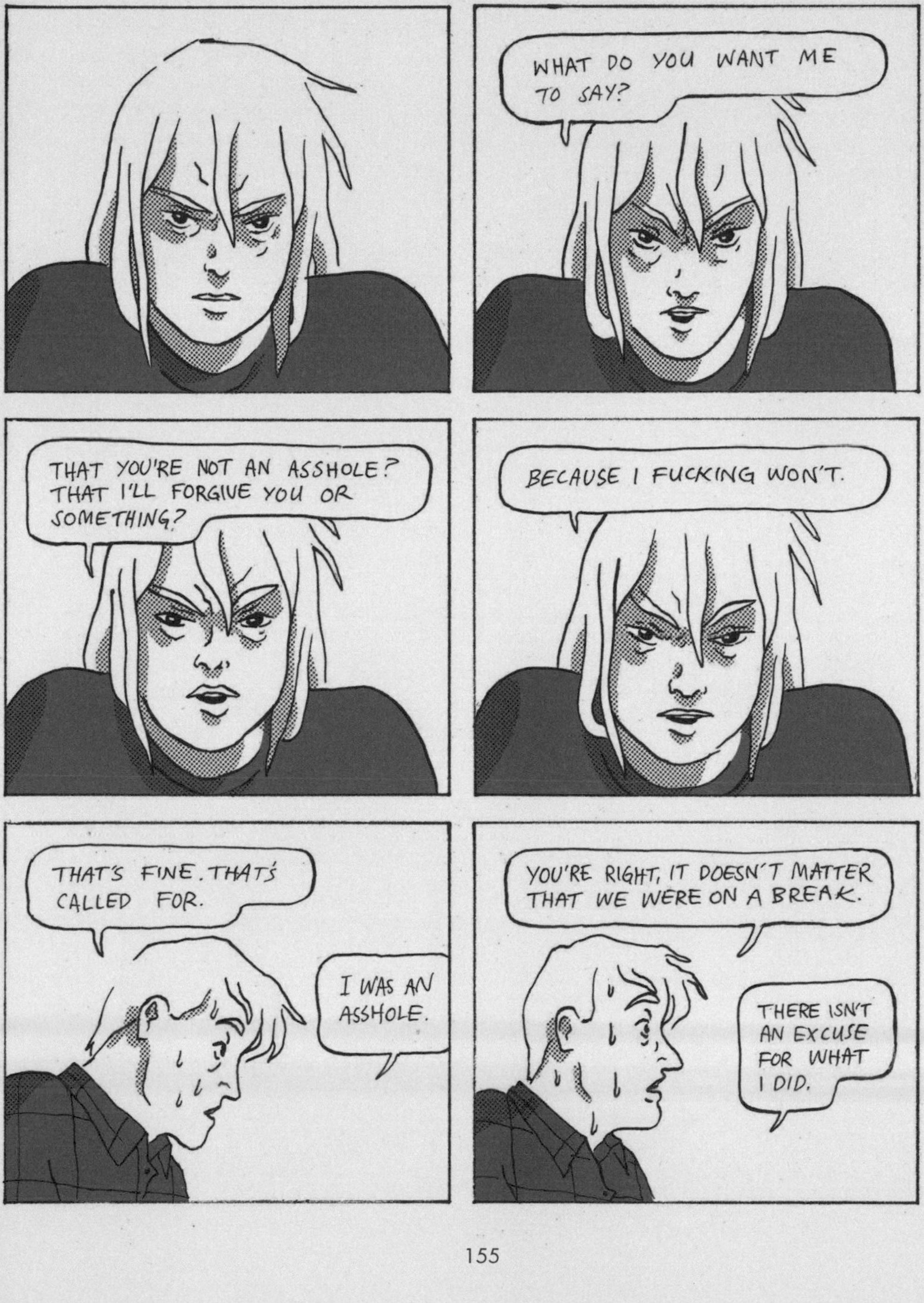
WHAT DO YOU WANT ME TO SAY?
THAT YOU'RE NOT AN ASSHOLE? THAT I'LL FORGIVE YOU OR SOMETHING?
BECAUSE I FUCKING WON'T.
THAT'S FINE. THAT'S CALLED FOR.
I WAS AN ASSHOLE.
YOU'RE RIGHT, IT DOESN'T MATTER THAT WE WERE ON A BREAK.
THERE ISN'T AN EXCUSE FOR WHAT I DID.

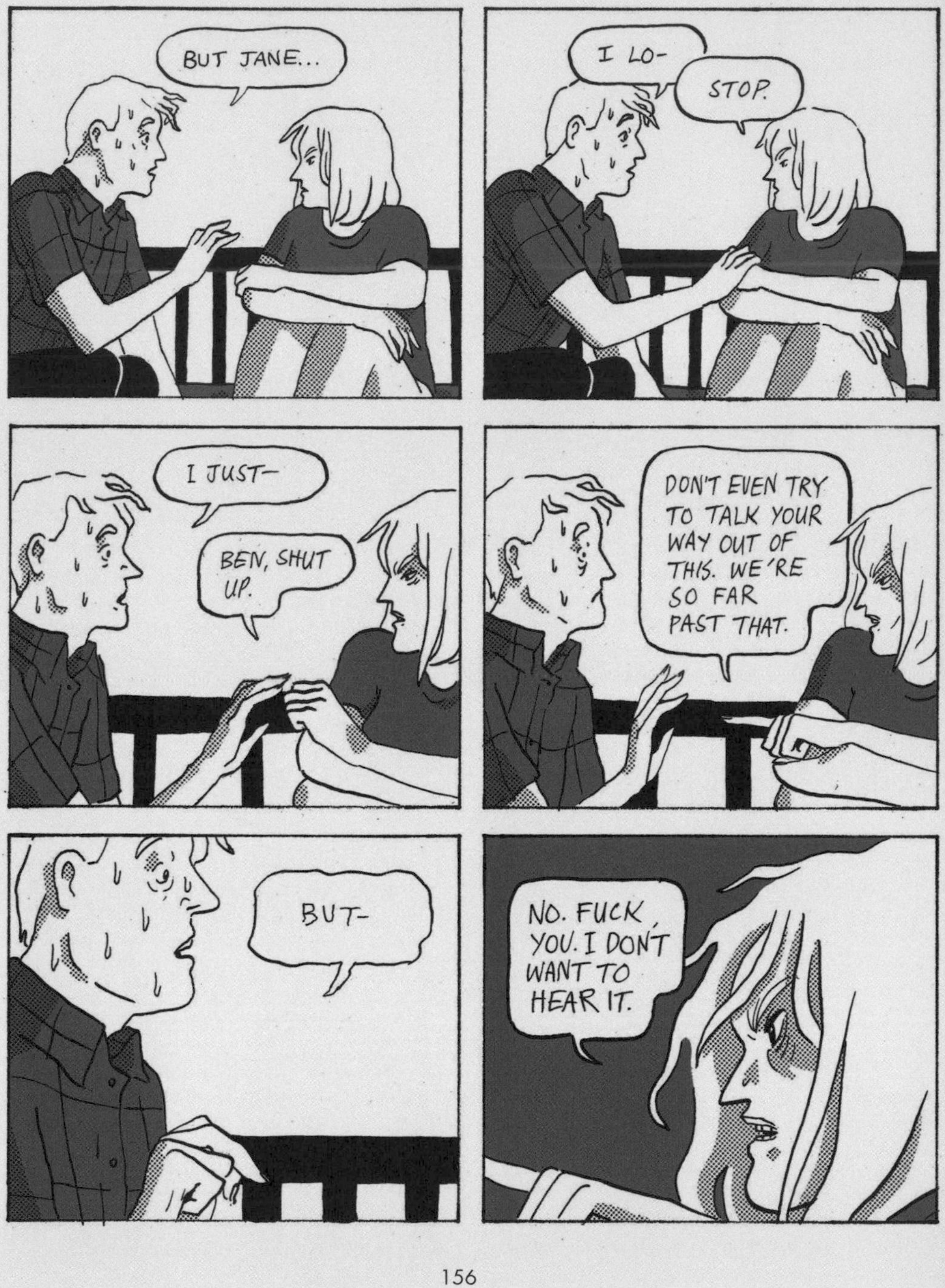
BUT JANE...
I LO-
STOP.
I JUST-
BEN, SHUT UP.
DON'T EVEN TRY TO TALK YOUR WAY OUT OF THIS. WE'RE SO FAR PAST THAT.
BUT-
NO. FUCK YOU. I DON'T WANT TO HEAR IT.

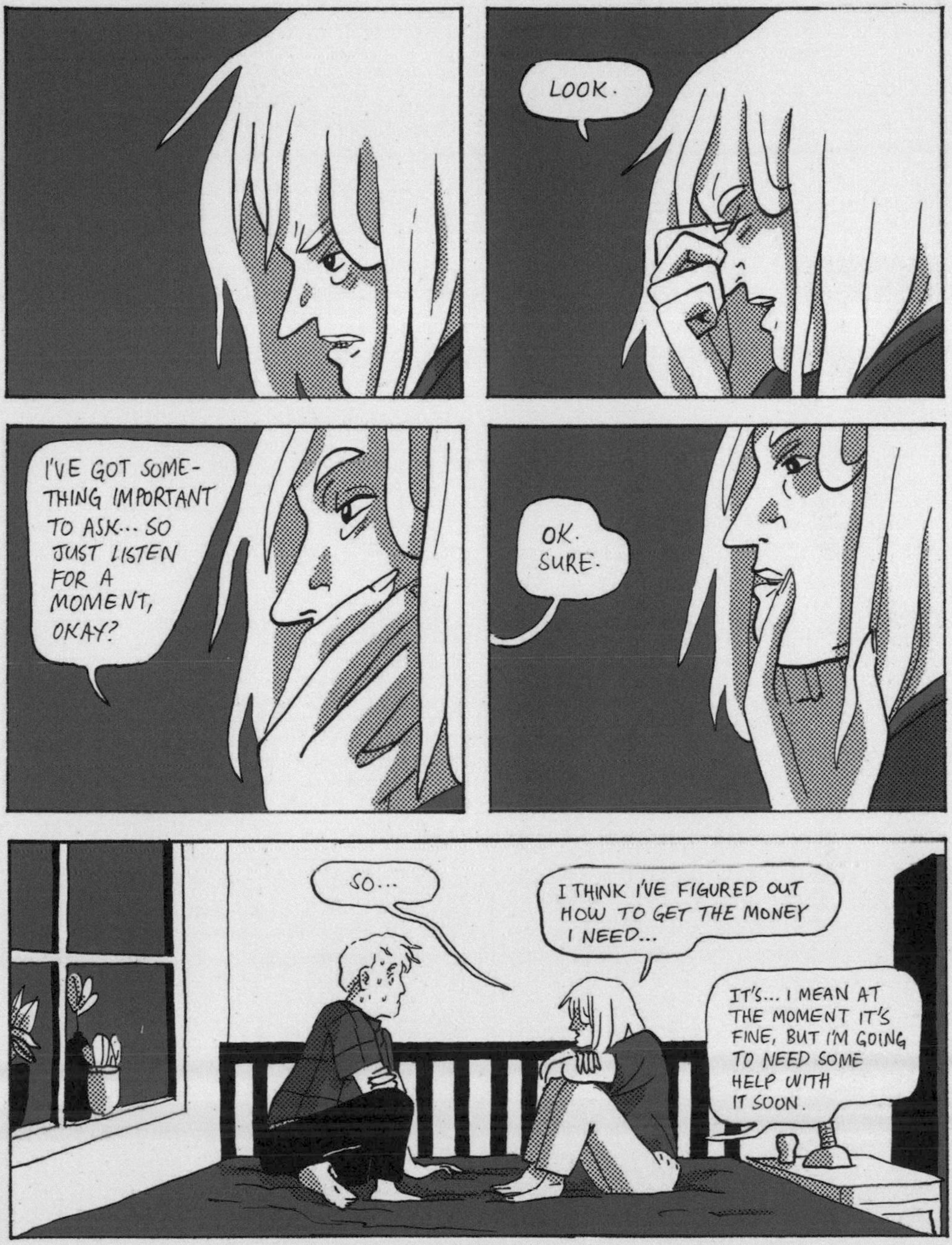
LOOK.
I'VE GOT SOMETHING IMPORTANT TO ASK... SO JUST LISTEN FOR A MOMENT, OKAY?
OK. SURE.
SO...
I THINK I'VE FIGURED OUT HOW TO GET THE MONEY I NEED...
IT'S... I MEAN AT THE MOMENT IT'S FINE, BUT I'M GOING TO NEED SOME HELP WITH IT SOON.

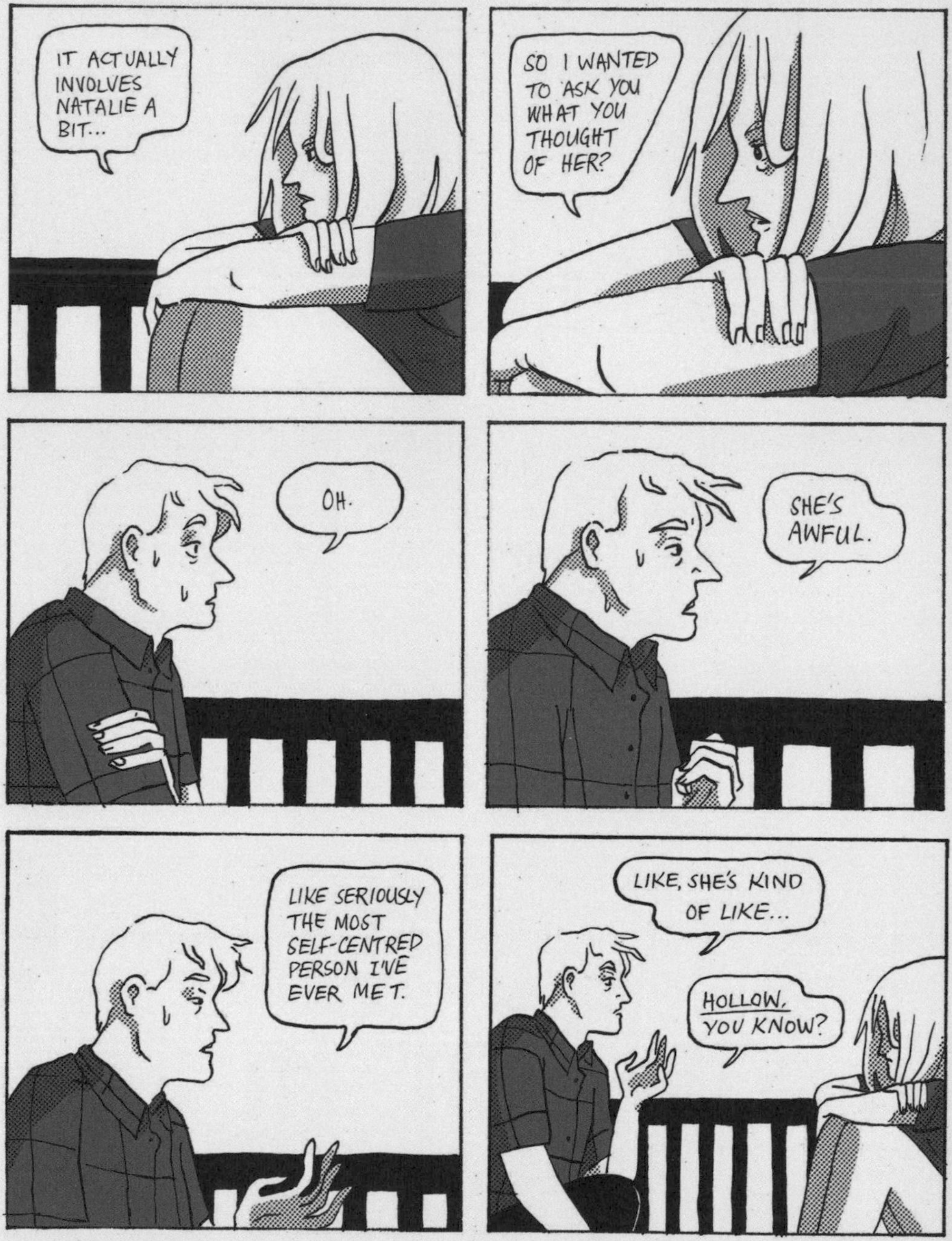
IT ACTUALLY INVOLVES NATALIE A BIT...
SO I WANTED TO ASK YOU WHAT YOU THOUGHT OF HER?
OH.
SHE'S AWFUL.
LIKE SERIOUSLY THE MOST SELF-CENTRED PERSON I'VE EVER MET.
LIKE, SHE'S KIND OF LIKE...
HOLLOW, YOU KNOW?

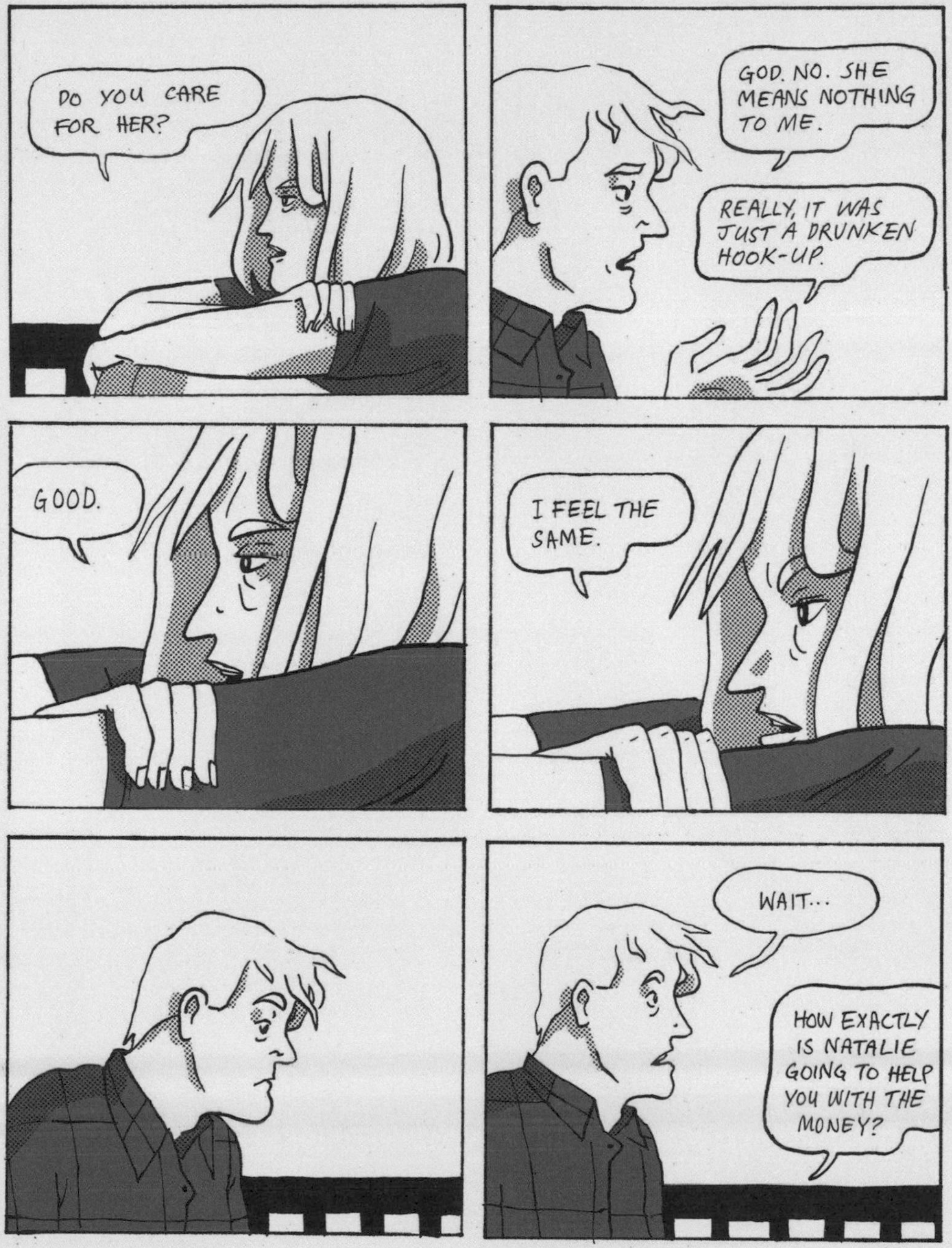
DO YOU CARE FOR HER?
GOD. NO. SHE MEANS NOTHING TO ME.
REALLY, IT WAS JUST A DRUNKEN HOOK-UP.
GOOD.
I FEEL THE SAME.
WAIT...
HOW EXACTLY IS NATALIE GOING TO HELP YOU WITH THE MONEY?

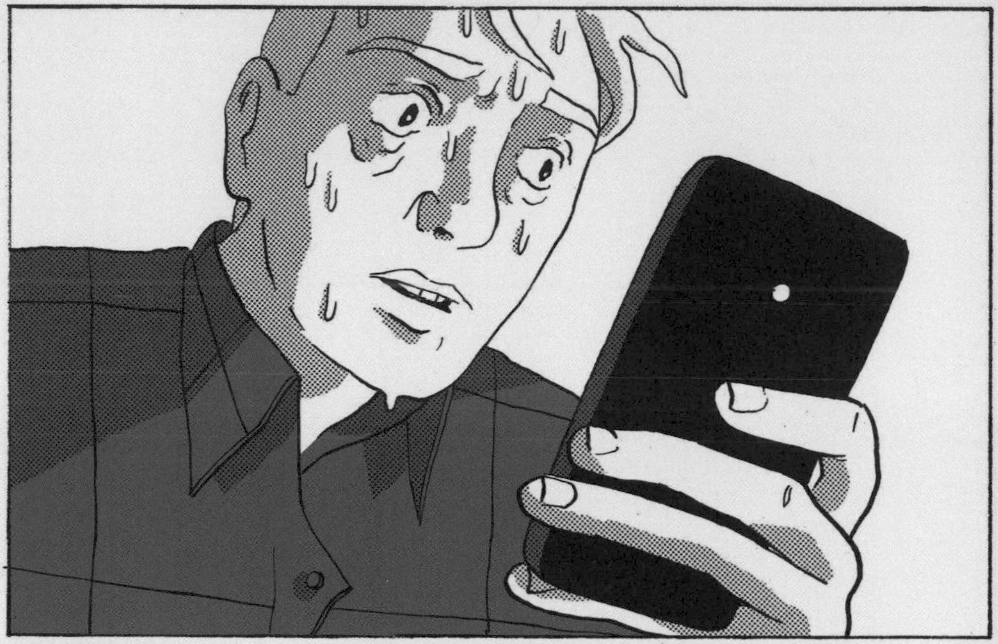

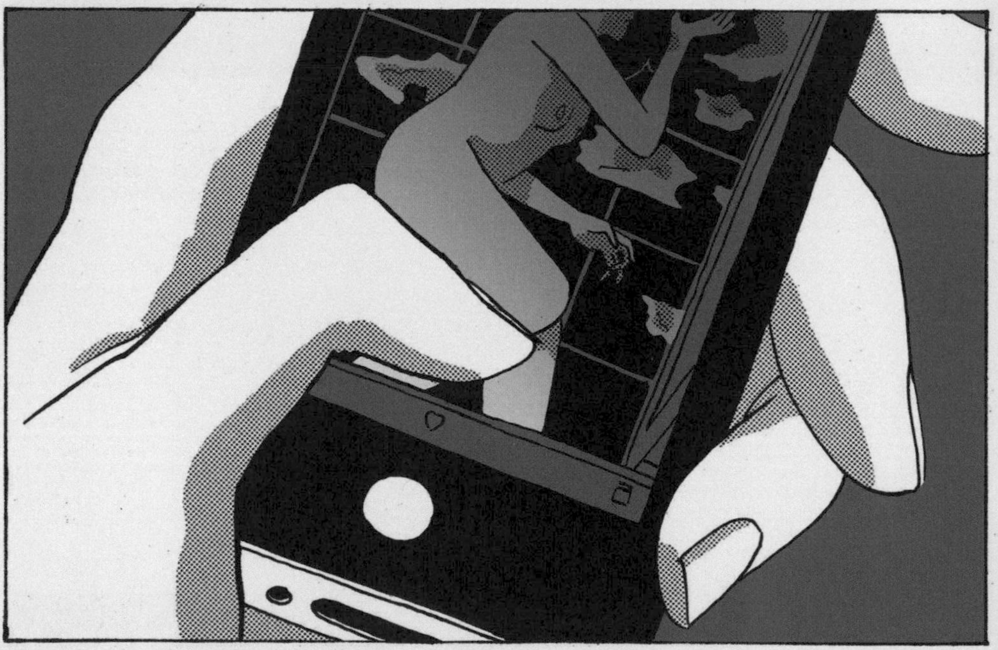

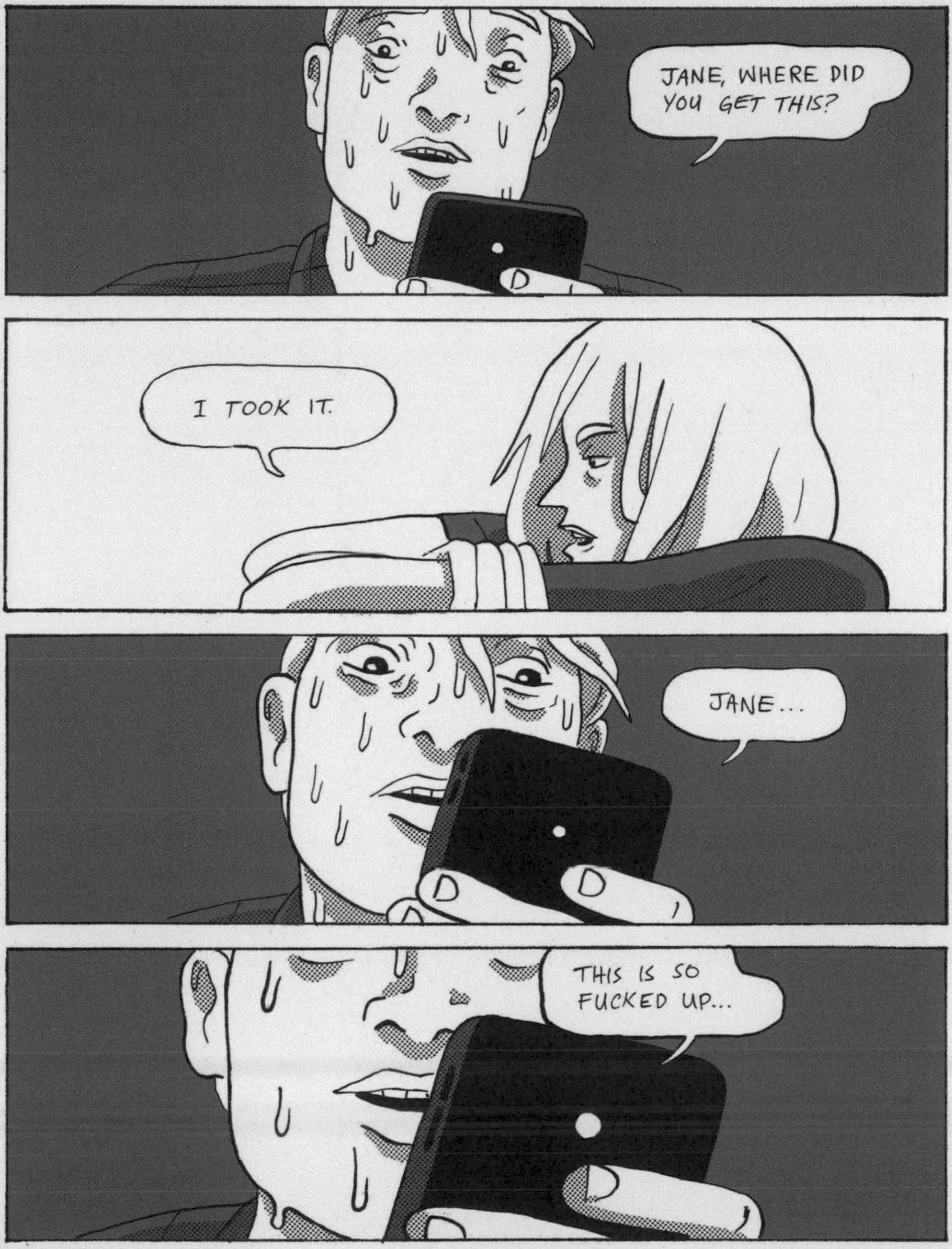
JANE, WHERE DID YOU GET THIS?
I TOOK IT.
JANE...
THIS IS SO FUCKED UP...

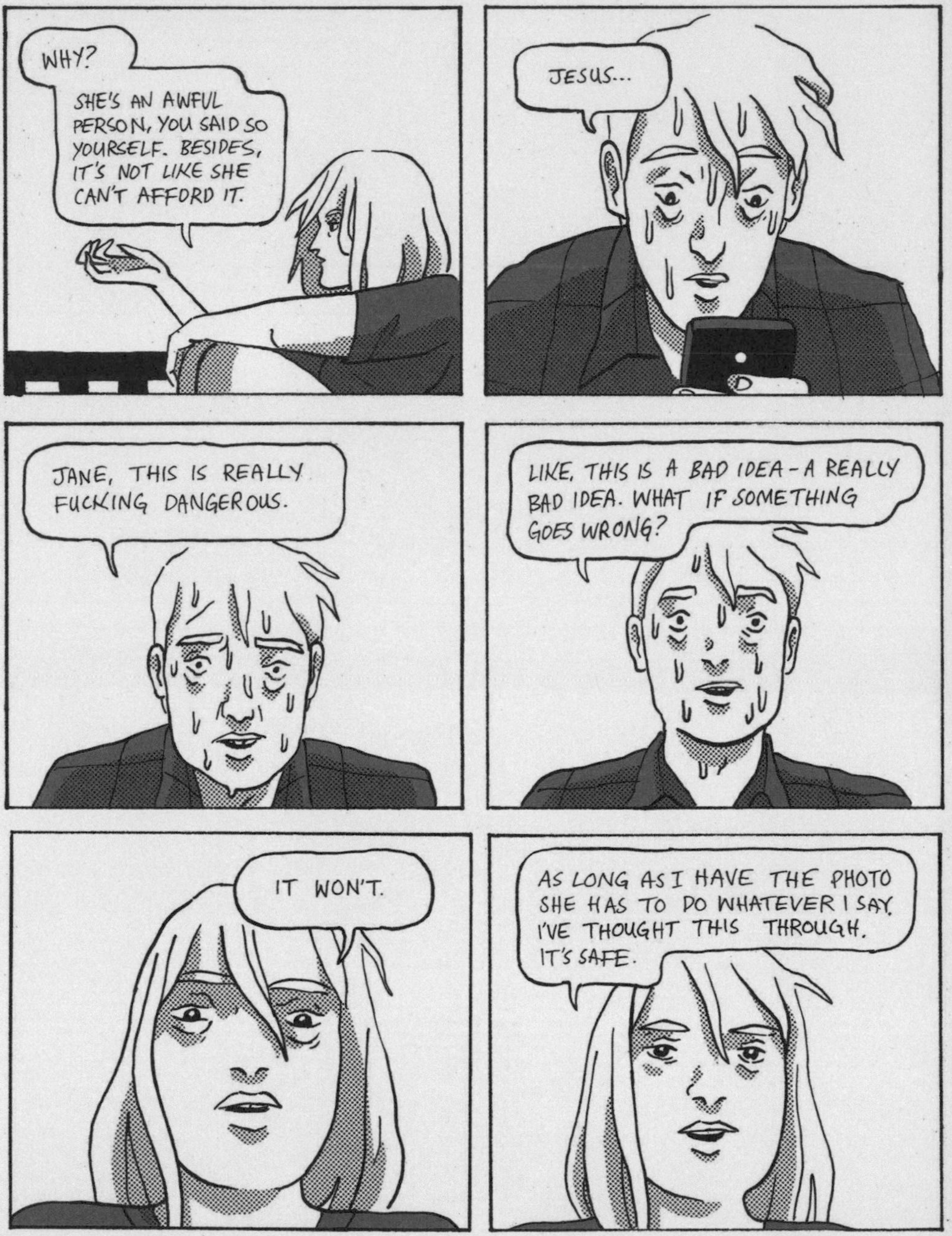
WHY?
SHE'S AN AWFUL PERSON, YOU SAID SO YOURSELF. BESIDES, IT'S NOT LIKE SHE CAN'T AFFORD IT.
JESUS...
JANE, THIS IS REALLY FUCKING DANGEROUS.
LIKE, THIS IS A BAD IDEA - A REALLY BAD IDEA. WHAT IF SOMETHING GOES WRONG?
IT WON'T.
AS LONG AS I HAVE THE PHOTO SHE HAS TO DO WHATEVER I SAY. I'VE THOUGHT THIS THROUGH. IT'S SAFE.

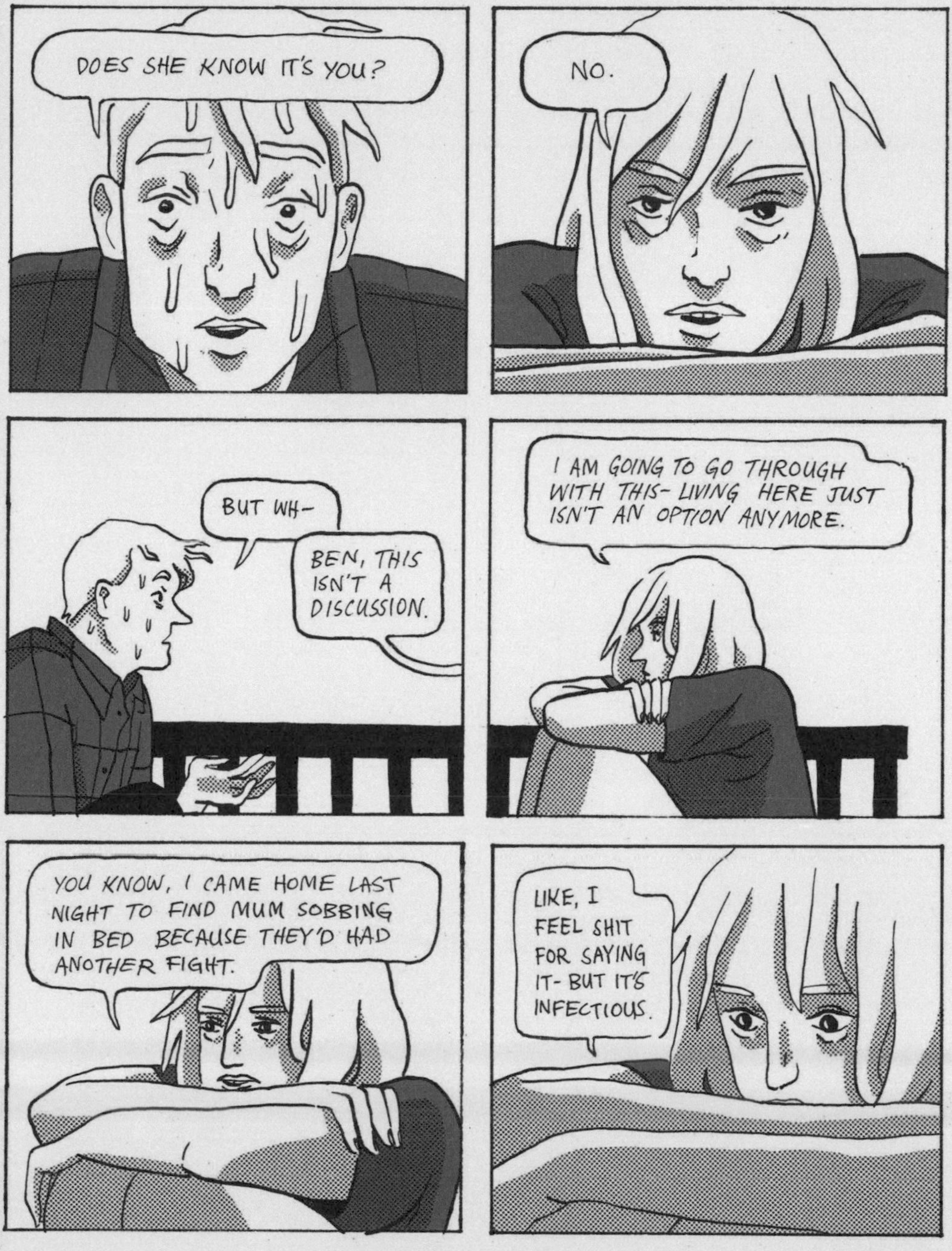
DOES SHE KNOW IT'S YOU?
NO.
BUT WH-
BEN, THIS ISN'T A DISCUSSION.
I AM GOING TO GO THROUGH WITH THIS- LIVING HERE JUST ISN'T AN OPTION ANYMORE.
YOU KNOW, I CAME HOME LAST NIGHT TO FIND MUM SOBBING IN BED BECAUSE THEY'D HAD ANOTHER FIGHT.
LIKE, I FEEL SHIT FOR SAYING IT- BUT IT'S INFECTIOUS.

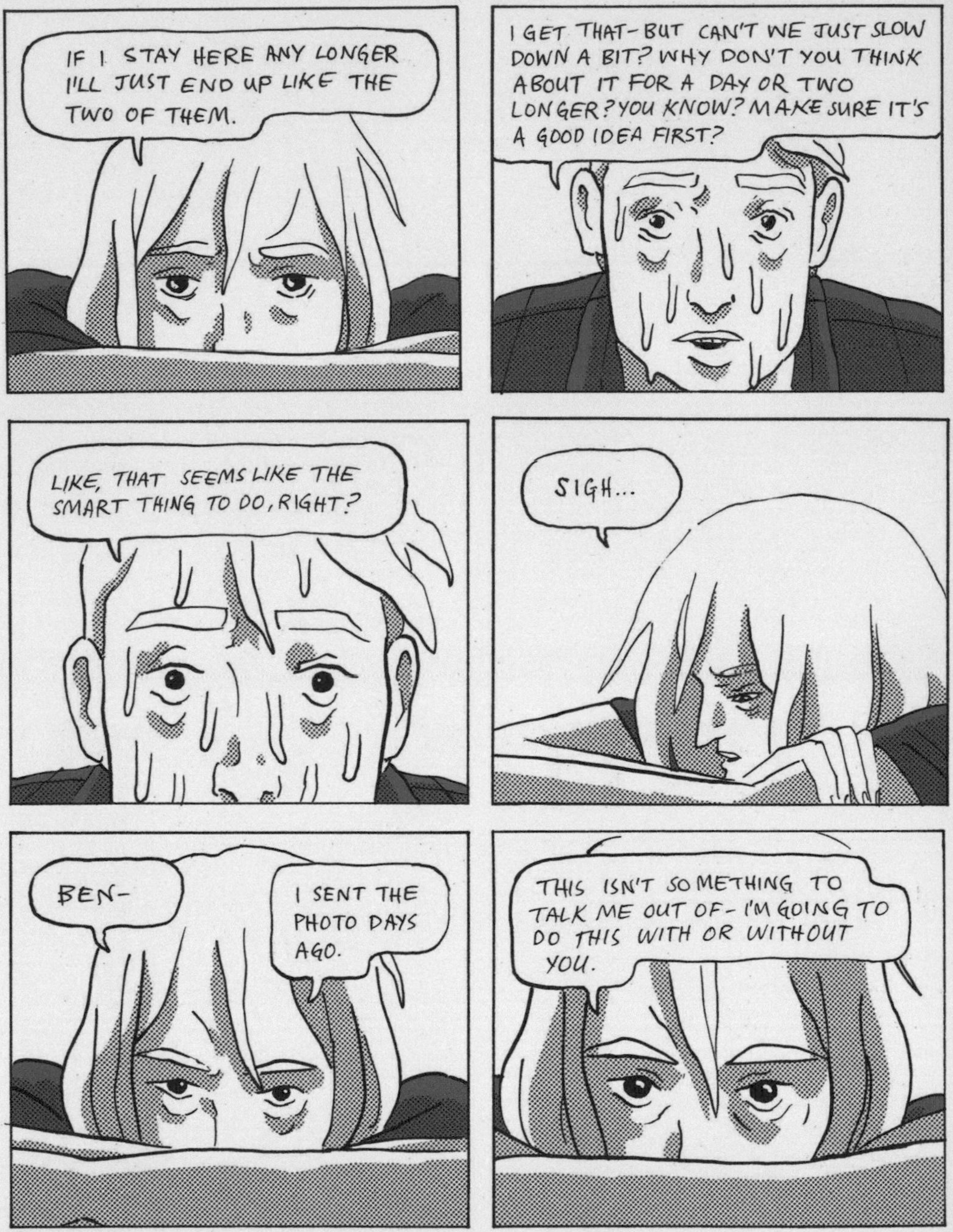
IF I STAY HERE ANY LONGER I'LL JUST END UP LIKE THE TWO OF THEM.
I GET THAT- BUT CAN'T WE JUST SLOW DOWN A BIT? WHY DON'T YOU THINK ABOUT IT FOR A DAY OR TWO LONGER? YOU KNOW? MAKE SURE IT'S A GOOD IDEA FIRST?
LIKE, THAT SEEMS LIKE THE SMART THING TO DO, RIGHT?
SIGH...
BEN-
I SENT THE PHOTO DAYS AGO.
THIS ISN'T SOMETHING TO TALK ME OUT OF- I'M GOING TO DO THIS WITH OR WITHOUT YOU.

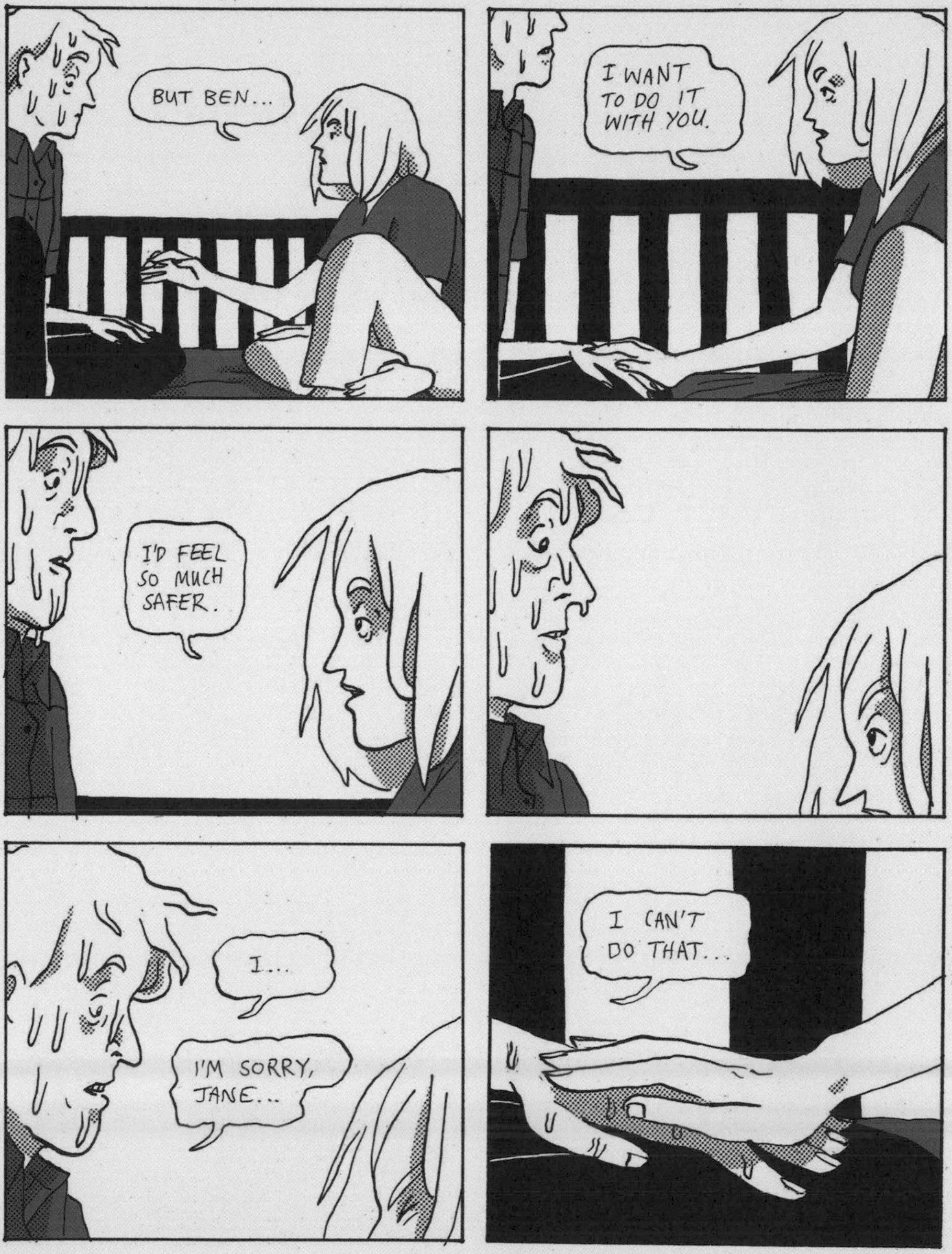
BUT BEN...
I WANT TO DO IT WITH YOU.
I'D FEEL SO MUCH SAFER.
I...
I'M SORRY, JANE...
I CAN'T DO THAT...

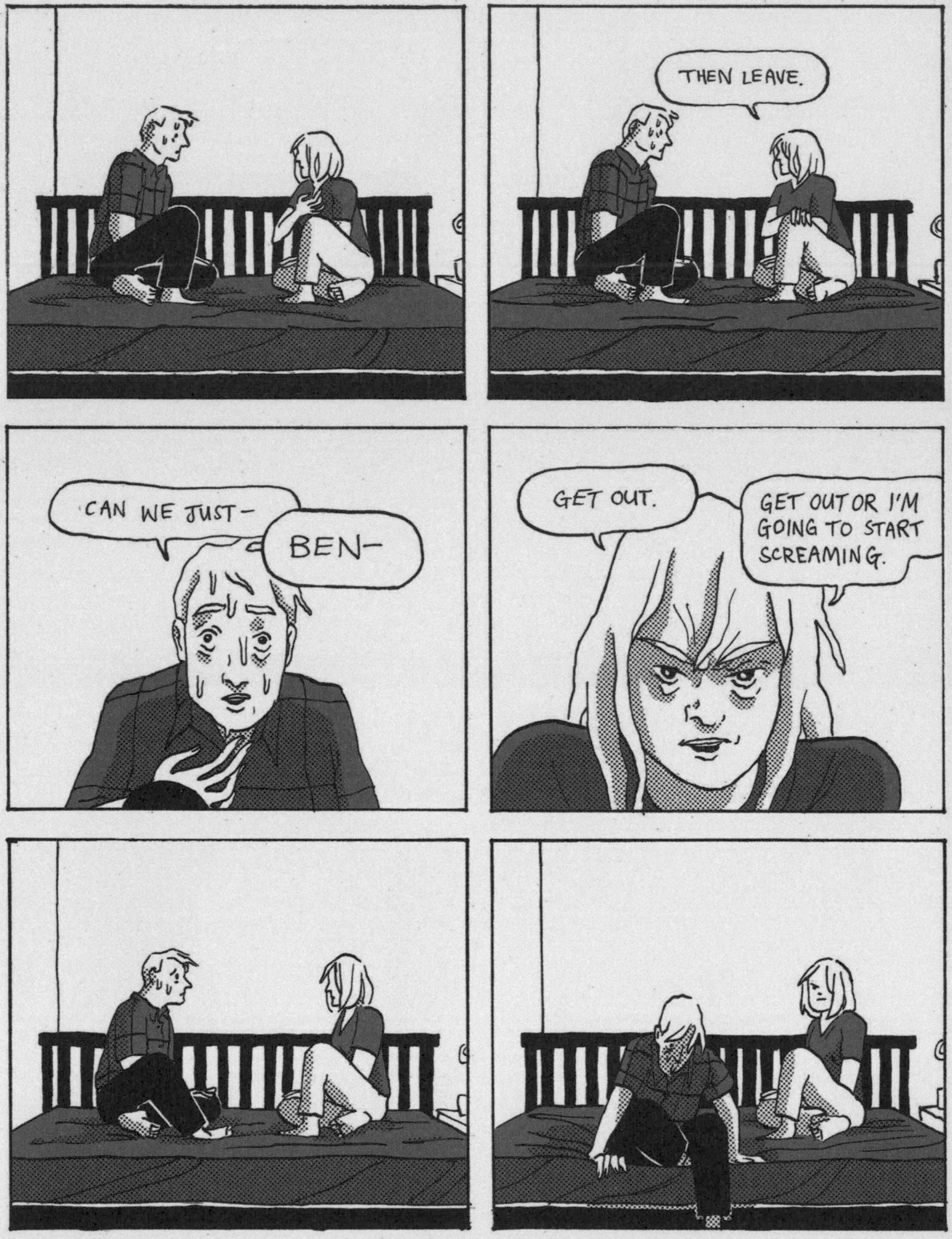
THEN LEAVE.
CAN WE JUST-
BEN-
GET OUT.
GET OUT OR I'M GOING TO START SCREAMING.

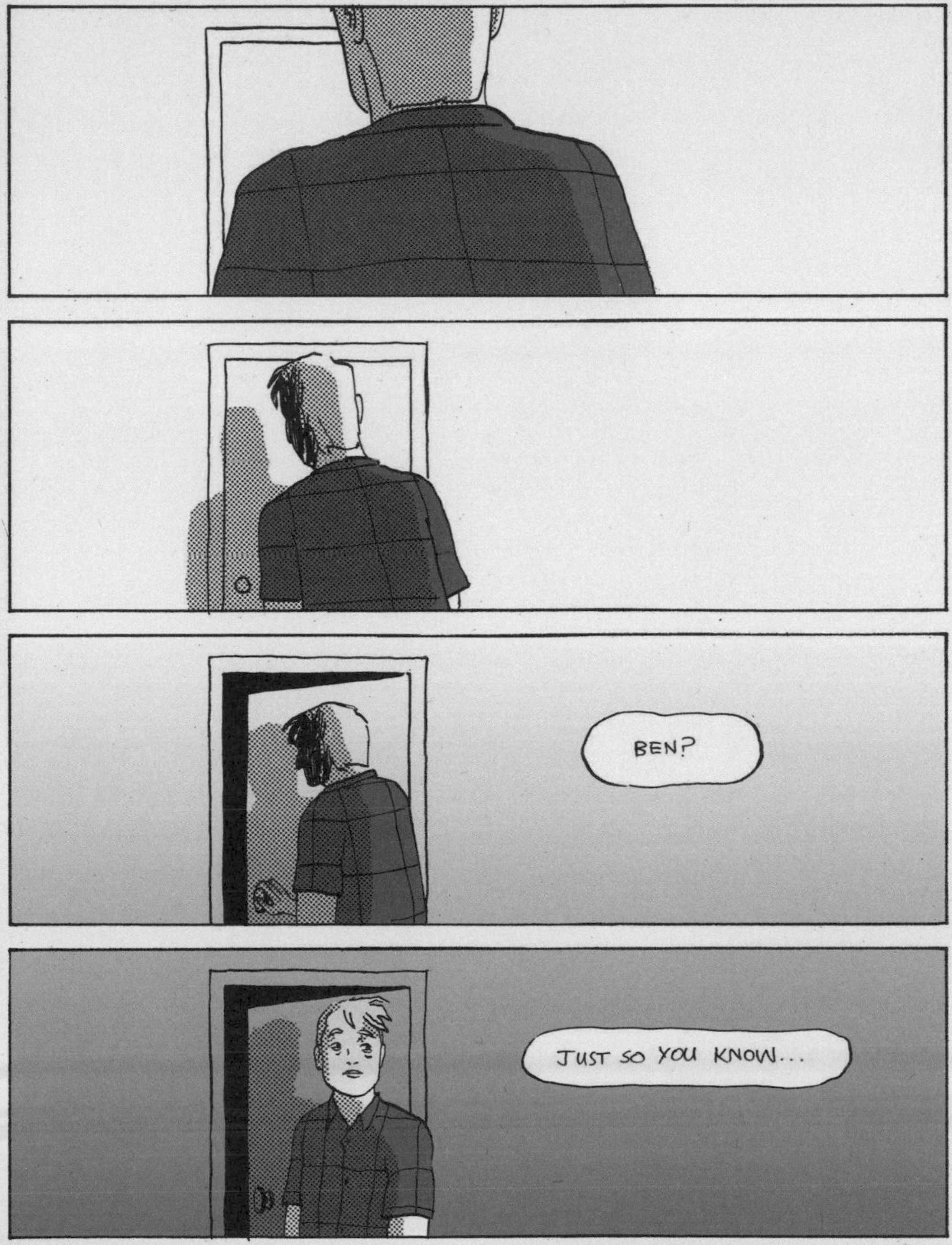
BEN?
JUST SO YOU KNOW...

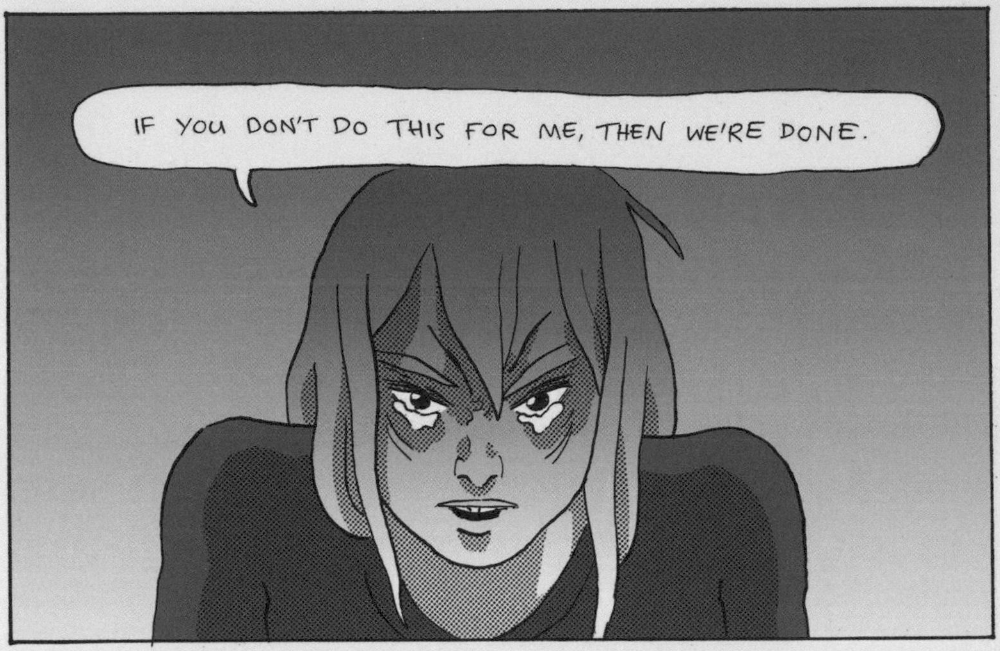
IF YOU DON'T DO THIS FOR ME, THEN WE'RE DONE.

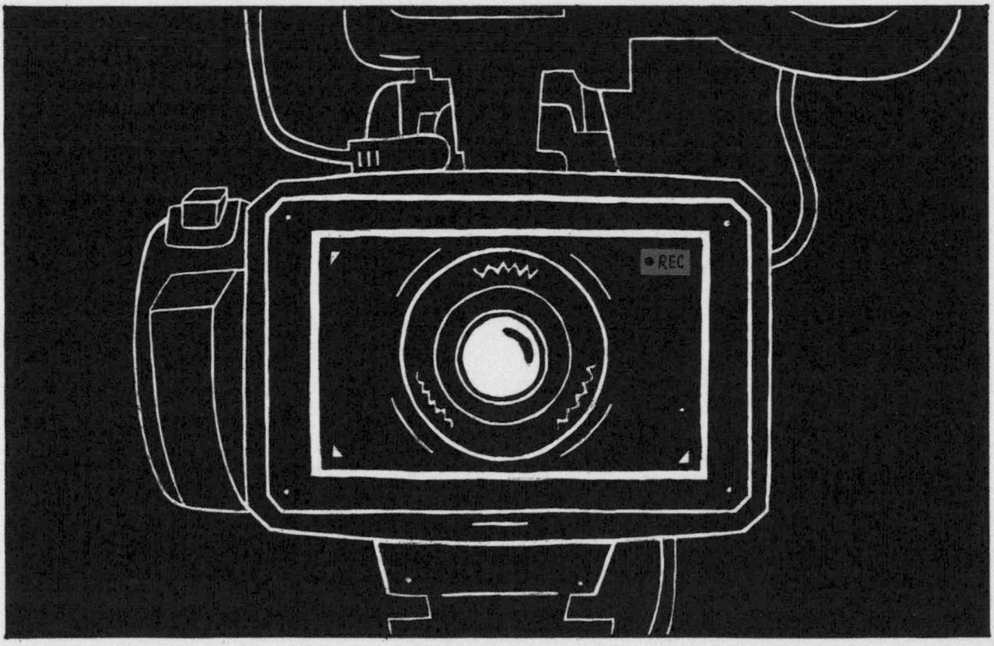
REC

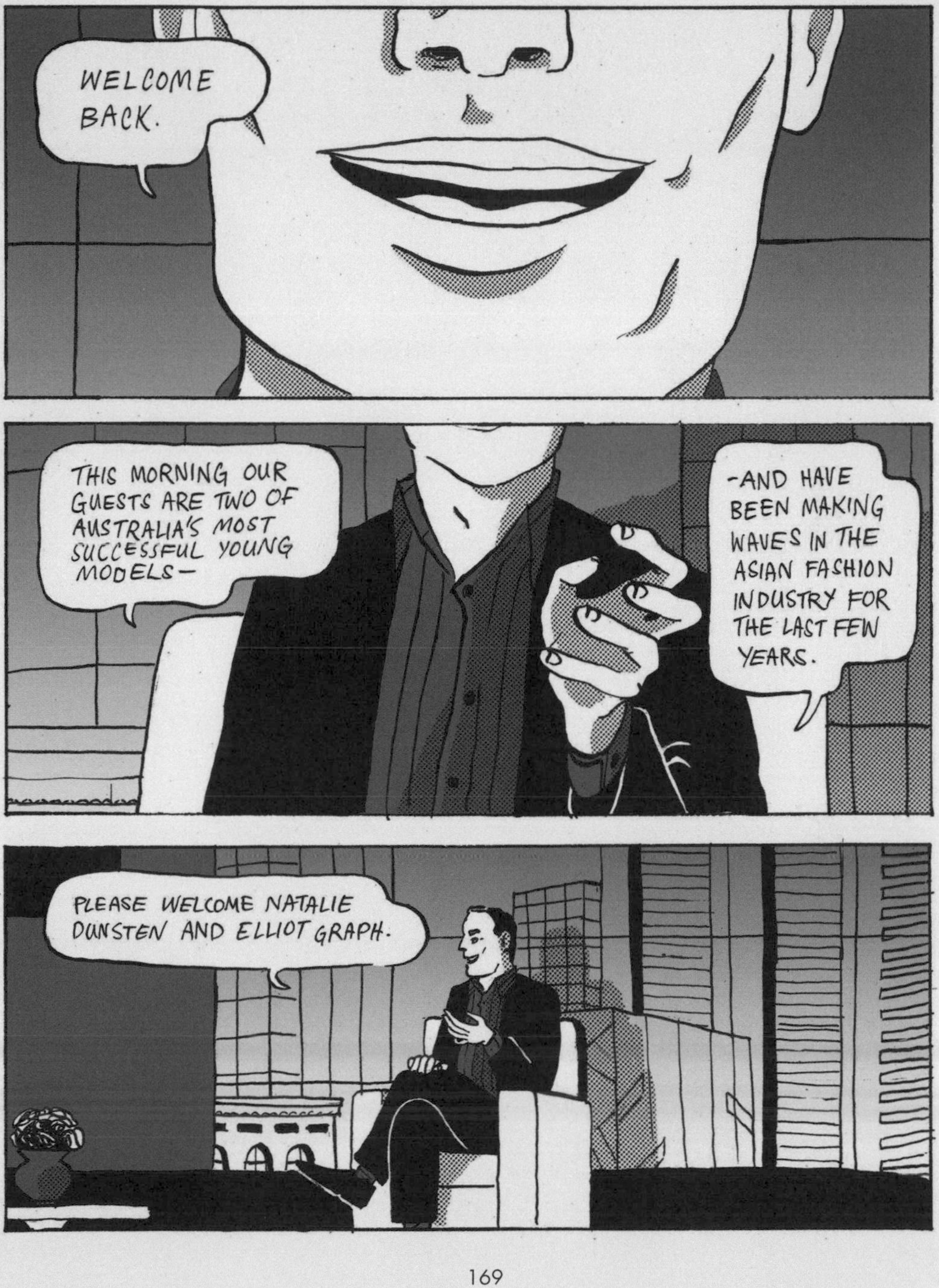
WELCOME BACK.
THIS MORNING OUR GUESTS ARE TWO OF AUSTRALIA'S MOST SUCCESSFUL YOUNG MODELS—
-AND HAVE BEEN MAKING WAVES IN THE ASIAN FASHION INDUSTRY FOR THE LAST FEW YEARS.
PLEASE WELCOME NATALIE DUNSTEN AND ELLIOT GRAPH.

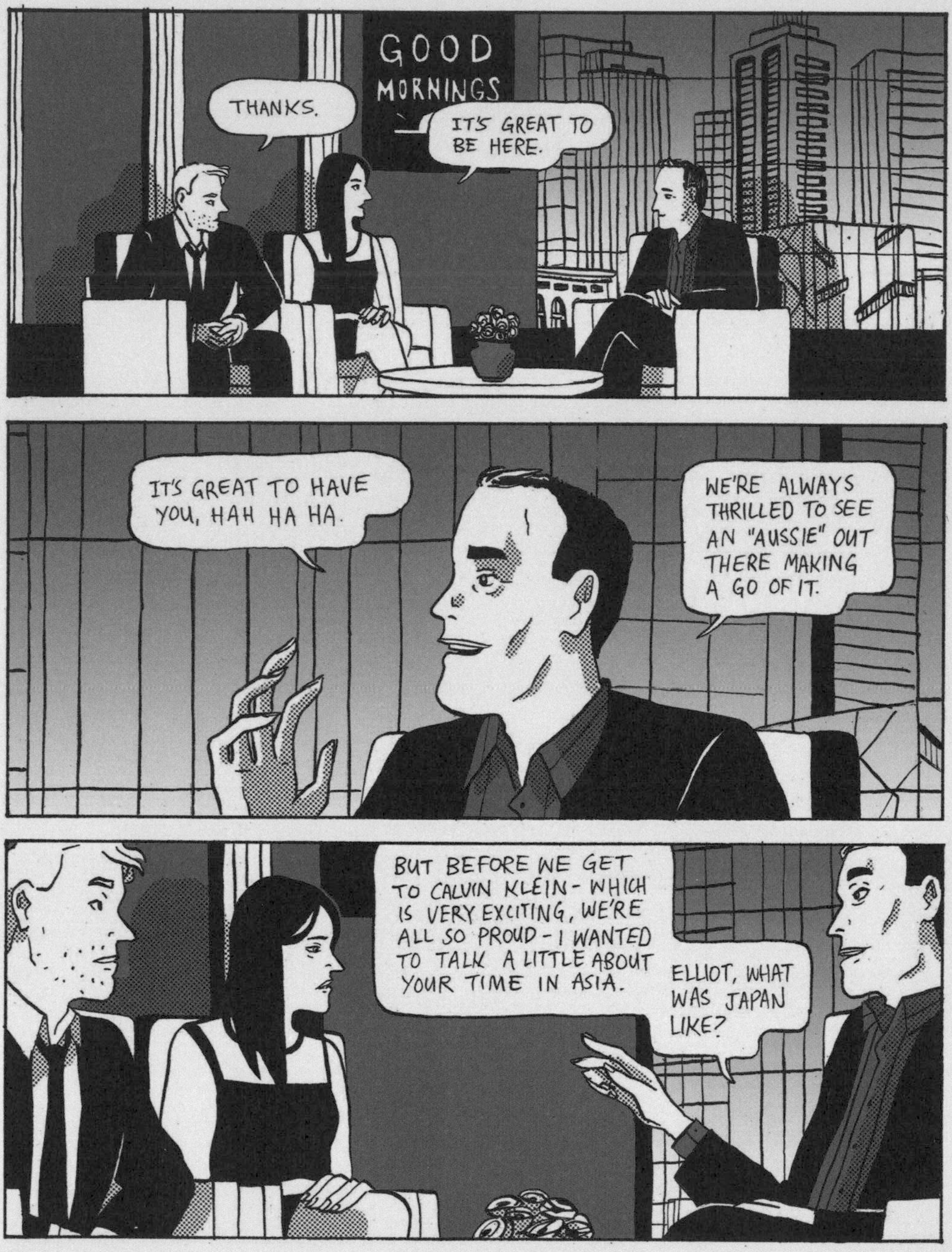
GOOD MORNINGS
THANKS.
IT'S GREAT TO BE HERE.
IT'S GREAT TO HAVE YOU, HAH HA HA.
WE'RE ALWAYS THRILLED TO SEE AN "AUSSIE" OUT THERE MAKING A GO OF IT.
BUT BEFORE WE GET TO CALVIN KLEIN - WHICH IS VERY EXCITING, WE'RE ALL SO PROUD - I WANTED TO TALK A LITTLE ABOUT YOUR TIME IN ASIA.
ELLIOT, WHAT WAS JAPAN LIKE?

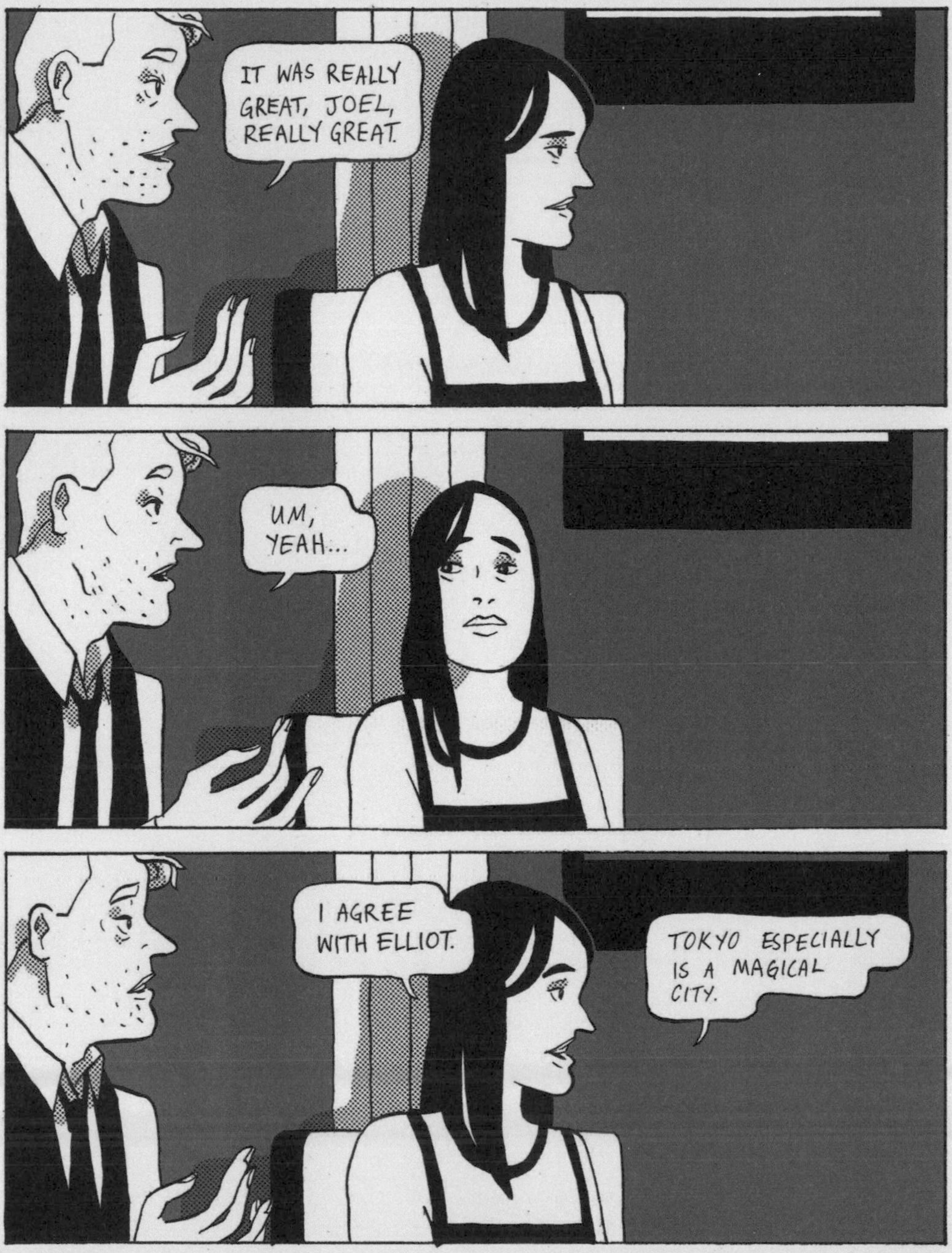
IT WAS REALLY GREAT, JOEL, REALLY GREAT.
UM, YEAH...
I AGREE WITH ELLIOT.
TOKYO ESPECIALLY IS A MAGICAL CITY.

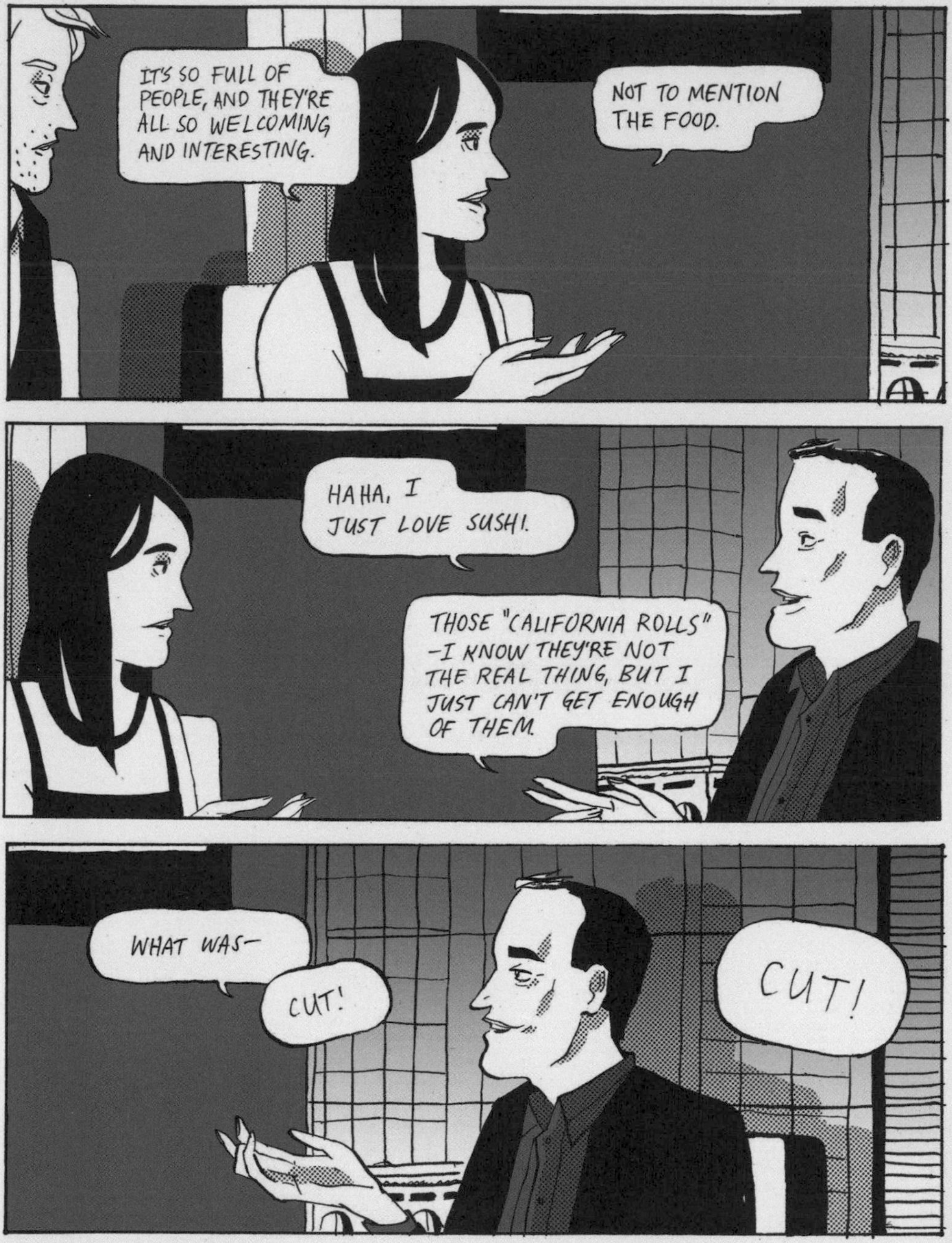
IT'S SO FULL OF PEOPLE, AND THEY'RE ALL SO WELCOMING AND INTERESTING.
NOT TO MENTION THE FOOD.
HAHA, I JUST LOVE SUSHI.
THOSE "CALIFORNIA ROLLS" —I KNOW THEY'RE NOT THE REAL THING, BUT I JUST CAN'T GET ENOUGH OF THEM.
WHAT WAS—
CUT!
CUT!

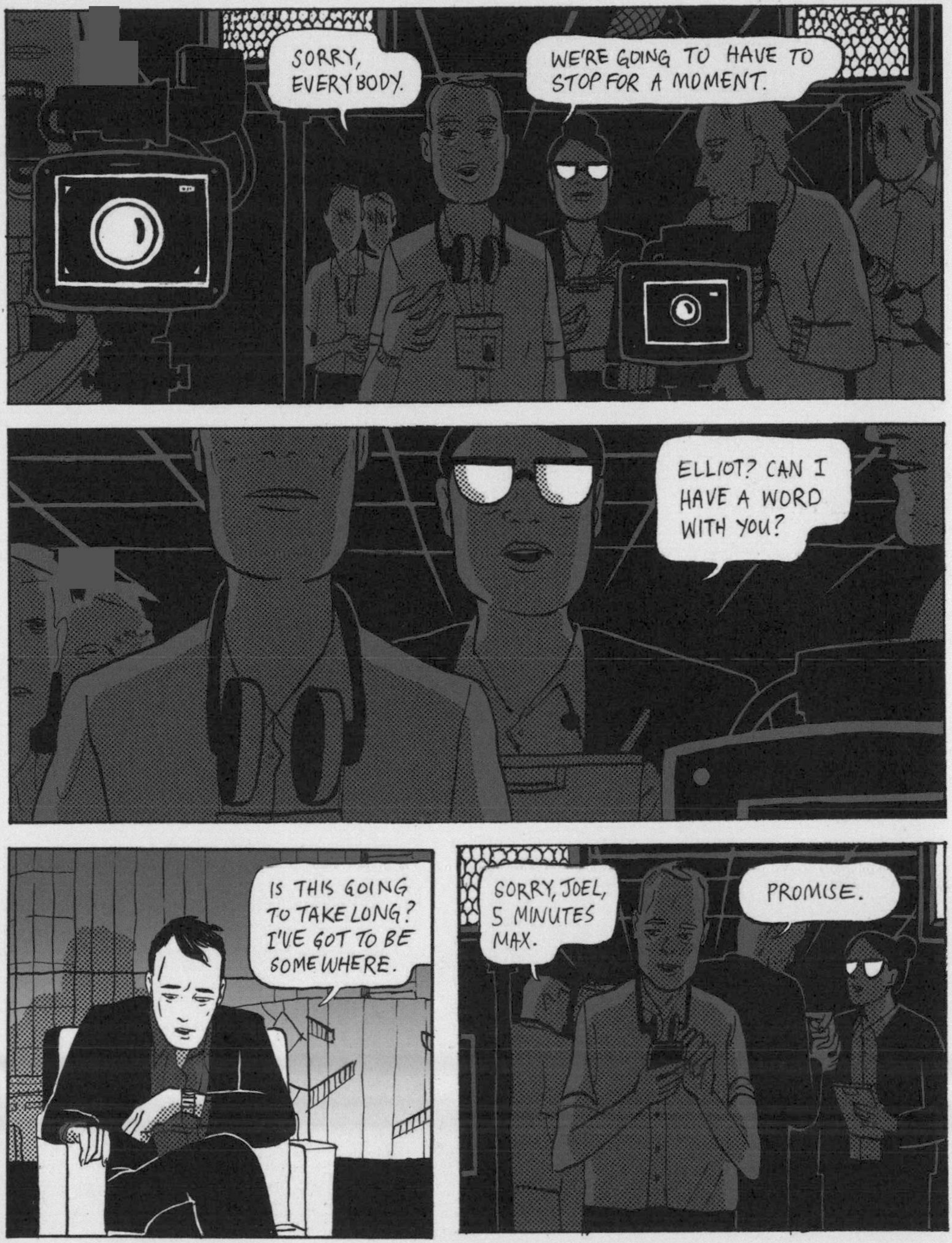
SORRY, EVERYBODY.
WE'RE GOING TO HAVE TO STOP FOR A MOMENT.
ELLIOT? CAN I HAVE A WORD WITH YOU?
IS THIS GOING TO TAKE LONG? I'VE GOT TO BE SOMEWHERE.
SORRY, JOEL, 5 MINUTES MAX.
PROMISE.

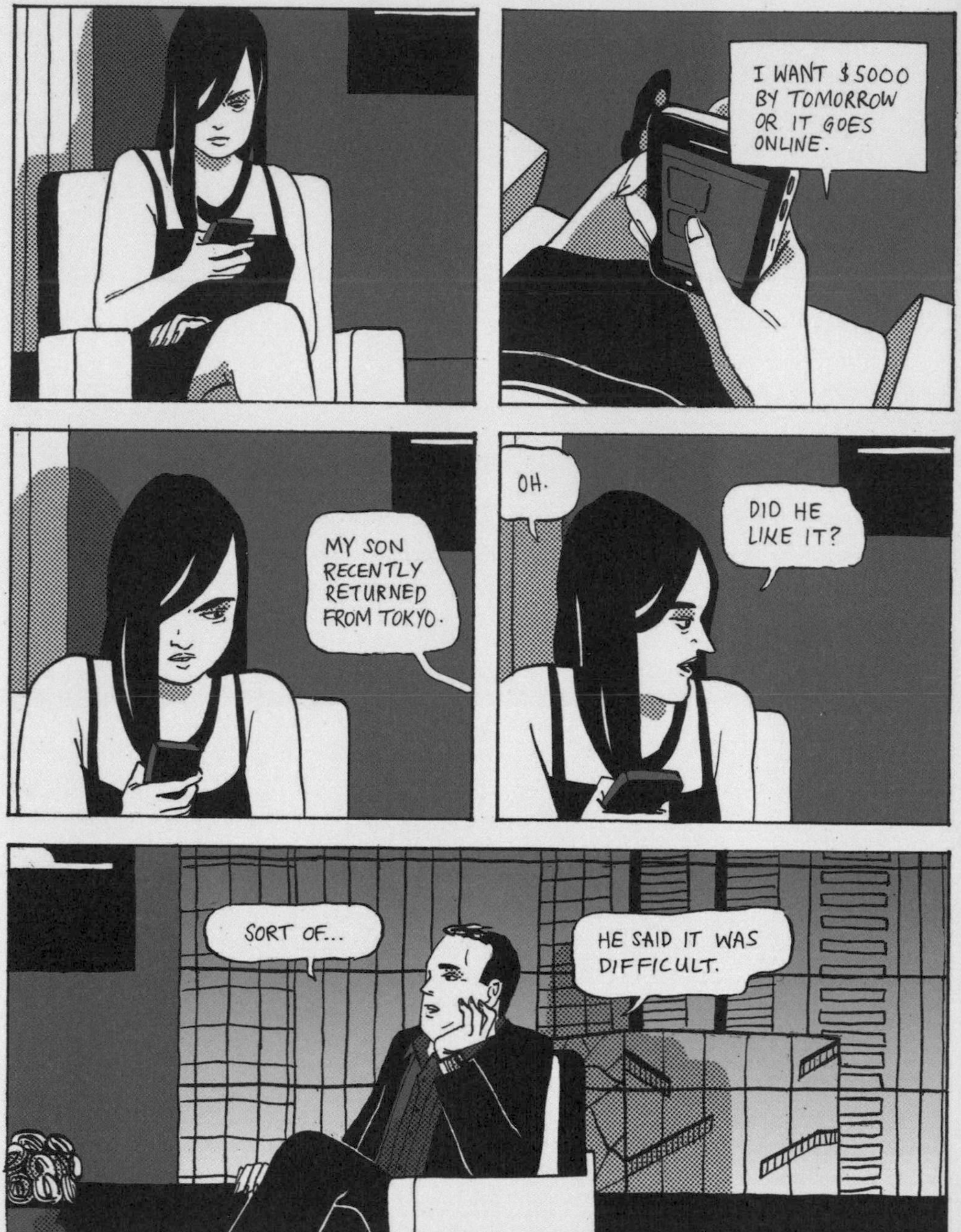
I WANT $5000 BY TOMORROW OR IT GOES ONLINE.
MY SON RECENTLY RETURNED FROM TOKYO.
OH.
DID HE LIKE IT?
SORT OF...
HE SAID IT WAS DIFFICULT.

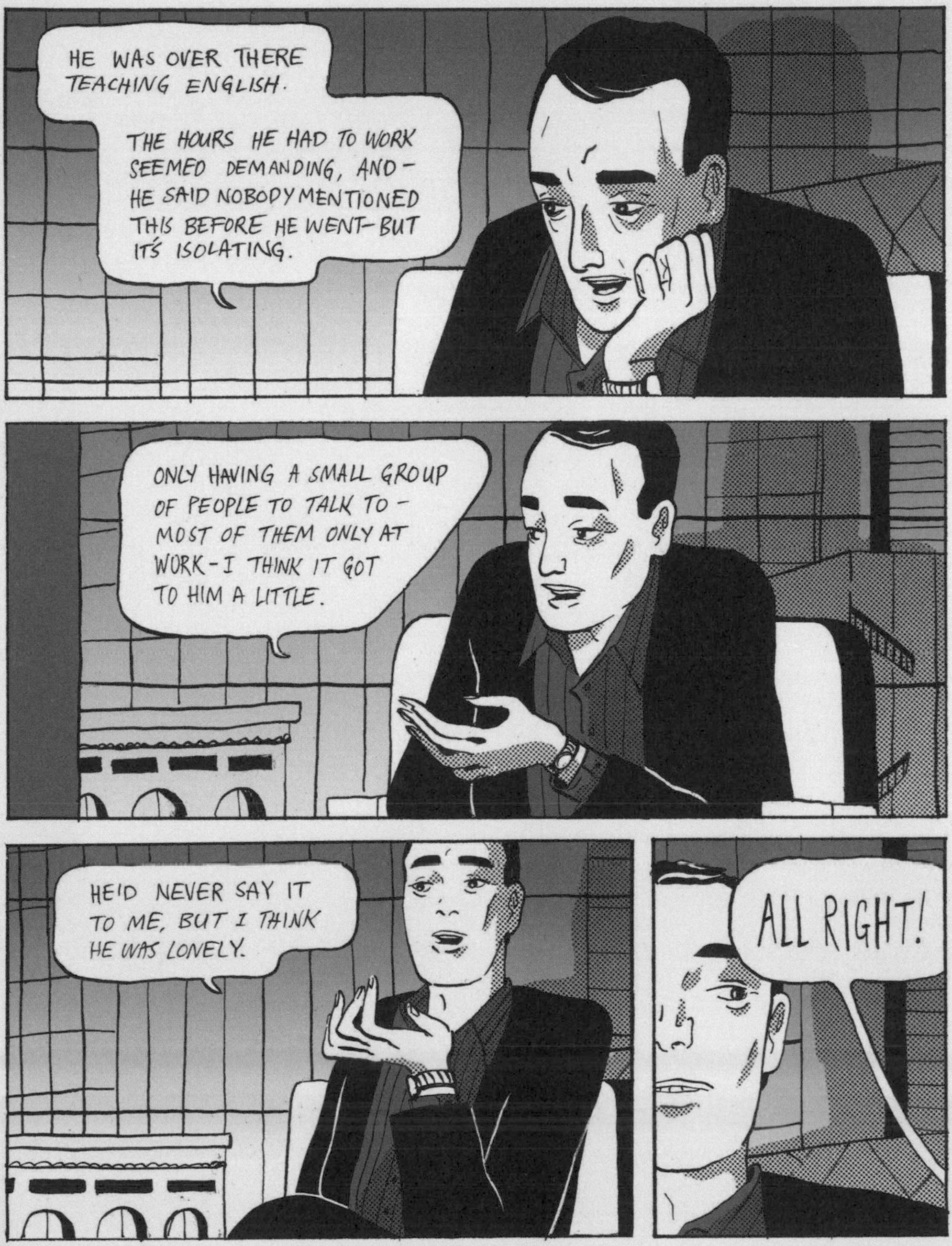
HE WAS OVER THERE TEACHING ENGLISH.
THE HOURS HE HAD TO WORK SEEMED DEMANDING, AND- HE SAID NOBODY MENTIONED THIS BEFORE HE WENT- BUT IT'S ISOLATING.
ONLY HAVING A SMALL GROUP OF PEOPLE TO TALK TO - MOST OF THEM ONLY AT WORK - I THINK IT GOT TO HIM A LITTLE.
HE'D NEVER SAY IT TO ME, BUT I THINK HE WAS LONELY.
ALL RIGHT!

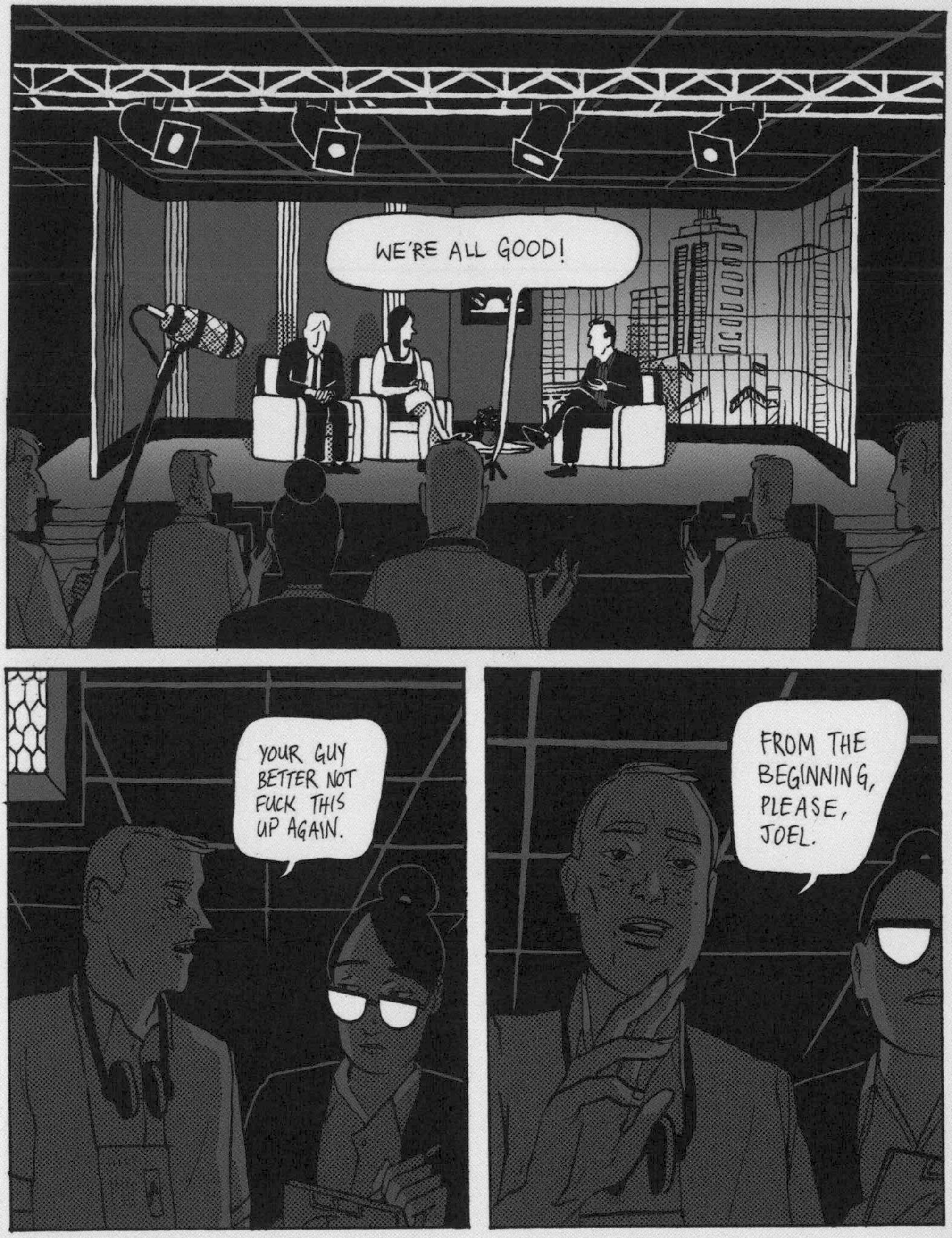
WE'RE ALL GOOD!
YOUR GUY BETTER NOT FUCK THIS UP AGAIN.
FROM THE BEGINNING, PLEASE, JOEL.

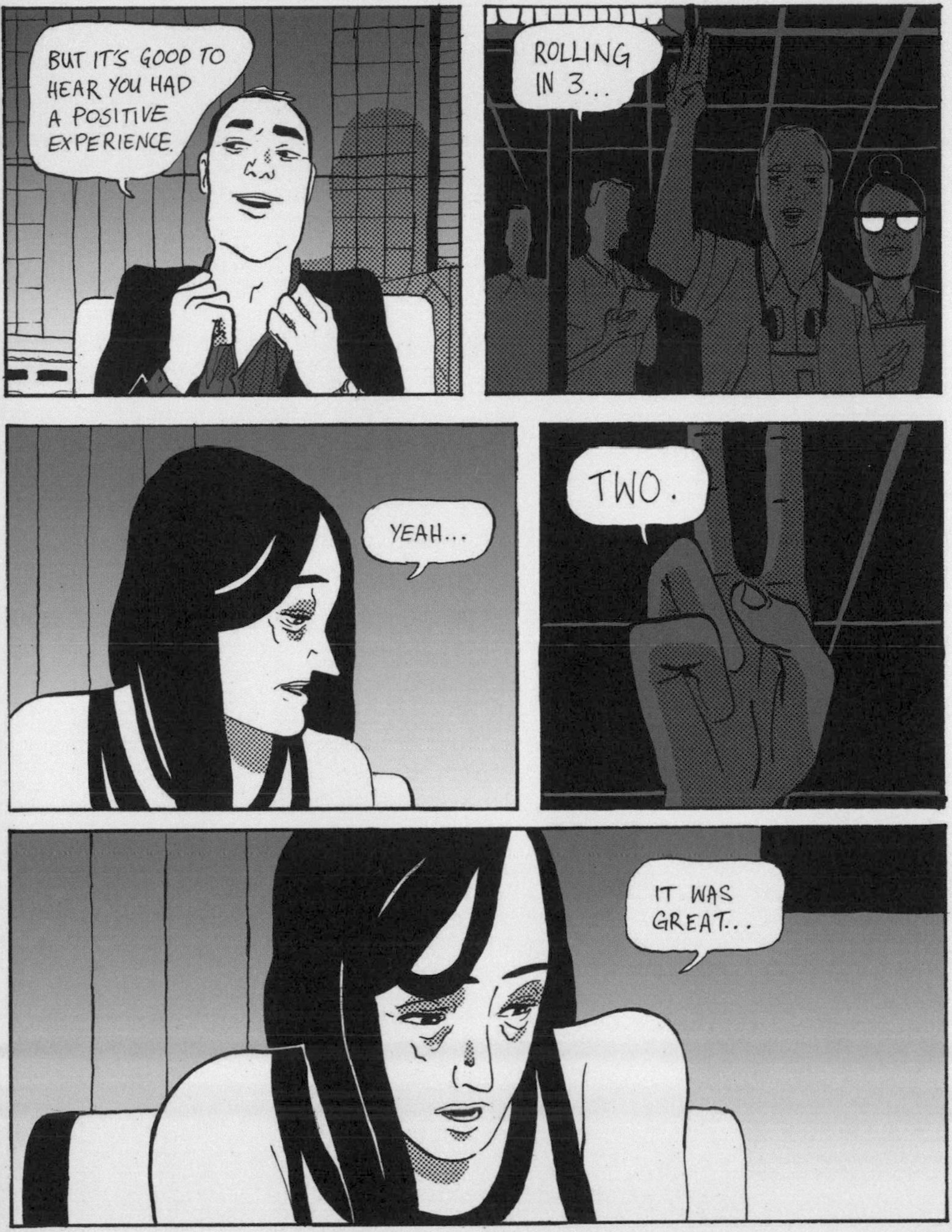
BUT IT'S GOOD TO HEAR YOU HAD A POSITIVE EXPERIENCE.
ROLLING IN 3...
YEAH...
TWO.
IT WAS GREAT...

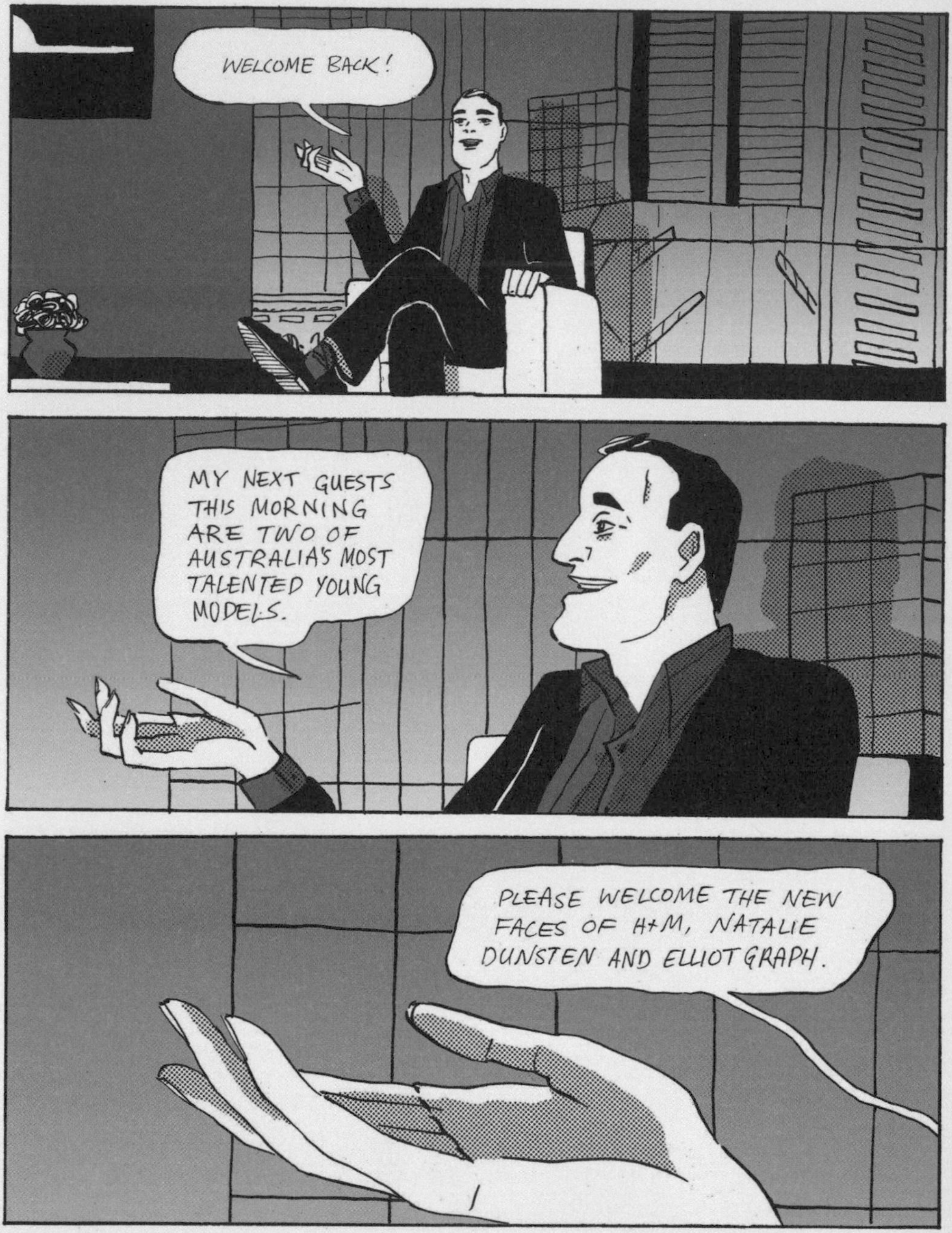
WELCOME BACK!
MY NEXT GUESTS THIS MORNING ARE TWO OF AUSTRALIA'S MOST TALENTED YOUNG MODELS.
PLEASE WELCOME THE NEW FACES OF H+M, NATALIE DUNSTEN AND ELLIOT GRAPH.

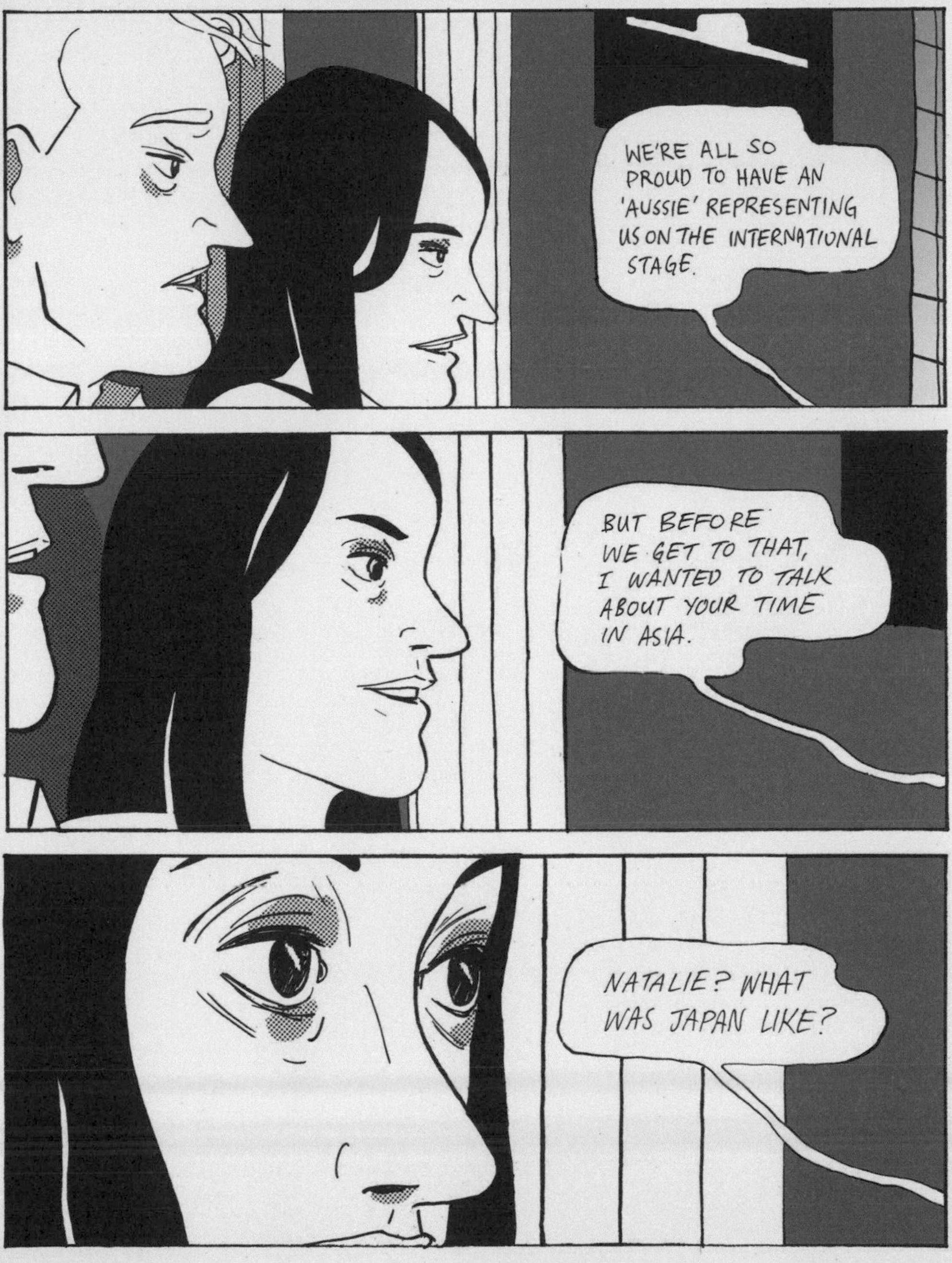
WE'RE ALL SO PROUD TO HAVE AN 'AUSSIE' REPRESENTING US ON THE INTERNATIONAL STAGE.
BUT BEFORE WE GET TO THAT, I WANTED TO TALK ABOUT YOUR TIME IN ASIA.
NATALIE? WHAT WAS JAPAN LIKE?

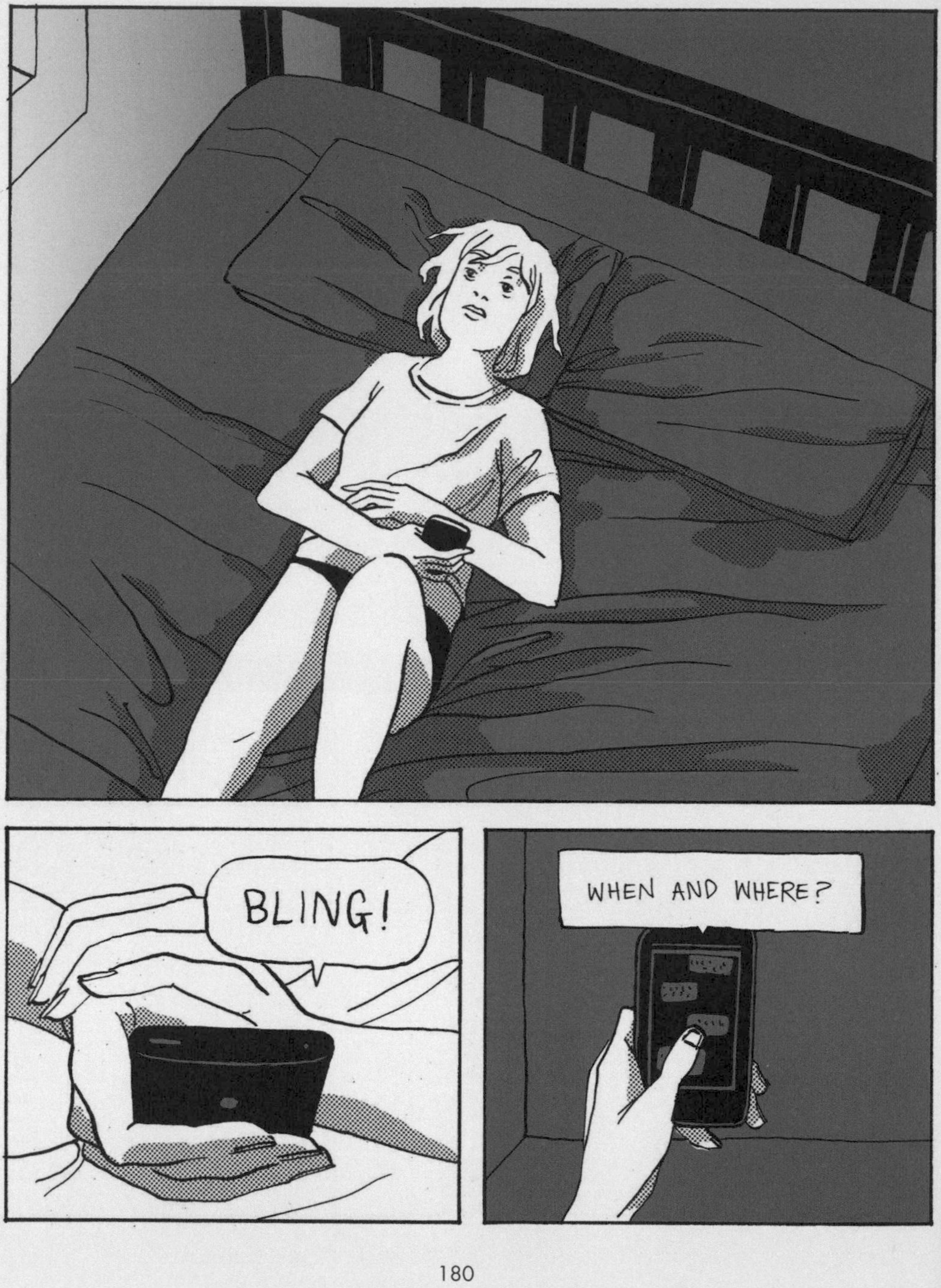
BLING!
WHEN AND WHERE?

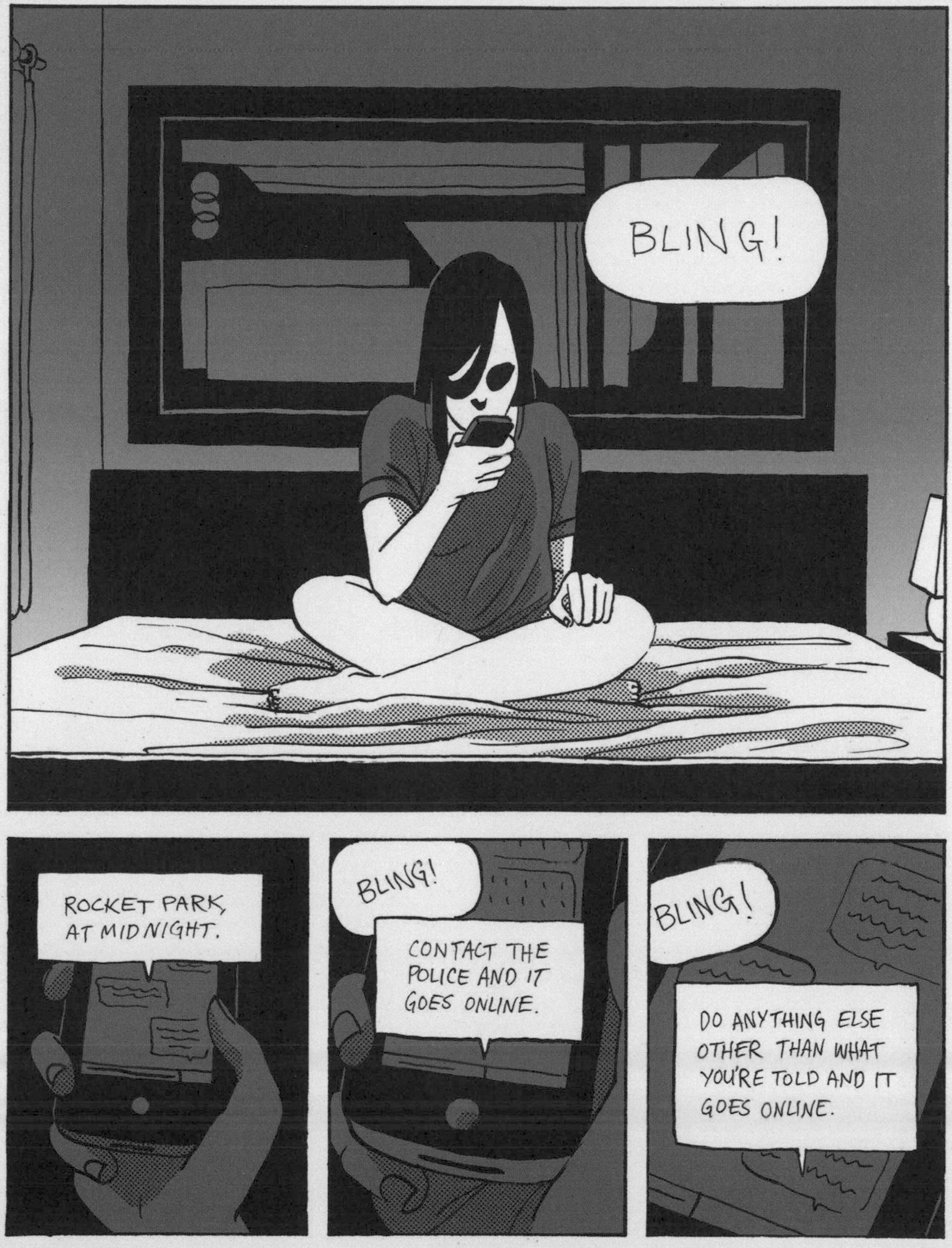
BLING!
ROCKET PARK, AT MIDNIGHT.
BLING!
CONTACT THE POLICE AND IT GOES ONLINE.
BLING!
DO ANYTHING ELSE OTHER THAN WHAT YOU'RE TOLD AND IT GOES ONLINE.

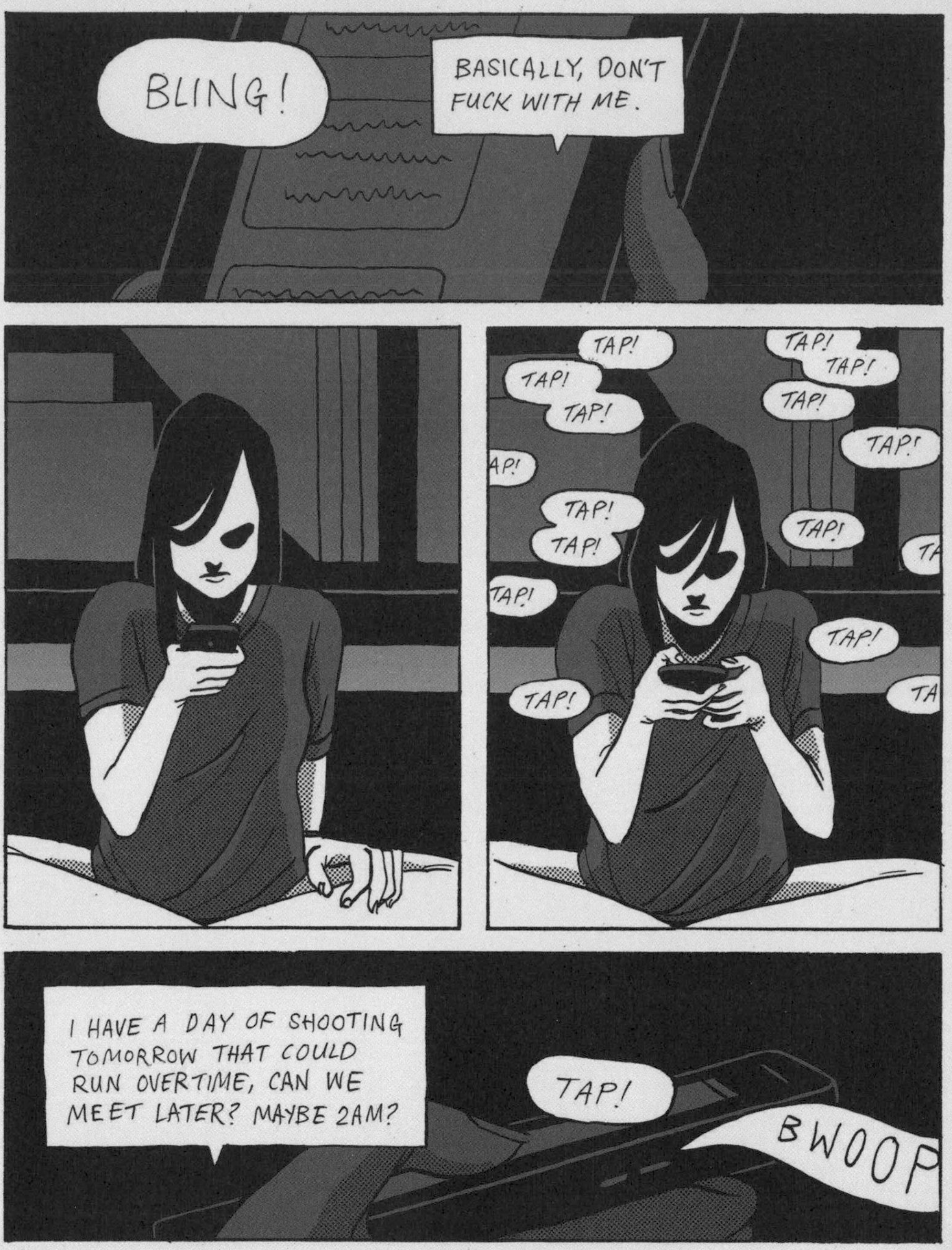
BLING!
BASICALLY, DON'T FUCK WITH ME.
TAP!
TAP!
TAP!
TAP!
TAP!
TAP!
TAP!
TAP!
TAP!
TAP!
TAP!
TAP!
I HAVE A DAY OF SHOOTING TOMORROW THAT COULD RUN OVERTIME, CAN WE MEET LATER? MAYBE 2AM?
TAP!
BWOOP

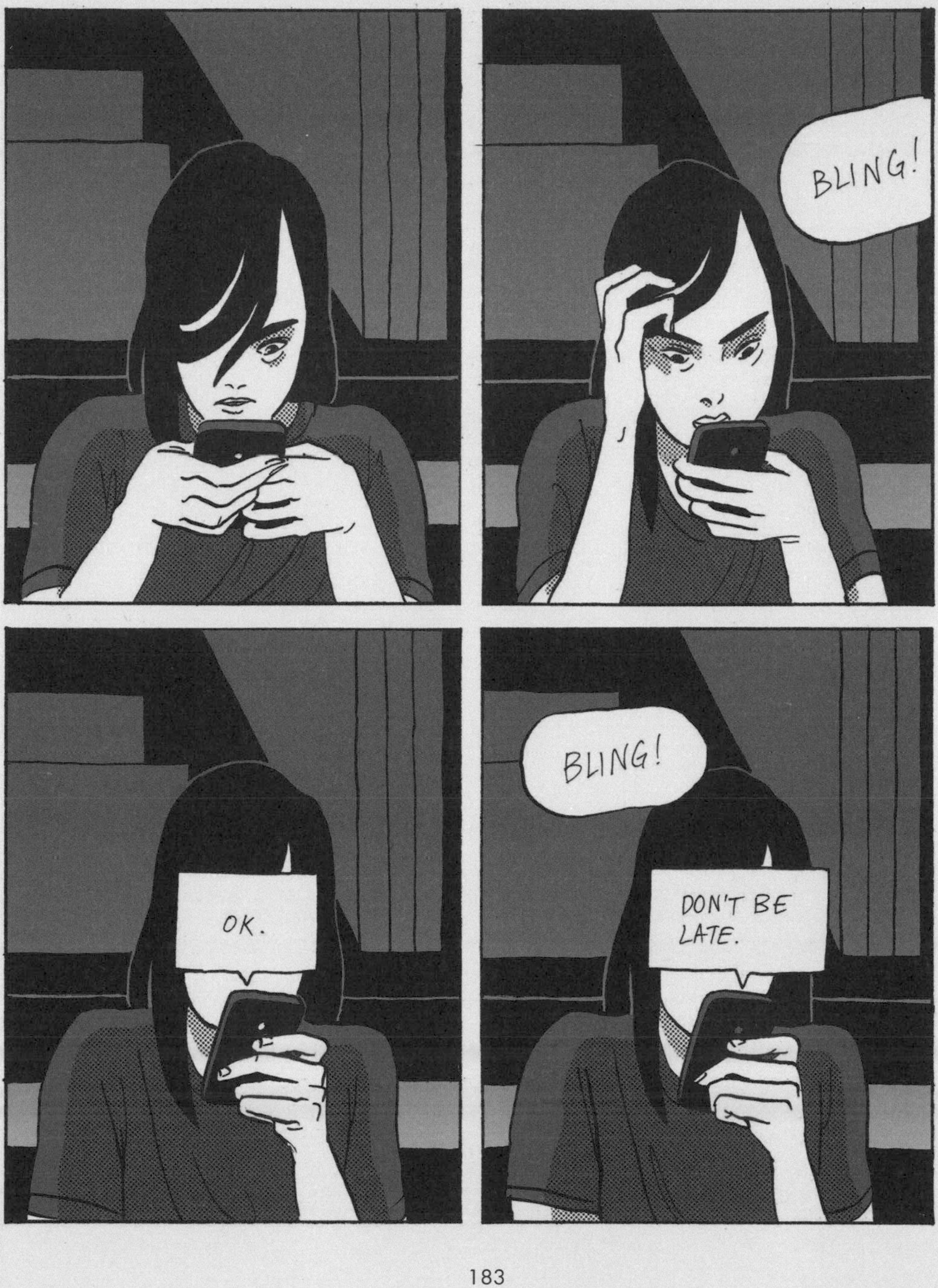
BLING!
OK.
BLING!
DON'T BE LATE.

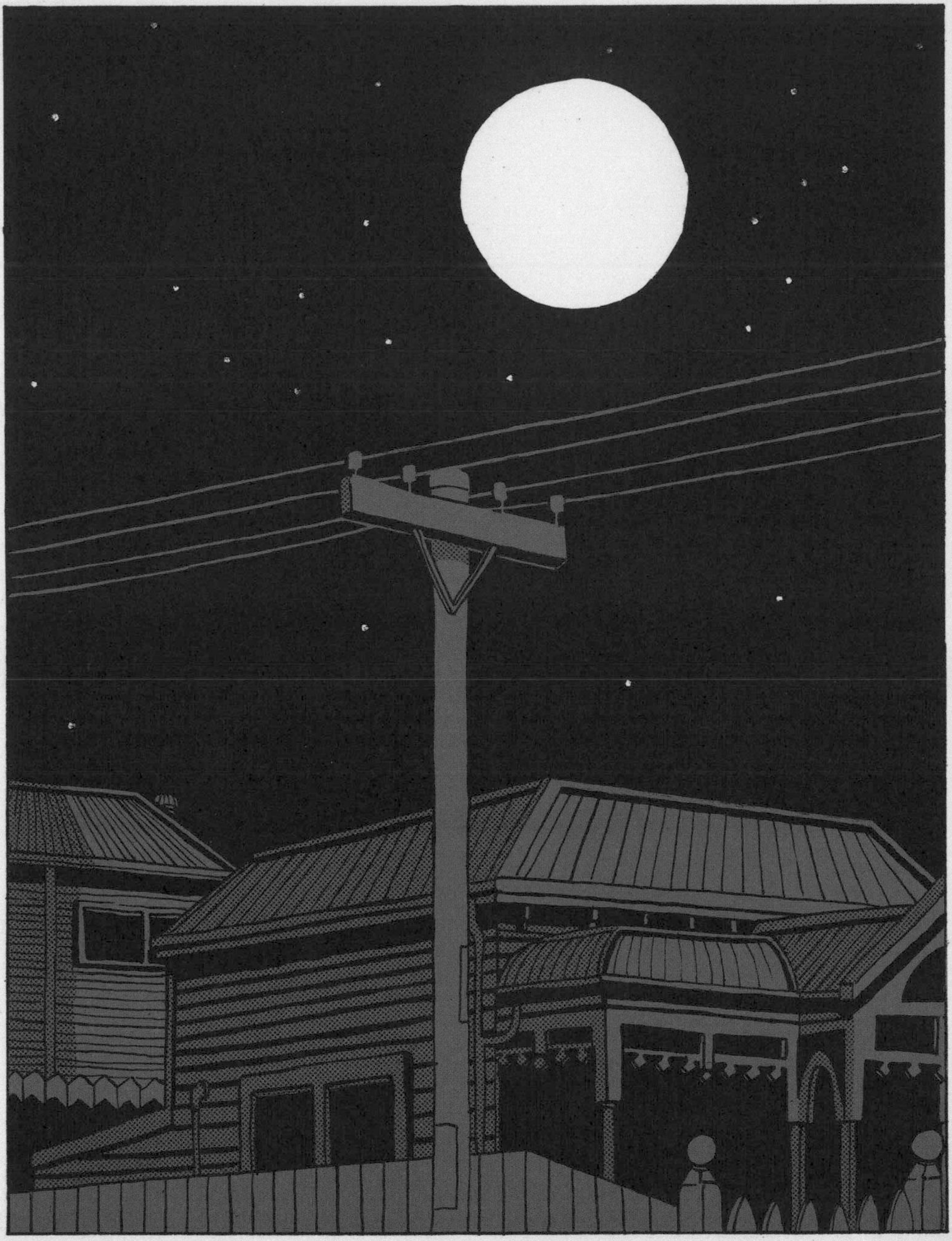

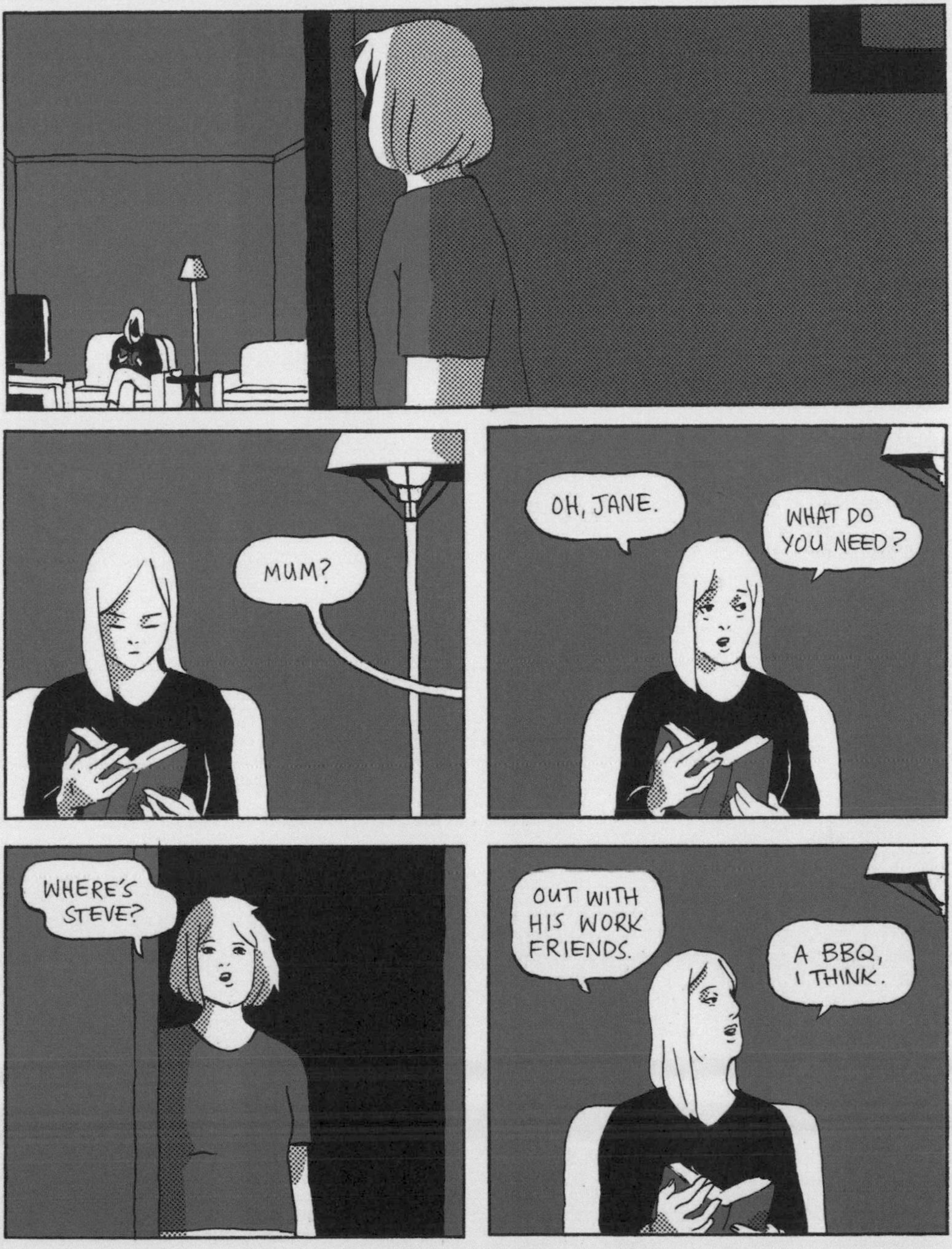
MUM?
OH, JANE.
WHAT DO YOU NEED?
WHERE'S STEVE?
OUT WITH HIS WORK FRIENDS.
A BBQ, I THINK.

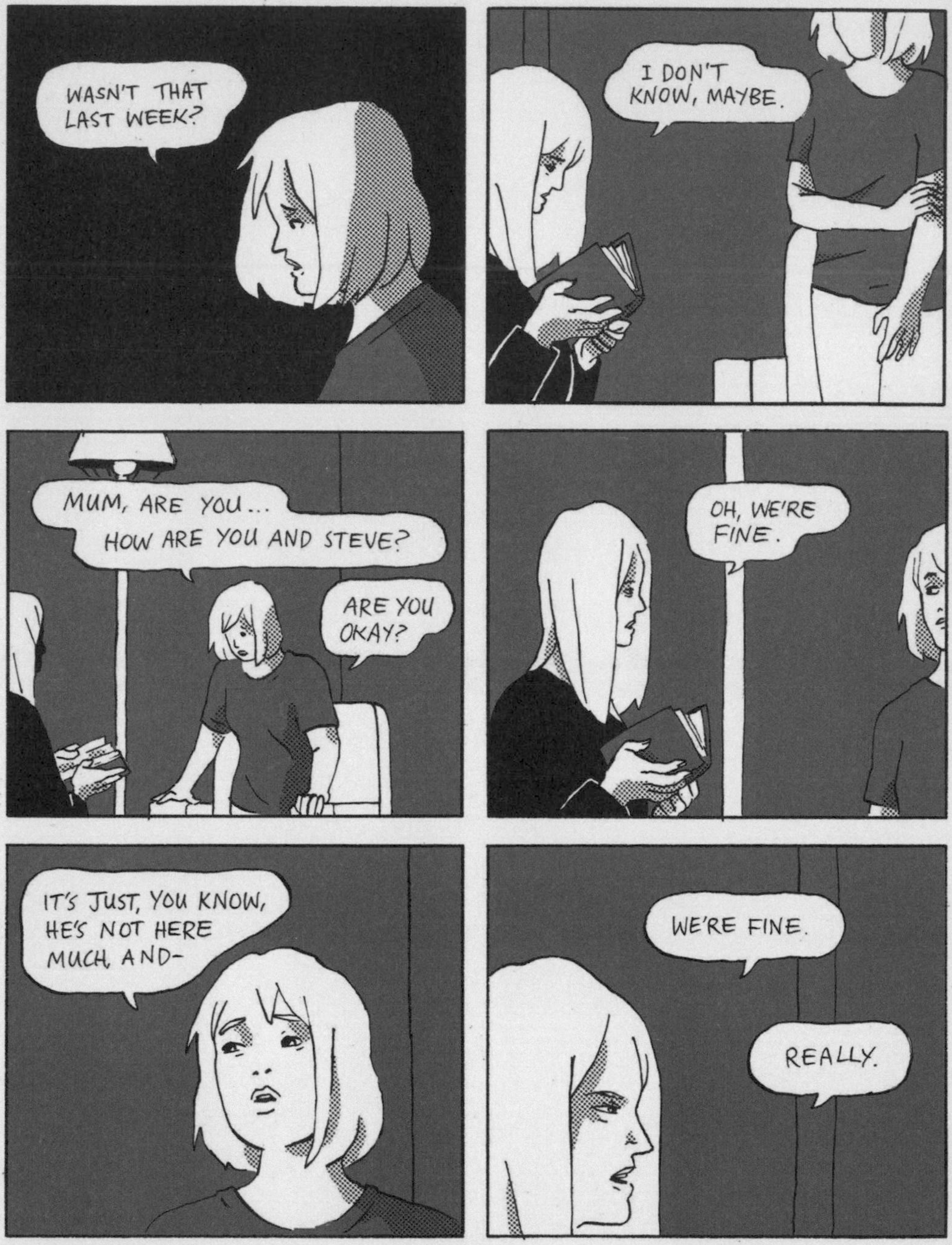
WASN'T THAT LAST WEEK?
I DON'T KNOW, MAYBE.
MUM, ARE YOU... HOW ARE YOU AND STEVE?
ARE YOU OKAY?
OH, WE'RE FINE.
IT'S JUST, YOU KNOW, HE'S NOT HERE MUCH, AND-
WE'RE FINE.
REALLY.

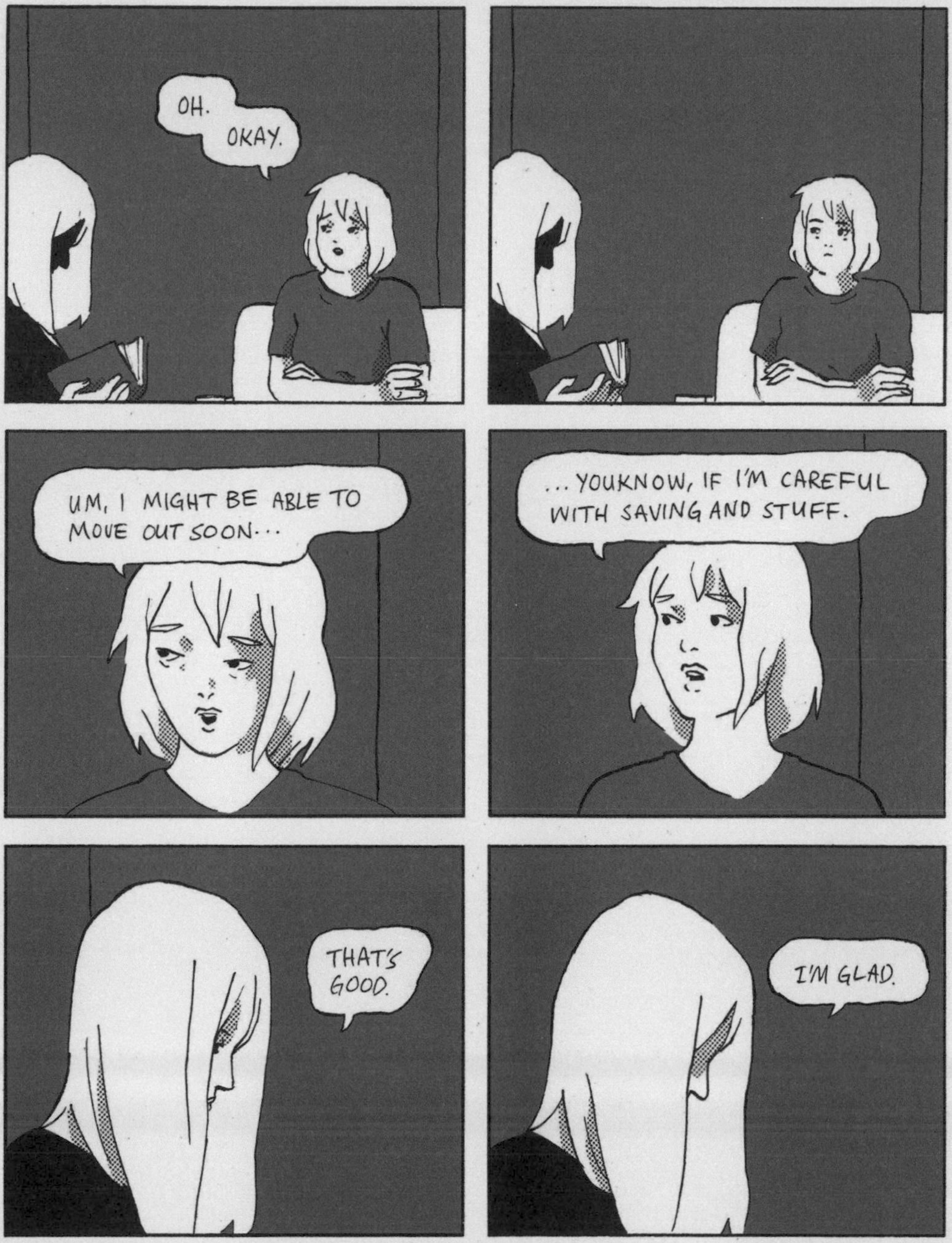
OH.
OKAY.
UM, I MIGHT BE ABLE TO MOVE OUT SOON...
... YOUKNOW, IF I'M CAREFUL WITH SAVING AND STUFF.
THAT'S GOOD.
I'M GLAD.

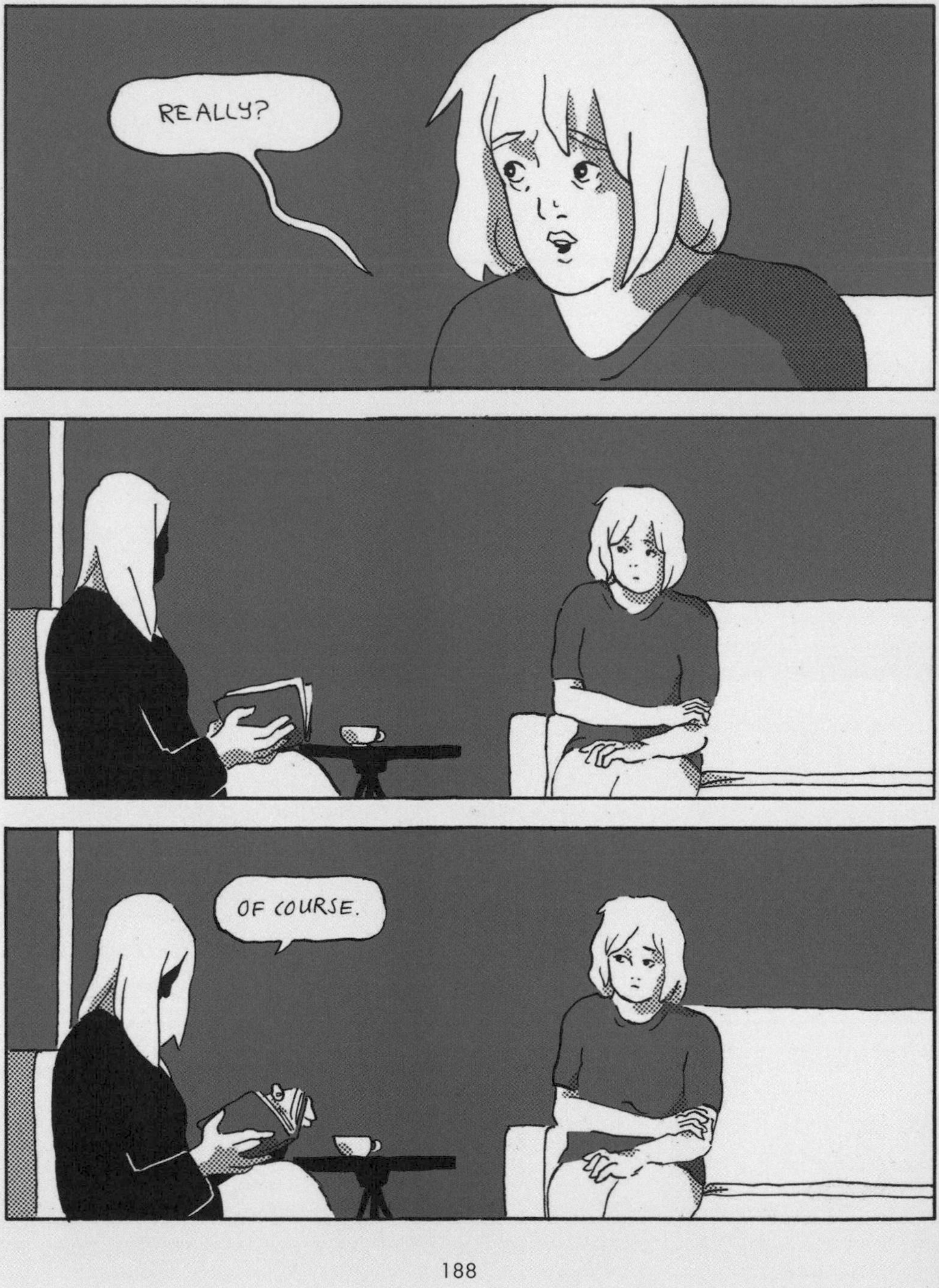
REALLY?
OF COURSE.

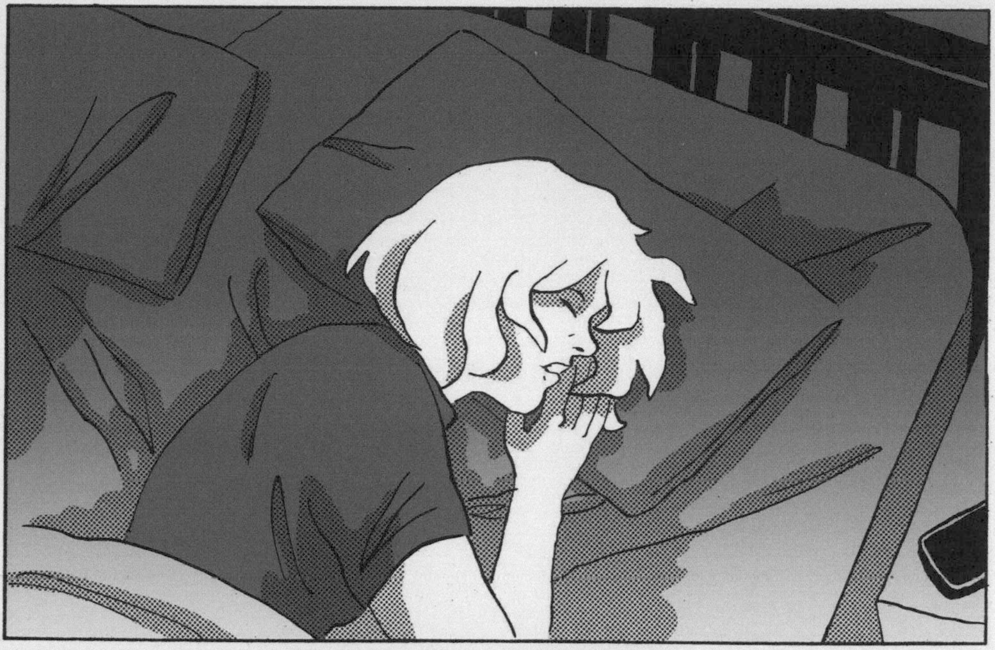

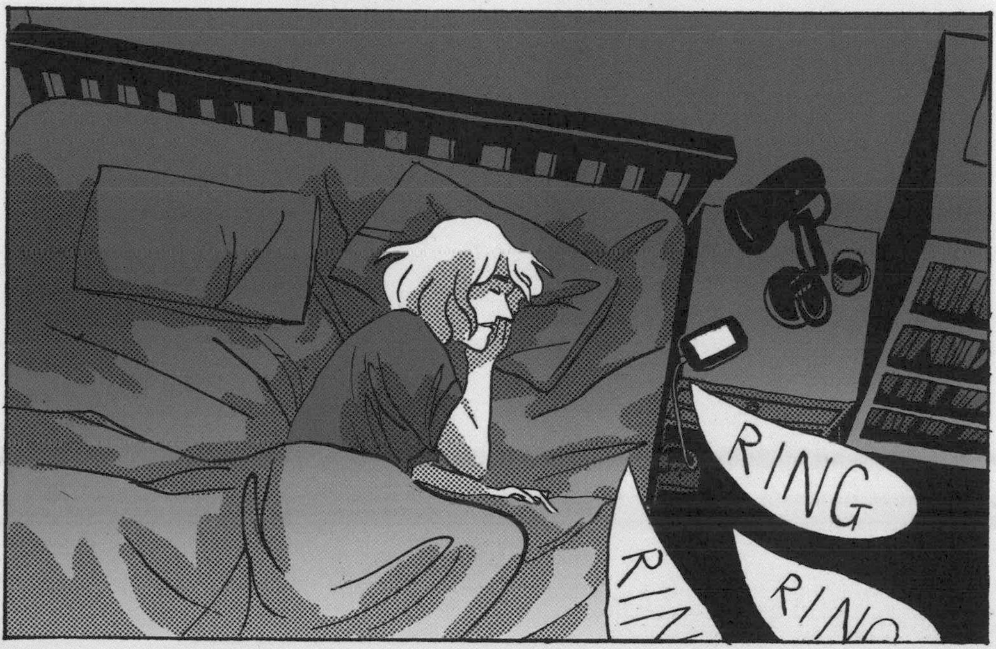
RING

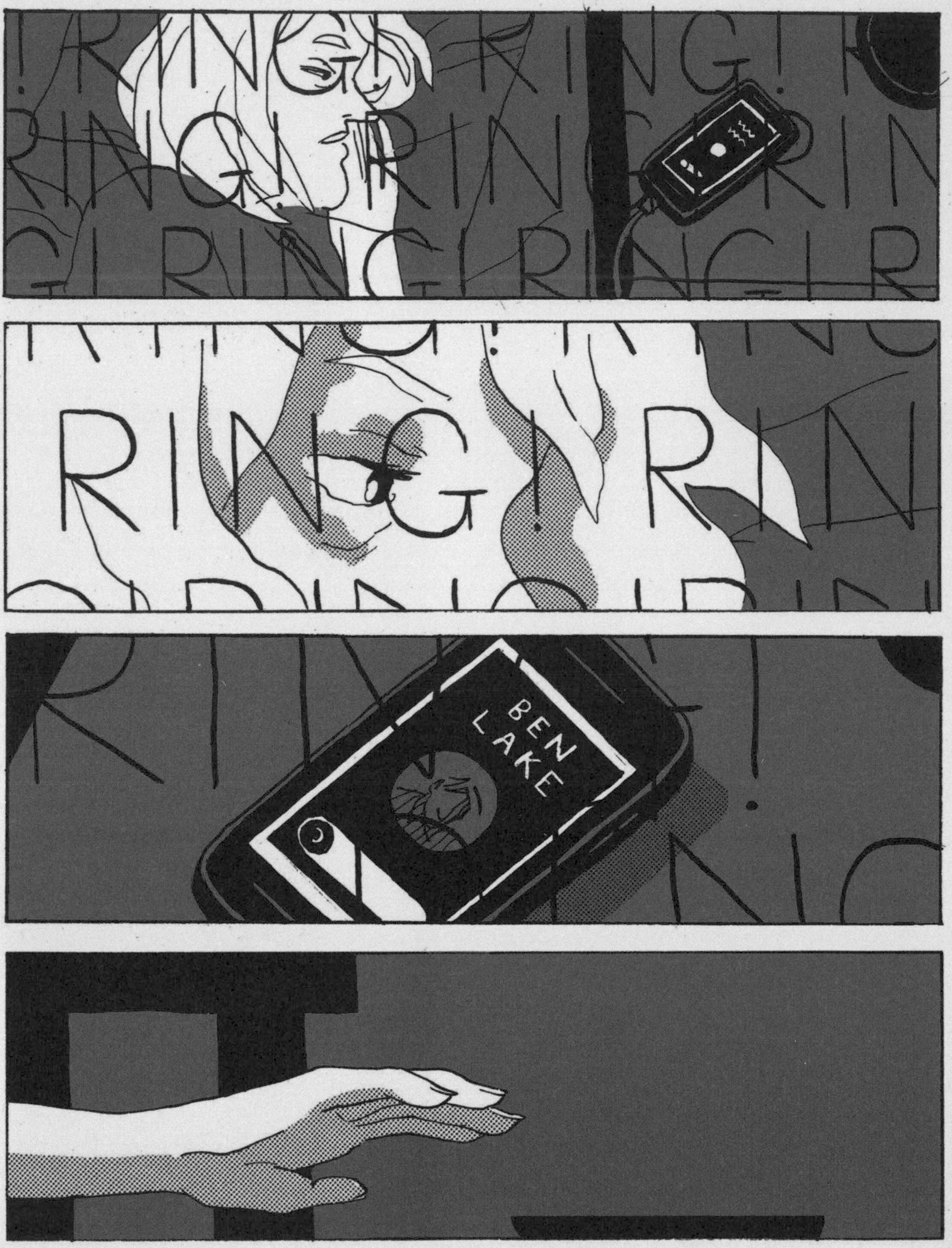
RING! RING!
RING!
BEN LAKE

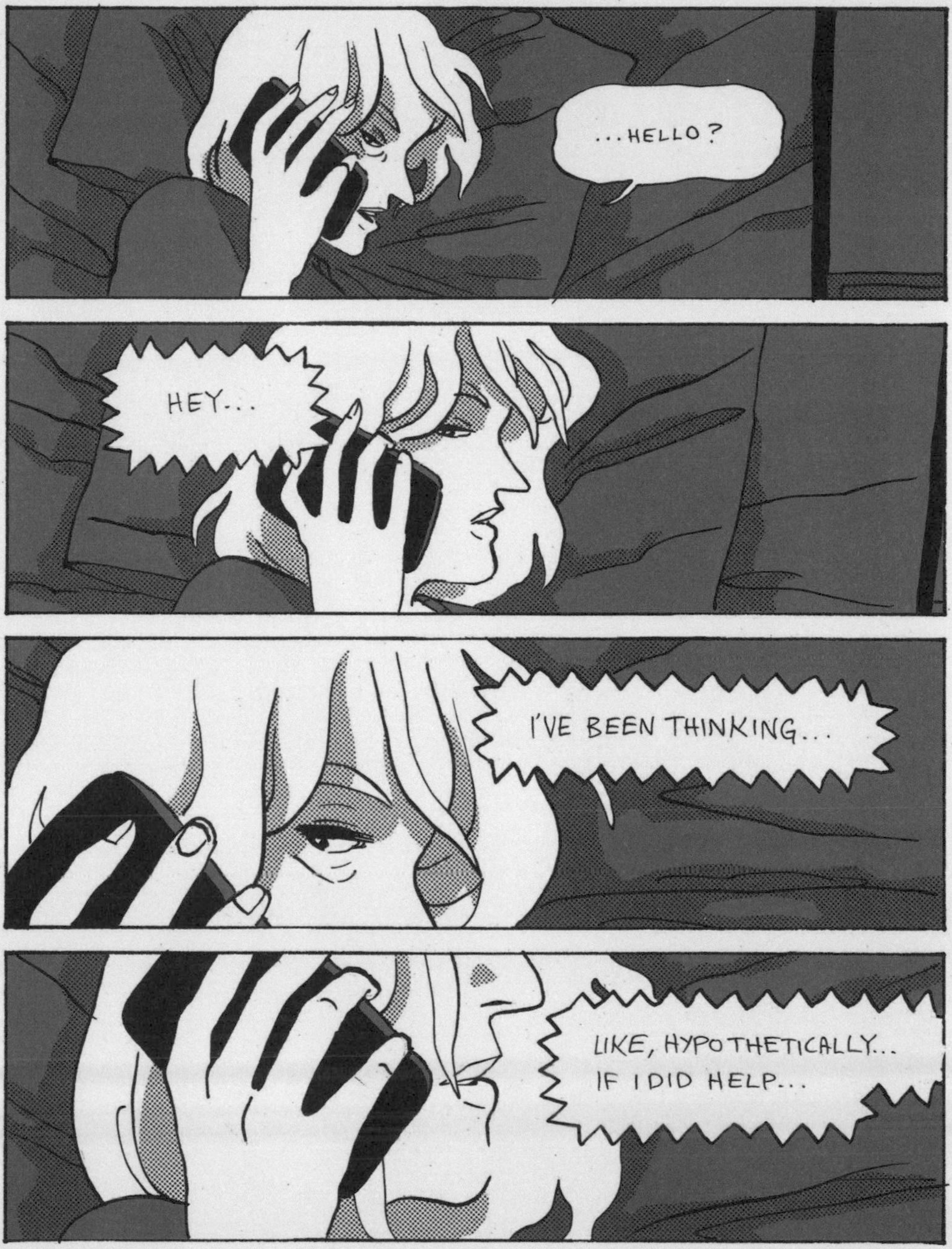
...HELLO?
HEY...
I'VE BEEN THINKING...
LIKE, HYPOTHETICALLY...
IF I DID HELP...

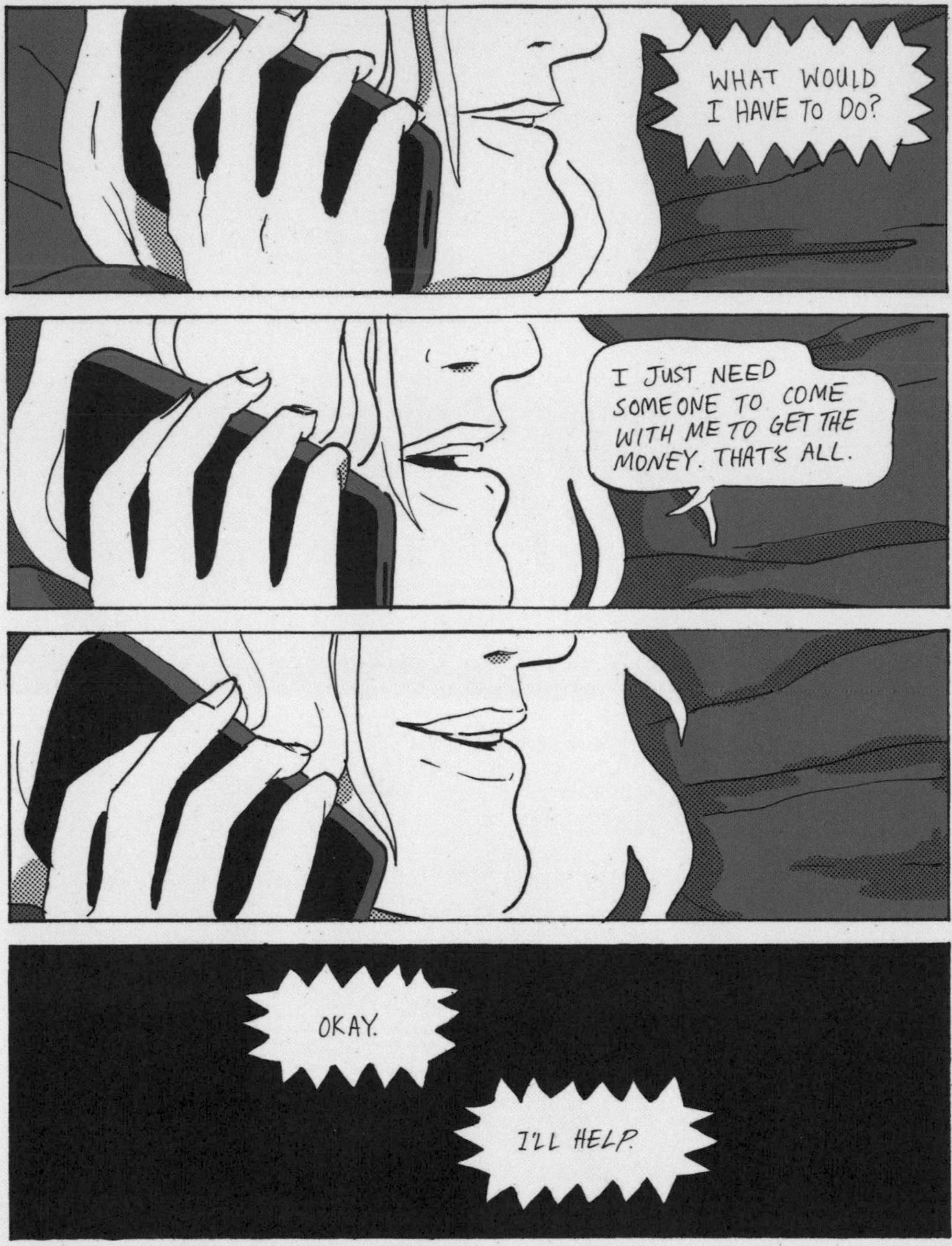
WHAT WOULD I HAVE TO DO?
I JUST NEED SOMEONE TO COME WITH ME TO GET THE MONEY. THAT'S ALL.
OKAY.
I'LL HELP.

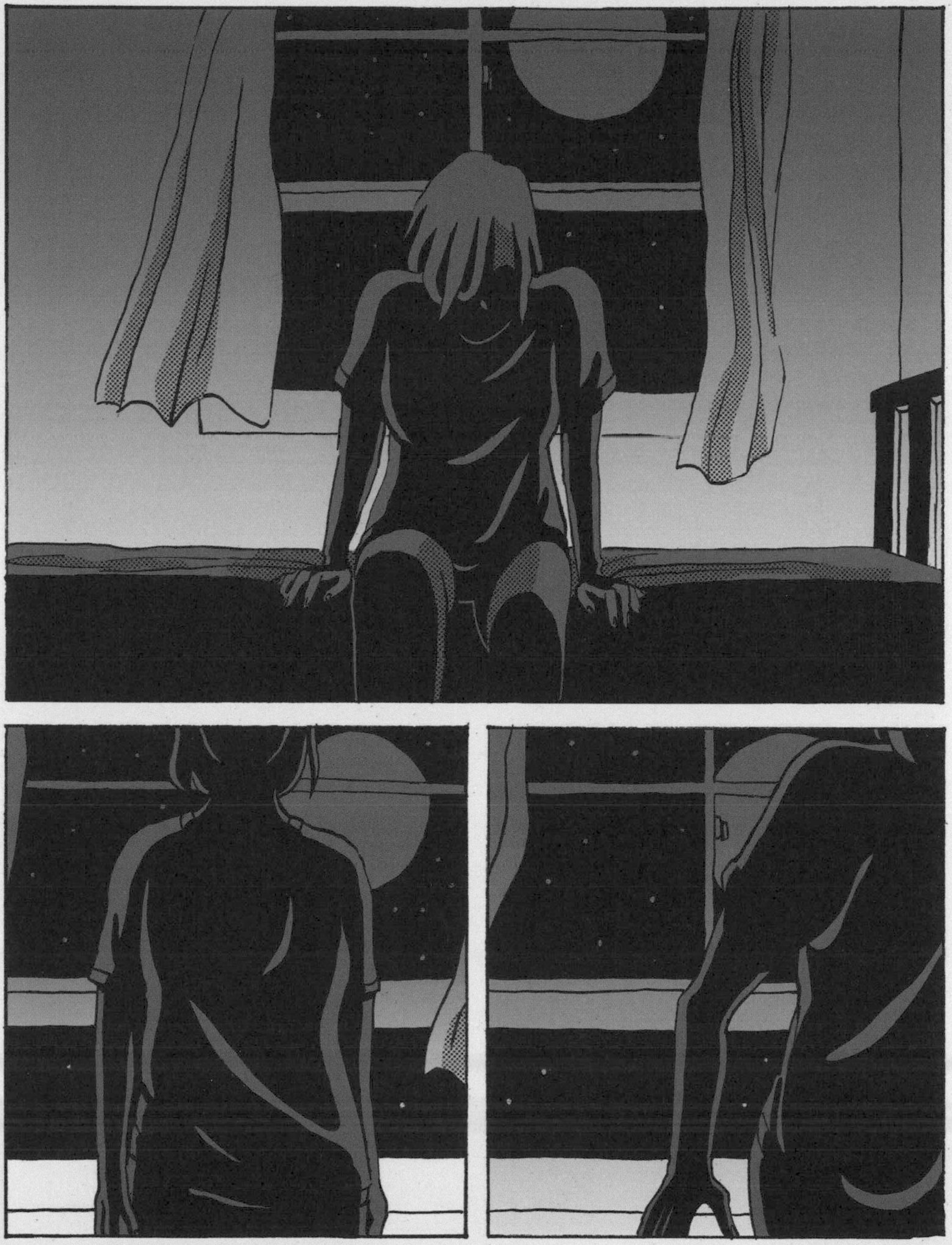

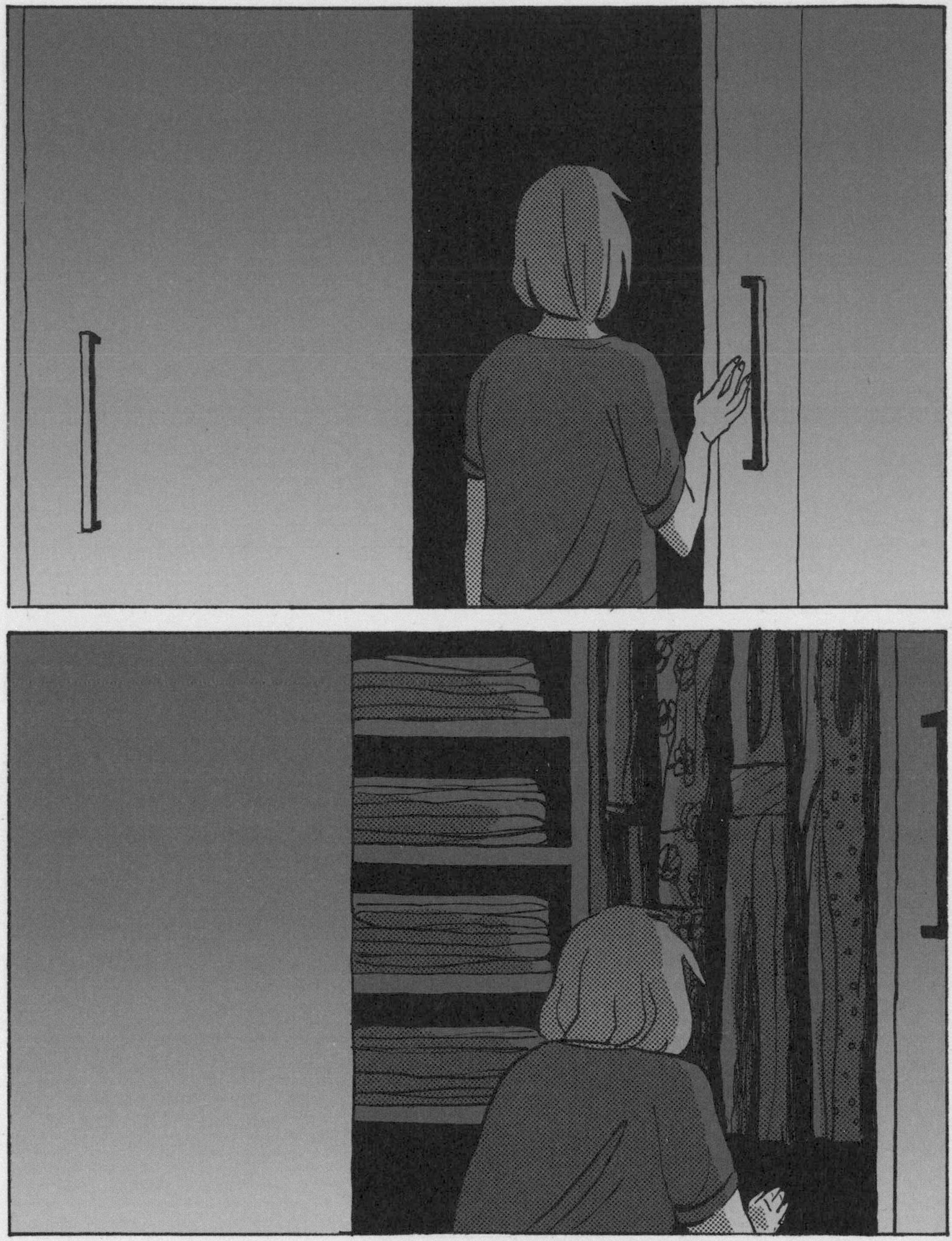

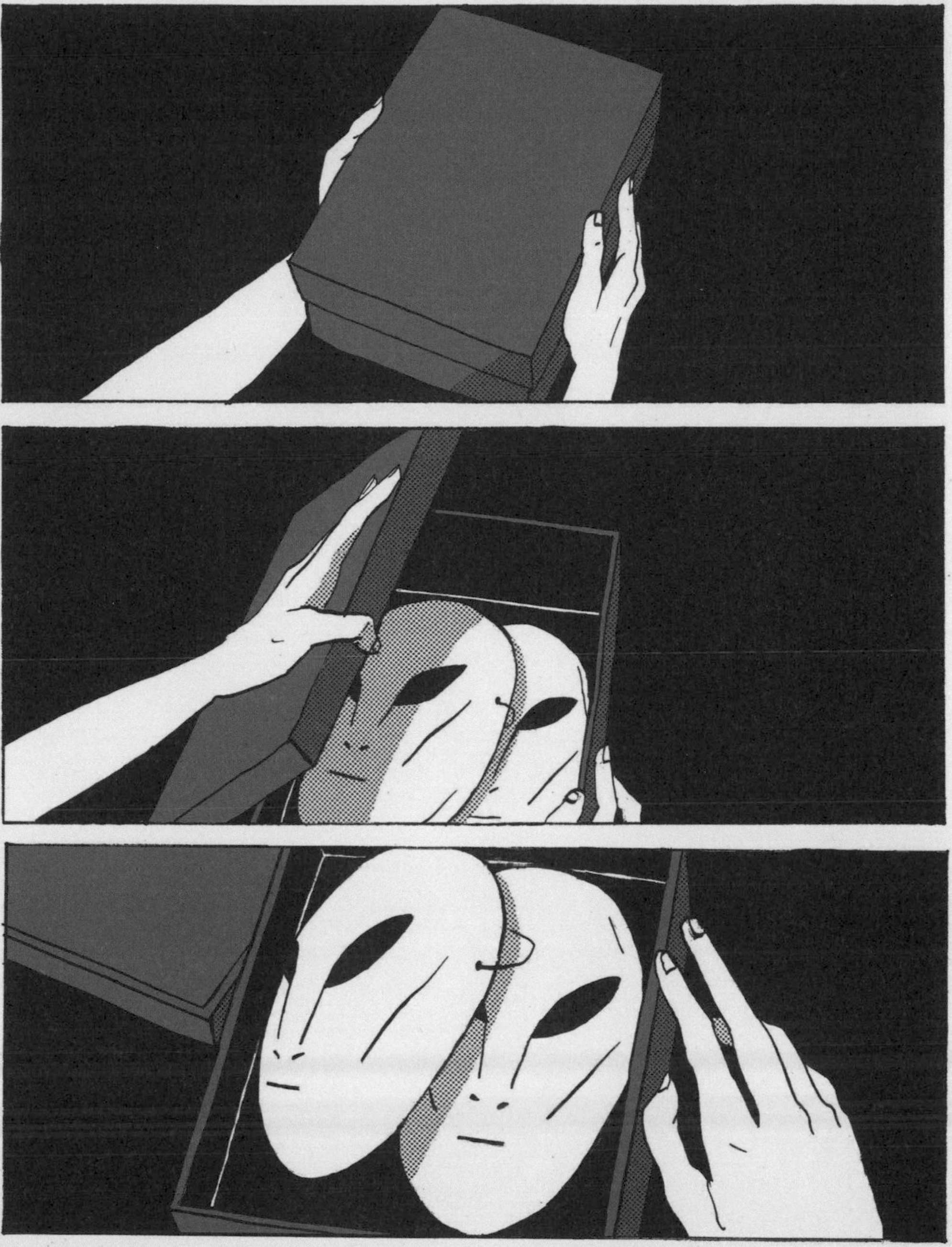

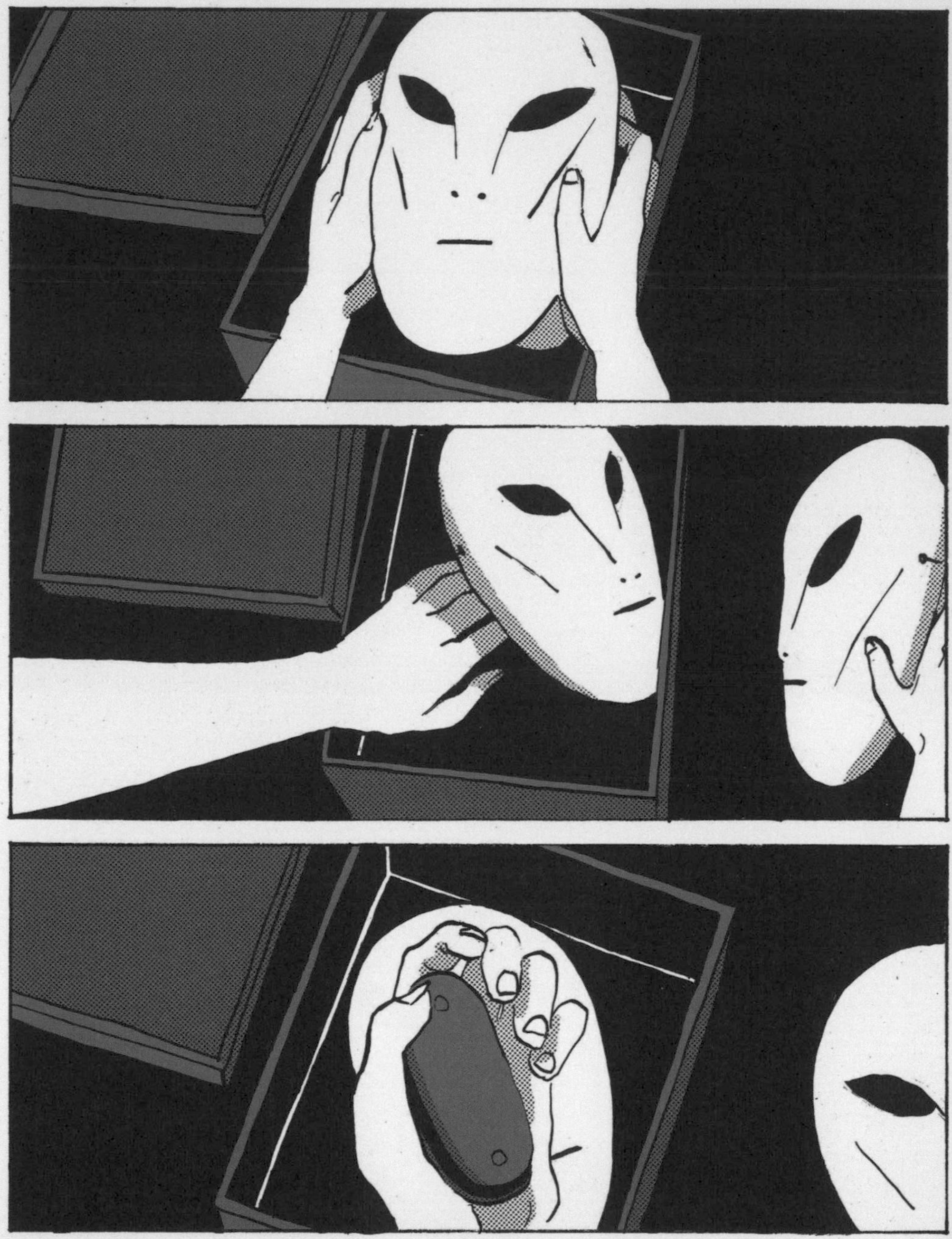

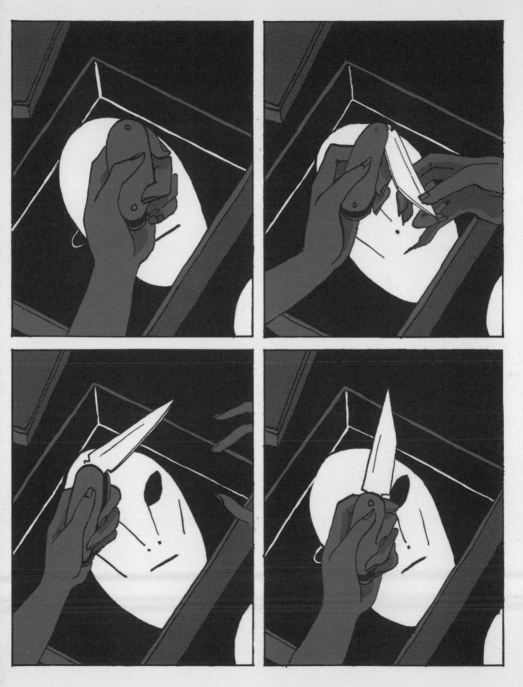

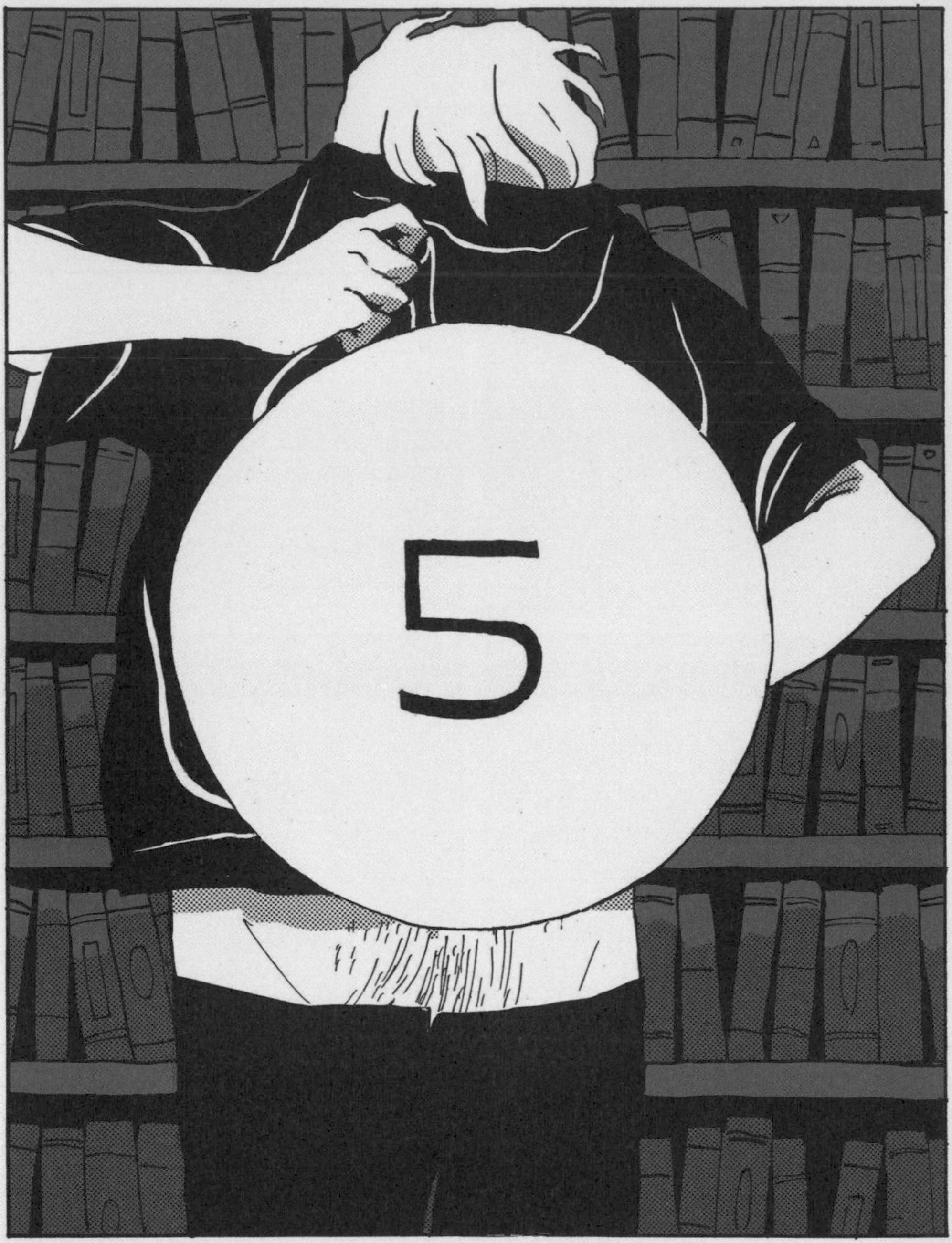
5

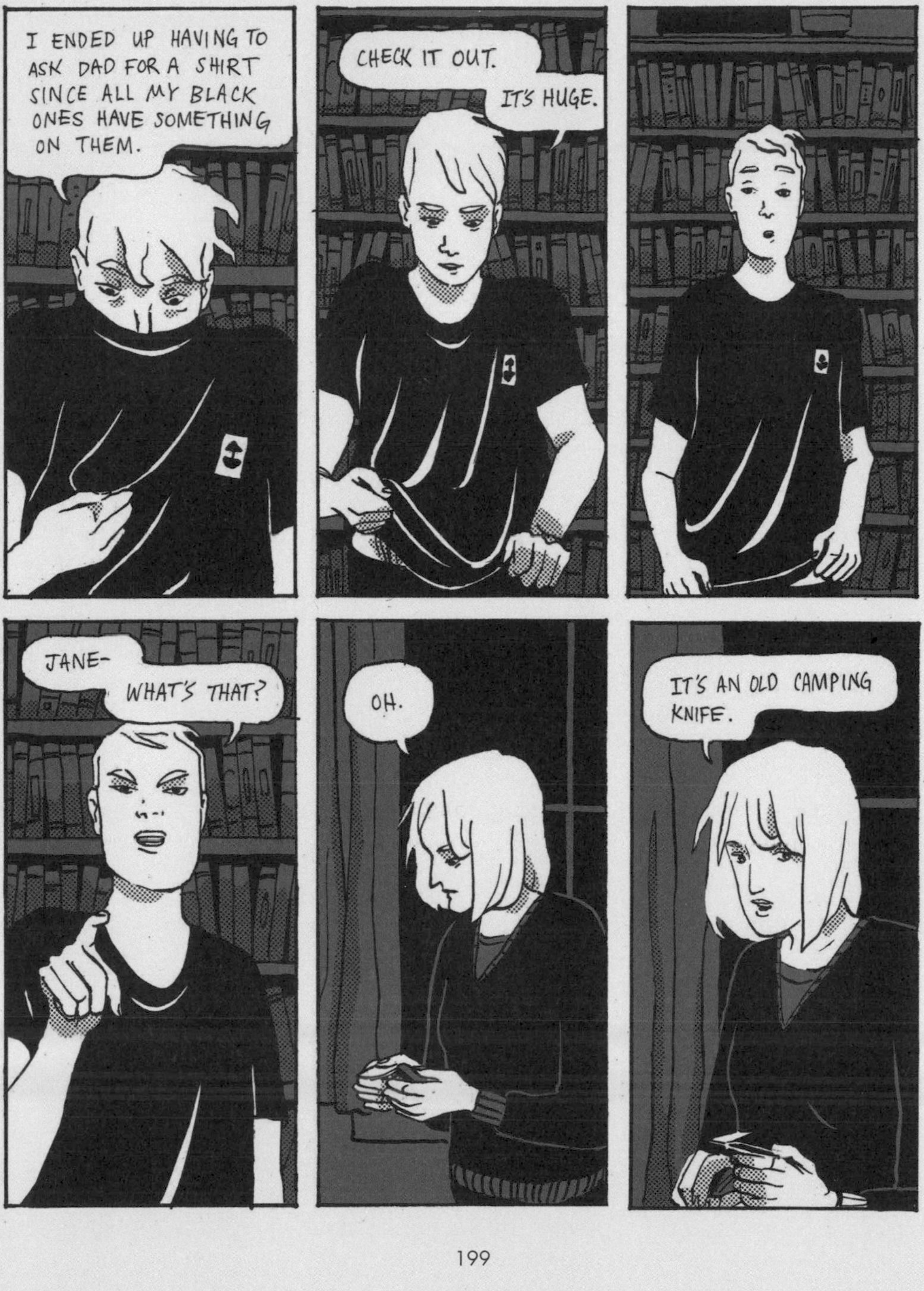
I ENDED UP HAVING TO ASK DAD FOR A SHIRT SINCE ALL MY BLACK ONES HAVE SOMETHING ON THEM.
CHECK IT OUT.
IT'S HUGE.
JANE-
WHAT'S THAT?
OH.
IT'S AN OLD CAMPING KNIFE.

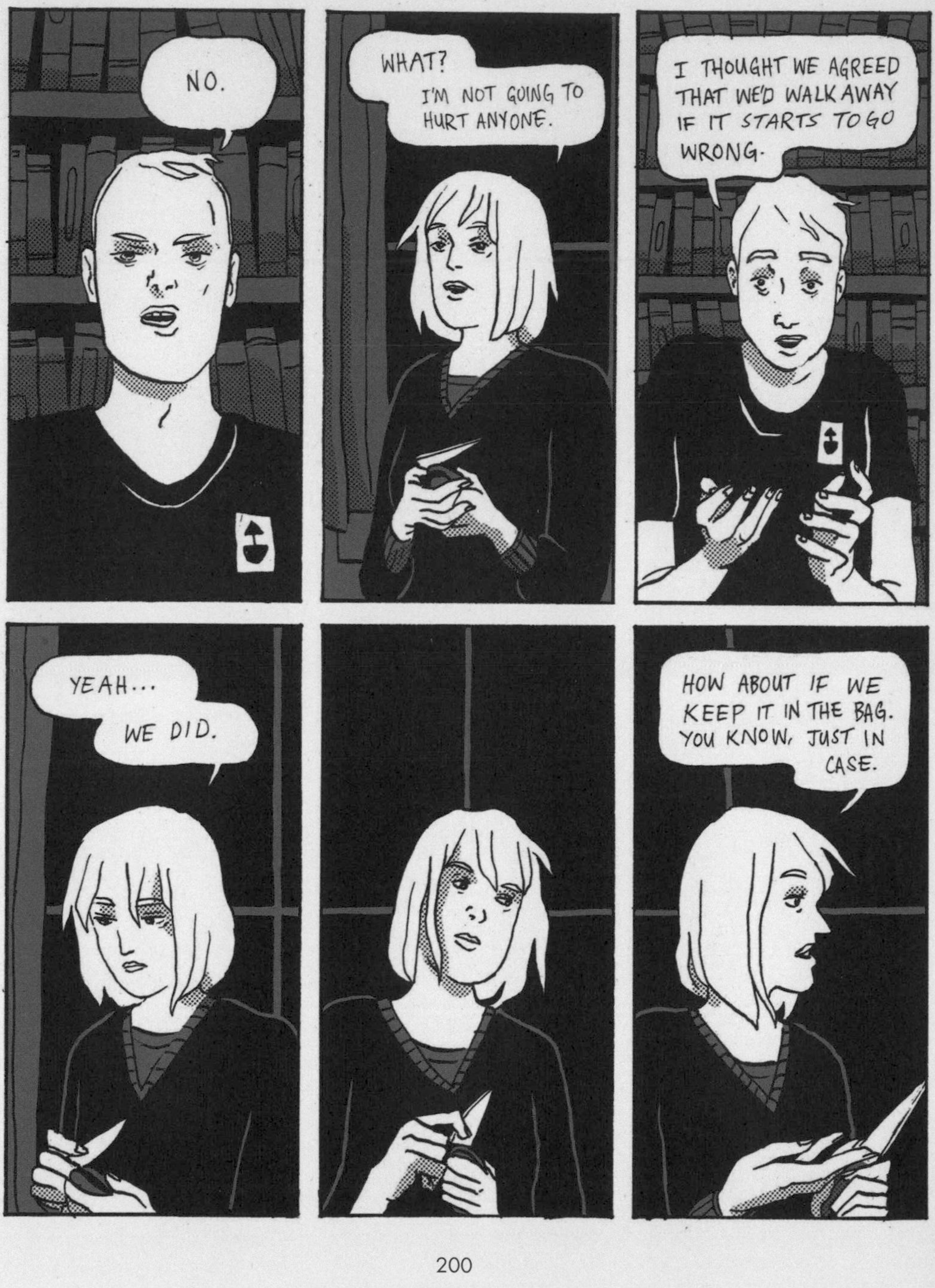
NO.
WHAT?
I'M NOT GOING TO HURT ANYONE.
I THOUGHT WE AGREED THAT WE'D WALK AWAY IF IT STARTS TO GO WRONG.
YEAH...
WE DID.
HOW ABOUT IF WE KEEP IT IN THE BAG. YOU KNOW, JUST IN CASE.

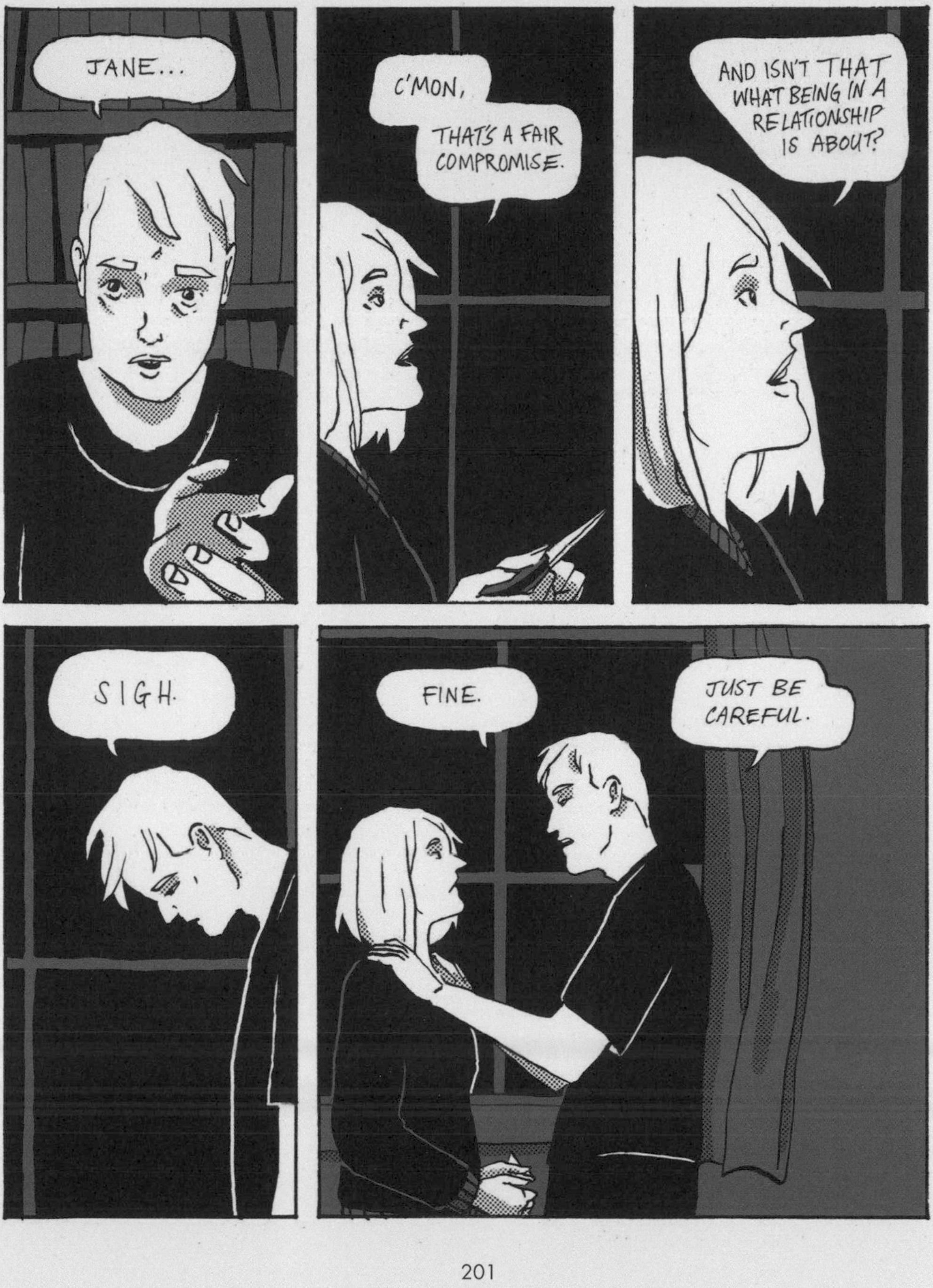
JANE...
C'MON,
THAT'S A FAIR COMPROMISE.
AND ISN'T THAT WHAT BEING IN A RELATIONSHIP IS ABOUT?
SIGH.
FINE.
JUST BE CAREFUL.

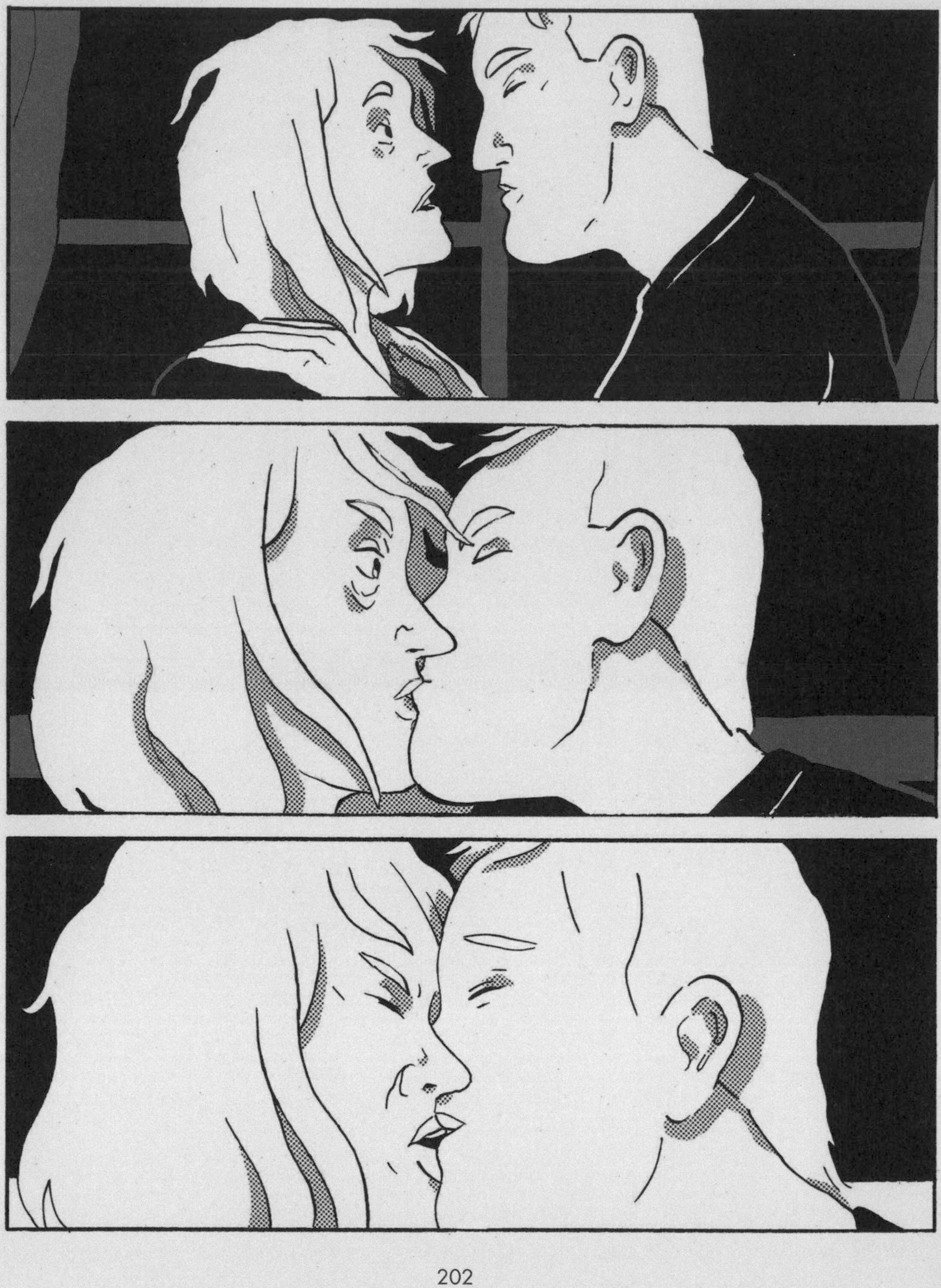

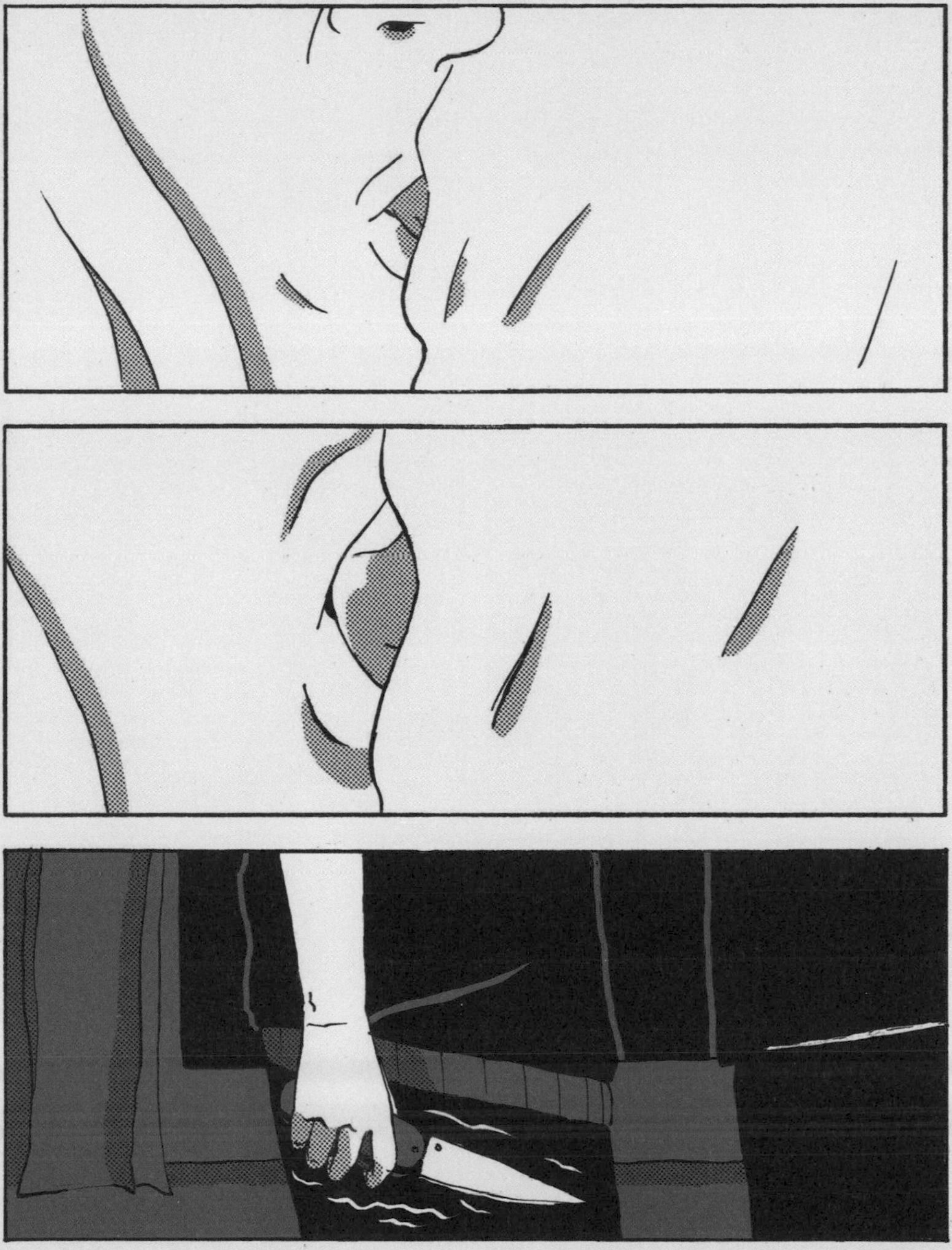

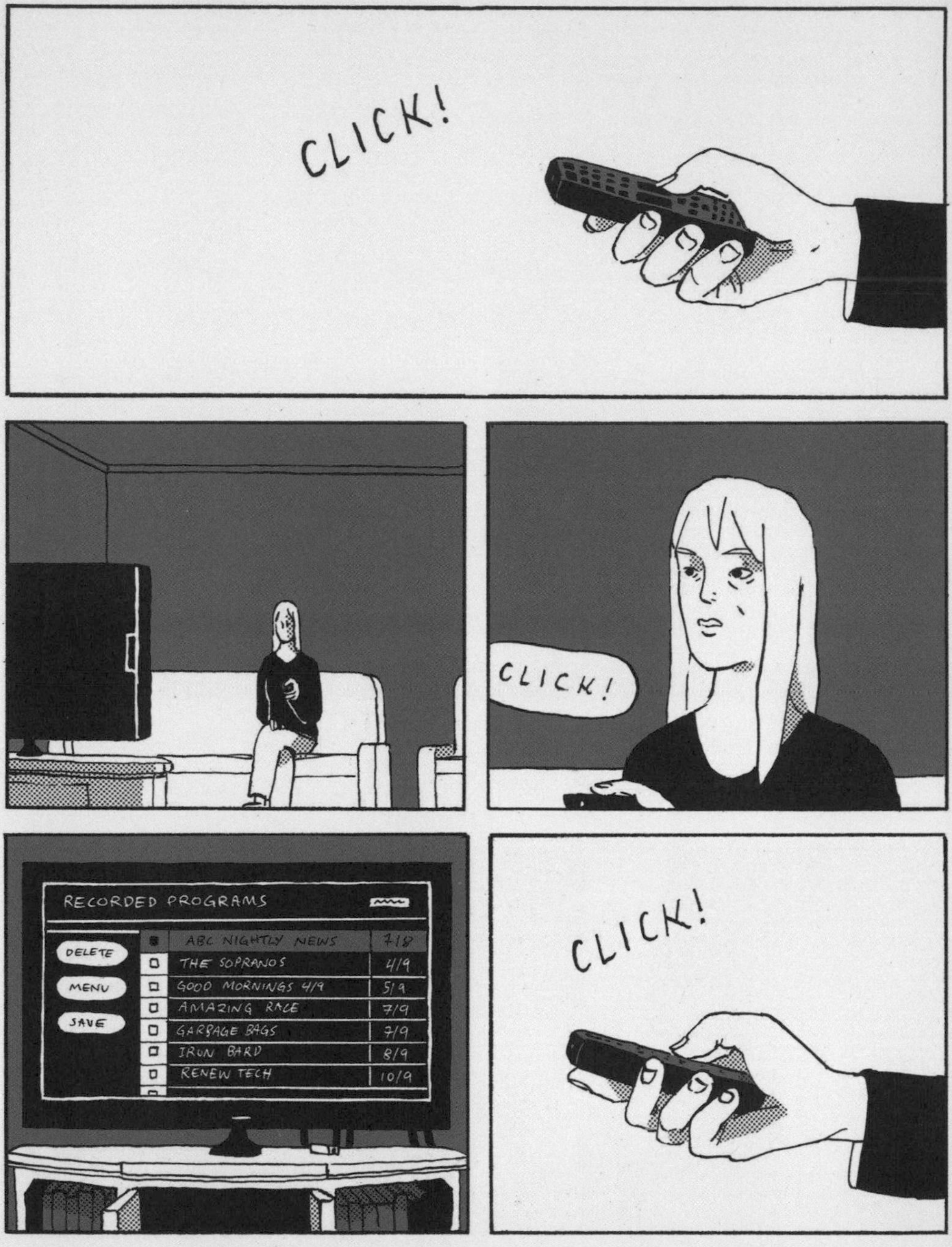
CLICK!
CLICK!
RECORDED PROGRAMS
DELETE
MENU
SAVE
ABC NIGHTLY NEWS 7/8
THE SOPRANOS 4/9
GOOD MORNINGS 4/9 5/9
AMAZING RACE 7/9
GARBAGE BAGS 7/9
IRON BARD 8/9
RENEW TECH 10/9
CLICK!

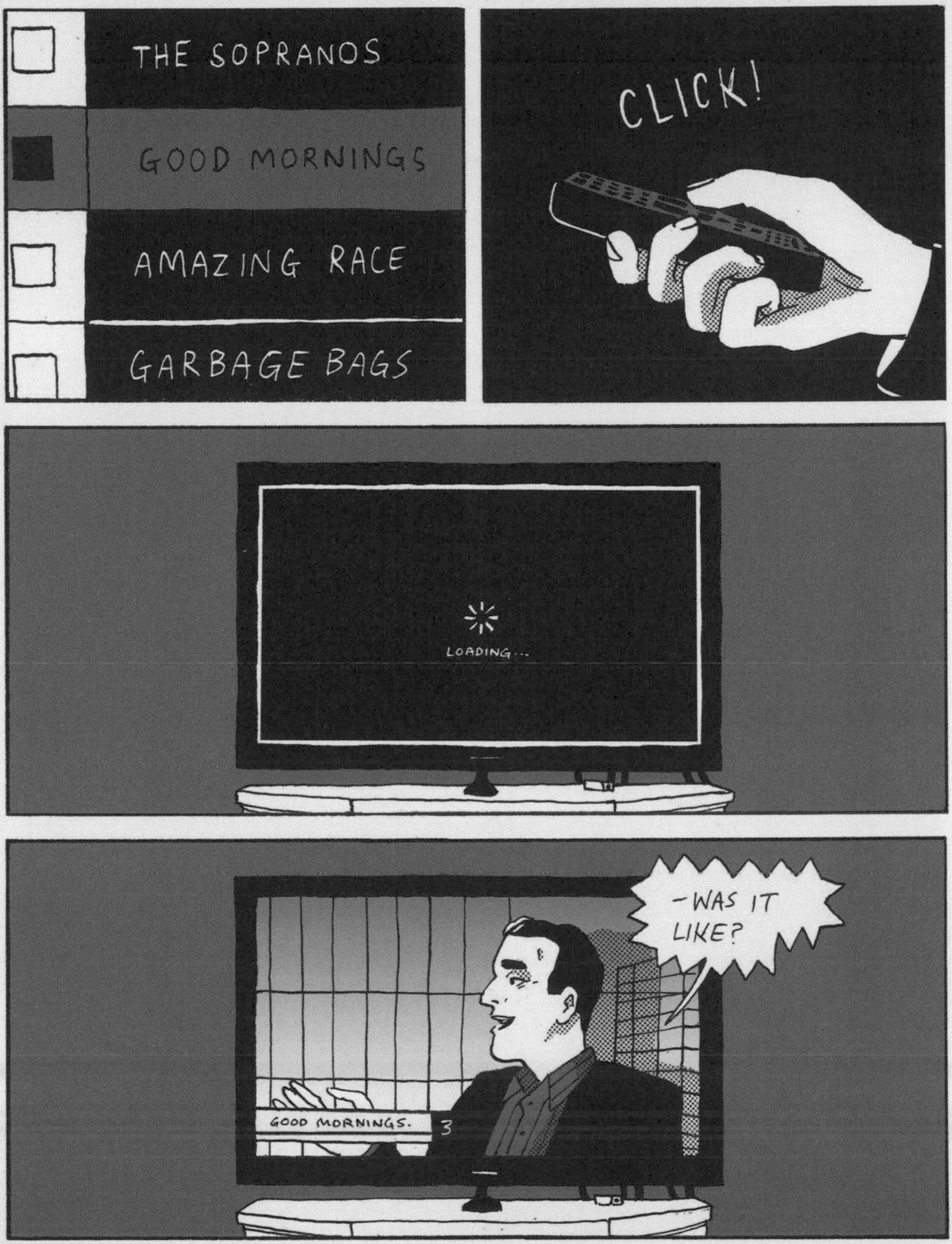
THE SOPRANOS
GOOD MORNINGS
AMAZING RACE
GARBAGE BAGS
CLICK!
LOADING...
-WAS IT LIKE?
GOOD MORNINGS.
3

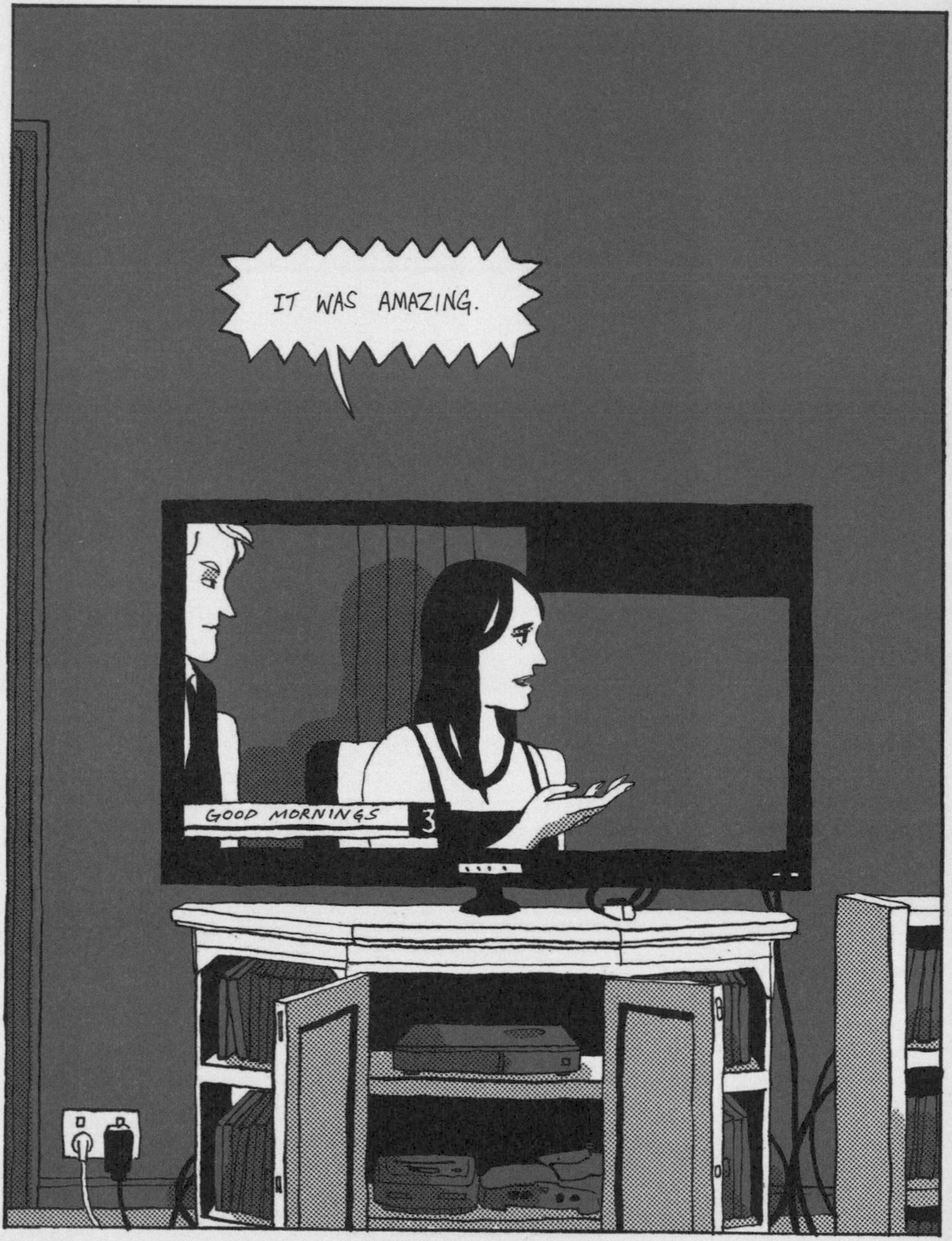
IT WAS AMAZING.
GOOD MORNINGS
3

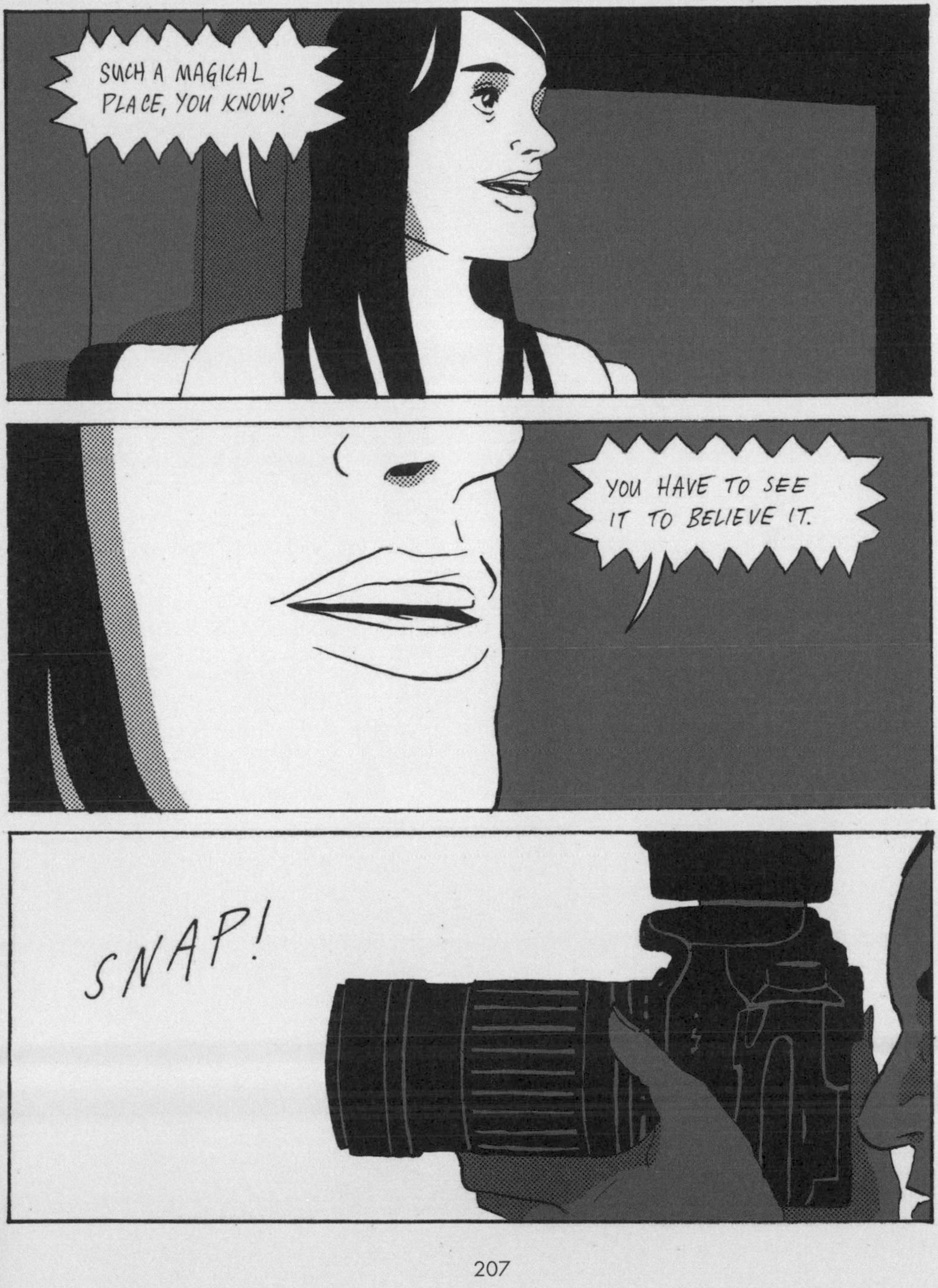
SUCH A MAGICAL PLACE, YOU KNOW?
YOU HAVE TO SEE IT TO BELIEVE IT.
SNAP!

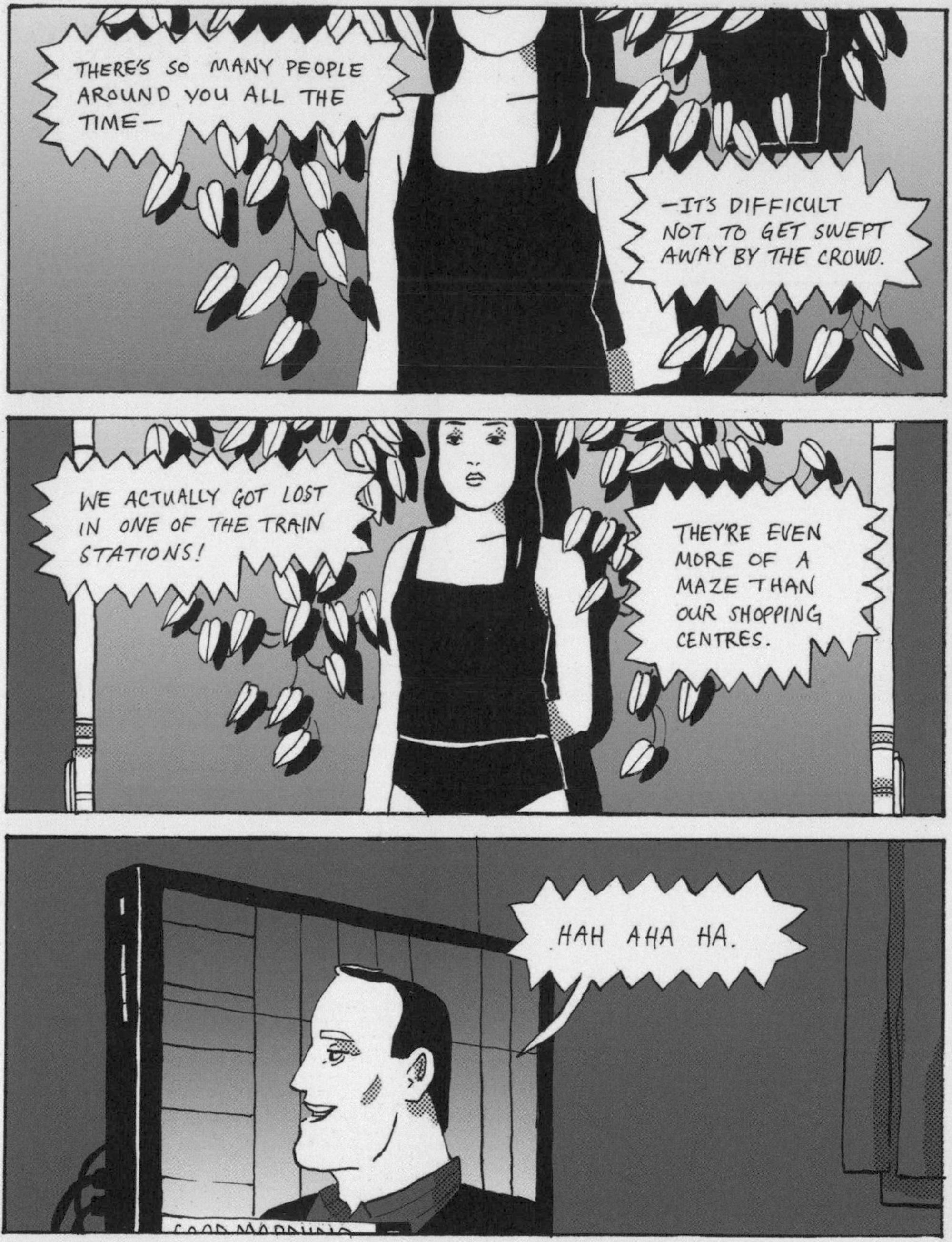
THERE'S SO MANY PEOPLE AROUND YOU ALL THE TIME—
—IT'S DIFFICULT NOT TO GET SWEPT AWAY BY THE CROWD.
WE ACTUALLY GOT LOST IN ONE OF THE TRAIN STATIONS!
THEY'RE EVEN MORE OF A MAZE THAN OUR SHOPPING CENTRES.
HAH AHA HA.

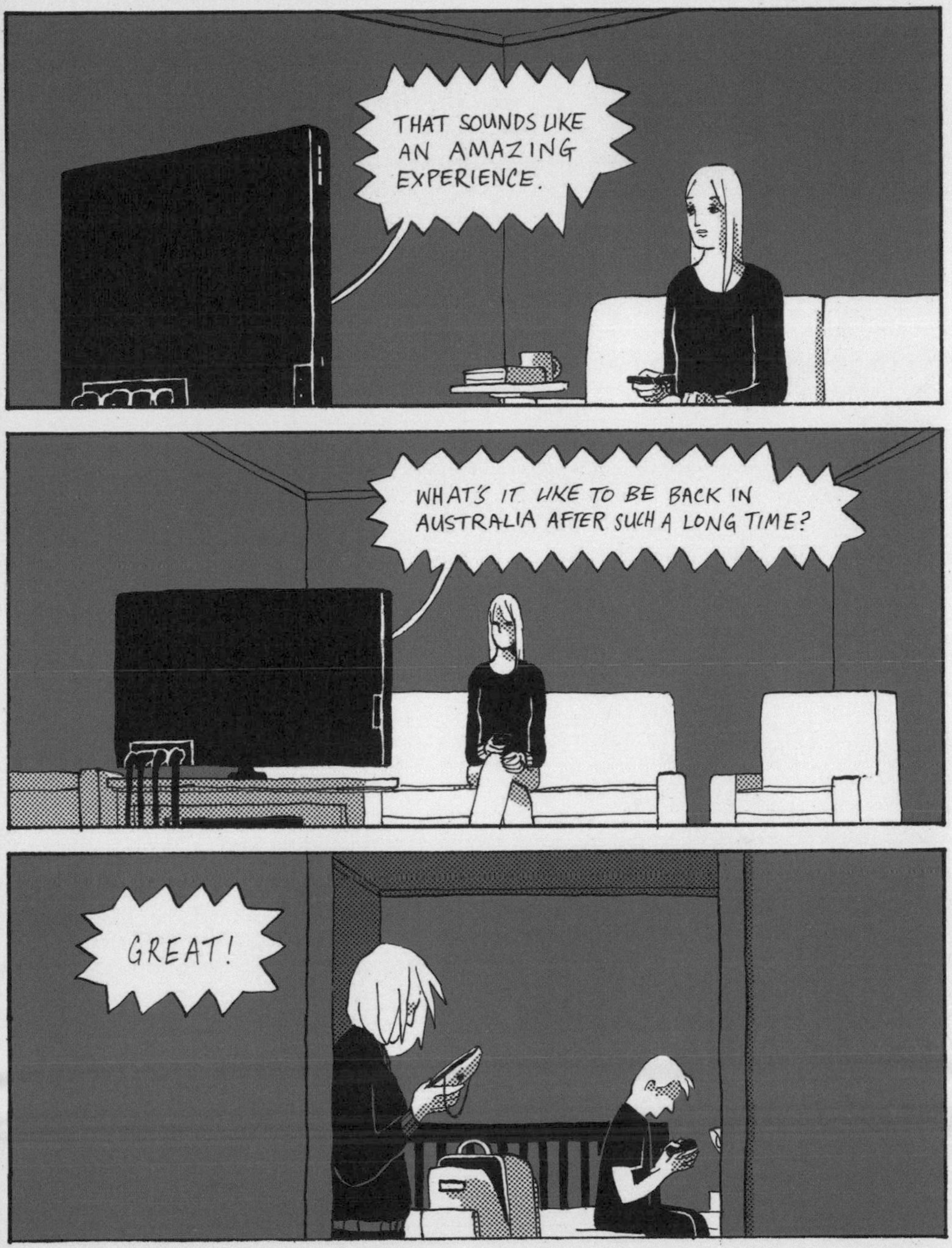
THAT SOUNDS LIKE AN AMAZING EXPERIENCE.
WHAT'S IT LIKE TO BE BACK IN AUSTRALIA AFTER SUCH A LONG TIME?
GREAT!

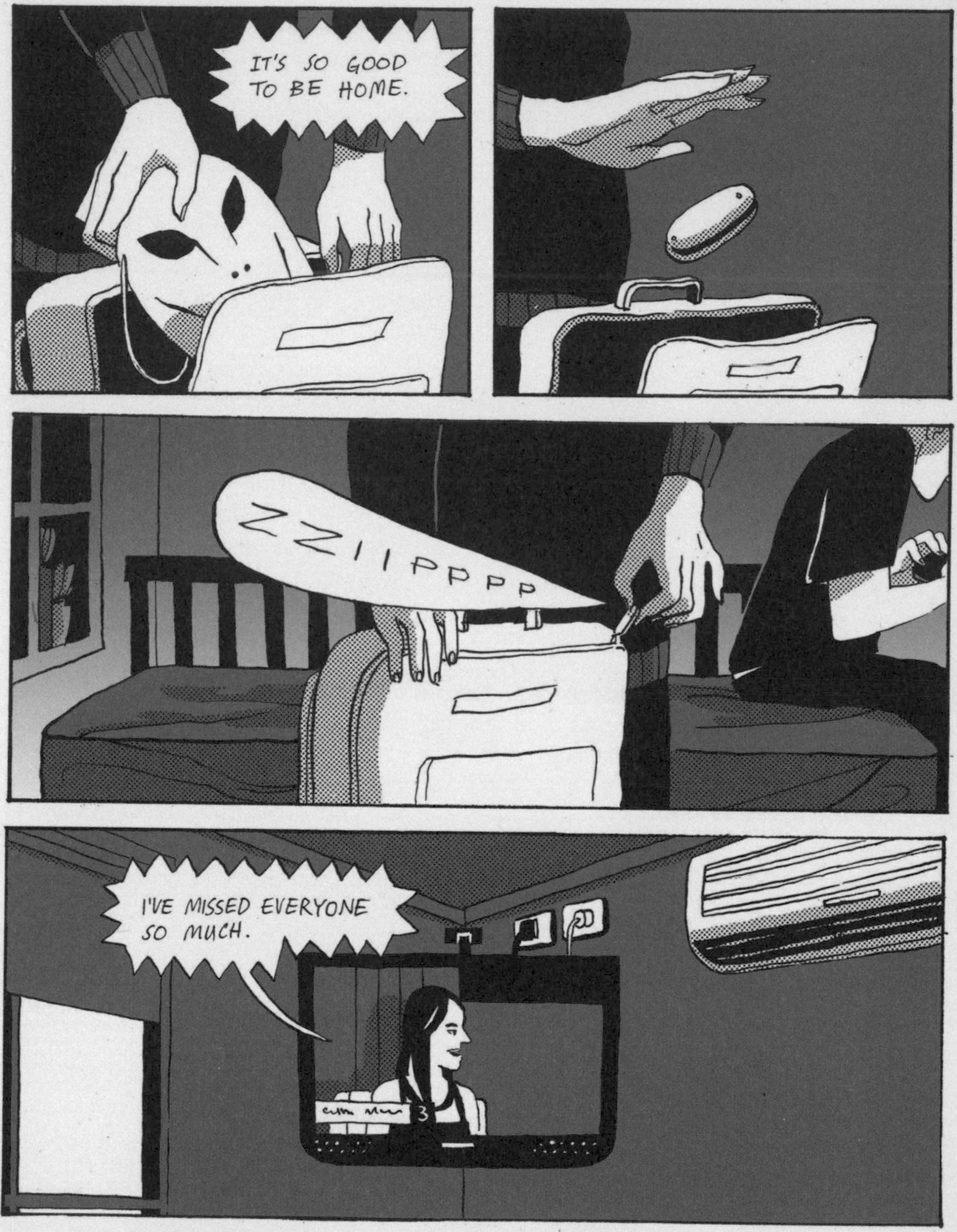
IT'S SO GOOD TO BE HOME.
ZZIIPPPPP
I'VE MISSED EVERYONE SO MUCH.

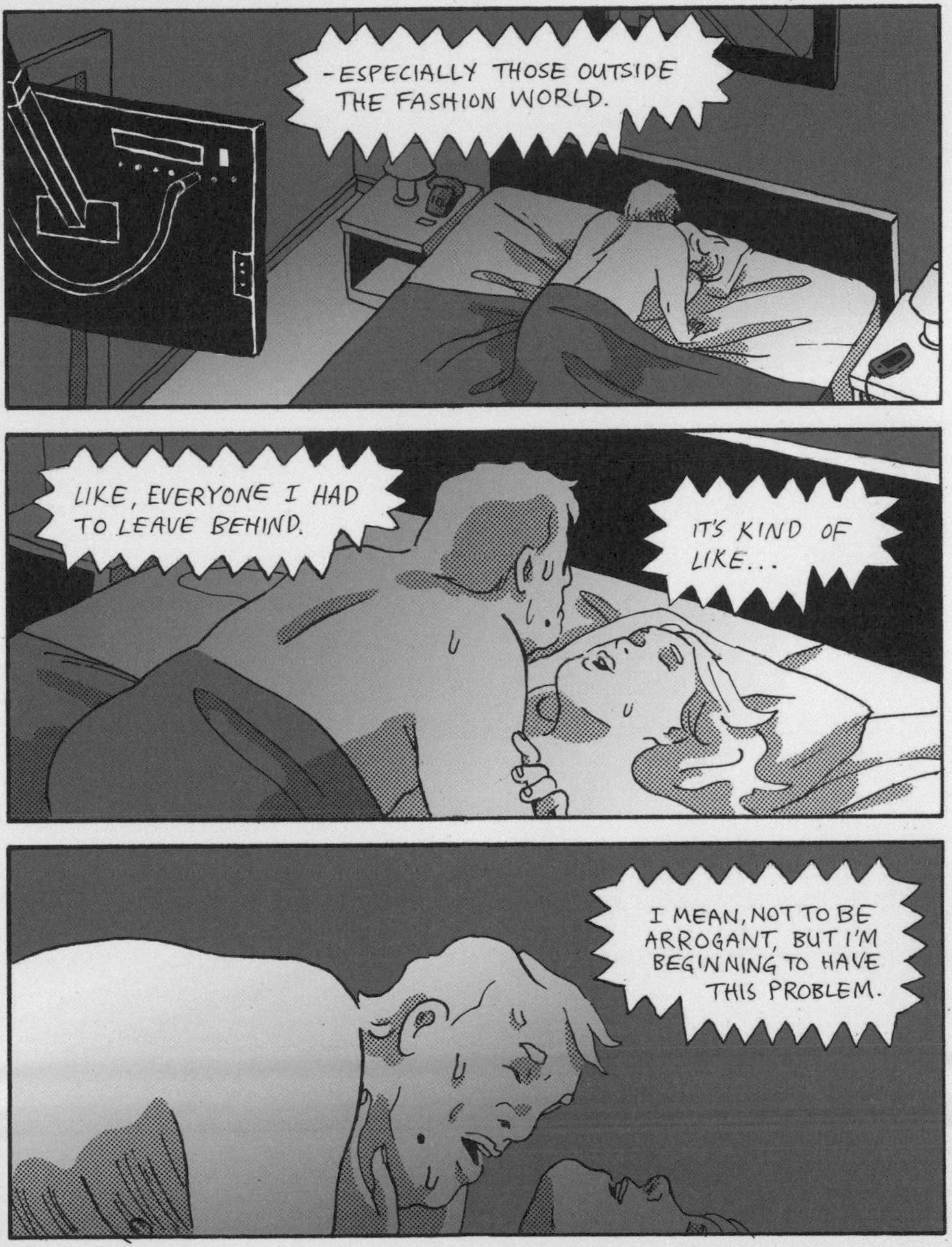
-ESPECIALLY THOSE OUTSIDE THE FASHION WORLD.
LIKE, EVERYONE I HAD TO LEAVE BEHIND.
IT'S KIND OF LIKE...
I MEAN, NOT TO BE ARROGANT, BUT I'M BEGINNING TO HAVE THIS PROBLEM.

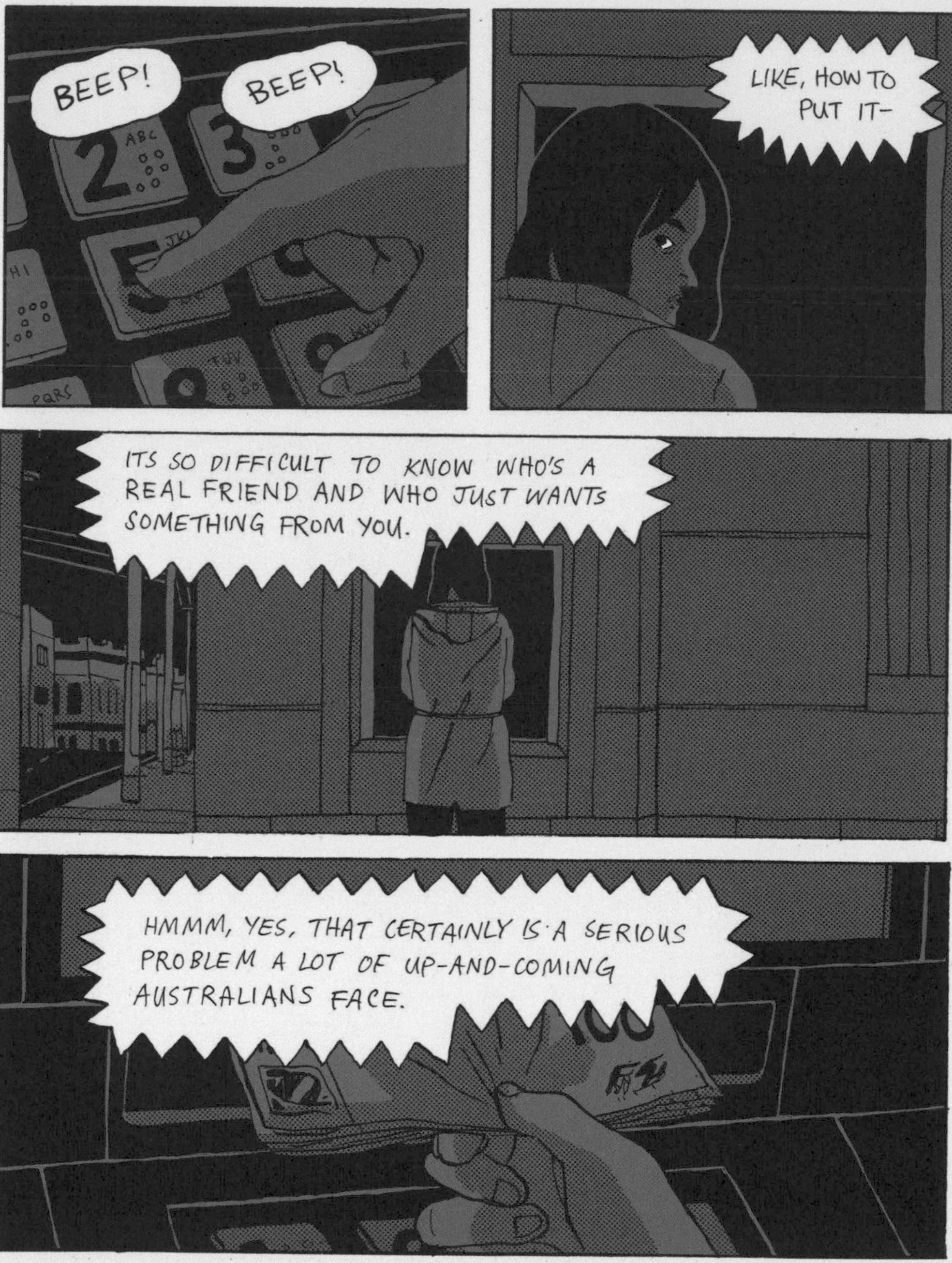
BEEP!
BEEP!
LIKE, HOW TO PUT IT-
ITS SO DIFFICULT TO KNOW WHO'S A REAL FRIEND AND WHO JUST WANTS SOMETHING FROM YOU.
HMMM, YES, THAT CERTAINLY IS A SERIOUS PROBLEM A LOT OF UP-AND-COMING AUSTRALIANS FACE.

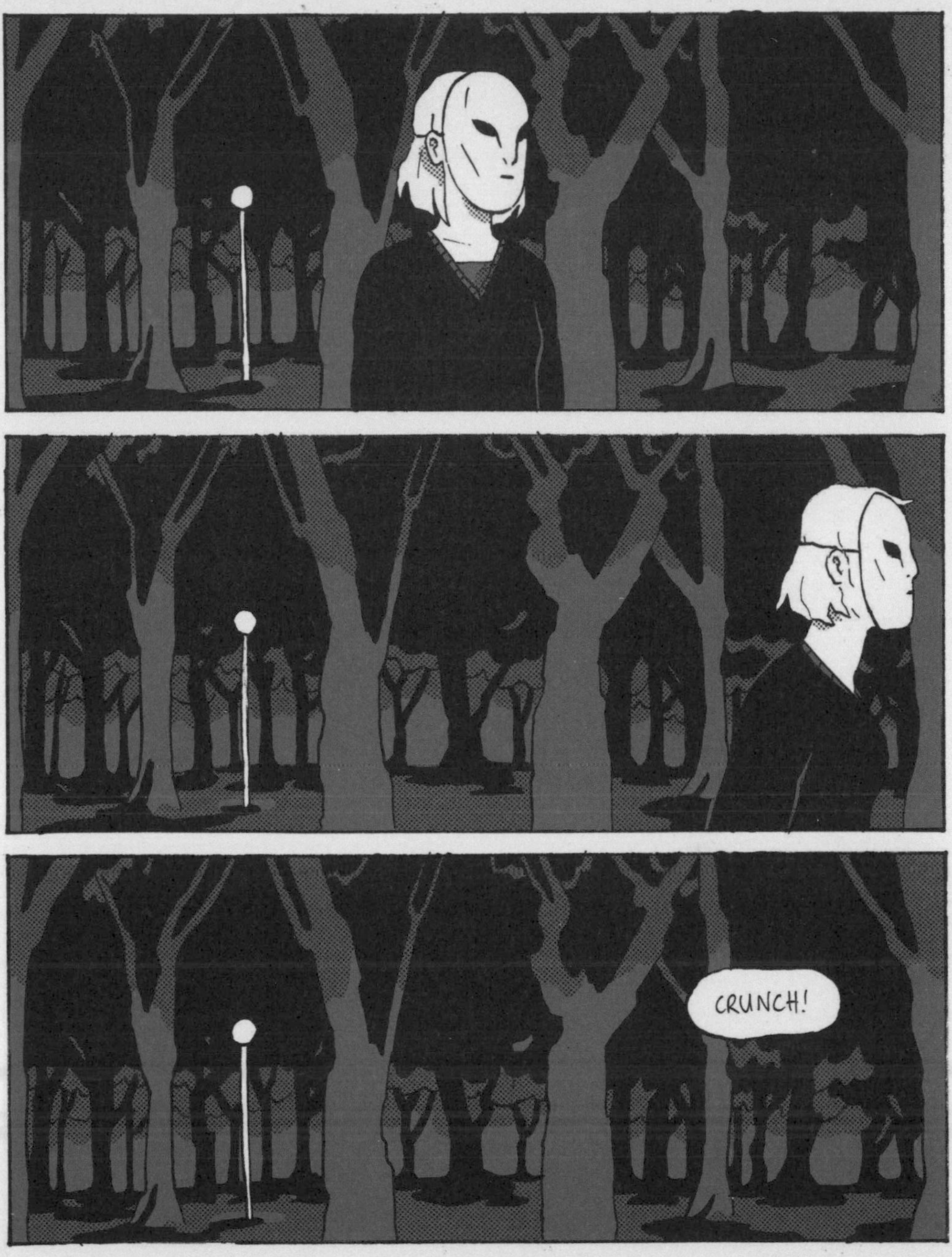
CRUNCH!

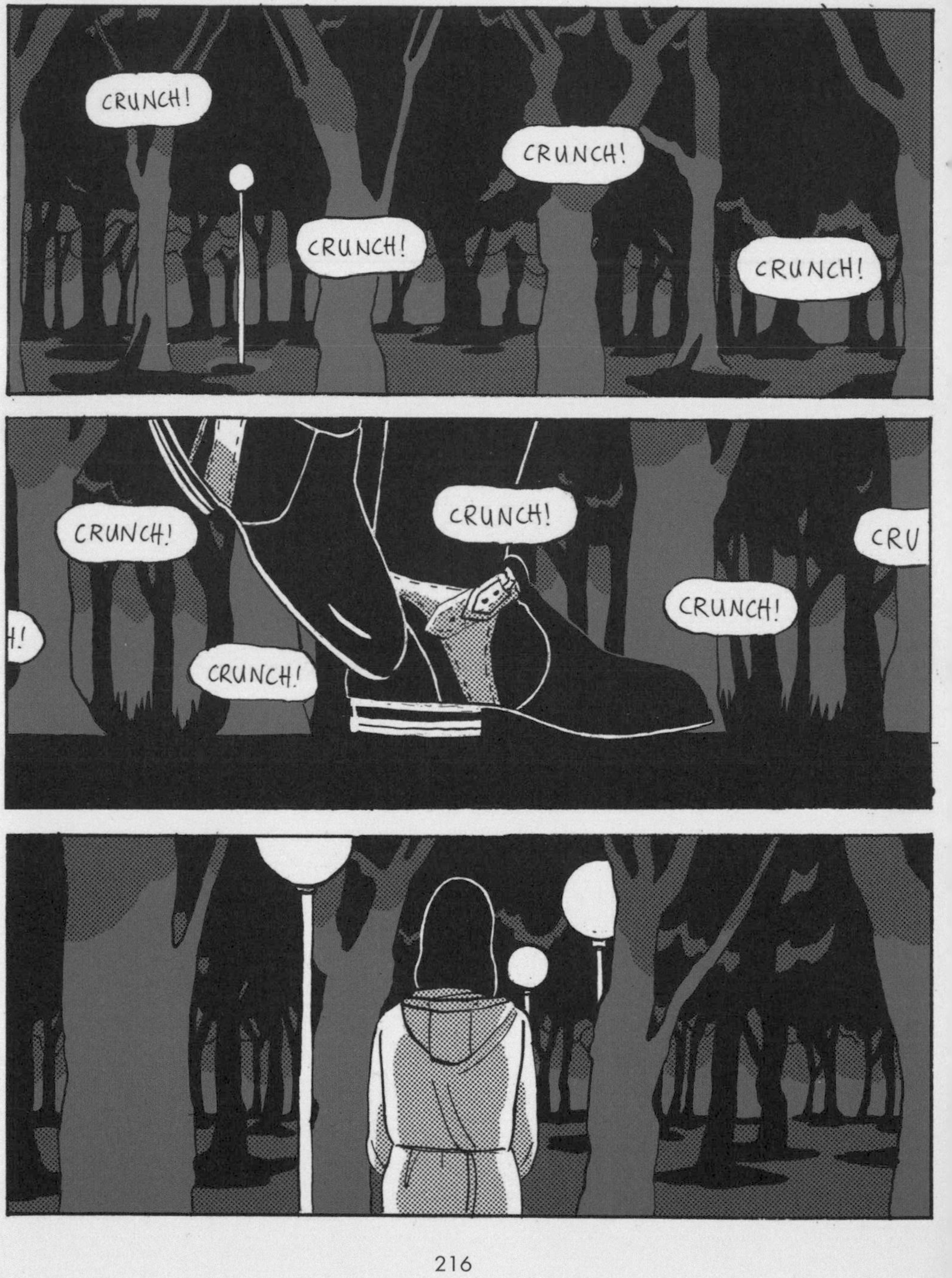
CRUNCH!
CRUNCH!
CRUNCH!
CRUNCH!
CRUNCH!
CRUNCH!
CRU
H!
CRUNCH!
CRUNCH!

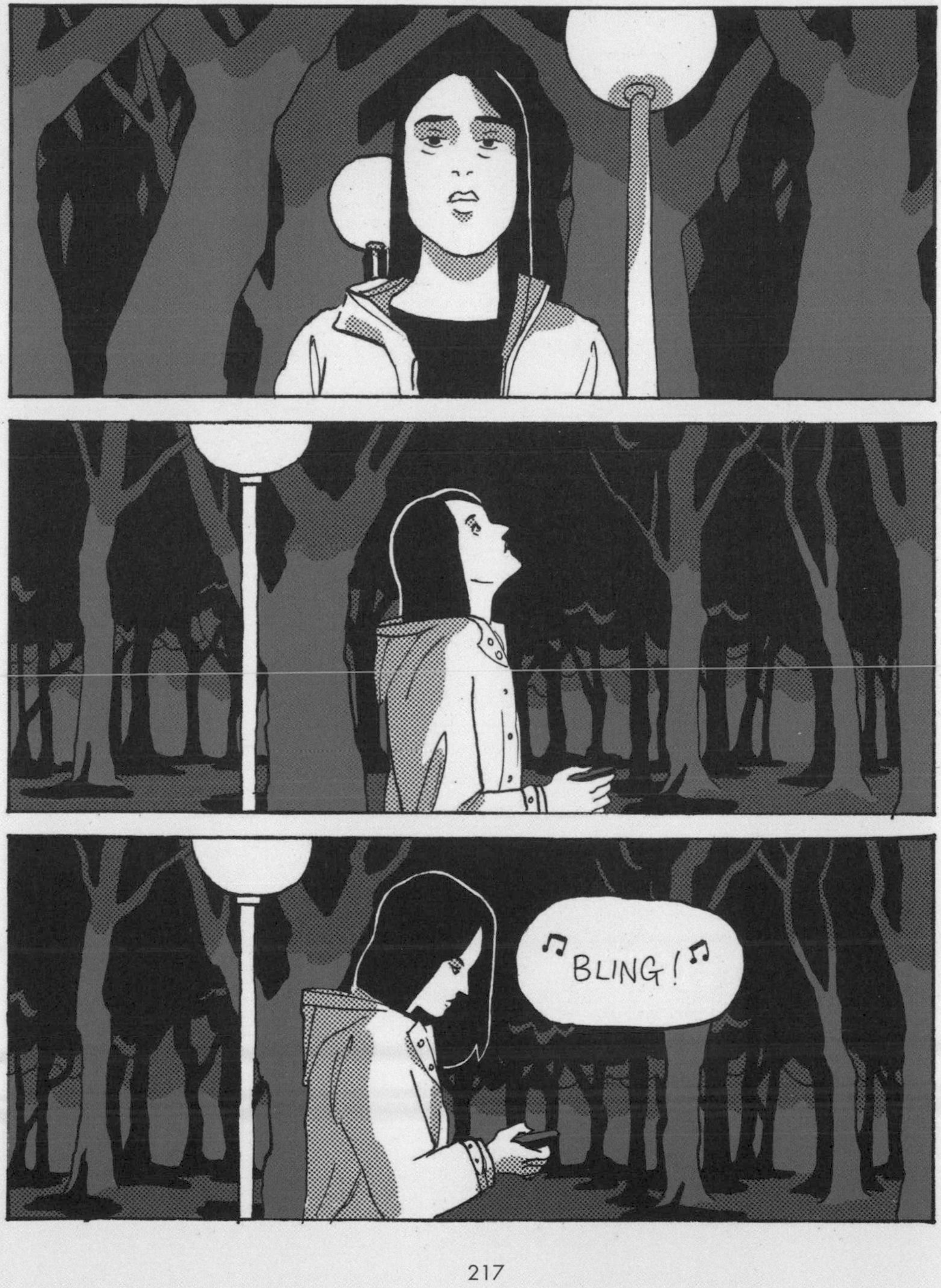
♫ BLING! ♫

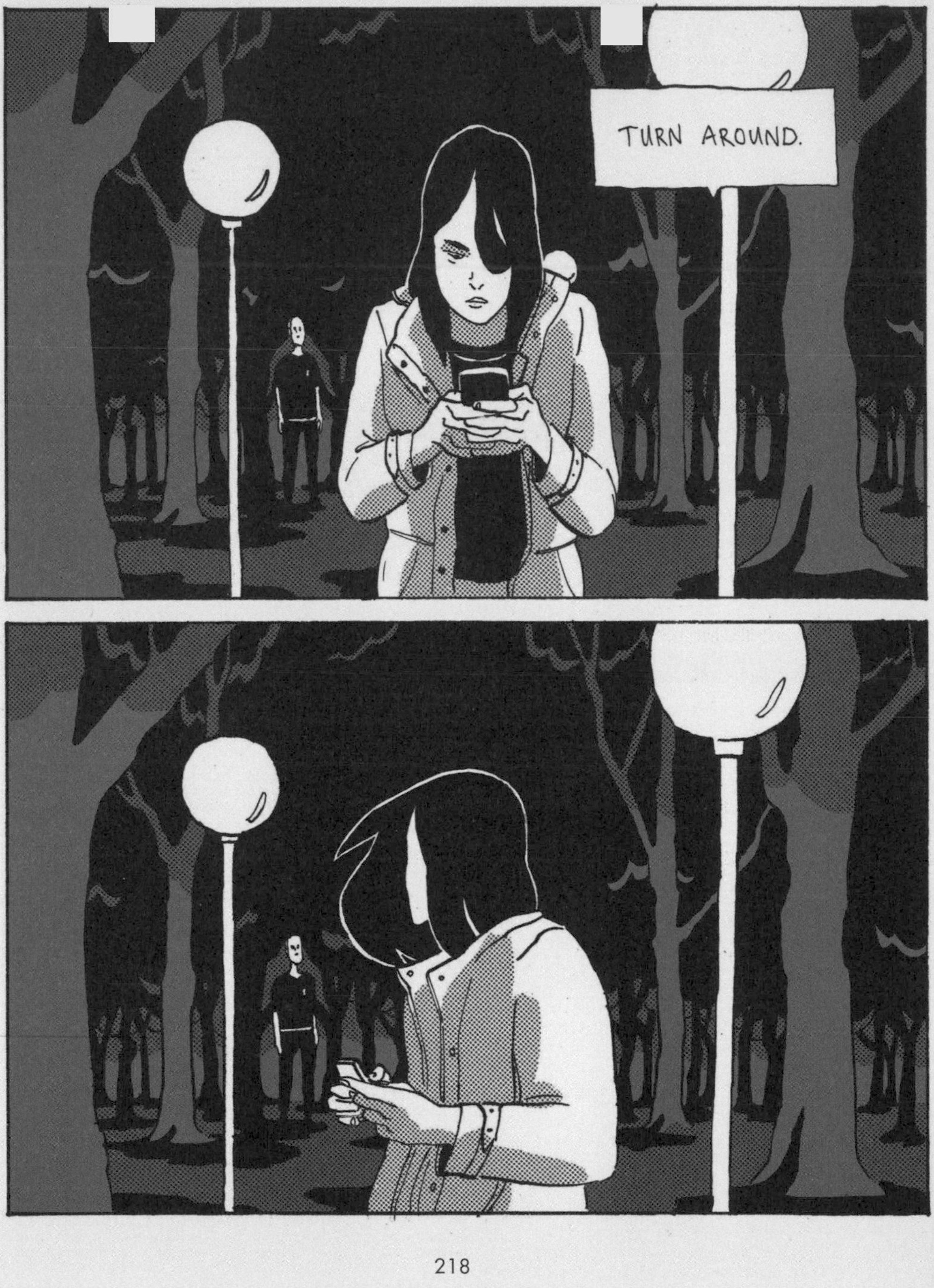
TURN AROUND.

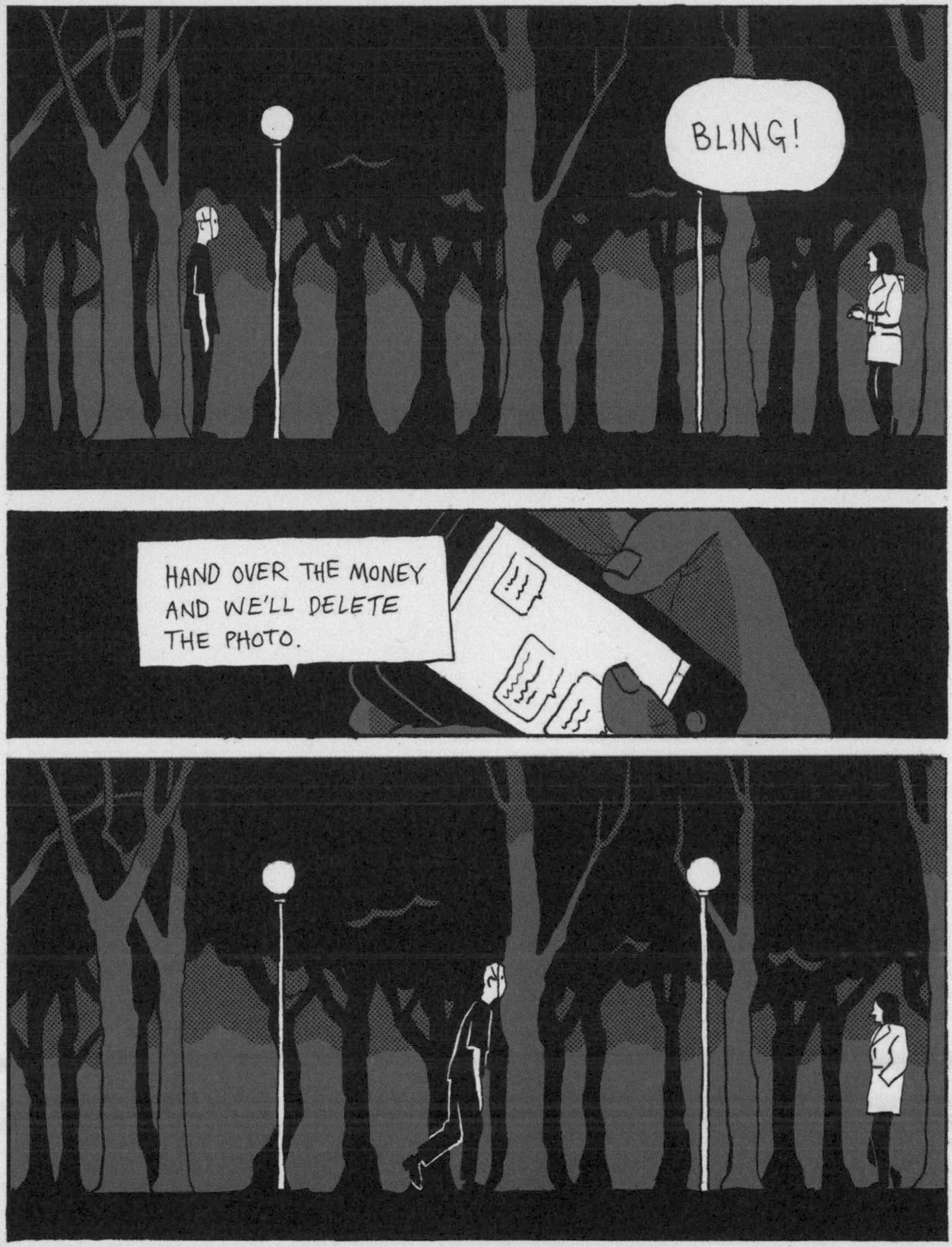
BLING!
HAND OVER THE MONEY AND WE'LL DELETE THE PHOTO.

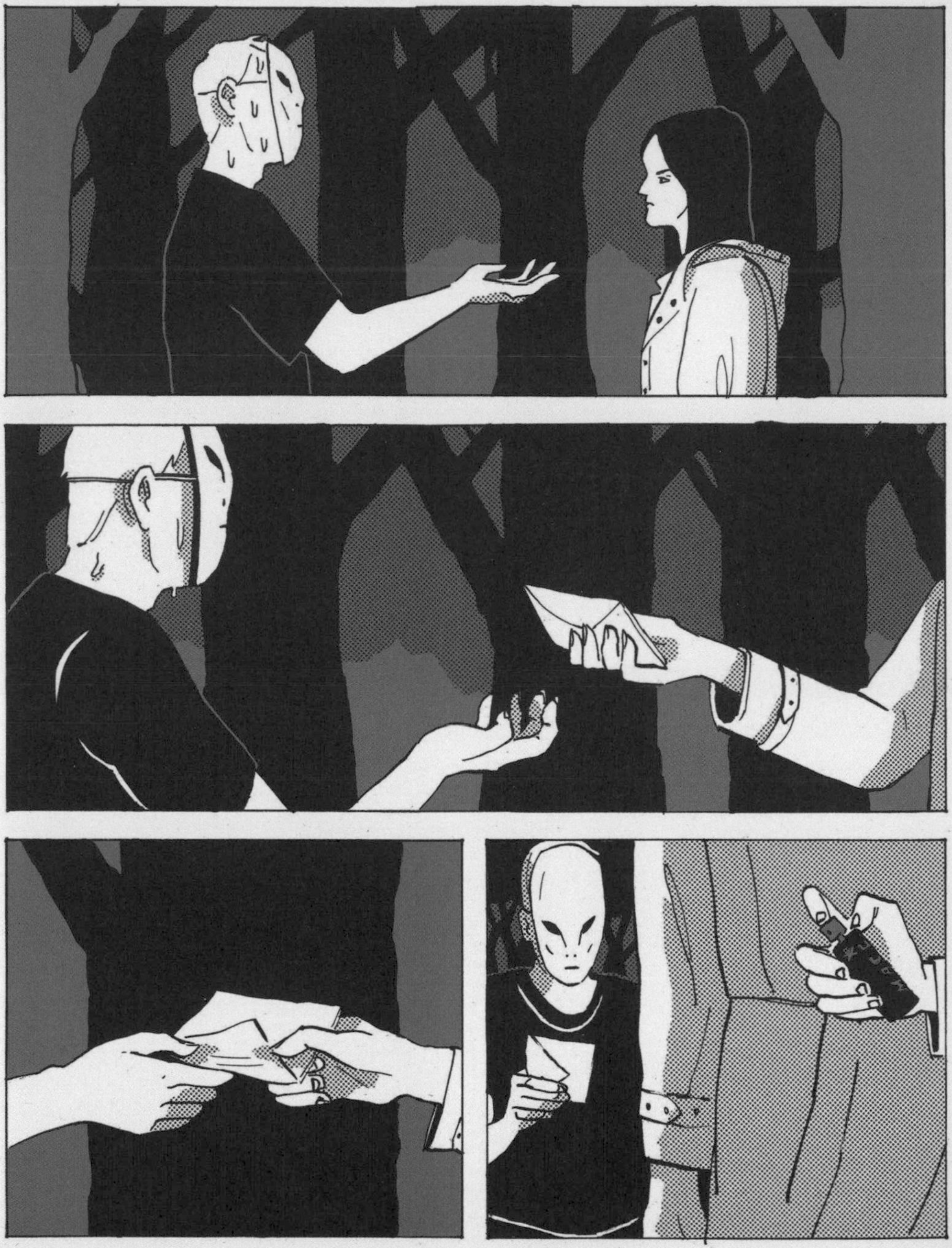

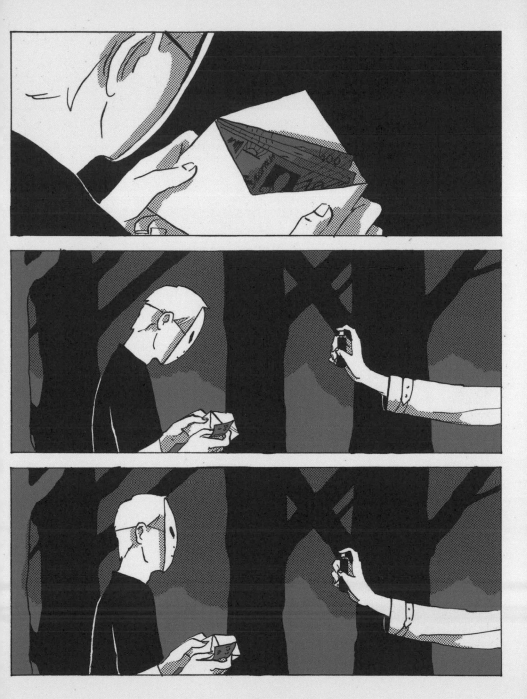

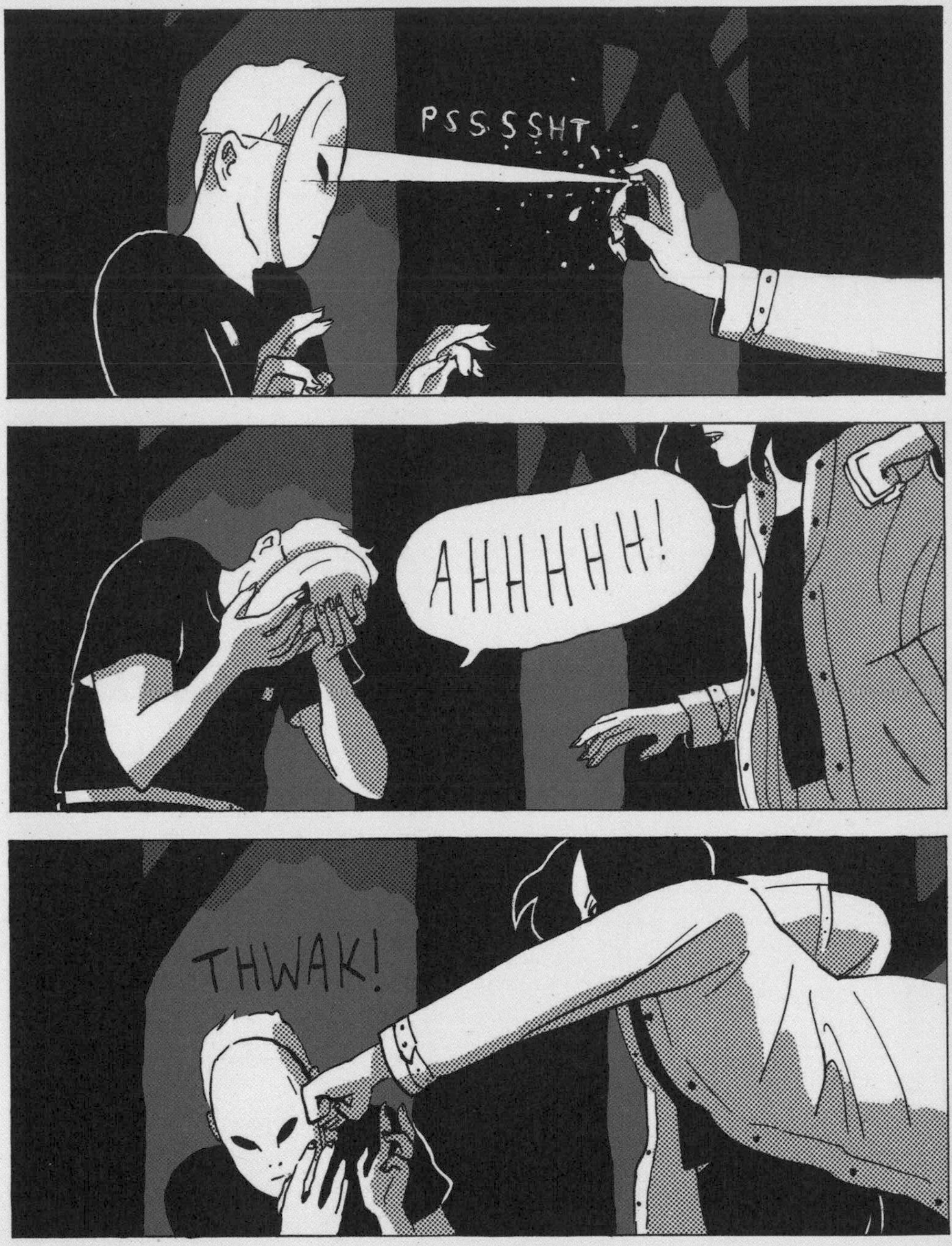
PSSSSHT
AHHHHH!
THWAK!

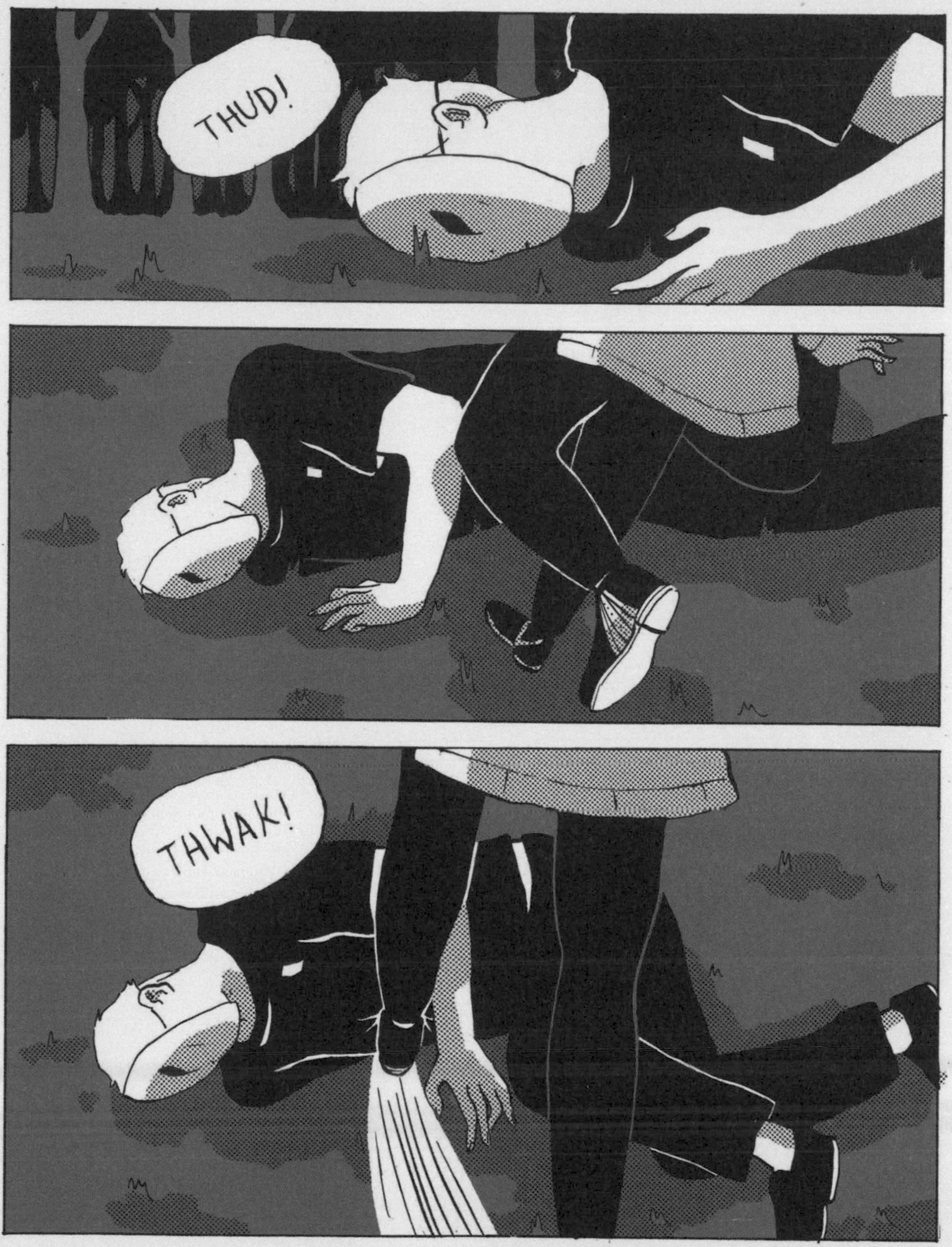
THUD!
THWAK!

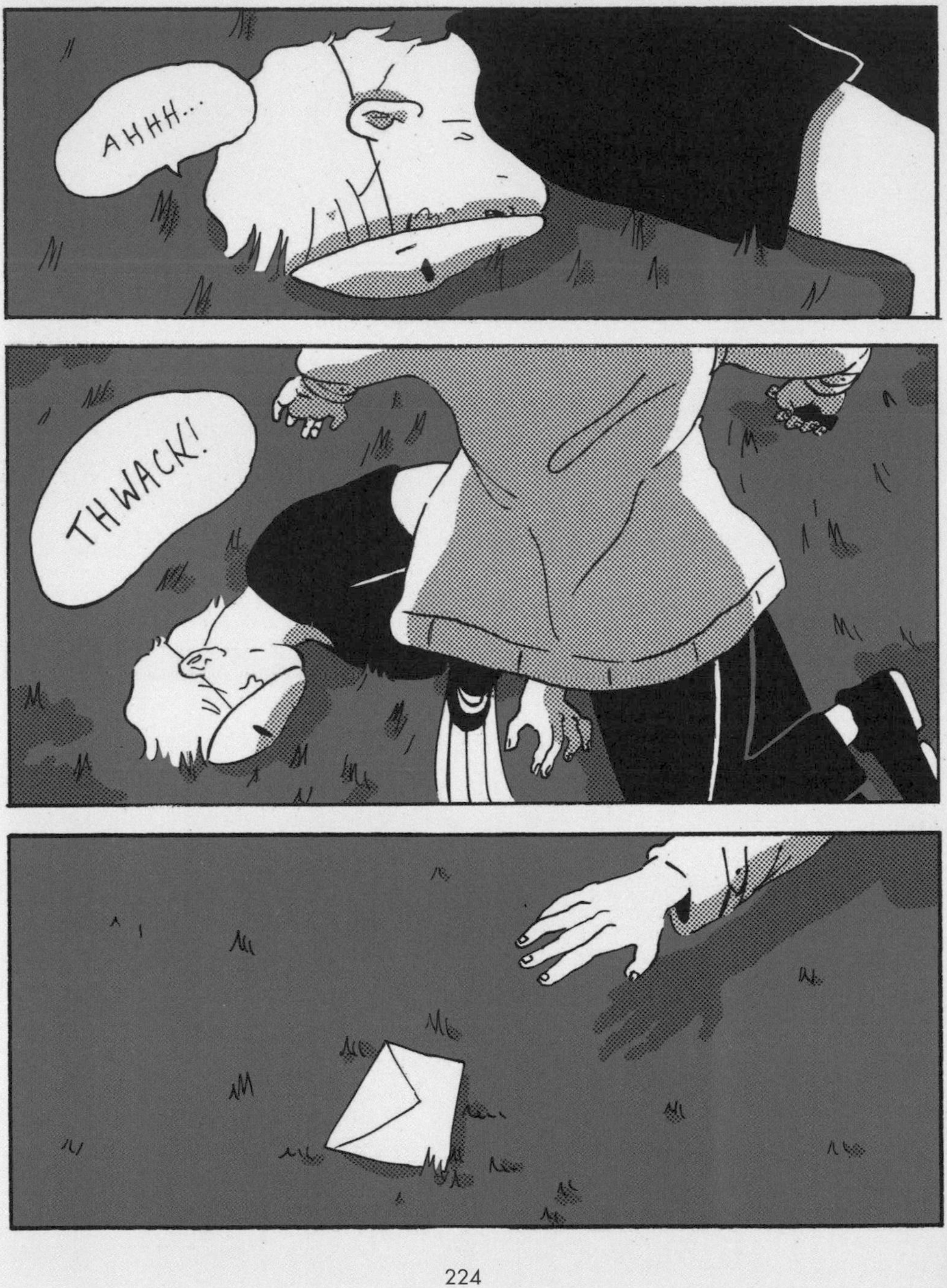
AHHH...
THWACK!

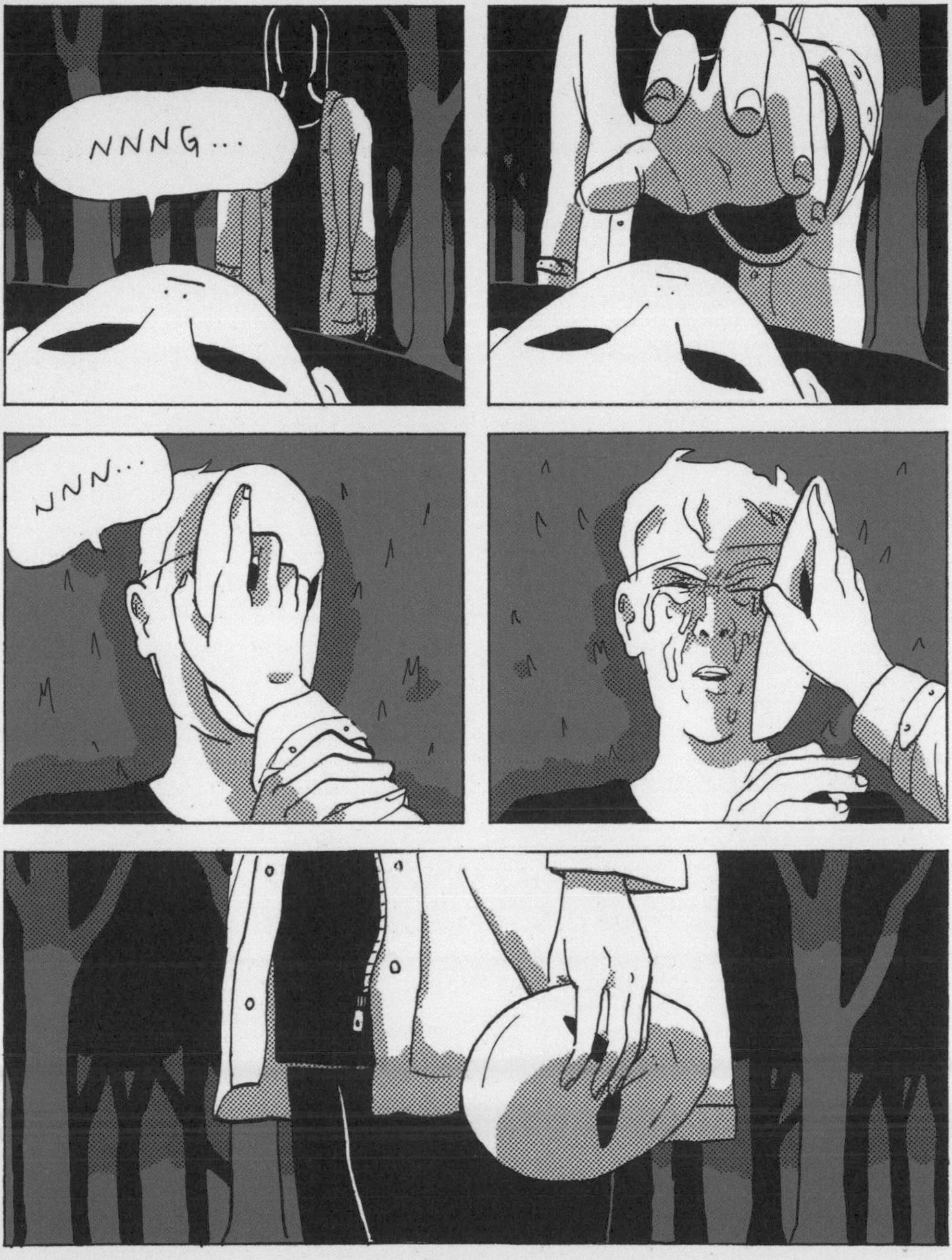
NNNG...
NNN...

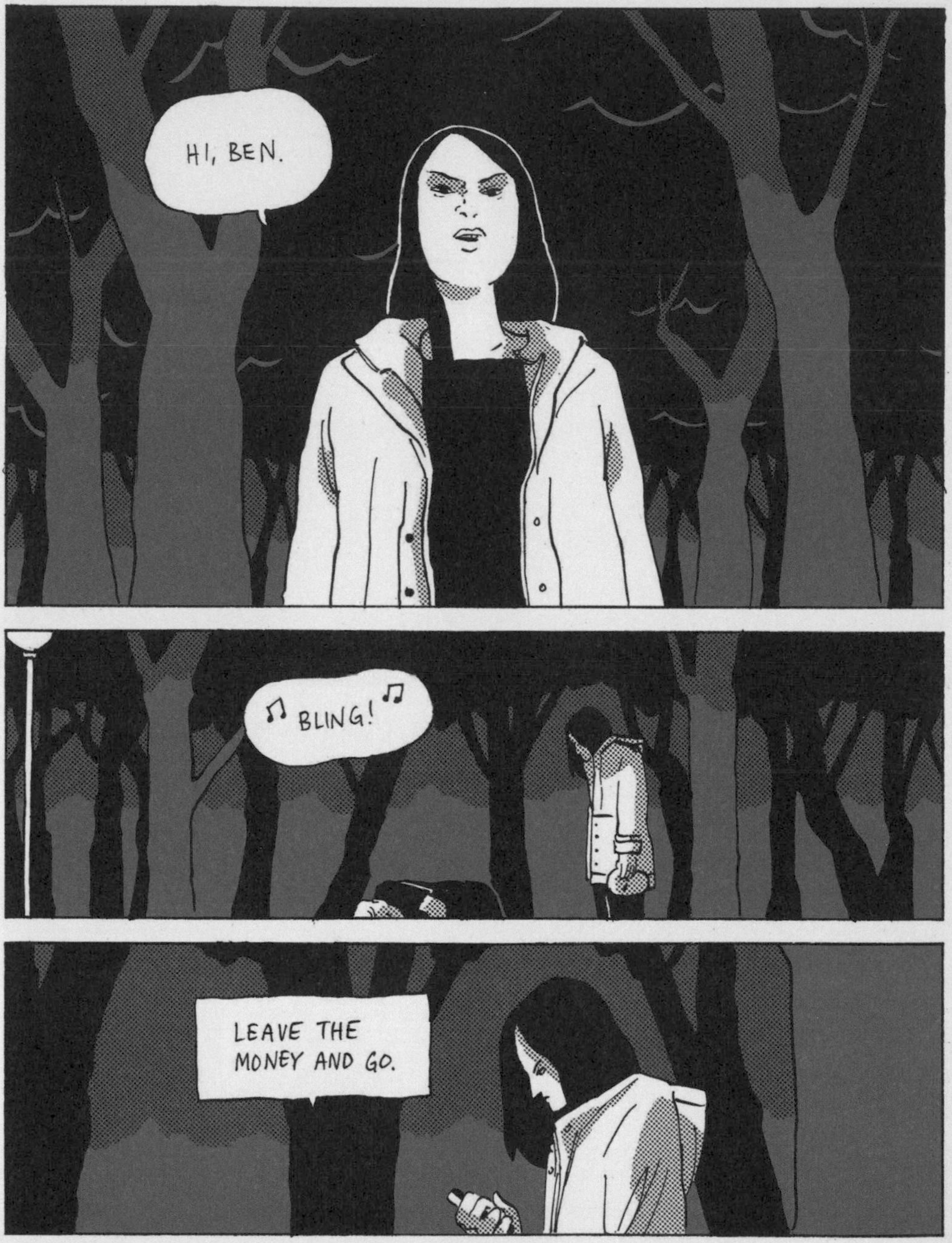
HI, BEN.
♫ BLING! ♫
LEAVE THE MONEY AND GO.

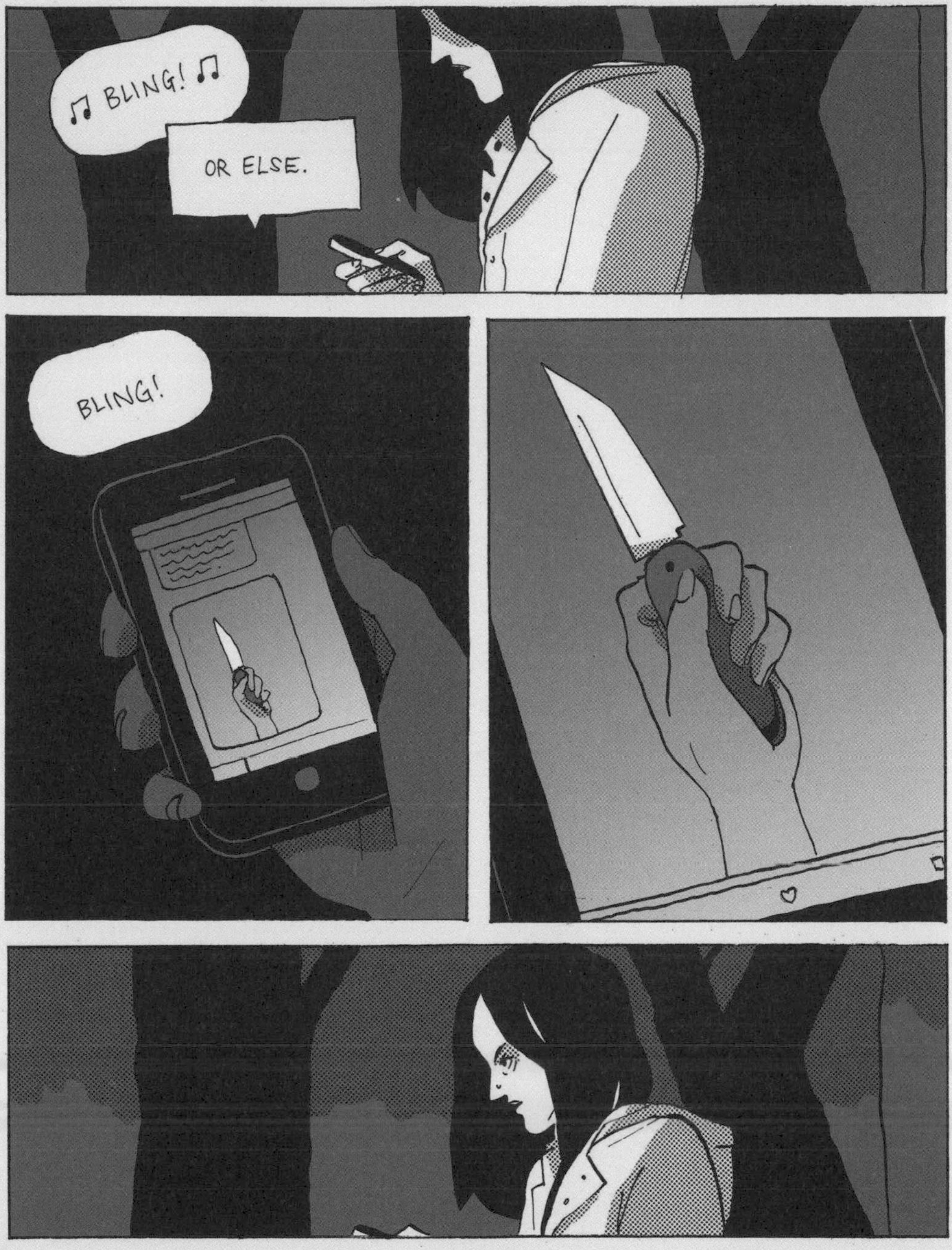
♫ BLING! ♫
OR ELSE.
BLING!

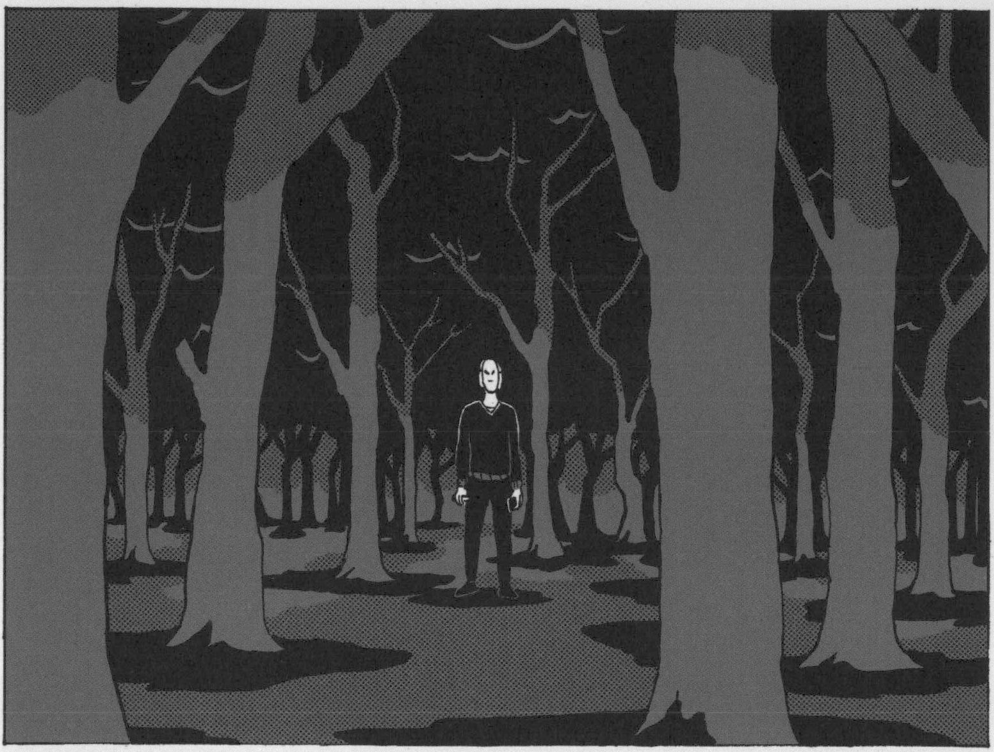

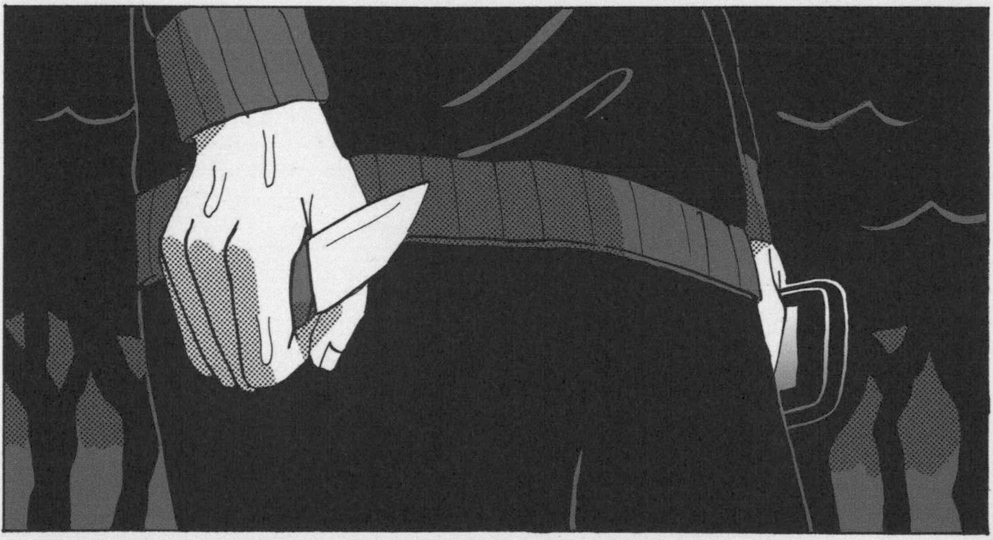

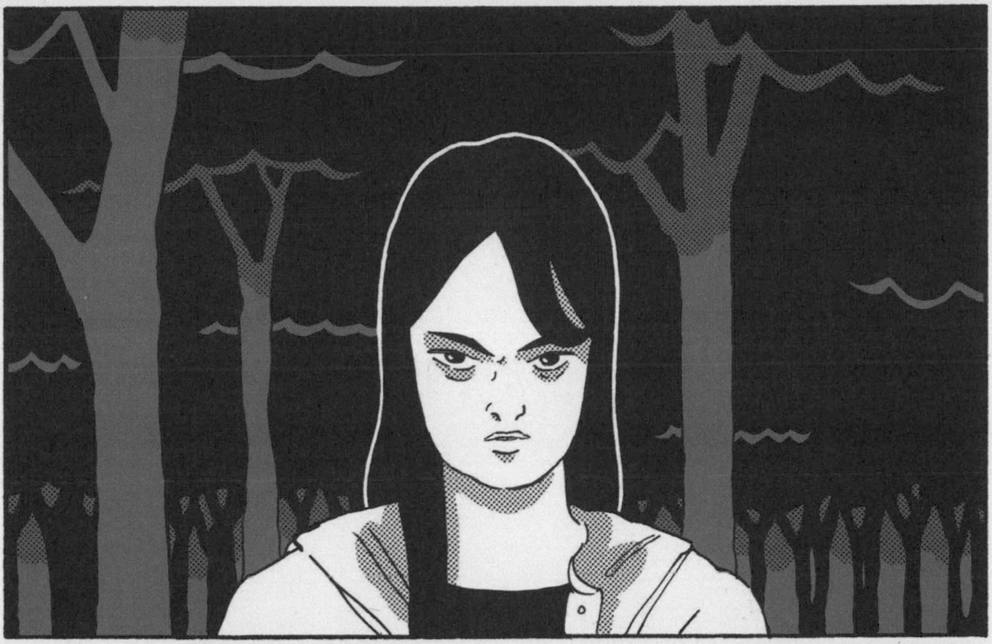

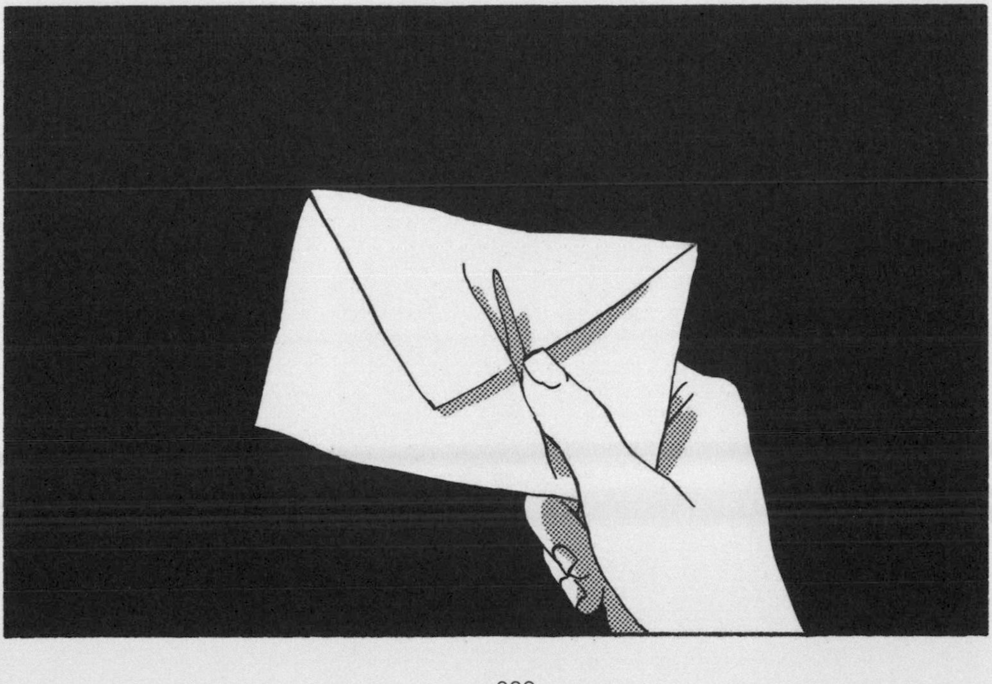

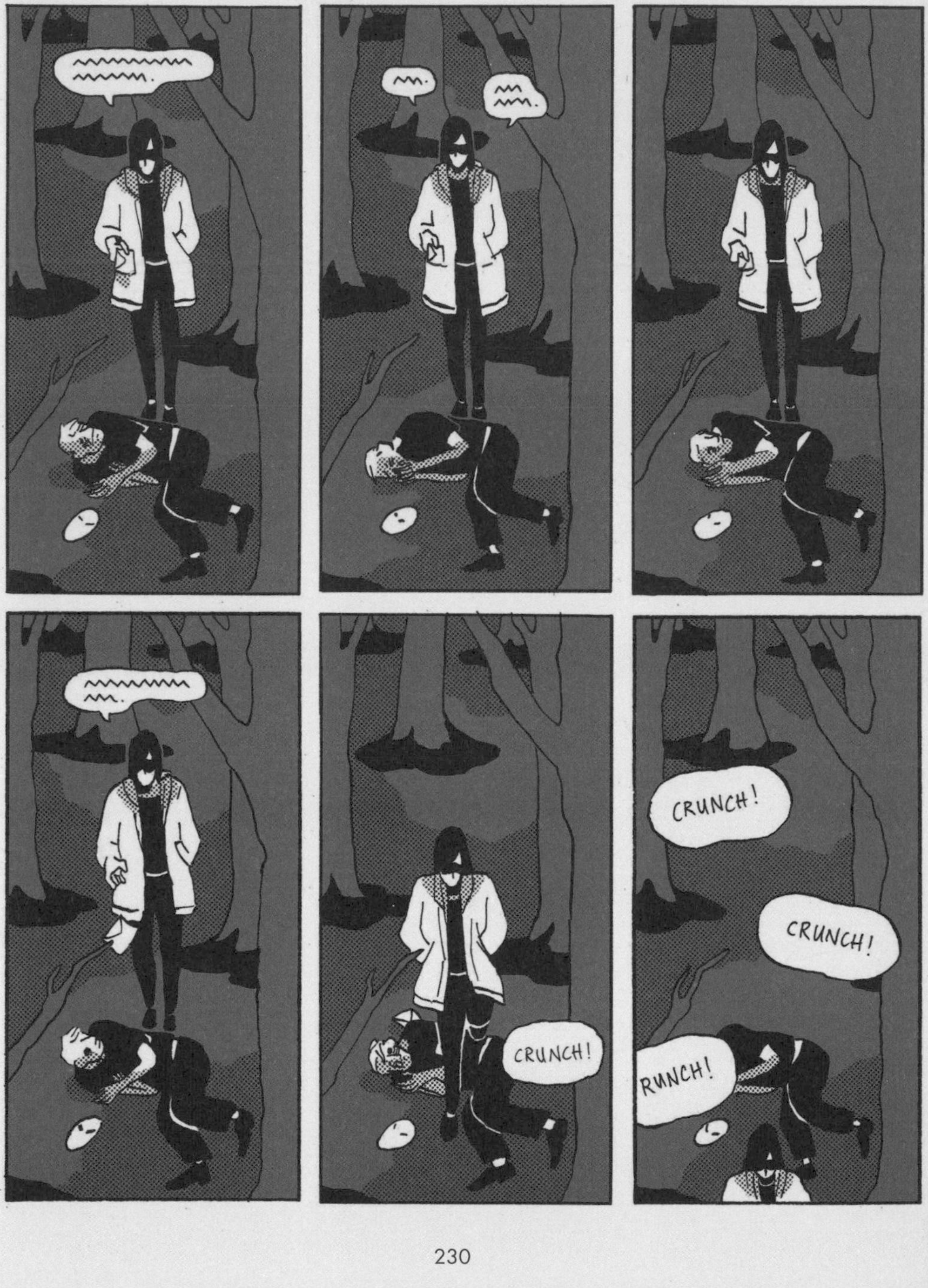
CRUNCH!
CRUNCH!
CRUNCH!
RUNCH!

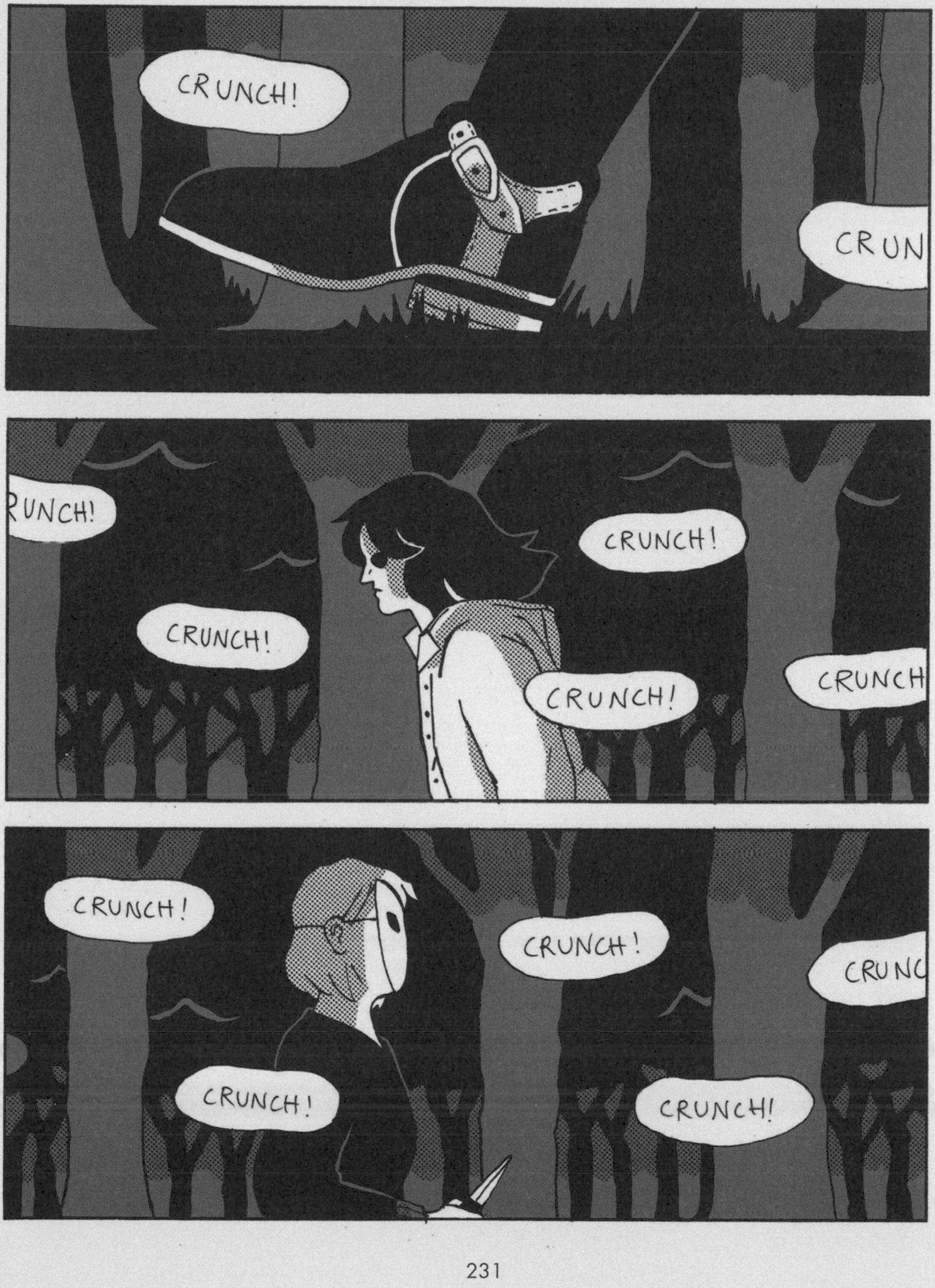
CRUNCH!
CRUN
RUNCH!
CRUNCH!
CRUNCH!
CRUNCH!
CRUNCH
CRUNCH!
CRUNCH!
CRUNC
CRUNCH!
CRUNCH!

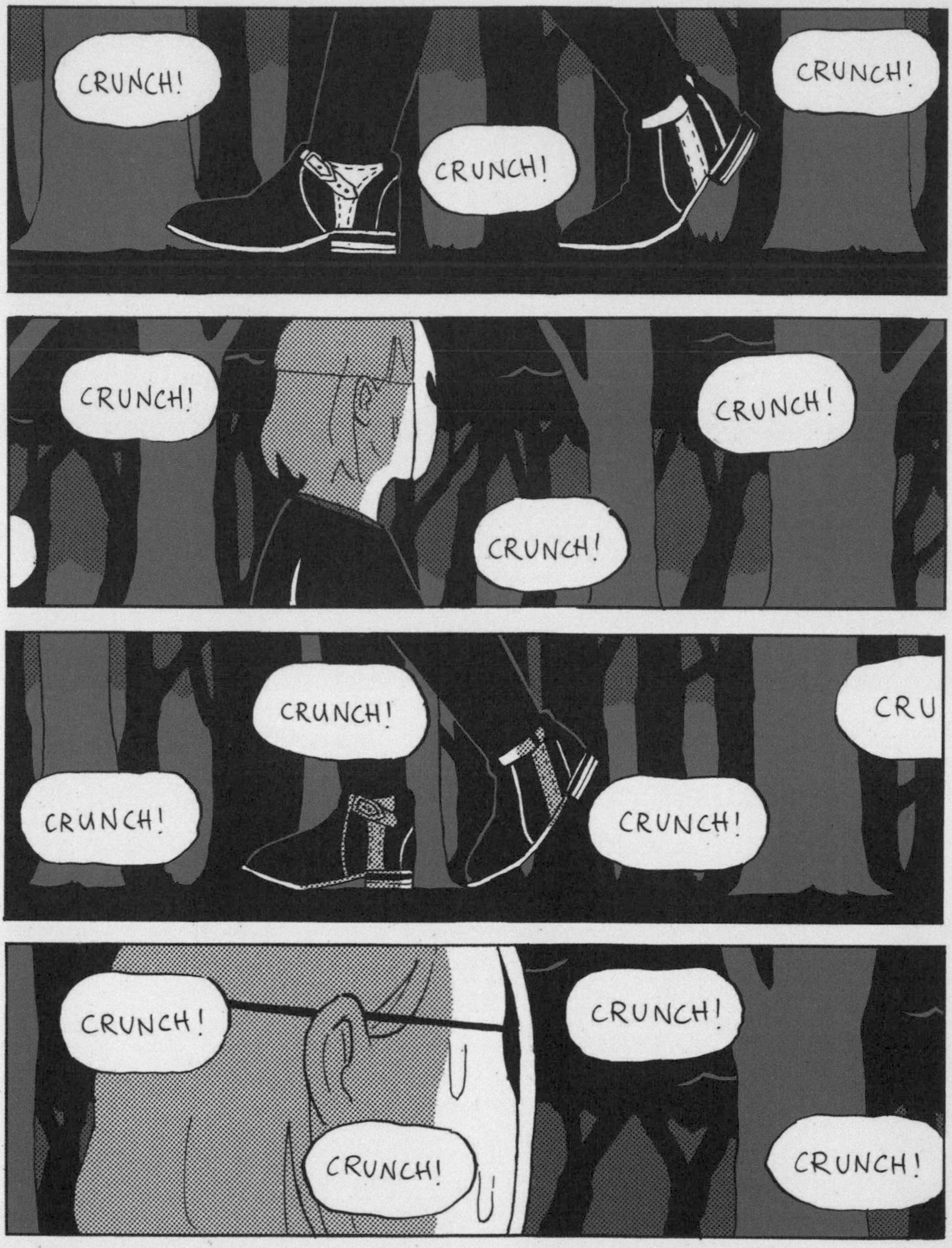
CRUNCH!
CRUNCH!
CRUNCH!
CRUNCH!
CRUNCH!
CRUNCH!
CRUNCH!
CRUNCH!
CRUNCH!
CRU
CRUNCH!
CRUNCH!
CRUNCH!
CRUNCH!

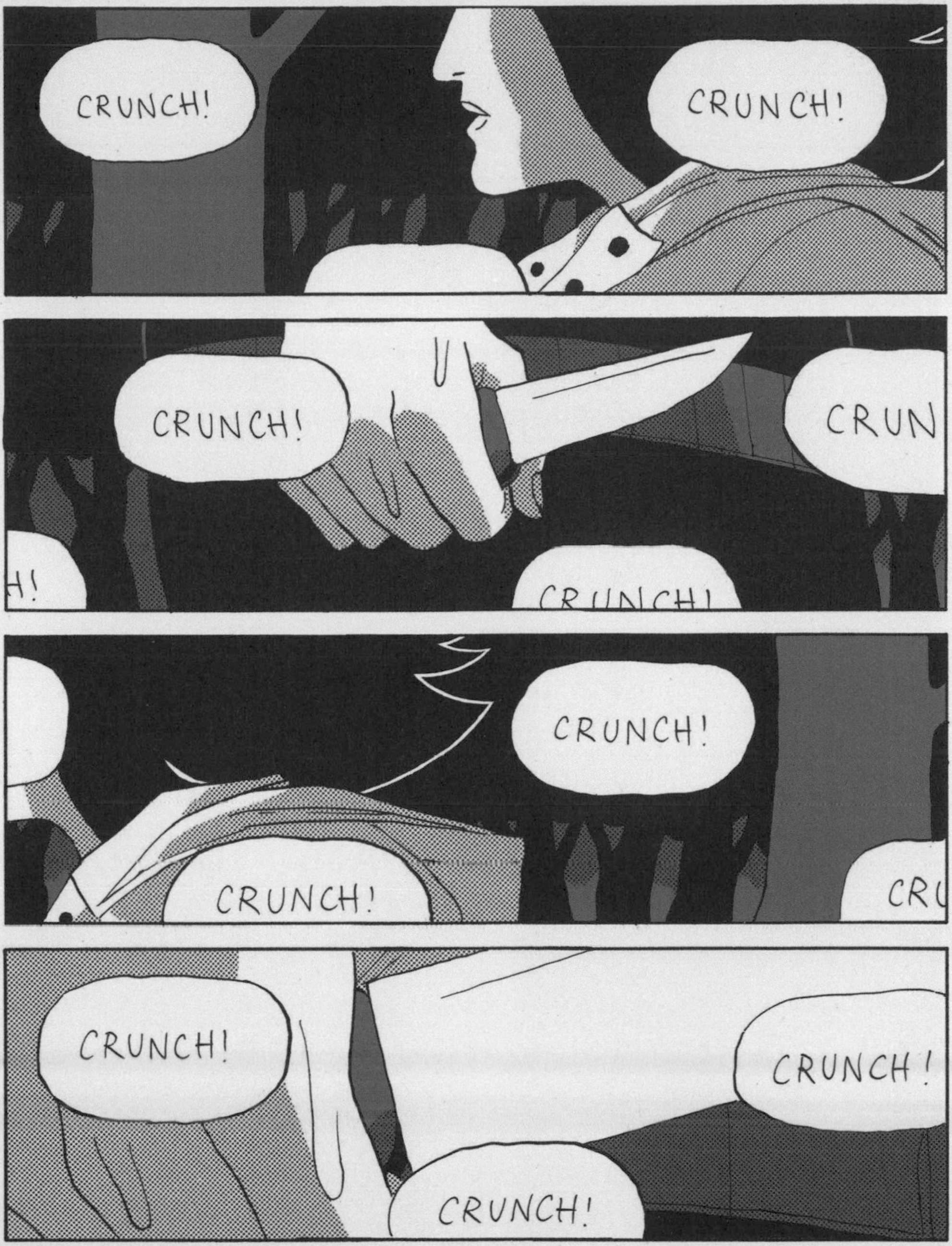
CRUNCH!
CRUNCH!
CRUNCH!
CRUNCH!
CRUNCH!
CRUNCH!
CRUNCH!
CRUNCH!

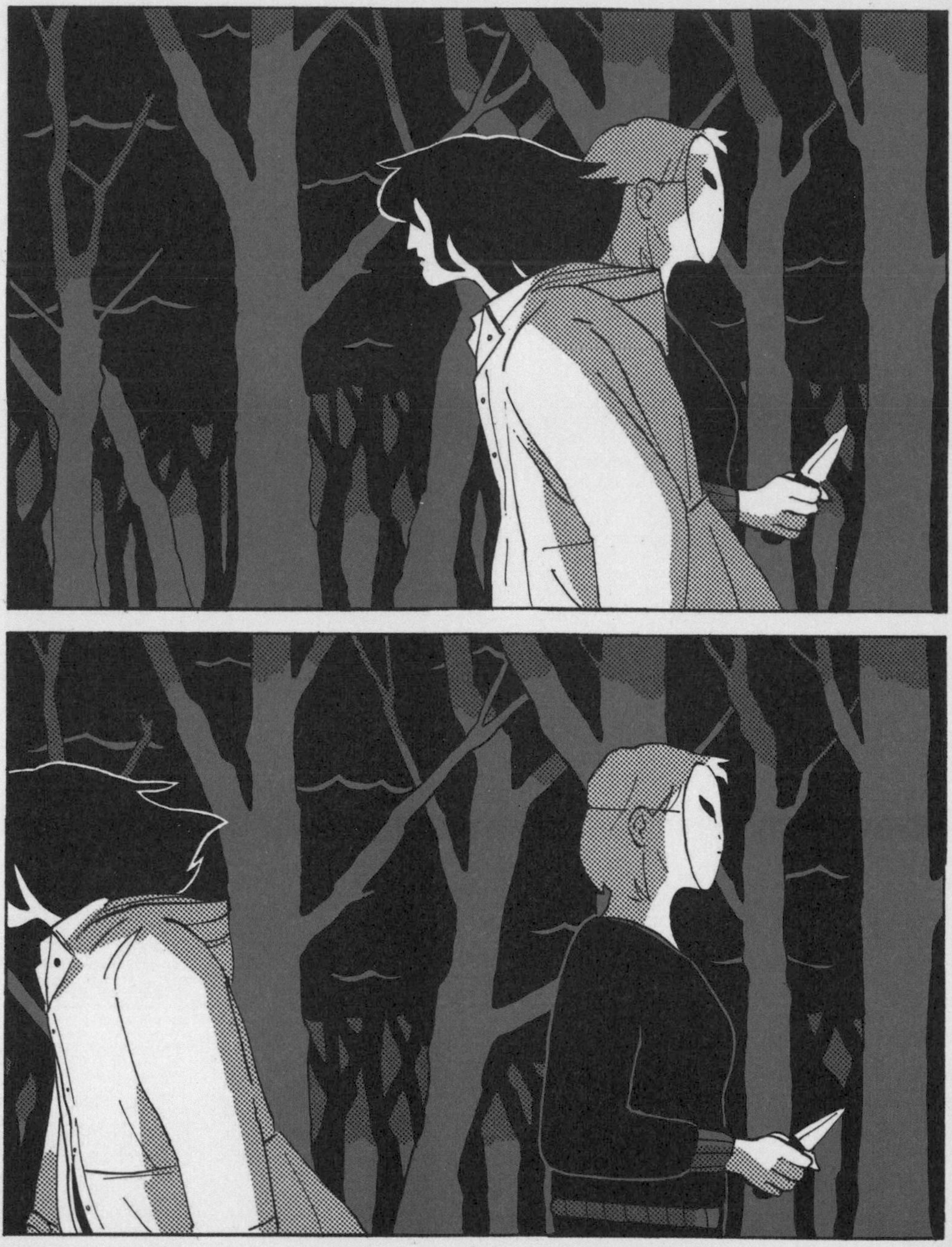

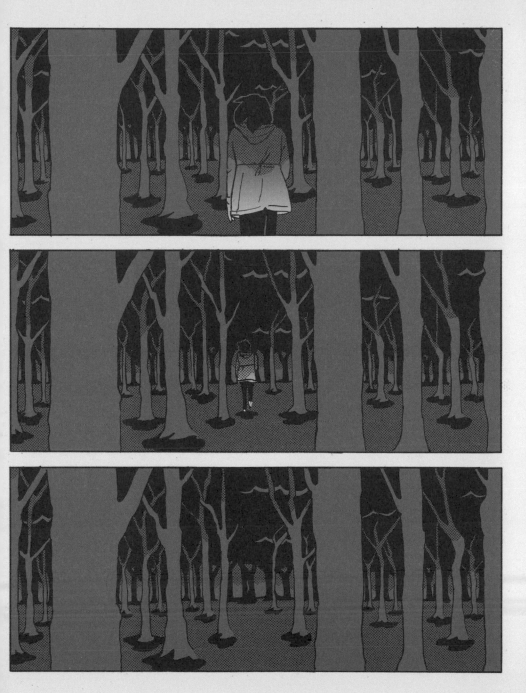

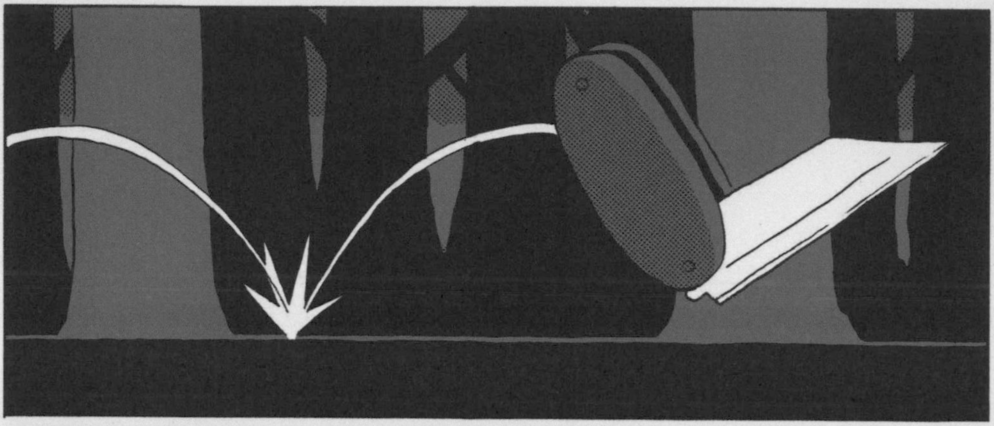

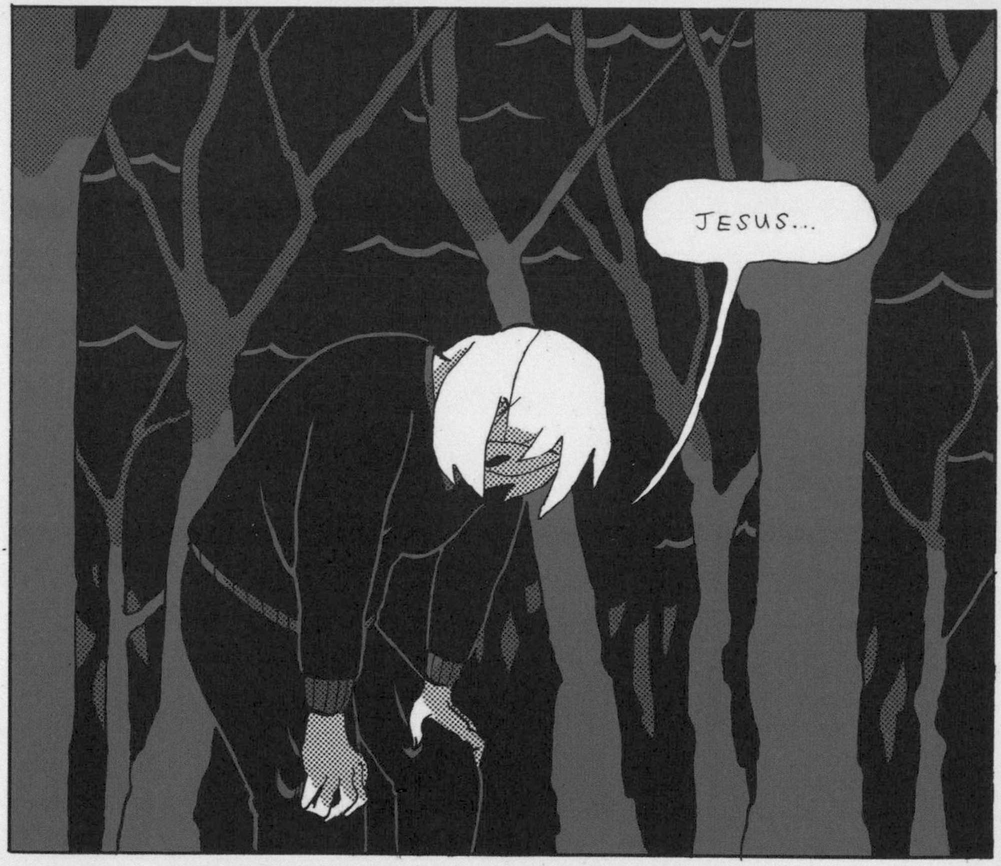
JESUS...

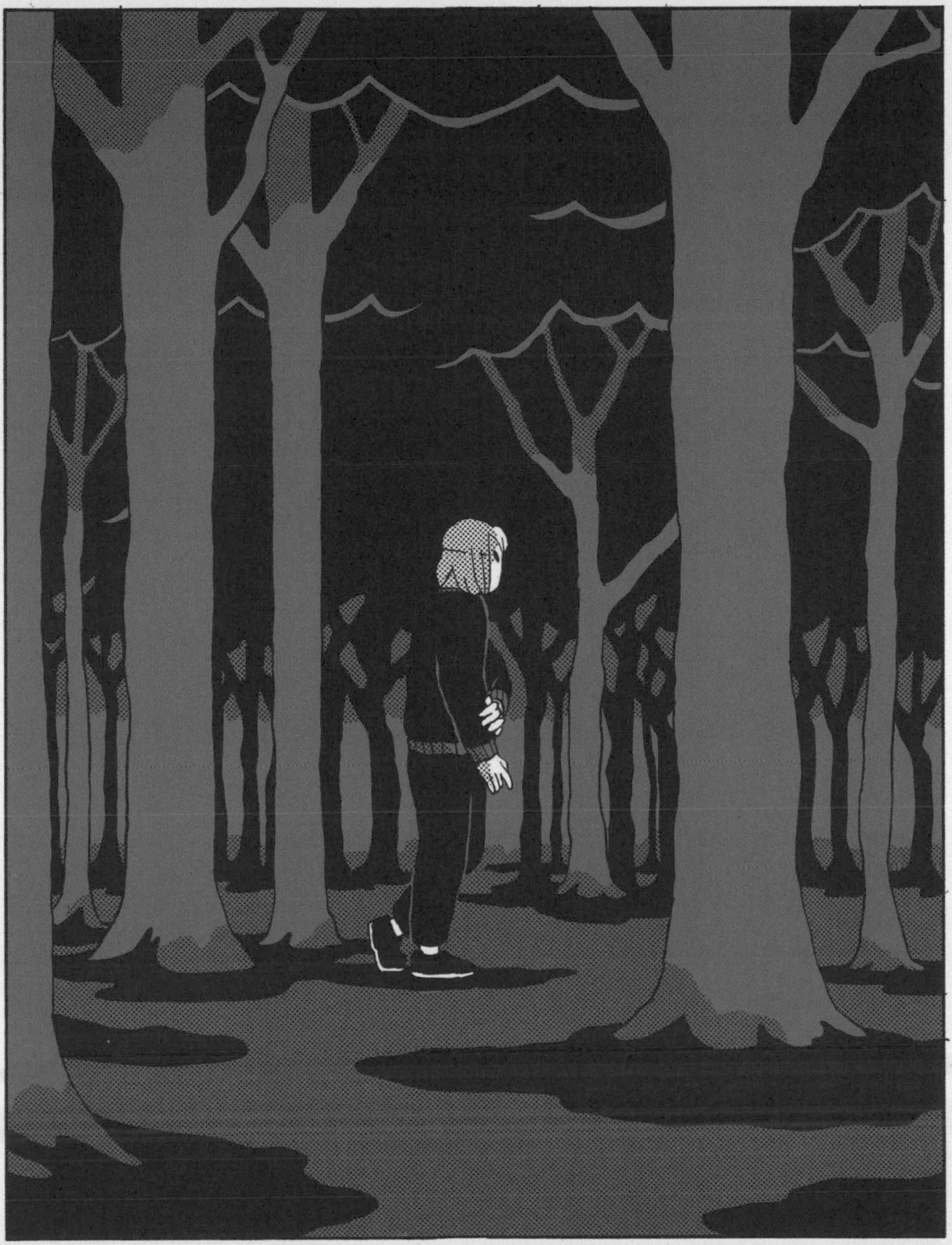

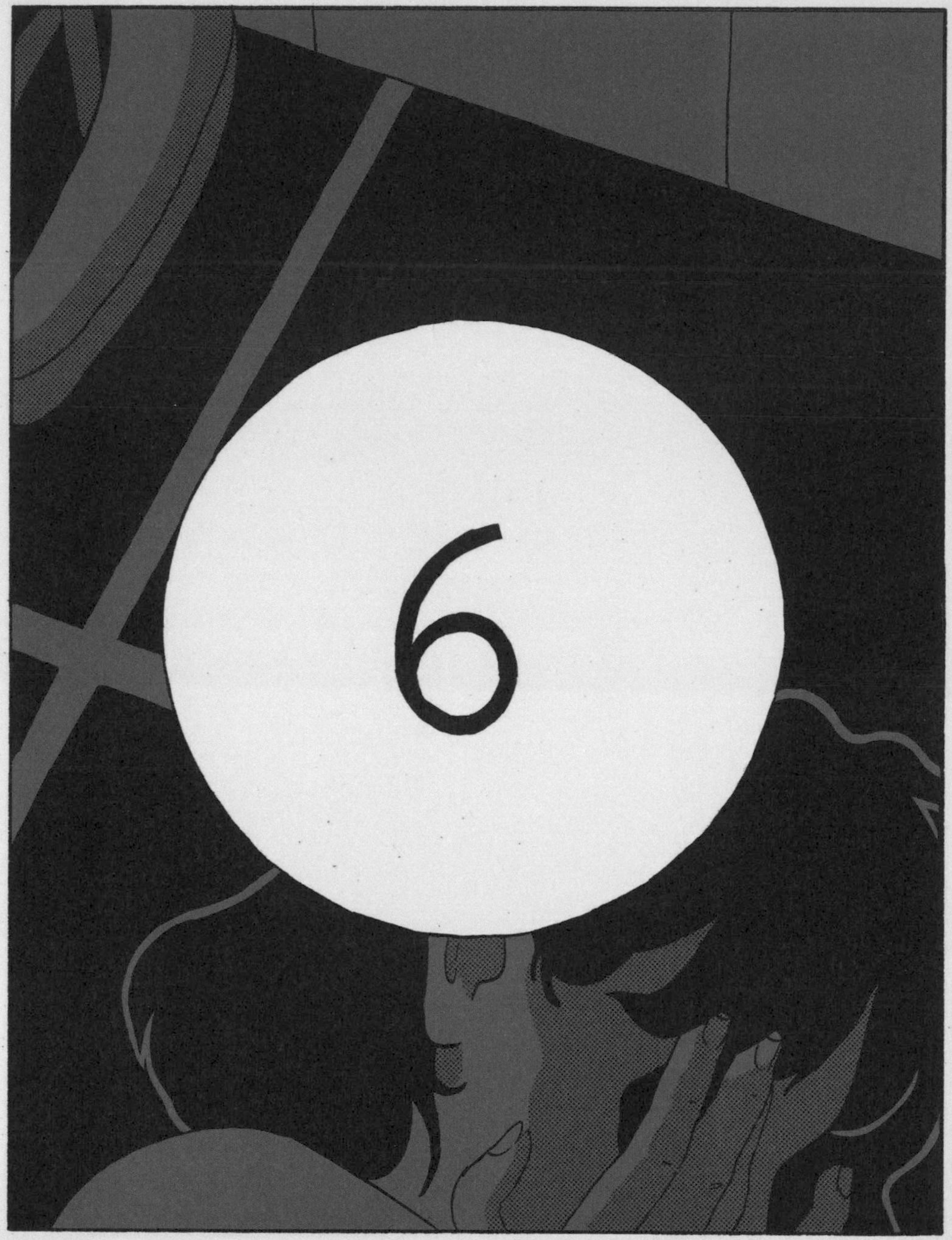
6

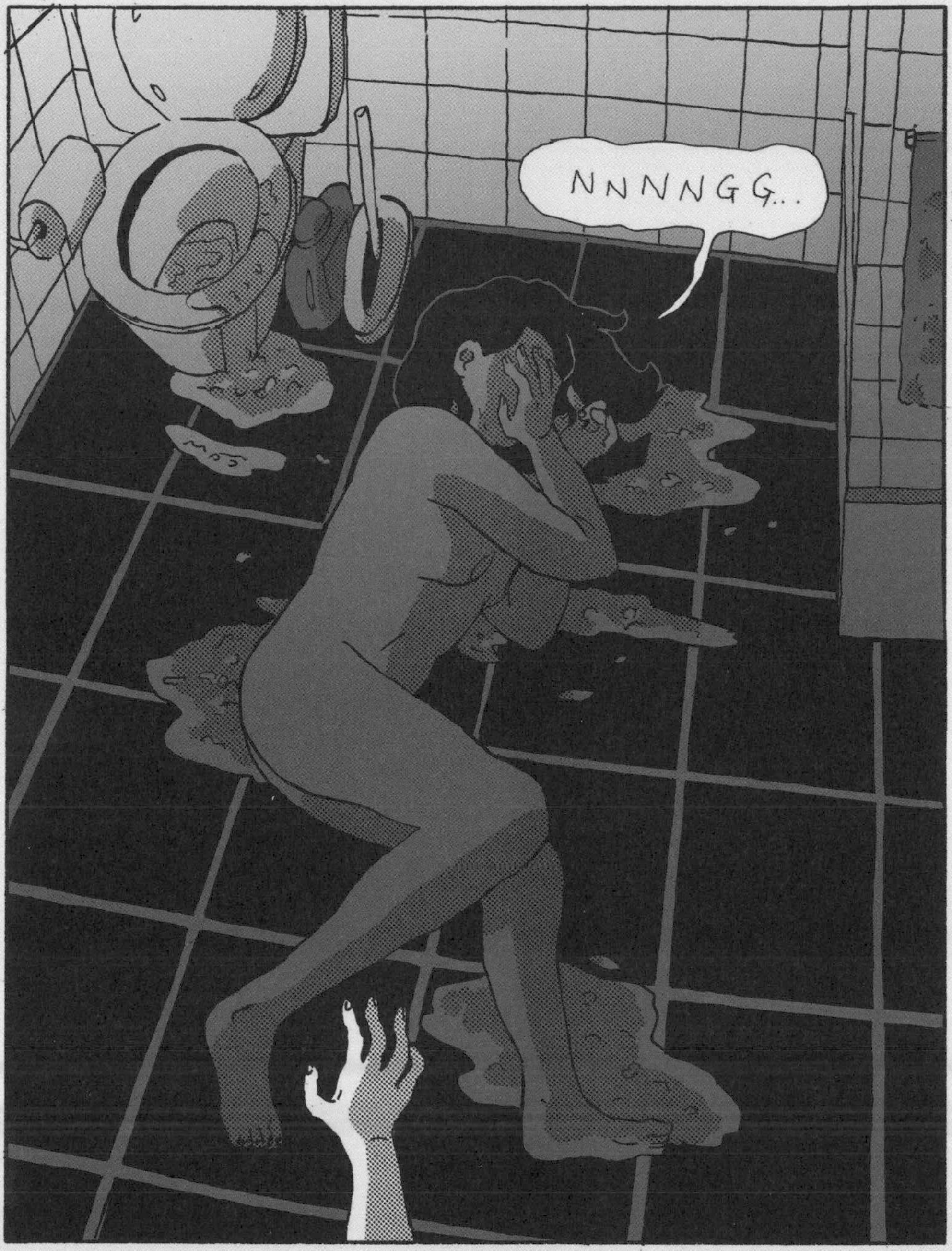
NNNNGG...

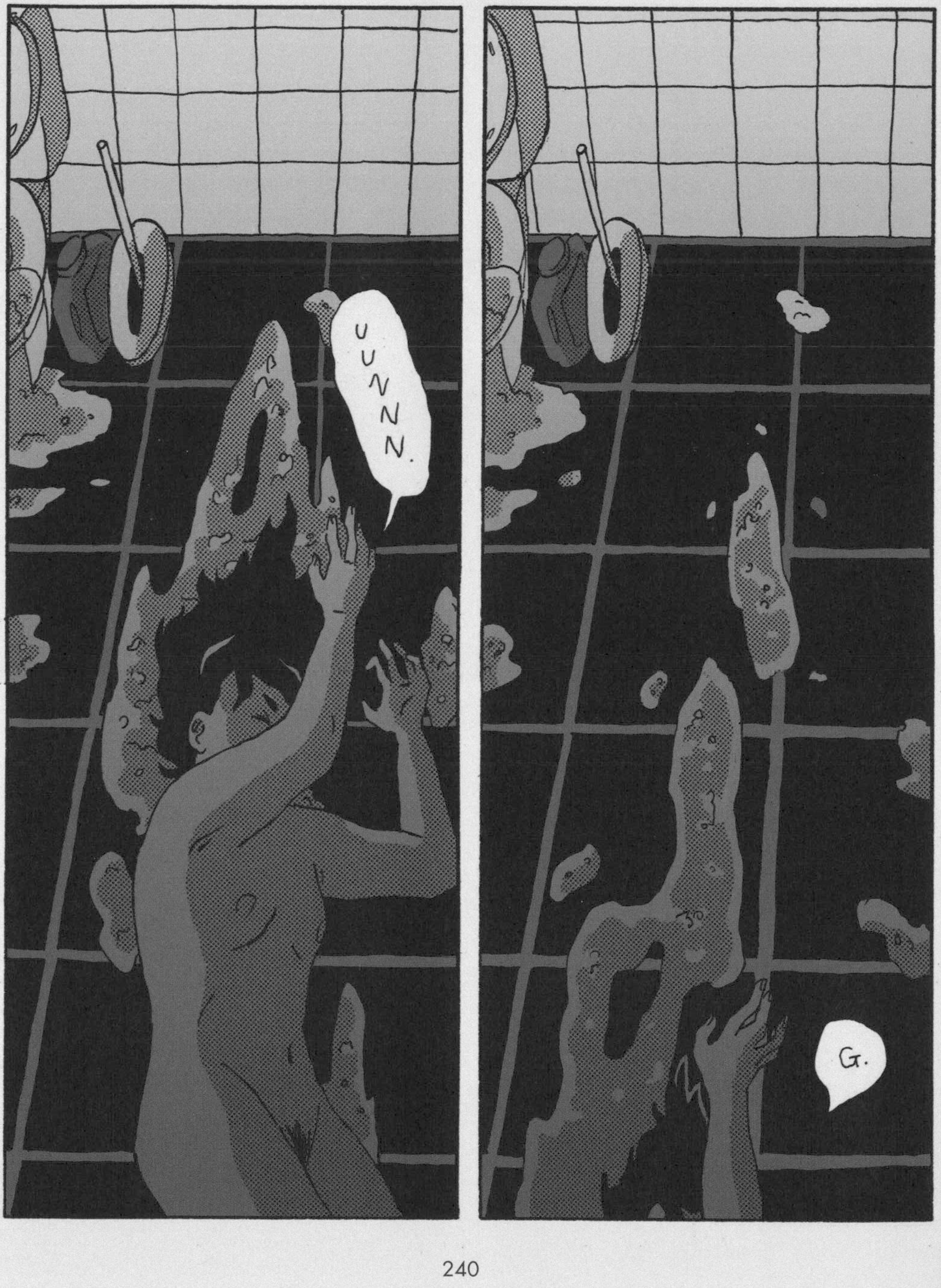
UUNNN.
G.

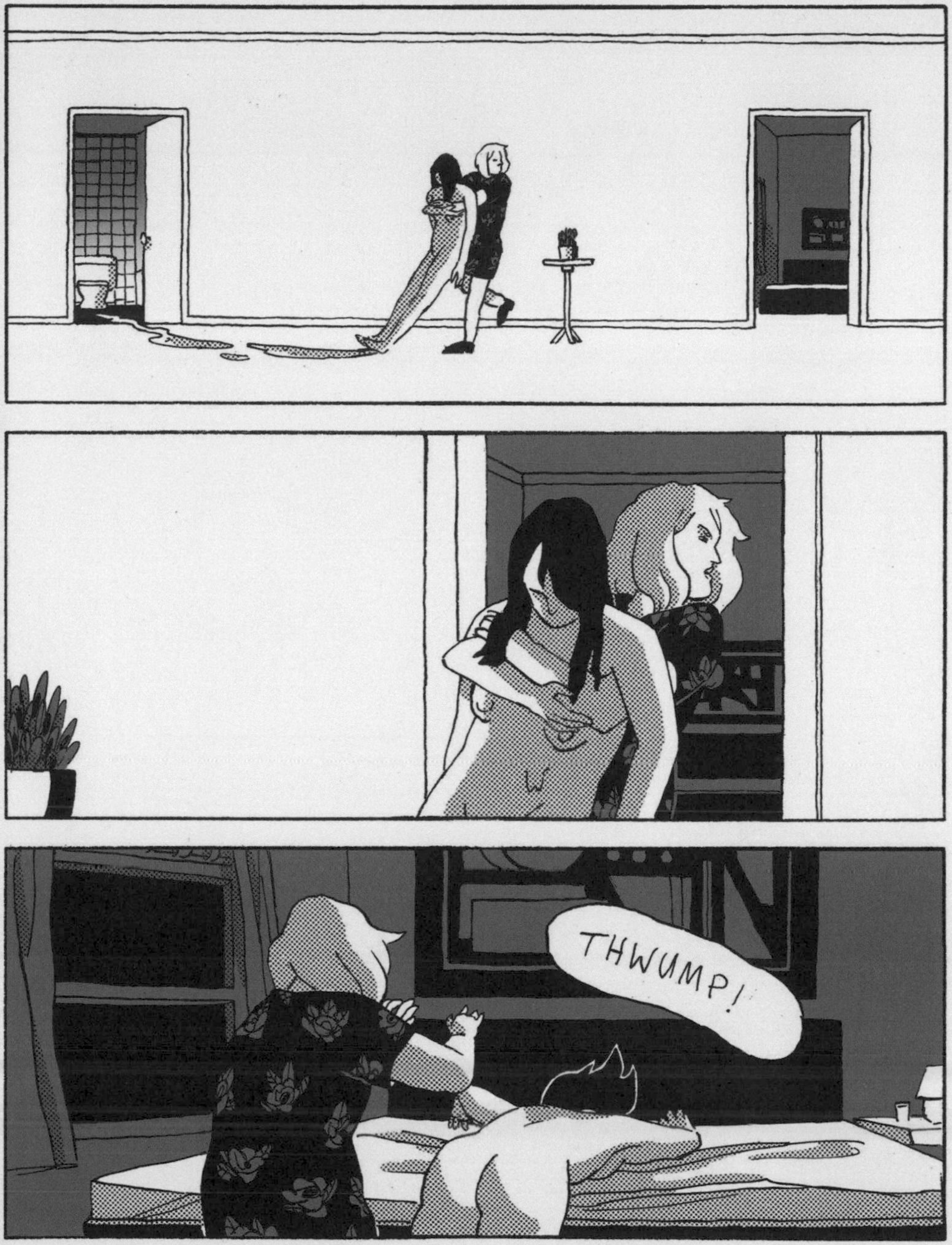
THWUMP!

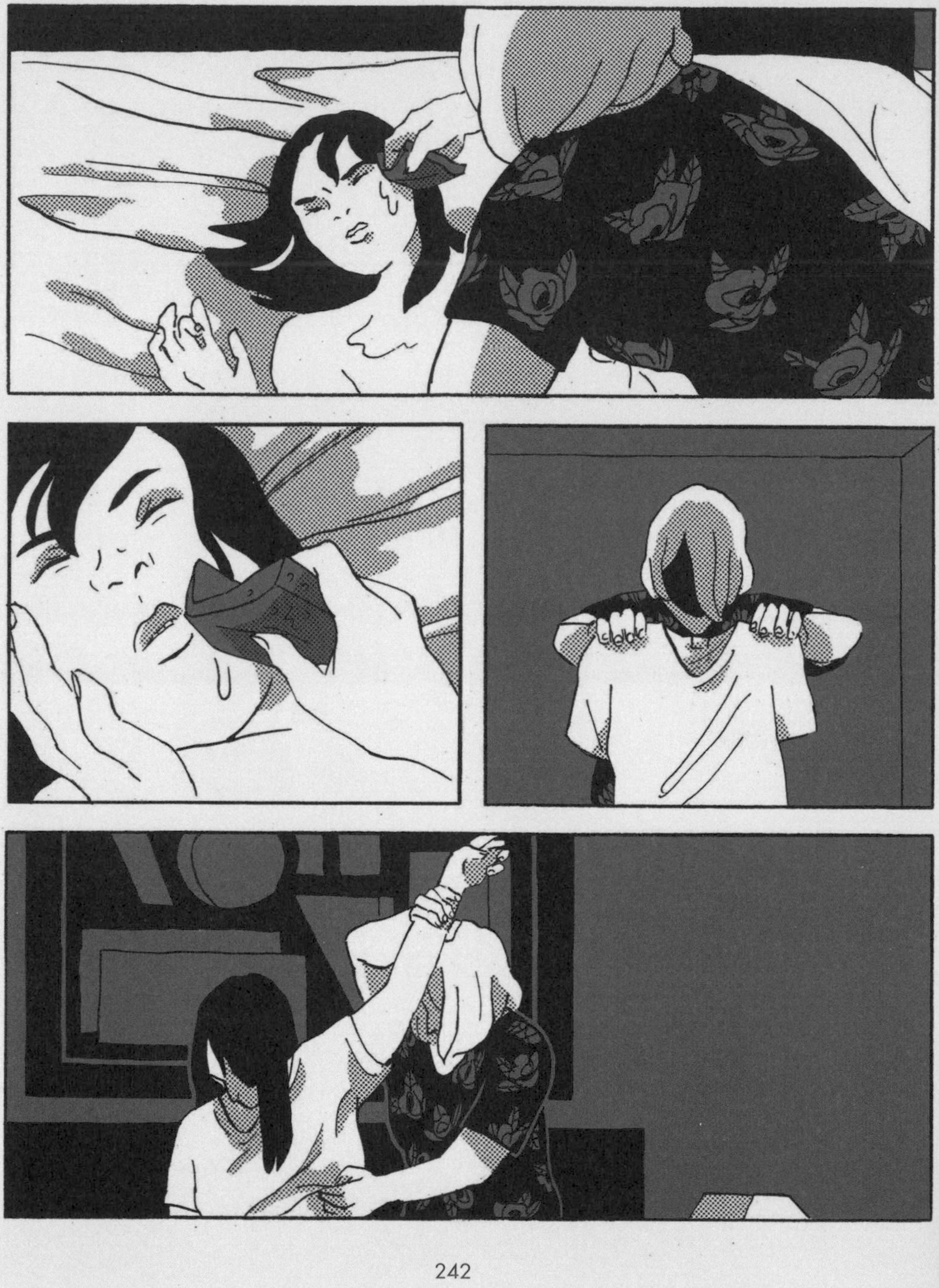

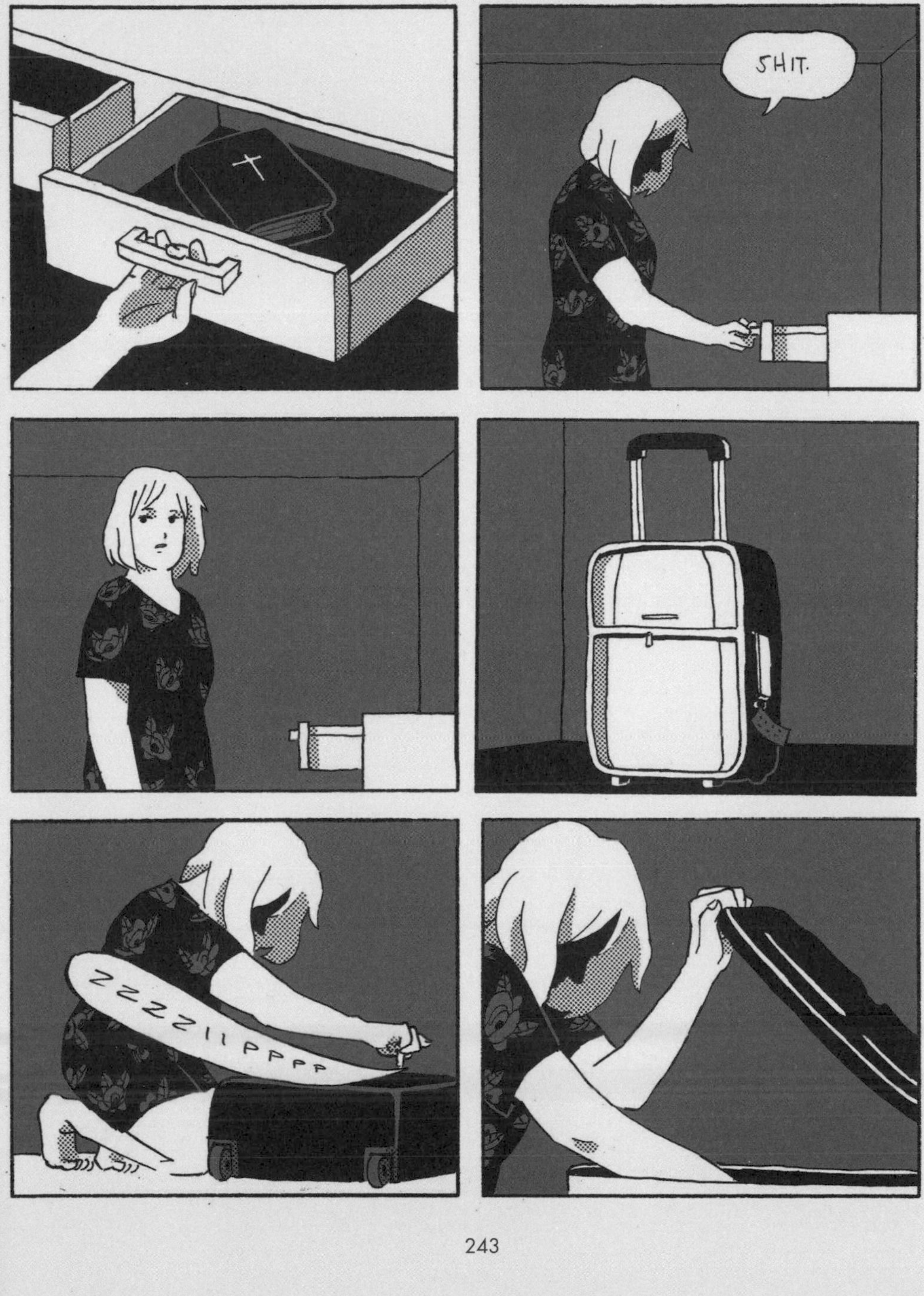
SHIT.
ZZZZZIIPPPP

12 regular

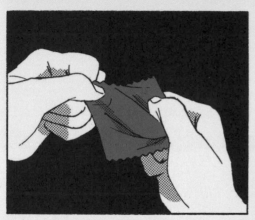

UGH. FUCKING THING.

RIP

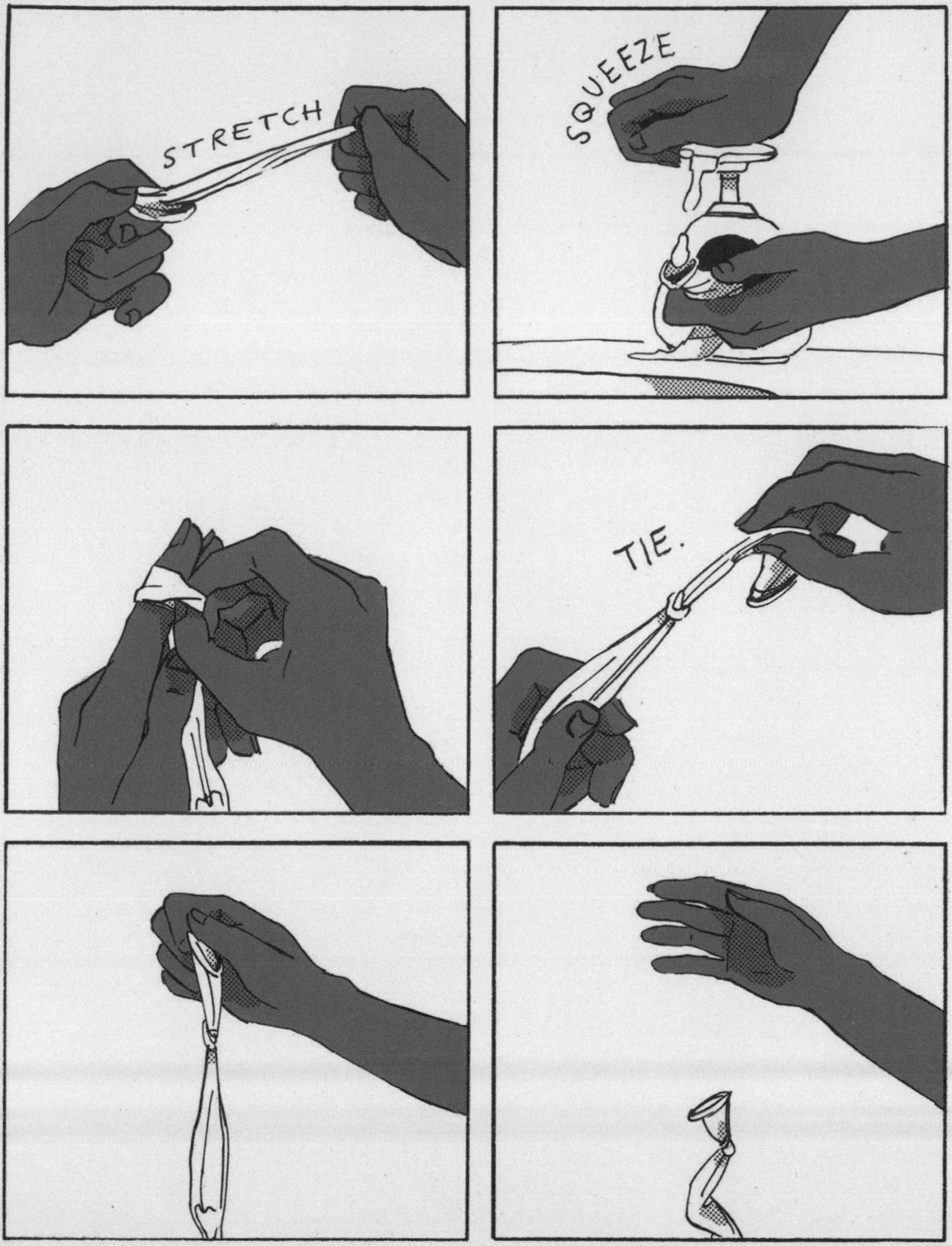
STRETCH
SQUEEZE
TIE.

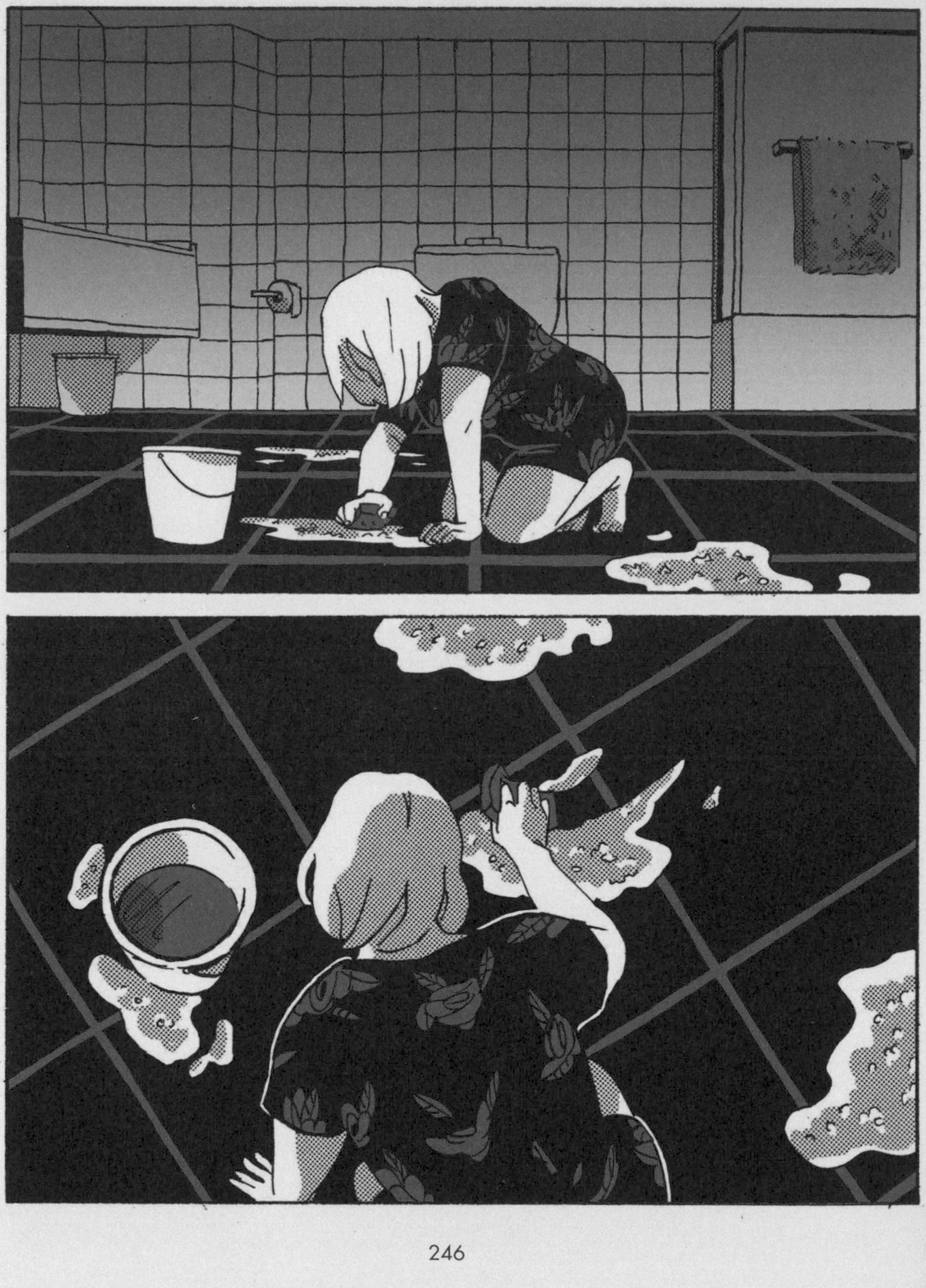

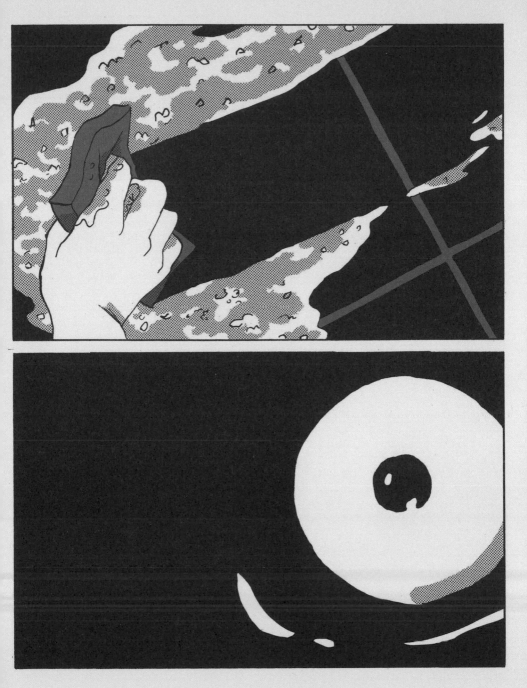

247

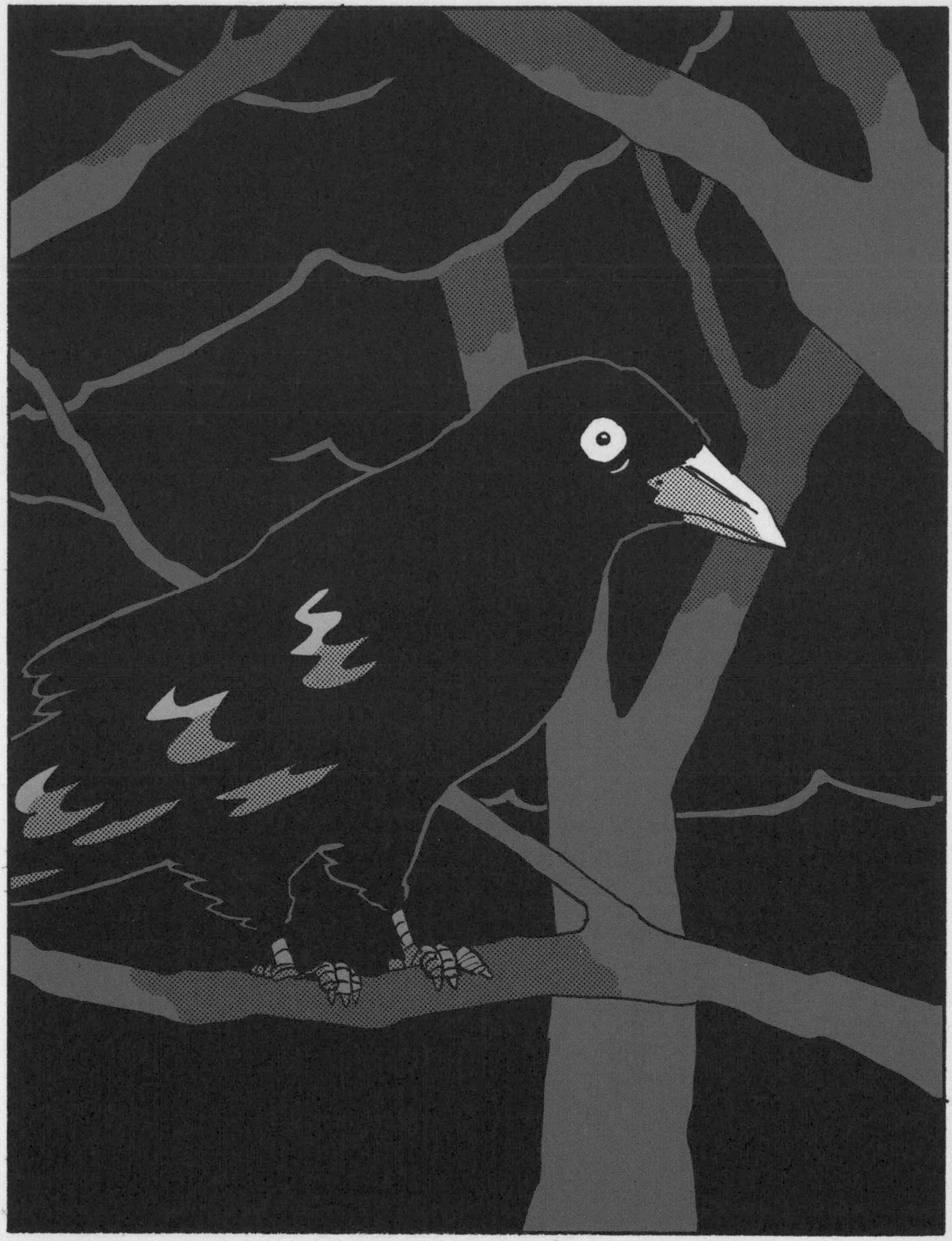

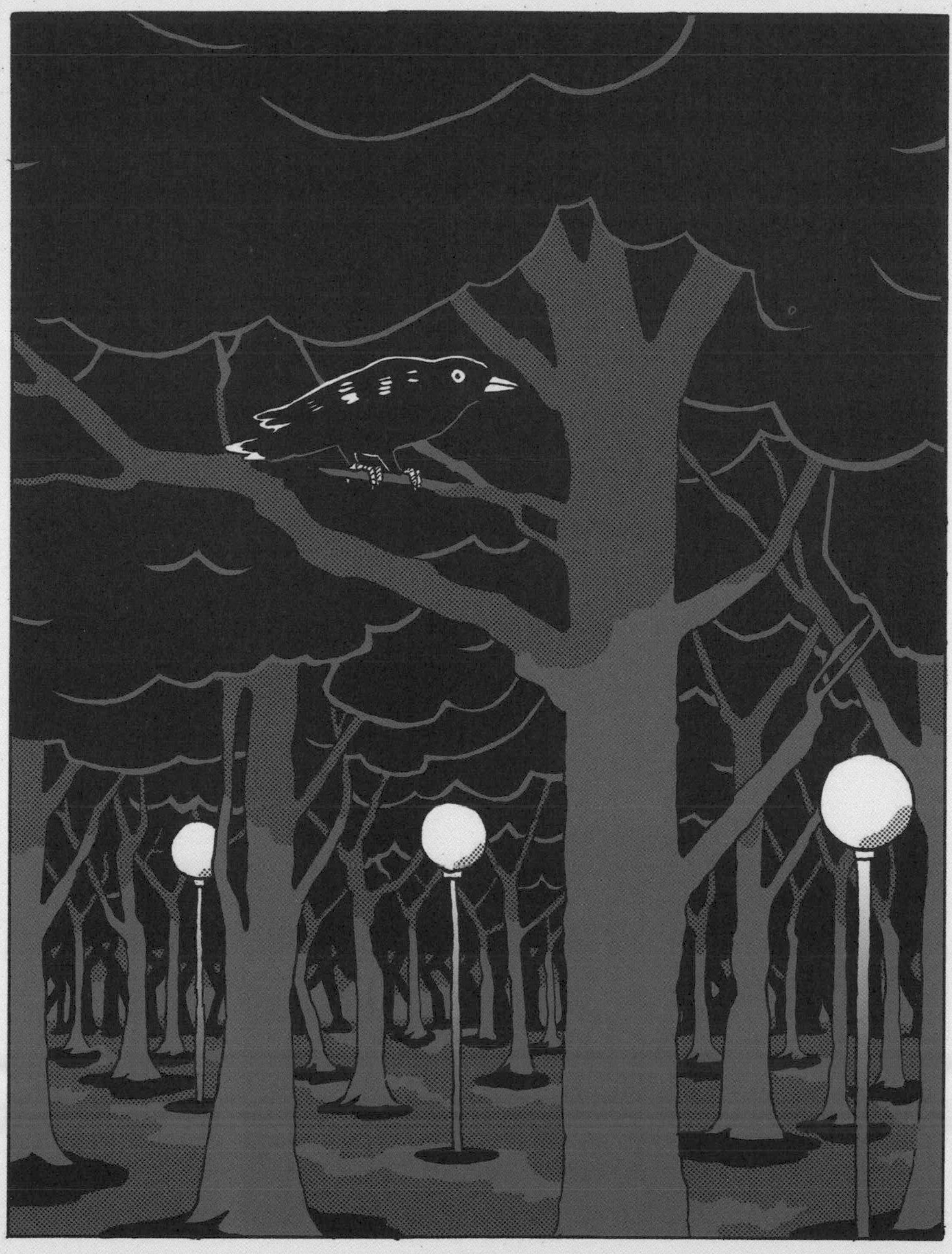

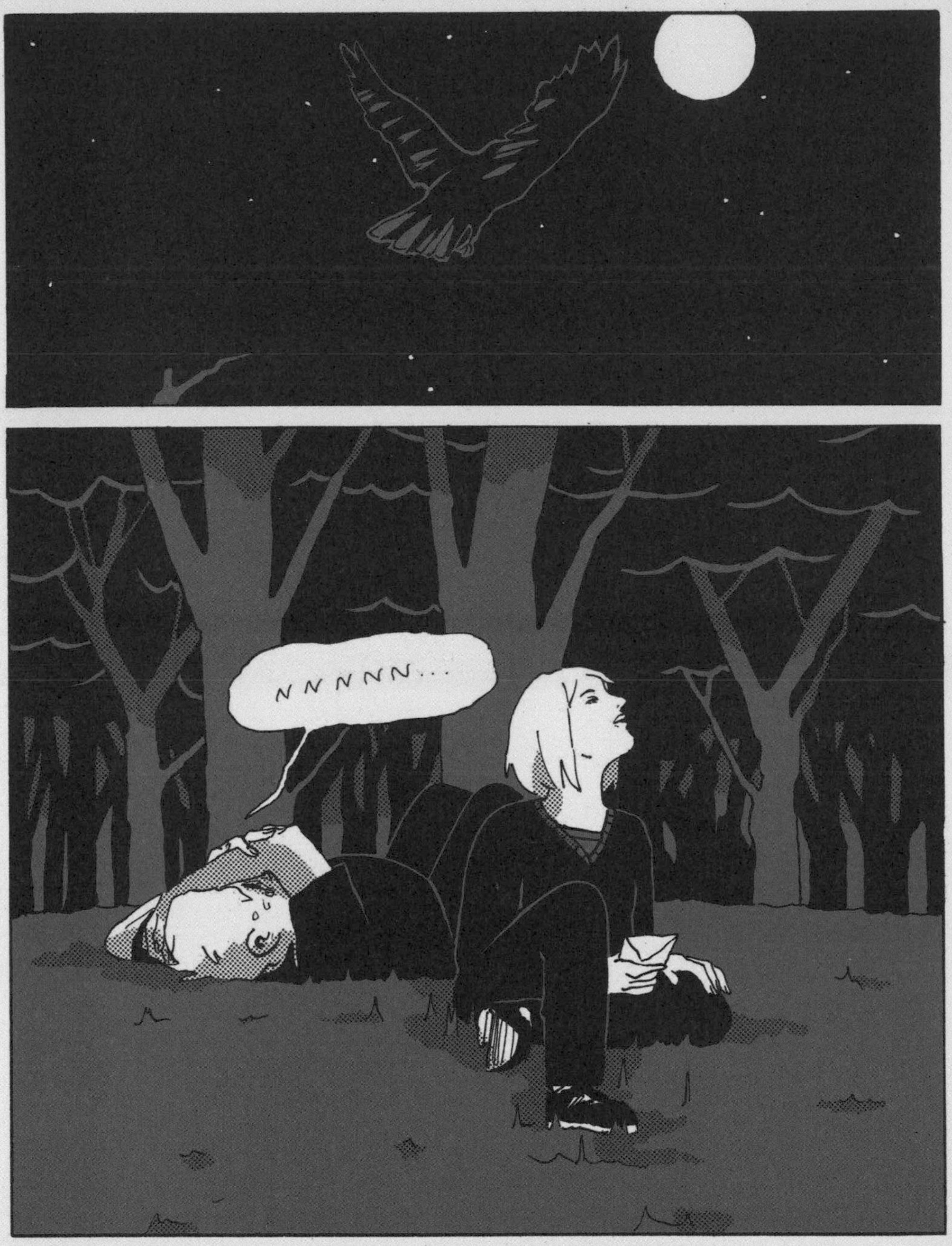
NNNNN...

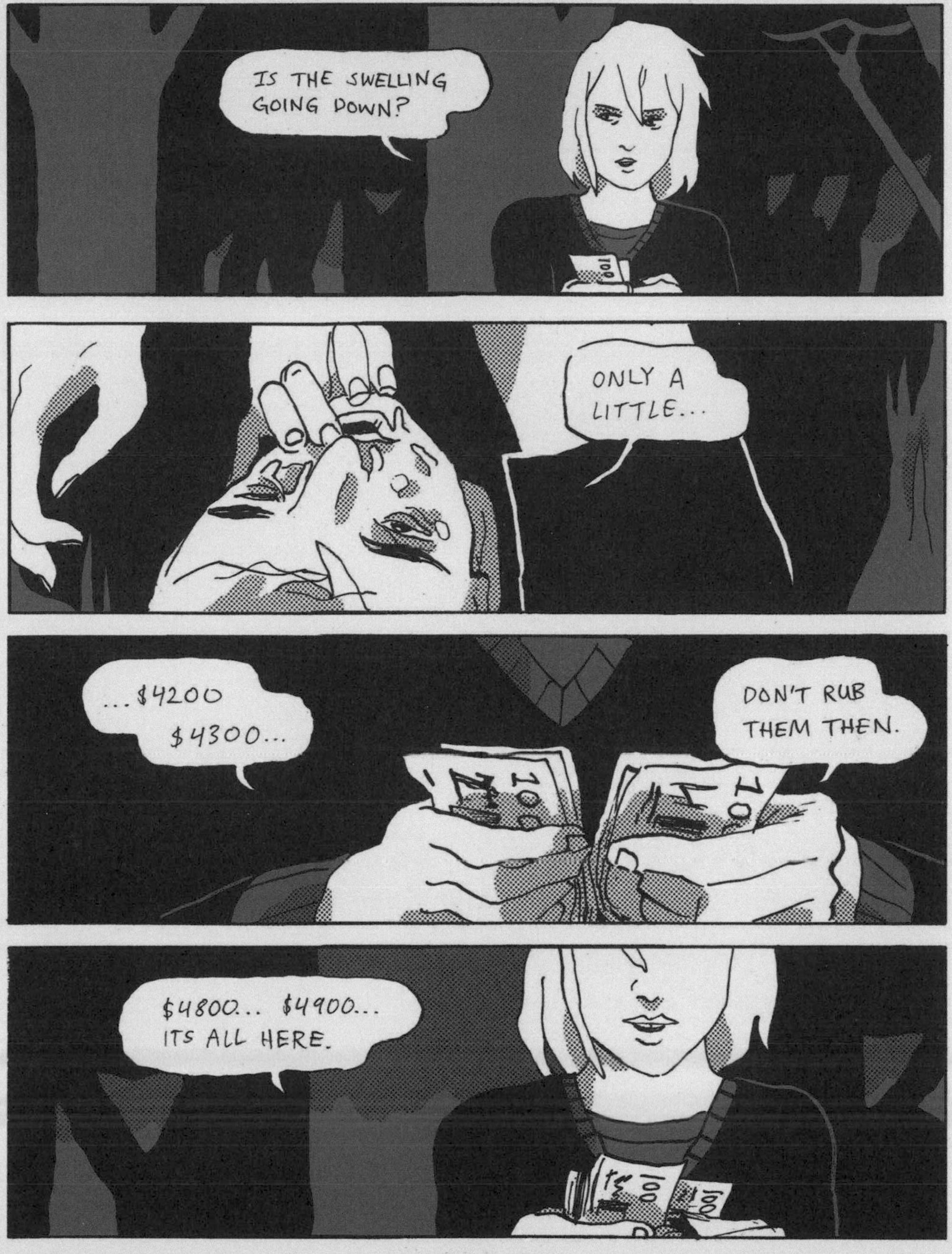
IS THE SWELLING GOING DOWN?
ONLY A LITTLE...
...$4200 $4300...
DON'T RUB THEM THEN.
$4800... $4900... ITS ALL HERE.

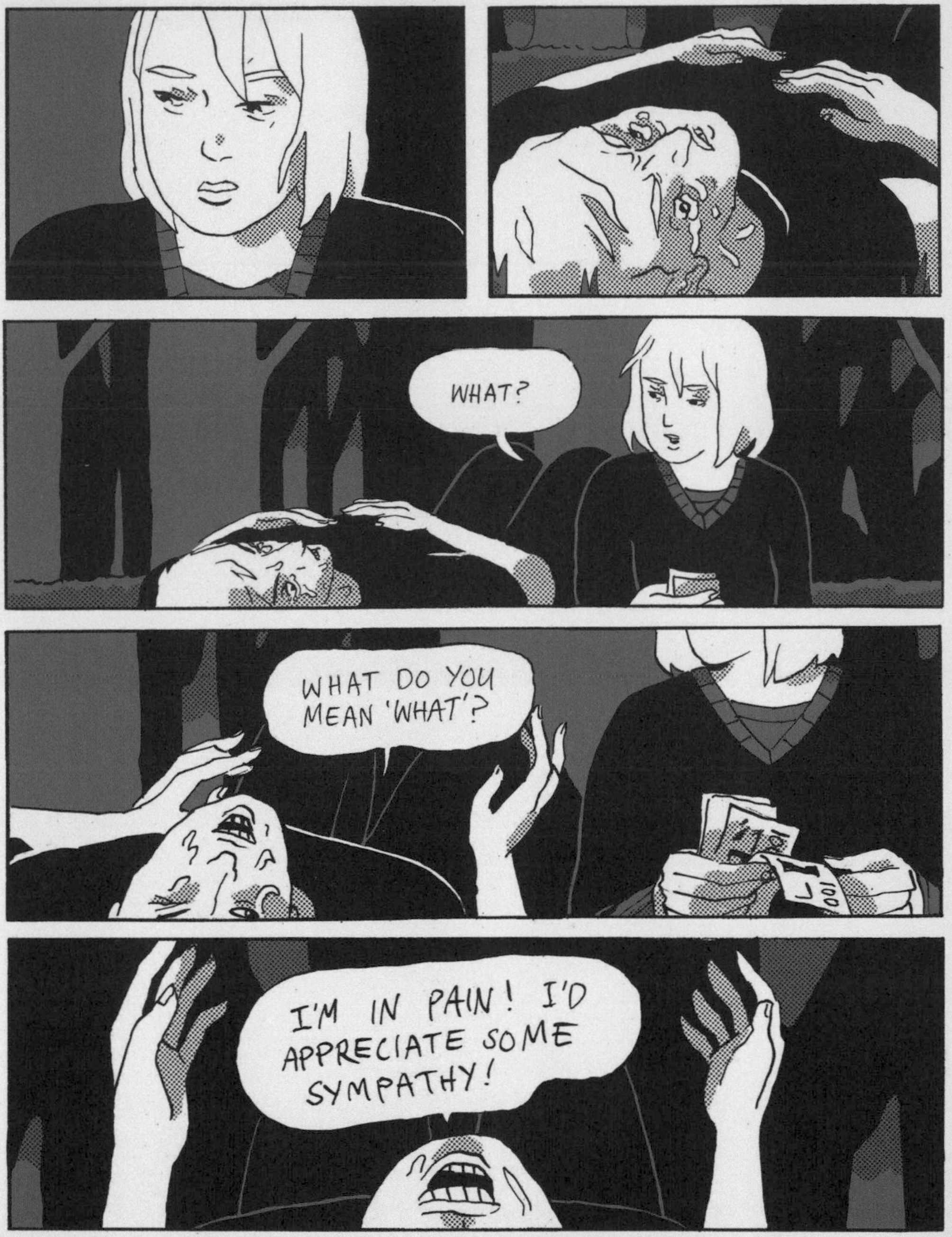
WHAT?
WHAT DO YOU MEAN 'WHAT'?
I'M IN PAIN! I'D APPRECIATE SOME SYMPATHY!

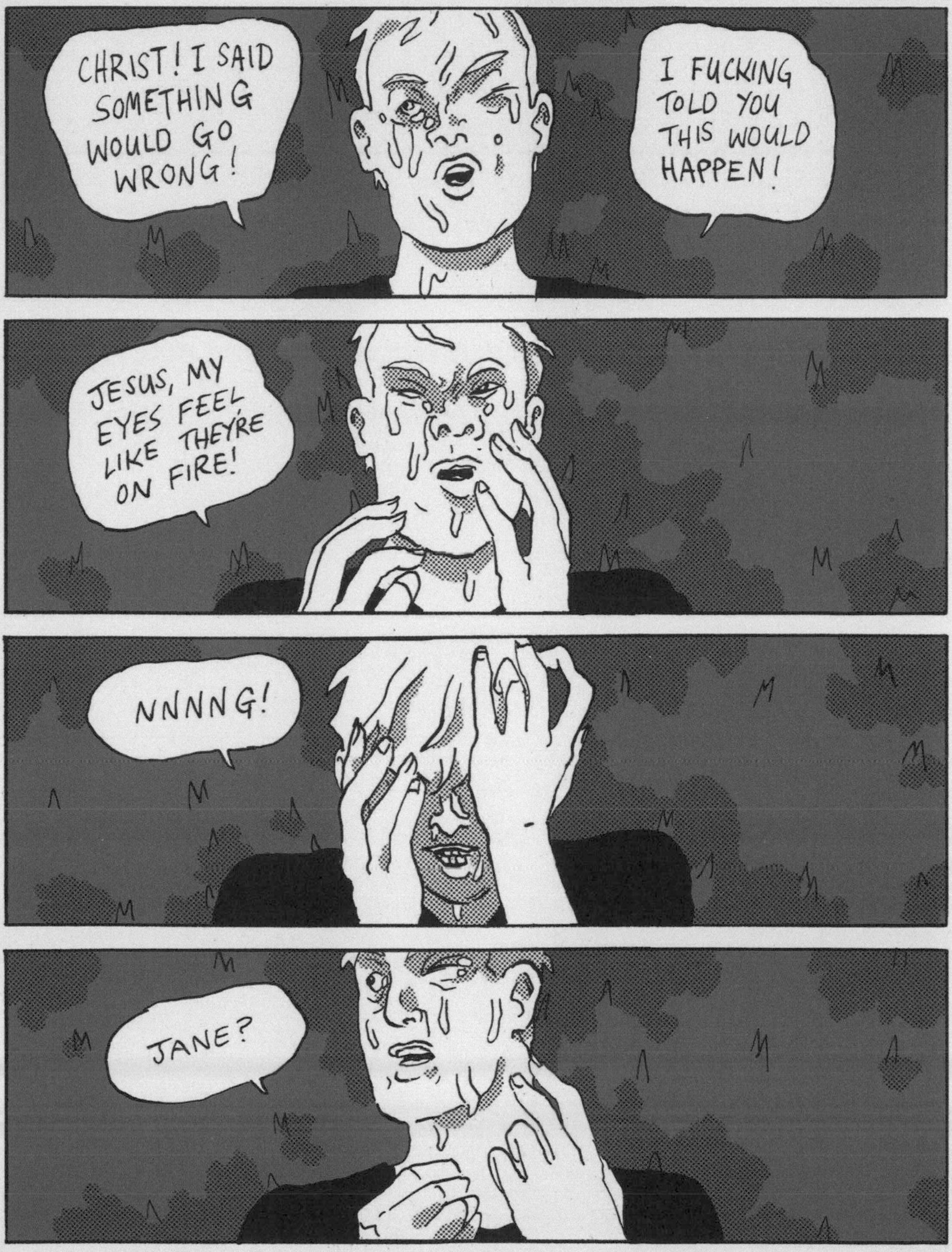
CHRIST! I SAID SOMETHING WOULD GO WRONG!
I FUCKING TOLD YOU THIS WOULD HAPPEN!
JESUS, MY EYES FEEL LIKE THEY'RE ON FIRE!
NNNNG!
JANE?

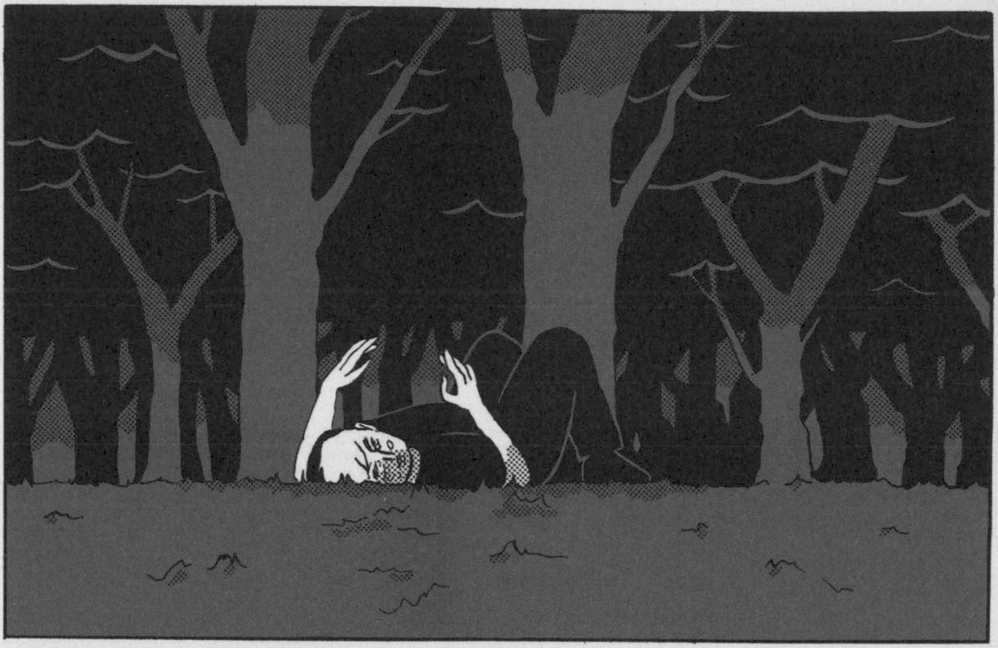

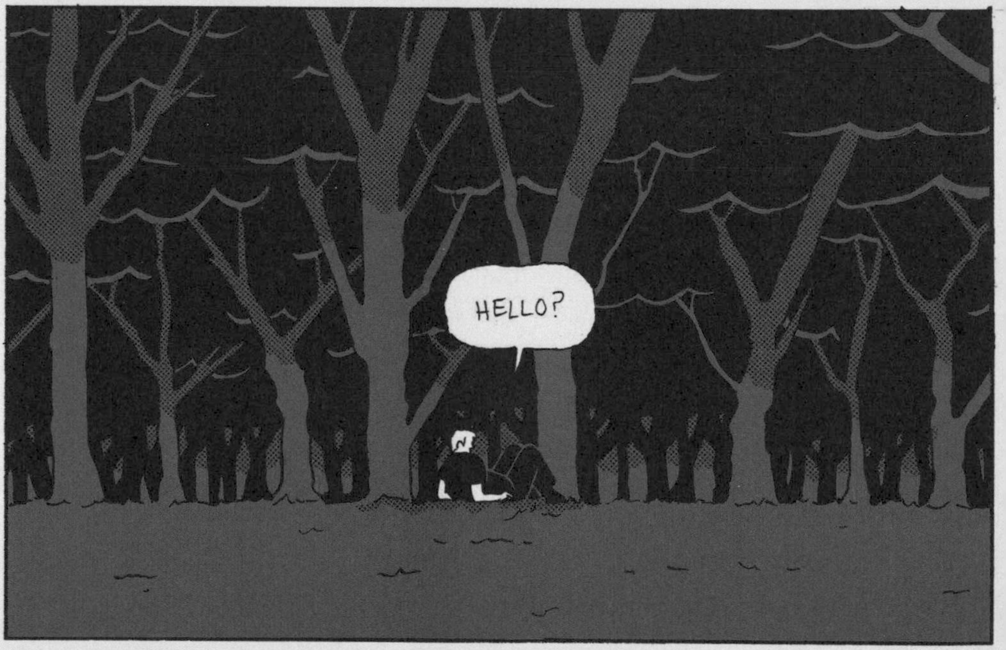
HELLO?

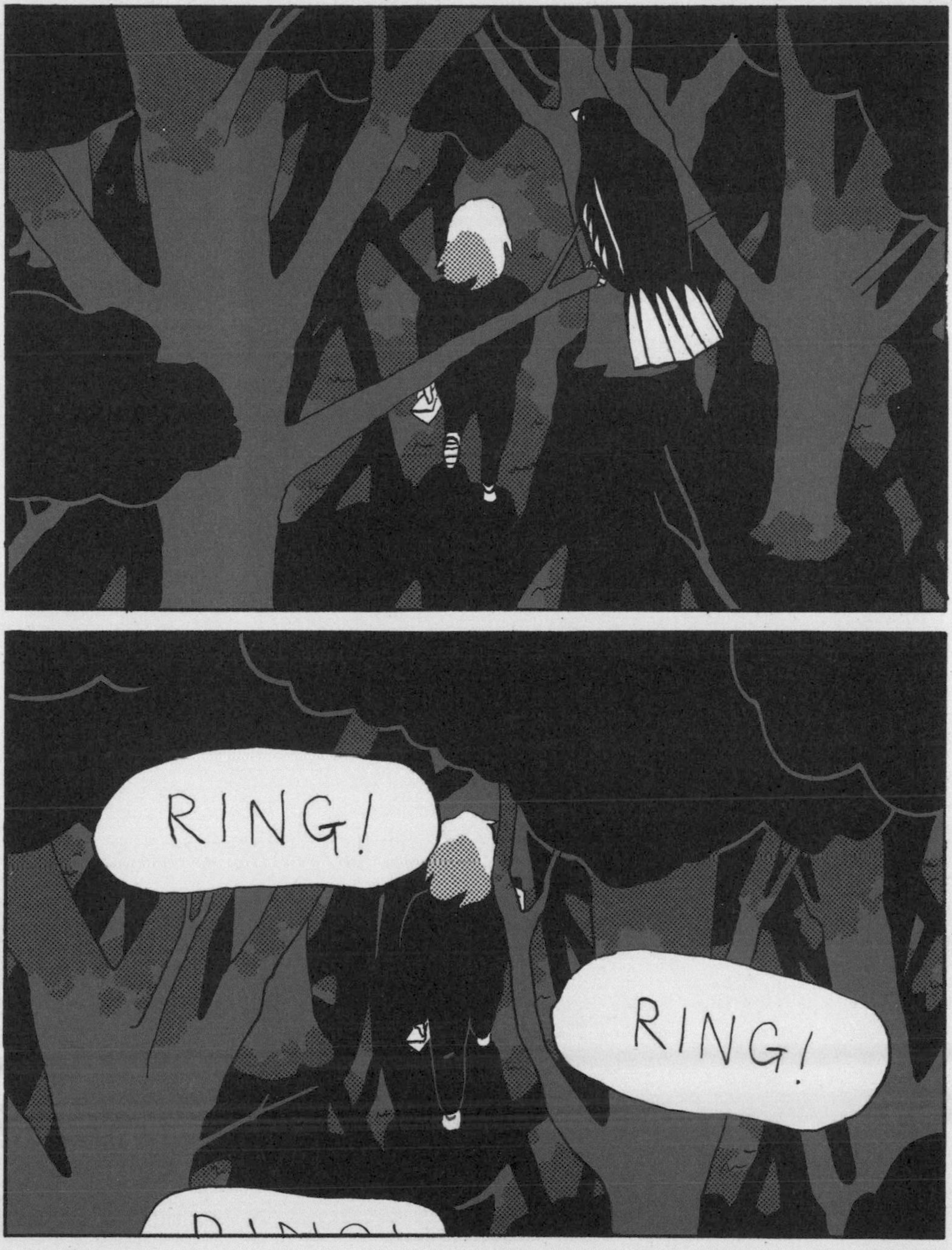
RING!
RING!

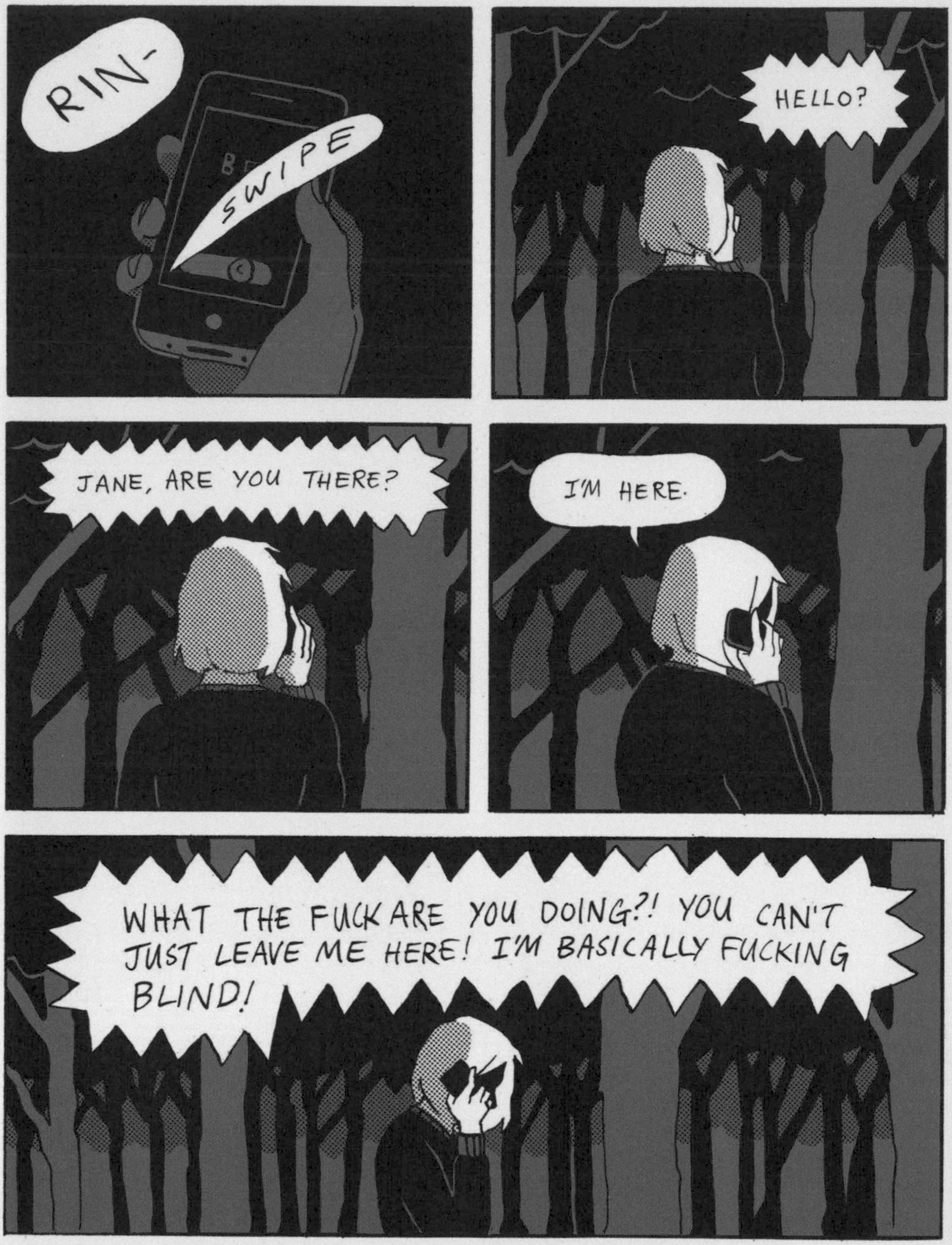
RIN-
SWIPE
HELLO?
JANE, ARE YOU THERE?
I'M HERE.
WHAT THE FUCK ARE YOU DOING?! YOU CAN'T JUST LEAVE ME HERE! I'M BASICALLY FUCKING BLIND!

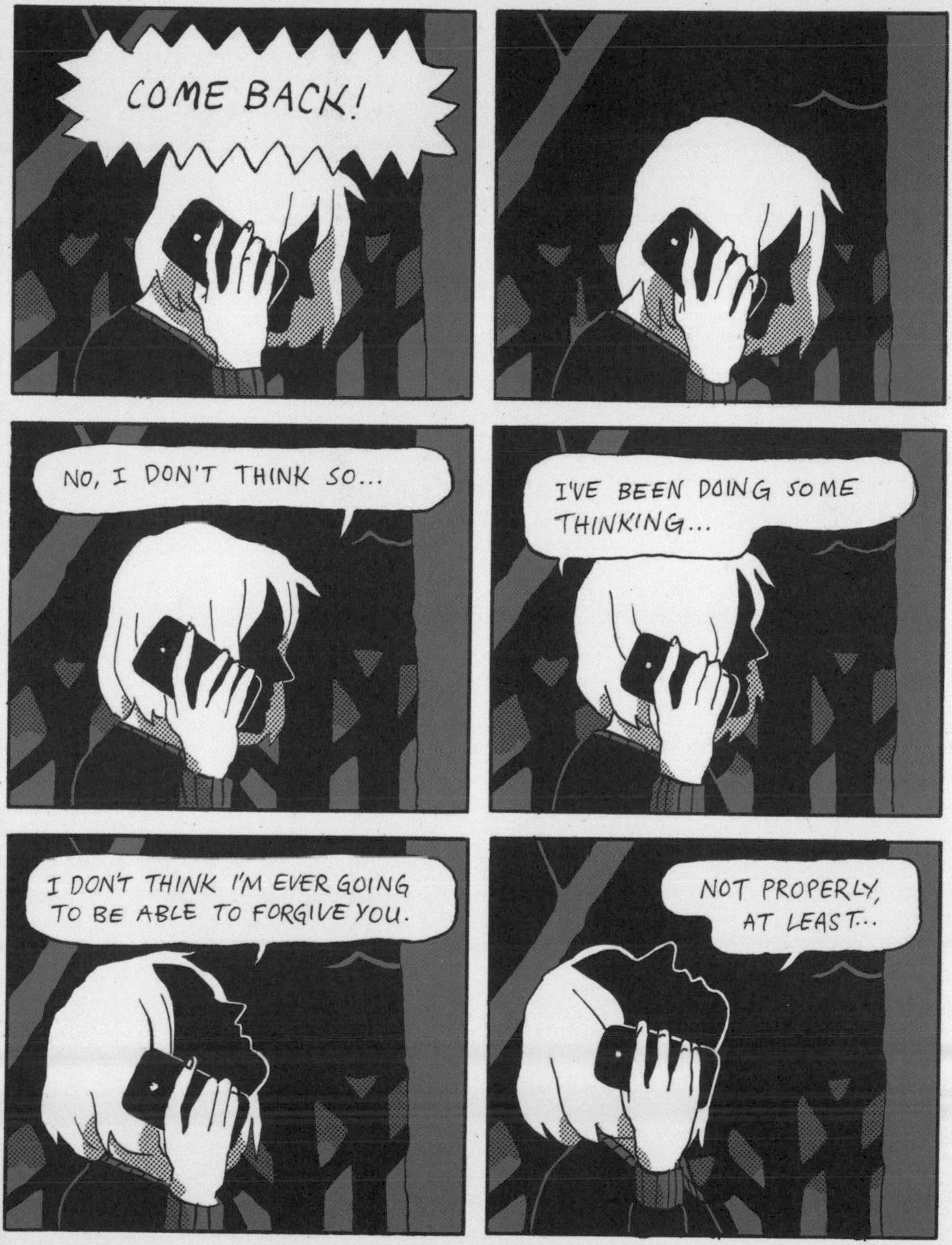
COME BACK!
NO, I DON'T THINK SO...
I'VE BEEN DOING SOME THINKING...
I DON'T THINK I'M EVER GOING TO BE ABLE TO FORGIVE YOU.
NOT PROPERLY, AT LEAST...

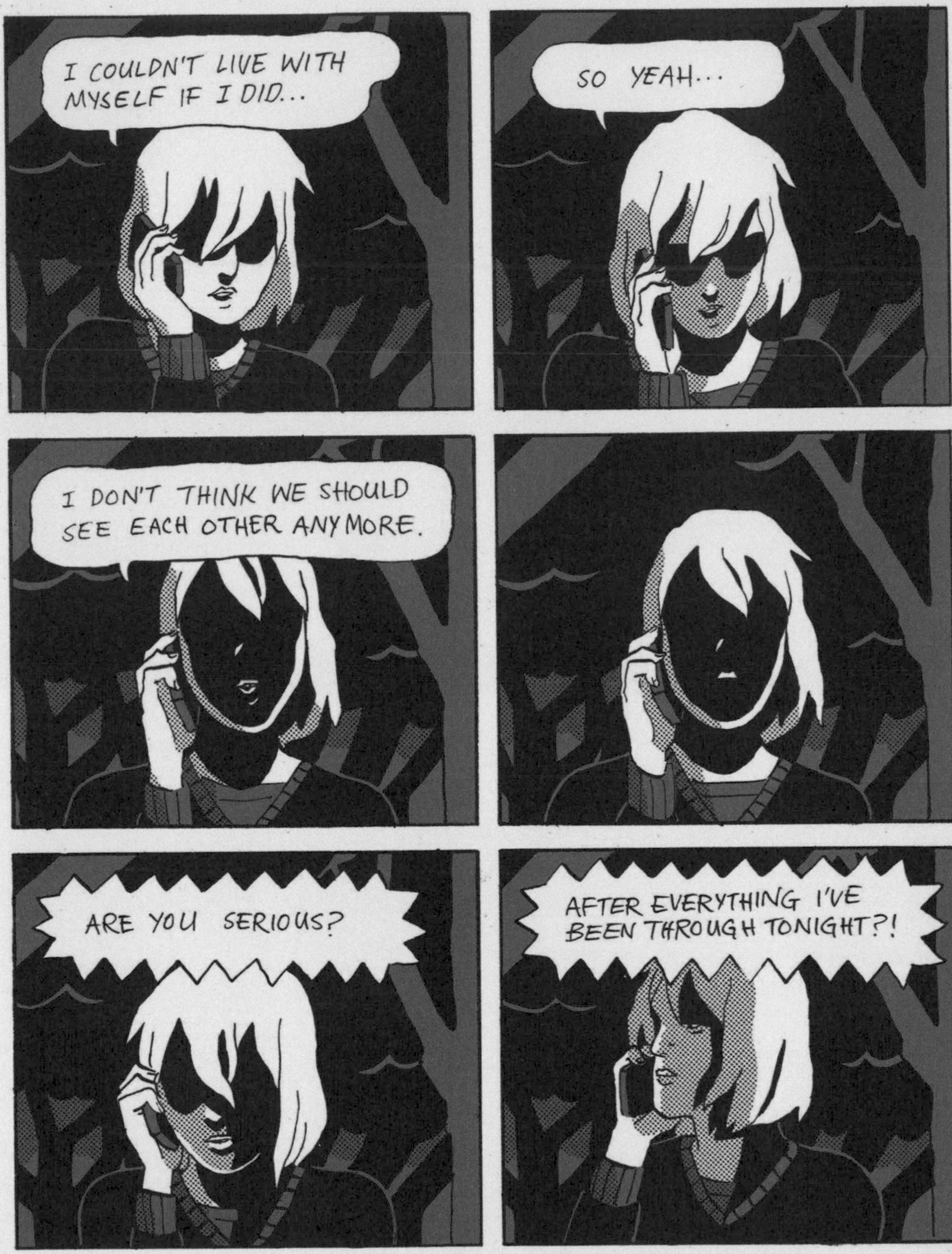
I COULDN'T LIVE WITH MYSELF IF I DID...
SO YEAH...
I DON'T THINK WE SHOULD SEE EACH OTHER ANYMORE.
ARE YOU SERIOUS?
AFTER EVERYTHING I'VE BEEN THROUGH TONIGHT?!

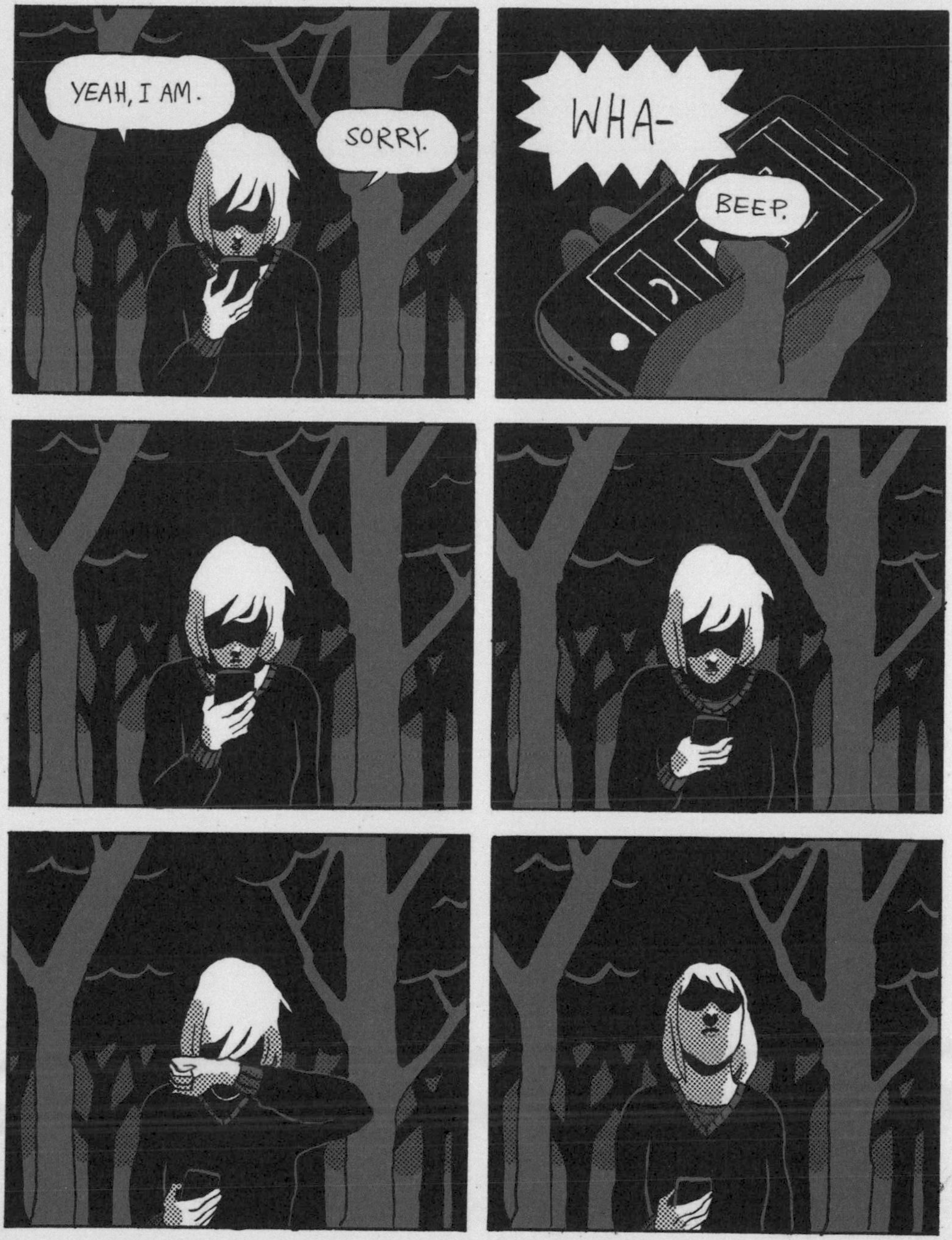
YEAH, I AM.
SORRY.
WHA-
BEEP.

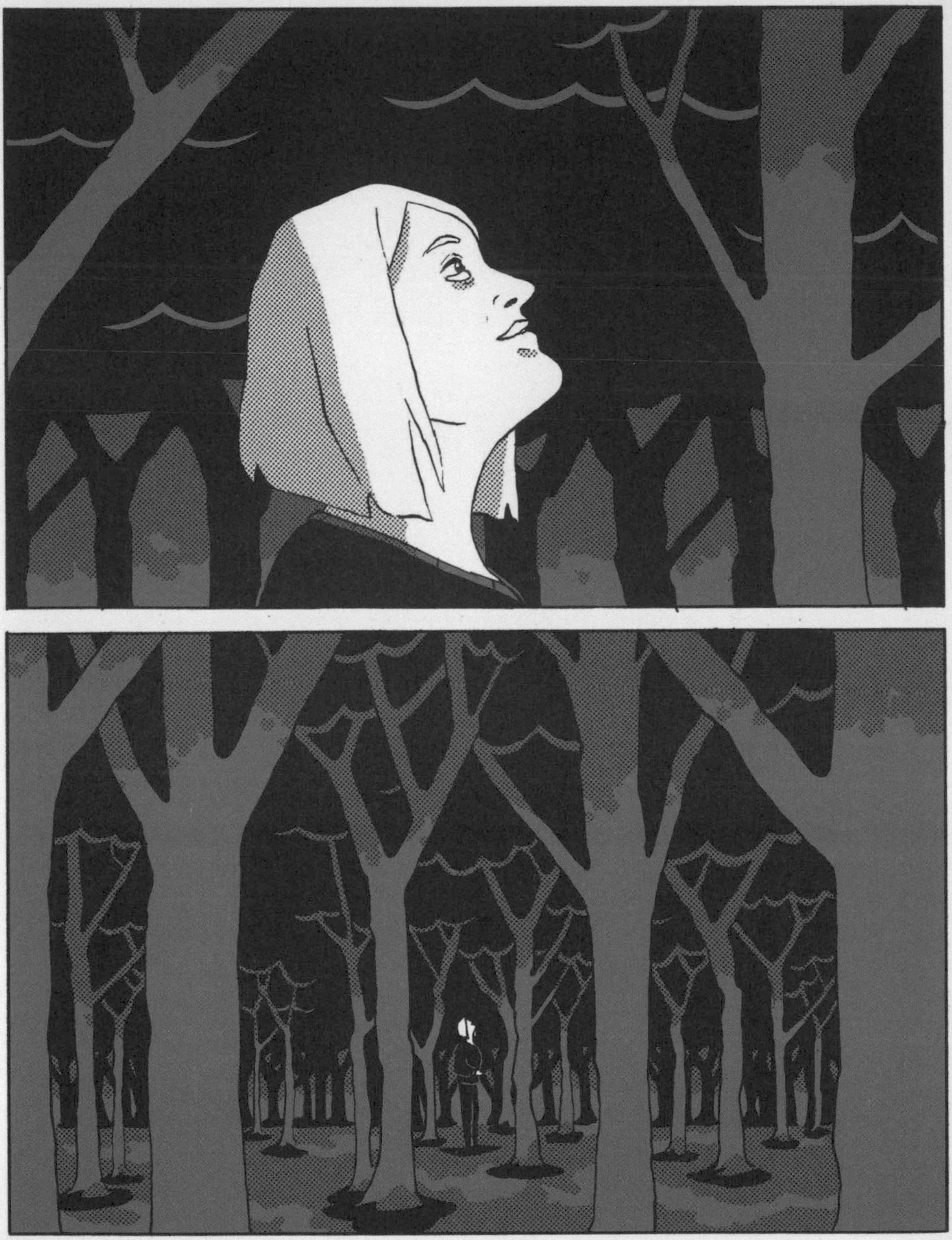

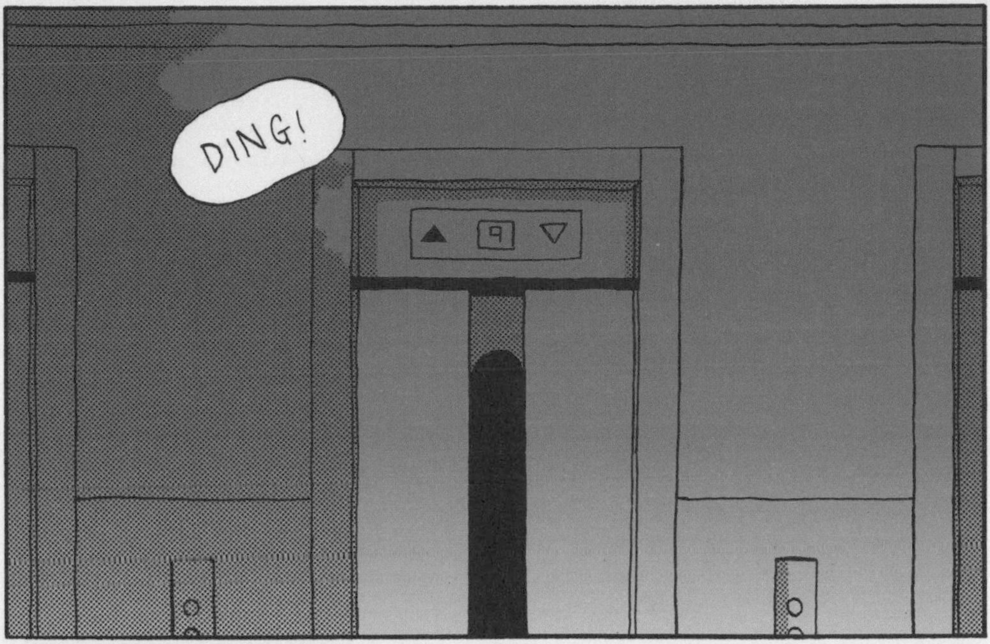
DING!

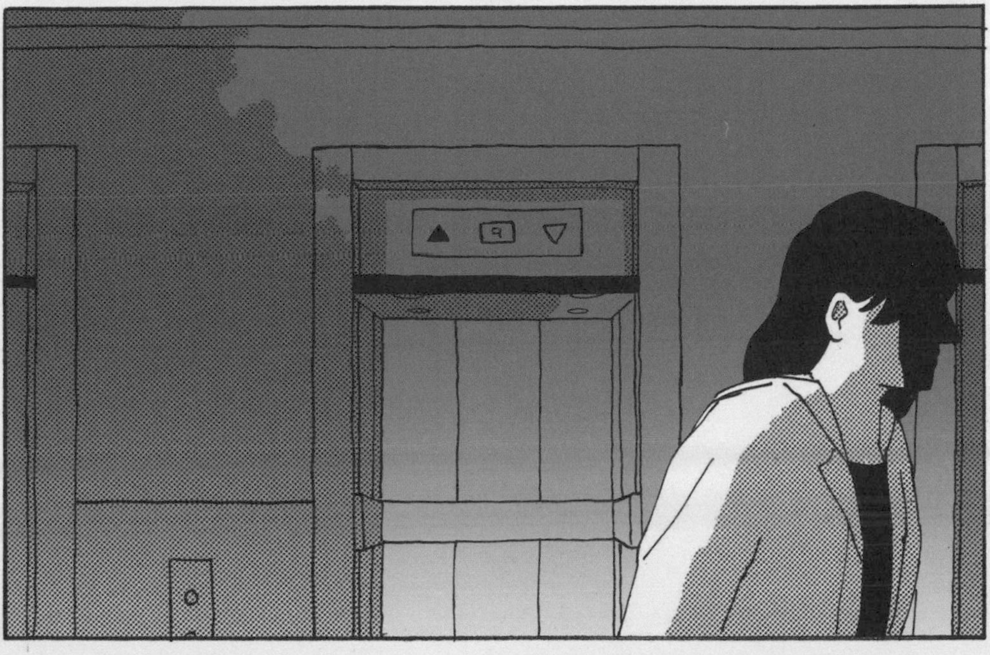

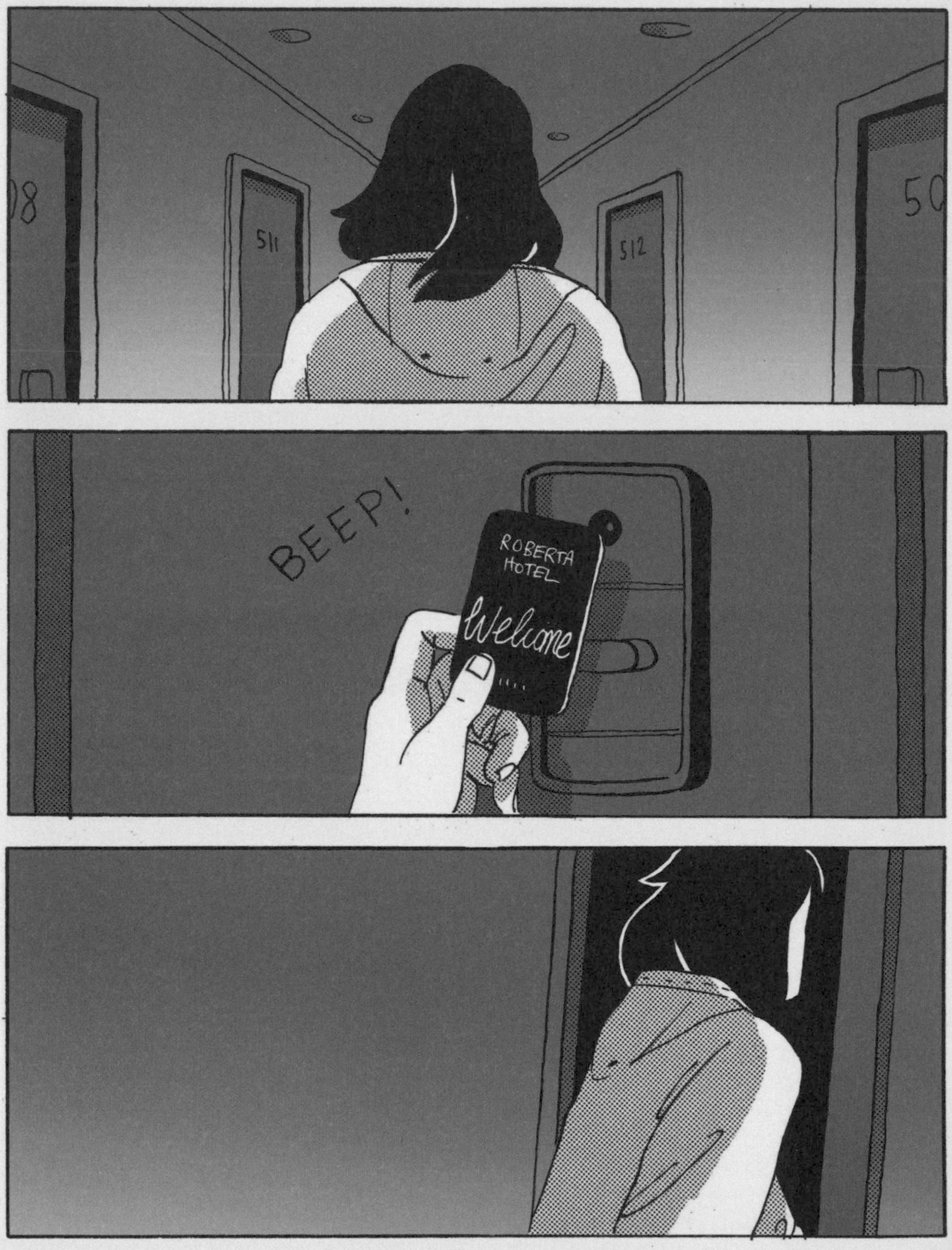
511
512
BEEP!
ROBERTA
HOTEL
Welcome

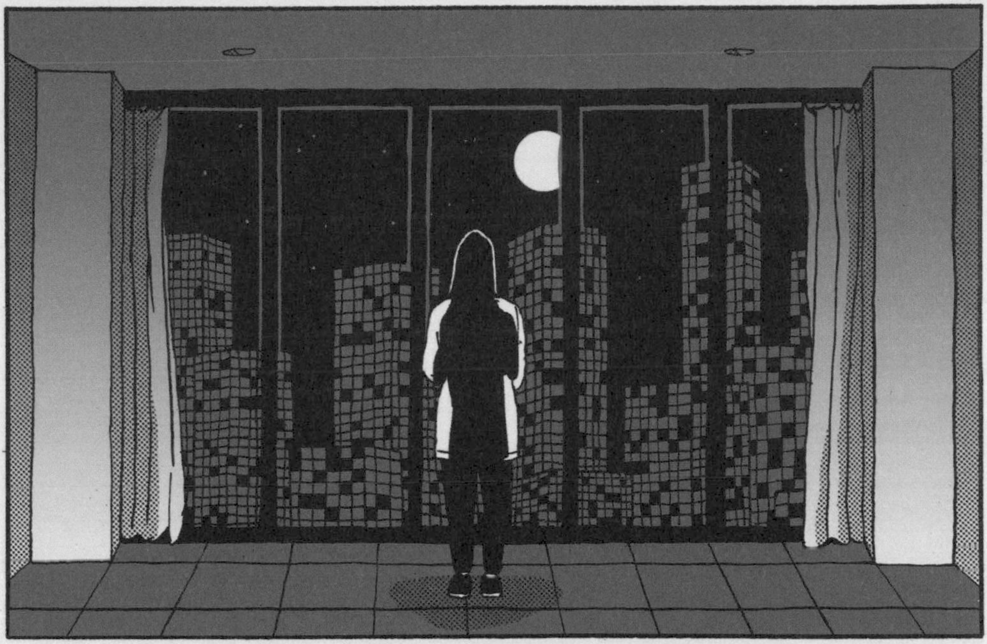

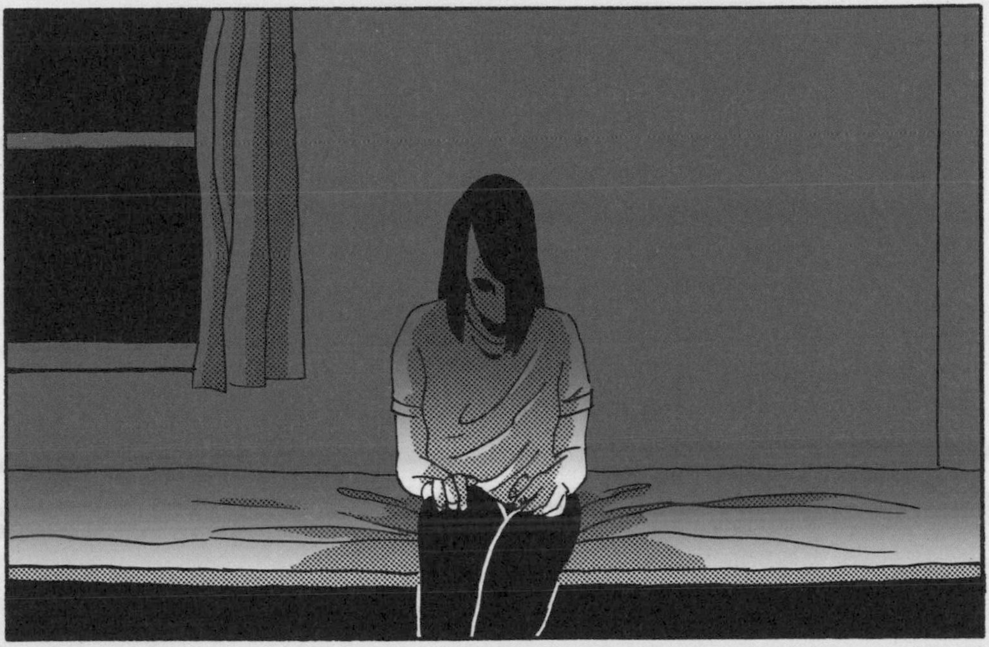

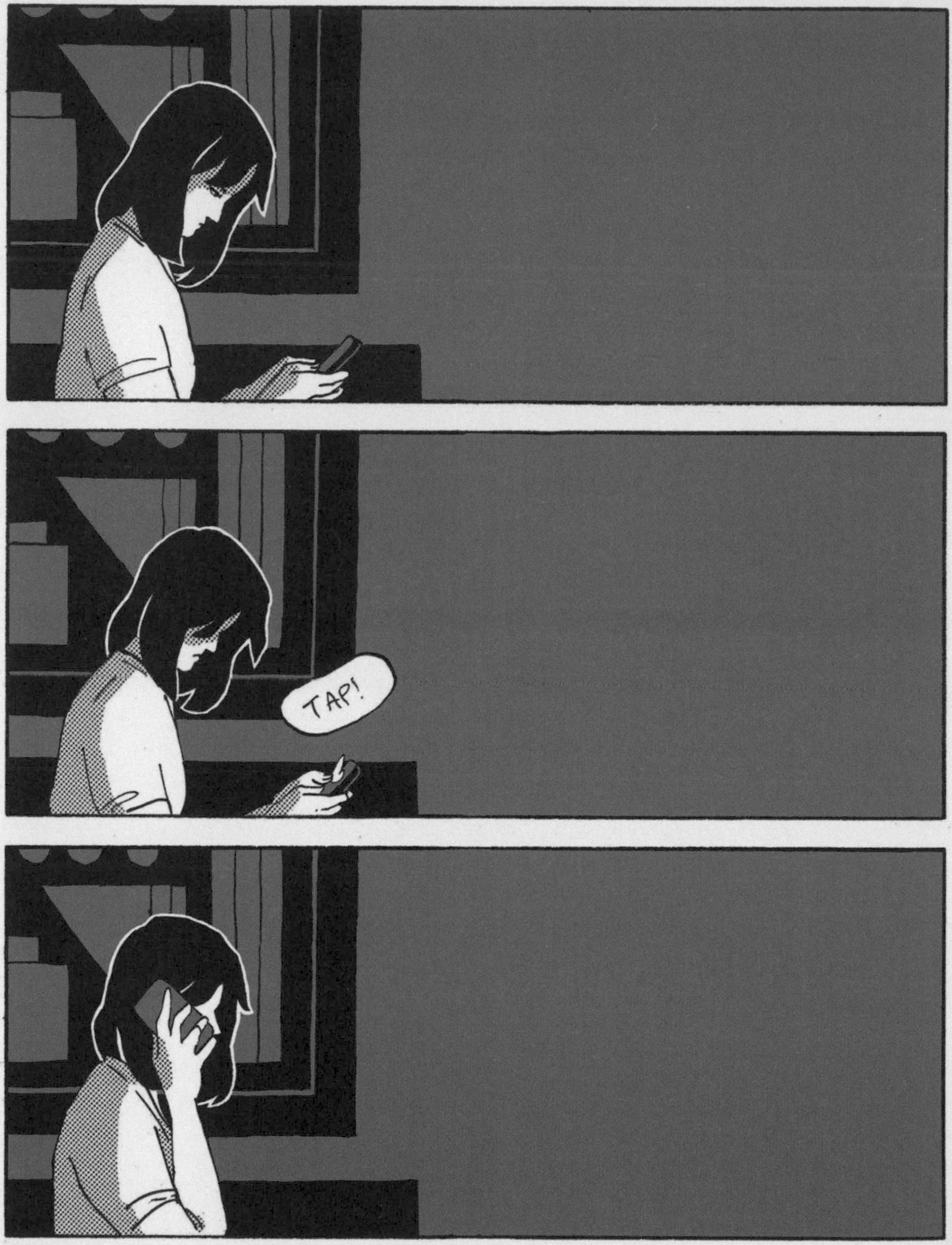
TAP!

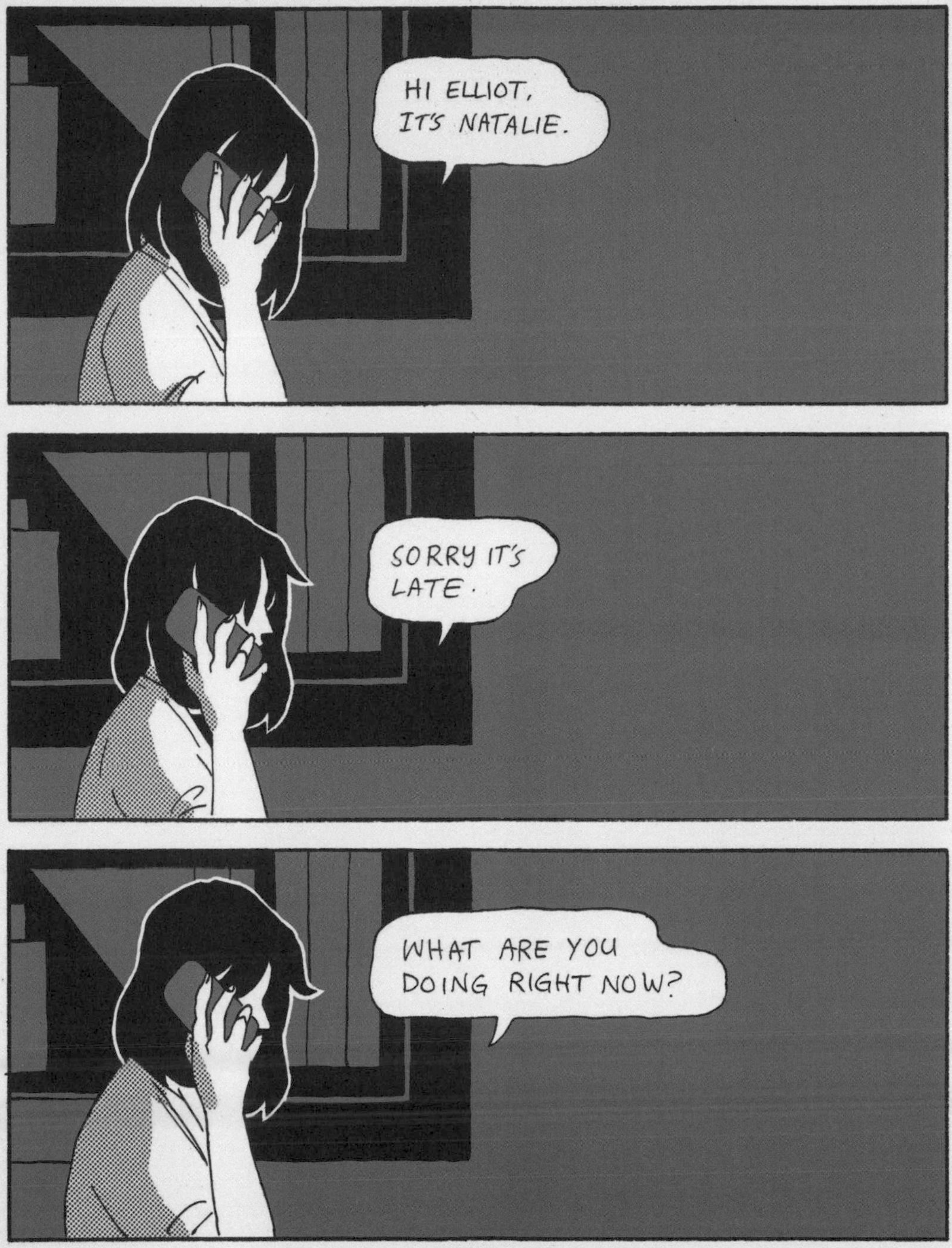
HI ELLIOT,
IT'S NATALIE.
SORRY IT'S LATE.
WHAT ARE YOU DOING RIGHT NOW?

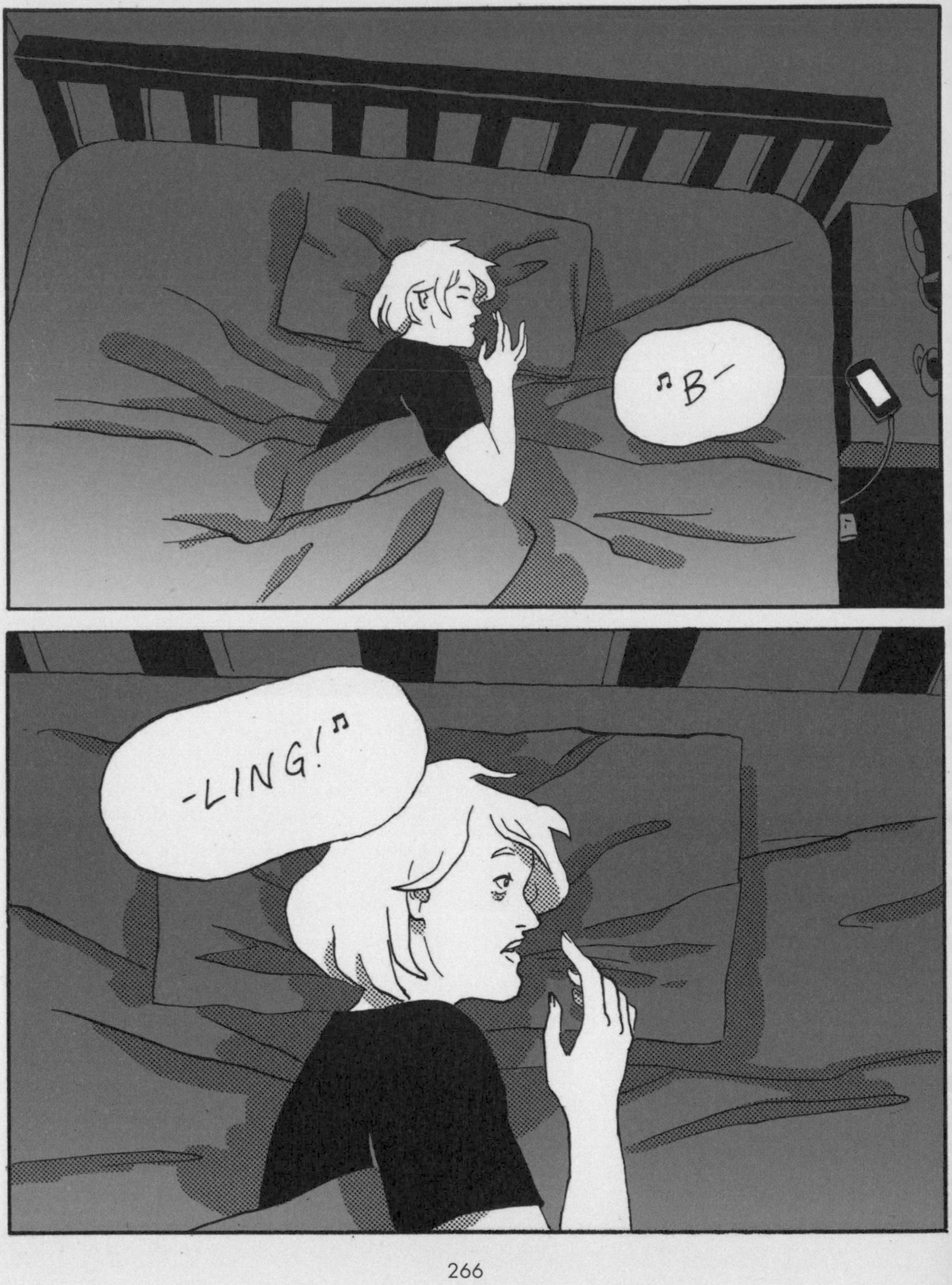
♫B–
-LING!♫

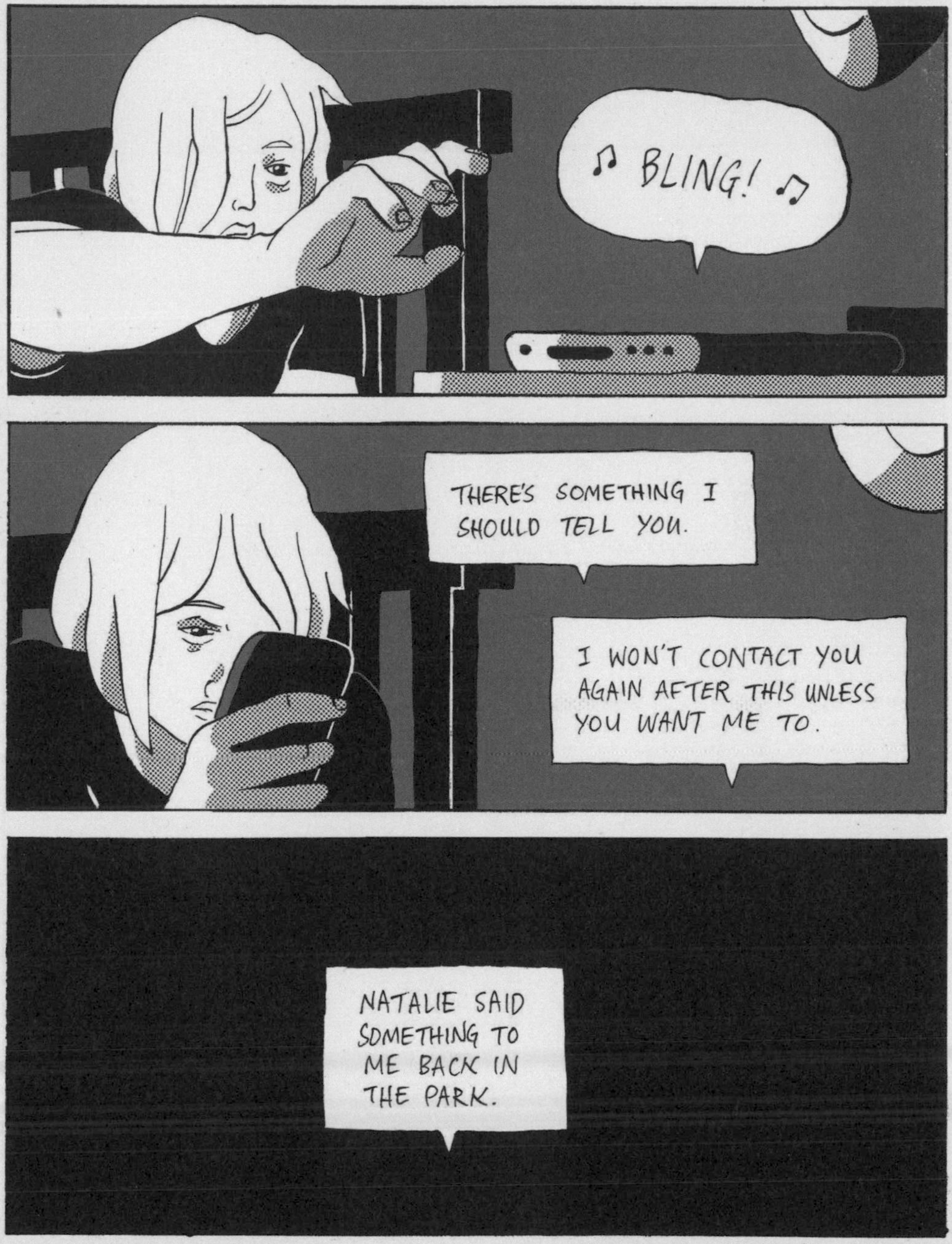
♫ BLING! ♫
THERE'S SOMETHING I SHOULD TELL YOU.
I WON'T CONTACT YOU AGAIN AFTER THIS UNLESS YOU WANT ME TO.
NATALIE SAID SOMETHING TO ME BACK IN THE PARK.

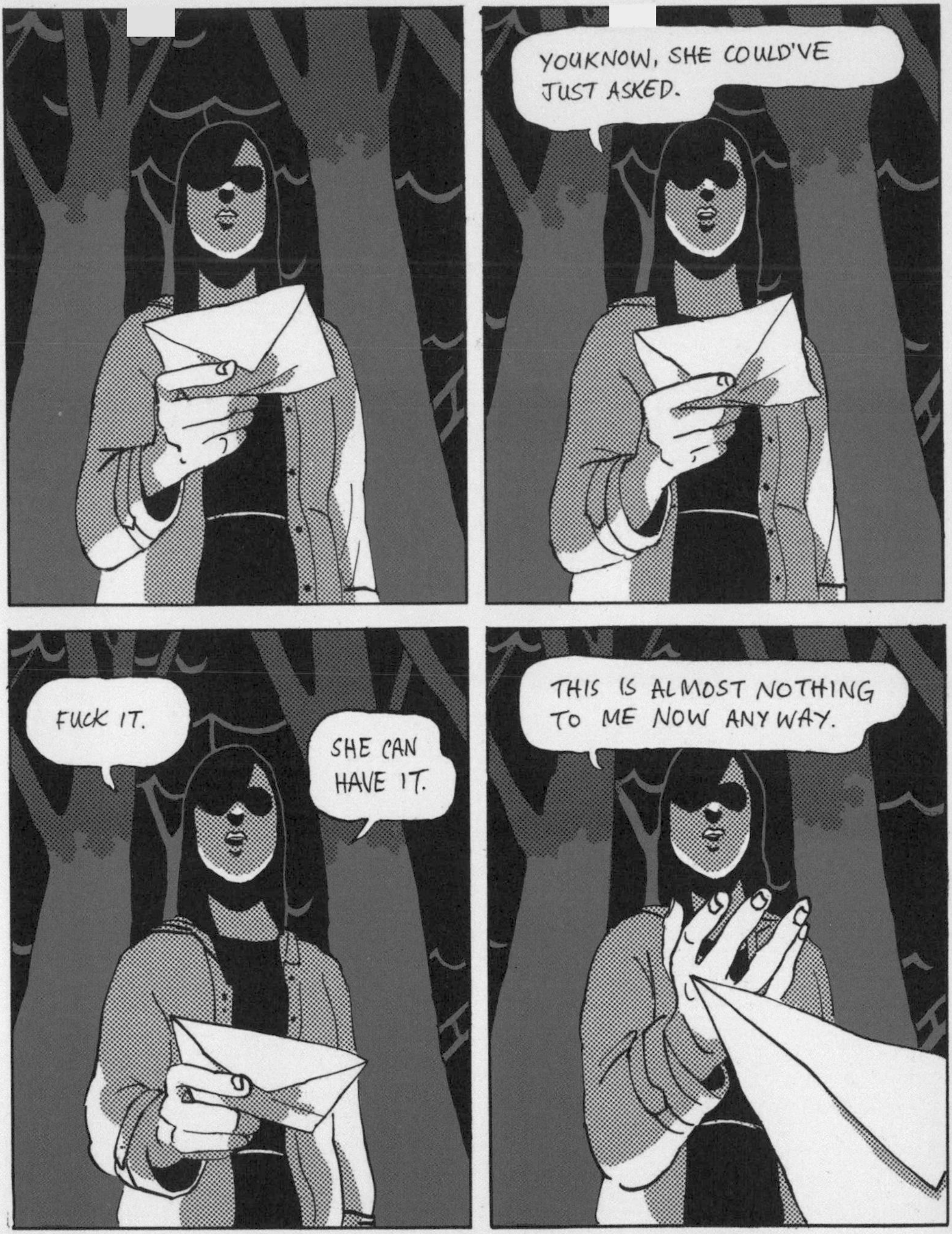
YOUKNOW, SHE COULD'VE JUST ASKED.
FUCK IT.
SHE CAN HAVE IT.
THIS IS ALMOST NOTHING TO ME NOW ANYWAY.

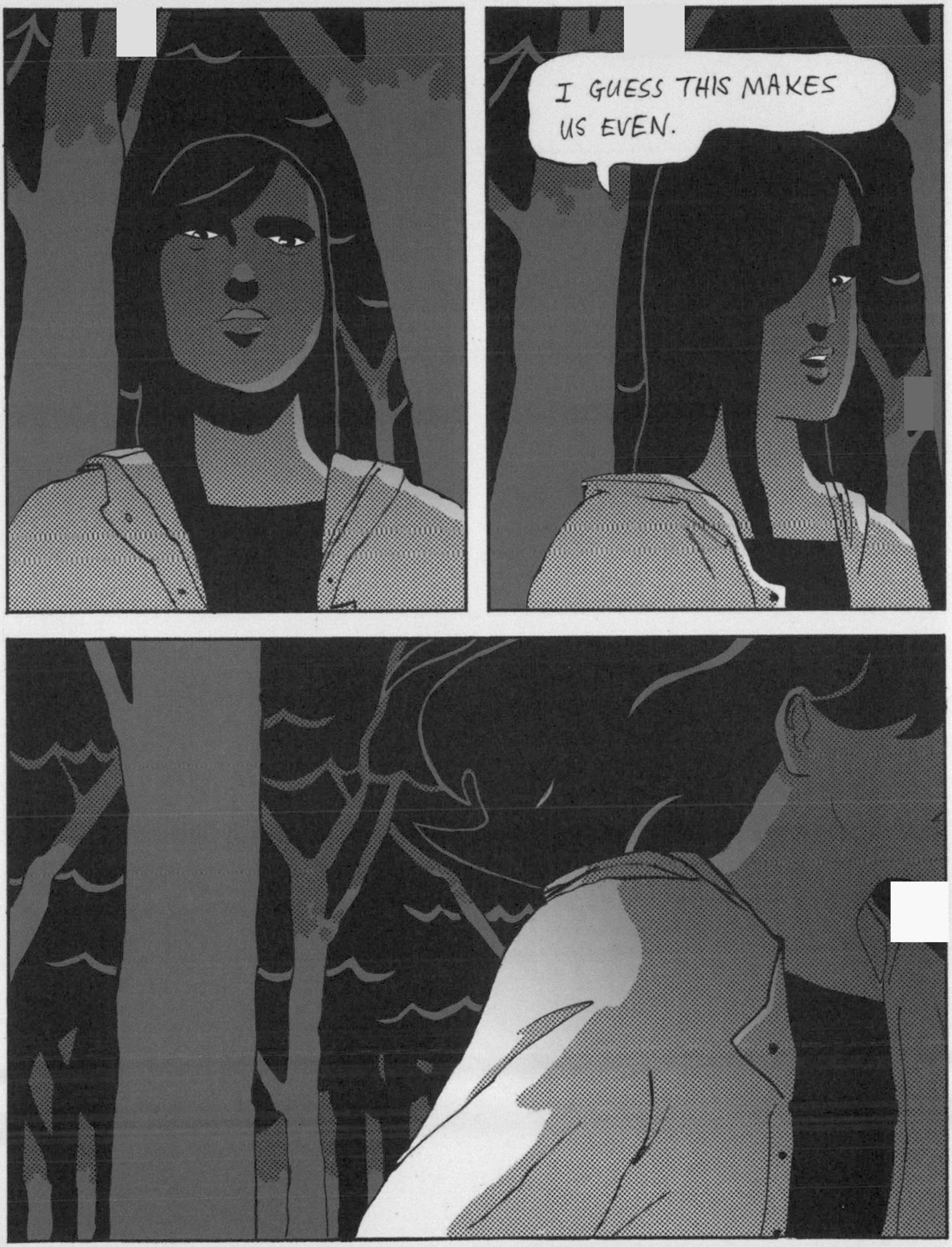
I GUESS THIS MAKES US EVEN.

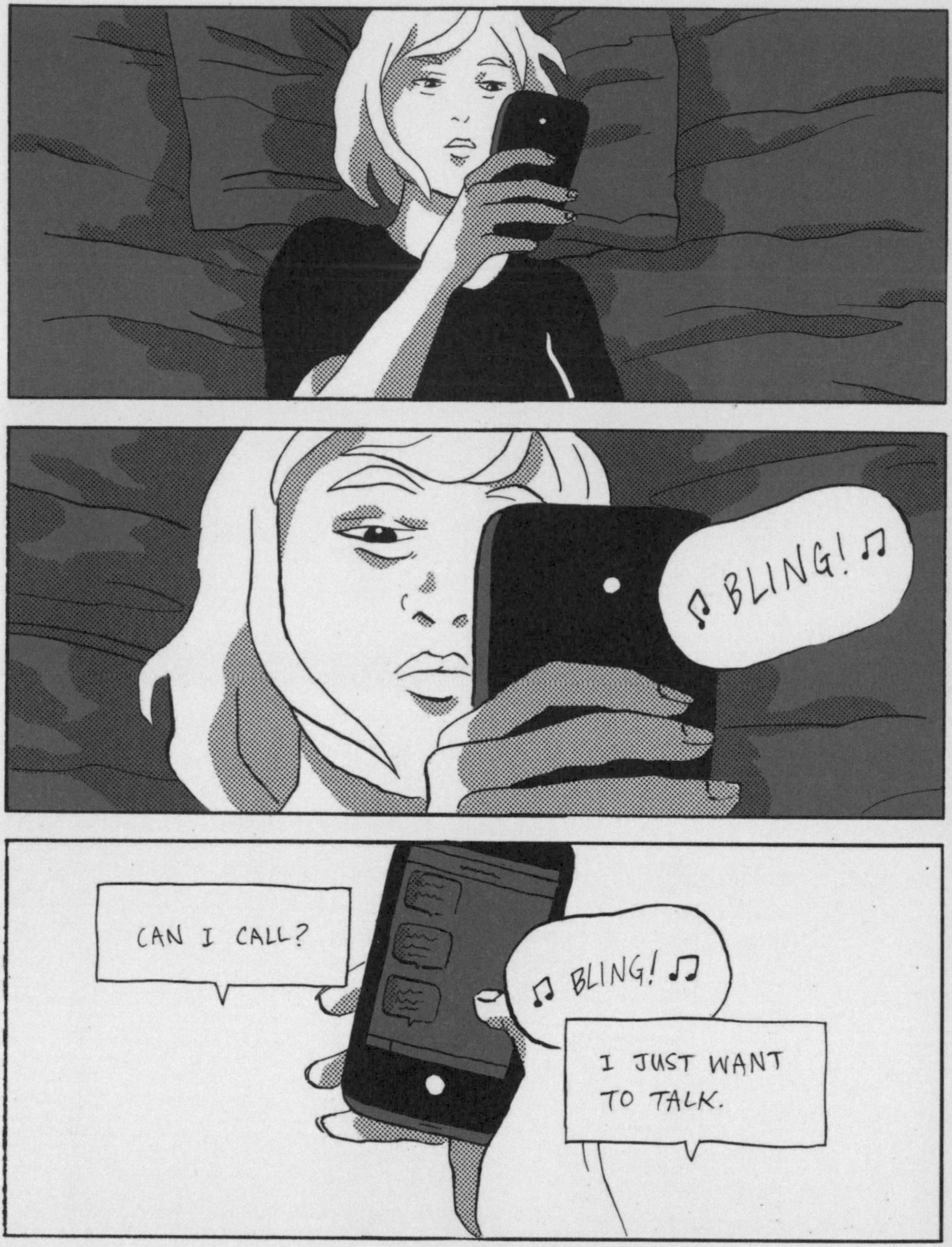
♫ BLING! ♫
CAN I CALL?
♫ BLING! ♫
I JUST WANT TO TALK.

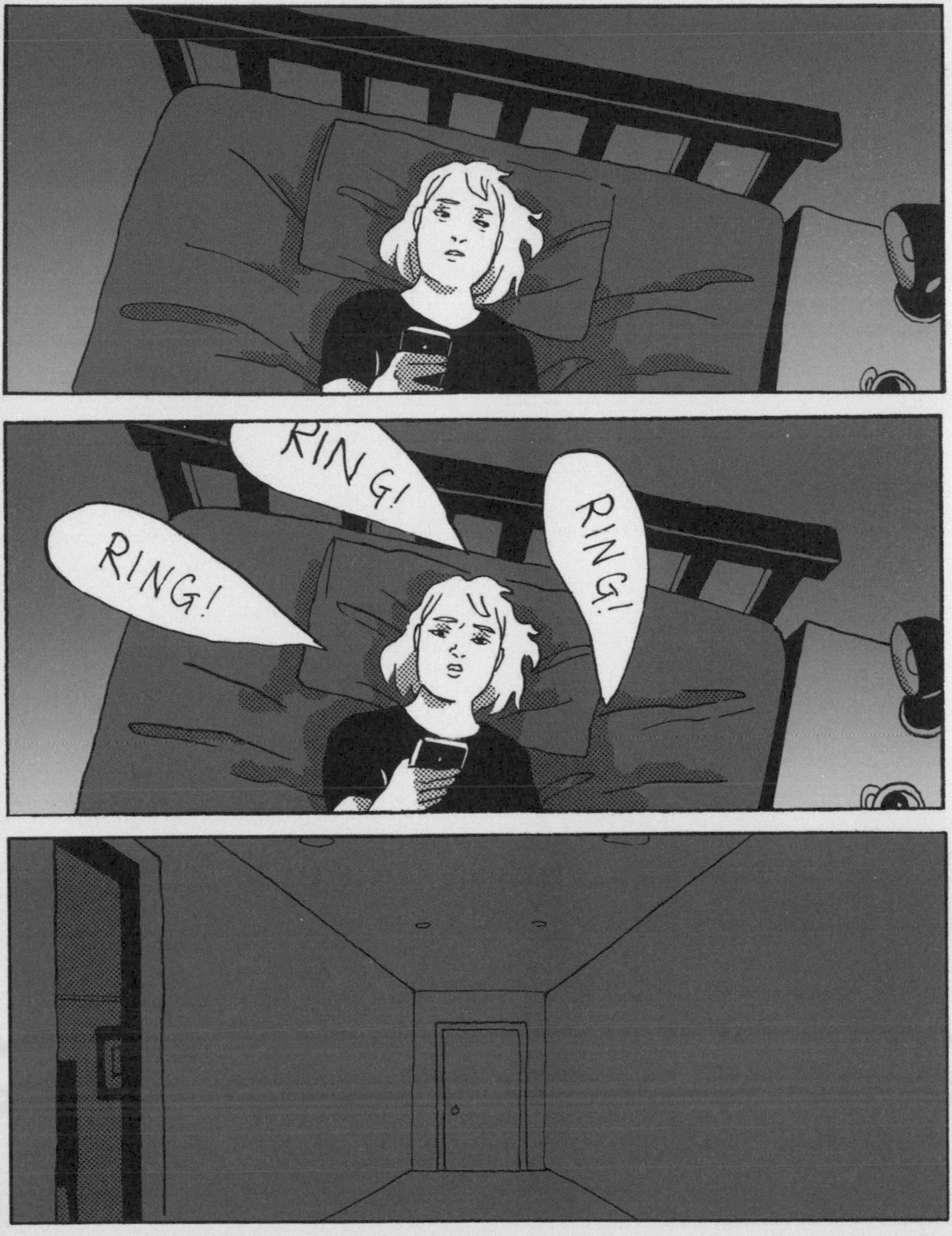
RING!
RING!
RING!

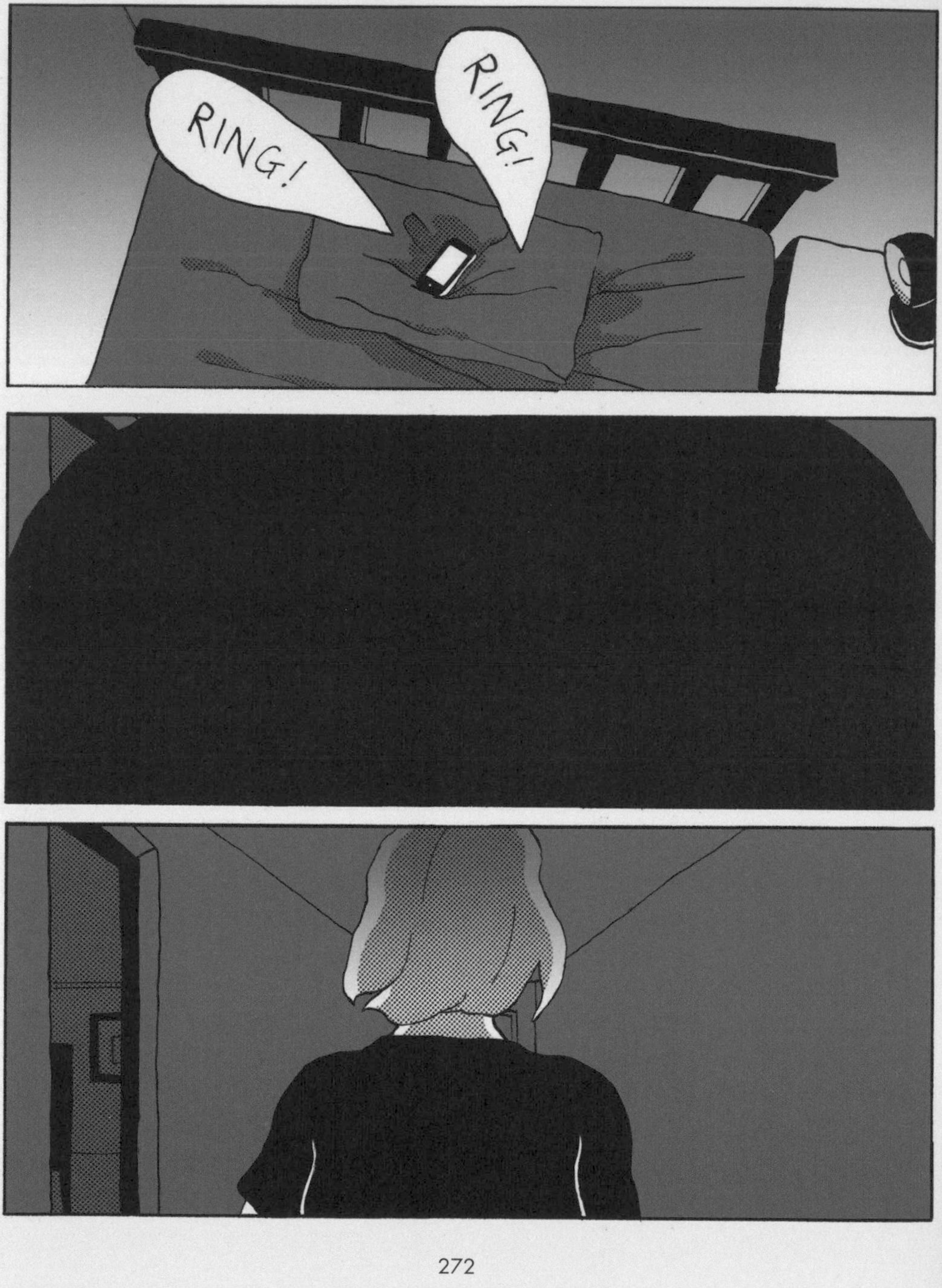
RING!
RING!

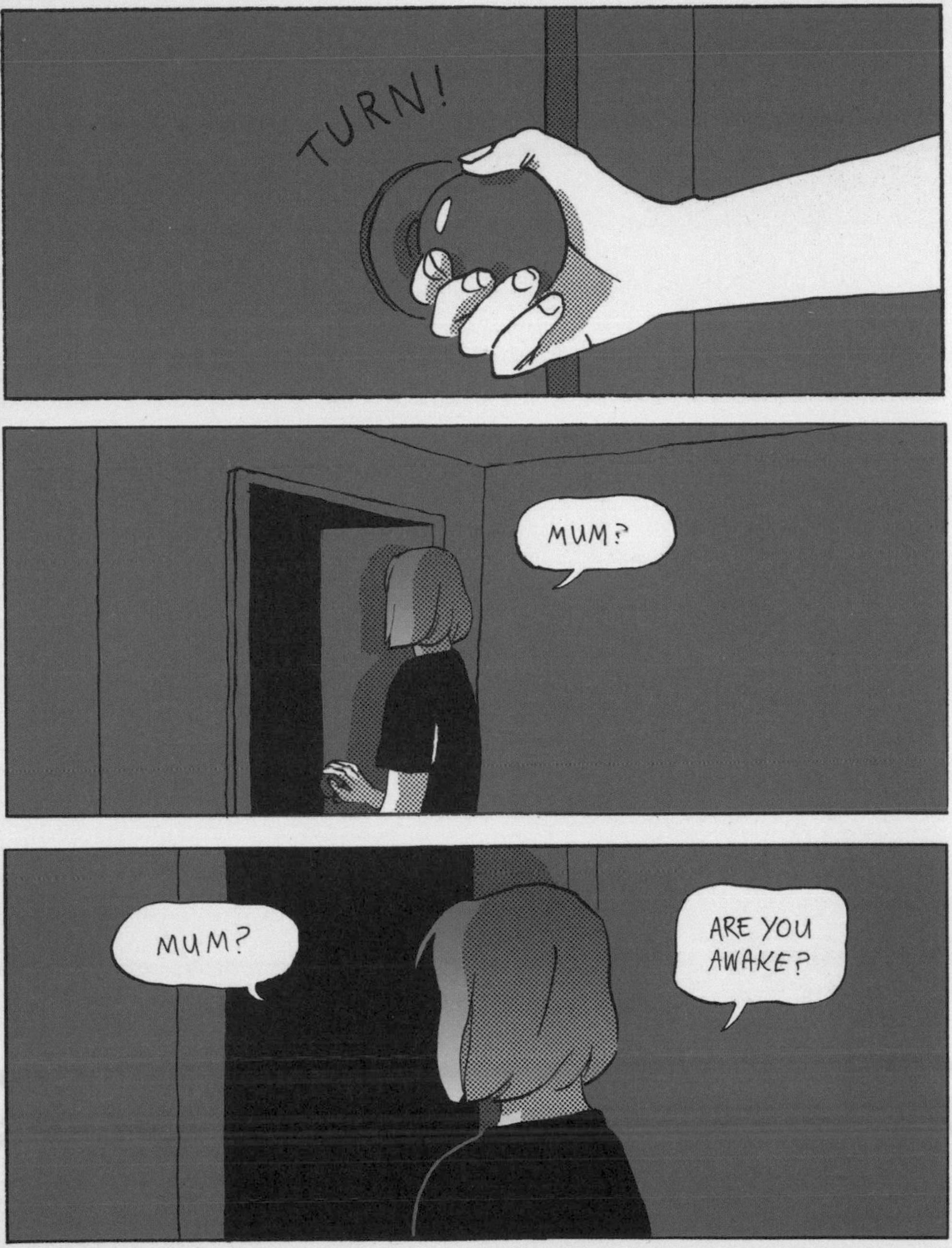
TURN!
MUM?
MUM?
ARE YOU AWAKE?

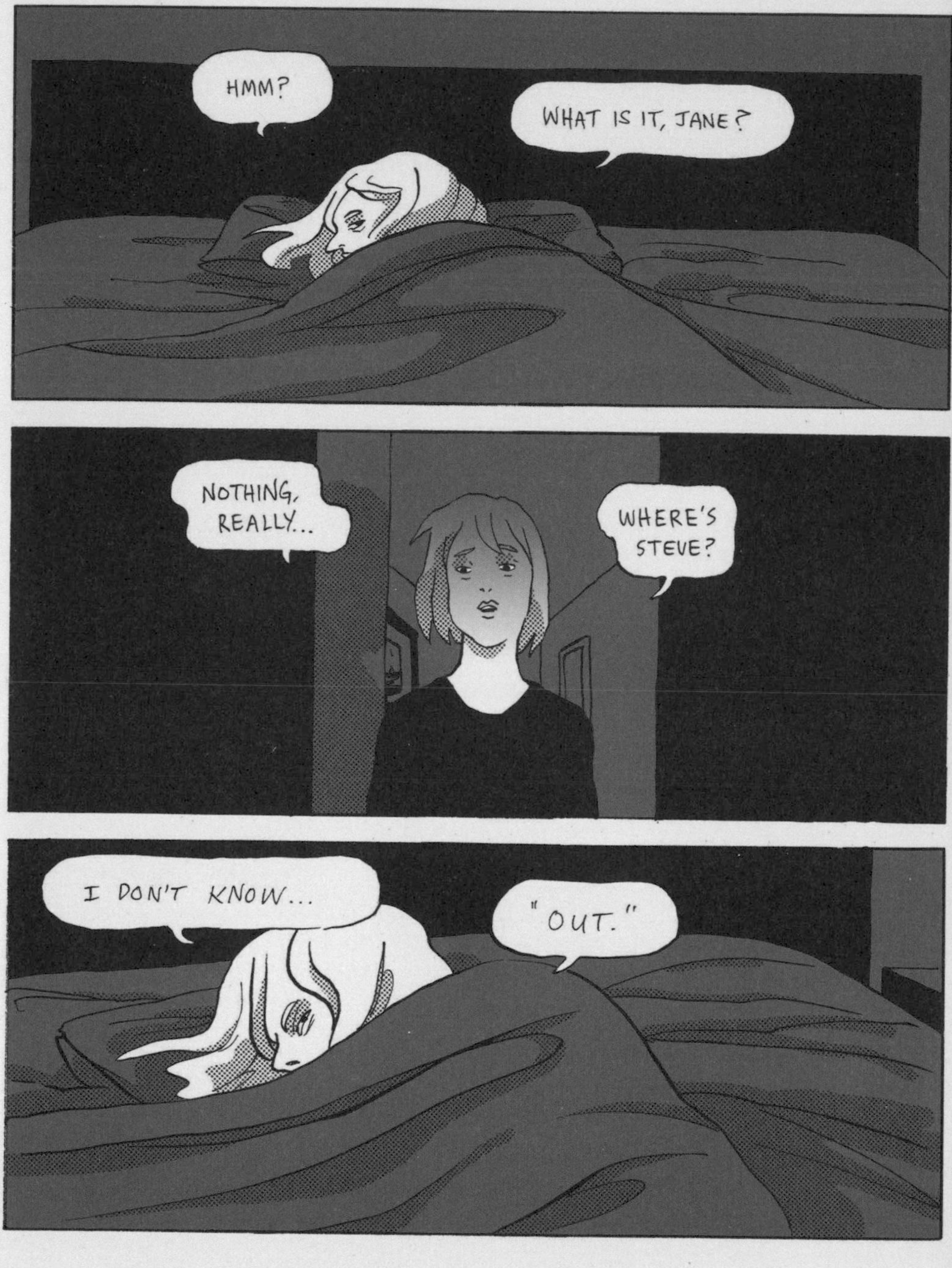
HMM?
WHAT IS IT, JANE?
NOTHING, REALLY...
WHERE'S STEVE?
I DON'T KNOW...
"OUT."

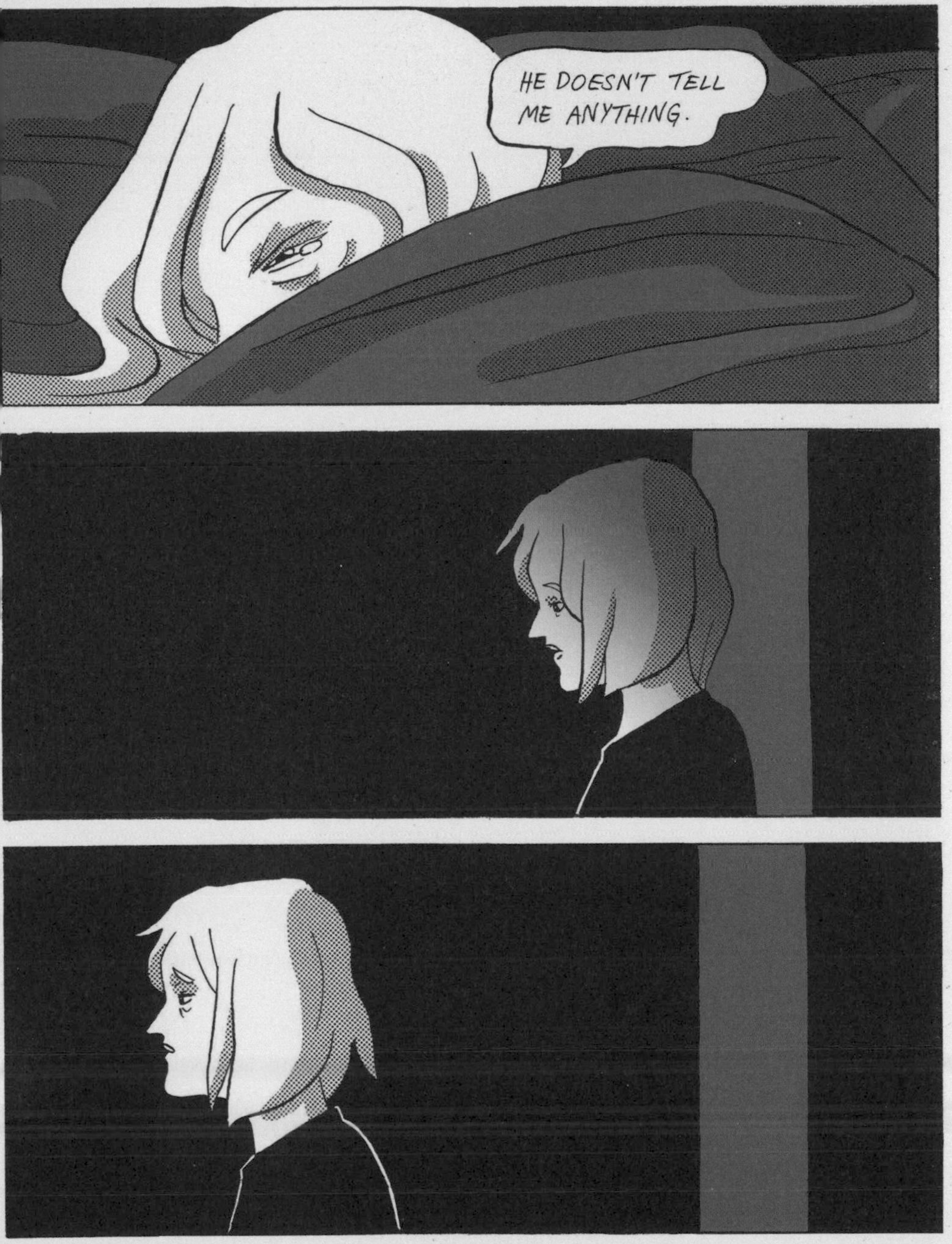
HE DOESN'T TELL ME ANYTHING.

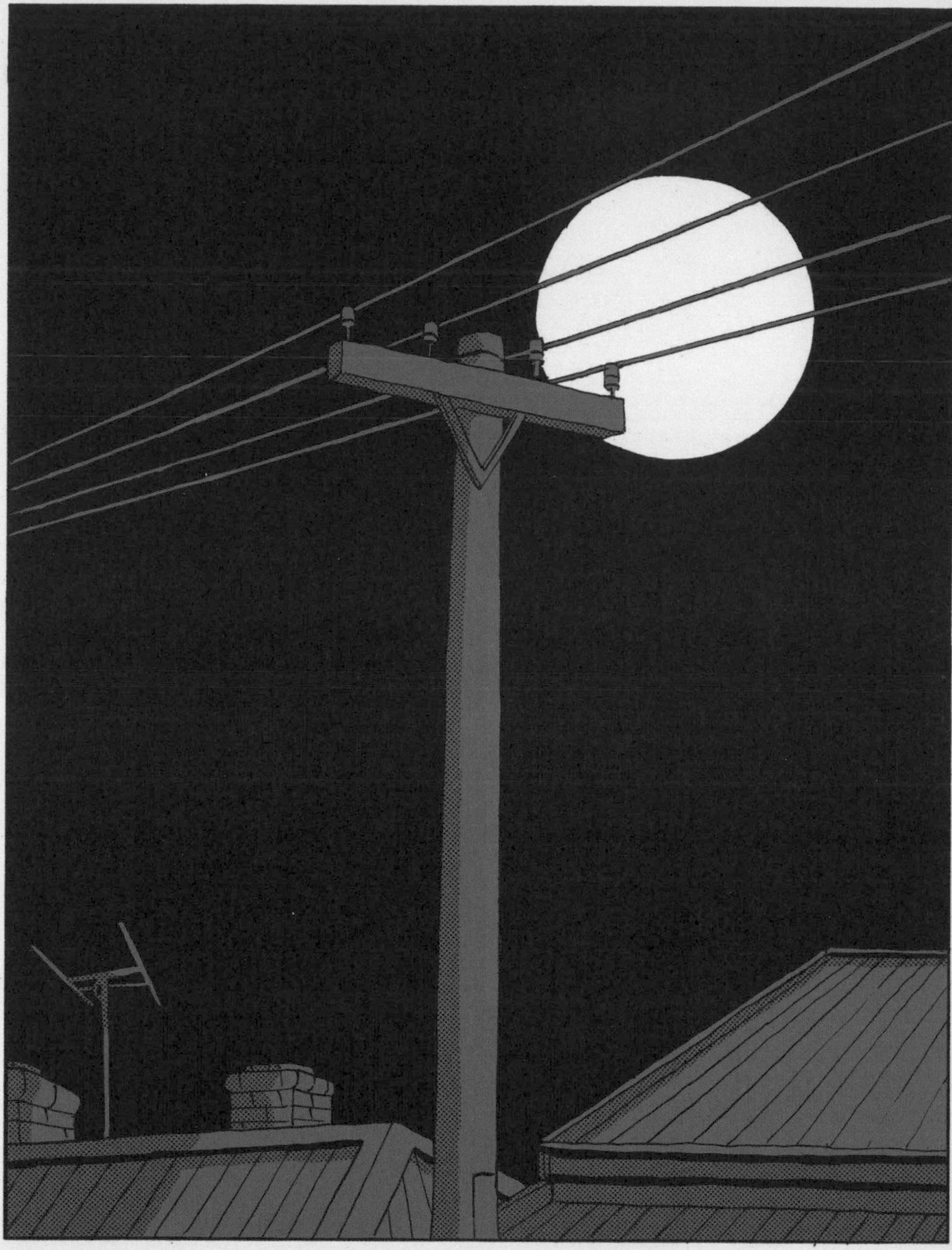

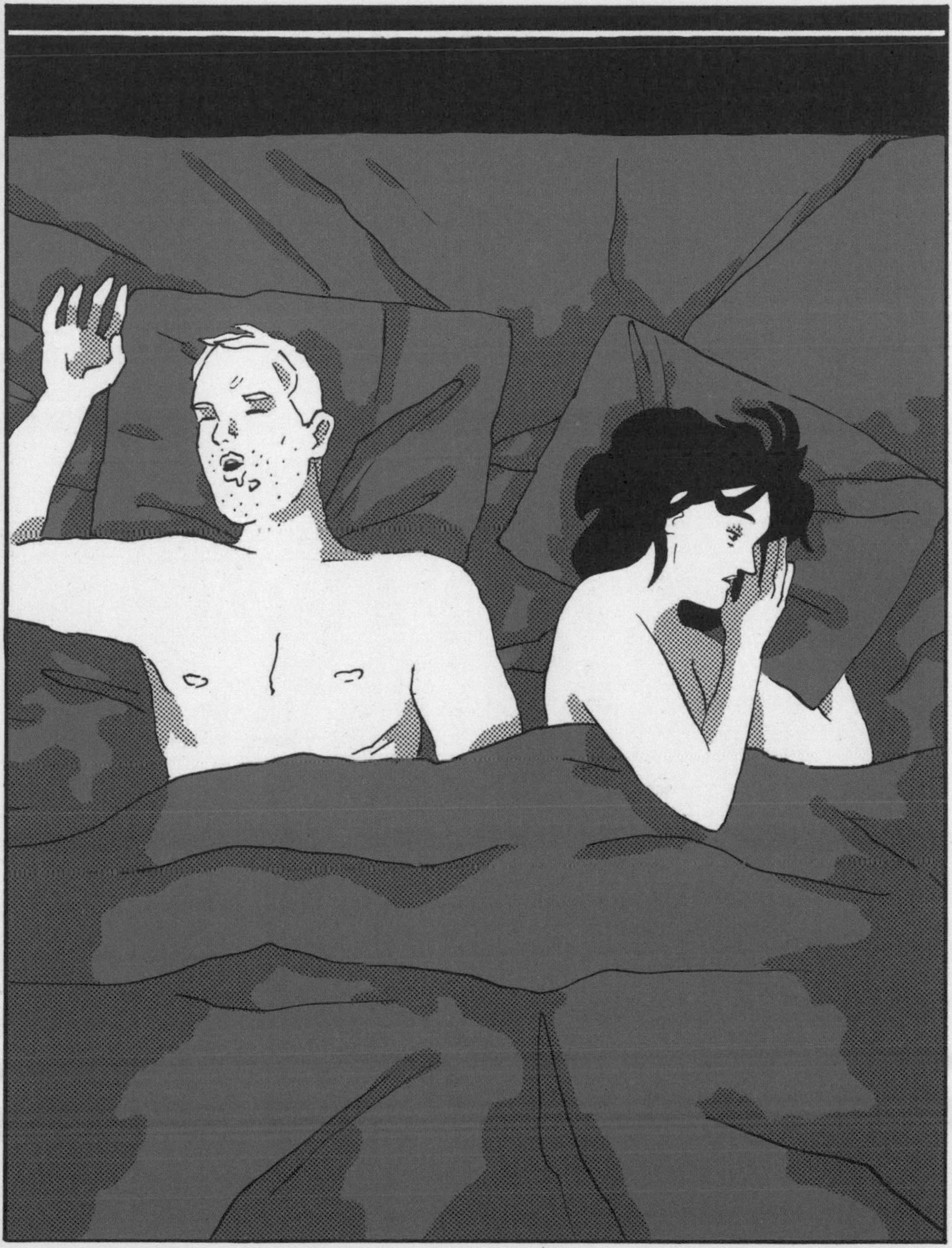

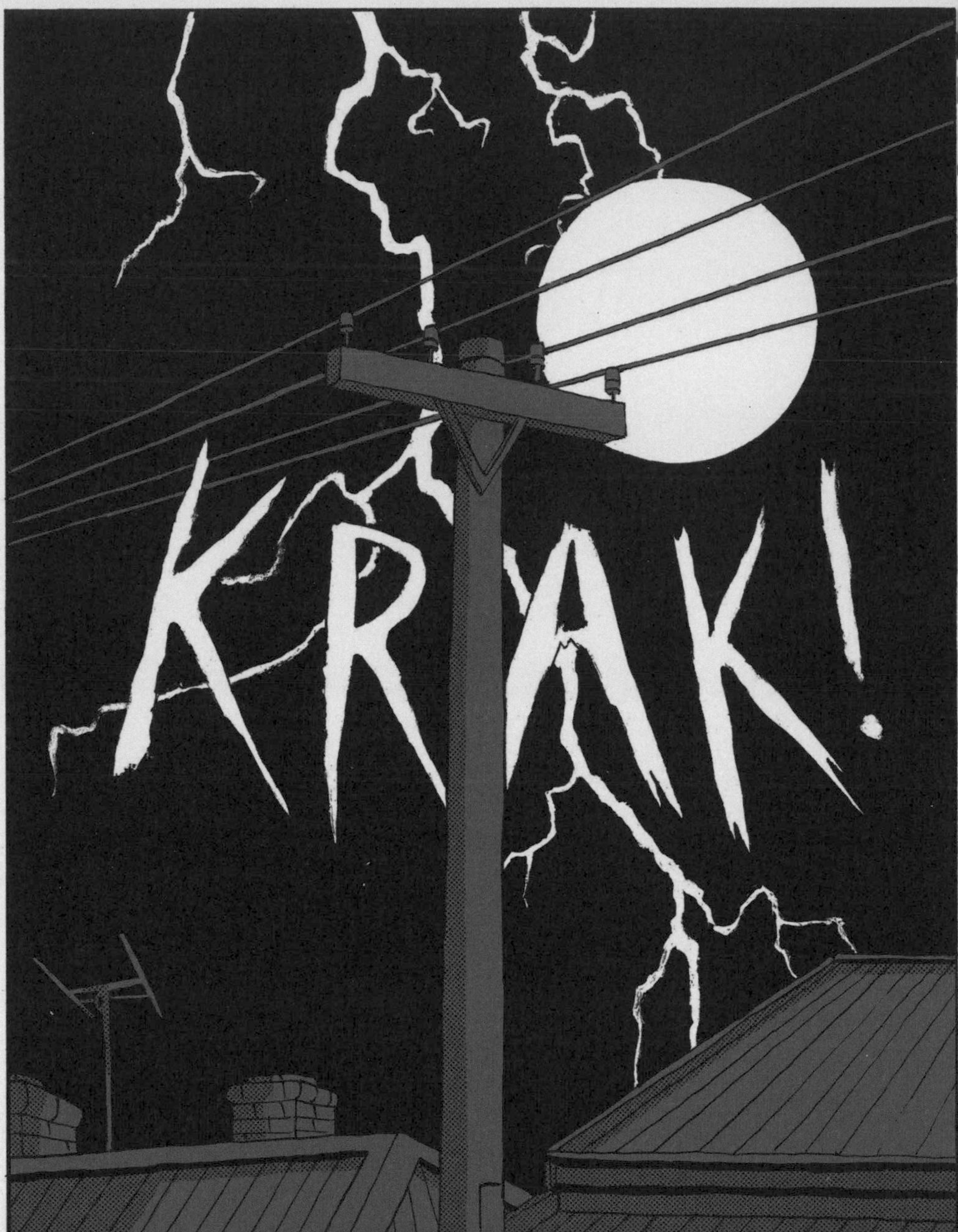
KRAK!

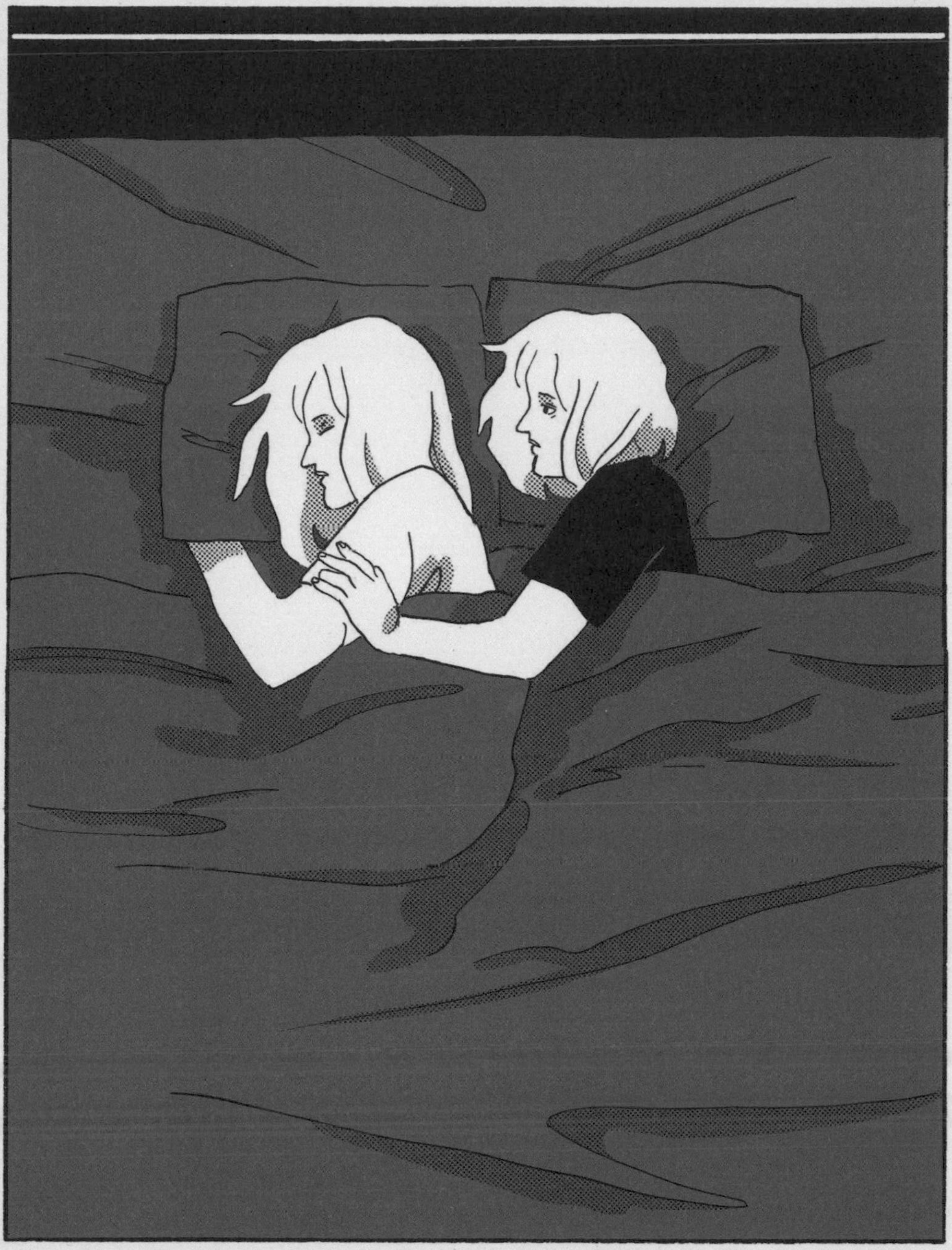

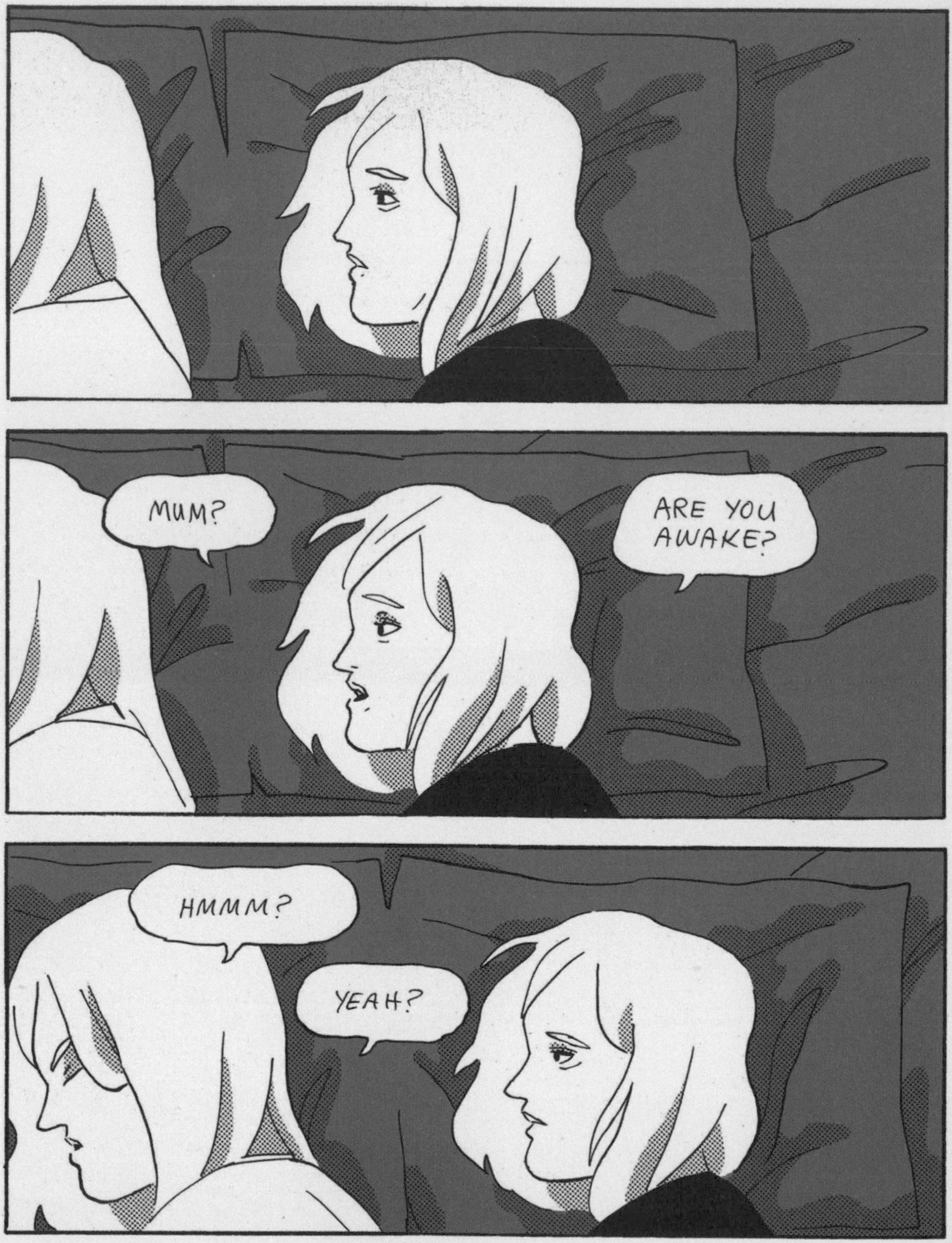
MUM?
ARE YOU AWAKE?
HMMM?
YEAH?

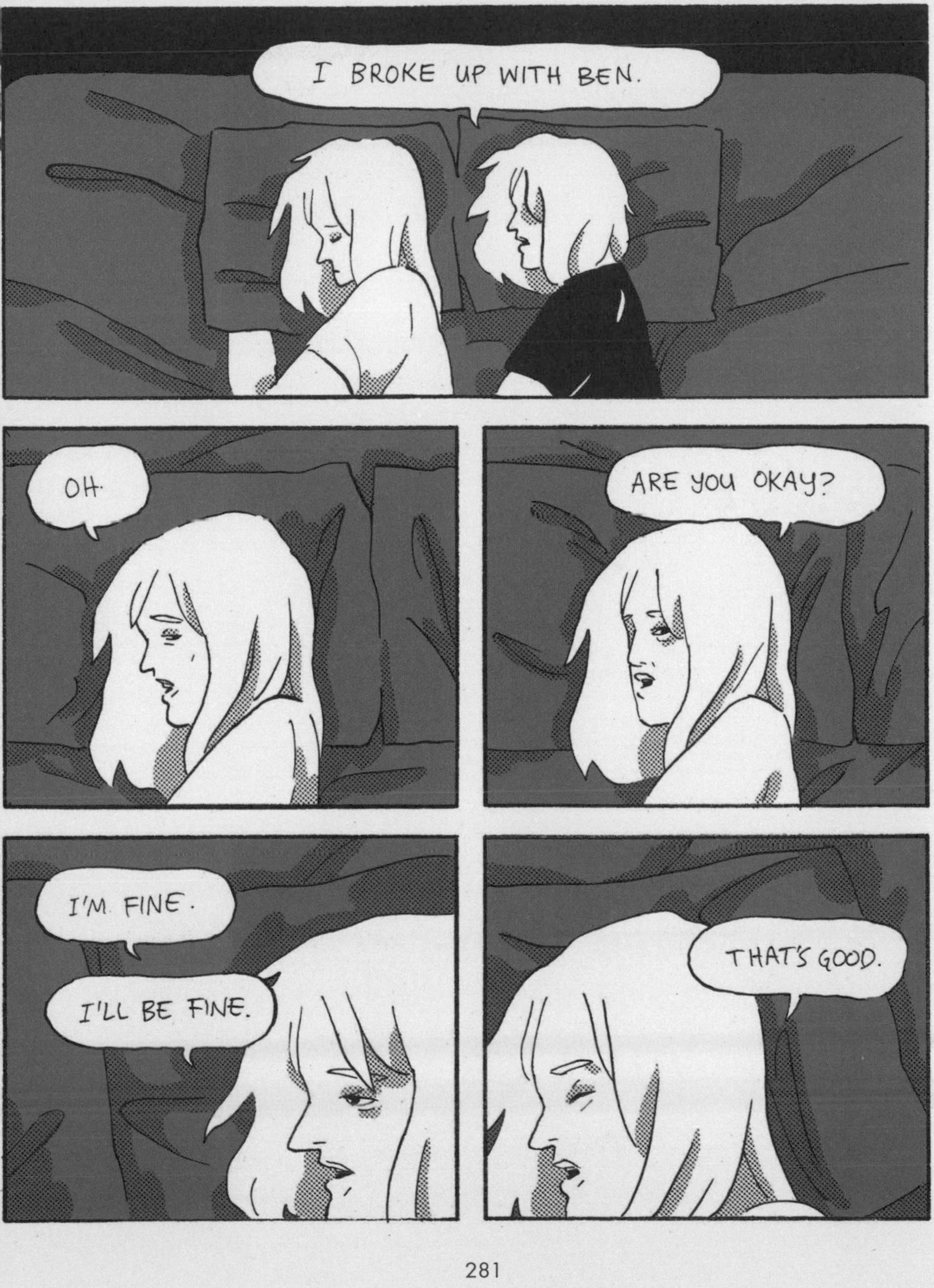
I BROKE UP WITH BEN.
OH.
ARE YOU OKAY?
I'M FINE.
I'LL BE FINE.
THAT'S GOOD.

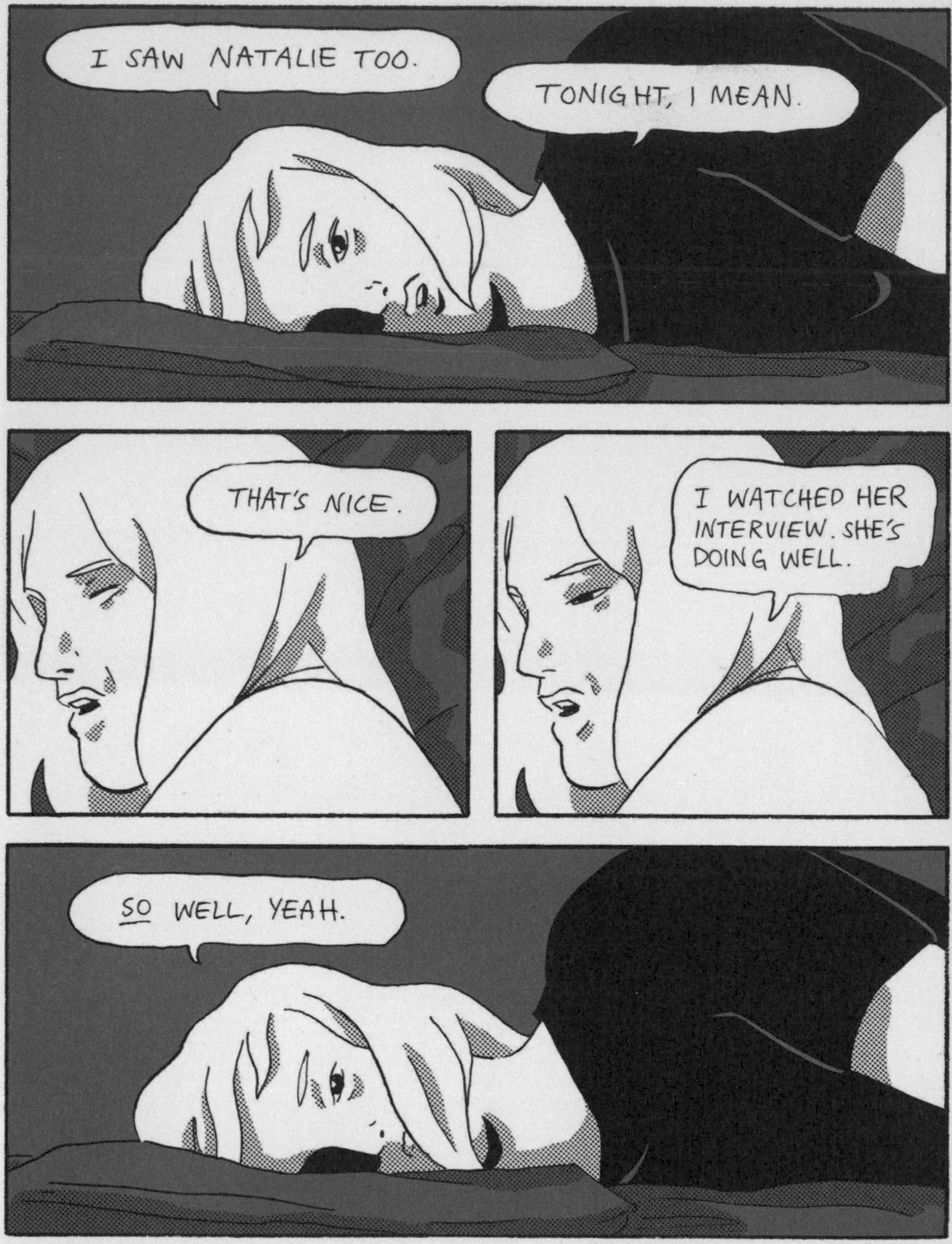
I SAW NATALIE TOO.
TONIGHT, I MEAN.
THAT'S NICE.
I WATCHED HER INTERVIEW. SHE'S DOING WELL.
SO WELL, YEAH.

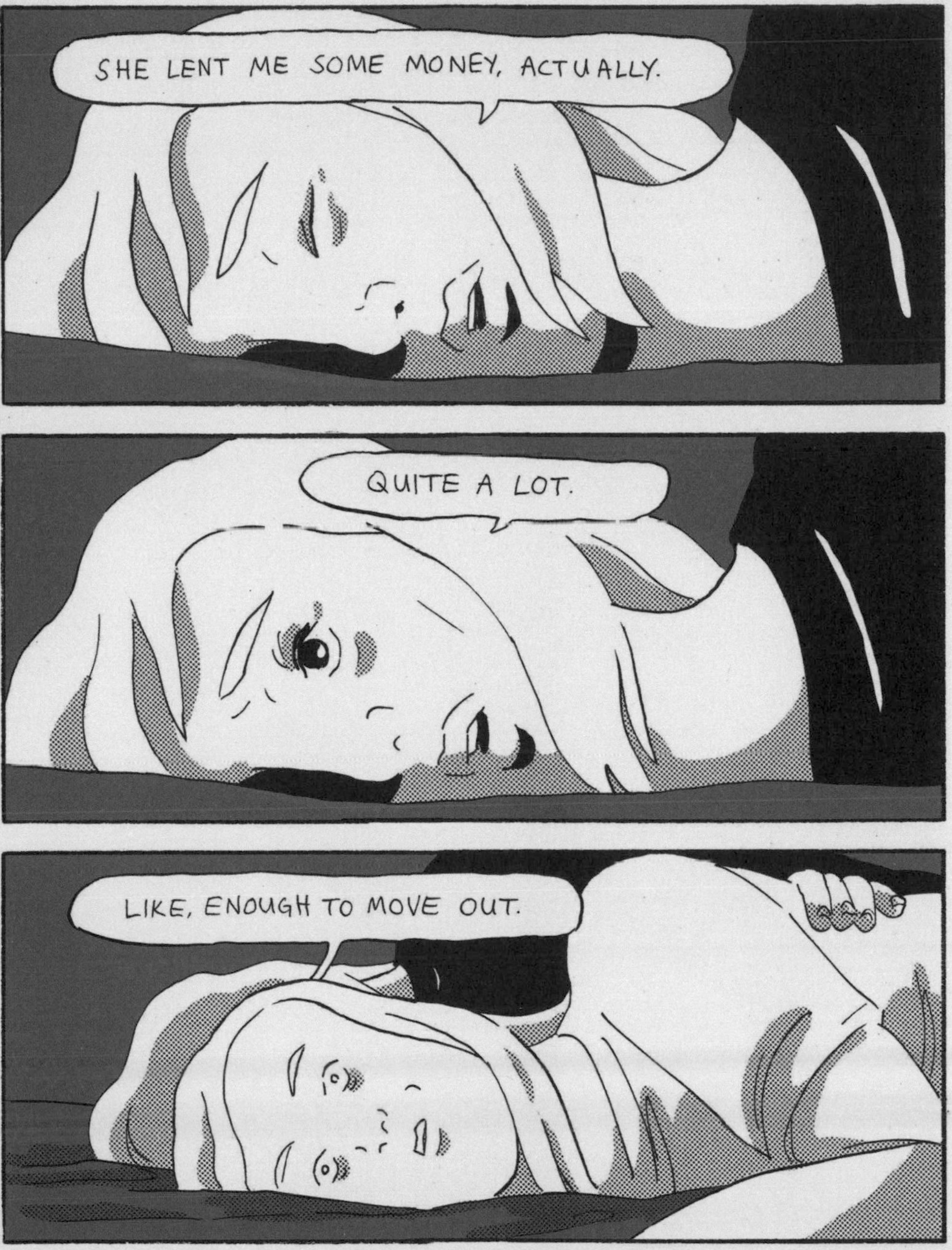
SHE LENT ME SOME MONEY, ACTUALLY.
QUITE A LOT.
LIKE, ENOUGH TO MOVE OUT.

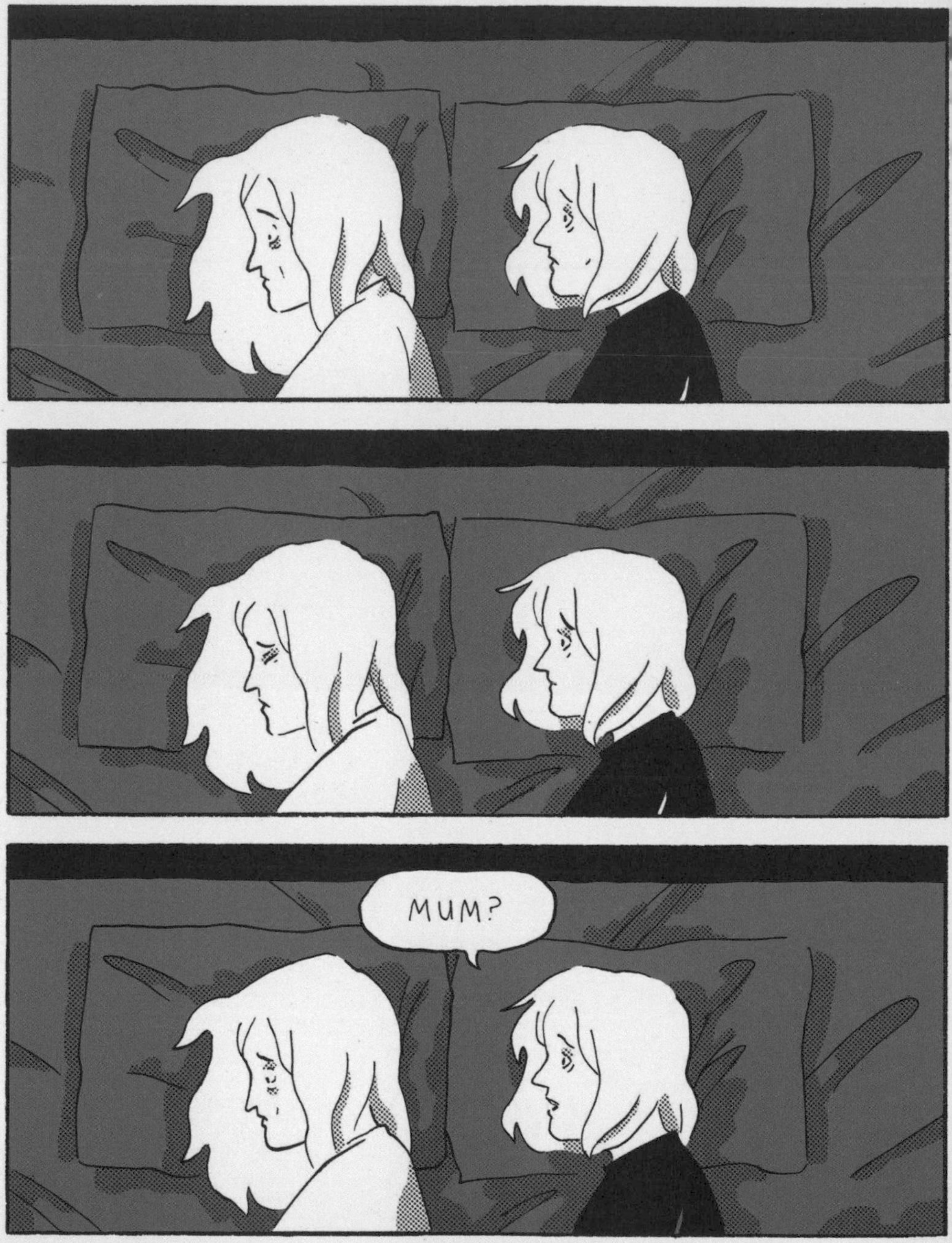
MUM?

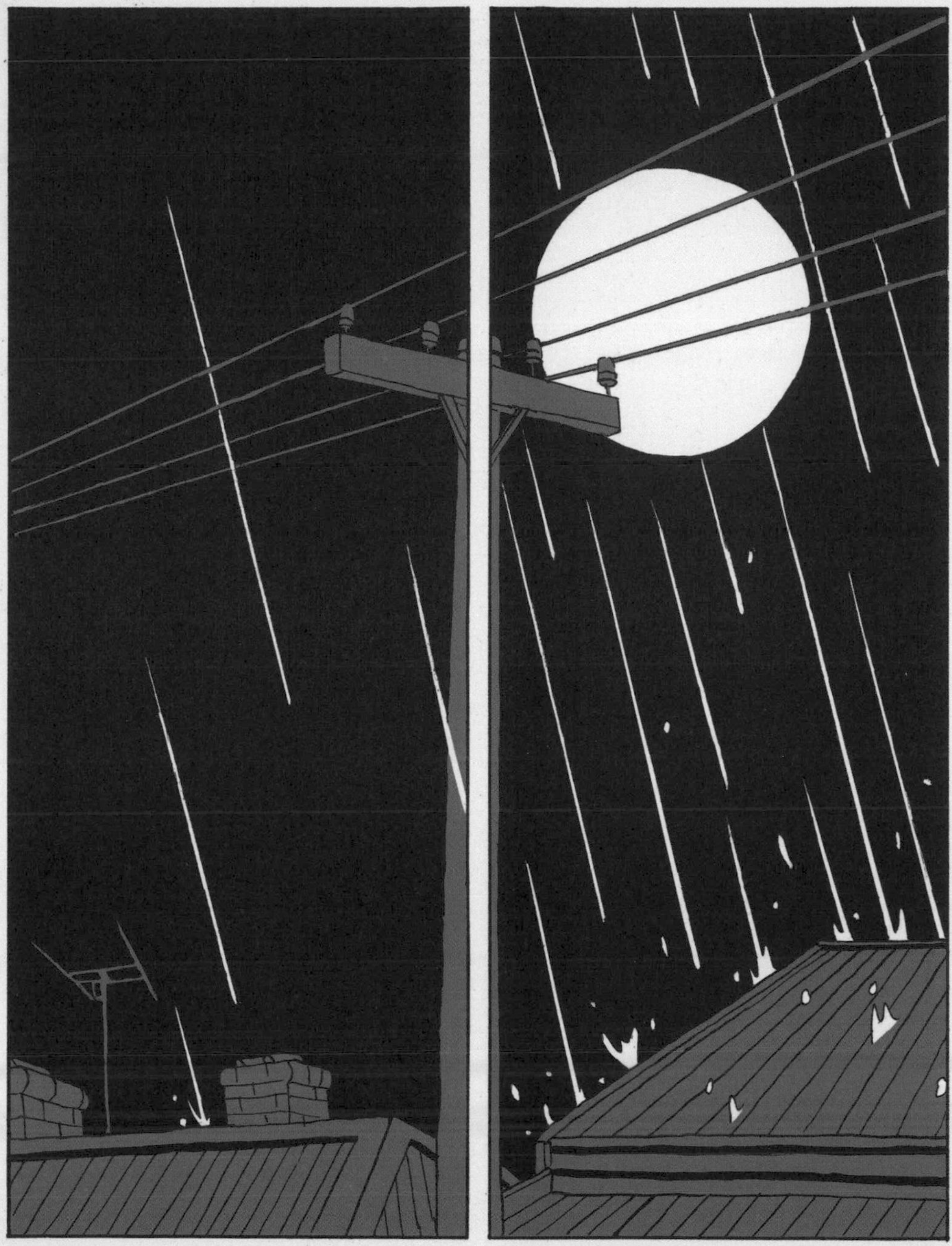

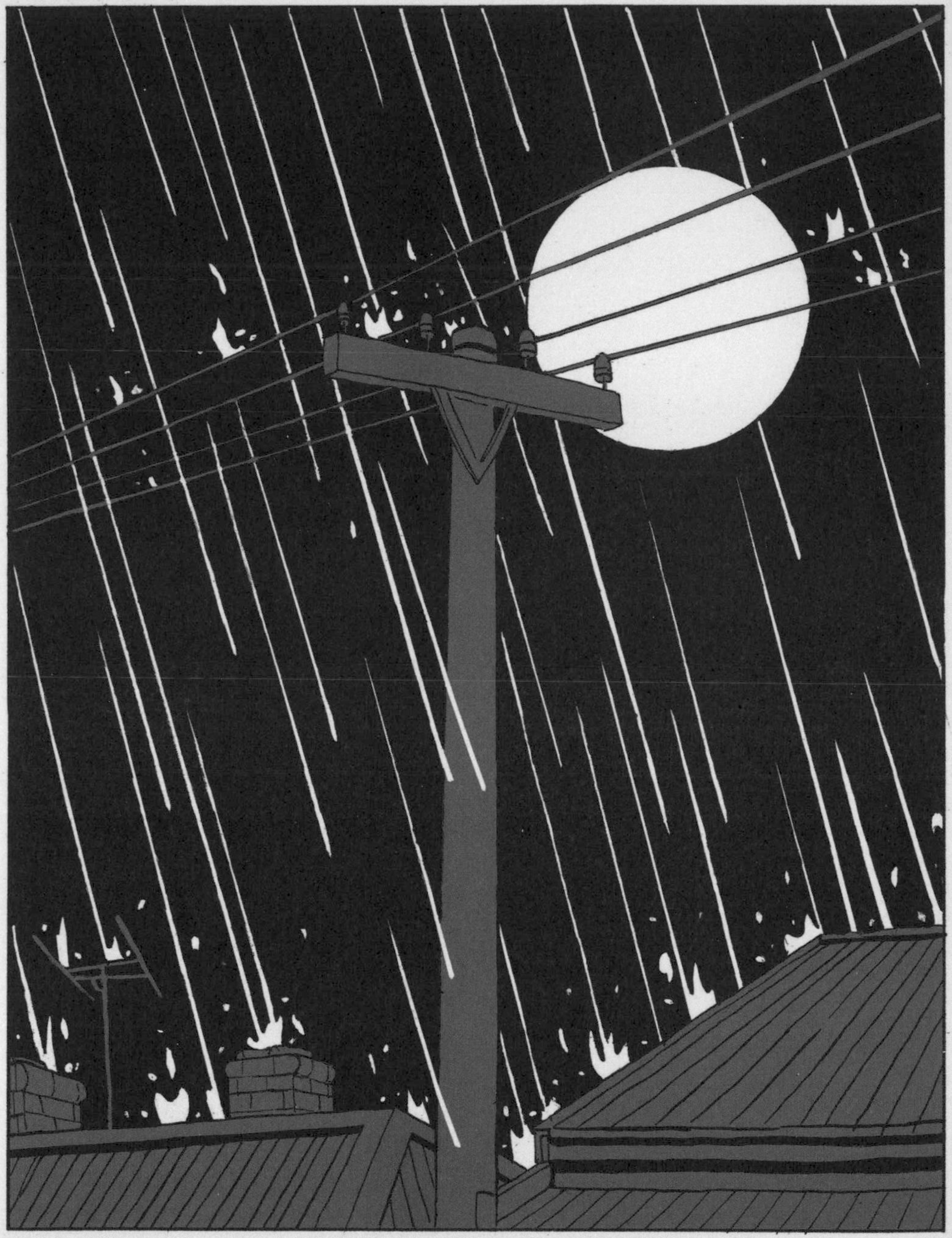

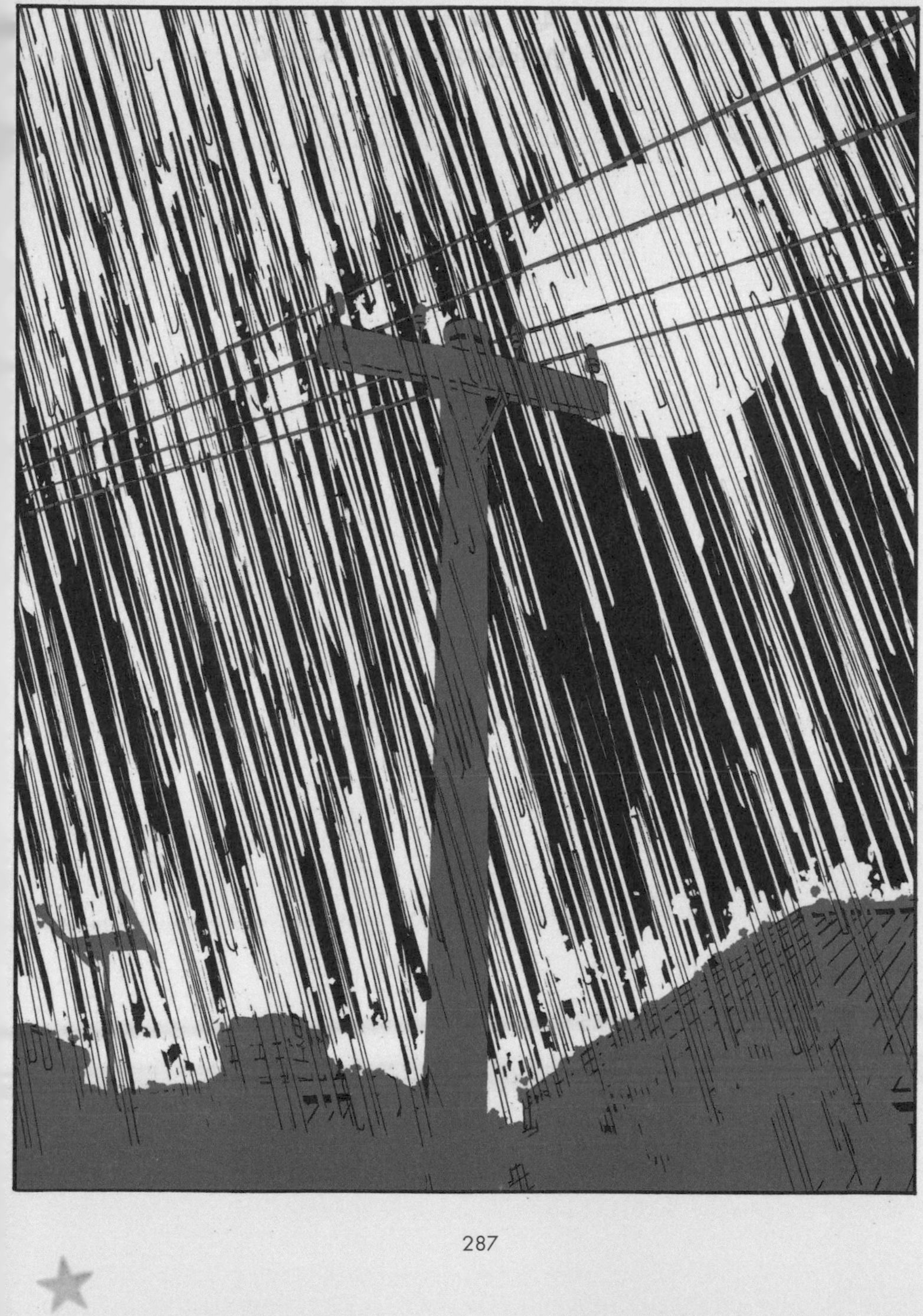

Many thanks to Mum, Dad, Nicholas, Jess,
Brendan, Sarah, Pat, Pandy; everyone from
Squishface Studio, CAW, and Top Shelf;
and anybody who gave me feedback or
said nice things.